"Information through Innovation"

dBASE Programming

Robert A. Wray
Philip J. Pratt

boyd & fraser
bf
boyd & fraser publishing company

Credits:

Senior Acquisitions Editor: James H. Edwards
Production Coordinator: Pat Stephan
Director of Production: Becky Herrington
Interior Design: Design Works
Cover Design: Mike Fender Design
Composition: Huntington & Black Typography
Cover Photo: Randy Braaten, The Image Bank

Registered Trademark Listing:

dBASE II®, dBASE III®, dBASE III PLUS®, dBASE IV®, dCONVERT®, RUNTIME+®, dBRUN®, dBCODE®, dBLINKER®, Network dBASE III PLUS®, and Multiplan® are registered trademarks of the Ashton-Tate Corporation
UNIX® is a registered trademark of Bell Laboratories
GENIFER® is a registered trademark of the Bytel Corporation
Compaq® is a registered trademark of the Compaq Corporation
IDMS® and IDMS/R® are registered trademarks of the Cullinet Corporation
FoxBASE+® is a registered trademark of Fox Software
Intel 8086®, Intel 80286®, and Intel 80386® are registered trademarks of the Intel Corporation
IMS®, DL/I®, DB2®, QBE®, SQL®, SQL/DS®, IBM-PC®, IBM/XT®, IBM/AT®, IBM Personal System/2®, PC-DOS®, and IBM-PC Network Program® are registered trademarks of International Business Machines Corporation
Lotus 1-2-3® is a registered trademark of Lotus Development Corporation
R:BASE SYSTEM V® is a registered trademark of Microrim, Inc.
MS-DOS® and OS/2® are registered trademarks of the Microsoft Corporation
Clipper® is a registered trademark of Nantucket Corporation
NOMAD® is a registered trademark of MUST Software International
Visicalc® is a registered trademark of Software Arts, Inc.
PFS® is a registered trademark of Software Publishing Corporation
TANDY 1000® and TRS-80® are registered trademarks of the Tandy Corporation
Quicksilver® is a registered trademark of Wordtech Systems

© 1992 by boyd & fraser publishing company
A Division of South-Western Publishing Company
Danvers, MA 01923

All rights reserved. No part of this work may be reproduced or used in any form or by any means—graphic, electronic, or mechanical, including photocopying, recording, taping, or information and retrieval systems—without written permission from the publisher.

Manufactured in the United States of America

Library of Congress Cataloging-in-Publication Data

Wray, Robert A.
dBASE programming / Robert A. Wray, Philip J. Pratt.
p. cm.
Includes index.
ISBN 0-87835-794-7
1. Data base management. 2. dBase IV (Computer program)
I. Pratt, Philip J., 1945- . II. Title.
QA76.9.D3W74 1992
005.75'65--dc20 91-33669
CIP

3 4 5 6 7 8 9 10 D 5 4

Contents in Brief

CONTENTS

CHAPTER 3 WORKING FROM THE DOT PROMPT 61

CHAPTER 4 INITIAL PROGRAMMING SKILLS 91

CHAPTER 5 THE DO WHILE/ENDDO LOOP 119

PREFACE

dBASE Programming serves a critical need in the contemporary business environment. There is a serious lack of business professionals trained to create microcomputer database systems. Every effort has been made in this book to provide all the elements one would expect in an introductory programming course and include required database and structured programming concepts. Students who successfully complete this course will possess a marketable skill that will serve them well for years to come.

OBJECTIVES

1. To describe the use of all of the features of dBASE IV.
2. To teach useful interactive commands to effectively manage and use database files.
3. To present sound, structured programming fundamentals using dBASE IV.
4. To develop the ability to design systems.
5. To survey relational aspects of database theory.

Although this book was developed for a one-semester introductory course in dBASE IV programming, it offers maximum flexibility for rapidly changing curriculum needs. There is sufficient support for the solo learner as well. Since it is comprehensive, the text can be used as a component in courses that survey DBMSs. There is enough database theory to satisfy an introduction to the subject. The reading ability and problem level are appropriate for undergraduate students with little or no programming experience.

ORGANIZATION

The organization of the book is based on a spiral approach. New concepts and skills build upon the work in previous chapters. This provides reinforcement while motivating the reader with new challenges. The first four chapters introduce the interactive use of dBASE IV. Commands used in programming are emphasized. The student is led toward writing programs as quickly as possible. The remaining eleven chapters present every aspect of programming required to develop a working business system.

DISTINGUISHING FEATURES

REALISTIC BUSINESS PROBLEM SOLVING

The concepts and techniques presented in this book have been tested in working systems many times. Examples are based on actual business situations. Mastery will enable the student to "hit the ground running."

NUMEROUS PROGRAM EXAMPLES

An abundance of figures includes programs, screens, diagrams, and reports. Students can easily see the relationship between the program and its results. Abstract concepts such as nested loops are illustrated by easily understood analogies and drawings.

STRUCTURED PRINCIPLES

The principles of structured programming are presented and constantly reinforced throughout the text. All program examples are documented and indented for emulation by the student.

INTRODUCTION TO DATABASE THEORY

Important aspects of database theory are treated from a practical standpoint. Students are exposed to the normalization of data through a problem. The benefits of the relational model and its comparison with other DBMS types are explored. Many important terms are defined and explained.

IN-DEPTH COVERAGE OF THE CONTROL STRUCTURES

The DO WHILE/ENDDO, IF/ELSE/ENDIF, and DO CASE/ENDCASE are not merely presented; the structures are analyzed so the student understands how they operate and can predict their behavior.

SUPERIOR COVERAGE OF MULTIPLE FILE PROGRAMMING

Chapter 11 provides coverage of an often neglected topic, the programming of multiple file systems. System planning is discussed, and a complex program example clearly illustrates how several database files can be accessed simultaneously.

dBUG dBASE SECTIONS

Most chapters include a dBUG dBASE feature containing valuable hints that relate to the chapter topics. These tips generally originate from practical experience.

SPECIAL dBASE IV FEATURES

User-defined functions; horizontal bar, pull-down, and pop-up menus; windows; erase; and the on-line debugger are introduced and explained.

NUMEROUS EXERCISES, PROBLEMS, AND PROJECTS

Chapters include Self-check Questions that review important chapter material, Try It Yourself exercises that provide hands-on practice of techniques, and Programming Projects that require the student to plan and code comprehensive programs.

CHAPTER OBJECTIVES AND SUMMARIES

Preceding an introduction to motivate further study, students are presented with clearly stated chapter objectives that provide purpose and direction. Each chapter concludes with concise summaries for each section, a list of key terms, and a command summary including definitions. This is convenient for reference while working in the chapter.

COMPLETE CASE STUDY/MAJOR PROJECT

As an optional tool, the text includes a complete, comprehensive Case Study/Major Project. A working version is included on the Instructor's Diskette. Suggestions for using the Case Study are provided in the Instructor's Manual.

STUDENT DATA DISK

Many programs and files are contained on a convenient data disk packaged with each book. This saves the student and the instructor a great deal of time. In a lab setting the students can run the programs to reinforce lecture concepts. The programs and files can be modified for individual study.

INSTRUCTOR'S MANUAL

An Instructor's Manual will be provided to all adopters. Lecture notes and hints, answers to exercises, a complete test bank, and helpful suggestions will aid the instructor in delivering the course.

ACKNOWLEDGEMENTS

This book includes the valuable ideas and suggestions of several individuals who took the time and interest to review the manuscript. I wish to thank the following educators: Albert (Jack) Atkins, Greenville Technical College; Chris Carter, Indiana Vocational Technical College; Marvin L. Harris, Lansing Community College; Mary Z. Last, Grand Valley State University; and Vince Yen, Wright State University.

Thank you also to the staff at boyd & fraser for their special efforts.

Robert A. Wray
Philip J. Pratt
January 1992

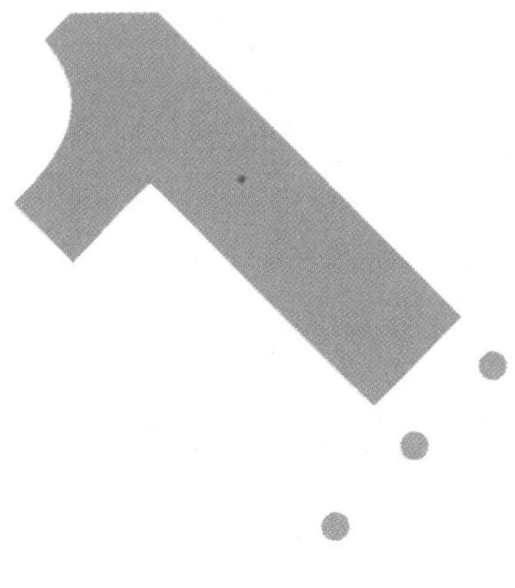

LEARNING OBJECTIVES

To define a database management system (DBMS) in terms of its capabilities.

To define several relevant computer terms.

To examine some relevant concepts of database theory.

To properly execute several essential DOS commands.

To identify the capacities of dBASE IV.

To become familiar with the basic operation of dBASE IV.

An Overview

Introduction

In our world today, information is power. It is certainly true that as society evolves, people are evermore dependent on timely information to participate in a complex but rewarding environment. The business world recognizes that success often relies on managing information better than the competition, and most often uses the computer to meet this goal. The challenge lies in effectively and efficiently designing the instructions that direct the computer's activities. This chapter introduces a popular product for meeting that challenge: dBASE IV.

1.1 WHAT IS A DBMS?

These are exciting times in the business world. Recent technological developments are improving computers dramatically. Speed and storage capacity are increasing while size and cost dwindle. Parallel improvements in software (the instructions that operate the computer) are providing power, flexibility, and accessibility to a swiftly growing proportion of society. The businesses that provide these products and services will prosper because they meet a critical need—the effective management of information. Amid these realistically optimistic projections only one deficiency is apparent: an inadequate number of skilled business professionals who are capable of designing systems that can solve complex business problems effectively and profitably.

The combination of a microcomputer system, a powerful database management system (DBMS) such as dBASE IV, and a knowledgeable user is all that is required for the effective management of astonishing amounts of stored information. This book is designed to help you become a knowledgeable user of this technology. You will learn to manage information and to program in dBASE IV. As you might expect, these are highly prized abilities in the business world. All businesses today depend on the availability of timely information. Those who are responsible for maintaining that information rely on computers because of the unsurpassable accuracy and efficiency they afford when they are properly programmed.

Businesses use various types of information systems, but no matter which type a particular business has selected, an information system must perform three critical tasks:

1. Collecting and storing information.
2. Organizing and maintaining the information in a way that will increase its usefulness.
3. Responding to requests for information in a natural and convenient manner.

Any information that has been centralized and organized can be considered a database. Telephone directories, encyclopedias, dictionaries, and card files all store information in a central place in an organized way so that it can be easily retrieved. Since the essence of most business activities can be described as the processing of information, databases are critical to the daily functioning of most businesses. Table 1.1 lists just a few of the functions that are routinely performed by dBASE IV in the area of accounting.

TABLE 1.1 Accounting uses of dBASE IV

General Ledger	Time and Billing
Accounts Receivable	Personnel
Accounts Payable	Sales Tracking
Inventory	Fixed Asset Manager
Payroll	Customer-Account System

In the computer industry, information is often referred to as *data*. Data consists of raw facts such as account numbers, account balances, and dates. Some data is used for calculations such as gross pay, whereas other data identifies such things as names, addresses, and catalog numbers.

Data is organized within several commonly used categories. The smallest of these is the single *character*, or symbol. Characters that are grouped together to form a single piece of information, such as a Social Security number, are called *fields*. When several fields are used to represent an entity such as a person, business, product, or city, the grouped fields are called a *record*. A *file* is a collection of records. Figure 1.1 illustrates this hierarchy of data.

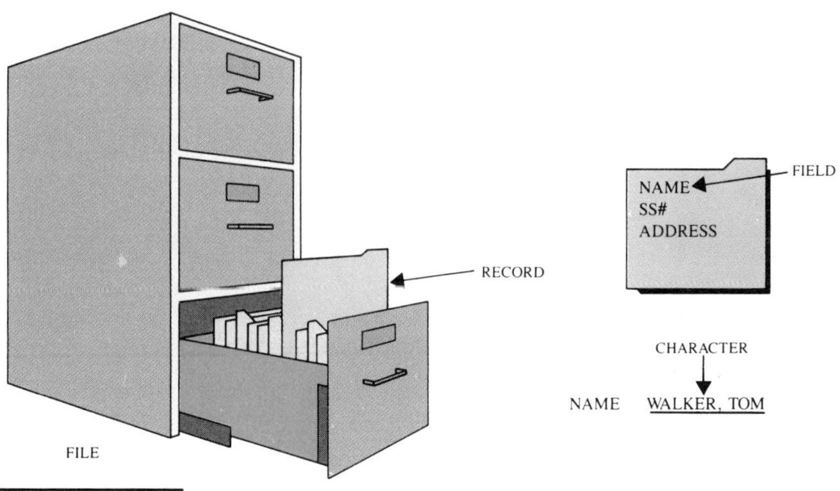

Figure 1.1 HIERARCHY OF DATA

The terms character, field, record, and file are familiar in the office environment. To categorize data in computer systems, we use these terms and others. A *byte* is a unit of storage in the computer. It usually represents one character of data such as a number, a comma, or a letter. Files are often measured in terms of the number of kilobytes they occupy. A *kilobyte* contains 1024 bytes. A *database* is a collection of organized data and other related information that is stored in the computer as a database file. Computer programs that are designed to create, maintain, and use databases are called *database management systems (DBMSs)*, the most powerful software products available to manage stored information. These computer programs collect, store, retrieve, and report information neatly and precisely. There are many DBMS products on the market. Some are designed for large computer systems, others for microcomputers such as the IBM Personal System/2.

The advantages of a DBMS include:

- It offers rapid access to and flexible use of information. A DBMS uses sophisticated methods of organization and retrieval.
- The incidence of redundancy (repetition) is limited and information is kept current. An efficient computer program stores only pertinent information and keeps the information it does store up to date.
- The cost/benefit ratio is good. Compared to the value of the benefits it affords, set-up costs for a DBMS are negligible.
- Storage of information is compact, compared to paper storage.
- Mundane, repetitive tasks such as searching for information and preparing reports can be automated.
- A DBMS imposes an organized structure that would be difficult to attain manually. Once a DBMS has been established, its maintenance encourages efficiency in office procedures.

The disadvantages of a DBMS include:

- Operations and programming require skill in the use of the system as well as a knowledge of DBMS concepts.
- Because information is stored in a complex way, it can be difficult to back up or reconstruct.

- Information is centralized, and it requires maintenance. Someone must assume responsibility for administering the DBMS.
- As the power and features of the DBMS are utilized, more complex information management is required, and this generates new administrative problems.

As you can see, the advantages of a DBMS far outweigh its disadvantages. Although some business situations do not require the use of DBMS products, all mid- to large-sized companies (and even many small businesses) use them extensively. In fact, these products pervade the entire spectrum of modern business activity, which suggests that DBMS technology will eventually affect the jobs of most business professionals. Let's take a brief look at the history and basic characteristics of dBASE IV.

1.2 HISTORY AND CHARACTERISTICS OF dBASE IV

In the mid-1970s, Wayne Ratliff became acquainted with data management while working on mainframes for NASA. In the late 1970s, Ratliff, drawing on this mainframe experience, wrote one of the first microcomputer database management systems. He marketed the product, which he called Vulcan, by placing an ad in *Byte* magazine. The extremely encouraging response to his ad exceeded his expectations.

In 1980, he sold the rights for Vulcan to Ashton-Tate. He also became a vice president of the company responsible for new product development. Ashton-Tate enhanced the product and renamed it dBASE II (there was no dBASE I). dBASE II sold more than 200,000 copies worldwide.

In 1984, under Ratliff's direction, Ashton-Tate brought out dBASE III, the first major upgrade to dBASE II. dBASE III was easier to use, faster, and more flexible than dBASE II. It was also much more accessible to nonprogrammers. An upgrade, dBASE III PLUS, was brought out one year later and further expanded the program's ease of use, speed, and flexibility.

The late 1980s saw another major upgrade, dBASE IV. Like each of its predecessors, it represented major improvements in convenience, speed, and flexibility. The use of the various dBASE products has now become so widespread that there are attempts underway to develop a standard based on the dBASE language.

Table 1.2 gives some of the important specifications for dBASE IV.

TABLE 1.2 dBASE IV specifications

FEATURE	LIMIT
Number of records per database file	1,000,000,000
Record size	4000 bytes
Number of fields per record	255
Open files	99
Open database files	10
Length of command at dot prompt	255
Memory variables	15,000
Procedures per program	963
Procedure size	64K
Work areas	10
Programmable function keys	29

1.3 DATABASE THEORY

DBMSs provide access to data by responding to requests, or *queries*. Besides the ability to manipulate data by appending, retrieving, modifying, and deleting, a DBMS performs other functions including:

Data definition
Programming language
Report writing (formatting and printing data)
File catalogs
Indexing (to locate data)
Views
Security
Integrity
Locking

As you might expect, users can obtain many products that perform the preceding functions. Most of these products were developed on mainframes, using languages like COBOL. As *minicomputers* (smaller mainframes) and microcomputers became common in business, software developers provided DBMSs to satisfy that market. DBMSs are often categorized by the form in which they organize and access data. The three most common categories are *hierarchical*, *network*, and *relational*.

Hierarchical DBMSs establish relationships among data items by using sets of pointers, links, and lists. It is as if each piece of data carries a set of directions for access. Because hierarchical DBMSs require large memories and powerful processing units, they are found on mainframe computers, often in a COBOL environment. Good examples are IMS, IBM's hierarchical DBMS, with its associated programming language, DL/I; RAMIS; and FOCUS.

Network databases are constructed on an underlying foundation of records and relationships. Besides being popular for use on mainframes, they also appear on minicomputers like the Hewlett-Packard HP-3000. IDMS, by Cullinet, is a network-type DBMS that conforms to an industry standard called the CODASYL model.

In the relational model, information is stored in related data *tables* in separate files. It can be accessed and manipulated interactively or in batch (program) mode. A table organizes data into rows and columns. The rows are records, and the columns are fields. Programmers call the rows *tuples* and the columns *attributes*.

Since dBASE IV is a relational DBMS, we will explore this type more closely. Imagine a simple table of two columns and four rows. Label the first column NAME and the second column PHONE. Each row then provides a position in each column for individual records. If we were to add some data, the table might look like the one in Table 1.3. Accessing data from either dimension, row or column, is the strength of the relational DBMS. In a relational DBMS such as dBASE IV, records are thought of as rows and fields as columns. For example, you could work with only the phone numbers and ignore the names, or vice versa. By positioning yourself at the proper row, you can retrieve all the fields in that row.

TABLE 1.3 A sample table

	NAME	PHONE
1	Cecil Wright	555-3964
2	Ray Porter	555-9385
3	Jay Vollink	555-9359
4	Mary Hughes	555-2051
5	↓	↓
6	↓	↓
7	↓	↓

A relational DBMS has the following characteristics:

1. Records must be unique in order to provide access by row.
2. A table does not depend on order in either dimension because relationships are established through the DBMS structure, not through the physical order of the data. This allows a great deal of flexibility when one is accessing the data.
3. Columns produce consistency in the rows by maintaining a strict format for each field.

Other examples of relational DBMSs include Oracle, Ingres, Paradox, and R:base for DOS.

SQL (which stands for Structured Query Language and is pronounced "sequel") is a very popular language for manipulating relational databases. It was developed by IBM. It is included in SQL/DS and DB2, two relational DBMSs designed for mainframe computers by IBM, as well as many other DBMSs.

1.4 IMPORTANT DOS COMMANDS

An important part of any computer system is the *operating system*. This is a set of programs that is designed to allow the user to control the organization and use of the data that is stored on the disk. The most widely used microcomputer operating system is *MS-DOS*, also called *PC-DOS*. Microsoft Corporation developed the system and sells it as MS-DOS. PC-DOS is the same product, marketed by IBM. The latest version of DOS as of this writing is 5.0, released for the IBM Personal System/2. A powerful new operating system called OS/2 was also introduced for the IBM Model 80 in 1987. To run dBASE IV under the MS-DOS operating system, you must use a version of DOS labeled 3.3 or higher.

You will need some knowledge of the MS-DOS commands to perform tasks such as checking the contents of the disk or copying files from one disk to another. An understanding of DOS is essential for the general operation of the computer and for using dBASE IV.

DOS STARTUP

DOS must be read from the default disk drive when the system is turned on or rebooted with the Ctrl-Alt-Del keys. A prompt for the date and time may appear on the screen. You can enter the date and time or simply press Enter twice. DOS then displays a prompt like this:

```
A> or C>
```

The letter indicates which drive is currently active. All commands that don't explicitly indicate otherwise will refer to that drive. The "greater than" sign, >, identifies DOS. You can access another disk drive by typing the letter of the drive and a colon and then pressing Enter.

```
A>B:
B>
```

Notice that the prompt now shows B as the active drive.

Data is organized and stored on the disk in separate sections called files. A file can contain any kind of information including programs like dBASE IV or the data it uses. A portion of DOS itself is stored in a file called COMMAND.COM.

(**Note**: DOS commands can be typed in either uppercase or lowercase.)

THE DIR COMMAND

The DIR command (for directory) displays information about all the files on the disk, as shown in Figure 1.2.

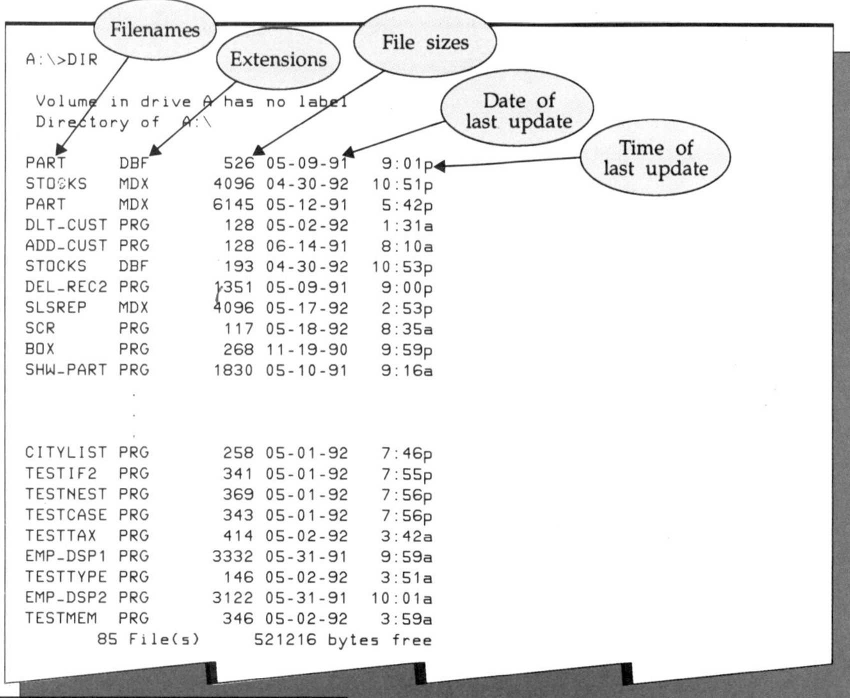

Figure 1.2 RESULTS OF THE DIR COMMAND

DOS provides the name of the file (filename), its size in bytes, and the time and date when it was created or updated on the disk. It is possible to be selective when referring to files with DIR and other commands. For example, you can type the filename after DIR to see if it exists on the disk. (See Figure 1.3.)

```
A:\>DIR CUSTOMER.DBF

 Volume in drive A has no label
 Directory of  A:\

CUSTOMER DBF          808 05-14-92  11:02a
        1 File(s)     521216 bytes free
```


Figure 1.3 USING DIR FOR A SPECIFIC FILE

The asterisk (*) can be used as an ambiguous character or "wild card" to group files, as in the example in Figure 1.4. The command issued in Figure 1.4 displays all the files with DBF as the second section, or *extension*, of the filename regardless of the first section of the name.

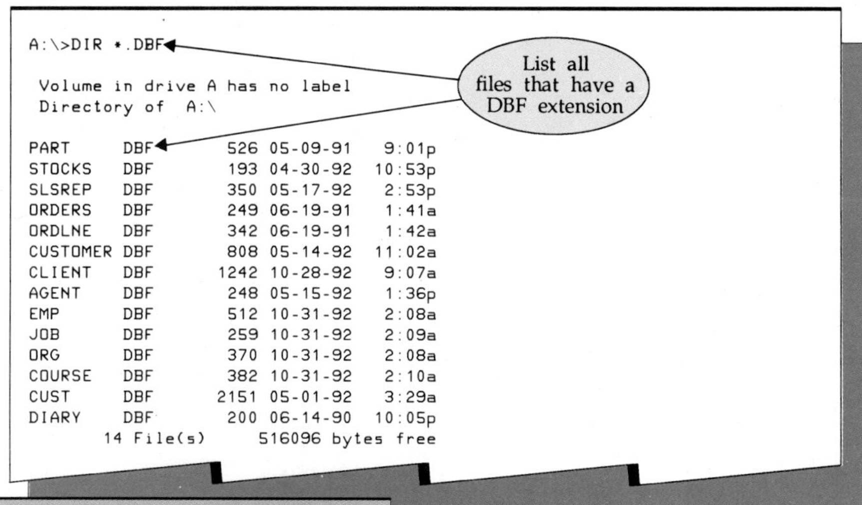

```
A:\>DIR *.DBF

 Volume in drive A has no label
 Directory of  A:\

PART     DBF          526 05-09-91   9:01p
STOCKS   DBF          193 04-30-92  10:53p
SLSREP   DBF          350 05-17-92   2:53p
ORDERS   DBF          249 06-19-91   1:41a
ORDLNE   DBF          342 06-19-91   1:42a
CUSTOMER DBF          808 05-14-92  11:02a
CLIENT   DBF         1242 10-28-92   9:07a
AGENT    DBF          248 05-15-92   1:36p
EMP      DBF          512 10-31-92   2:08a
JOB      DBF          259 10-31-92   2:09a
ORG      DBF          370 10-31-92   2:08a
COURSE   DBF          382 10-31-92   2:10a
CUST     DBF         2151 05-01-92   3:29a
DIARY    DBF          200 06-14-90  10:05p
       14 File(s)     516096 bytes free
```


Figure 1.4 USING DIR FOR A GROUP OF FILES

DIR also provides some useful switches for changing the screen display. You can use /W to place the filenames in columns so that many names may be viewed at once, as shown in Figure 1.5, or you can use /P to display one screenfull of names in the normal format. Then you can continue by pressing Enter.

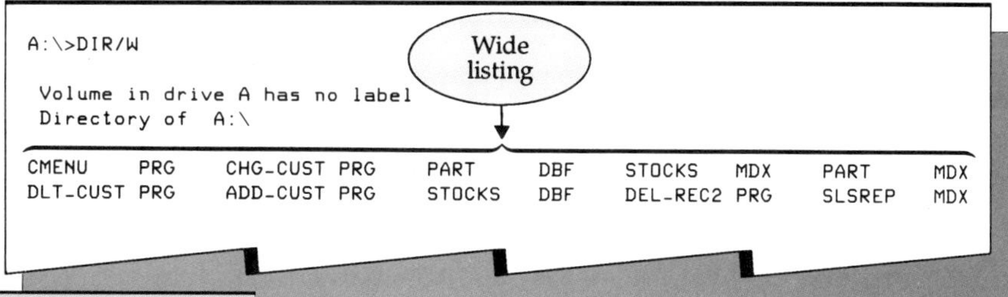

Figure 1.5 USING /W WITH DIR

DOS COMMANDS FOR MANIPULATING FILES

The COPY command transfers copies of files to other disks. The asterisk can be used effectively with COPY to move groups of files with one command. For example, the command

```
A>COPY *.DBF B:
```

writes an exact duplicate of all the DBF files on the A drive to the B drive.

FORMAT is a DOS utility program that prepares a new disk for the disk drive to use. The process magnetically encodes circular tracks divided into sectors on the disk. The following command executes the FORMAT program on the A drive, which prepares the disk in the B drive.

```
A>FORMAT B:
```

You can remove a file from a disk with the DEL or ERASE command:

`A>DEL TEST.DBF` or `A>ERASE TEST.DBF`

You can display the contents of some files with the TYPE command. (An example is given in Figure 1.6.) This is useful with dBASE IV PRG and TXT files. However, most files you are likely to encounter will not respond well to this command because they contain program information that is coded in a special format.

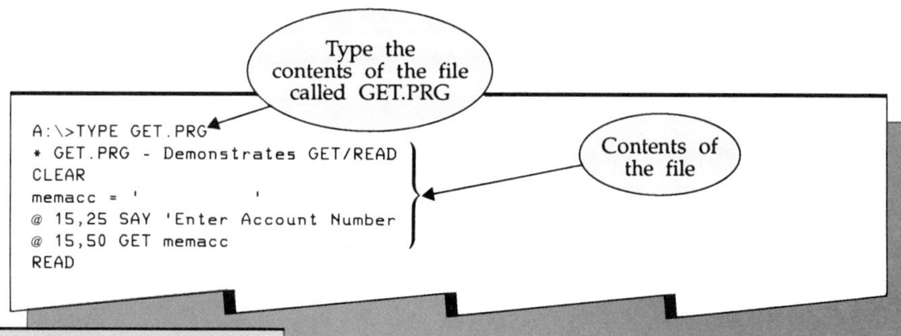

Figure 1.6 CONTENTS OF GET.PRG

DOS UTILITY COMMANDS

The F1 key retypes one character from the last DOS command entered in order to duplicate portions of the command. The F3 key displays the complete command.

^P (Ctrl-P) toggles on the printer and echoes any screen displays to the printer. Another ^P turns it off again.

CLS clears the screen and places the cursor in the upper left corner.

CHKDSK is a DOS utility program that, like FORMAT, can be found on the DOS disk. It provides the status of the capacities of both the disk and the computer's memory. (See Figure 1.7.)

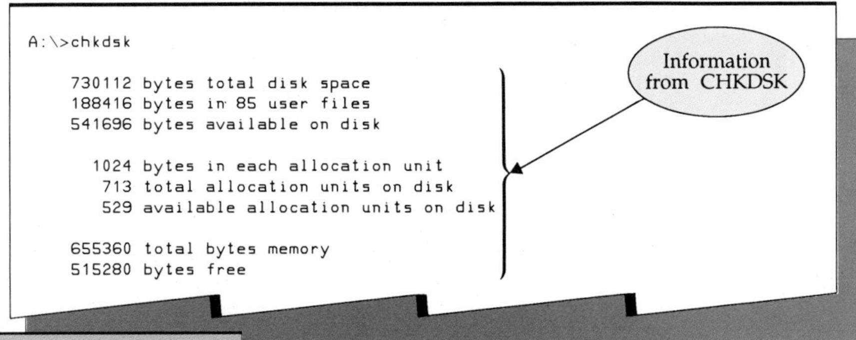

A:\>chkdsk
730112 bytes total disk space
188416 bytes in 85 user files
541696 bytes available on disk
1024 bytes in each allocation unit
713 total allocation units on disk
529 available allocation units on disk
655360 total bytes memory
515280 bytes free
Information from CHKDSK

Figure 1.7 RESULTS OF CHKDSK

DOS COMMANDS FOR MANIPULATING SUBDIRECTORIES

As computer technology advances and becomes more price-competitive, hard drive systems are more common. Users of hard drives require a means of organizing the large number of files that tend to accumulate. The solution is to partition the drive into subdirectories. Each subdirectory is named and then separated from the other subdirectories on the disk.

MD (or MKDIR) creates a new subdirectory. The following MD command creates a subdirectory called DBASE.

```
A>MD DBASE
```

CD or CHDIR changes to the new DBASE subdirectory. Files can now be copied into and out of the subdirectory as if it were another disk. RD (or RMDIR) removes an empty subdirectory. Figure 1.8 illustrates the use of these commands.

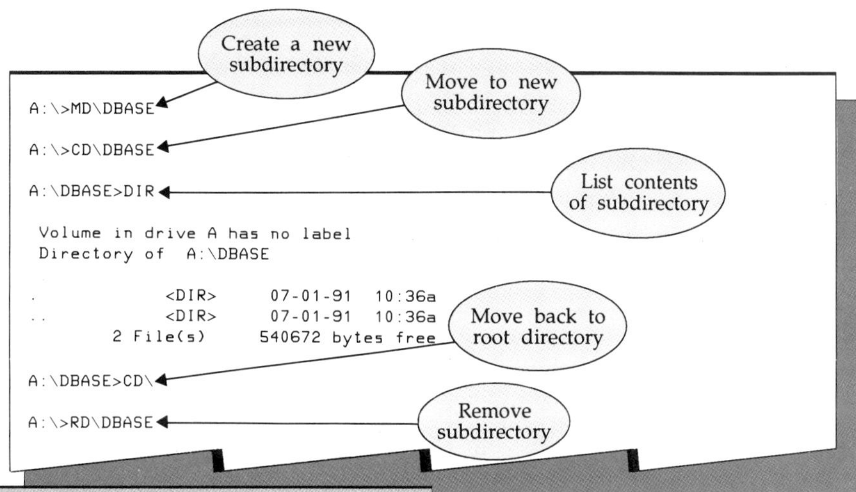

Figure 1.8 CREATING AND USING SUBDIRECTORIES

1.5 FILES IN dBASE

Filenames in dBASE IV follow the same conventions as those in DOS. The rules for creating names are as follows:

1. The name must be at least one but not more than eight characters long.
2. Acceptable characters include:
   a. Uppercase or lowercase letters A through Z
   b. Numerals 0 through 9
   c. Certain special characters: $ & # @ () – [] _ / \
3. Following a dot, a three-character extension may be included.

In creating names, you should avoid:

1. DOS or dBASE IV commands, filenames, or device names.
2. The individual letters A through I, which are used for ALIAS names (a special concept in dBASE).
3. Special characters other than those listed in the preceding rules.
4. The space, which is an invalid character.

For purposes of simplicity and clarity, it is best to limit filenames to the alphanumeric characters and the hyphen. These limitations allow DOS to work with files generated in dBASE IV. Some examples of acceptable filenames follow:

```
ACCT-REC
QRT-1-88
VENDOR
```

The second part of a filename, the *extension*, contains a dot and three letters. It is assigned by dBASE IV according to the function of the file. Thirteen types of files are used in dBASE IV. The DBF, PRG, MDX, and FMT are the most important file types in the programming environment. You will be working with these file types as you use dBASE IV in future chapters. For now, it will be helpful to be familiar with their names and functions (see Table 1.4).

TABLE 1.4 **dBASE IV file types**

FILE EXT.	FILE TYPE	FILE DESCRIPTION
CAT	Catalog	Stores names of dBASE IV files grouped by usage.
DBF	Database	Contains most of the dBASE IV source data in an organized format. A dBASE IV file contains a header, which is stored in several formats; the data; an end-of-file marker; and a section of scrambled data.
DBT	Database	Contains large amounts of text data related to records in the DBF file through a memo-type field. The data would be too bulky to store in the DBF file, so it is stored in and accessed from the DBT file.
FMT	Format	Contains commands to produce a custom data entry screen for use in programs.
FRM	Form	Stores the specifications for the formatted printing of data; created by the Report Generator.
LBL	Label	Stores formatting information for labels.
MEM	Memory	Saves information generated by programs that would otherwise be temporarily stored in file format.
MDX	Index	Contains the sorting order for records in a DBF file; important for finding data quickly and for displaying data in order.
PRG	Program	Contains dBASE IV commands that automatically perform tasks. MODIFY COMMAND stores a program in a PRG file.
TXT	Text	Contains simple text material stored as in a word processing file; important in the transfer of files into or out of dBASE IV.
QRY	Query	Stores filtering commands that allow selective use of data; specified with the CREATE QUERY command.
SCR	Screen	Supports FMT files. SCR files are internally generated and maintained by Painter.
VUE	View	Establishes a relationship linking databases by a common field. These files can be used to perform powerful functions without programming.

1.6 SETTING A CUSTOM ENVIRONMENT

If you are using a computer owned by your school, someone has already installed dBASE IV for you. If you are using your own computer, you will need to install dBASE IV by following the instructions in the booklet called *Getting Started with dBASE IV*. This booklet is part of the documentation that comes in the box with your dBASE IV disks. It contains all the information you need to install and customize dBASE. Part of the installation process modifies two very important files: CONFIG.DB and CONFIG.SYS.

CONFIG.DB

The *CONFIG.DB* file contains a number of settings that take effect automatically when dBASE IV is started. This is very convenient because these settings would otherwise have to be typed in before each work session. The CONFIG.DB file created by the installation procedure, for example, typically contains the following two commands:

```
STATUS = ON
COMMAND = ASSIST
```

These commands display the status bar at the bottom of the screen and automatically start the Control Center feature, a feature designed to *assist* users in interacting with dBASE.

If you later decide you would like to customize dBASE IV by changing some of the settings in CONFIG.DB, follow the instructions in the same *Getting Started with dBASE IV* booklet you used when you installed dBASE. (If you are working on a computer at your school, any customization should be done by a lab assistant or instructor, since customizing dBASE will affect all students who use the computer.)

CONFIG.SYS

The *CONFIG.SYS* file must be present on the disk during a power-up or reboot. DOS looks for it and makes internal settings according to the specifications contained in the file. DOS allows commands in CONFIG.SYS to control the number of disk drives and the format of the date, among other things. The installation process for dBASE IV modifies CONFIG.SYS to include the following two commands, which are necessary for dBASE IV to operate properly:

```
FILES = 40
BUFFERS = 15
```

Failure to set the number of files high enough produces a "too many files are open" message. If you ever get such a message, there is probably a problem with CONFIG.SYS.

If you are working on a computer owned by your school, ask a lab assistant or your instructor to look into the problem. If you are working on your own computer, check your DOS diskette (if you boot from a floppy disk) or the root directory on your hard disk to make sure there is a file called CONFIG.SYS. Assuming there is, check to make sure it contains a FILES statement and a BUFFERS statement. The number in the FILES statement should be at least 40 and the number in the BUFFERS statement should be at least 15. If you are absolutely sure there is no CONFIG.SYS file, use any word processor or text editor to create one. It should have the FILES = 40 and BUFFERS = 15 commands in it.

1.7 WORKING WITH dBASE

STARTING dBASE

You need three commands to start dBASE. The commands and their functions are as follows:

Command	**Function**
`path c:\dbase`	Creates the required path to the directory containing dBASE. This command assumes that dBASE is located in a directory called dbase on drive C. (**Note:** If dBASE has been installed in the normal manner, such a path command will be executed automatically for you when you boot your computer. In that case, you can skip this first step. Check with your instructor to see if this is the case.)
`a:`	Makes the drive where you place your data files the default drive. It assumes that your data files are placed on a diskette in drive A. If this is not the case, you need to change this command accordingly.
`dbase`	Loads and starts dBASE.

These commands can be typed in uppercase or lowercase. Remember to press Enter after each command.

After you have completed these steps, dBASE will be loaded into main memory, and the dBASE license agreement will be displayed on the screen. To proceed, press the Enter key again. (If you don't press Enter, dBASE will take you on to the next screen after a short period of time. Pressing Enter at this point simply speeds up the process.)

Before we proceed, you should be aware of the following information when you are working with dBASE:

1. In general, filenames can contain a three-character extension (the characters following the period in the name of the file). dBASE has its own extensions that it adds to filenames. This is nothing for you to worry about. You just indicate the regular part of the name, and dBASE will do the rest automatically. On some screens you will see these extensions, but you need not do anything with them.
2. The *NumLock* key on your keyboard switches your keyboard in and out of NumLock mode. In NumLock mode, you can use the numeric keypad on your keyboard to enter numbers. If you are not in NumLock mode, you use the keypad for cursor movement. (If your keyboard does not have separate cursor movement keys, you will not want to use NumLock. If you have separate cursor movement keys, you can decide to be in NumLock mode; it's up to you.) If you are in NumLock mode, the letters "Num" appear on some screens. The screens shown in the text include these letters. If you are not in NumLock mode, your screen will not include them. This is not a problem. Just be aware of this slight difference between what appears on your screen and what is shown in the text.
3. Most relational database management systems use the terms *table*, *row*, and *column*. dBASE, however, uses the terms *database file*, *record*, and *field*. As you read through the dBASE material, be aware of this difference. The correspondence between the two sets of terms is as follows:

General Term	dBASE Term
table	database file
row	record
column	field

THE CONTROL CENTER

Your screen should now look similar to the one shown in Figure 1.9 on the next page. This is called the Control Center. It is designed to allow nonprogrammers to tap much of the power of dBASE. Although, as programmers, we will work in a different environment, it's worth gaining a general familiarity with the Control Center. In particular, even though you won't work from the Control Center, you will encounter situations in which you will need to select options from menus. You'll do it the same way that you would at the Control Center.

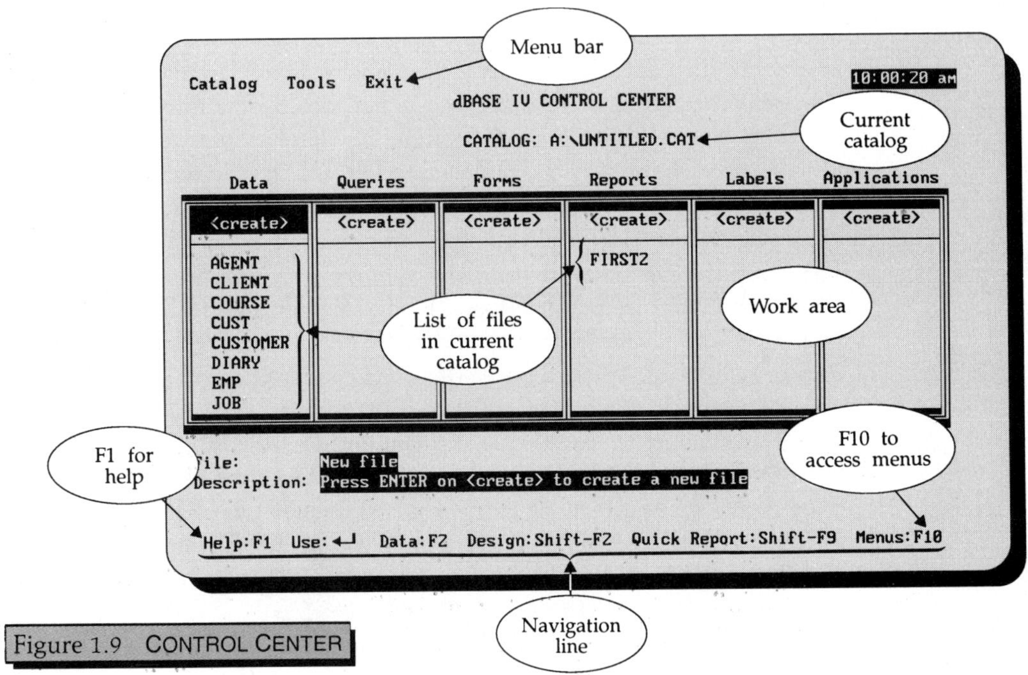

Figure 1.9 CONTROL CENTER

Let's take a look at the various portions of the Control Center. The area at the top of the screen where you see the words "Catalog," "Tools," and "Exit" is called the menu bar. Each of the three terms (Catalog, Tools, and Exit) represents a *menu*. A menu is simply a list of actions from which you can choose. As you work with dBASE, you will encounter times when the row of words at the top of the screen changes, but the menu bar always plays the same role—a collection of menus that you can access to take some desired action. You will see how to use these menus shortly.

Moving down the screen you come to a line that begins CATALOG:. A *catalog* is a collection of related files. (The concept of a catalog is very important at the Control Center, but is not particularly useful in dBASE IV programming.) The CATALOG line on the screen indicates which catalog is currently in use.

The big box on the screen is called the *work area*. It contains a list of files of various types that are in the current catalog. At any given point, either one of these files or <create> will be highlighted. If a file is highlighted, the filename appears after the word File (below the work area) and a description of it appears after the word Description. If <create> is highlighted, the filename and description will appear as shown in Figure 1.9.

Finally, the line at the bottom of the screen is called the *navigation line*. It helps to explain the effect of some special keys. The navigation line in Figure 1.9, for example, shows you that you can press Function key 1 (the key labeled F1 on your keyboard) to obtain help and you can press F10 to use the menus.

PRESSING ESC

The key labeled Esc is called the *Escape key*. Sometimes you might find that you inadvertently choose the wrong option, or that you might not want to proceed with some action you have started, but you're not sure how to get out of it. When this happens, simply press the Esc key. In some cases, this immediately returns you to the Control Center. In others, you may be asked a question first, in which you will indicate whether you really want to escape from the task on which you are working. In yet other situations, you may need to press the Esc key more than once to return to the Control Center.

To illustrate the use of the Esc key, press F10. Your screen should now look like the one in Figure 1.10. You have selected the Catalog menu and, if you desired to, you could choose an option from this menu. Let's suppose that you decide not to make a choice after all.

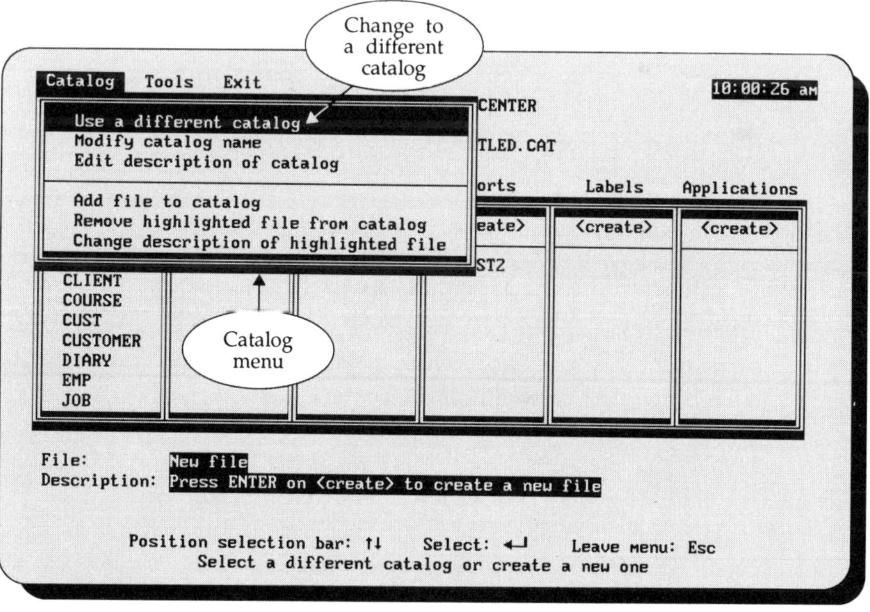

Figure 1.10 CATALOG MENU

Press Esc. The menu is removed from your screen. You are returned to the same state in which you were before you pressed F10. The function of the Esc key is a handy thing to know if you are ever unsure of how to proceed.

USING MENUS

Next, let's examine the way you use menus in dBASE. Press F10. This produces the screen shown in Figure 1.10. You are now in the Menu mode, where you indicate the option you want by selecting it from a menu. Don't worry about the meaning of the specific choices for now. We will get into these later.

The menu currently visible on the screen is the Catalog menu. The possible options, "Use a different catalog," "Modify catalog name," and so on, are listed in the box. Notice that the first choice, "Use a different catalog," is currently highlighted. Press the Down Arrow twice.

You will see the highlight move down through other choices. Whenever an option is highlighted, a brief description of the option appears near the bottom of the screen. Depending on what actions you have taken before you pressed F10, some of these options may not be currently available to you. You don't need to worry about this, however, since the highlight automatically skips over such options.

Press the Up Arrow twice. The highlight will move back up through the choices.

Press the Right Arrow once. Your screen should look like the one in Figure 1.11. You now see a different menu, the Tools menu. Press the Right Arrow again. You see the Exit menu (Figure 1.12).

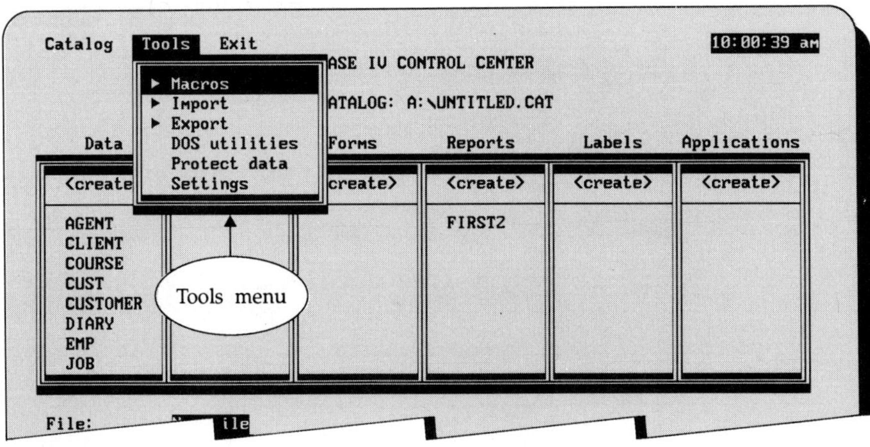

Figure 1.11 TOOLS MENU

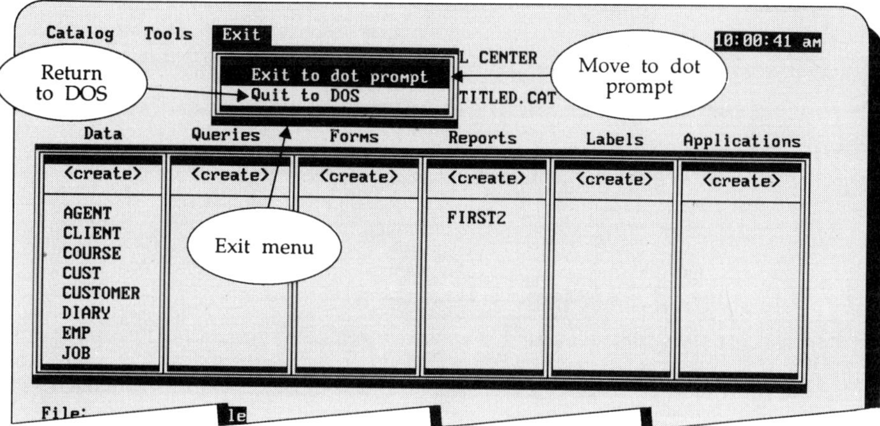

Figure 1.12 EXIT MENU

To recap,

1. To bring the menus to the screen, press F10.
2. To move from one menu to another, use the left and right arrows.
3. To move from one option to another within a menu, use the up and down arrows.

The final step in the process is to actually make the selection. First, make sure the option you want to select is highlighted. Use the appropriate arrow keys to make any necessary adjustments, and press Enter.

(**Note**: There is a shortcut you can use. Hold the Alt key down and type the first letter of the menu (for example, Alt-C for the Catalog menu). The options will then be displayed. Release the Alt key and type the first letter of the option you want.)

THE DOT PROMPT

In addition to the Control Center, there is another way to use dBASE. This other mode, called the *dot prompt*, is the one we will use throughout the text.

If you are at the Control Center and press Esc, you first see a screen similar to the one in Figure 1.13 on the next page. The question in the box asks if you are sure you want to abandon the operation. You will encounter such boxes frequently. Notice that since the "No" choice is already highlighted, you will not abandon what you are doing if you inadvertently press Enter. You would just return to the regular Control Center screen. For now, however, press the Left Arrow to move the highlight to "Yes" and then press Enter.

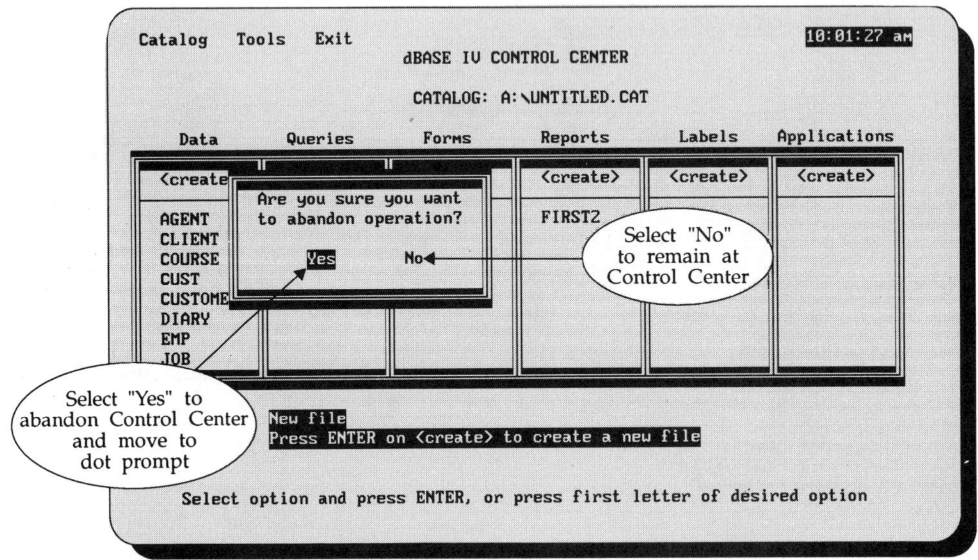

Figure 1.13 "ABANDON OPERATION" QUESTION

Your screen will now look like the one in Figure 1.14. This is the dot prompt. This is the screen we will use throughout the text. If you ever want to move from the dot prompt mode back to the Control Center, press F2. You will again see the Control Center on your screen. **Remember:** Pressing F2 returns you from the dot prompt to the Control Center.

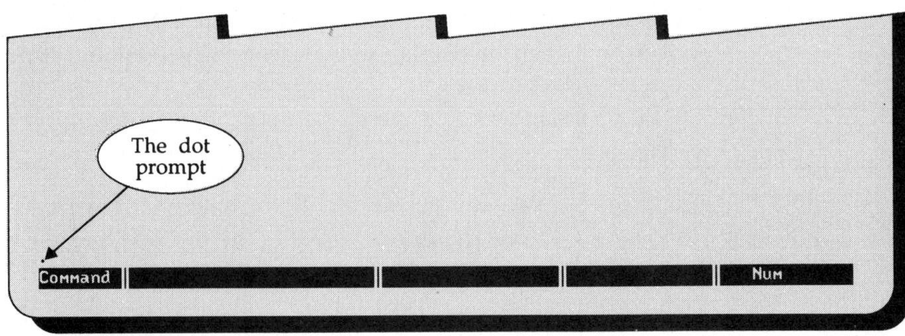

Figure 1.14 DOT PROMPT

"PRESS ANY KEY TO CONTINUE..."

The simplest message you will encounter in dBASE is "Press any key to continue...". It means exactly what it says. Press any key on the keyboard and you can continue what you are doing. This message typically appears when you are displaying a report on the screen. dBASE displays one screenful of the report and then this message. You can look at the displayed portion of the report for as long as you want. When you are ready to move on, press any key and view the next portion of the report.

GETTING HELP

dBASE has an extensive help facility. You can get help on a variety of topics while you are at the computer by simply pressing F1 or by typing HELP at the dot prompt and pressing Enter. If you are at the dot prompt and request help using either approach, you will see a screen similar to the one in Figure 1.15.

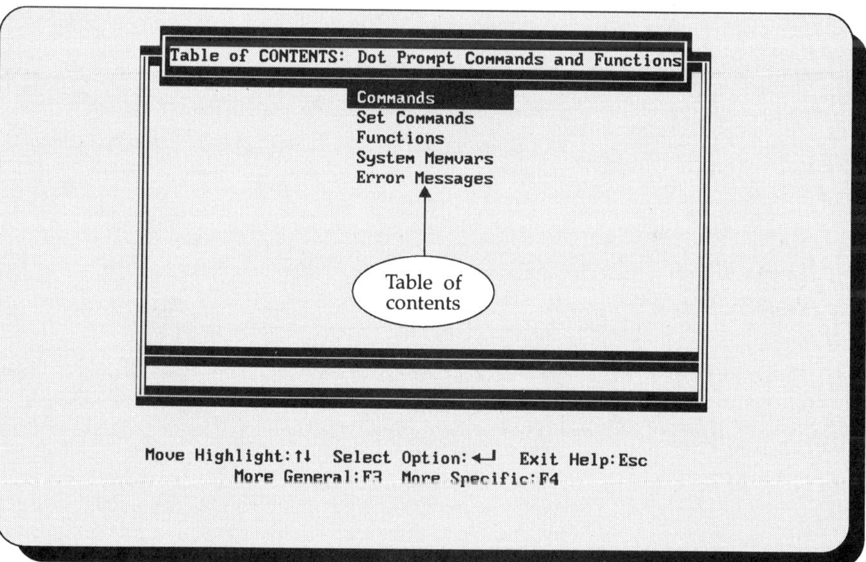

Figure 1.15 INITIAL HELP SCREEN

This is the initial help screen. From here you can browse through the various topics to find the specific information you need. Let's suppose, for example, that you want help on a command and you know the command starts with DISP.

The first step would be to select "Commands" from the list shown in Figure 1.15. Your screen would then look like the one shown in Figure 1.16. You can use the down arrow to move through all the available commands. Alternatively, you could type a letter and immediately move to the section of commands that begin with that letter. In any case, once you move the highlight far enough, you see that the command you want is DISPLAY (Figure 1.17).

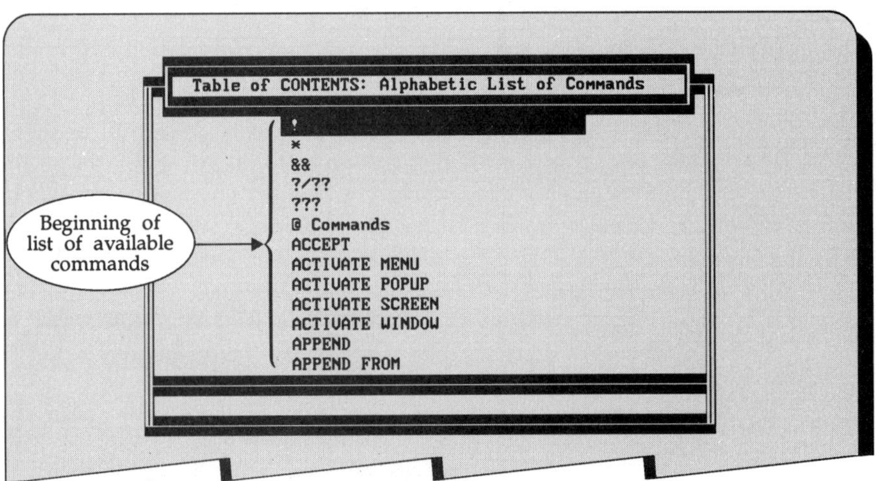

Figure 1.16 GETTING HELP ON COMMANDS—INITIAL SCREEN

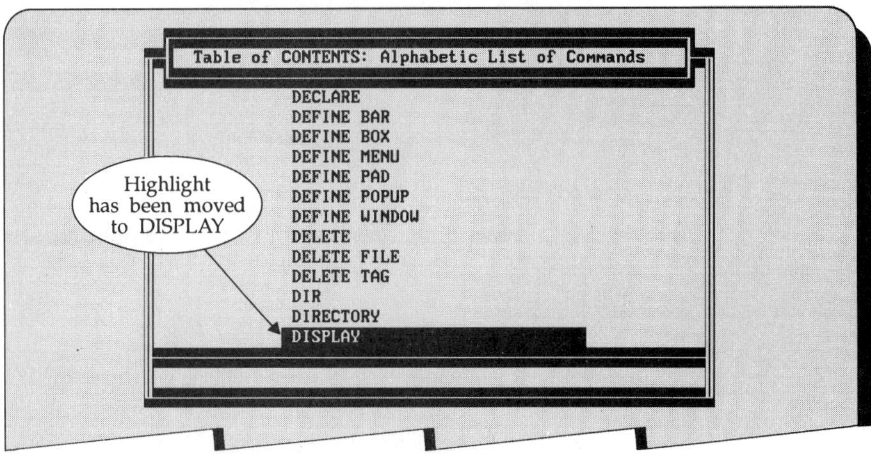

Figure 1.17 GETTING HELP ON THE DISPLAY COMMAND

Once you have highlighted the command in which you are interested, press Enter. You will then see the help information (Figure 1.18). At this point, you have a number of alternatives.

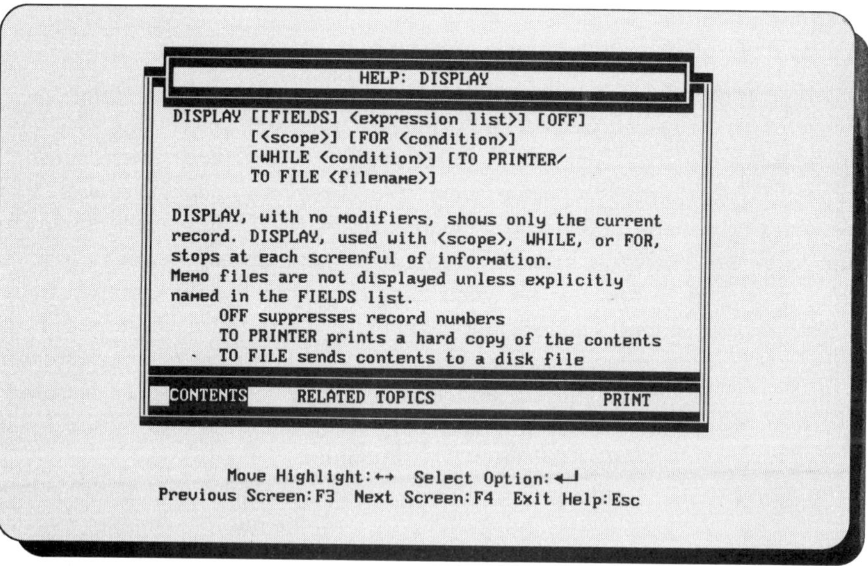

Figure 1.18 HELP ON DISPLAY COMMAND

You can select "Contents" to see a table of contents of help information or "Related Topics" to get information on other topics that are related to the topic at which you are currently looking. You can also select "Print" to get a printed copy of the information (assuming you have a printer attached to your computer). To select any of these, move the highlight to the option you want and press Enter. When you have finished looking, press Esc.

If you happen to know the particular command on which you want help, there is a shortcut. Simply type the word HELP followed by the command. To obtain help on the DISPLAY command, for example, you would type

```
HELP DISPLAY
```

at the dot prompt. You would immediately see information on the DISPLAY command. The remainder of the process would be the same as before.

LEAVING dBASE

To leave dBASE from the dot prompt, type `QUIT` (in either uppercase or lowercase) and press Enter. To leave dBASE from the Control Center, select the "Quit to DOS" option of the Exit menu.

COMMAND CONSTRUCTION

A few guidelines should help you construct commands correctly. Commands in dBASE IV always start with one of the reserved words such as LIST, CREATE, or REPLACE. They are limited in length to 255 characters. Once you have typed the command, you execute it by pressing Enter. dBASE IV ignores blanks or spaces. You can abbreviate commands to the first four letters or more, but you may not misspell them.

You can use certain editing keys to edit commands before you press Enter. The Left and Right Arrow keys move the cursor one character within a command. The Home and End keys move one word forward or backward. The Up and Down Arrow keys redisplay previous commands or move forward to the current command. You can use the Backspace, Insert, or Delete keys to edit commands.

Commands in dBASE IV are constructed in a pattern. In addition to each verb command itself, you may include optional *scopes, expressions,* and *conditions.* Scopes describe the limit of the records affected by the command, such as NEXT 5. Expressions can include field names, constants or literals, variables, and operators or functions. Conditions act as filters to select certain records on the basis of some criterion.

SCOPE examples

NEXT 5—The next five records from the current record
ALL—All the records
REST—The remaining records after the current record

EXPRESSIONS

Any combination of:
Field names—from the structure of the database
Variables—the current contents of variables
Arithmetic operators: + , –, *, /, ^
Logical Operators—.AND., .OR., .NOT.
Relational operators— = , <, > , < > , # , < = , > =
String operators— + , -
Constants—specific data

CONDITIONS

Conditions compare contents of items to test whether a particular relationship is true or false. Records are affected by the command on the basis of this comparison. Chapter 5 discusses conditions more fully.

CHAPTER SUMMARY

1. The effective management of information is critical to businesses. Several terms are associated with the organization of data in a computer system: field, record, file, and database. Database management systems, or DBMSs, collect, store, and report information in an organized way. Advantages of a DBMS include rapid access and flexible use of information, relatively low redundancy, compact storage, and reasonable cost. Its disadvantages include a required level of skill, increased complexity, and required maintenance for centralized information.
2. One of the more popular DBMSs is dBASE IV, with its useful features, widely used programming language, and very large capacity for storing different types of information.
3. Of the three types of DBMSs, dBASE IV is relational, which means that data is accessed by its relative position in a table containing rows and columns. Data is categorized into characters, fields, records, and files. A DBMS can append, modify, delete, and retrieve data. Other types of DBMSs are hierarchical and network.
4. The MS-DOS operating system performs critical functions both in general use and with dBASE IV. Important commands include DIR, COPY DEL, TYPE, and FORMAT.
5. dBASE IV uses several different types of files, which are identified by a file extension. You must follow DOS rules when assigning the first part of the filename.

6. CONFIG.DB and CONFIG.SYS are included on the system disks and can be altered to customize your copy of dBASE IV. Some settings such as FILES and BUFFERS are critical, whereas others make use of the software more convenient.
7. The Control Center allows users to access databases by selecting operations from menus. It is convenient for interactive operation. At the dot prompt, users type commands to access data or to write and execute programs.
8. The on-line HELP feature, which is accessed by pressing F1 or typing HELP, gives explanations of the various commands and features.

KEY TERMS

data
database
network
character
database management system (DBMS)
relational
field
table
record
mainframe
tuple
file
query
attribute
byte
hierarchical
SQL
filename
extension
NumLock key
CONFIG.DB
Escape key
CONFIG.SYS
dot prompt
operating system
scope
MS-DOS
expression
PC-DOS
condition
menu
catalog
work area
navigation line

COMMAND SUMMARY

Command Name	Use
DIR	Display the contents of a directory or disk.
COPY	Copy files.
FORMAT	Format disks.
DEL	Remove a file from a disk.
TYPE	Display contents of a readable file.
CLS	Clear the screen.
CHKDSK	Display disk and memory usage and capacity.
MD	Make a new directory.
CD	Change to another directory.
RD	Remove an empty directory.
QUIT	Close all files and leave dBASE IV.
ASSIST	Return to the Control Center from the dot prompt (typing ASSIST is like pressing F2).
HELP	Start the HELP feature.

SELF-CHECK QUESTIONS

1. List three functions of information management.
2. What is a DBMS? What does it do?
3. Describe three features of dBASE IV.
4. Name two field types and describe how they might be used.
5. If mainframe computers are more powerful than microcomputers, why aren't they used for all business problems? When is it best to use a mainframe?
6. What are some of the disadvantages of using a language like COBOL?
7. Which product, dBASE IV or a mainframe DBMS, would be most suitable for each of the following applications?
   a. A major corporation has to handle the payroll for over 8000 employees.
   b. A health club wants to keep track of its members.
   c. The business department of a community college wants to schedule fourteen classrooms over a five-day period.
   d. A small consulting firm is trying to keep track of its clients and the various services they use.

8. Give some practical examples of a character, a field, a record, and a file.
9. A database file occupies 64 kilobytes. What is the actual number of bytes in the file?
10. What are the four data manipulation functions?
11. What are the three types of DBMSs? What type is dBASE IV?
12. Describe how a relational DBMS stores data.
13. Write five correct filenames for DOS or dBASE IV.

TRY IT YOURSELF

1. Load DOS and issue a command to display all files on your data disk which have a PRG extension.
2. Display all disk files on your data disk, with a pause for each screen.
3. Format a new disk in the drive (or the A drive on a hard disk system) and copy COMMAND.COM from the C drive or a DOS diskette to the new disk. Display the name of the copied file to verify the copy.
4. Delete the file from Exercise 3 and check the space usage on the disk and the status of the computer's memory.
5. Make a subdirectory on the new disk called TEST, and then change to this subdirectory and display the files. Change back to the root directory. Remove the TEST subdirectory.
6. Start dBASE IV. Use the Escape key to leave the Control Center and move to the dot prompt. Leave dBASE from the dot prompt.
7. Use CHKDSK to examine disk and memory usage.
8. In dBASE, type DOR instead of DIR at the dot prompt and then press Enter. Select "Cancel" when you see an error message. Correct and reexecute the command.

9. Leave dBASE IV and return to DOS. List all the files with a PRG extension. List all the files that begin with the word PART and have any extension.
10. Start dBASE IV. Move to the dot prompt. Type a DIR command and compare the result to the display you would get if you typed DIR at the DOS prompt. List the differences between the two commands.
11. Use the HELP feature to answer the following questions:
    a. What does the DELETE FILE command do? What is another name for it?
    b. What does the DATE() function do?
    c. What does the ZAP command do?
    d. List three error messages that start with the word ALIAS.

LEARNING OBJECTIVES

To use the CREATE command to establish a database.

To use the APPEND command to add records.

To use the MODIFY STRUCTURE command to alter the structure of a database.

To modify records with EDIT, BROWSE, and REPLACE.

To remove records with DELETE and PACK.

To display data using the LIST command and the ? command.

2 Interactive Skills

Introduction

As you know, the goal of this text is to help you learn to program. Since programs are actually lists of dBASE IV commands, the first thing you need to understand is how each command operates. Some commands, for example, can be executed only from the dot prompt. Many users who work with data every day use nothing beyond the commands presented here. Mastery of these commands will provide you with an excellent background for the concepts presented in the chapters to follow.

2.1 ESTABLISHING THE DATABASE

DETERMINING THE STRUCTURE OF THE DATABASE

Using dBASE IV to establish a database is a simple process. However, using your computer is only the end of this task. We have all heard Thomas Edison's quote, "Genius is one percent inspiration and ninety-nine percent perspiration." Although the percentages may be somewhat closer together for the creation of a database, the principle is the same. You should spend a reasonable amount of time planning the structure of the database before you begin to enter your specifications into dBASE IV.

You need to have a clear idea of what pieces of information, or data, will be included; for example, a name, a zip code, or an account balance. These data items are referred to as fields. A field can be as short as one letter (M for male, F for female) or in the case of a memo field, thousands of characters in length. These fields must be very rigidly formatted in order for dBASE IV to do its work. This is accomplished by grouping the fields and their individual characteristics into a record. Once the record format has been established, all records stored in the database have this same format. Think of the record format as a blank questionnaire. Each person has to fill in the same "blanks" because they are preprinted on the form, but the information will certainly vary from person to person. You will be guided through the actual process by dBASE IV, but you must know what you want before you begin. Figure 2.1 shows some examples of filled-in fields for each type of data.

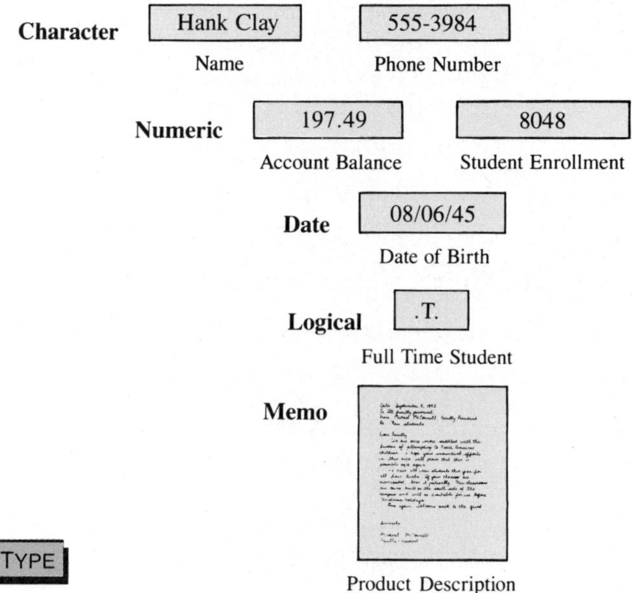

Figure 2.1 dBASE DATA TYPE

You need three or four pieces of information for each field that you plan to include. First, you must give the field a name to which dBASE IV can refer. The rules for dBASE IV field names are more strict than those for DOS filenames. The only special character allowed is the underscore. However, the name may be up to ten characters long. The CREATE screen does not permit you to use illegal characters in your field names nor to enter names that are more than ten characters in length.

Before you consider the other requirements, you should know that computers treat *numeric* values quite differently from *character* or *alphanumeric* data. This is because numeric values are used in arithmetic operations and are stored and handled in a special way by the computer and by dBASE IV. Other than being sure to identify any fields that might be used for calculation as numeric, you need not be concerned about this. There are three other important field types: *date*, *logical*, and *memo*. These will be discussed in Chapter 3. What is important for you to know now is that the second piece of information needed by dBASE IV is the field type. The third thing you must specify is the maximum length of the field. In the event that the field is numeric, you will also need to specify the number of decimal places to be used by dBASE IV.

It is best to plan this structure on paper first. Table 2.1 illustrates how this might be done. The example is a design for a database that can store the names of cities, the state in which the city is located, the population of the city in 1970, and the population of the city in 1982.

TABLE 2.1 Sample database design

FIELD NAME	TYPE	WIDTH	DECIMAL PLACES	INDEX?
CITY	Character	20	—	Y
STATE	Character	2	—	N
POP_70	Numeric	7	0	N
POP_82	Numeric	7	0	N

The width of the CITY field is an educated guess. Some cities' names could be longer than 20 characters, but you are unlikely to encounter them. Note that any extra characters will be truncated (cut off) from the end of the name should the size of the name be larger than the field width. Names with fewer than 20 characters will be filled out to 20 with blanks. The STATE field is easy because we can use the two-letter postal abbreviations.

Since numeric fields contain only digits and decimal points, we can calculate their widths by allowing enough positions to accommodate the largest numeric value we anticipate. Seven digits can represent any value up to 9,999,999, which is more than enough for any city in the United States. The POP_70 and POP_82 fields did not require a decimal point, but an extra position would be needed if a decimal point was required. For example, the dollar value 2187.52 also occupies seven positions: four dollar digits, a decimal point, and two digits for cents. Do not include commas or dollar signs in numeric fields, and allow enough positions for the largest possible number. dBASE IV will not display a number that is too large for its established length.

(**Note:** In Table 2.1 there is a column labeled "Index." We will examine indexes in detail later in the text. We will see how to determine whether to enter a Y or an N in this column. For now, simply make the entries as you see them in the table.)

CREATING THE DATABASE

Now that we have determined these specifications, we are ready to instruct dBASE IV to set up or CREATE the file format on your disk. Start dBASE IV in the same manner you did in Chapter 1 and make sure you are at the dot prompt. (If you see the Control Center, select the "Exit to dot prompt" option of the Exit menu.)

Before we can create our database file, we need to determine a name for it. The filename can be no longer than eight characters and cannot contain blanks or certain special characters. These are the same rules listed for DOS filenames in Chapter 1. Let's use the name CITIES. To begin the process, type

```
CREATE CITIES
```

and press Enter.

You will now see the screen shown in Figure 2.2. This is the CREATE screen (also referred to as the Database Design screen). You use this screen to describe the fields in your database. Table 2.2 provides information concerning the use of some special keys during the CREATE process. Experiment with these as you enter the field information. Most of the keys are self-explanatory, except for those beginning with Ctrl. This symbol means that you should hold down the Control key (Ctrl) while you press the next key. For example, to delete an entire field, hold down the Ctrl key while you type the letter U.

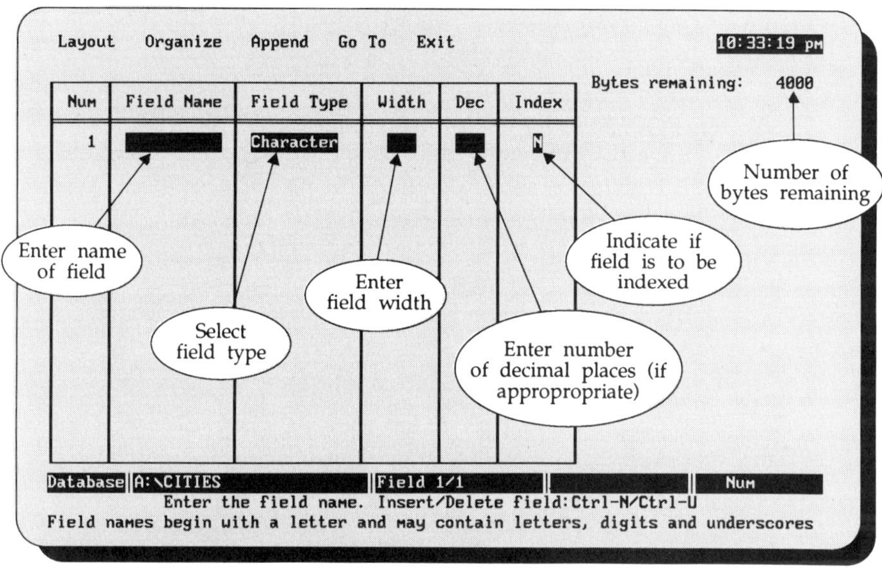

Figure 2.2 THE CREATE SCREEN

TABLE 2.2 Special keys used when designing a database

KEY	PURPOSE
↑	Moves the highlight up one row
↓	Moves the highlight down one row
→	Moves the cursor one position to the right
←	Moves the cursor one position to the left
[Tab]	Moves the cursor one column to the right
[Shift-Tab]	Moves the cursor one column to the left
[Backspace]	Moves cursor one position to the left and erases character that was in that position
[Enter]	Completes current entry and moves cursor to the next column. If you are in the last column in a row, moves to the first column in the next row
[Ctrl-N]	Inserts a blank row at current cursor position
[Ctrl-U]	Deletes row at current cursor position
[Ctrl-End]	Saves your work
[Esc]	Abandons your work without saving. (As a safety feature, dBASE will ask you if you wish to do so)

At the bottom of the CREATE screen, dBASE IV includes some useful information. The active disk drive, the filename, and the current field number are displayed above a message area where you are prompted for your next task. Below the prompt is a description of the task.

You will discover while working with the CREATE screen that you can move easily among the highlighted blocks to enter, edit, or delete your entries. Enter information following the steps listed in Table 2.3 until your screen looks the same as the one in Figure 2.3.

TABLE 2.3 Completing the CREATE screen

1. Type CITY in the Field Name block and press Enter.
2. Press the Enter key in the Type block.
3. Type 20 in the Width block and press Enter.
4. Type Y in the Index block.
5. Type STATE in the Field Name block and press Enter.
6. Press the Enter key in the Type block.
7. Type 2 in the Width block and press Enter.
8. Type N in the Index block.
9. Type POP_70 in the third Field Name block.
10. Press the space bar to change the Type to Numeric and press Enter.
11. Type 7 in the Width block and press Enter.
12. Press Enter in the Decimal Places block to accept 0.
13. Type N in the Index block.
14. Complete the blocks for POP_82 as in steps 9 through 13.

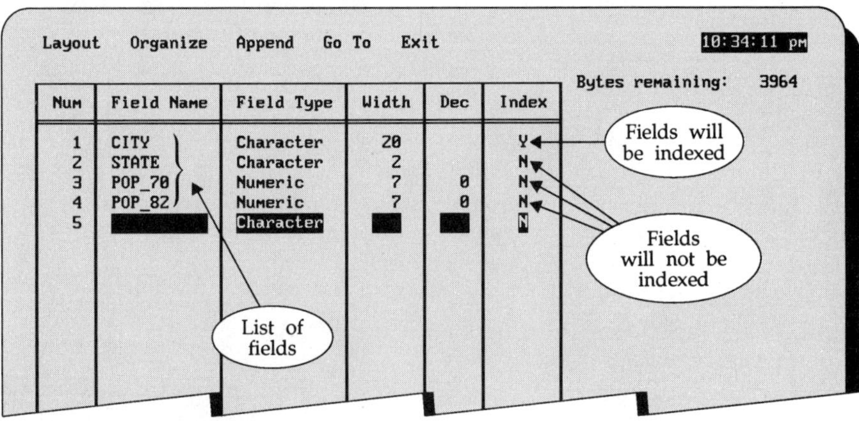

Figure 2.3 THE FINISHED CREATE SCREEN

After you have made all the entries, you can save the information and leave the CREATE screen by selecting the "Save changes and exit" option of the Exit menu. You can also do so by simply pressing the Enter key on the Field Name portion of a new field. In this case, you will see this message:

```
Press ENTER to confirm. Any other key to resume
```

Press Enter in response to the message. dBASE IV will then save the file. It will add an extension *DBF* (*database file*) to the name you selected. The actual name of your database on disk will thus be CITIES.DBF.

USING A DATABASE

Now that you have created the CITIES.DBF database file, you need to be able to access it. To do so, you must open it (activate it). The command to open a database is USE followed by the name of the database file (you do not need to include the DBF extension). To open the CITIES database, at the dot prompt type

```
USE CITIES
```

Once the CITIES.DBF file is in use, you can view the structure by typing DISPLAY STRUCTURE as shown in Figure 2.4. Notice that the total of the lengths of the four fields appears to be overstated by one (the total should be 36). This is because one position is reserved in case the record must be marked for deletion later.

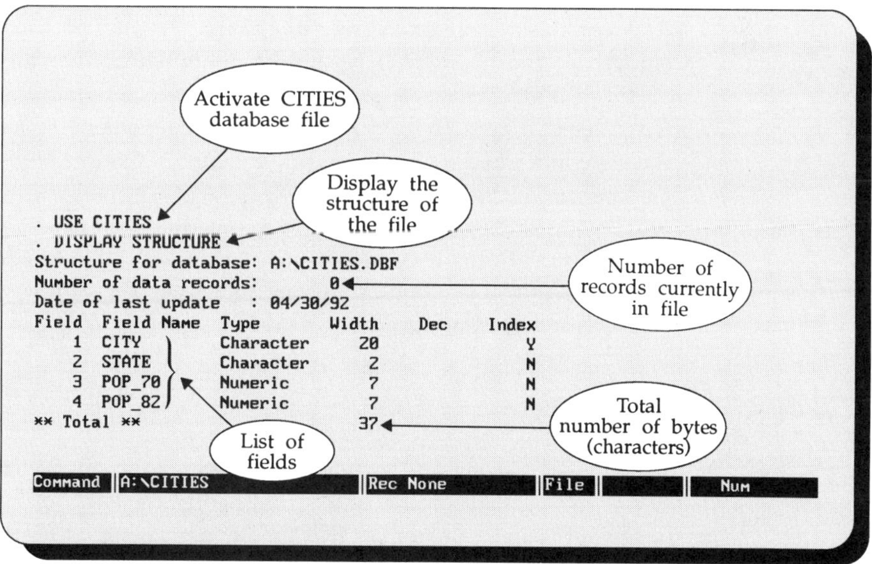

Figure 2.4 THE STRUCTURE OF CITIES.DBF

It may be helpful to think of a database file as a drawer full of record cards in a file cabinet. To use the record cards, you must, of course, open the drawer. It is also wise to close the drawer when you are finished in order to avoid accidental damage to the information. To close a database, either open another or simply type the word USE and immediately press Enter.

UPDATING A DATABASE

Three essential tasks keep the file properly updated: APPENDing, or adding; EDITing, or modifying; and DELETE(ing) record cards. We will consider the order of the record cards later; for now, think of the record cards as being numbered in the order in which they are added to the file.

Let's use the analogy of a drawer in a file cabinet to describe the three tasks for updating a file. To APPEND, or add, a record card to the file, you might have to allow some room at the end of the drawer and then insert the new record card when the information has been filled in. You could, of course, APPEND a record card that was only partially complete or even empty, and then complete it later.

Changing (EDITing) existing information on a record card would require searching through the numbers, pulling out the proper card, and making the change. You could replace the card in its correct numeric position within the file when you finished.

The records would be easier to work with if they were numbered both sequentially and consecutively; that is, in order with no numbers missing. However, this system of numbering would present a problem: anytime you removed a record, a number would be eliminated from the file. The only solution, as difficult as it sounds, would be to renumber the file anytime you deleted a record. It might be more convenient to first "mark" the records you wished to delete, and then actually remove and renumber them at a later time.

These tasks are performed upon your database file in a similar fashion by dBASE IV. In the following sections you will learn to add, modify, and delete records. You will also gain an understanding of how these functions operate in programming.

2.2 ADDING RECORDS

The APPEND command provides the means to add records to a database. To use this or any of the other commands we will be investigating, the database file must be active. If it is not, activate it with a USE command.

Once the database file is active, type

```
APPEND
```

at the dot prompt and press Enter. A pointer will then be positioned at the next available physical record number. For example, if there are currently ten records in the database file and you issue an APPEND command, the record pointer is placed at eleven. You are then presented with a screen that reflects the structure CREATEd earlier (Figure 2.5 on the next page). You will use this screen to enter or edit records. Table 2.4 shows special keys you can use when you enter data.

TABLE 2.4 **Special keys used when entering data**

KEY	PURPOSE
↑	Moves the cursor up one row
↓	Moves the cursor down one row
→	Moves the cursor one position to the right
←	Moves the cursor one position to the left
[Tab]	Moves to the next field
[Shift-Tab]	Moves to the previous field
[Page Down]	Moves to next record if you are on "Edit" screen. Moves down one screenful if you are on "Browse" screen
[Page Up]	Moves to previous record if you are on "Edit" screen. Moves up one screenful if you are on "Browse" screen
[Home]	Moves to beginning of field if you are on "Edit" screen. Moves to first field in record if you are on "Browse" screen
[End]	Moves to end of field if you are on "Edit" screen. Moves to last field in record if you are on "Browse" screen
[Backspace]	Moves cursor one position to the left and erases character that was in that position
[Delete]	Deletes character at current cursor position
[Enter]	Completes current entry and moves cursor to the next field
[Ctrl-Y]	Deletes all characters to the right of the cursor
[F2]	Changes between "Edit" and "Browse" screens
[Insert]	Switches between Insert mode and Replace mode. If in Insert mode "Ins" will be displayed on the status line
[Esc]	Leaves the entry process without saving changes to the current record (other changes have already been saved)
[Ctrl-End]	Leaves the entry process saving changes to the current record (other changes have already been saved). If you are on the first field of a new record, this will save a blank record in your database file

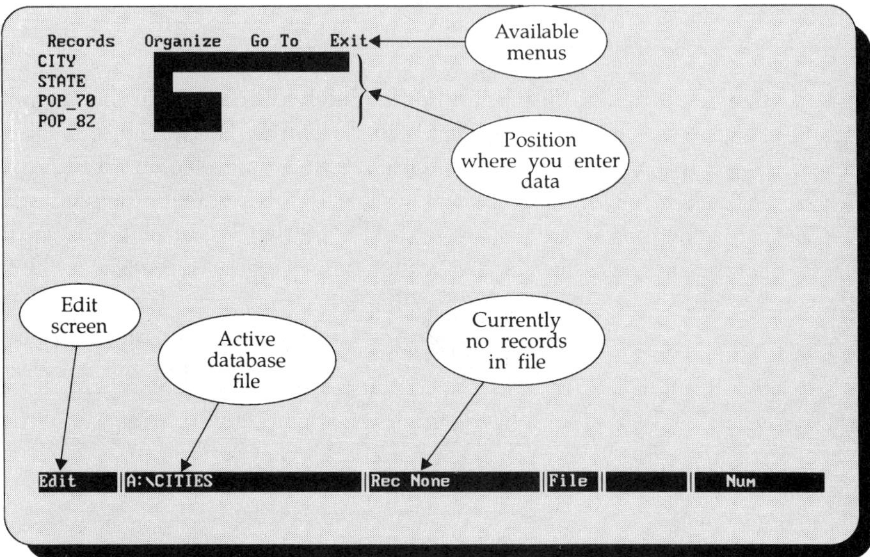

Figure 2.5 THE APPEND SCREEN

Your field names are listed to the left of the highlighted blocks. You may now enter data in the fields and modify the data using the keys shown in the table. The data is shown in Figure 2.6. When you have completely entered the data for a record, dBASE stores that record, advances to the next record number, and gives you an empty form for data entry. At this point you may enter additional data. When you have entered all the records you wish to enter, select the "Exit" option of the Exit menu.

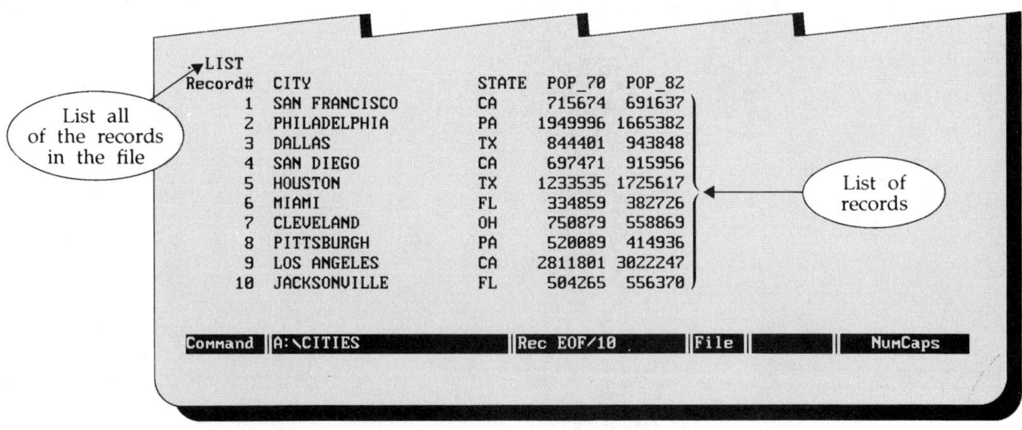

Record#	CITY	STATE	POP_70	POP_82
1	SAN FRANCISCO	CA	715674	691637
2	PHILADELPHIA	PA	1949996	1665382
3	DALLAS	TX	844401	943848
4	SAN DIEGO	CA	697471	915956
5	HOUSTON	TX	1233535	1725617
6	MIAMI	FL	334859	382726
7	CLEVELAND	OH	750879	558869
8	PITTSBURGH	PA	520089	414936
9	LOS ANGELES	CA	2811801	3022247
10	JACKSONVILLE	FL	504265	556370

Figure 2.6 RESULT OF THE LIST COMMAND

Since the file is still open, you can LIST the records by typing LIST from the dot prompt, as shown in Figure 2.6.

2.3 MODIFYING THE STRUCTURE

On occasion, you may have to change the structure of a database file. Perhaps a new field will be required or one will have to be deleted. You may need to increase or decrease the length of a field or change the number of decimal positions. These changes can be accomplished with the MODIFY STRUCTURE command. Make sure the database file you wish to change is active and then type

```
MODIFY STRUCTURE
```

You will then see the same Database Design (CREATE) screen you used when you first created the file. You can now make changes to the structure. Just as when you created the file, you can use the keys shown in Table 2.2. It's a good idea to avoid changing the name of a field since dBASE may not be able to retain the data in a field whose name has been changed.

To illustrate the process, create a database file called STOCKS. Its structure is shown in Figure 2.7.

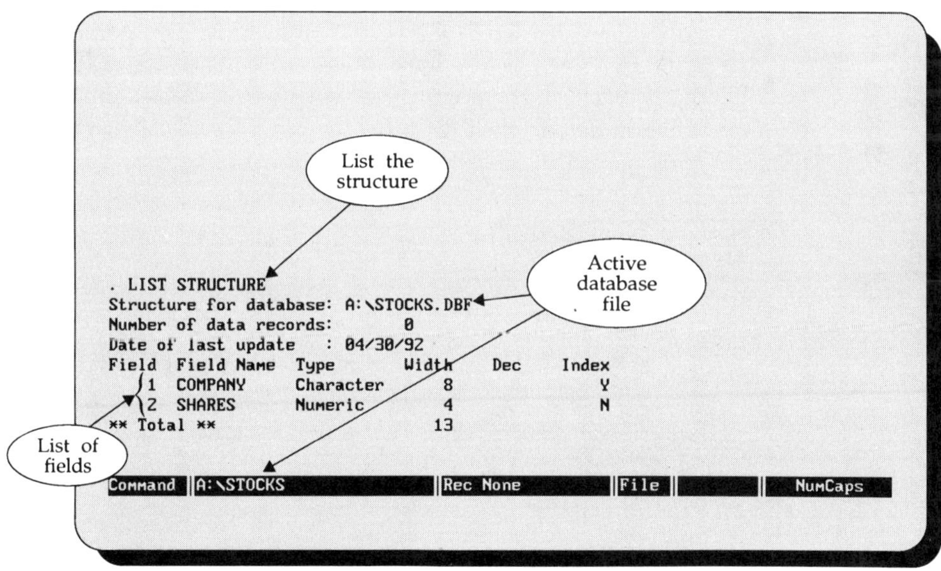

Figure 2.7 STRUCTURE FOR STOCKS.DBF

Next use APPEND to add the records shown in Figure 2.8. Once you have done so, type

```
MODIFY STRUCTURE
```

and press Enter. You will now see the same CREATE screen you saw earlier.

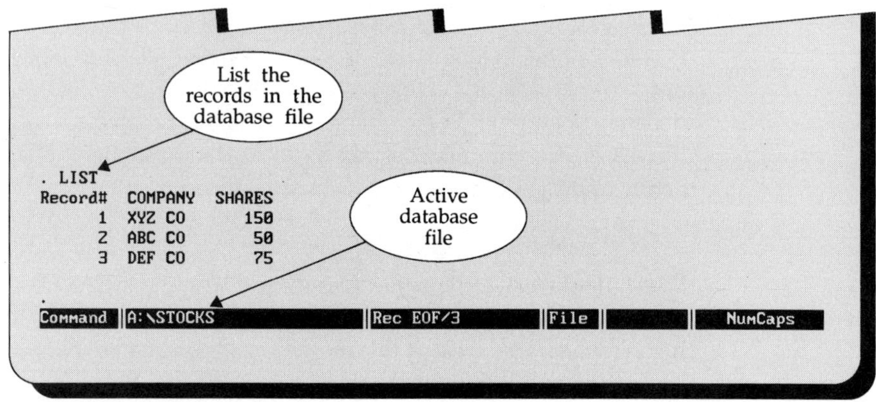

Figure 2.8 DATA IN STOCKS.DBF

Change the length of COMPANY to 10 and add the PRICE field shown in Figure 2.9 with MODIFY STRUCTURE. Once you have done so, leave the CREATE screen as you have done before. Then type LIST as shown in Figure 2.9 to check the accuracy of your work. (**Note:** In the next section you will add data to the PRICE field.)

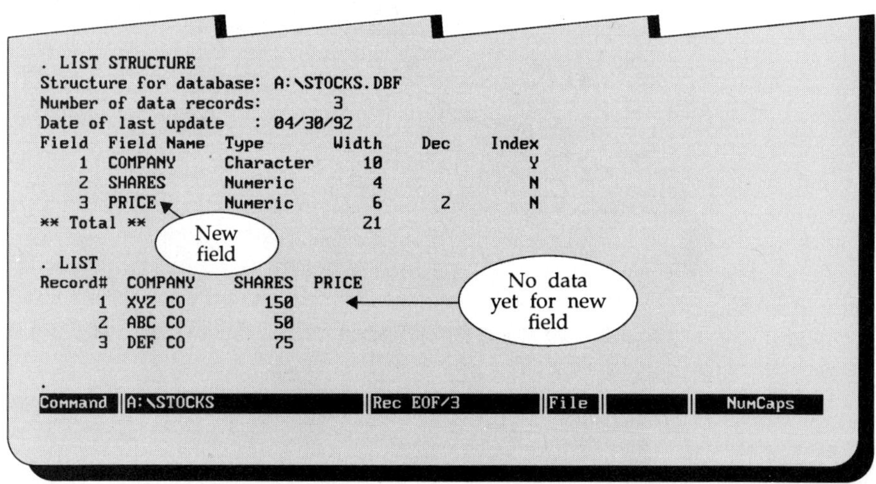

Figure 2.9 RESULTS OF MODIFY STRUCTURE

2.4 RECORD MODIFICATION

dBASE IV provides several methods to modify the data in existing records. These include EDIT, BROWSE, REPLACE, and GET/READ. Of these, the main commands used in programming are REPLACE and GET/READ, which will be covered in Chapter 10. All of these commands act upon records that are already part of the database file and all are important.

To begin, activate the CITIES database with the USE command. It would be best to work with a copy of the database while working with the next few commands in order to preserve the original data in CITIES. To create such a copy, type the following two commands:

```
COPY TO TEMP WITH PRODUCTION
USE TEMP
```

The first command makes a copy of the structure and data in CITIES and names the copy TEMP. (The WITH PRODUCTION clause causes dBASE to make a copy of an important related file called the *production index file*. The details concerning this related file are not important for this discussion. We will investigate them later.)

The second command activates the TEMP database file that the COPY command just created. The following commands will now act upon the TEMP file rather than the CITIES file. You can list the data in TEMP.DBF to reassure yourself that this copy of your file is identical to the original.

USING EDIT TO CHANGE RECORDS

To edit records, you use the EDIT command. You may access a specific record by including the proper record number in the EDIT command. This positions a special internal marker called the *record pointer* at a specific point in the file. For example, to edit record 3, type

```
EDIT 3
```

After you press Enter, you are presented with a screen like the one in Figure 2.10 on the next page. This is the same screen you used when you added records. This time, however, the form will not be blank but will instead contain the data for record 3. (If you do not include a record number in the EDIT command, the record you see will be the record at which you happen to be currently positioned.)

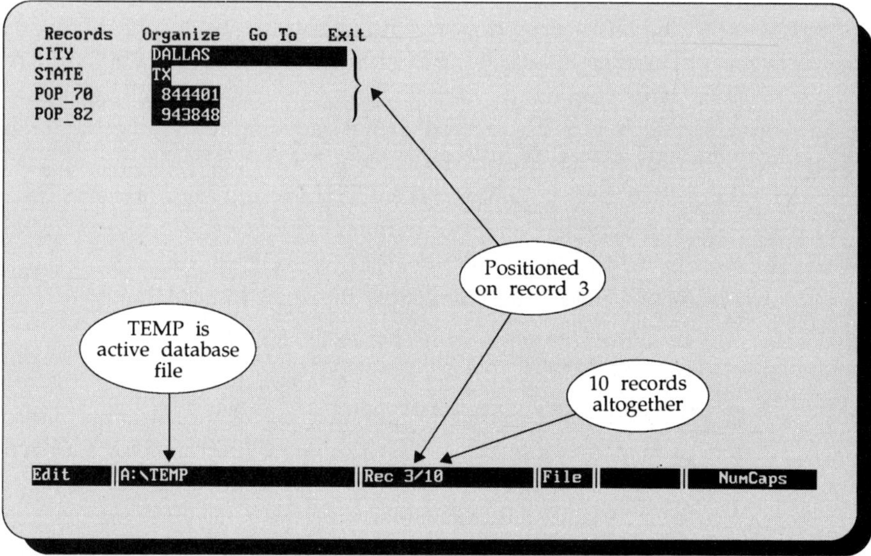

Figure 2.10 THE EDIT SCREEN

If the record on the screen is not the record you want to change, you can move to another record by pressing either Page Up (which moves you to the previous record) or Page Down (which moves you to the next record). Since the number of the record currently on the screen is always displayed on the status line and since your database file is very small, this is not a problem. (This would be very cumbersome if your file were large. Fortunately there are other ways to move between records. For now, however, simply follow this procedure.)

In any case, once the desired record is on the screen, repeatedly press the Tab key until the cursor is on the field to be changed. One way to correct the data in the field is to completely retype the contents of the field with the correct data. Another way is to use the keys shown in Table 2.4. Use whichever seems simplest to you.

After you have corrected the data in the field, press Enter. If you need to make other changes to this record, make them in the same way. If you need to correct other records, use Page Up or Page Down to move to them and make the corrections. When you are done, select the "Exit" option from the Exit menu.

Use this technique to change the name of the city in record 3 to AUSTIN, change the value in POP_70 to 156905 and the value in POP_82 to 168107. Once you have done so, list the data in the database file to make sure your changes were made correctly.

USING BROWSE TO CHANGE RECORDS

Another way to change data is to use BROWSE. When you use BROWSE, several records are displayed on the screen in the form of a list. To use BROWSE, make sure your database file is active and type BROWSE. To change the price data in the STOCKS database file, for example, type

```
USE STOCKS
BROWSE
```

You will now see the BROWSE screen (Figure 2.11). To change any record it must be highlighted. You can move the highlight to another record by using the Up and Down Arrow keys. Once you have moved the highlight to the correct record, you need to move it to the field to be changed. To move the highlight one field to the right, press the Tab key. To move it to the left, press Shift-Tab (hold down the Shift key while you press the Tab key). You can then correct the data in the field by typing the correct data over the old data. After you have made all your corrections, select the "Exit" option of the Exit menu.

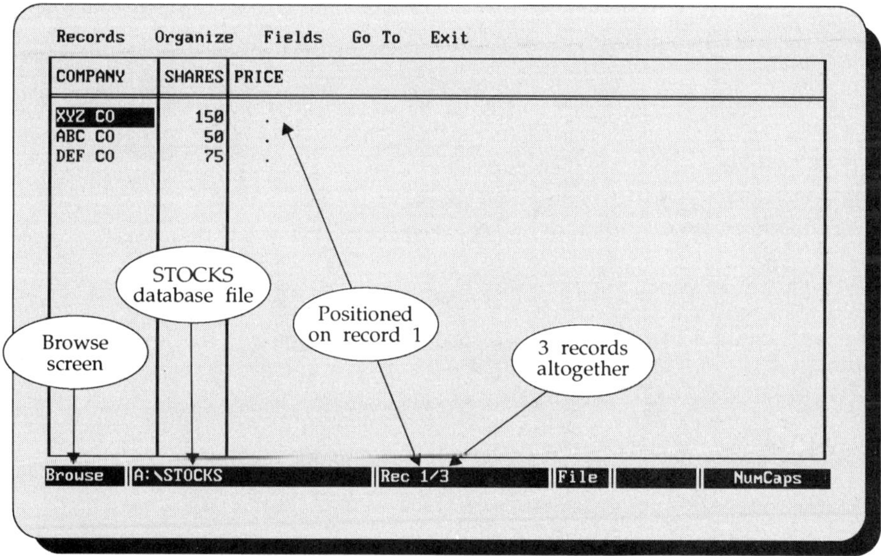

Figure 2.11 THE BROWSE SCREEN

(**Note:** If you make a change to the last field of the last record, dBASE will ask you if you wish to add records. Assuming you don't want to add any records, simply press N.)

Use this technique now to add the prices in the STOCK database file, so that your screen looks like the one shown in Figure 2.12. After you have completed this process, use the same technique to change the data on the third record of the TEMP database file back to its original state (DALLAS, 844401, and 943848 for CITY, POP_70, and POP_82, respectively).

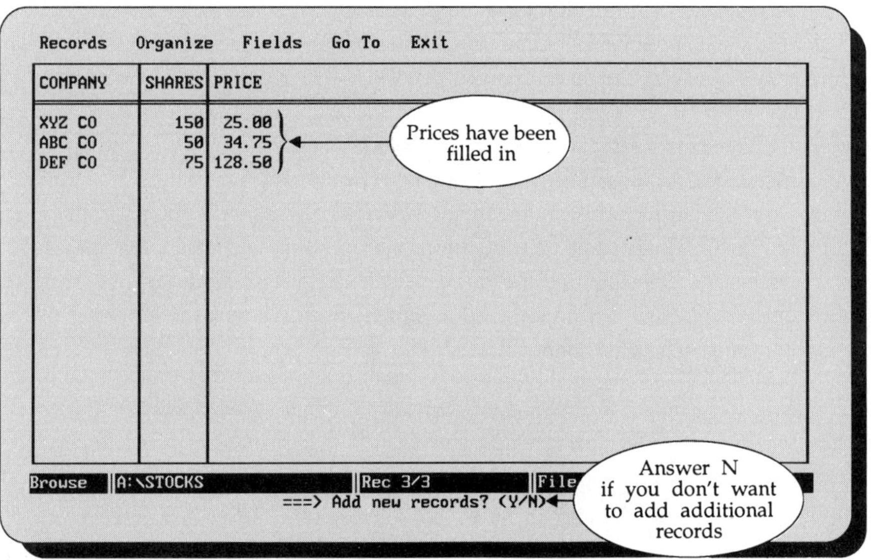

Figure 2.12 THE BROWSE SCREEN: ADDING VALUES

USING REPLACE TO CHANGE RECORDS

REPLACE is useful both in programs and at the dot prompt. To illustrate the use of REPLACE, be sure the TEMP database is open and access record 6 by typing GO 6. Next type a DISPLAY command to display the record (see Figure 2.13).

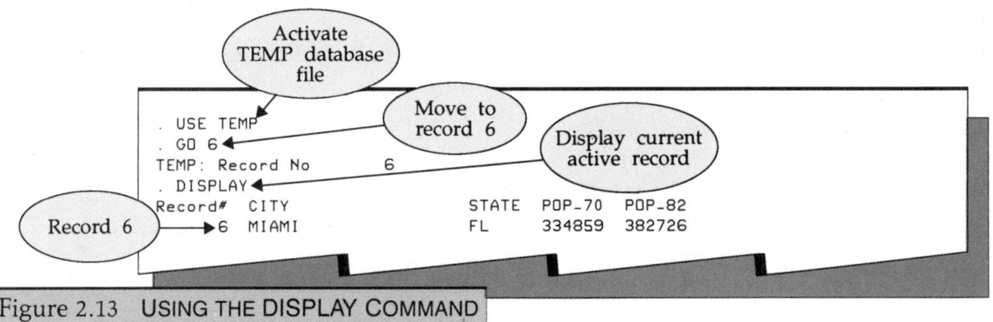

Figure 2.13 USING THE DISPLAY COMMAND

Let's change the CITY on this record to GREATER MIAMI. To do so, type the REPLACE command shown in Figure 2.14 and then type the word DISPLAY to see that the change has been made.

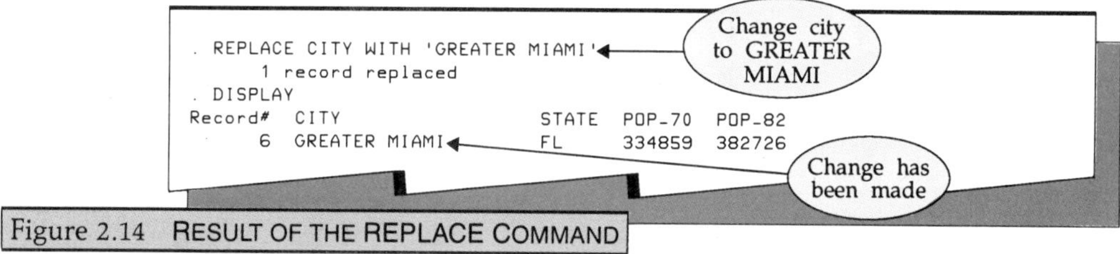

Figure 2.14 RESULT OF THE REPLACE COMMAND

2.5 REMOVING RECORDS

Removing records is a two-step process in dBASE. The first step is to *mark records for deletion*. The second step is to *physically remove the marked records*.

We will illustrate the process by removing the sixth record from the TEMP database file. Since this is just a copy of the original file, there is no harm in doing so. The command to delete (mark) this record is shown in Figure 2.15.

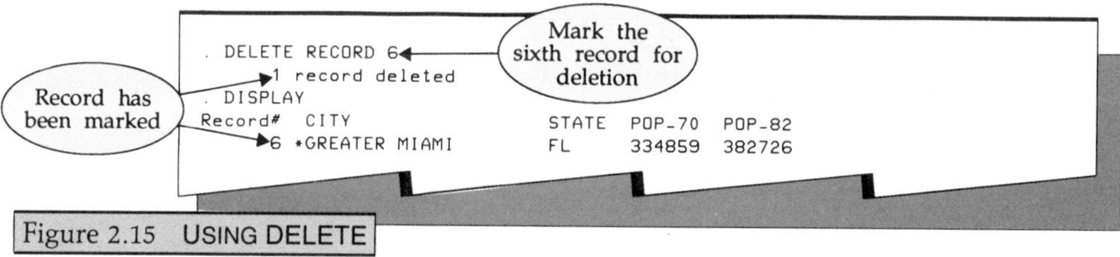

Figure 2.15 USING DELETE

If you use the LIST command, you can see the results of the DELETE, which are shown in Figure 2.16 on the next page. Notice that record 6 contains an asterisk (*). You can use the RECALL command to remove the asterisk from a deleted record. (See Figure 2.17 also on the next page.) This prevents the record from being deleted during the PACK operation.

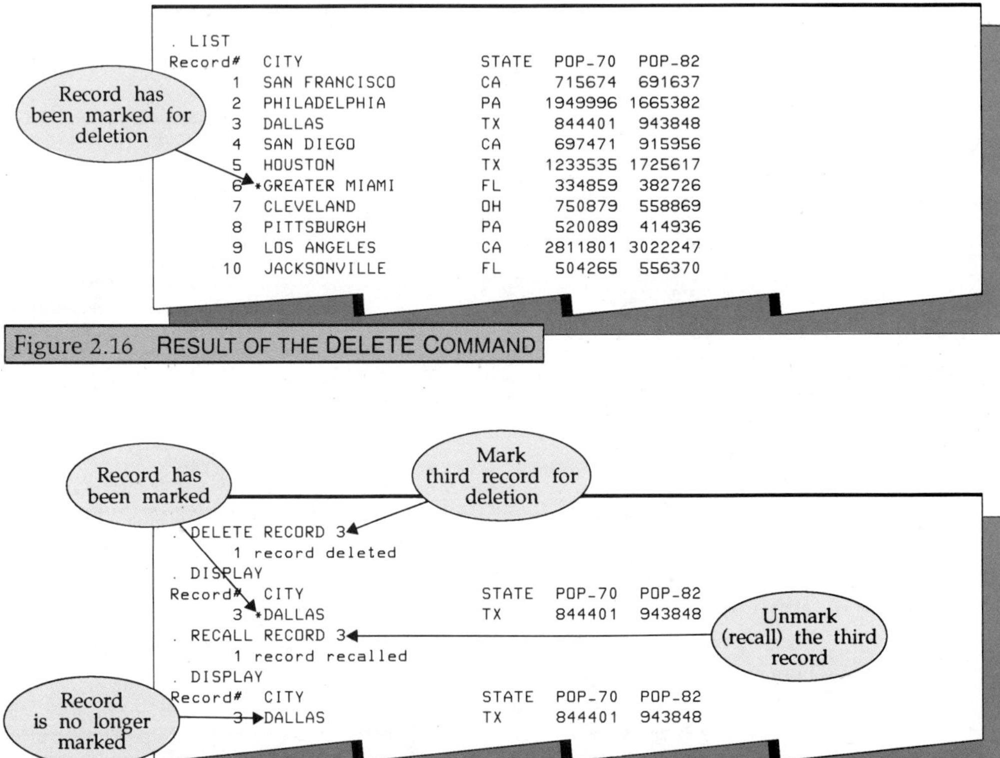

. LIST
Record# CITY STATE POP_70 POP_82
1 SAN FRANCISCO CA 715674 691637
2 PHILADELPHIA PA 1949996 1665382
3 DALLAS TX 844401 943848
4 SAN DIEGO CA 697471 915956
5 HOUSTON TX 1233535 1725617
6 *GREATER MIAMI FL 334859 382726
7 CLEVELAND OH 750879 558869
8 PITTSBURGH PA 520089 414936
9 LOS ANGELES CA 2811801 3022247
10 JACKSONVILLE FL 504265 556370
Record has been marked for deletion

Figure 2.16 RESULT OF THE DELETE COMMAND

. DELETE RECORD 3
1 record deleted
. DISPLAY
Record# CITY STATE POP_70 POP_82
3 *DALLAS TX 844401 943848
. RECALL RECORD 3
1 record recalled
. DISPLAY
Record# CITY STATE POP_70 POP_82
3 DALLAS TX 844401 943848
Record has been marked
Mark third record for deletion
Unmark (recall) the third record
Record is no longer marked

Figure 2.17 USING RECALL

Once you have made sure that you have marked the correct set of records, you remove them with the PACK command. The results are shown in Figure 2.18. Notice that the "Greater Miami" record is now missing and that the records that had followed it have changed their positions in the file to eliminate the gap.

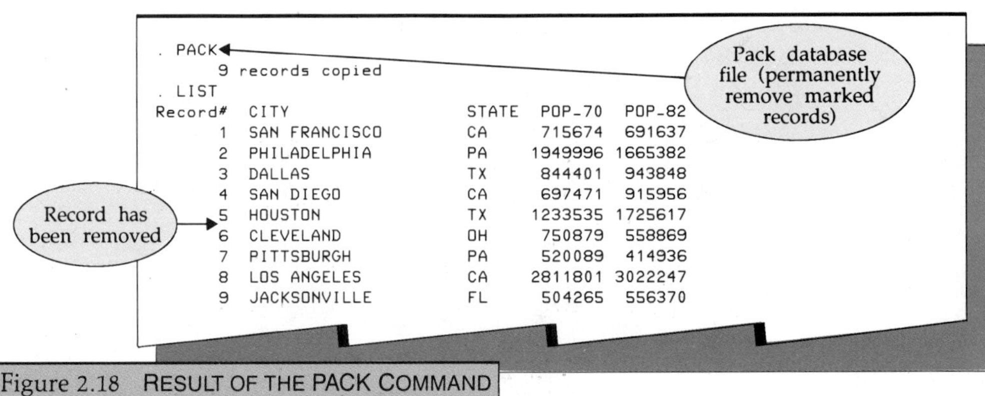

. PACK
9 records copied
. LIST
Record# CITY STATE POP_70 POP_82
1 SAN FRANCISCO CA 715674 691637
2 PHILADELPHIA PA 1949996 1665382
3 DALLAS TX 844401 943848
4 SAN DIEGO CA 697471 915956
5 HOUSTON TX 1233535 1725617
6 CLEVELAND OH 750879 558869
7 PITTSBURGH PA 520089 414936
8 LOS ANGELES CA 2811801 3022247
9 JACKSONVILLE FL 504265 556370
Pack database file (permanently remove marked records)
Record has been removed

Figure 2.18 RESULT OF THE PACK COMMAND

2.6 DISPLAYING DATA

You have seen how the LIST command was used earlier in this chapter to display all the data in a database file on the screen. Although LIST is more flexible and powerful than earlier examples indicate, like EDIT, it is of limited use in programs. It is helpful to be skilled in using LIST from the dot prompt, however, and the following examples illustrate its use.

Before using the LIST command, the file CITIES.DBF must be active. If it is not, type

```
USE CITIES
```

and press Enter.

You can specify the fields you want to LIST, as shown in Figure 2.19.

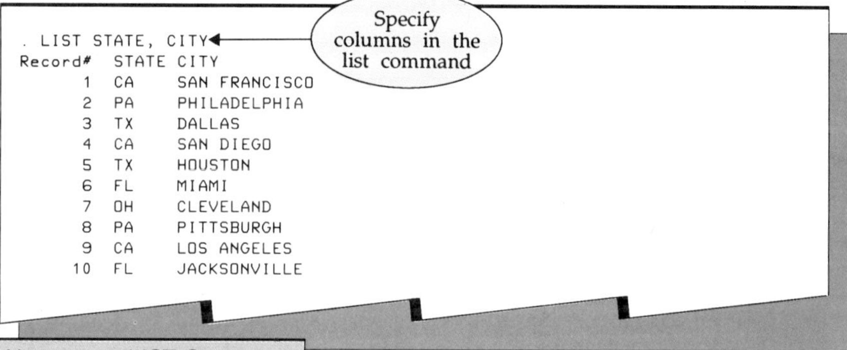

Figure 2.19 USING THE LIST COMMAND

Performing an arithmetic operation on numeric fields while LISTing can produce interesting results. For example, you can compare the population growth of all the cities. Figure 2.20 shows the results of this comparison. You will find that you can LIST fields in any combination.

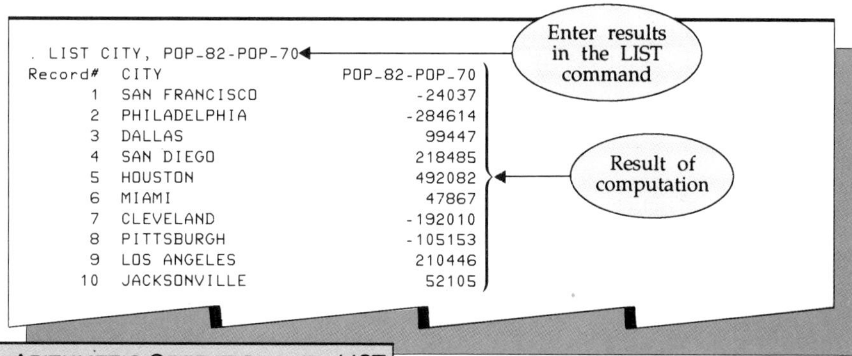

Figure 2.20 ARITHMETIC OPERATION WITH LIST

If you wish to be selective while LISTing records, specify a criterion by placing one of the *relational operators* between a field name and a specific expression. The expression will contain a piece of data that dBASE IV can use for comparison. Character (alphanumeric) data must be placed within a set of quotation marks (' ' or " "). Never use quotes with numeric information, and avoid nonnumeric symbols such as the dollar sign and the comma. Effectively writing these comparison expressions, or conditions, is a skill that you will use frequently when programming. The relational operators are shown in Table 2.5.

TABLE 2.5 **The relational operators**

OPERATOR	MEANING
=	Equal to
<	Less than
>	Greater than
< =	Less than or equal to
> =	Greater than or equal to
# or < >	Not equal to

Notice how the conditions in the next few examples are constructed, and observe the results on the displayed data in Figure 2.21. In this example, dBASE IV tested the first three characters of the CITY field of each record and displayed the records that matched, regardless of what was contained in the subsequent characters. Sometimes this kind of test may be helpful, but a more specific comparison may be required on occasion.

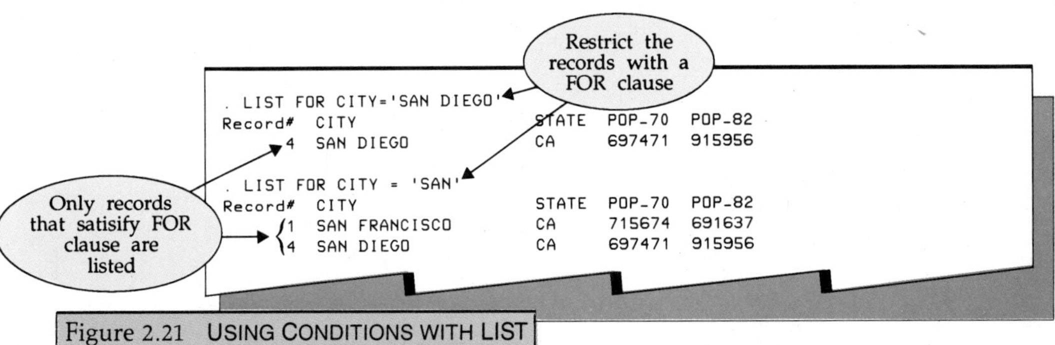

Figure 2.21 USING CONDITIONS WITH LIST

The SET EXACT ON command allows only the fields that match perfectly to be displayed. In the example in Figure 2.22, none of the city names matched 'SAN' exactly, so no records are displayed.

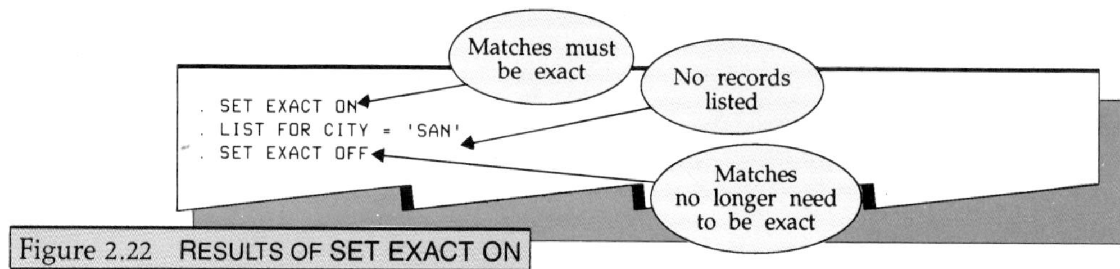

Figure 2.22 RESULTS OF SET EXACT ON

An example of a numeric comparison is shown in Figure 2.23. Notice that only cities with a 1982 population of fewer than 1,000,000 are displayed. If you were interested in Pennsylvania cities in this category, you might do another LIST and compare, as shown in Figure 2.24.

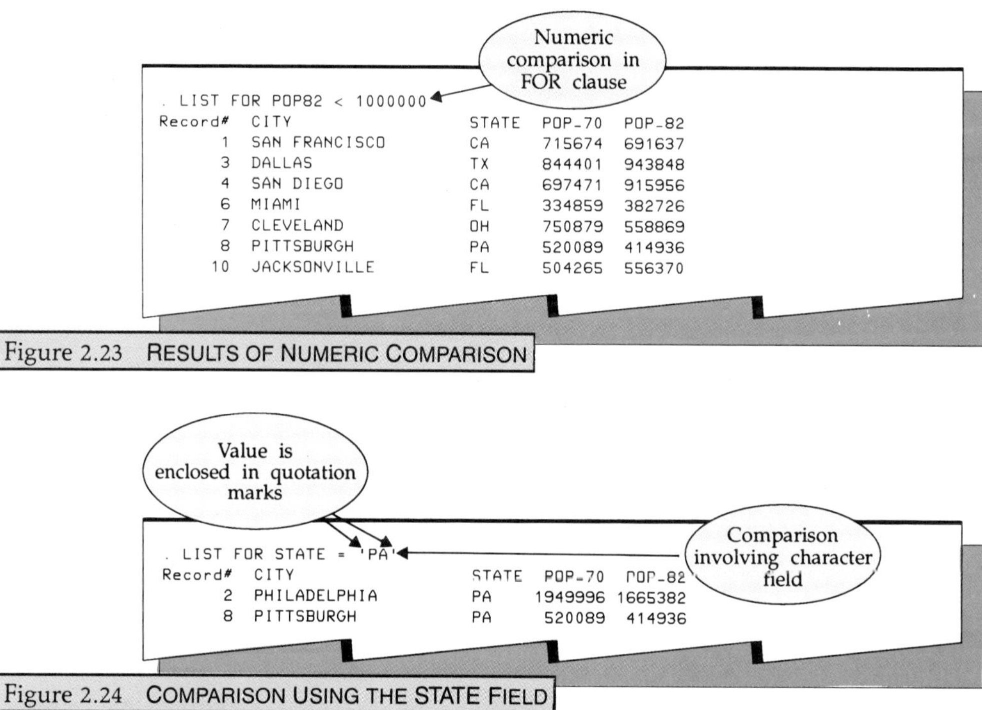

Figure 2.23 RESULTS OF NUMERIC COMPARISON

Figure 2.24 COMPARISON USING THE STATE FIELD

A more convenient way to accomplish the same result is to combine the two tests with .AND., a *logical operator*. Logical operators (.AND., .OR., and .NOT.) combine the effects of logical tests. (See Figure 2.25 on the next page.) This will prove to be a useful technique in Chapter 6. Notice that logical operators must be enclosed between periods.

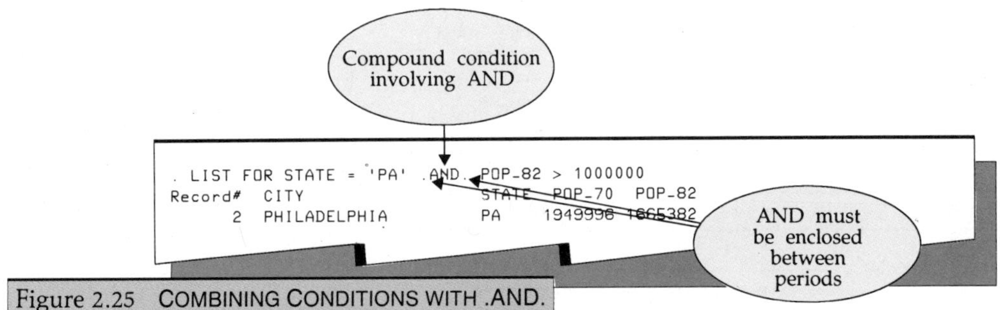

Figure 2.25 COMBINING CONDITIONS WITH .AND.

Another way to display data is to use the question mark (?). The ? allows you to display a string of characters, data in a field, or an expression. In Figure 2.26, the ? is used to display the string of characters 'METROPOLITAN AREA IN RECORD 3 - ' followed by the contents of the CITY field. You can also perform calculations by including an expression as shown in Figure 2.27.

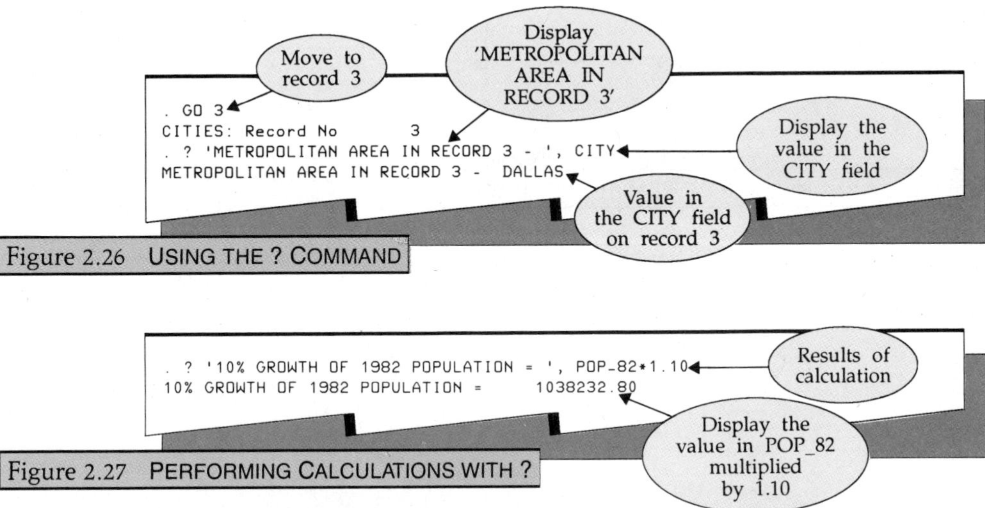

Figure 2.26 USING THE ? COMMAND

Figure 2.27 PERFORMING CALCULATIONS WITH ?

Perhaps you are wondering about the decimal portion that appears in the result. The fraction appeared because of the two decimal places in the multiplier, 1.10. You will learn to round or remove fractions in a later chapter.

Fields can be printed in any order, as shown in the example in Figure 2.28. The values in any fields listed will, of course, come from the *current record* (the record on which you are currently positioned).

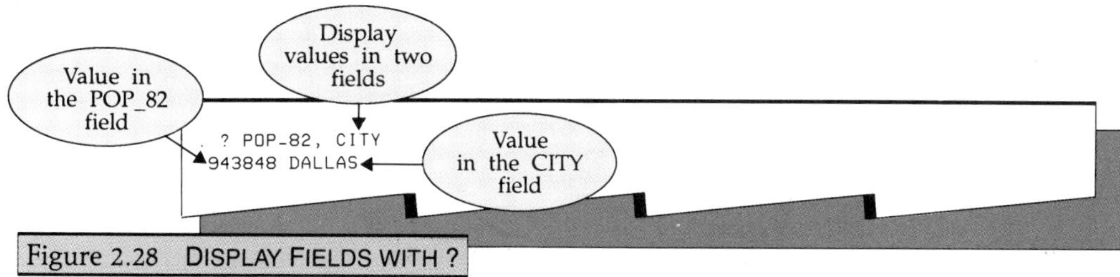

Figure 2.28 DISPLAY FIELDS WITH ?

The exercises at the end of this chapter are designed to develop your ability to use ? and LIST. These skills will be applied again when you begin to program in dBASE IV.

CHAPTER SUMMARY

1. After you have planned the format of the database, including such details as the name, type, and length of each field, you can use CREATE to establish the structure of the database file. A convenient screen is used to set up the specifications for each field. A database file must be opened with USE before you can access the data in it.
2. The APPEND command allows you to add records to the active database file. A screen is displayed that prompts you to enter data into each field.
3. The structure of a database file can be altered with the MODIFY STRUCTURE command, which displays a screen similar to CREATE. The data is rewritten to the file following the alterations.
4. Existing records can be modified with several commands, including EDIT, BROWSE, REPLACE, and GET/READ. EDIT allows any changes to the data in an individual record. If many records require modification, the BROWSE command is more convenient. REPLACE changes the data in the current record from the dot prompt. REPLACE is useful for programming, whereas EDIT and BROWSE typically are not.
5. The removal of a record is a two-command process using DELETE and PACK. The DELETE command marks the record with an asterisk, and PACK actually removes the marked record and rewrites the file. Before the PACK operation takes place, marked records can be unmarked with the RECALL command.
6. LIST is a flexible command that displays any combination of fields from selected records. Comparative expressions using relational operators can be linked logically to perform the selection.
7. The ? displays fields from the current record, and messages. LIST is useful from the dot prompt, and ? is used in programs.

KEY TERMS

numeric type
character type
DBF (database file)
alphanumeric type
record pointer
relational operator
logical operator
current record

COMMAND SUMMARY

Command Name	**Use**
CREATE	Establish a database file.
USE	Open a database file for use.
DISPLAY STRUCTURE	Show the structure of a database file.
APPEND	Add a record to a database file.
MODIFY STRUCTURE	Change the structure of a database file.
LIST	Display the data in a database file.
EDIT	Modify the data in a record.
BROWSE	Change the data in several records.
REPLACE	Substitute the data in the fields.
PACK	Remove deleted records.
RECALL	Unmark a record for deletion
LIST FOR	Display data with a condition.
SET EXACT ON	Display data that matches a condition exactly.
?	Display data.

SELF-CHECK QUESTIONS

1. Why is it important to consider the characteristics of a field, such as length?
2. What is the difference between numeric data and character data?
3. How can we determine the length of a numeric field?
4. What does Ctrl-U do? How is this done on the keyboard?
5. What happens when you USE a file?
6. What happens when an APPEND command executes?
7. What piece of information is required in order to EDIT a record?
8. Why is the deletion process done in two steps?

9. Provide a field name and determine the type and length (include decimal positions if appropriate) for each of the following examples:
   a. A Social Security number with hyphens.
   b. The hourly pay rate at a fast-food restaurant.
   c. The price of a new car.
   d. The date on which an employee was hired.
   e. A product description.
   f. A code for marital status.
   g. An interest rate, such as 9.25%.
10. When would SET EXACT ON be useful?

TRY IT YOURSELF

1. Plan a database structure for the following body of information. Consider the name, type, and length of each field. (**Note:** Only the name of the contributor should have a Y for the Index entry.)

   A charity wishes to record the name of the contributor, the amount of the contribution, and the date on which the contribution was made. Amounts of $1000 or more are not included, but change (a cents figure) is often given. Only last names are required.
2. Use CREATE to establish and name a DBF file for Exercise 1. Display the structure.
3. APPEND these records to your file:

```
Garcia,21.50,March 8, 1992
Nelson,120,January 12, 1992
Gordon,58.75,April 19, 1992
Zucco,325,February 3, 1992
```

   LIST the records.
4. Make the following modifications to the appropriate records:
   a. Nelson's name is incorrect. Change it to Neilson.
   b. Gordon contributed 158.75, not 58.75.
   c. The contribution shown for February 3 was actually made on February 13.
5. Remove the Gordon record from the file. LIST the records and note the change in record numbers. Add a record for Norton's contribution of 34.50 on March 15, 1991.

6. LIST the records with the following conditions:
   a. The dates first and then the amounts without the names.
   b. The original amounts and then the amounts increased by 10%.
   c. The names that begin with 'N' and the dates of those records.
   d. The names of those who contributed more than $100.
   e. The entire record of those whose names begin with 'N' and who gave more than $100.
7. Place the record pointer at record 3. Display this message: `LAST NAME IS - ZUCCO`
8. Modify the structure of the database in Exercise 1 so that it includes a field to represent the status of the contributions (P = pledged, R = received). Use REPLACE to place a P in all the records.
9. Using the CITIES database file, print a LIST of the names of the cities whose population in 1970 was 600,000 or less.
10. Print a list of city names and the difference in population between 1982 and 1970 for cities in California.
11. Print the city, the state, and a population projection that is based on a 10% increase over the 1982 population.
12. CREATE a daily log database, including the date and a 20-character field for the event. Add several records from your daily life during the last week. (**Note:** The date is the only field that should have a Y as the index entry.)
13. Using the database in Exercise 12, edit several records, delete one record, and PACK.
14. An office manager wants to automate a card file of business contacts. CREATE a DBF file to store the following fields. (**Note:** Only the field for last name should have a Y as the index entry.) Make your own decisions concerning the field name, data type, width, and decimal places. Close the file.

```
Last name
First name
Street address
City
State
Zip code
Area code and phone number
Company
Value of last contract (no larger than 9000.00)
Date of last contract
```

15. Open the file from Exercise 14. Display the structure and add ten records. Be sure to vary the contents as much as possible. List all the records.

16. Use either BROWSE or EDIT to change the data in records 3, 6, and 10. List the records and note the changes. Position the record pointer on record 3. Use the command to display the last name and phone number of record 3. Close the file to save the changes.
17. Open the file from Exercise 14. Type LIST commands that will display approximately half the records in the file using conditions for each field. For example, list the records having contracts of $5000.00 or more. You will have to create conditions that work with the data in your file.
18. Delete record 6. List the file and note the asterisk. Remove the asterisk and list the file again. Delete the record and permanently remove it from the file. List the file and note the record numbers.
19. Replace all the records with the code for your state. For example, make all the states PA. Replace all the contract amounts with an amount reflecting a 10% increase. List the file and note the changes. Close the file.

LEARNING OBJECTIVES

To use the report and label generators.

To use utility commands such as COPY, DIR, and ERASE.

To learn the characteristics of date-, memo-, and logical-type fields.

To control the record pointer with GOTO and SKIP.

To place data in order with the INDEX command.

3 WORKING FROM THE DOT PROMPT

INTRODUCTION

Now that you have acquainted yourself with dBASE IV, you will want to take advantage of some of the powerful commands and features that are available from the dot prompt. For example, you can easily produce attractive reports and useful labels by means of convenient generator programs. You will also find that a knowledge of the various utility commands will be helpful when you are maintaining files. Further, you will learn to move through the database and place records in order. As you learn to harness these and other commands, you will gain an excellent preparation for programming, which we begin in Chapter 4.

3.1 CREATING REPORTS AND LABELS

There are tools within dBASE to allow you to quickly and easily create reports and labels. They are called the report generator and the label generator, respectively. In this section, you will become acquainted with their basic use. Later in the text you will also see how to write programs to produce reports.

The report generator in dBASE is especially powerful. If you would like to investigate it further, Appendix B examines it in much more detail.

USING THE REPORT GENERATOR

To create a report, you must first activate the database file for which the report is intended. You then use the CREATE REPORT command. When you do, you will specify a filename. This is the name of the file that will contain the details you specify concerning your report. dBASE automatically assigns this file an extension of FRM. In addition, dBASE also creates a program for us. When we print the report, it is this program that will actually do the job.

Let's examine the basic use of the report generator by creating a report for the CITIES database file. Before you use the generator, you should have an idea of the layout you want for your report. We'll assume we want to produce a report like the one shown in Figure 3.1. To begin, type

```
USE CITIES
CREATE REPORT FIRST
```

(FIRST is the name of the report.)

Page 1
04/30/92

Report of U.S. Cities

San Francisco	CA	691637
Philadelphia	PA	1665382
Dallas	TX	943848
San Diego	CA	915956
Houston	TX	1725617
Miami	FL	382726
Cleveland	OH	558869
Pittsburgh	PA	414936
Los Angeles	CA	3022247
Jacksonville	FL	556370
		10877588

Figure 3.1 DESIGN FOR A REPORT

You should now see the screen shown in Figure 3.2. This is the Report Design screen. On this screen you will see a number of bands. These correspond to the various portions of the report. In this discussion we will focus on the Page Header band, the Detail band, and the Report Summary band.

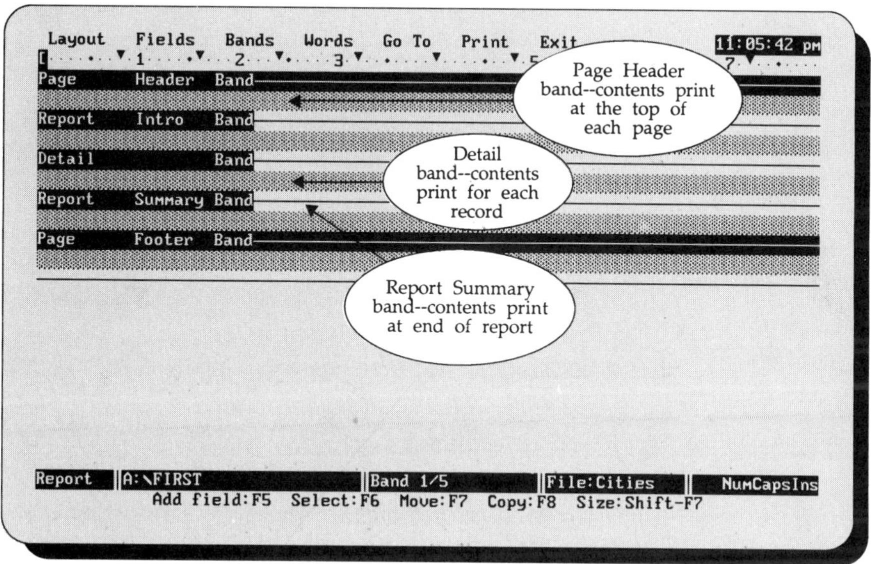

Figure 3.2 REPORT DESIGN SCREEN

The contents of the Page Header band print at the top of each page in the report. The contents of the Detail band print once for each record in the database file. Finally, the contents of the Report Summary band print once at the end of the report. We typically use the Report Summary band to print some grand totals of one or more of the numeric fields in the report.

The easiest way to begin working with the report generator is to let it create an initial report layout. To do so, select the "Quick layout" option of the Layout menu and then select "Column layout." You will then see the screen shown in Figure 3.3 on the next page. This is the "quick layout." We will now modify this layout, gradually transforming it into the one we want.

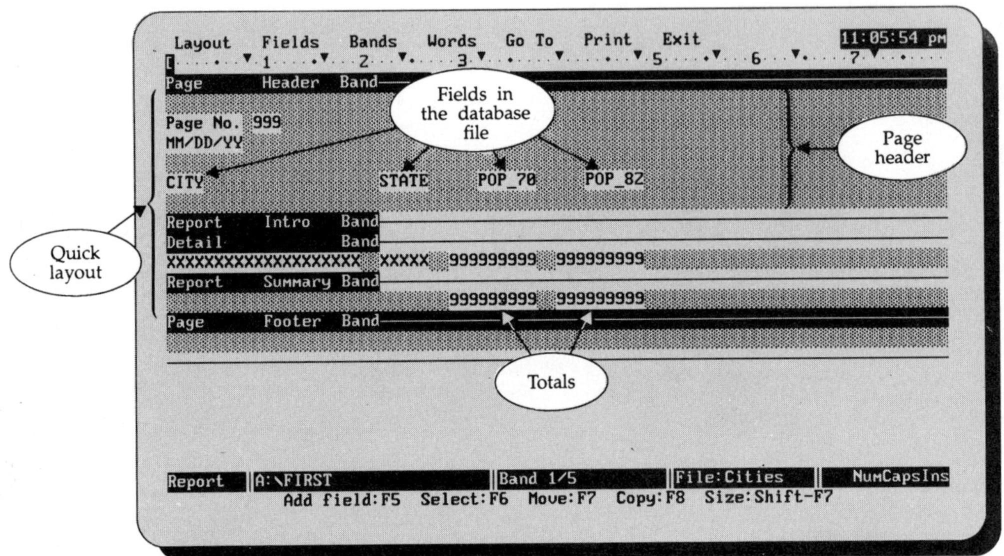

Figure 3.3 REPORT DESIGN SCREEN: QUICK LAYOUT

The screen visually indicates where the various items on the report will be placed. "Page No.," "CITY," "STATE," "POP_70," and "POP_82" will all print in the page header at the positions where they appear on the screen. The "999" that follows "Page No." is where the page number will print. The "MM/DD/YY" under "Page No." is where the date will print.

The Xs and 9s in the other bands indicate where the various fields will print. Although you cannot tell simply by looking at a group of Xs or 9s what fields they represent, there is an easy way to tell. Simply move the cursor into the Xs or 9s. The field represented by the group will be displayed near the bottom of your screen.

There is another way to tell what the report will look like. Select the "View report on screen" option of the Print menu. The Report Design screen will disappear and you will see a sample of your report. With the current layout, the report would look like the one shown in Figure 3.4. Once you have finished looking at the report, simply follow the directions on the screen to return to the Report Design screen.

(**Note:** As you transform the report, the keys shown in Table 3.1 will prove useful.)

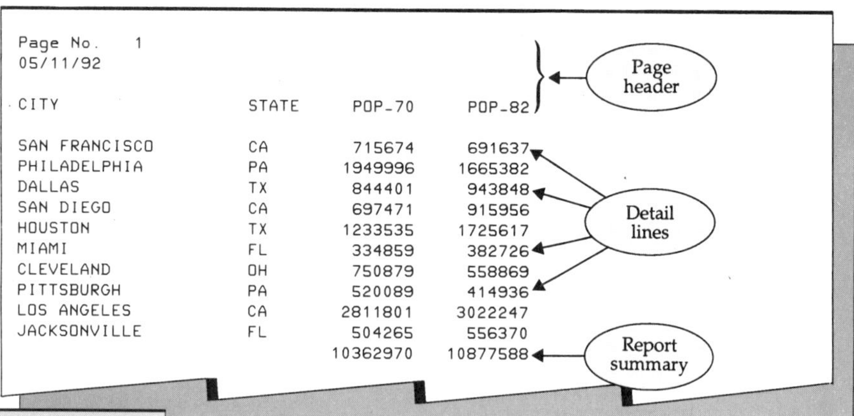

Page No. 1
05/11/92
CITY STATE POP_70 POP_82
SAN FRANCISCO CA 715674 691637
PHILADELPHIA PA 1949996 1665382
DALLAS TX 844401 943848
SAN DIEGO CA 697471 915956
HOUSTON TX 1233535 1725617
MIAMI FL 334859 382726
CLEVELAND OH 750879 558869
PITTSBURGH PA 520089 414936
LOS ANGELES CA 2811801 3022247
JACKSONVILLE FL 504265 556370
10362970 10877588
Page header
Detail lines
Report summary

Figure 3.4 QUICK REPORT

TABLE 3.1 Special keys used when creating labels and reports

KEY	PURPOSE
↑	Moves the cursor up one row
↓	Moves the cursor down one row
→	Moves the cursor one position to the right
←	Moves the cursor one position to the left
[Tab]	Moves to the next tab setting
[Shift-Tab]	Moves to the previous tab setting
[Page Down]	Moves to bottom of screen
[Page Up]	Moves to top of screen
[Home]	Moves to beginning of line
[End]	Moves to end of line
[Backspace]	Moves cursor one position to the left and erases character that was in that position
[Insert]	Switches between Insert mode and Replace mode
[Enter]	In Insert mode, moves down one line and inserts a new line. Otherwise, simply moves down one line
[Ctrl-Y]	Deletes the line the cursor is on
[Ctrl-N]	Inserts new line at the cursor
[F5]	Adds a new field at the current cursor position
[F6]	Selects field or block for subsequent work
[F7]	Moves selected field or block
[F8]	Copies selected field or block
[Delete]	Deletes selected field or block. If none selected, deletes character at current cursor position

The first step in transforming the report is to remove the POP_70 field from the Detail band and the total of the POP_70 field from the Report Summary band (Figure 3.5). To remove a field, move the cursor to it, press F6 and then Enter to select it, and then press the Delete key.

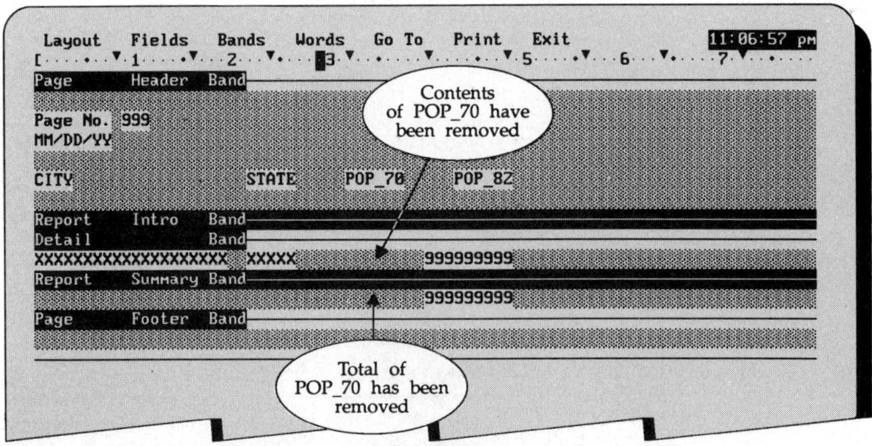

Figure 3.5 REPORT DESIGN SCREEN: REMOVING A FIELD

Next move the POP_82 field in the Detail band into the position shown in Figure 3.6. Also move the field that represents the total of POP_82 in the Report Summary band into the position shown in the figure. To move a field, move the cursor to it, select it (F6 and then Enter), press F7 (Move), move the cursor to the new position and then press Enter.

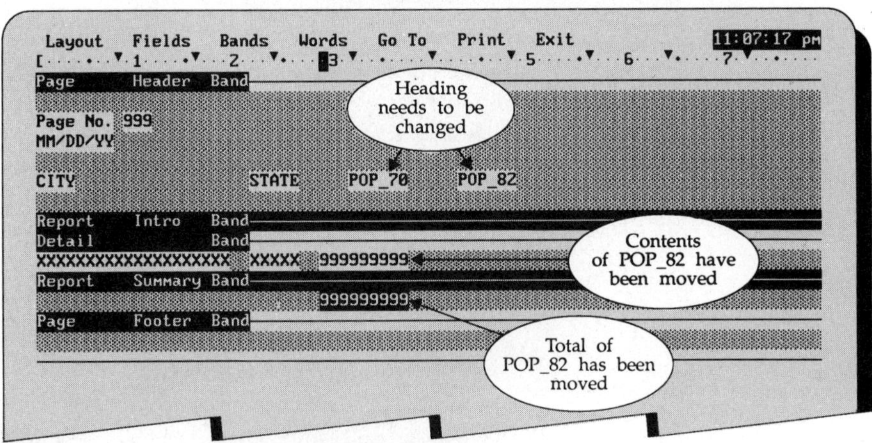

Figure 3.6 REPORT DESIGN SCREEN: MOVING A FIELD

Finally, let's change the Page Header band so that it matches the one shown in Figure 3.7. The simplest way is to move the cursor to the line that begins with "CITY," press Ctrl-Y to delete this line, and then press Ctrl-N twice to add two blank lines. Then add the various items shown in the Page Header in the figure by moving the cursor to the indicated position and typing the entry.

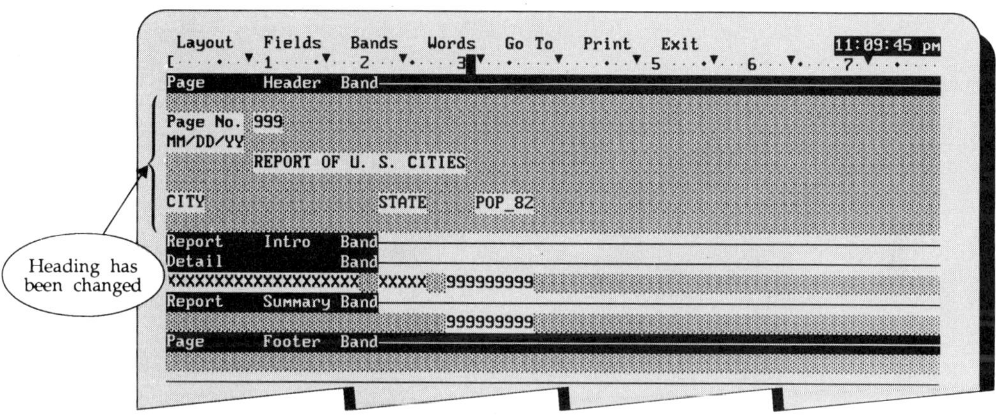

Figure 3.7 REPORT DESIGN SCREEN: CHANGING PAGE HEADER BAND

The report design is now complete, so save your work by selecting the "Save changes and exit"option of the Exit menu. To print the report, make sure the CITIES database file is active and then type the command

```
REPORT FORM FIRST TO PRINT.
```

The results are shown in Figure 3.8.

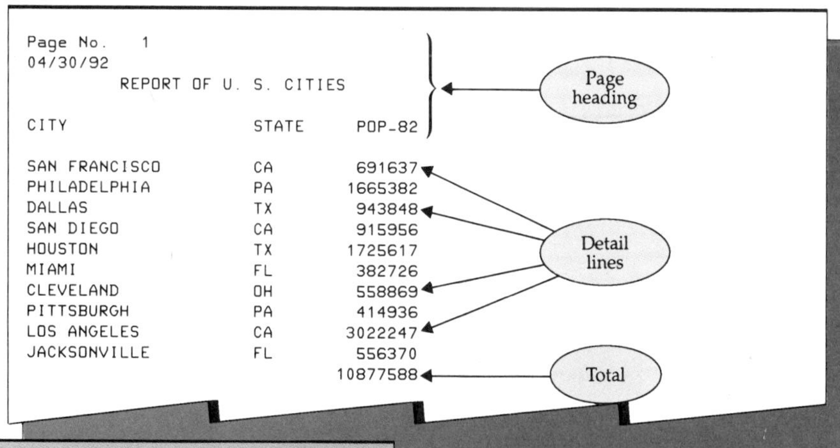

Figure 3.8 RESULT OF THE REPORT GENERATOR

USING THE LABEL GENERATOR

Your experience with the report generator will be helpful in learning to produce paper labels with the label generator, since both features use pull-down menus and input screens for convenience. The label generator is started with the CREATE LABEL command as in Figure 3.9. As with the report generator, you must enter a valid filename for the label file. You should have a database file active; if one isn't, you will be prompted to indicate which database file you wish to activate.

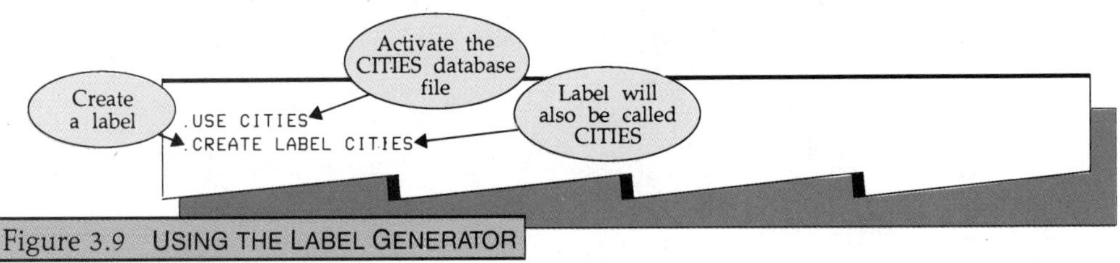

Figure 3.9 USING THE LABEL GENERATOR

Figure 3.10 shows the Label Design screen. The first step in creating a label is to indicate the label size. To do so, select the "Predefined size" option of the Dimensions menu (Figure 3.11). You then select the size corresponding to the particular labels you need to print. Let's assume the size we want is "15/16 × 3-1/2 by 1" (15/16 inches by 3-1/2 inches and 1 label across), a very common size. We would then select that size from the list.

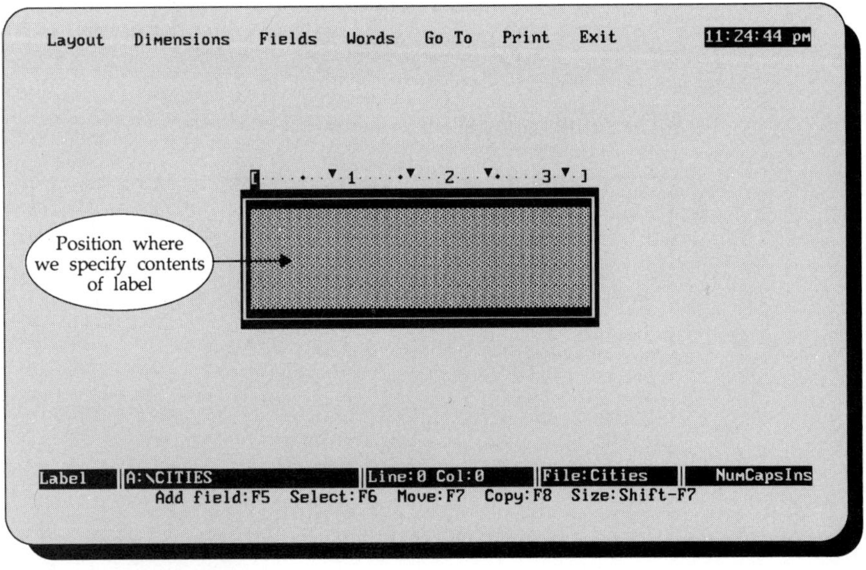

Figure 3.10 LABEL DESIGN SCREEN

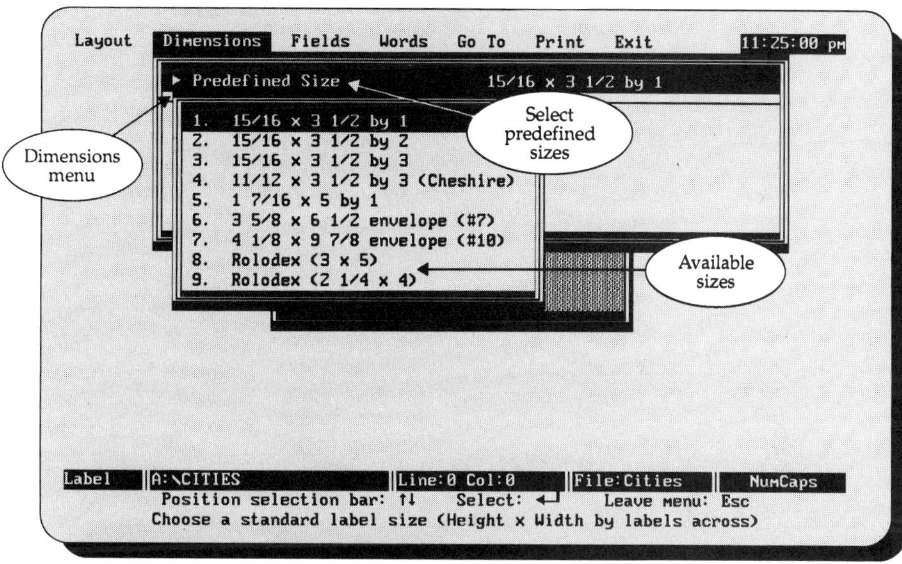

Figure 3.11 LABEL DESIGN SCREEN: DIMENSIONS MENU

Next we add the fields we want at the appropriate positions in the box in the middle of the screen. To add a field, first position the cursor at the desired location. Then select the "Add field" option of the Fields menu. You will then see a list of available fields. Select the one you want and then press Ctrl-End. In Figure 3.12 we have added the CITY field on the first line and the STATE field on the second. When you have completely specified fields for your label, select the "Save changes and exit" option of the Exit menu.

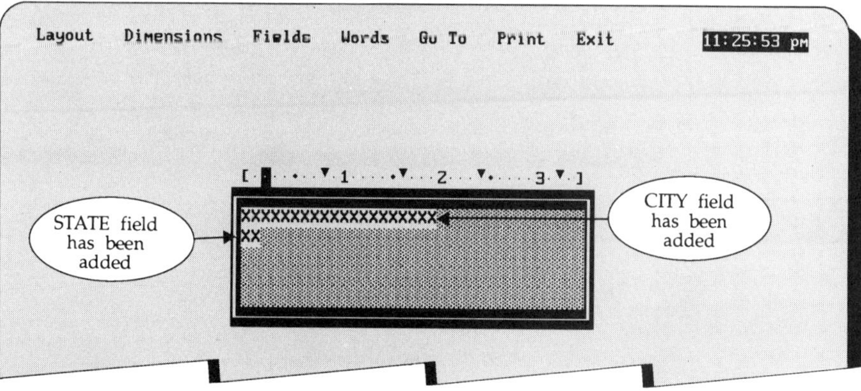

Figure 3.12 LABELS DESIGN SCREEN: ADDING FIELDS

Once we have created a label file, we can produce labels with the LABEL FORM command. The labels can be produced on the screen with the LABEL FORM CITIES command (Figure 3.13). To direct the output to the printer, simply add the TO PRINT clause at the end of the command. If we also add the word SAMPLE, dBASE will print a facsimile of a label, using an X for each character, so you can adjust the printer before starting to print the labels (Figure 3.14). Figure 3.15 illustrates the labels produced using the CITIES database file and the labels file we just created.

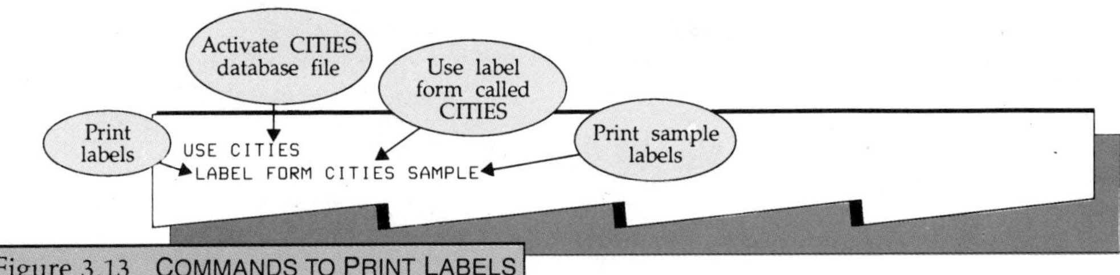

Figure 3.13 COMMANDS TO PRINT LABELS

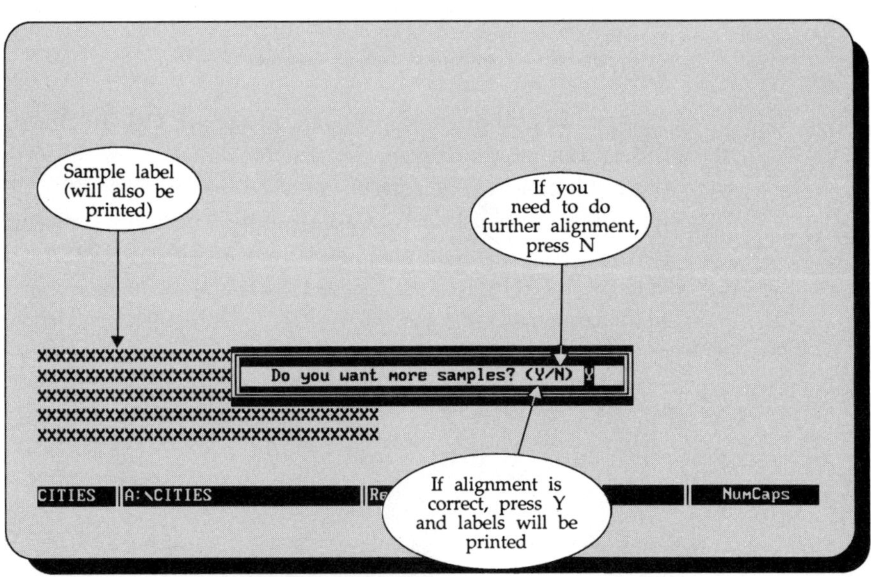

Figure 3.14 RESULT OF LABEL FORM ... SAMPLE

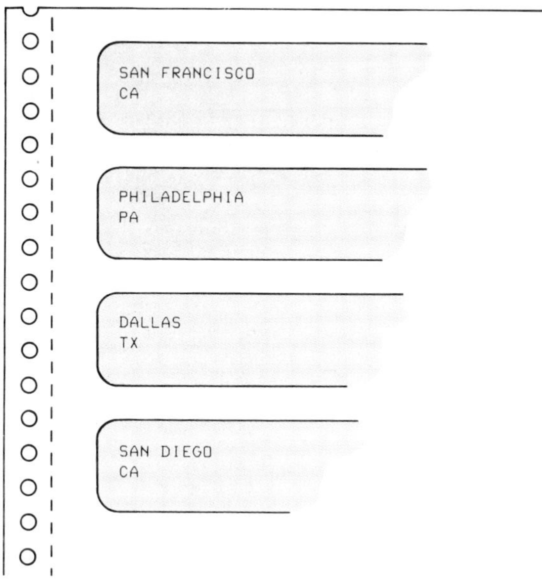

Figure 3.15 PRINTED LABELS

You learned how to use the LIST command with a FOR clause in Chapter 2. The same clause can be used with the LABEL FORM and REPORT FORM commands to print labels or reports on the basis of a condition. The command in Figure 3.16, for example, prints labels only for cities that are in Pennsylvania.

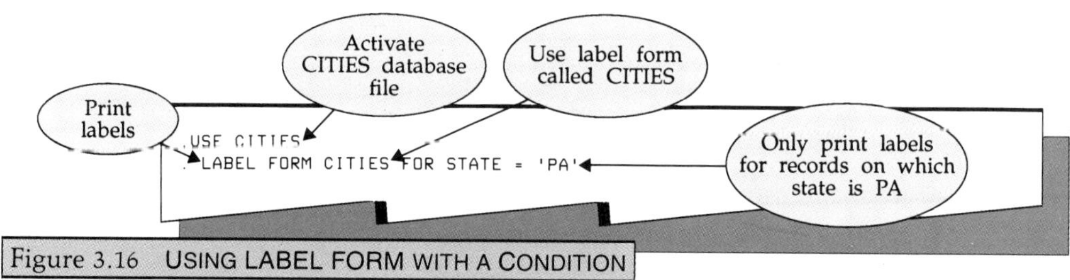

Figure 3.16 USING LABEL FORM WITH A CONDITION

3.2 UTILITY COMMANDS

Several commands in dBASE IV can be used to save time and effort when you are performing housekeeping chores with your files. Some of these commands are presented here, with brief descriptions and examples. Try each of them with the TEMP.DBF file in order to understand how they operate.

COPY TO The COPY TO command is used to produce an identical copy of the database file currently in use. (See Figure 3.17.)

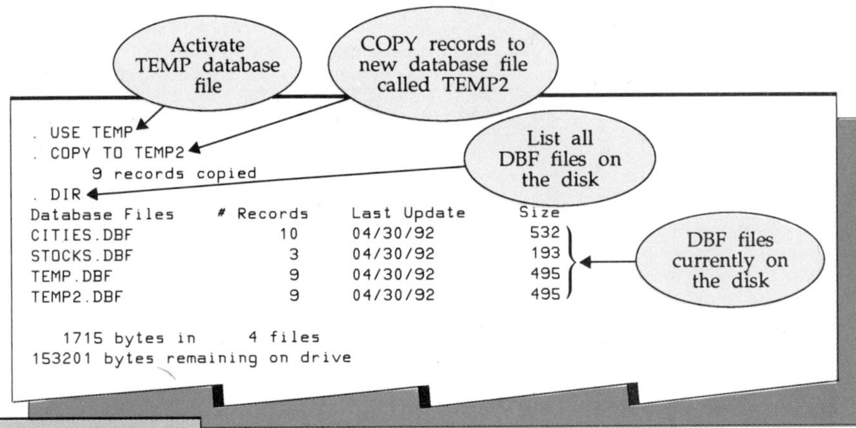

Figure 3.17 USING COPY TO

COPY STRUCTURE The COPY STRUCTURE command can be used to copy the structure of a database file without the records. This may prove useful when testing programs or sharing file structures with others. (See Figure 3.18.)

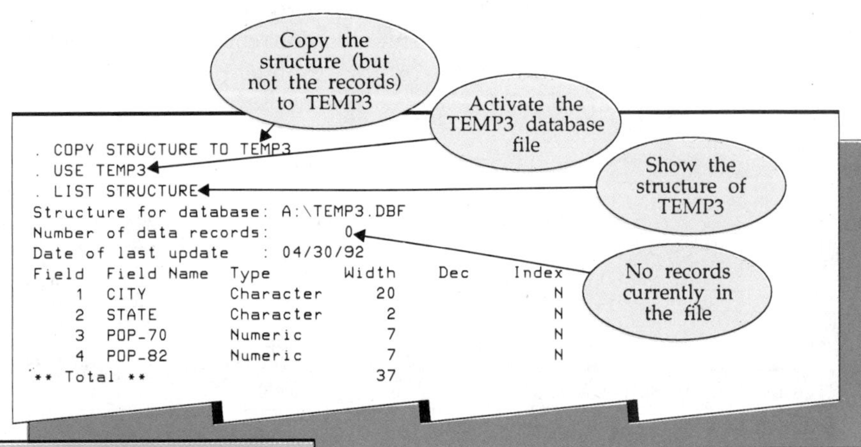

Figure 3.18 USING COPY STRUCTURE

COPY FILE If you need to perform a COPY on other types of files, use the COPY FILE command. (See Figure 3.19.)

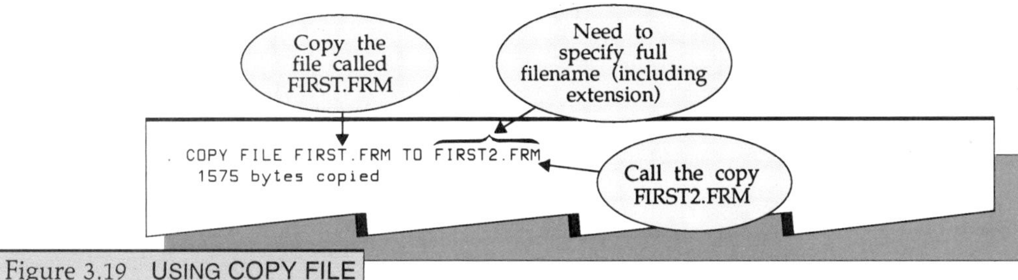

Figure 3.19 USING COPY FILE

COUNT The COUNT command is combined with a condition to return the number of records that satisfy the criteria. (See Figure 3.20.)

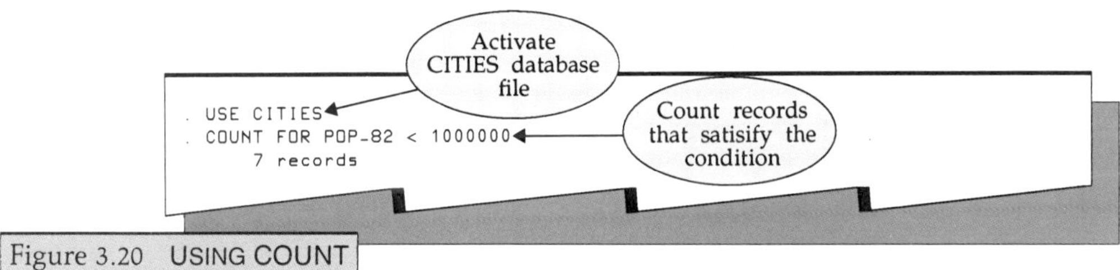

Figure 3.20 USING COUNT

SUM If there are numeric fields in the database file, they can be totaled with the SUM command. (See Figure 3.21.)

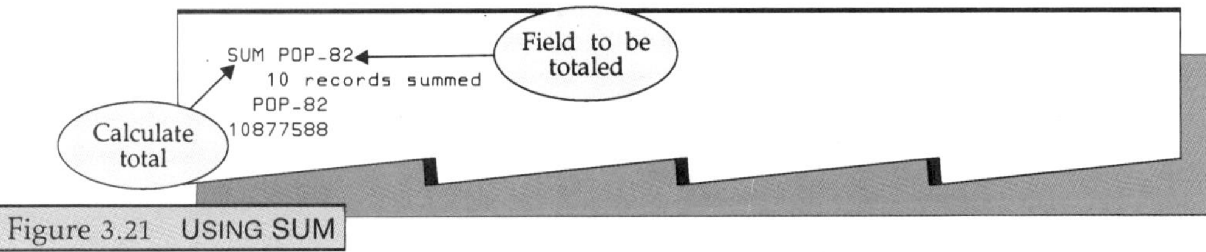

Figure 3.21 USING SUM

AVERAGE The AVERAGE command calculates an average on any or all numeric fields. (See Figure 3.22.)

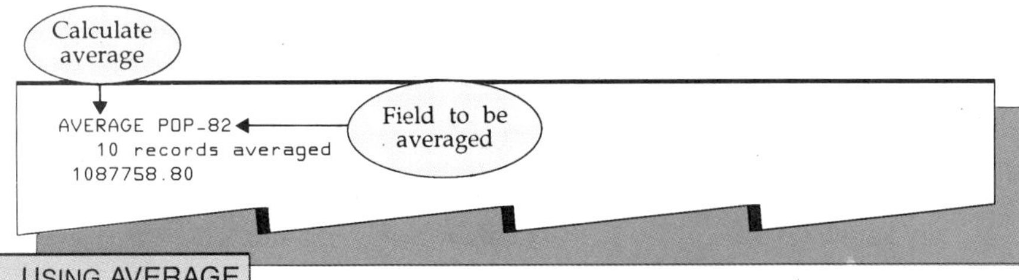

Figure 3.22 USING AVERAGE

DIR This DOS command checks the directory of the disk and displays any database (DBF) files. The filenames can also be displayed by means of the *. (A sample of this is shown in Figure 3.23. Your listing will be different.)

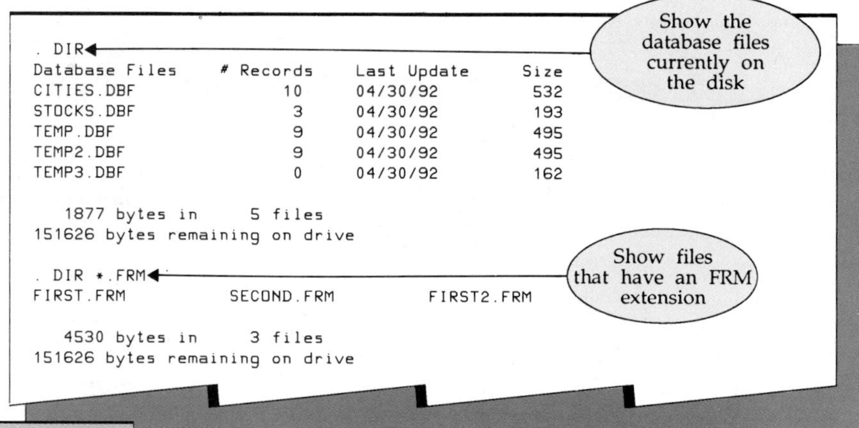

Figure 3.23 USING DIR

DISPLAY STATUS or **LIST STATUS** This command provides a variety of useful information about the files being used and about dBASE IV itself. This includes a listing of open files, the status of the SET commands, and the commands issued by the function keys. This feature is useful when debugging programs because you can determine the status of files and features. (See Figure 3.24.)

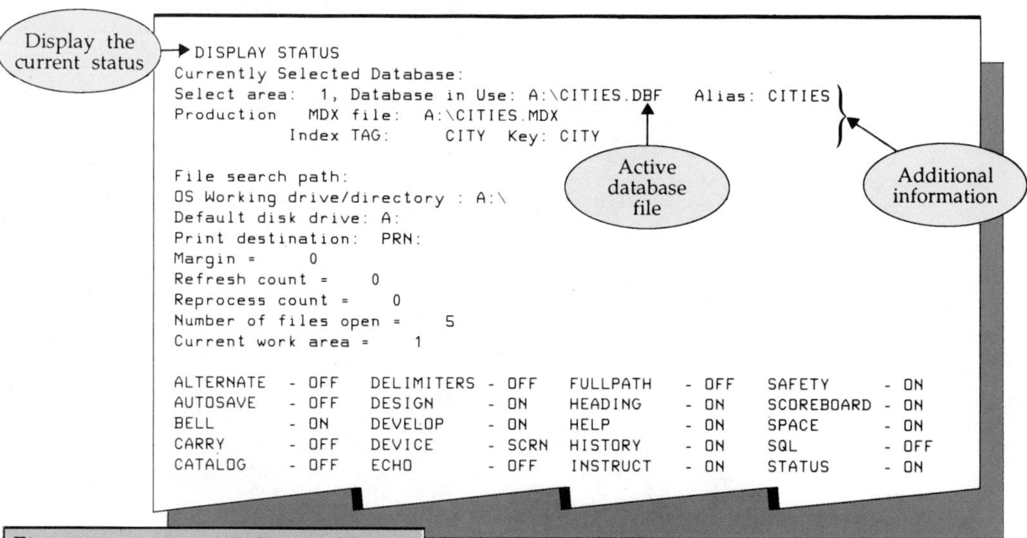

Figure 3.24 USING DISPLAY STATUS

DISPLAY HISTORY This command displays the most recent commands that have been typed. (See Figure 3.25.) Pressing the Up Arrow key displays them one at a time. Pressing Enter allows a command to be executed again without retyping.

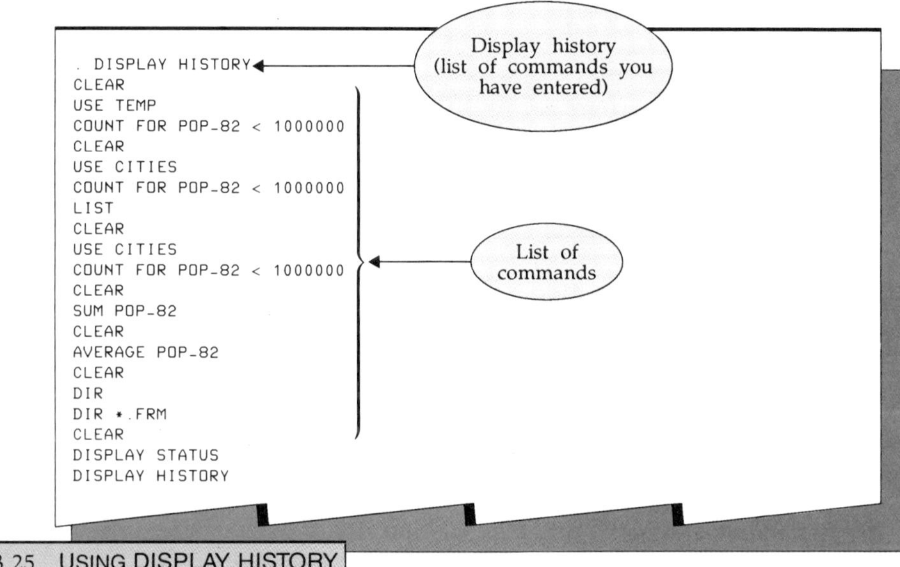
. DISPLAY HISTORY
CLEAR
USE TEMP
COUNT FOR POP_82 < 1000000
CLEAR
USE CITIES
COUNT FOR POP_82 < 1000000
LIST
CLEAR
USE CITIES
COUNT FOR POP_82 < 1000000
CLEAR
SUM POP_82
CLEAR
AVERAGE POP_82
CLEAR
DIR
DIR *.FRM
CLEAR
DISPLAY STATUS
DISPLAY HISTORY
Display history (list of commands you have entered)
List of commands

Figure 3.25 USING DISPLAY HISTORY

SKIP Using the SKIP command moves the record pointer to the next record. (See Figure 3.26.)

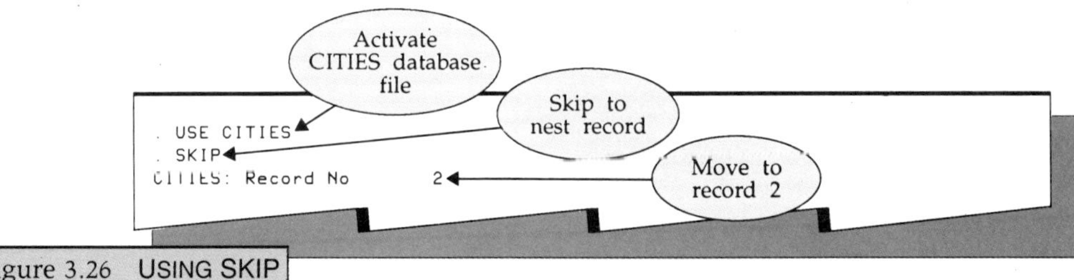
Activate CITIES database file
Skip to nest record
Move to record 2
. USE CITIES
. SKIP
CITIES: Record No 2

Figure 3.26 USING SKIP

RENAME You can change the DOS directory name of a file with this command. Make certain that the file is closed using CLEAR ALL or CLOSE ALL before using RENAME. In this case, the old filename, TEMP2.DBF is changed to NEW.DBF. (See Figure 3.27 on the next page.)

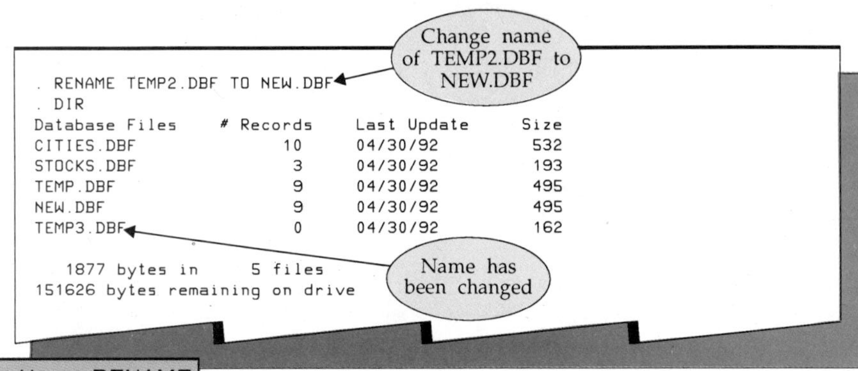

Figure 3.27 USING RENAME

ERASE Use the ERASE command to remove files from the disk as shown in Figure 3.28.)

Figure 3.28 USING ERASE

ZAP ZAP is useful when the structure of a database file is to be retained, but the data is no longer wanted. (See Figure 3.29.) This procedure can be risky since the data loss is permanent. dBASE IV provides a Y/N prompt for safety.

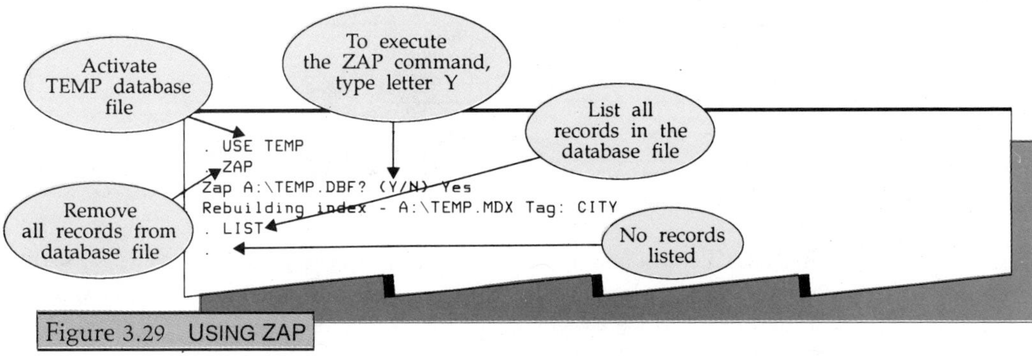

Figure 3.29 USING ZAP

EJECT EJECT causes the printer to produce a *page eject,* that is, to advance to the top of a new page. This will be useful in report programs. It is also useful at the dot prompt since many commands (like LIST) do not automatically advance to the top of a new page after they have printed all the data. If you want the printer to advance, simply type EJECT after the LIST command has completed.

You have seen only a selection of the commands that are available in dBASE IV. However, you will find that they are the ones that are most frequently used. As you grow in skill, you should note which commands are useful for programming and which are not. To fully use the considerable power of dBASE IV, you must be competent both as an interactive user (typing commands from the dot prompt) and as a programmer. In Chapter 4 you will begin to write programs with many of the commands that were presented here.

3.3 OTHER FIELD TYPES

In Chapter 2 you learned the critical difference between character- and numeric-type data fields. Although these two types work well with most of the data you will encounter, you need to be familiar with the three other data types that are used in dBASE IV. The first, the *date* type, is a convenient way to handle dates. Exactly six numeric digits are required to fill in a date-type field, with two extra positions provided for the slashes. To be certain that they are reasonable, dBASE IV checks the digits. For example, since there are only twelve months in a year, you cannot enter the number 13 in the month position. Date fields accept data in the format shown in Figure 3.30.

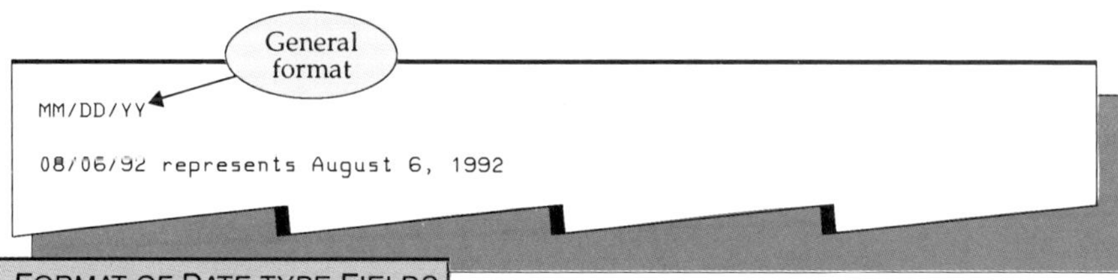

General format
MM/DD/YY
08/06/92 represents August 6, 1992

Figure 3.30 FORMAT OF DATE-TYPE FIELDS

If you enter an invalid date during an APPEND or EDIT, dBASE IV sounds a beep that prompts you to press the space bar in order to correct the data. Date fields also enable you to calculate the number of days between dates, which is information that you should find useful when programming.

Memo-type fields, which require special handling, are used when large fields of character-type data are needed in records. If you define a field as a memo type in the CREATE operation, you must use Ctrl-Home to enter data into the memo field during APPEND or EDIT operations. You will then be taken to a separate screen where you can enter the data into the field. When you are done, pressing Ctrl-End will return you to the normal EDIT screen. The data you entered into the memo field is stored in a separate file on your disk with a DBT extension. Unfortunately these and other factors limit the practical use of memo fields during programming.

The other important field type is *logical*. Fields of this type can contain only two possible values: T (for true) and F (for false). (When you enter data for such fields you can enter either T or Y for true and F or N for false. Regardless of how you enter the data, however, dBASE will store T or F.)

Suppose, for example, that in a CUSTOMER database file, you needed to keep track of whether each customer's account was current or not. You could include a field called CURRENT, whose type was logical. For those customers whose account is current, you would store a T in CURRENT. For those customers whose account is not, you would store an F. The only special thing you need to know about this type of field is the way you use it in a test. Remember that a condition is simply an expression that is either true or false. The condition PAY_RATE = 6.00, for example, is true for some records and false for others. A logical field (a field whose type is logical), like CURRENT, on the other hand, is either true or false *by itself*; that is, it does not need to be compared with some value. Thus you will not need to enter a comparison operator or value when you use logical fields. To list customers whose account is current, the command would be

```
LIST FOR CURRENT
```

To list customers whose account is not current, the command would be

```
LIST FOR .NOT. CURRENT
```

It is sometimes more useful to include a character-type field with a length of 1. For example, rather than the logical field CURRENT, we might include a character field called STATUS that can take on one of the following four values: O = Overdue, A = active, C = current, S = sent to collection. This approach often gives more flexibility than using logical fields.

Most data that you will encounter can be stored effectively in numeric-, character-, or date-type fields. On occasion, the memo and logical fields will be useful.

3.4 GETTING AROUND IN THE DATABASE

As you learned in Chapter 2, all database files contain a *record pointer*. This is an internal "bookmark" that can be moved from record to record. For example, after a USE command has been issued, the record pointer is positioned at the first record. Since the DISPLAY command always references the current record, it is useful for examining the behavior of the record pointer, as Figure 3.31 illustrates. Try each of the commands to become familiar with the behavior of the record pointer because its use is critical in later chapters.

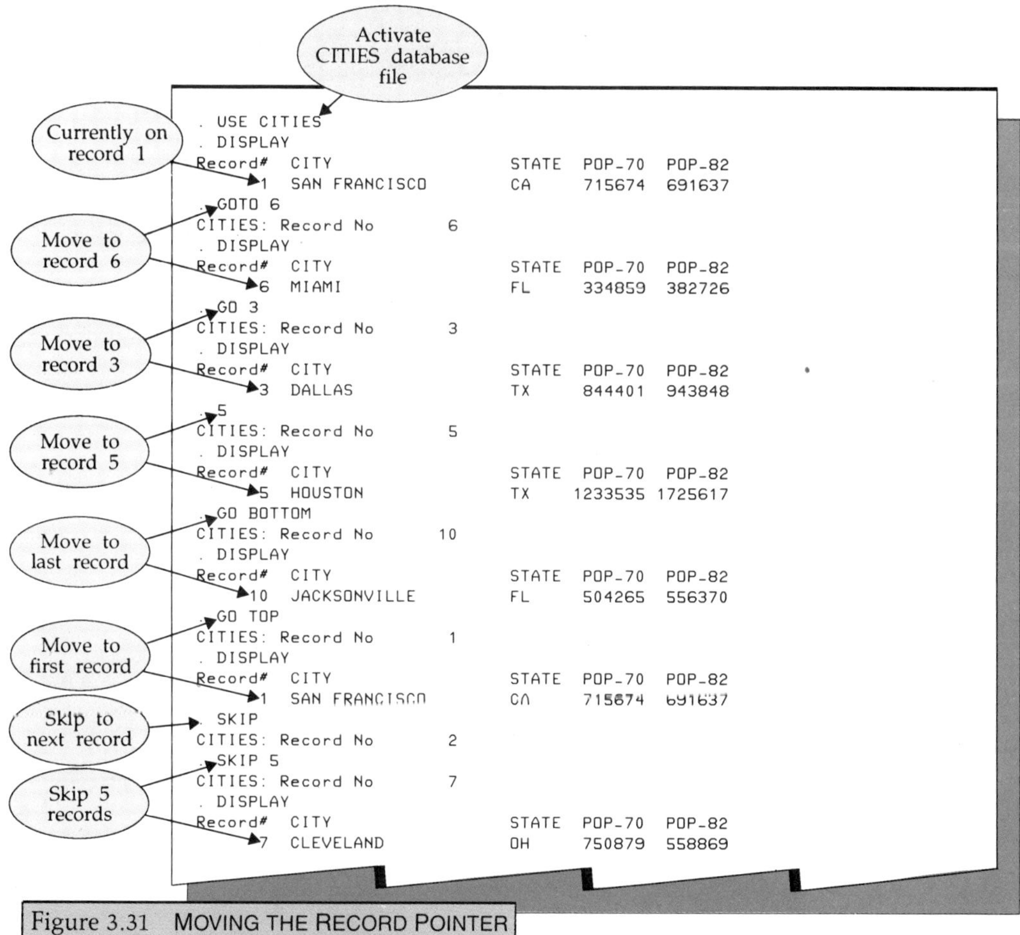

Figure 3.31 MOVING THE RECORD POINTER

Several commands enable you to move the record pointer to any location in the file. A specific record number can be placed after the GOTO command to position the record pointer on that record. In Figure 3.31, the GOTO 6, GO 3, and 5 commands place the record pointer on the sixth, third, and fifth records, respectively. As you can see, this command has three variations. GO BOTTOM moves the pointer to the last record in the file, record 10. GO TOP returns the pointer to the first record. The SKIP command moves the record pointer a specified number of records away from the current location. The SKIP in Figure 3.31 moves the record pointer from the current location, record 1, to record 2. Other numbers such as 5 and -3 can be used with the SKIP as the figure illustrates.

The GOTO command requires the user to know which record number contains the desired data. It is unlikely that the record numbers would be useful since they have no relevance to the data but are simply sequential numbers. The LOCATE command positions the record pointer on the basis of selected data placed in the command. For example, if you issued the LOCATE command in Figure 3.32, the record pointer would be positioned at the first record that met the condition CITY = 'PHILADELPHIA'. If the specified condition could be true for more than one record, the CONTINUE command could be used to advance to the next record that satisfied the condition. Since there are three California cities in the database, the CONTINUE command can be used to display the second and third as in Figure 3.32.

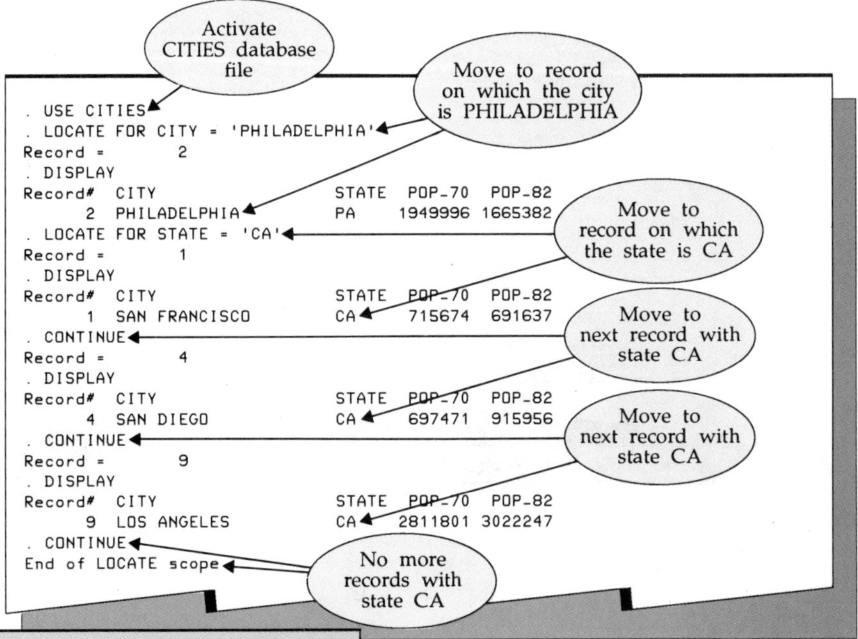

Figure 3.32 USING LOCATE AND CONTINUE

3.5 USING AN INDEX TO ORDER RECORDS

You may have noticed that the data you have been using never appears in alphabetical order. In fact, you may have thought that the order was random. It was not, however; the records appeared in the same order in which they were originally entered. It is possible to order data on the basis of a field. The CITIES database could appear in order by CITY or STATE, for example. A field that is used for this purpose is often called the *key field*.

Key fields are put to use through a process called *indexing*. This is accomplished by means of a special file that is related to the database file. This special file is called the *production index file*. This file has the same name as the database file, but has an extension of MDX rather than DBF. It is created and maintained automatically by dBASE. It will hold all the indexes we create for the database file. (Actually, it is limited to 47 indexes. We should never come close to this number, however. Practically, there is no limit.)

Remember that on the CREATE screen there is a column labeled "Index." When you put a Y in this Index column for some field, dBASE will create an index for the field. The command to use such an index is SET ORDER TO. When we created the CITIES database file, we put a Y in the Index column for the CITY field so dBASE created an index on CITY. To use this index to order records, the command would be

```
SET ORDER TO CITY
```

as shown in Figure 3.33. Notice that when the records are listed they are ordered by city. If you look at the Record # column, however, you can see that this is not the order in which they occur in the database file.

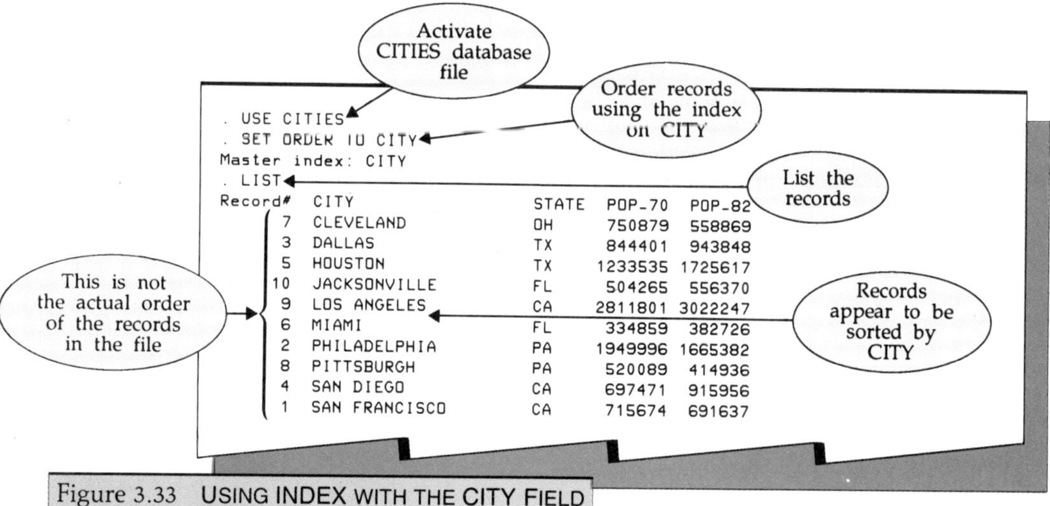

Figure 3.33 USING INDEX WITH THE CITY FIELD

The INDEX ON command creates a new index. The syntax of the command requires the key field following the word ON and a name for the index (dBASE calls this name a *tag*) at the end as in this example:

```
INDEX ON STATE TAG STATE
```

The first STATE refers to the field, whereas the second gives the name (tag) for the index. Wherever possible, it is a good idea to give the index the same name as the key field. Figure 3.34 shows the results of creating an index on STATE and then listing the records. Notice that when the records are listed they are ordered by state.

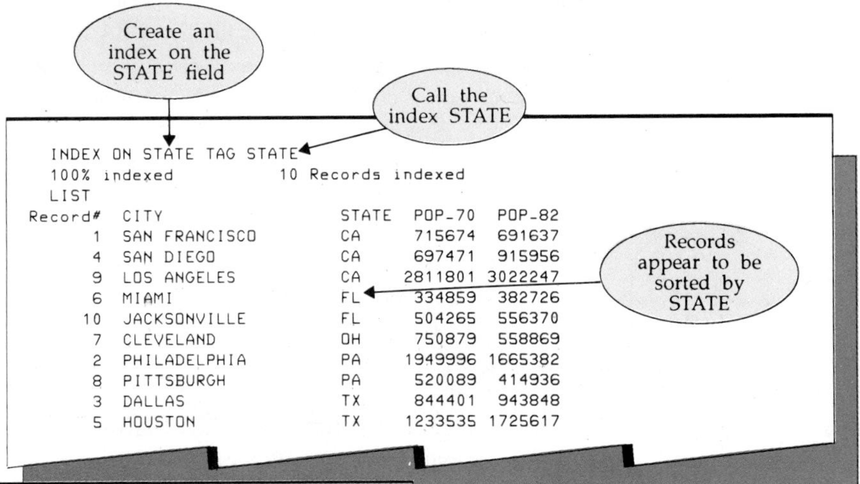


```
INDEX ON STATE TAG STATE
100% indexed          10 Records indexed
LIST
Record#  CITY                    STATE  POP_70   POP_82
      1  SAN FRANCISCO           CA      715674  691637
      4  SAN DIEGO               CA      697471  915956
      9  LOS ANGELES             CA     2811801 3022247
      6  MIAMI                   FL      334859  382726
     10  JACKSONVILLE            FL      504265  556370
      7  CLEVELAND               OH      750879  558869
      2  PHILADELPHIA            PA     1949996 1665382
      8  PITTSBURGH              PA      520089  414936
      3  DALLAS                  TX      844401  943848
      5  HOUSTON                 TX     1233535 1725617
```

Figure 3.34 USING INDEX WITH THE STATE FIELD

You may be wondering why we didn't also need to use the SET ORDER TO command. When you first create an index, that index is considered to be active; that is, it will be used to order records. As soon as you create another index, order records by another index, activate another database file, or leave dBASE, the index is no longer active. Thus at any point in the future, to order records by STATE, we would need the SET ORDER TO command. It would be entered as

```
SET ORDER TO STATE
```

We can also use a numeric field as a key field. Figure 3.35 illustrates this by using POP_70 as the key field.

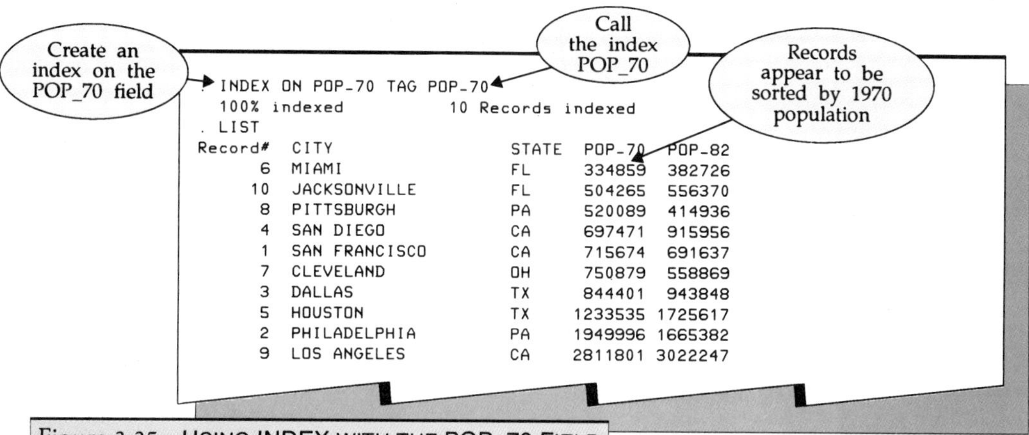

Figure 3.35 USING INDEX WITH THE POP_70 FIELD

When we use the SET ORDER TO command, the records are ordered by the index we specify for anything we do. If we use BROWSE, for example, the records will be ordered in the order we have selected. This proves especially useful when we print reports or labels. If we want the report or the labels to be sorted in some particular fashion, we first make sure we have created an appropriate index. (If not, we would create one). Then, when it is time to print the report or labels, we first enter the necessary SET ORDER TO command.

Suppose, for example, that we want the report of CITIES to be ordered by city. We would execute the

```
SET ORDER TO CITY
```

command before printing the report. (The results are displayed in Figure 3.36.) If we wanted the same report to appear in a different order, we would just execute a different SET ORDER TO command.

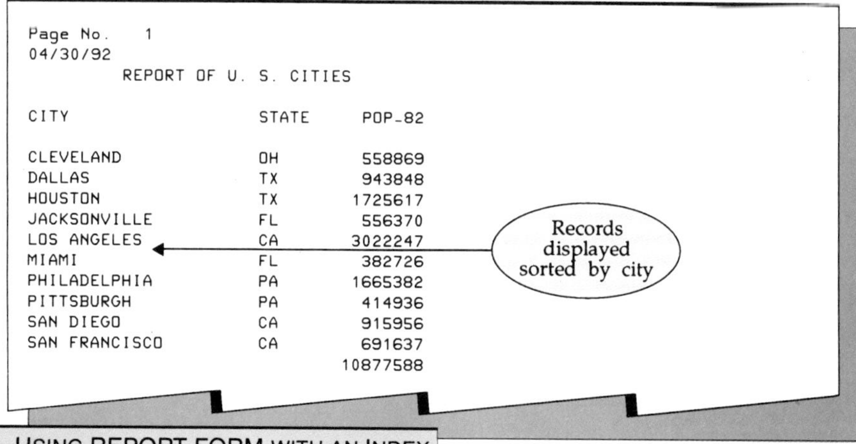

Page No. 1
04/30/92
REPORT OF U. S. CITIES
CITY STATE POP_82
CLEVELAND OH 558869
DALLAS TX 943848
HOUSTON TX 1725617
JACKSONVILLE FL 556370
LOS ANGELES CA 3022247
MIAMI FL 382726
PHILADELPHIA PA 1665382
PITTSBURGH PA 414936
SAN DIEGO CA 915956
SAN FRANCISCO CA 691637
10877588
Records displayed sorted by city

Figure 3.36 USING REPORT FORM WITH AN INDEX

If an index does not appear to be working properly, for example, if it is not displaying certain records, simply recreate it with another INDEX ON command. You will be asked if you wish to overwrite the existing index. If you respond Y, the file is replaced with a correct version. Indexing is obviously quite useful, and it will be addressed in much more detail in Chapter 9. The summary in Table 3.2 should help you to work with indexes until you have an opportunity to learn more about them.

TABLE 3.2 Using INDEX

1. Use INDEX ON <field name> TAG <tag name> to establish the index, which is then part of the production index file.
2. Activate the index, if necessary, with the SET ORDER TO command.
3. You can index on any type of field except memo or logical.
4. The records remain in their original physical order but appear to be in order by the selected field.
5. Commands such as REPORT FORM and LIST are affected by the index.
6. An index file can be recreated if it does not work properly.

CHAPTER SUMMARY

1. Attractive reports can be generated from the dot prompt by means of the report generator. The report generator places details concerning a report in an FRM file. It also creates a program that will be run to actually produce the report. A similar tool, the label generator, can be used to create mailing labels.
2. A number of utility commands make dBASE IV easier to use. Among these are COPY, DIR, DISPLAY STATUS, DISPLAY HISTORY, RENAME, SKIP, ERASE, ZAP, and EJECT.
3. Dates may be stored in date-type fields. Although they are employed infrequently in programs, memo- and logical-type fields are used to store large amounts of text and true/false conditions, respectively.
4. The record pointer can be used to DISPLAY a particular record. The GOTO command positions the record pointer when a record number is specified. The SKIP command moves the record pointer a specified number of records away from its current location. The LOCATE command positions the record pointer by attaching the data to a specified condition. The CONTINUE command moves to other records that match the condition.
5. An index can be used to display records in alphabetical or numerical order on the basis of a selected field. The INDEX ON command establishes an index that can be reactivated with the SET ORDER TO command. Records are displayed in index key order with commands such as REPORT FORM and LIST.

KEY TERMS

report generator
label generator
record pointer
key field
index file (MDX)
indexing
production index file
memo type
date type
logical type
tag

COMMAND SUMMARY

Command Name	**Use**
CREATE REPORT	Establish a REPORT format.
REPORT FORM	Produce a report.
CREATE LABEL	Establish a LABEL format.
LABEL FORM	Produce labels.
COPY TO	Copy a database file.
LIST FILES	Display database filenames.
COPY STRUCTURE	Copy the structure of the active database file.
COPY FILE	Copy non-database files.
COUNT	Count the number of records that meet a condition.
SUM	Sum numeric fields.
AVERAGE	Average numeric fields.
DIR	Display filenames.
DISPLAY STATUS	Show statistics concerning environment.
DISPLAY HISTORY	Show recently executed commands.
DELETE RECORD	Mark a record for deletion.
SKIP	Move the record pointer.
DISPLAY	Show the contents of the current record.
RENAME	Change the filename.
ERASE	Remove a file from the disk.
ZAP	Remove all records from a file.
EJECT	Causes a page eject.
GOTO	Move the record pointer.
GOTO TOP	Place the record pointer at the top of the file.
GOTO BOTTOM	Place the record pointer at the bottom of the file.
LOCATE	Place the record pointer on the first record that satisfies a given condition.
CONTINUE	Place the record pointer on the next record that satisfies the condition.
SET ORDER TO	Activates a particular index.
INDEX ON	Establish index file on key field.

SELF-CHECK QUESTIONS

1. Why is it important to be familiar with DOS commands?
2. Is it possible to have more than one FRM file per database file?
3. Why is the SAMPLE option in the LABEL FORM especially useful?
4. When is it helpful to use the COPY STRUCTURE command?
5. What is the difference between DISPLAY STATUS and LIST STATUS?
6. Why would you want to use RENAME?
7. What are the disadvantages of the memo-type field?
8. Is it useful to be able to move around the database by record number? Why?
9. Can a LOCATE command be used with a numeric field?
10. How do you create an index? What purpose does it serve?
11. How can an index be useful when you are printing reports or labels?
12. Do you think it would be a good idea to create indexes for all the fields in a database just in case they are needed? Why?
13. Can the LOCATE command be employed with a file that is utilizing an index?
14. What would happen if you issued the following two commands while a database file was open?

    ```
    GOTO BOTTOM
    SKIP
    ```

15. Some accounting procedures require the aging of accounts, which means calculating the number of days between the current date and a due date. Which feature of dBASE IV could be used for this purpose?

TRY IT YOURSELF

1. Produce a report that is similar to the following. It uses the CHARITY database from the Try It Yourself exercises in Chapter 2.

```
Page No. 1

04/03/92                       DONATIONS

DATE              NAME OF PATRON          AMOUNT
03/08/92          GARCIA                   21.50
01/12/92          NEILSON                 120.00
02/13/92          ZUCCO                   325.00
03/15/92          NORTON                   34.50

*** Total ***                             501.00
```

2. Execute the following commands:
   a. COPY the structure of the database file created in Try It Yourself Exercise 2 in Chapter 2 to a file named TEMP.DBF.
   b. COUNT the number of records with contributions over $25. Then SUM and AVERAGE the contributions.
   c. Show a directory of all FRM files.
   d. Display the settings for the programmable function keys.
3. Print a set of labels for the data in Try It Yourself Exercise 2 in Chapter 2. Include only the names of the patrons in alphabetical order. Print a sample first.
4. Produce labels, as in the preceding exercise, for those patrons who contributed more than $100. Make a copy of the label file under a different name.
5. Display a list of all the commands you have issued while completing these exercises.
6. Erase the file copy you made in Exercise 4.
7. Make a copy of the CITIES database. Add a date-type field called FOUNDED. Practice putting data in the new field by means of BROWSE. (You can make up the dates the cities were founded.)
8. Add a logical field called INCORP and add data the way you did in Exercise 7.
9. Use the CITIES database. Move the record pointer in the following ways:
   a. Move to record 4.
   b. Skip to record 7.
   c. Move to the top of the file.
   d. Skip backward one record.

10. Move the record pointer to any city in Pennsylvania. Move the record pointer to all other Pennsylvania cities.
11. Index the CITIES database by state and then list the contents of the database. Are the cities in alphabetical order within each state?
12. Attempt to index by the FOUNDED field and then LIST.
13. Add your city to CITIES.DBF. Reactivate the state index and LIST. Does your city appear? Attempt to LOCATE your city by name.
14. Move the record pointer to the bottom of the file and DISPLAY. What appears on the screen? Why?
15. Attempt to index by the logical field in Exercise 8 and LIST. Can you LOCATE by INCORP?
16. Create a report showing the state, then the city, then the 1970 population. There should be a total of the 1970 population at the end of the report. (**Hint:** Be careful when you move the fields around. If you cover an existing field during a move, the field will be deleted.)
17. Activate the STATE index and run the report created in Exercise 16. Note the order of the resulting report. Display the report on the printer.
18. Establish indexes for all three fields in the CHARITY file from Chapter 2. Run the report created in Exercise 1 using each index and observe the results.
19. Issue a DISPLAY STATUS command with the date index created in Exercise 18 active. Note the first portion of the display.
20. Issue a DIR command to list all files of each extension type present on your disk. For example, list all database files.

LEARNING OBJECTIVES

To understand the procedures and advantages of programming.

To use the features of MODIFY COMMAND.

To use pseudocode and debugging procedures in program development.

To examine the principles of structured programming.

To use the STORE command in order to create and use memory variables.

To identify the differences between numeric-type and character-type data.

INITIAL PROGRAMMING SKILLS

INTRODUCTION

You have learned a great deal about dBASE IV in the last three chapters. All the powerful functions and operations you have performed have been in the interactive mode, or from the dot prompt. Your experience may make it difficult to believe that programming will increase the range of tasks you can perform and at the same time make dBASE IV easier to use. In addition to these benefits, however, programming also offers others. You will learn to approach problems in a more effective way and to plan in a logical sequence. Finally, you will enjoy the satisfaction of creating something useful and of watching it in action.

4.1 ADVANTAGES OF PROGRAMMING

In Chapter 3 you operated at command level, or from the dot prompt. This means that the commands that you type execute immediately after you press Enter. The command must be retyped for each repetition. You also learned that the Control Center can relieve you from having to retype any commands at all. You can use menus that prompt you for your intentions. Although many people regularly work with their data in this way, you will surely want to take advantage of the power and flexibility of the extensive programming capability of dBASE IV.

Programming in dBASE IV is the process of grouping normal dBASE IV commands in a special file called a *command file* or *program*. Such a file has a PRG extension. Once you have created and saved a command file, you can execute the commands in it by typing DO followed by the name of the file. (You don't need to type the PRG extension in the DO command.)

This chapter explains how to plan, code, revise, and debug (find problems in) programs in dBASE IV. In later chapters, you will see how several programs can be organized into a system to perform a number of useful functions.

Let's return now to the PRG file. dBASE IV reads and executes the commands stored in this file one at a time. The computer is operating in *batch mode* at this point. This means that predefined tasks are being performed in a set order. As an analogy, you might think of a player piano. When a set of instructions, encoded on the piano roll, is inserted and run, the player piano appears to play itself. But the roll must be encoded with music that the listener wishes to hear. Similarly, if the instructions are correct and the needs of the user are met, the computer program will be successful.

Some formal methods and procedures associated with the proper construction of programs are addressed later in this chapter. For your first efforts, it may be more helpful to use the following strategy:

1. List the actions you wish to perform, step by step, in plain English.
2. Translate the actions into dBASE IV commands that you already know.
3. Type the commands into a file (Section 4.2).
4. Test the program by running it with a DO command.
5. Evaluate the performance and consider modifications.
6. Change the program as necessary.
7. Repeat steps 4, 5, and 6 until you are satisfied.

An experienced programmer once commented that a good program is never finished. Step 7 seems to reinforce this idea, which expresses the essence of what programmers do much of the time. You will find that adjusting to this cycle of development is a familiar process. You did something very similar when you learned how to use note cards, outlines, drafts, and, of course, revisions to write a term paper. In the next few pages you will see how a programmer, faced with the need to perform a series of steps over and over again, designs and codes programs in dBASE IV. First, though, you need to learn about the text editor in dBASE IV, which is called MODIFY COMMAND.

4.2 USING MODIFY COMMAND

The purpose of MODIFY COMMAND is to allow you to create programs (command files). You can access MODIFY COMMAND from the dot prompt by typing MODIFY COMMAND followed by the name of the file you wish to create or modify. If you do not specify a file, dBASE IV prompts you for a name. If you do not include a DOS extension, dBASE assigns an extension of PRG to your filename on the disk. To create a program called TEST, for example, you would type:

```
MODIFY COMMAND TEST
```

or

```
MODIFY COMMAND
ENTER FILE NAME: TEST
```

You are presented with the MODIFY COMMAND screen (Figure 4.1).

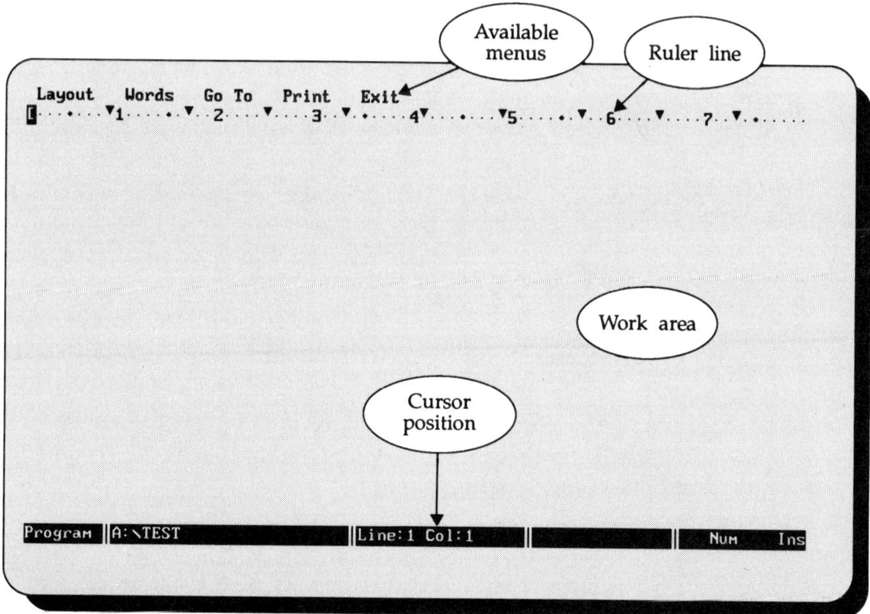

Figure 4.1 THE MODIFY COMMAND SCREEN

When you enter or modify programs using this screen, you can use any of the menus at the top or the special keys shown in Table 4.1. As you create your first program, it would be useful to experiment with the various keys shown in the table.

TABLE 4.1 Special keys used with MODIFY COMMAND

KEY	PURPOSE
↑	Moves the highlight up one row
↓	Moves the highlight down one row
→	Moves the cursor one position to the right
←	Moves the cursor one position to the left
[Page Down]	Moves down one screen's worth
[Page Up]	Moves up one screen's worth
[Backspace]	Moves cursor one position to the left and erases character that was in that position
[Tab]	Moves cursor to next Tab
[Shift-Tab]	Moves cursor to previous Tab
[Home]	Moves cursor to beginning of line
[End]	Moves cursor to end of line
[Insert]	Switches between Insert mode and Replace mode
[Ctrl-Y]	Deletes the line the cursor is on
[Ctrl-T]	Deletes word under cursor
[Ctrl-N]	Inserts new line at the cursor
[F6]	Begins selection of a block (finish with Enter)
[F7]	Moves selected block
[F8]	Deletes selected block
[Delete]	Deletes selected field or block. If none selected, deletes character at current cursor position

You must press Enter at the end of each line. You can type in uppercase or lowercase. In this text, we will use uppercase and lowercase in a special way. Words that are part of the dBASE language will be in uppercase. Words that we have assigned, such as names for database files and fields, will be in lowercase. Following this approach, the command to activate the CITIES database file would be

```
USE cities
```

USE is uppercase since this is a dBASE command. The word "cities" is lowercase since that is a name that we assigned.

There are times when we would like to split a command over two lines to improve readability. To do so, we just end the first line with a semicolon. This indicates to dBASE that the command is not complete, and that the rest of the command is found on the next line. For example, to split the command

```
LIST city, pop_82 FOR state = 'CA'
```

over two lines, we could type

```
LIST city, pop_82 FOR ;
 state = 'CA'
```

When we do this, we will often indent the second line a few spaces. This visually emphasizes the fact that the second line is really part of the command that began on the first line rather than a new command.

With this introduction, let's create our first program. Use MODIFY COMMAND to create a program named TEST. Once you are at the MODIFY COMMAND screen, type in the program shown in Figure 4.2. The first line of the program begins with an asterisk (*), which identifies the line as a *comment* or note. This simply means that dBASE will ignore the remainder of the line when it executes the program; it will not treat it as a command to be executed. You should get in the habit of placing comments in your programs to identify and document what is occurring. This comment indicates the name of the program.

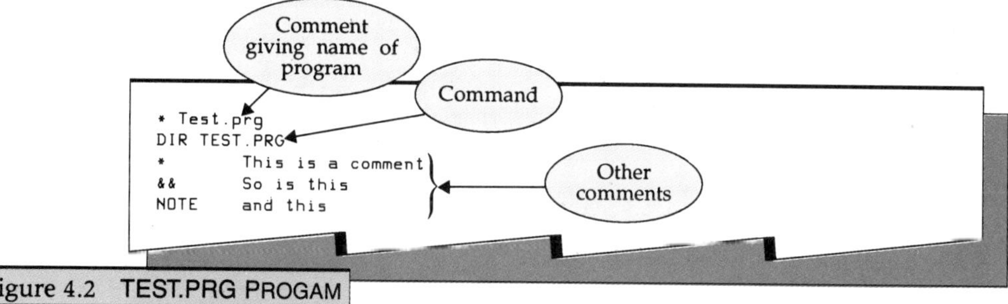

Figure 4.2 TEST.PRG PROGAM

Comments can be placed in a PRG file by preceding the line with an asterisk, two ampersands (&&), or the word NOTE. The two ampersands can be placed at the end of a command line, whereas the asterisk or NOTE declare the entire line a comment. Thus, if you want a comment on the same line as a command, you must use two ampersands. For full-line comments, any of the three will work. While it is really a matter of personal preference, most dBASE programmers use the asterisk.

Once you have typed the complete program, save it by selecting the "Save changes and exit" option of the Exit menu. The program is stored on the disk as TEST.PRG. Execute the program by typing `DO TEST` at the dot prompt. As you might expect, the program does nothing with the comment lines, but it does display a directory of PRG files, as shown in Figure 4.3.

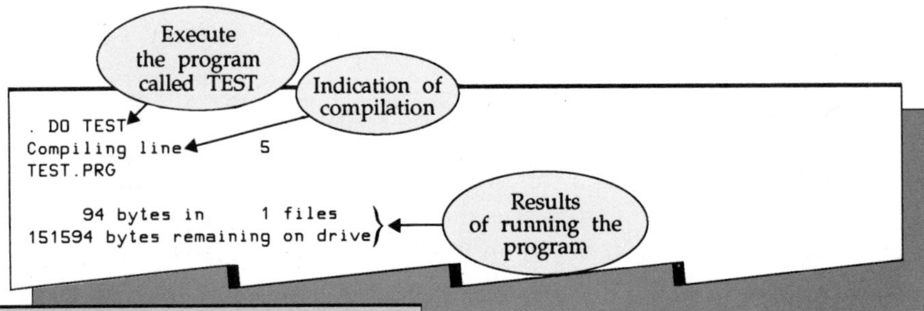

Figure 4.3 EXECUTING A PRG FILE (PROGRAM)

(**Note:** In the figure and on your screen, you will see the message "Compiling". This is an indication that a special process called *compilation* is taking place. dBASE is translating your program into a special form that it will execute. This is nothing for you to worry about. dBASE does it automatically.)

You can make changes to the program by typing MODIFY COMMAND TEST again. When the screen appears, you can add, delete, or change commands at will, and then save the program in the same manner you did before. Use this technique to add two commands to the program that will turn on communications with the printer before the DIR and then turn them off after the command. (See Figure 4.4.) Make certain that the printer is ready before you execute the program with the DO command.

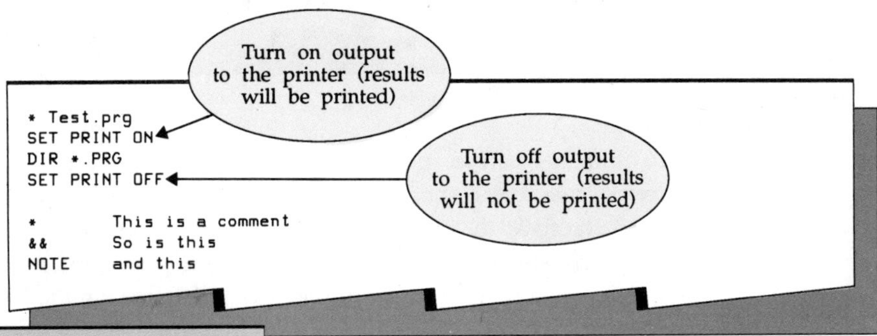

Figure 4.4 MODIFYING A PRG FILE

(**Note:** If you enter MODIFY COMMAND and decide not to change the program, press the Escape key (Esc) to exit without saving. You will be asked if you want to abandon your changes. Answer Yes and you will be returned to the dot prompt.)

You will repeat this process of changing, saving, and testing until you are satisfied with the performance of your program. Try to become comfortable with the procedure by adding, deleting, and changing comment lines in the TEST.PRG file and experimenting with the keys in the MODIFY COMMAND menu.

It is sometimes helpful to have a printed copy (also called a *hard copy*) of your program for study when you are away from the computer. If the program is less than one full screen, you could simply press the PrintScreen key. A snapshot of the screen's contents will print, providing the printer is on and is correctly set. Longer programs can be printed through the use of either of the following command sequences:

```
TYPE TEST.PRG TO PRINT
```

or

```
SET PRINT ON
TYPE TEST.PRG
SET PRINT OFF
```

Notice that the PRG extension was required in the TYPE command. This is because TYPE can be used to print other types of files. DOS, which actually executes the command, requires the full filename.

The steps just outlined are only the means for putting commands in the file. A great deal more than this is involved in building a program. Before you begin, you need to complete a clear and effective plan.

4.3 PLANNING A PROGRAM

After you have written a number of programs (and made a few mistakes), you will begin to develop both a style and an organized way of working. Some tips and techniques on good programming standards are presented in this chapter. Further tips and techniques are included in Chapter 8.

A convenient way to begin planning a program is to briefly state in plain language the tasks that the program must perform. Although you may have to add, delete, or change some steps later, you should be able to specify most of the required tasks. A list of tasks in logical order is often called *pseudocode*. The example in Figure 4.5 on the next page illustrates how pseudocode might be written. Note that since this is a first effort, it contains errors.

```
Clear the screen
Open database
Remove unwanted records
Close database
Display names of cities < 500000 in 1982
Display names of cities < 500000 in 1982
Turn off printer
```

Figure 4.5 EXAMPLE OF PSEUDOCODE

Figure 4.5 is an example of pseudocode for a program that attempts to clean up a database by PACKing it and that then displays some data on the printer. The programmer thought through the pseudocode and made the changes shown in the pseudocode in Figure 4.6.

```
XXXXXXXXXXXXXXX
Open database
Remove unwanted records
Close database
Turn on printer ←
Display cities < 500000 in 1982
Display cities < 500000 in 1970 ←
Turn off printer
```

Figure 4.6 MODIFYING PSEUDOCODE

Figure 4.6 shows how easily pseudocode can be changed. Steps can be added, deleted, moved, or modified until the purpose of the program appears to be satisfied. Then the pseudocode must be translated into acceptable dBASE IV commands and tested. Figure 4.7 illustrates the translation.

```
XXXXXXXXXXXXXXX
Open database                       USE CITIES
Remove unwanted records                PACK
Close database                      CLOSE
Turn on printer                     SET PRINT ON
Display cities < 500000 in 1982        LIST FOR POP-82<500000
Display cities < 500000 in 1970        LIST FOR POP-70<500000
Turn off printer                    SET PRINT OFF
```

Figure 4.7 CONVERTING PSEUDOCODE TO COMMANDS

You can place the dBASE IV commands in Figure 4.7 in a PRG file with MODIFY COMMAND and then execute the program with DO from the dot prompt. This step in the process is referred to as *coding*. The simple fact that you have entered the commands does not mean that the resulting program is complete or correct. It is simply your first effort, and it must be tested. As you will discover, programs very rarely run correctly the first time. When the program in Figure 4.7 is executed, dBASE IV detects an error, as shown in Figure 4.8.

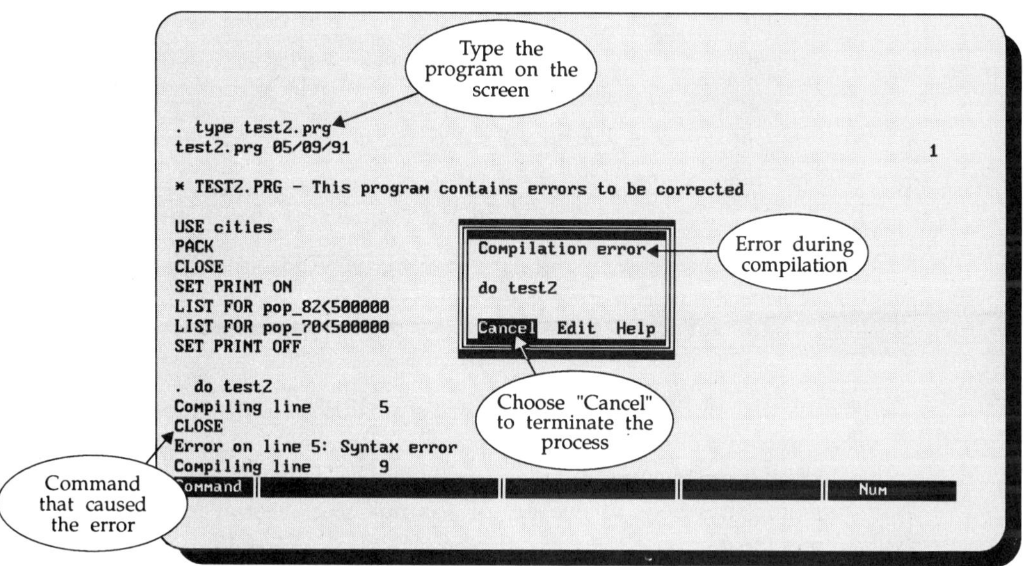

Figure 4.8 EXAMPLE OF A SYNTAX ERROR

TEST2.PRG will have to be changed and then tested again. Because this program is not complicated, it will probably not require many revisions. As you work through the process of finding errors, correcting them, and retesting, you will notice that some errors are the result of mistyping or misunderstanding the *syntax* (rules) of a command. This is what happened in Figure 4.8.

The CLOSE command must be written as CLOSE ALL or CLOSE DATABASES. When the program was being compiled, dBASE IV detected the error, paused, and asked if you would prefer to cancel, edit, or get help. Select Cancel. Then type MODIFY COMMAND TEST2 and change CLOSE to CLOSE ALL. Save your work and run the program again. The results of this rerun are shown in Figure 4.9 on the next page.

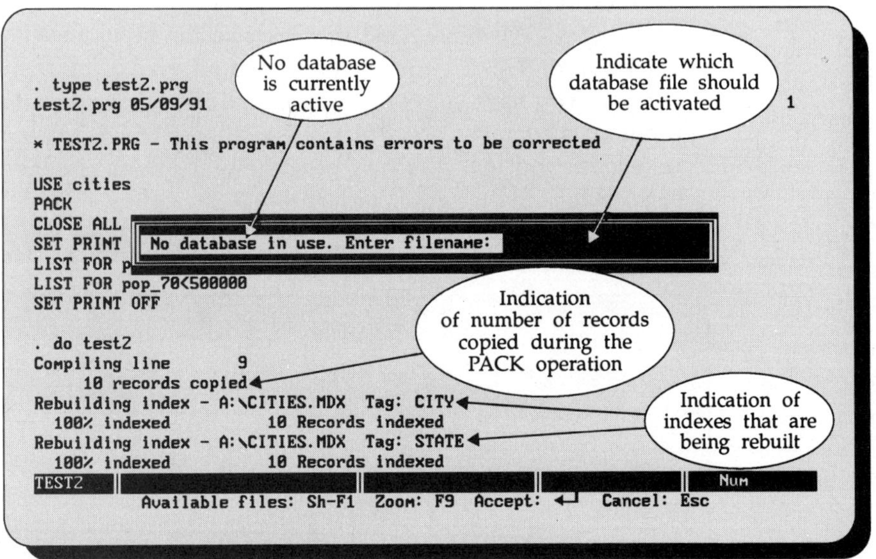
No database is currently active
Indicate which database file should be activated
. type test2.prg
test2.prg 05/09/91
1
* TEST2.PRG - This program contains errors to be corrected
USE cities
PACK
CLOSE ALL
SET PRINT
LIST FOR p
No database in use. Enter filename:
LIST FOR pop_70<500000
SET PRINT OFF
Indication of number of records copied during the PACK operation
. do test2
Compiling line 9
10 records copied
Rebuilding index - A:\CITIES.MDX Tag: CITY
100% indexed 10 Records indexed
Rebuilding index - A:\CITIES.MDX Tag: STATE
100% indexed 10 Records indexed
Indication of indexes that are being rebuilt
TEST2
Num
Available files: Sh-F1 Zoom: F9 Accept: ↵ Cancel: Esc

Figure 4.9 CORRECTING A LOGICAL ERROR

Although dBASE IV detected no errors this time, there does appear to be a problem. When a program runs but does not perform as expected, a logical error has probably been committed. This means that a command is missing, has been misplaced, or has not been used appropriately. In this case, the database file was closed after the PACK, and the LIST commands could not operate. The user (you, in this case) must type in the name of the DBF file in order to complete the execution of the program. The obvious solution is to move the CLOSE ALL command to a more appropriate location, and Figure 4.10 shows this correction.

Logical errors can be very difficult to find when programs are complicated. dBASE IV provides a way to obtain a step-by-step listing of the commands in your program as they execute. This listing can be compared with the program in order to study its behavior. SET ECHO ON displays each command in the PRG file as it executes. If you previously typed SET PRINT ON, the commands are sent to the printer as well. As you can see from Figure 4.11, you will have to separate the commands from the results of the program.

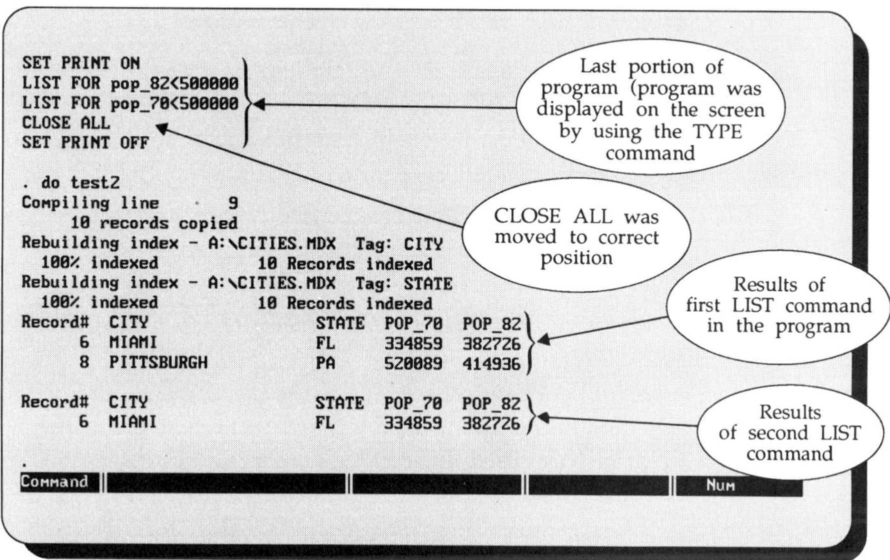

SET PRINT ON
LIST FOR pop_82<500000
LIST FOR pop_70<500000
CLOSE ALL
SET PRINT OFF
. do test2
Compiling line 9
10 records copied
Rebuilding index - A:\CITIES.MDX Tag: CITY
100% indexed 10 Records indexed
Rebuilding index - A:\CITIES.MDX Tag: STATE
100% indexed 10 Records indexed
Record# CITY STATE POP_70 POP_82
6 MIAMI FL 334859 382726
8 PITTSBURGH PA 520089 414936
Record# CITY STATE POP_70 POP_82
6 MIAMI FL 334859 382726
Command
Num
Last portion of program (program was displayed on the screen by using the TYPE command
CLOSE ALL was moved to correct position
Results of first LIST command in the program
Results of second LIST command

Figure 4.10 CORRECTING A COMMAND POSITION ERROR

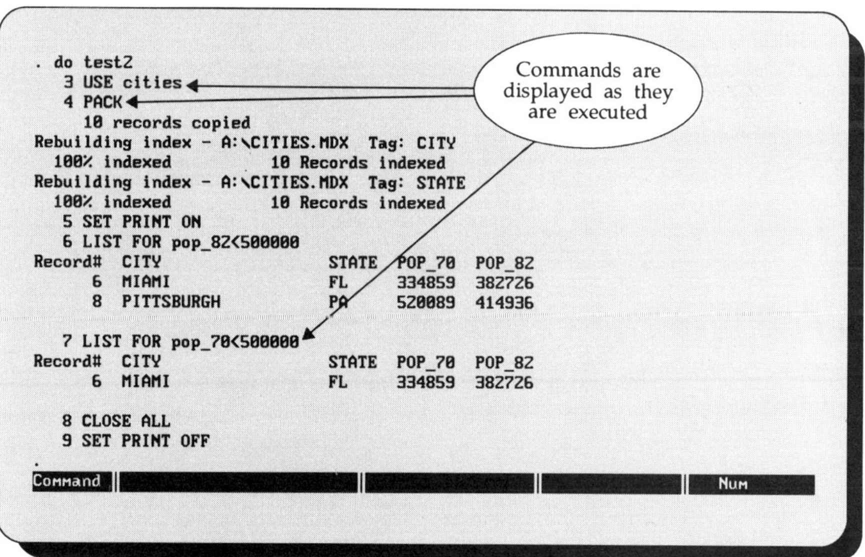

. do test2
3 USE cities
4 PACK
10 records copied
Rebuilding index - A:\CITIES.MDX Tag: CITY
100% indexed 10 Records indexed
Rebuilding index - A:\CITIES.MDX Tag: STATE
100% indexed 10 Records indexed
5 SET PRINT ON
6 LIST FOR pop_82<500000
Record# CITY STATE POP_70 POP_82
6 MIAMI FL 334859 382726
8 PITTSBURGH PA 520089 414936
7 LIST FOR pop_70<500000
Record# CITY STATE POP_70 POP_82
6 MIAMI FL 334859 382726
8 CLOSE ALL
9 SET PRINT OFF
Command
Num
Commands are displayed as they are executed

Figure 4.11 USING SET ECHO ON

Consider some of the potential advantages and benefits of this brief program, now that it is working as expected.

1. Future executions of the program will accurately reflect any changes in the data, including APPENDs, DELETEs, and EDITs.
2. A person who is not familiar with dBASE IV can run the program and produce results with very little instruction.
3. As the needs of the user change, modifications can be made to the existing program; it is not necessary to begin all over again.
4. Time is wasted on typing errors and on incorrect syntax when commands are typed interactively (from the dot prompt), especially if the same commands are used on a regular basis. Once the program is correct, this is no longer a problem.
5. The data in the files is safer if the standardized and tested procedures in the program are used instead of haphazard or poorly chosen interactive commands.

4.4 PROPER PROGRAMMING FORM

The work of innovators such as Edsger W. Dijkstra, Larry L. Constantine, Edward Yourdon, and others has produced some programming principles that enjoy wide acceptance among data processing professionals. These principles define what is known as *structured programming*. The general goals of structured programming are to ensure that programs will operate in an organized and predictable manner and that programmers can understand each other's work.

Although much can be said for individuality and creativity in programming, the business environment requires accountability. This means that projects must be completed in a cost-effective manner. It is difficult, if not impossible, to estimate the amount of time and money a program will consume if only the programmer understands the programming methods to be used. Structured programs are developed in less time and are more easily maintained than those that are written freestyle.

Table 4.2 describes some of the common features of structured programming. Some of these may not make much sense to you at this point, since we have not studied the corresponding programming topic. Keep this table in mind, however. You may want to periodically refer back to it as we encounter these other concepts later in the text. When you do, you should be able to appreciate the importance of these principles.

TABLE 4.2 **Common features of structured programs**

FEATURE	DESCRIPTION
Comments	It is always preferable to include enough comments so that the reader can follow the logic of the program, without cluttering the listing.
Indentation	Since dBASE IV ignores spaces, indent where appropriate and include blank lines between sections.
Design	The primary consideration is the design of the program, which should be complete before coding can begin. If the design is flawed, the program can never perform satisfactorily.
Top-down design	Proceed from the general to the specific when designing the program. Large tasks should be broken down into subtasks.
Modularity	Each section should be a freestanding module that can be tested and that can function on its own.
No direct branching	Since dBASE IV has no direct branching statement such as the GOTO in BASIC or COBOL, and since it uses block-structured commands, it encourages structured programming.
No infinite loops	Looping must be controlled so that no loop will proceed endlessly.

Large organizations depend on structured programming because teams of programmers are often assigned to one project. A common structure allows programs to be universally understood, so one programmer can substitute for another if necessary. It has also been demonstrated that structured programs require less "debugging" than programs that are written in a loose, haphazard manner.

Some of these features may not be clear to you at this time; they will be discussed in later chapters. Other features such as the use of comments, indentation, and top-down design can become part of your programming practice immediately.

4.5 MEMORY VARIABLES

An essential part of any programming environment is the capability to store data in the computer's *random access memory (RAM)* for temporary use while a program is executing. The way in which this storage is accomplished is the same in most programming languages. The data is stored in a memory location, which must be labeled. The name provided allows the program to reference the data location by the memory variable name regardless of what specific data happens to be stored there at the moment. The STORE command is used for this purpose in dBASE programs. Memory variable names may be between one and ten characters long. They should generally follow the same restrictions as dBASE field names (Chapter 2). The only special character you can use in the name is the underscore.

Figure 4.12 illustrates how the STORE command can be used to place a numeric value in a memory variable. By displaying the contents, dBASE IV verifies the operation.

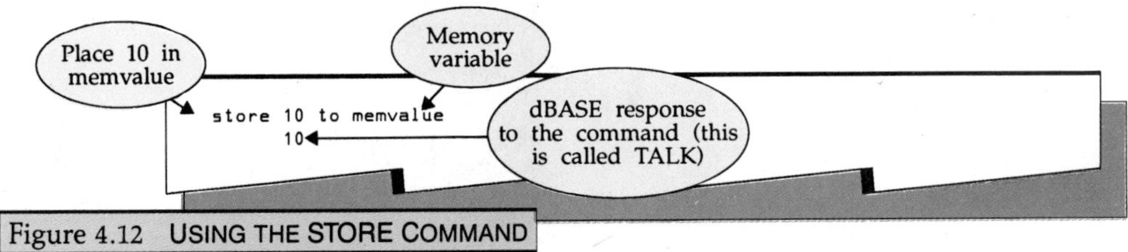

Figure 4.12 USING THE STORE COMMAND

As shown in Figure 4.13, LIST MEMORY or DISPLAY MEMORY can provide the current status of all memory variables that are currently active. Either command is useful for studying how memory variables operate, and either can be used as a debugging tool. The output of these commands is a fairly lengthy report. The portion of the report that is of most interest comes first. For this reason, we will usually use DISPLAY MEMORY since DISPLAY causes dBASE to pause after each screenful of data. With LIST MEMORY, on the other hand, the entire report will rapidly scroll by on the screen. The portion of interest to you will disappear before you have a chance to study it.

The contents of a memory variable can be redefined with a second STORE command, as illustrated in Figure 4.14. Figure 4.15 illustrates the use of the STORE command in assigning the same value to several memory variables. Notice that the names must be separated by commas.

Show contents of memory
Current value
. DISPLAY MEMORY
User Memory Variables
MEMVALUE pub N 10 (10.00000000000000000)
1 out of 500 memvars defined (and 0 array elements)
Only memory variable we have created
User MEMVAR/RTSYM Memory Usage
2800 bytes used for 1 memvar blocks (max=10)
850 bytes used for 1 rtsym blocks (max=10)
0 bytes used for 0 array element memvars
0 bytes used for 0 memvar character strings
Display continues
3650 bytes total

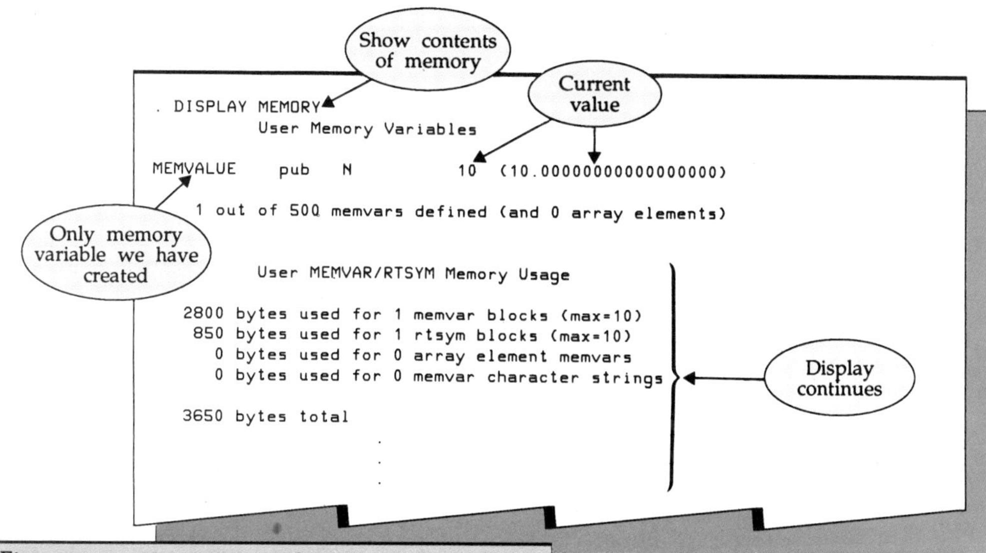

Figure 4.13 VIEWING THE CONTENTS OF MEMORY

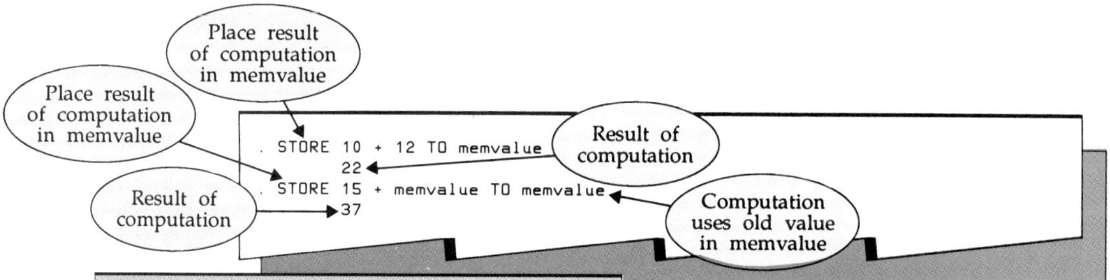

Place result of computation in memvalue
Place result of computation in memvalue
. STORE 10 + 12 TO memvalue
22
. STORE 15 + memvalue TO memvalue
37
Result of computation
Result of computation
Computation uses old value in memvalue

Figure 4.14 REDEFINING A MEMORY VARIABLE

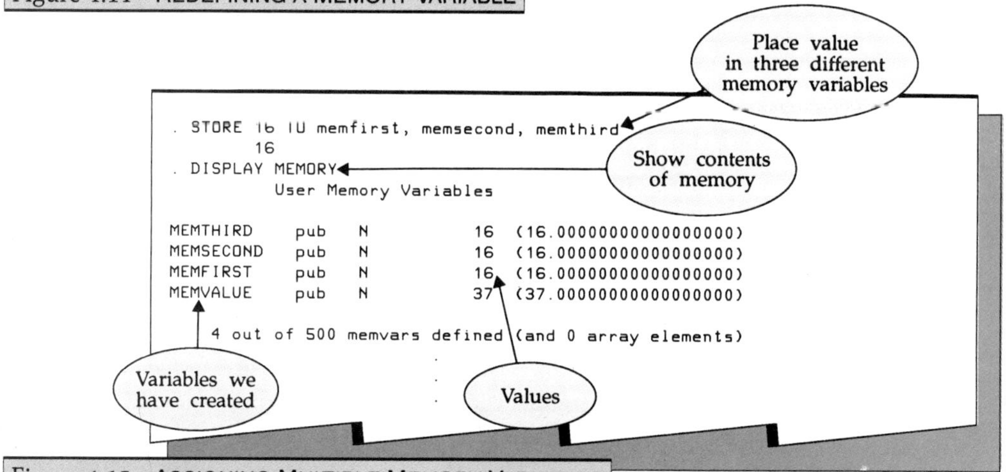

Place value in three different memory variables
. STORE 16 TO memfirst, memsecond, memthird
16
. DISPLAY MEMORY
Show contents of memory
User Memory Variables
MEMTHIRD pub N 16 (16.00000000000000000)
MEMSECOND pub N 16 (16.00000000000000000)
MEMFIRST pub N 16 (16.00000000000000000)
MEMVALUE pub N 37 (37.00000000000000000)
4 out of 500 memvars defined (and 0 array elements)
Variables we have created
Values

Figure 4.15 ASSIGNING MULTIPLE MEMORY VARIABLES

A memory variable's type is determined by the data that is being stored. In Figure 4.16, a character value defines the type of the memory variable memcapitol.

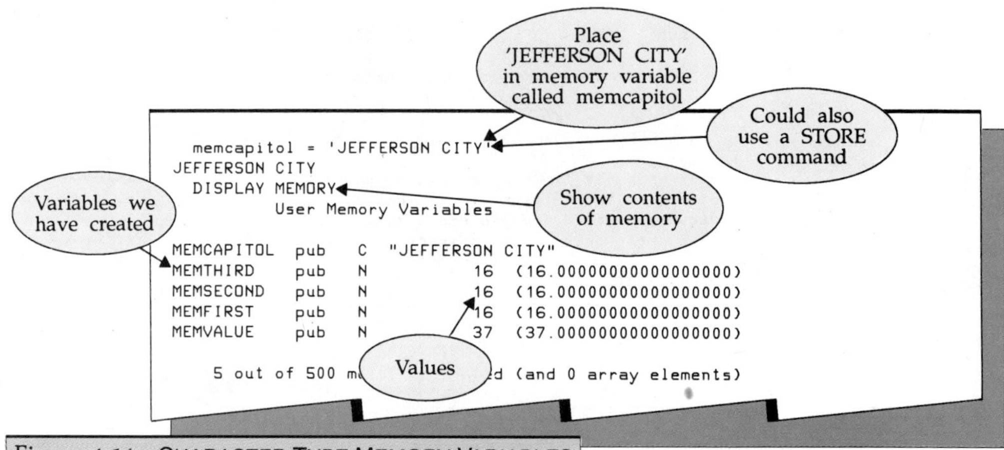

Figure 4.16 CHARACTER-TYPE MEMORY VARIABLES

(**Note:** Programmers often use lowercase letters for memory variables in order to distinguish them from commands. The prefix m or mem is also often used for this purpose.)

As shown in Figure 4.17, the ? can be used to print the contents of memory variables on the screen or to the printer (with SET PRINT ON). If the + sign is used between character variables, the two will be "pasted" together; this is a process known as *concatenation*. Of course, when the + sign is used between numeric variables, it represents addition.

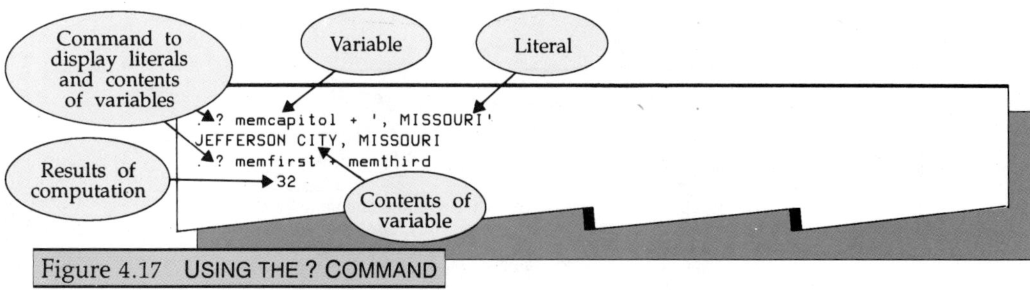

Figure 4.17 USING THE ? COMMAND

Data that is stored in memory variables is easily lost since it is in the computer's memory rather than in a file on a disk. **NOTE:** If you leave dBASE IV or turn off the power, memory variables are erased.

4.6 NUMERIC VERSUS CHARACTER DATA TYPES

Although a variety of data (or field) types are available in dBASE IV, character and numeric are the ones you will use most frequently. It is essential that you understand the purpose of and the differences between these two data types.

In Chapter 2 you learned fields that might be used in an arithmetic operation should be declared as numeric during CREATE. In a business environment, this means such things as money or an inventory of items. It may be difficult on occasion to decide which type a certain field should be. Consider the following examples and explanations of the proper choice of field type.

- **111-11-1111 (Social Security number).** Although this field contains no letters, it does contain hyphens. These would not be interpreted as negative (minus) signs because they do not precede the field and because there is more than one of them. Further, a Social Security number would probably not be used in a calculation. Given these reasons, the field should be declared as character type.
- **12/27/92 (December 27, 1992).** Dates are always stored in date-type fields that include the month, day, and year. (Chapter 12 explains how to do arithmetic with dates.)
- **SKU-101-24636 (Furniture inventory number).** The letters SKU and the hyphens require this to be a character-type field.
- **22 (Person's age).** It is usually best to record age as the date of birth in a date-type field. However, it would be possible to store 22 as a numeric field and use it in a calculation, such as the average age of a group.
- **.007 (Tolerance in a manufacturing process).** This field would probably be useful for calculation and should be declared as numeric type.
- **200000.00 (Salary of the president of the United States).** Money is almost always declared as numeric. It is primarily because the last three examples could be used in an arithmetic operation that they should be numeric-type fields.

When specific data is used in dBASE IV, some rules must be followed for expressing it. A specific piece of character data, which may be referred to as a *string*, a *label*, an *alphanumeric constant*, or an *alphanumeric literal* must always be enclosed in a matched set of quotation marks. You can use single or double quotes provided you use the same symbol both before and after the data. You can also use square brackets. For example,

```
'SOUTH DAKOTA'
"Wayne Ratliff"
[dBASE IV]
```

If the symbols surrounding a string do not match, dBASE IV generates an error message, as shown in Figure 4.18. To correct the error, make sure both quotation marks are the same (Figure 4.19). Conversely, when specific numeric data is being referenced, it is never enclosed in quotation marks or square brackets. This type of data is sometimes called a *value,* a *numeric constant,* or a *numeric literal.* Care must be taken not to include stray symbols such as letters, dollar signs, or commas in numeric data.

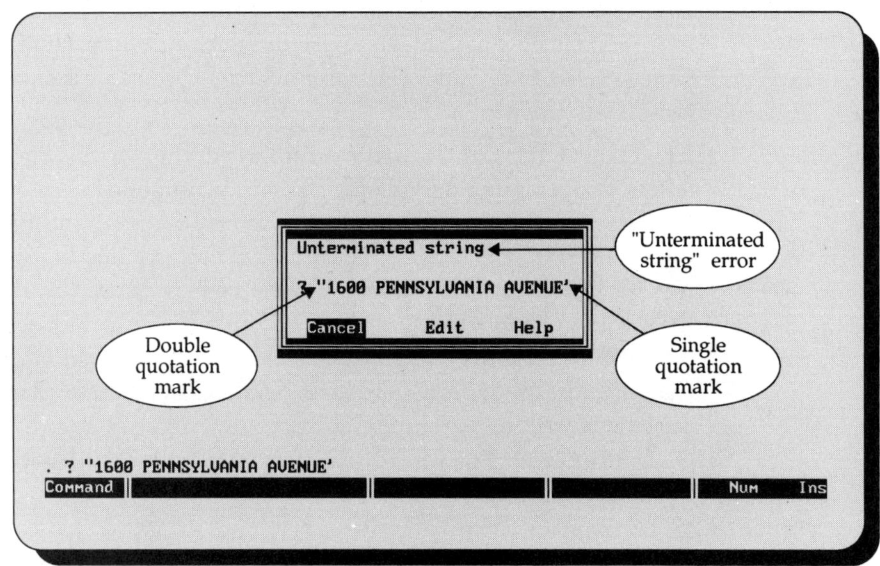

Figure 4.18 RESULT OF UNMATCHED QUOTATION MARKS

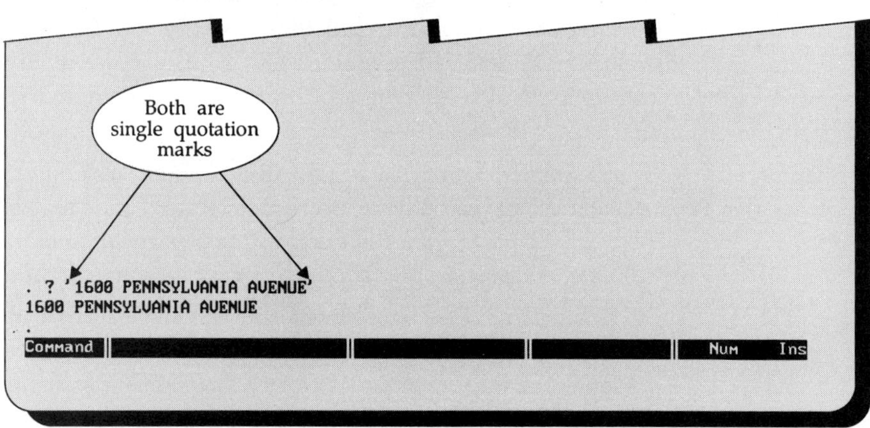

Figure 4.19 MATCHED QUOTATION MARKS

The quotation marks in the example in Figure 4.20 express the character symbol '3,' not the numeric value 3. dBASE IV detected the problem and could not perform the calculation. The corrected statement appears in Figure 4.21.

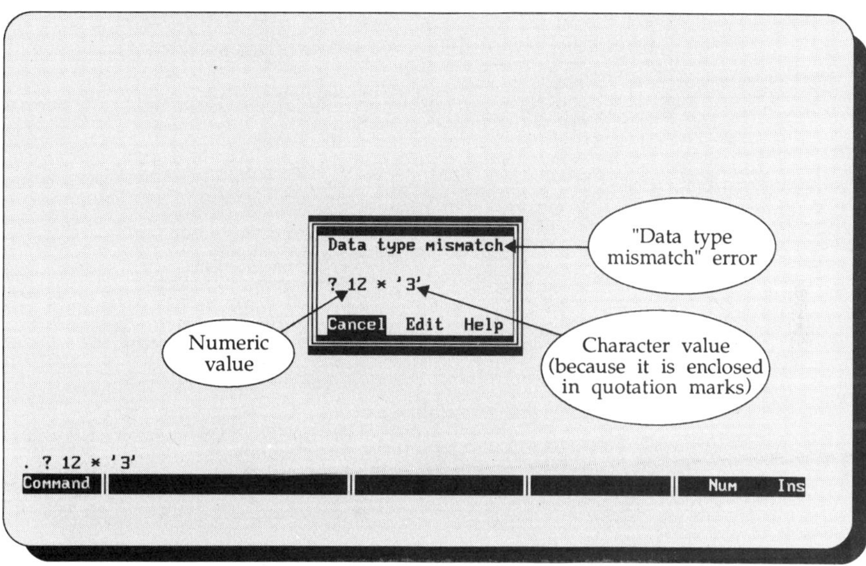

Figure 4.20 DATA TYPE MISMATCH

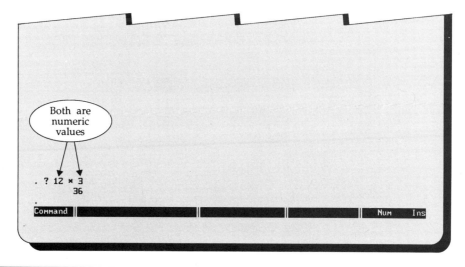

Figure 4.21 CORRECTED NUMERIC FIELDS

Usually we include dollar signs and commas when we deal with money, but these characters are not permitted in numeric fields. Figure 4.22 shows what happens when you use these two characters. Again, dBASE IV has detected the problem and has issued the appropriate message. The value should be expressed as 4500.00, as shown in Figure 4.23.

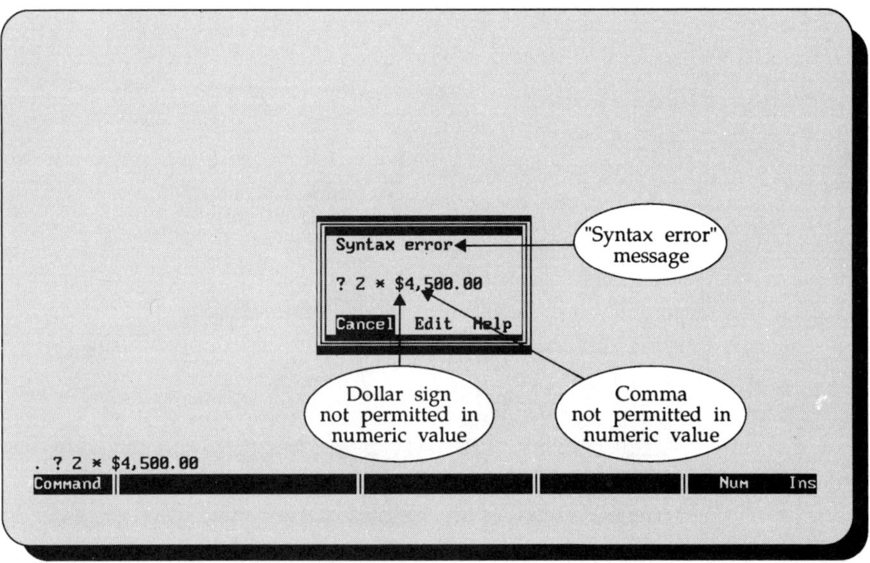

Figure 4.22 EFFECT OF $ AND , IN NUMERIC FIELDS

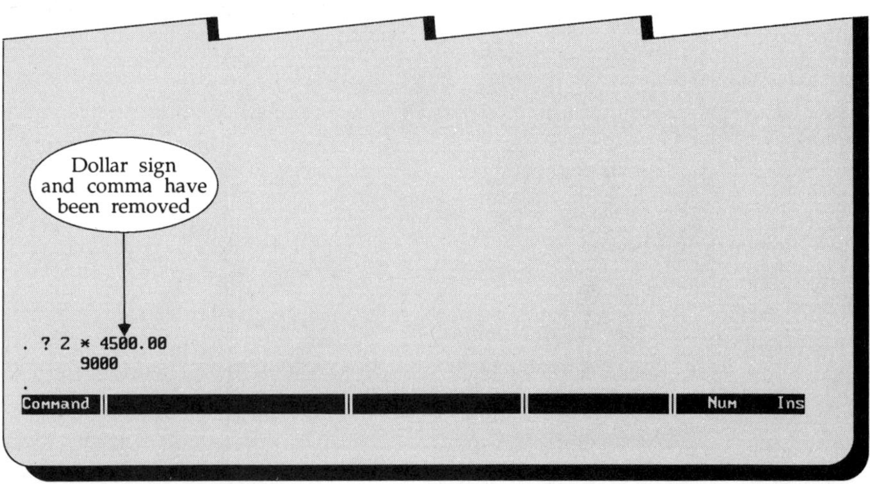

Figure 4.23 CORRECTED NUMERIC FIELD

Although *pi* is often used in mathematics, dBASE IV does not recognize it (Figure 4.24). You must use a special function for *pi* [PI()] as shown in Figure 4.25. The parentheses shown in Figure 4.25 are part of the format for a function and are essential.

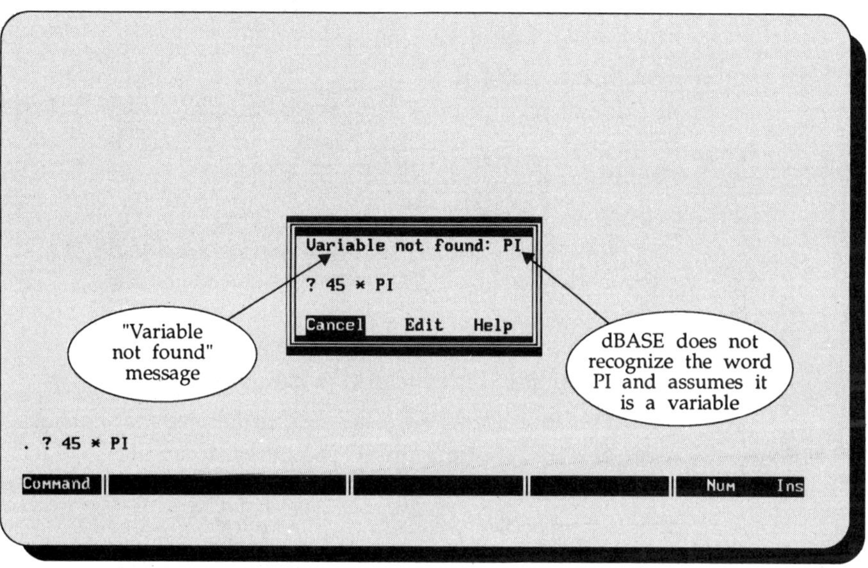

Figure 4.24 UNRECOGNIZED ARITHMETIC FUNCTIONS

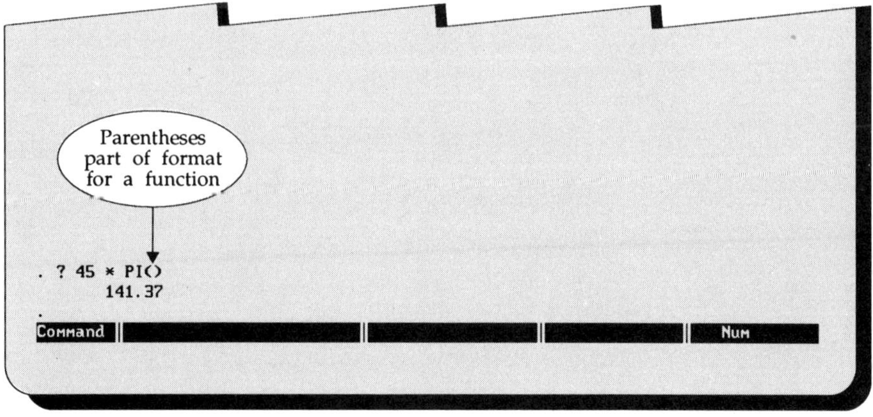

Figure 4.25 USING THE FUNCTION FOR PI

Being careless with data types when expressing field names, memory variables, or specific data in programs produces annoying errors.

CHAPTER SUMMARY

1. Sets of dBASE IV commands that are saved on the disk with a PRG extension and that can be executed with the DO command are called programs or command files. Programs increase efficiency, flexibility, and power, and they are an effective way of solving complex business problems. An organized method of modifying and testing programs is essential.
2. MODIFY COMMAND is a text editor that facilitates the creation and modification of programs. Several key combinations are available to manipulate commands within the PRG file. Comments can be included by preceding the line with * or NOTE. TYPE <filename> TO PRINT displays a program on the printer.
3. Programs should be written in pseudocode before the actual dBASE IV commands are coded. This helps prevent logical errors caused by misplaced or missing commands. Syntax errors (commands spelled or expressed incorrectly) will halt the program. SET ECHO ON displays the commands as they execute; this is helpful in debugging.
4. Structured programming is a set of principles that encourages the development of clear, well-organized programs. Comments, indentation, and top-down design are some of the features of this important concept.
5. Memory variables are used to hold data temporarily during the execution of a program. They may be examined with LIST MEMORY or DISPLAY MEMORY. The STORE command requires a name and a specific piece of data in order to establish the memory variable.
6. Data should be declared numeric if it is going to be used in an arithmetic operation. Numeric data can contain digits, a decimal point, and a negative sign. Character data is always enclosed in a matched set of quotation marks, whereas numeric data is not.

KEY TERMS

command file
compilation
batch mode
comment
pseudocode
coding
syntax
hard copy
structured programming
random access memory (RAM)
concatenation
string
label
alphanumeric constant
alphanumeric literal
value
numeric constant
numeric literal
debugging

COMMAND SUMMARY

Command Name	**Use**
MODIFY COMMAND	Edit a file with the MODIFY COMMAND text editor.
*	Comment.
&&	End-of-line comment.
NOTE	Comment (like *).
CLOSE ALL	Close all open files.
SET ECHO ON	Display commands as they execute.
SET PRINT ON	Activate the printer.
STORE	Place a value in a memory variable.
DISPLAY MEMORY or LIST MEMORY	Display the contents of memory.

dBUG dBASE

Debugging is the process of finding errors in a program and correcting them. Since the debugging of a program can consume as much as half of the programmer's development time, it is wise to learn to use the available techniques and features. You will find helpful dBUG dBASE sections at the end of most of the remaining chapters.

- It is very important to keep backup copies of your programs in case something should happen to your work disk. Making a backup copy takes only a few minutes with the COPY FILE command in dBASE IV or with the COPY command in DOS. Many hours of work can be lost in an instant as the result of having no backup.
- You can examine a "play-by-play" listing of the commands as they were typed at the dot prompt by using LIST HISTORY. The default is twenty commands, but you can increase the size of the HISTORY buffer with SET HISTORY TO 100, for example. Use SET PRINT ON to obtain a printed copy.
- Get in the habit of constantly monitoring the dBASE IV environment with the following commands. You can often spot an unanticipated problem simply by frequently checking the disk, memory, structure, and status.

```
DIR                 LIST STRUCTURE
DISPLAY FILES       LIST FILES
DISPLAY MEMORY      LIST MEMORY
DISPLAY STATUS      LIST STATUS
DISPLAY STRUCTURE
```

SELF-CHECK QUESTIONS

1. What are some of the advantages of programming?
2. Is writing a program always the best way to use dBASE IV?
3. How can you tell when a program is finished?
4. Why are comment lines important?
5. Why would you want to exit MODIFY COMMAND without saving the file?
6. Why is a printed copy of a program useful?
7. Why is pseudocode useful? Wouldn't it be easier to immediately type the program into the computer?
8. If a program has a significant number of syntax errors, is it fair to say that it was poorly designed? Would you say that a program containing many logical errors had been poorly designed?
9. Why is data safer when it is maintained and accessed by good programs as opposed to interactive use?
10. What is the danger in planning bottom-up rather than top-down, in other words, in programming details first and then moving on to the larger aspects of the program?
11. Why is it important to be aware of the data type when working with memory variables?
12. What is the danger in holding data in memory variables?
13. Is there a way to include quotation marks when printing a character string (for example, "Garbage In, Garbage Out")?

TRY IT YOURSELF

1. Use MODIFY COMMAND to create the following PRG file:

```
* EX.PRG
```

   * This will illustrate how MODIFY COMMAND is used.

   After saving EX.PRG on your disk, use MODIFY COMMAND and the available key functions to change the program as follows:

```
* EX.PRG
```

   * This is a program modification.
   * This program will illustrate how MODIFY COMMAND is used.

2. Use the DIR command to display all PRG files on your disk. Display a copy of the program in Exercise 1 on the screen and then on the printer.
3. Use the memrate and memhour memory variables to STORE 4.75 and 37, respectively. Write another STORE statement to calculate the product in memgross. List the memory variables. Change memrate to 5.25 and calculate memgross again.
4. Here is a section of pseudocode. Study the sequence of tasks and determine whether the pseudocode will execute properly when converted to dBASE IV commands. Make corrections if necessary.

```
Open the database
Display cities in California
Direct output to the printer
Display names of DBF files
Clear the screen
```

5. Write a dBASE IV program on paper using the pseudocode in Exercise 4. Evaluate and modify the program until you are satisfied that it works properly.
6. Write a short program that consists of several comment lines and that uses all three symbols for comment lines. Try all the features displayed in Table 4.1, including deleting and inserting lines and characters, and moving around the file by line, word, and character.

7. Store your first name to one memory variable and your last name to another. Display them together on the screen. Store both names to a single memory variable.
8. Store 28 in memone and 32 in memtwo. Store the sum in memtot. If you now store 15 in memone, will memtot change?
9. Store the perimeter and the area of a 9-by-12-foot room in two memory variables.
10. Decide what type of data each of the following examples should be. Create a memory variable for each value.

```
Car model number          - LX-70
Price of a stereo system  - $346.23 (be careful of the $)
Matriculation date        - May 10, 1993
Telephone number          - 555-1212
Zip code                  - 17055
Computer                  - IBM PS/2
```

11. Write a program using the following pseudocode:

```
Clear the screen
Open the CITIES database
List the cities in California
Direct the output to the printer
Print the cities in California
Turn off output to the printer
Close the database
```

12. Write a program using the following pseudocode:

```
Establish memory variables for each example in Exercise 12
Clear the screen
Display the contents of each variable using ?
List memory contents
```

PROGRAMMING PROJECTS

Write a program that will STORE your last name to the memlast memory variable and that will assign the first names of other members of your family to memfirst1, memfirst2, and so on. Include ? statements to print a list of the full names of the family members on the printer.

LEARNING OBJECTIVES

To construct and use the DO WHILE/ENDDO loop.

To examine the effect of DO WHILE/ENDDO on program control.

To code and test several types of DO WHILE/ENDDO loops.

The DO WHILE/ENDDO Loop

INTRODUCTION

Since computers are machines, they never become bored with their work. If you were asked to repeat the same menial task a hundred or a thousand times, you would probably not be pleased. The capability of computers to repeat operations is one of the features that make them so valuable to the business world. As you have learned, computers cannot operate without specific instructions for all activity, including repetition. This chapter presents the DO WHILE/ENDDO loop, the commands that control repetition, or *looping*, in dBASE IV. The ability to construct looping structures effectively is vital to a programmer's success.

5.1 CONSTRUCTING THE DO WHILE/ENDDO LOOP

The DO WHILE/ENDDO loop is the primary control structure in dBASE IV programming. Since it is, at minimum, a two-command structure, it can be used only in a program, not interactively (from the dot prompt).

Think of this structure as a sandwich. (See Figure 5.1.) The DO WHILE statement is the upper slice of bread and the ENDDO is the lower slice. The most important part of the sandwich (the meat, cheese, and so on) consists of normal dBASE IV commands that you wish to repeat a certain number of times. These commands are placed between the DO WHILE and ENDDO.

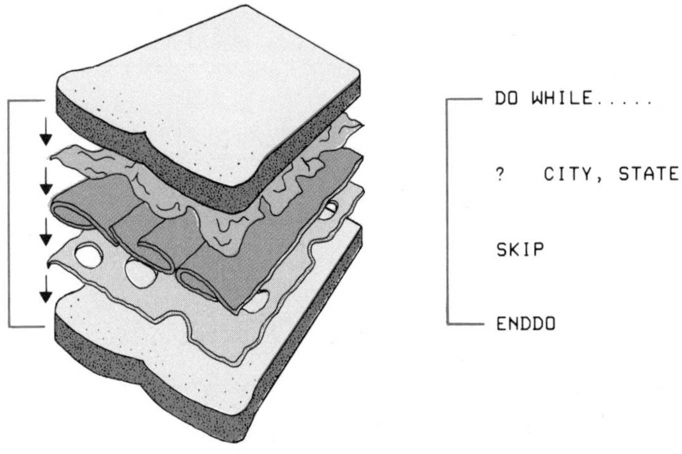
DO WHILE.....
? CITY, STATE
SKIP
ENDDO

Figure 5.1 THE DO WHILE/ENDDO SANDWICH

Notice that there is a space between the DO and the WHILE in the DO WHILE command but none in the ENDDO command. Another important thing to know is that these commands are always used as a pair (no open-faced sandwiches, please).

Before attempting to construct a DO WHILE loop, you should understand how it operates. Some sort of qualifying expression has to be placed after the DO WHILE command. This expression determines how many times the loop will execute or under what conditions the loop will cease to operate.

College students might express a spring vacation this way:

```
DO WHILE not in Florida
 Drive a mile
ENDDO
Enjoy the beach
```

This example would obviously not work in dBASE IV, but the same logic would apply in an actual program. The action placed between DO WHILE and ENDDO, "Drive a mile," must be repeated until the expression after DO WHILE, "not in Florida," is no longer true. This would mean that the students would have to be in Florida for the action following the ENDDO, "Enjoy the beach," to occur.

You will find that the expression following the DO WHILE is often stated in the negative because you want the action statements to continue to execute as long as the test to leave the loop is not true. Note also that this exit test is always at the top of the structure. This is an aspect of structured programming, and it also follows from common sense. Before commencing an activity, one needs to decide whether the activity is appropriate. This is why a structure should not execute unless the test condition is satisfied first.

A good illustration of the DO WHILE loop is a counting loop. The program we will discuss is called LOOP and is on your data disk. The complete program is shown in Figure 5.2.

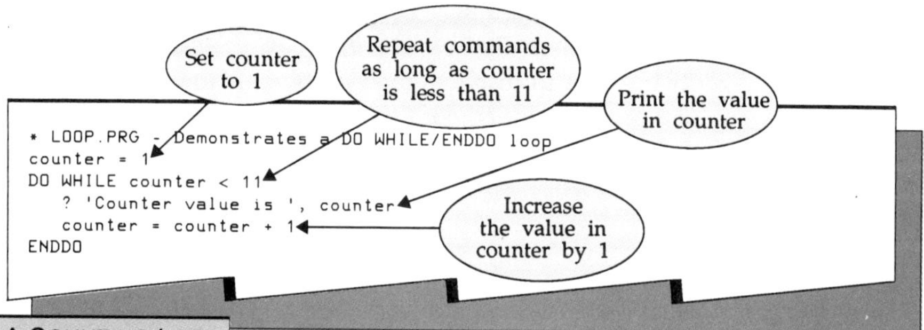

Figure 5.2 A COUNTING LOOP

The first step is to *initialize* (establish a value for) a variable called counter. We can use either of the following expressions:

```
STORE 1 TO counter
```

or

```
counter = 1
```

(The program on your disk uses the second version, `counter = 1`.) We then specify how many times you wish the loop to execute in the DO WHILE statement. The test to exit the loop should be expressed in a positive way:

```
DO WHILE counter < 11
```

This means that the loop will continue to operate as long as the variable called counter contains a value that is less than (<) 11. We need some means of *incrementing* (increasing) the value of counter each time the loop executes. This can be accomplished by including another STORE command. We can use either

```
STORE counter + 1 TO counter
```

or

```
counter = counter + 1
```

Although this command appears to be a formula, it is actually a means of assigning a value to the "new" counter by incrementing the value of the "old" counter.

Before this command, however we include a statement that will demonstrate that the loop is actually operating:

```
? 'Counter value is ', counter
```

The ? prints the literal, 'Counter value is ', on the screen, followed by the current value of counter (1, 2, 3, and so on). The comma separates the two parts of the print display. There will be a number of spaces between the two parts in order to display larger numbers. Finally, DO WHILE loops always conclude with an ENDDO command.

Execute the program by typing DO LOOP from the dot prompt. The display shown in Figure 5.3 should appear on your screen.

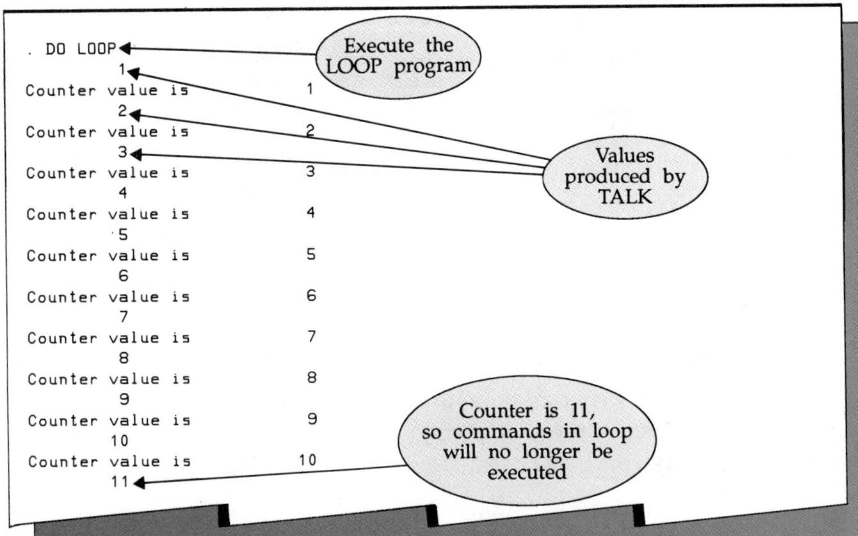

Figure 5.3 EXECUTION OF LOOP.PRG

The DO WHILE loop operates by testing the condition following the DO WHILE statement first. If the condition is true (counter is less than 11), all the statements between DO WHILE and ENDDO are executed. This execution continues until the ENDDO is encountered. Think of the ENDDO as a trampoline that bounces program control back to the DO WHILE, where the condition must be tested again. The extra numbers that you see between each line display the value of counter each time it is changed with the `counter = counter + 1` statement. You can remove this "system chatter" with the following command:

```
SET TALK OFF
```

In a properly constructed DO WHILE loop, the condition being tested will eventually not be true (counter will not be less than 11; it will be equal to 11). At that point, rather than executing the statements inside the loop as it did previously, control passes to the statement following ENDDO.

Since nothing follows the ENDDO in the LOOP program you will have to add a command to test the action of exiting the loop. Type MODIFY COMMAND LOOP from the dot prompt, and add the following statement after the ENDDO:

```
? 'Exit value of counter is ', counter
```

Save this modified version of the program and then execute it. This time you will see the following display after 'Counter value is 10':

```
Exit value of counter is 11
```

One of the fundamentals of structured programming is that programs must be *self-documenting*. Two ways to accomplish this with DO WHILE/ENDDO loops are indentation and the use of comments following the ENDDO. Indentation of the commands placed between the DO WHILE and the ENDDO is essential for clarity. Chapter 8 discusses *nesting*, a technique that places one loop within another. Without indentation, it becomes very difficult to determine which commands are part of which loop.

dBASE IV ignores comments that are placed after the ENDDO on the same line. This is another effective way to self-document a program because it establishes a visual connection between the DO WHILE and the ENDDO. The following two examples illustrate how effective these techniques can be.

(**Note:** During compilation, dBASE will produce a warning message for these comments placed after an ENDDO. You can ignore these messages. They do not affect compilation or execution of the program in any way. The benefits of including such commands far outweigh the inconvenience of seeing the messages during compilation.)

Notice how evident the two DO WHILE/ENDDO structures are in Figure 5.4. The indentations and the comments after the ENDDO contribute to the clarity of form. In the example in Figure 5.5, however, it is difficult to determine how the commands are related. If it is difficult in such a short program, think about how much more difficult it would be in programs that are substantially longer.

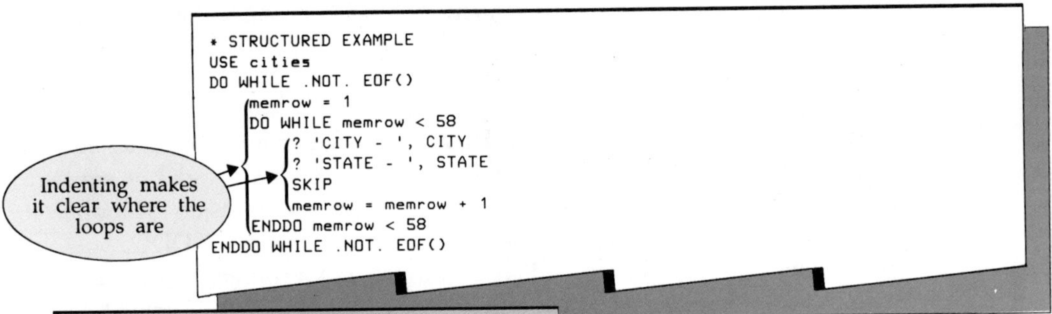

Figure 5.4 EXAMPLE OF STRUCTURED STYLE

Figure 5.5 EXAMPLE OF UNSTRUCTURED STYLE

Most DO WHILE commands require the use of a comparative expression. The effective construction of this portion of the DO WHILE/ENDDO unit is an essential skill. A *comparative expression* consists of two data items, which may be stored in memory variables or field names, separated by a relational operator. Once the expression has been established, dBASE IV can evaluate it and decide whether it is logically true or false. This true or false condition then becomes the basis for the continued execution of the DO WHILE/ENDDO loop.

The relational operators are used in mathematics and were presented in earlier chapters, so most of them will be familiar. dBASE IV accepts the following signs as valid:

=	Equal to
<	Less than
>	Greater than
< =	Less than or equal to
> =	Greater than or equal to
< >	Not equal to
#	Not equal to

Never place a space between any of the combined relational operators such as < =.

The following examples illustrate the variety of expressions that can be constructed.

- Memory variable compared to a literal (specific data):
  ```
  memcount > 100
  ```
- Field compared to a literal:
  ```
  CITY = 'KANSAS CITY'
  ```
- Memory variable compared to a memory variable:
  ```
  row <= max_row
  ```
- Field compared to a memory variable:
  ```
  pop_70 <= mempop
  ```

Any comparative expression is allowed in dBASE IV just as long as the items on either side of the relational operator are of the same data type. LOOP.PRG from Figure 5.2 has been modified in the following examples to illustrate how dBASE IV reacts to mismatches of data types in comparative expressions. In the version in Figure 5.6 on the next page, the memory variable counter has been initialized to the character literal '1' rather than the numeric value 1. Once counter has been established as a character-type variable with the quotes around the 1, it cannot be compared to the numeric literal 11 in the DO WHILE statement. In response, dBASE IV indicates a data-type mismatch error.

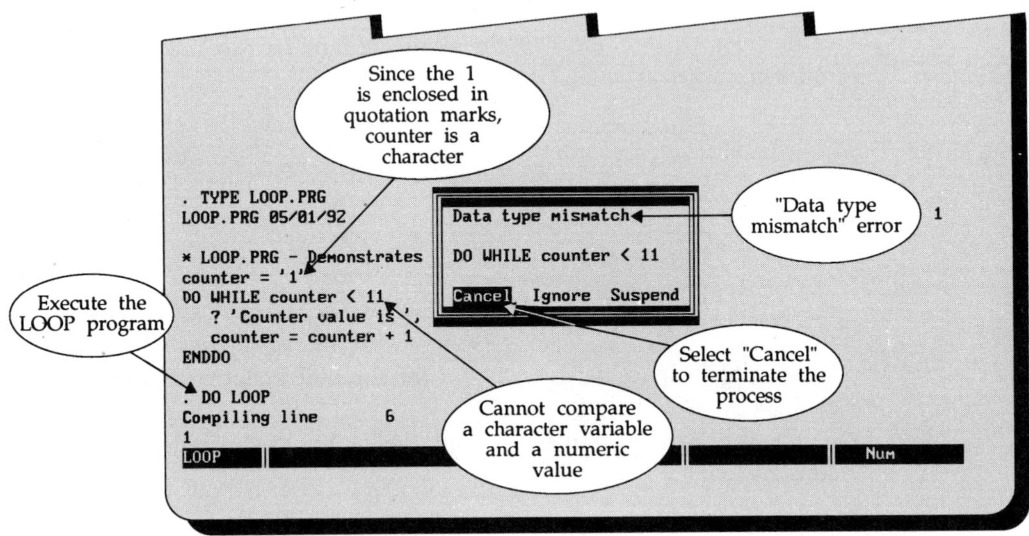

Figure 5.6 DATA-TYPE MISMATCH ERROR

An obvious example may be found in the modification of LOOP.PRG shown in Figure 5.7. Although counter has been initialized as numeric, the DO WHILE statement is comparing it to the character literal 'ELEVEN'. dBASE IV generates the data-type mismatch error in this case as well.

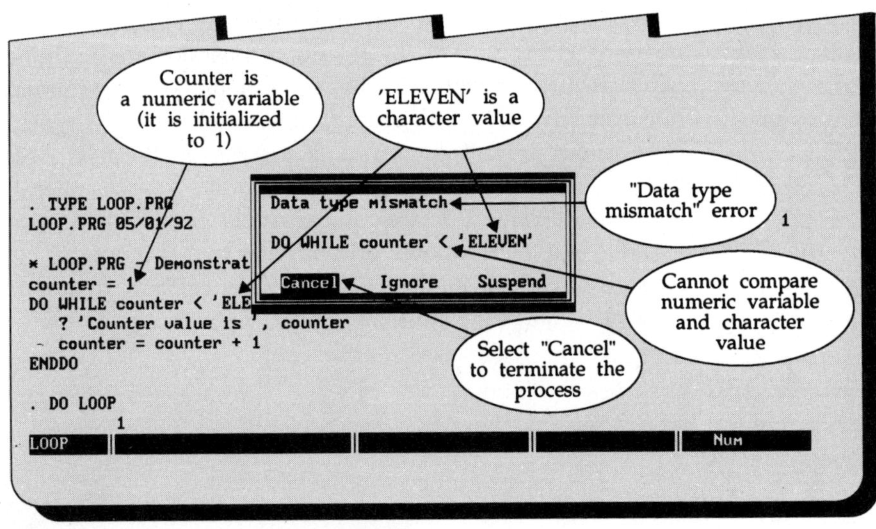

Figure 5.7 ANOTHER DATA-TYPE MISMATCH ERROR

Another common problem encountered in the construction of comparative expressions is inaccuracy in the use of the relational operator. Part of the difficulty is that the same comparison may often be made in several different ways. Consider the following examples:

```
AGE >= 18
AGE > 17

BALANCE < 500.01
BALANCE <= 500.00
```

People usually understand that when someone says, "You must be over 18 to vote," he or she means that you must be 18 or older to vote. We adjust to idiomatic usage of this type in everyday speech, but dBASE IV evaluates an expression quite literally. In general discourse it may not be essential to mean what you say, but when you are programming you must be certain to say what you mean.

5.2 THE DO WHILE/ENDDO LOOP AND PROGRAM CONTROL

Effectively writing the expression that is placed after DO WHILE is the key to using the structure for program control. In this section we will explore various possibilities for this expression and determine their effect on the execution of the program.

DO WHILE .T. LOOPS

In dBASE programs the letter T enclosed in periods (.T.) represents "True" and the letter F (.F.) represents "False." The next example shows a common type of loop that uses T (true) as the condition. Because the condition is always true, the DO WHILE loop will never end by itself! You would have to press the Escape key (Esc) to interrupt the loop and then choose Cancel to cancel the program's execution. (See Figure 5.8 on the next page.)

In Chapter 7 you will learn how to exercise control over an apparently endless loop by providing a "back door," or exit, within the program, and you will discover some practical applications of this technique. What is important to understand in the preceding example is that the DO WHILE/ENDDO structure can have a powerful effect on how a program behaves.

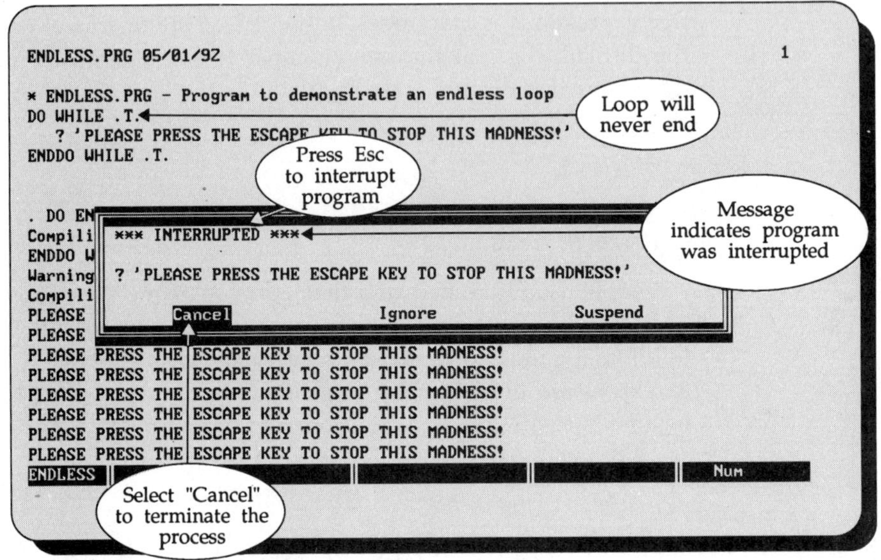

Figure 5.8 CANCELING AN ENDLESS LOOP

DO WHILE .NOT. EOF() LOOPS

It is often necessary to go through a database file record by record until all the records have been accessed. By checking for a special character that is found after the last record, dBASE IV can determine when the end of the file has been reached. The EOF() function can be used to control a DO WHILE loop when this is the case. Since we want to execute the commands in the loop as long as we have *not* reached the end of the file, we use the logical operator .NOT. in the condition. (See Figure 5.9.)

It appears that this program is behaving like the endless loop example, ENDLESS.PRG. The reason is that although the USE command set the file at the first record, there is no command in the program to advance to the next record. In previous chapters LIST did this automatically, but now you must place a SKIP command in the program for this purpose. The modified version of TEST_EOF.PRG shown in Figure 5.10 also includes a CLOSE ALL command to close CITIES.DBF.

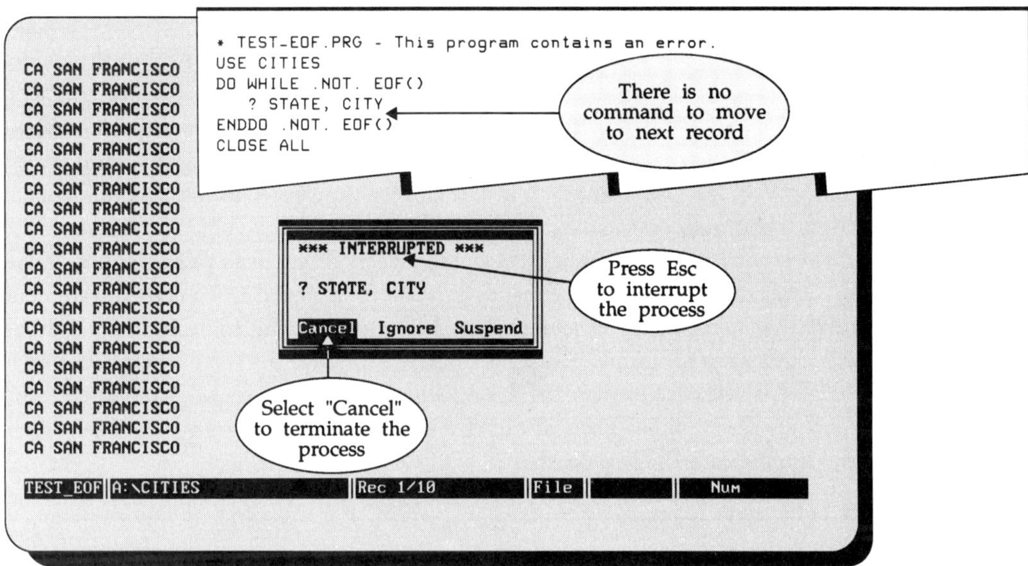

Figure 5.9 RESULT OF MISSING SKIP COMMAND

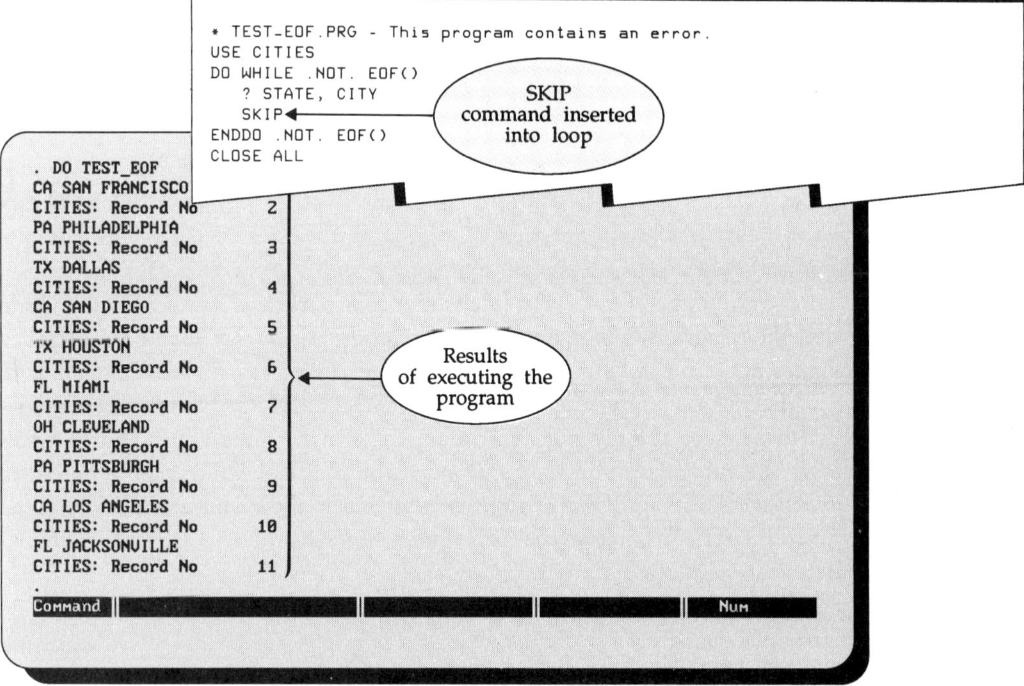

* TEST-EOF.PRG - This program contains an error.
USE CITIES
DO WHILE .NOT. EOF()
? STATE, CITY
SKIP
ENDDO .NOT. EOF()
CLOSE ALL
SKIP command inserted into loop
. DO TEST_EOF
CA SAN FRANCISCO
CITIES: Record No 2
PA PHILADELPHIA
CITIES: Record No 3
TX DALLAS
CITIES: Record No 4
CA SAN DIEGO
CITIES: Record No 5
TX HOUSTON
CITIES: Record No 6
FL MIAMI
CITIES: Record No 7
OH CLEVELAND
CITIES: Record No 8
PA PITTSBURGH
CITIES: Record No 9
CA LOS ANGELES
CITIES: Record No 10
FL JACKSONVILLE
CITIES: Record No 11
Results of executing the program
Command Num

Figure 5.10 PROPER USE OF THE SKIP COMMAND

This program accesses all the records in the file because the comparative expression in the DO WHILE statement does not branch to the statement after the ENDDO until EOF() is true, in which case .NOT. EOF() will be false. (The EOF() function is set to true when dBASE IV detects a special marker, Ctrl-Z (^Z), which always follows the last record in the file. When dBASE IV detects this marker, the EOF() function is set to true automatically. It is the programmer's responsibility, however, to test for this condition.) You also observed that dBASE IV must be instructed to move to the next record in the file when the current record has been processed.

The combination of the *test* to exit the loop in the DO WHILE statement and the *changing of factors* within the loop affecting that condition allows the DO WHILE loop to work properly. In Figure 5.11, DO WHILE .NOT. EOF() is the test to exit the loop, and SKIP is the factor that affects the condition. Being aware of these two aspects of the DO WHILE loop reveals its purpose and allows you to predict its behavior.

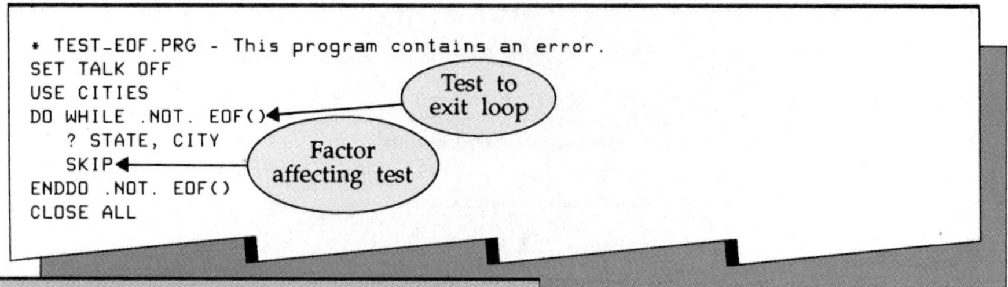

```
* TEST-EOF.PRG - This program contains an error.
SET TALK OFF
USE CITIES
DO WHILE .NOT. EOF()
   ? STATE, CITY
   SKIP
ENDDO .NOT. EOF()
CLOSE ALL
```


Figure 5.11 ANALYSIS OF A DO WHILE/ENDDO LOOP

USING SET ECHO ON TO TRACE A LOOP'S EXECUTION

dBASE IV actually "remembers" the test expression after the DO WHILE and recalls it when the ENDDO has been reached. You can observe the resulting loop action through the use of the SET ECHO ON command. This command displays each line from the program as it executes. The lines that the program would normally display on the screen have been offset in Figure 5.12 so that the program commands may be studied. Remember to SET ECHO OFF after the program has been run.

Notice how the program continues to branch to the command that follows the `DO WHILE` (`? STATE, CITY`), until the last valid record has been accessed. At this point the program branches to the command following the ENDDO. This branching action is the essence of the DO WHILE/ENDDO loop.

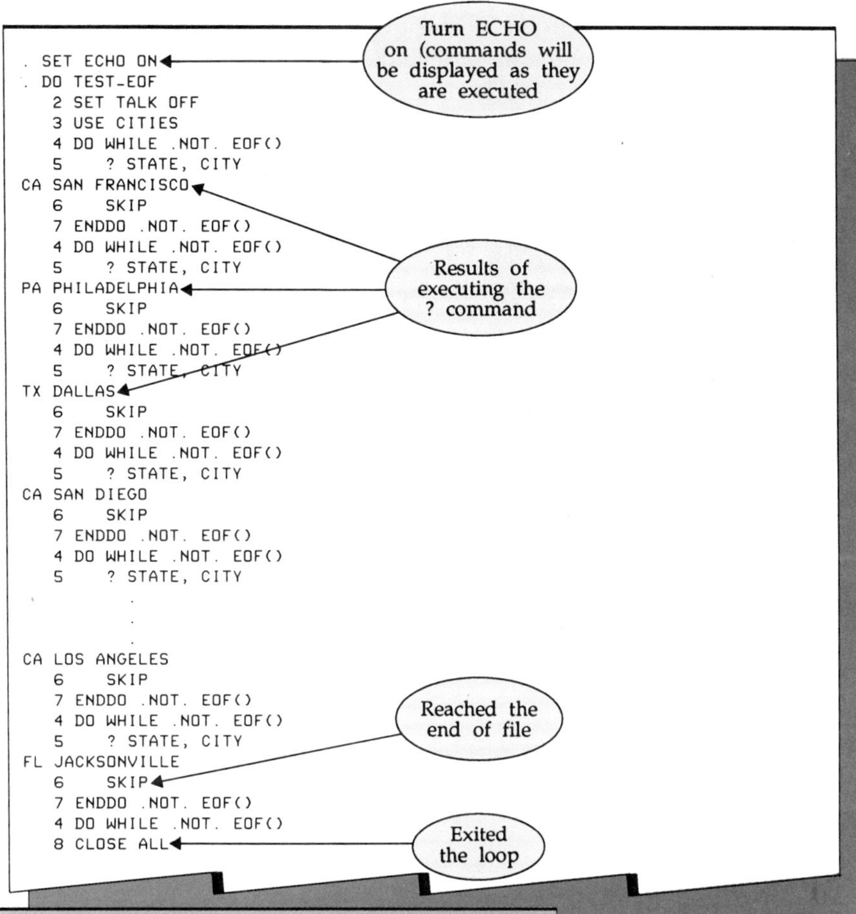
. SET ECHO ON
. DO TEST-EOF
2 SET TALK OFF
3 USE CITIES
4 DO WHILE .NOT. EOF()
5 ? STATE, CITY
CA SAN FRANCISCO
6 SKIP
7 ENDDO .NOT. EOF()
4 DO WHILE .NOT. EOF()
5 ? STATE, CITY
PA PHILADELPHIA
6 SKIP
7 ENDDO .NOT. EOF()
4 DO WHILE .NOT. EOF()
5 ? STATE, CITY
TX DALLAS
6 SKIP
7 ENDDO .NOT. EOF()
4 DO WHILE .NOT. EOF()
5 ? STATE, CITY
CA SAN DIEGO
6 SKIP
7 ENDDO .NOT. EOF()
4 DO WHILE .NOT. EOF()
5 ? STATE, CITY
CA LOS ANGELES
6 SKIP
7 ENDDO .NOT. EOF()
4 DO WHILE .NOT. EOF()
5 ? STATE, CITY
FL JACKSONVILLE
6 SKIP
7 ENDDO .NOT. EOF()
4 DO WHILE .NOT. EOF()
8 CLOSE ALL
Turn ECHO on (commands will be displayed as they are executed
Results of executing the ? command
Reached the end of file
Exited the loop

Figure 5.12 STUDYING LOOP EXECUTION WITH SET ECHO ON

5.3 OTHER TYPES OF DO WHILE/ENDDO LOOPS

It should be apparent at this point that DO WHILE/ENDDO is a versatile structure. The first portion of this chapter demonstrated the use of a counter and a test for the end of a file as exit conditions for the loop. This section presents some other types of loops.

USER-CONTROLLED LOOPS

The next example considers the intentions of the program user in determining when to discontinue the loop. More specifically, the user controls every pass of the DO WHILE/ENDDO structure.

The program is based on a variation of an old parable that is often used to illustrate the power of multiplication. In this case, an experienced salesperson managed to close a rather lucrative contract for his company. The sales manager asked him what he would like as a bonus for his outstanding performance. Hoping to take advantage of his supervisor's relative inexperience in business, the salesperson requested that the company grant him a bonus of one penny on the first of the month and double the amount every day for the remainder of the month. Fortunately for the company, the sales manager had recently completed a programming course in dBASE IV. She wrote the program shown in Figure 5.13. By running the program, she quickly discovered the devious nature of the scheme (Figures 5.14 and 5.15).

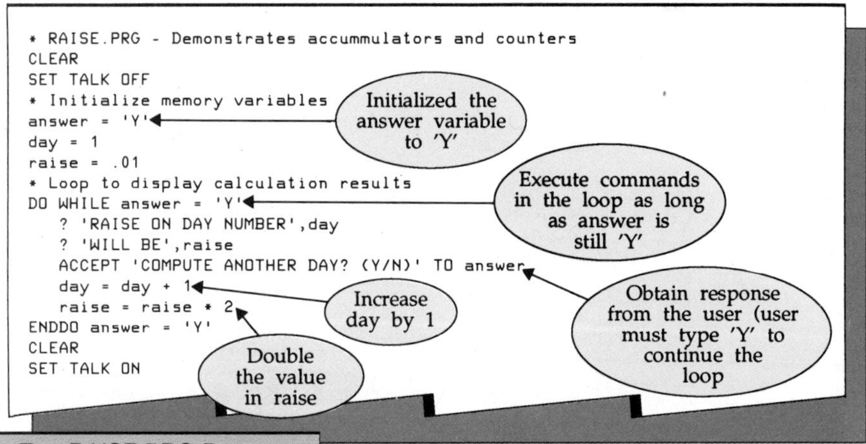

Figure 5.13 THE RAISE.PRG PROGRAM

After the comment line and SET TALK OFF, values are initialized for the three memory variables answer, day, and raise. Since the literal 'Y' is stored in the memory variable called answer and the DO WHILE loop is designed to continue as long as this memory variable contains a 'Y', it would appear that you have an endless loop. However, the ACCEPT command prompts the program user to store either 'Y' or 'N' in answer. Although another computation will occur as the result of the two commands that follow, the DO WHILE discontinues the loop if a comparison is made and 'Y' is not found in answer. The CLEAR command then clears the screen. The strategy illustrated here allows the user to control the number of executions of the loop. Again, it is the combination of the expression following the DO WHILE and the factor within the loop (the ACCEPT command) that provides the power and flexibility of the structure.

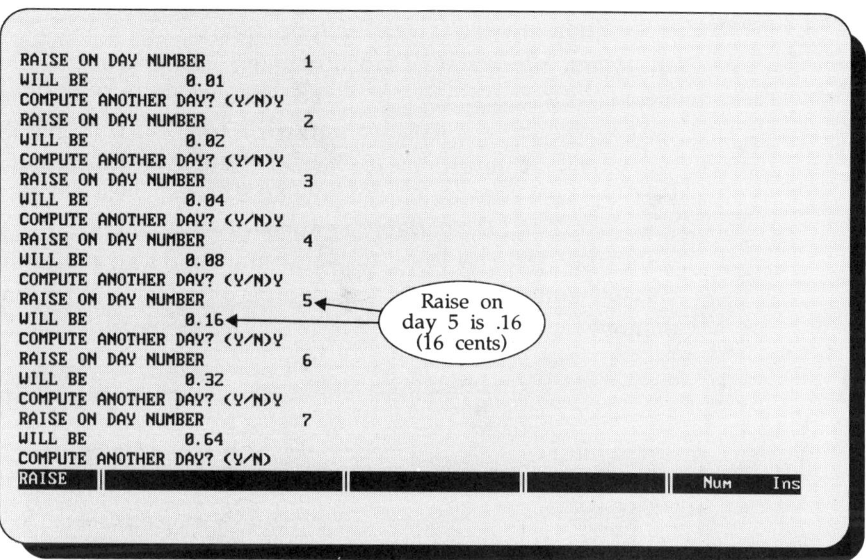

Figure 5.14 RAISES FOR FIRST SEVEN DAYS

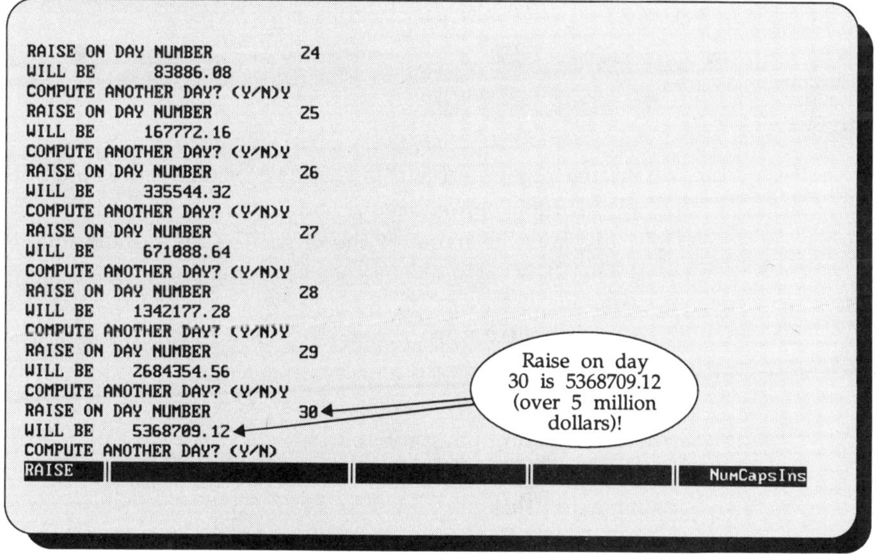

Figure 5.15 RAISES FOR DAYS 24 THROUGH 30

LOOPS WITH ACCUMULATORS

A variation of the DO WHILE loop in Figure 5.2 may be constructed using an *accumulator* rather than a counter. The principle is the same since a memory variable will be increased within the loop, and the expression after the DO WHILE will exit the loop when a certain limit has been reached.

Figure 5.16 illustrates a program that uses an accumulator in a DO WHILE loop. Notice that the pop_total memory variable is initialized to 0. This establishes the variable as numeric and ensures that it contains a base value of 0. The DO WHILE statement contains an expression that tests the variable and discontinues the loop once the value is no longer less than 5 million.

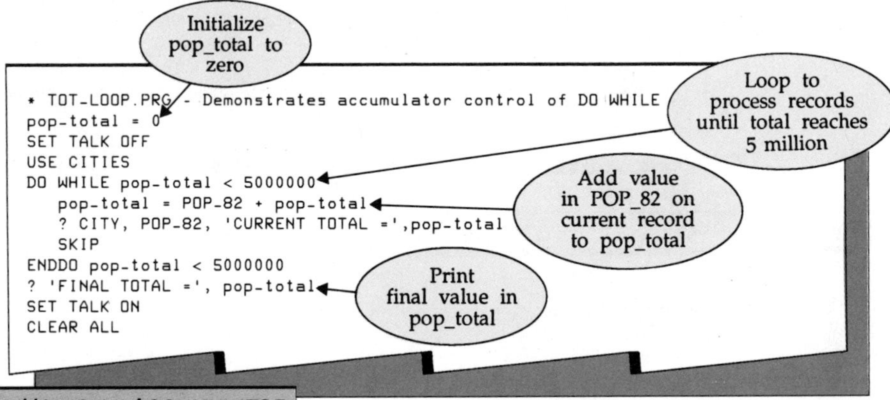

Figure 5.16 USING AN ACCUMULATOR

The first command within the loop increases the value of the accumulator by the 1982 population of the current record in the CITIES.DBF file. The ? displays the name of the city, the 1982 population, and the current total. The SKIP, as you have seen before, moves to the next record. After the ENDDO, a ? displays the value contained in the accumulator once the test in the DO WHILE statement is false (pop_total is not less than 5 million). The execution of the program is shown in Figure 5.17.

You can sometimes increase the effectiveness of a DO WHILE/ENDDO structure by combining two conditions in the DO WHILE statement. This may be accomplished with the .AND. logical operator. (The .OR. is also available for this purpose.) In Figure 5.18, both tests must be true: the memory variable answer must be equal to 'Y' and raise must be less than 350. This modification to the program would have allowed the manager to limit the executions of the loop to a reasonable amount.

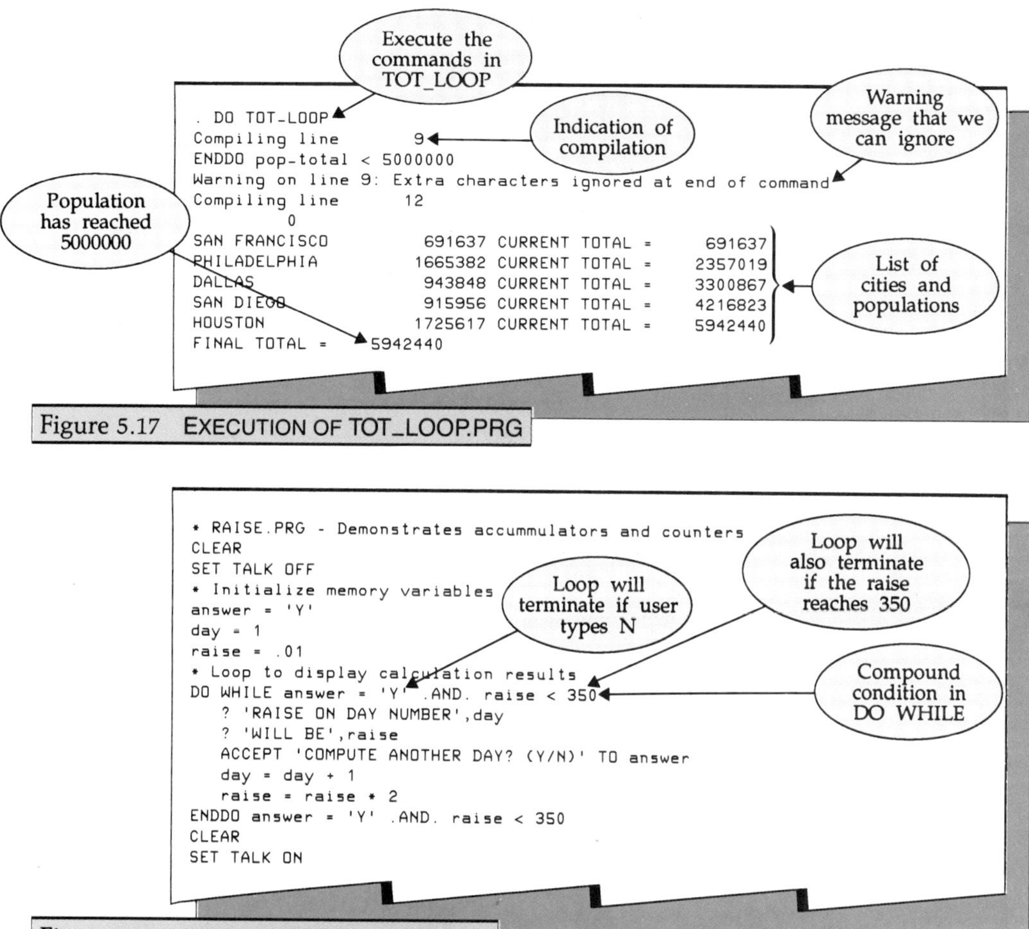


```
. DO TOT-LOOP
Compiling line        9
ENDDO pop-total < 5000000
Warning on line 9: Extra characters ignored at end of command
Compiling line       12
          0
SAN FRANCISCO          691637 CURRENT TOTAL =      691637
PHILADELPHIA          1665382 CURRENT TOTAL =     2357019
DALLAS                 943848 CURRENT TOTAL =     3300867
SAN DIEGO              915956 CURRENT TOTAL =     4216823
HOUSTON               1725617 CURRENT TOTAL =     5942440
FINAL TOTAL =        5942440
```

Figure 5.17 EXECUTION OF TOT_LOOP.PRG


```
* RAISE.PRG - Demonstrates accummulators and counters
CLEAR
SET TALK OFF
* Initialize memory variables
answer = 'Y'
day = 1
raise = .01
* Loop to display calculation results
DO WHILE answer = 'Y' .AND. raise < 350
   ? 'RAISE ON DAY NUMBER',day
   ? 'WILL BE',raise
   ACCEPT 'COMPUTE ANOTHER DAY? (Y/N)' TO answer
   day = day + 1
   raise = raise * 2
ENDDO answer = 'Y' .AND. raise < 350
CLEAR
SET TALK ON
```

Figure 5.18 USING A LOGICAL OPERATOR

The concepts presented in this chapter are vital to effective programming. Mastery of proper use of looping is an excellent foundation for the development of flexible and powerful programs.

CHAPTER SUMMARY

1. When a process requires repeating an action, the DO WHILE/ENDDO structure provides the repetition. Other commands are repeated in a controlled manner within the DO WHILE/ENDDO envelope. An expression is placed in the DO WHILE statement that determines the number of executions of the loop. A command must be included within the loop to affect the expression that follows the DO WHILE and allow an exit. Both the DO WHILE and the ENDDO lines must be present. Commands inside the loop should be indented for clarity, and a comment should be included at the end of the ENDDO line. Comparative or conditional expressions compare two pieces of data (literals, memory variables, or field names), using a relational operator. The data must be of the same type, and the operator should be selected carefully.
2. One type of DO WHILE/ENDDO loop employs the combination of a counter within the loop and a test for a specified condition to limit the number of executions. The combination of a test for end of file, .NOT. EOF(), and SKIP will access all records in a DBF file sequentially. In general, the DO WHILE statement establishes the criterion for ending the loop, and processing continues as long as the criterion is logically true. The ENDDO statement evaluates the test again and branches either to the first statement within the loop (.T.) or to the statement following the ENDDO (.F.).
3. A character-type literal such as 'Y' may be used as a criterion in a DO WHILE/ENDDO loop, allowing the program user to determine when the loop will cease. An accumulator provides a running total within the loop, which can be included in the comparative expression of the DO WHILE to exit the structure at a specified amount. Comparative expressions may also be combined, using logical operators (.AND.; .OR.) for certain applications.

KEY TERMS

looping
counting loop
incrementing
comparative expression
self-documenting
accumulator
nesting

COMMAND SUMMARY

Command Name	Use
DO WHILE	The first statement of the DO WHILE/ENDDO structure, which includes the condition.
ENDDO	The concluding statement of the DO WHILE/ENDDO structure.
EOF()	A logical function that indicates an end-of-file condition.
SKIP	Move the record pointer to the next record.
CLEAR ALL	Close files and release variables.

dBUG dBASE

- dBASE IV scans each command from left to right and stops if it finds an error. It looks for keywords first, and if the word or phrase that is delimited by blanks is not a keyword, it tries to determine whether it is a valid constant or a literal. It also tests for valid field names.
- SET TALK ON can be annoying when you are displaying data because it verifies and displays the results of commands such as REPLACE, STORE, and SKIP. However, this feature can be very useful if you are debugging and trying to monitor the results of commands.
- Loop problems usually fall into one of the following categories:
  1. *The loop executes only once.* There may be only one record in the file. Perhaps the condition controlling the loop exit is being changed at the bottom of the loop.
  2. *The loop executes continuously.* There is no SKIP or change of the exit condition in the loop.
  3. *The loop does not execute at all.* The control condition is not allowing execution; a control variable was not initialized or was changed before the loop executed; there are no records in the file.
- Create a PRG file containing the CLEAR ALL, SET commands, identifying documentation, and so on as a timesaver. Whenever you create a new program, you can then begin by simply copying this file. (To do so using MODIFY COMMAND, select the "Write/read text file" from the Words menu, select "Read text from file," and then enter the name of the file.)

SELF-CHECK QUESTIONS

1. What is the purpose of the ENDDO statement?
2. What is the reason for repeating the condition following the ENDDO?
3. Why is the indentation of commands within the DO WHILE/ENDDO loop important?
4. Under what conditions can a data-type mismatch error occur in a DO WHILE/ENDDO structure?
5. What is an endless loop?
6. What two elements in a DO WHILE/ENDDO unit determine when the loop will terminate?
7. Is it possible to allow the user to control the number of times a loop will execute? How?
8. What is an accumulator? How does it differ from a counter?
9. Where is the best position to place a test to exit a loop?
10. Which logical operator is more restrictive, .AND. or .OR.?

TRY IT YOURSELF

1. Construct a DO WHILE/ENDDO loop that counts to 12, incrementing by 2. Include a statement after the ENDDO that displays the exit value of the counter variable. Use indentation and comments.
2. Write a version of the program in Exercise 1 using no comments or indentation. Compare this with a version using structured style and observe the difference. Do not allow the results of the STORE command to display.
3. Write DO WHILE statements for the following conditions:
   a. BALANCE is less than 1000
   b. CITY is 'GRAND RAPIDS'
   c. CHOICE is not 9
   d. AGE is 16 or more
   e. 1500 or less is in TOTAL and ANSWER is 'Y'
   f. CHOICE is either 2 or 3
4. Assign the value 17 to a variable. Write a STORE command to increase the value by 12 and print the result with the ? command. Include a character literal that identifies the display.
5. Write a DO WHILE/ENDDO loop that displays your name on the screen seven times.
6. Rewrite the program in Exercise 5 using an "endless loop." Execute the program with SET ECHO ON and observe the results.

7. Display the 1982 population of the cities in the CITIES.DBF file using a DO WHILE/ENDDO loop. Remove the SKIP command and observe the results. Place the SKIP command after the DO WHILE and study the display.
8. Use a combination of an accumulator and an ACCEPT statement within a loop to generate the following list of interest rates. The user has the option to end the loop at any time. The rates begin at 9% (.09) but may not exceed 21%. They are incremented by 0.0025.

```
.0900
.0925
.0950
.0975
.1000
```

9. Write a program that processes each record in the CITIES database and displays the names of the cities and their 1970 populations on the printer.
10. Revise the program in Exercise 9 to allow the user to terminate the program after the city is displayed.
11. Type in the following incorrect program and run it. Debug as required.

```
USE CITIES
DO WHILE .NOT. EOF
SKIP
? POP1982
CLOSE ALL
SET PRINT OFF
```

12. Write a program that displays the names and amounts for each patron in the CHARITY database from Chapter 3. Display a running total of the contributions on each line.

PROGRAMMING PROJECT

Using structured style, write a program that displays all the states in CITIES.DBF followed by the message 'LIST COMPLETE'. Use SET ECHO ON to study the execution of the commands in the program.

Learning Objectives

To examine the procedures used by dBASE IV to make comparisons of data.

To construct IF/ENDIF structures.

To use ELSE and IIF().

To construct a program that selectively prints records.

DECISION MAKING WITH IF/ENDIF

INTRODUCTION

One of the most useful tasks that computers perform is the searching and sorting of data. Consider what is occurring in the background when a customer uses an ATM (Automatic Teller Machine). The customer inserts an ID card that contains an account number. The computer reads the number from the card, and the customer inputs a PIN (Personal Identification Number). Before any transaction can be completed, the computer at the bank must search all the relevant account numbers to find the customer's account. If the account is found, the PIN that the customer supplied must be compared to the PIN in the account. If they match, the customer can perform a transaction. If they do not match, the card is rejected. All of this searching and comparing occurs almost instantaneously. How does the computer make comparisons? How can it perform two separate tasks on the basis of one piece of data? This chapter focuses on learning to write programs that compare data and execute separate actions on the basis of the results.

6.1 HOW dBASE IV MAKES COMPARISONS

Computers must often compare two items of data in order to make clear the relationship between them. This process, sometimes called *selection* or *if-then-else,* is at the heart of a variety of useful functions, such as searching and sorting data or choosing between two courses of action. One important reason that computers are valuable to business operations is that their ability to compare is combined with both speed and endurance (computers rapidly perform the most boring and repetitive tasks endlessly, without complaint).

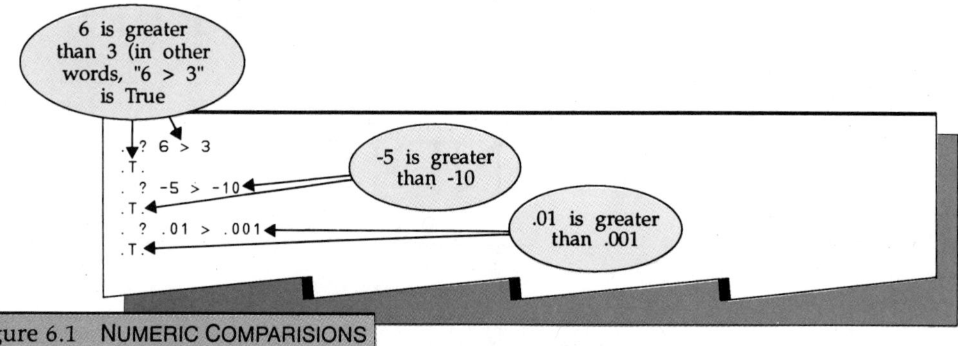

Figure 6.1 NUMERIC COMPARISIONS

In dBASE IV, numeric values are compared in the exact manner you would expect. Figure 6.1 demonstrates the process by using the ? command to print out the results of a number of such comparisons. The .T. or .F. on the following line indicates whether dBASE evaluated the condition as true or false. As you can see, dBASE IV evaluates expressions for their actual numeric value, just as you would using algebra. If you have any questions, try these examples and experiment with others until you are comfortable with this type of comparison.

When comparing character information, dBASE IV uses a different set of rules. The characters that appear on the monitor screen or that are stored on the disk are represented electronically or magnetically using the *ASCII* (American Standard Code for Information Interchange) code. This is a system of 256 codes that represent all the characters in common use, along with a number of other special characters such as the carriage return. A chart showing these codes appears in Appendix D. Although it is not necessary to memorize the codes, it is helpful to understand their "pecking order."

ASCII ranks the numerals 0 through 9 low on the scale, with values ranging from 48 for 0 through 57 for 9. Uppercase letters are represented by decimal values from 65 through 90. The higher values, 97 through 122, are reserved for the lowercase letters. Therefore, when any lowercase letter is compared to any uppercase letter, the lowercase letter always carries the greater value. Some of these codes and values are shown in Figure 6.2. Figure 6.3 illustrates the hierarchy of the ASCII characters in a dialog that uses the ? command.

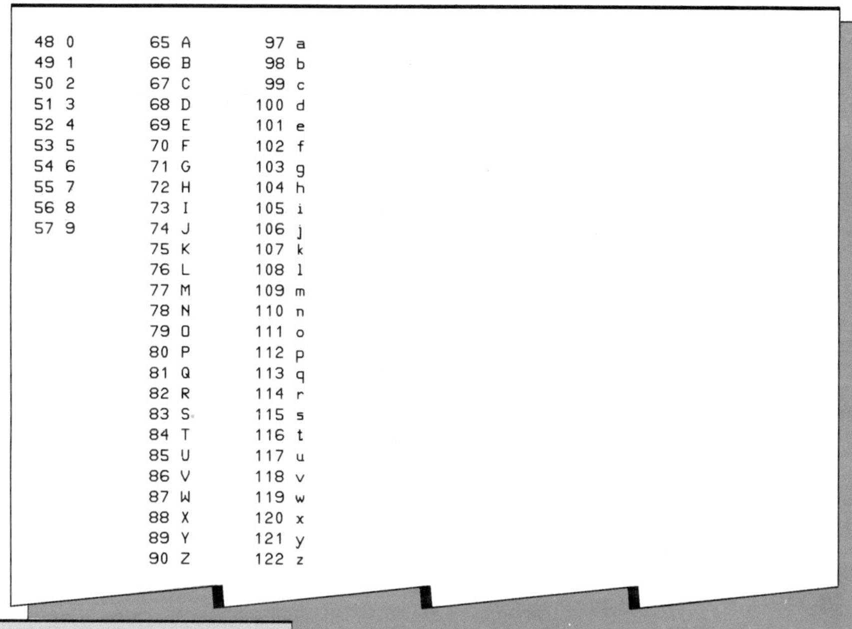

48	0	65	A	97	a
49	1	66	B	98	b
50	2	67	C	99	c
51	3	68	D	100	d
52	4	69	E	101	e
53	5	70	F	102	f
54	6	71	G	103	g
55	7	72	H	104	h
56	8	73	I	105	i
57	9	74	J	106	j
		75	K	107	k
		76	L	108	l
		77	M	109	m
		78	N	110	n
		79	O	111	o
		80	P	112	p
		81	Q	113	q
		82	R	114	r
		83	S	115	s
		84	T	116	t
		85	U	117	u
		86	V	118	v
		87	W	119	w
		88	X	120	x
		89	Y	121	y
		90	Z	122	z

Figure 6.2 ASCII CODES AND VALUES

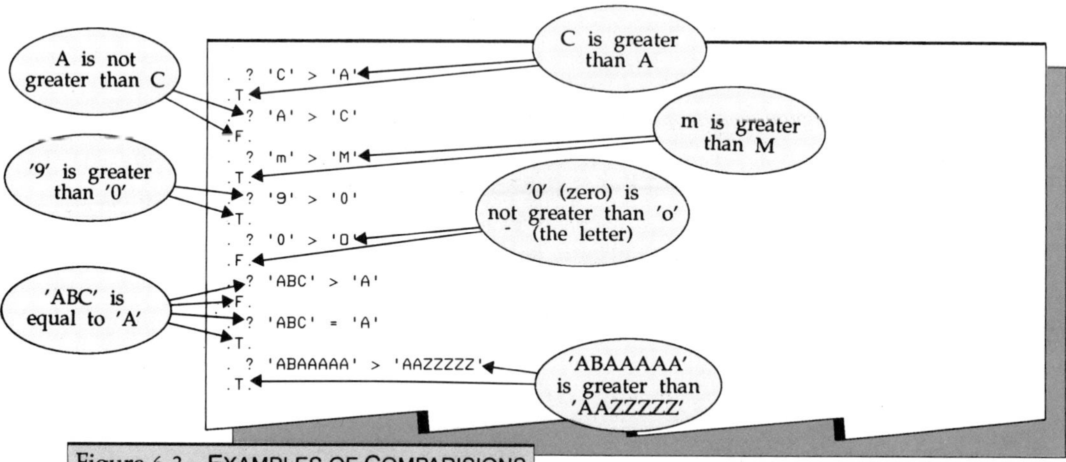

Figure 6.3 EXAMPLES OF COMPARISIONS

When characters are compared, the first character on either side that has the highest ASCII value is considered logically greater than the first character on the other side. If the condition cannot be determined, IF then compares the second character on each side. Eventually, either an inequality will be found or no more comparisons will be possible. In the former case, the two sides are obviously unequal; in the latter, they are equal as far as can be determined. Figure 6.3 uses ? commands to illustrate character comparisons. Again, try these examples and others until you are comfortable with the process.

It is important for you to understand the way in which dBASE IV compares both character and numeric values, fields, and variables. This enables you to write clear and accurate conditions for IF/ENDIF, DO WHILE/ ENDDO, and other structures. A major source of programming errors is the poor construction of comparative statements.

6.2 THE IF/ENDIF STRUCTURE

In Chapter 2, you used the FOR clause of the LIST command to decide which records should be displayed. This clause can also be used with other dBASE IV commands such as REPORT or COPY. When used in a command such as LIST FOR STATE = 'CA', the intention is to display records IF the state is California. We use exactly the same type of condition in the IF/ENDIF construction to make decisions in our programs.

Like DO WHILE/ENDDO, IF/ENDIF is a two-command structure, which means that it can be used only in programs. Both the IF and the ENDIF statements must be present. Note in the following example that the IF statement must include a comparative expression or condition. Also, as with the ENDDO, any text following the ENDIF is ignored. This provides an excellent means of self-documenting the structure.

```
IF STATE = 'CA'
     ? CITY
ENDIF STATE = 'CA'
```

The field name STATE is being compared to the constant 'CA'. This command could be paraphrased as "if it is true that the contents of the STATE field in the current record are equal to 'CA', print the contents of the CITY field."

If you place the preceding structure in a DO WHILE/ENDDO loop, you can print the name of only those cities that have 'CA' in the state field, as shown in Figure 6.4. Figure 6.5 shows the execution of this program.

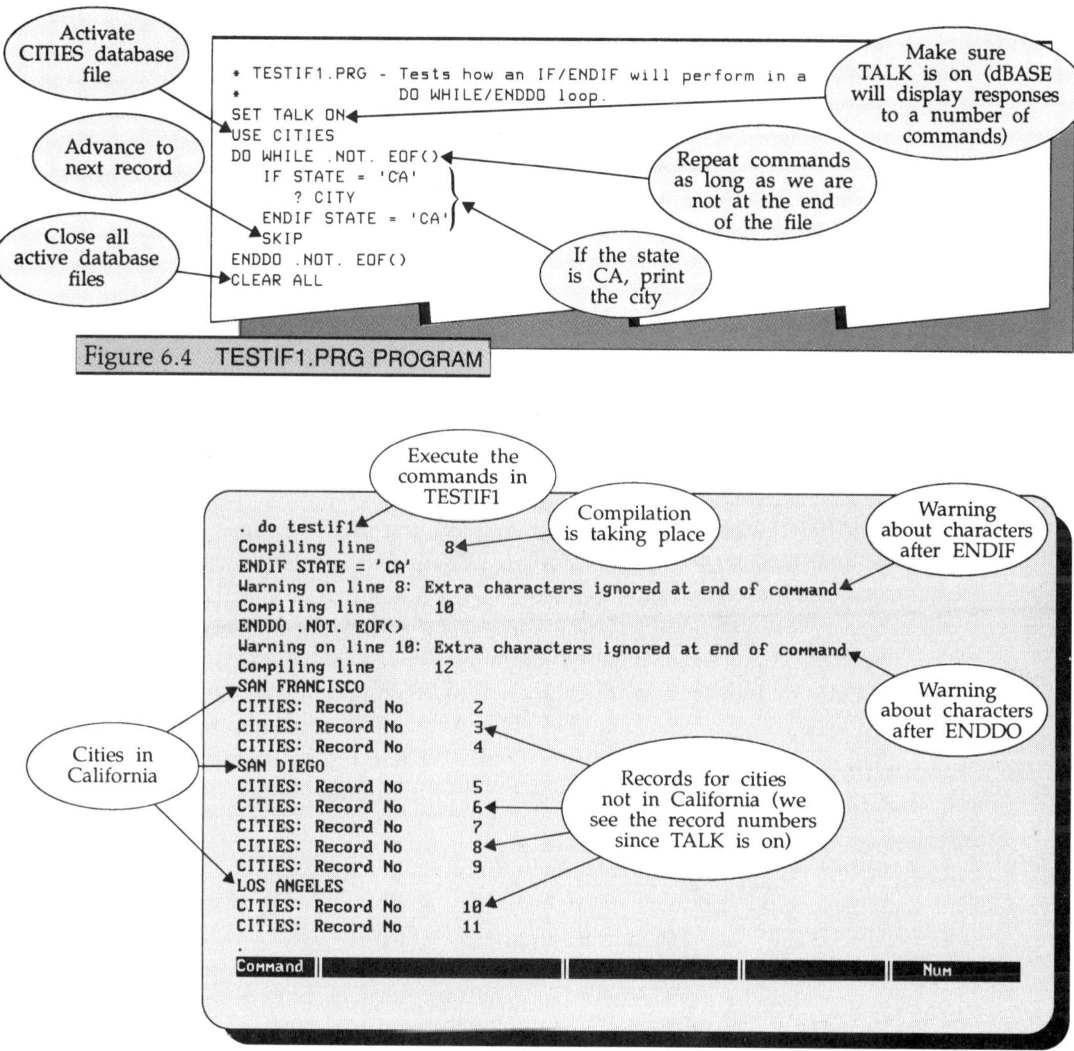

Figure 6.4 TESTIF1.PRG PROGRAM

Figure 6.5 EXECUTION OF TESTIF1.PRG

When the command USE CITIES is executed, the record pointer is positioned at record 1. As you learned in Chapter 5, the DO WHILE statement evaluates the condition, in this case, .NOT. EOF(). If the condition is false (in other words, if the end of file has been reached), the program branches to the statement following the ENDDO. At this point in the program, the record pointer is at record 1, so the command following the DO WHILE statement will be executed.

The program now enters the IF/ENDIF structure by evaluating the contents of the field STATE to determine whether it contains the characters 'CA'. This is the case in record 1, so the commands within the IF and ENDIF must be executed. This is why SAN FRANCISCO is displayed on the screen first (`? CITY`). (See Figure 6.6.)

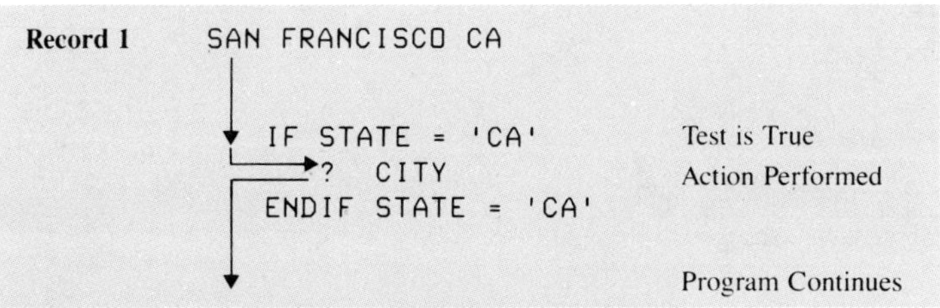

Figure 6.6 EVALUATING THE CONTENTS OF THE FIELD STATE

After the ENDIF command is passed, the SKIP command advances the pointer to record 2. (Since TALK is ON, dBASE displays the record number after each SKIP, so you can see when it has moved on to the next record.) The ENDDO command then loops, or passes control back to the DO WHILE. Since the end of the file has still not been reached, the commands within the loop are executed again. The IF command checks to see whether there is a 'CA' in the state field. This time there is not since the state is 'PA'. Thus, the command within the IF/ENDIF will not be executed (Figure 6.7). Control is passed to SKIP the command following ENDIF.

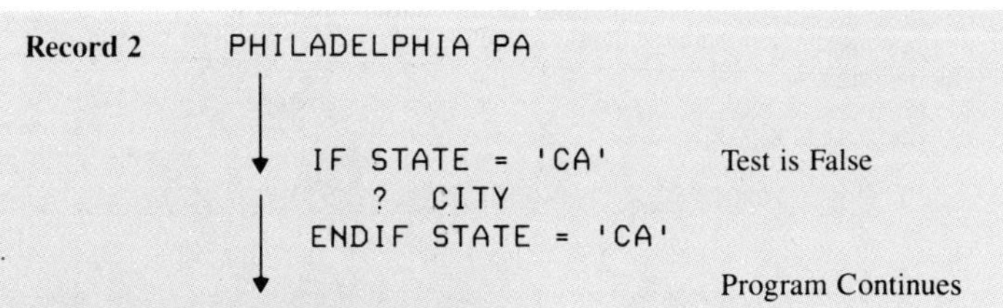

Figure 6.7 ANALYSIS OF IF/ENDIF EXECUTION

Let's change the IF statement in TESTIFI.PRG to test for 'C' instead of 'CA' and run the program. This modification is shown in Figure 6.8. Notice that the screen display is identical in Figures 6.5 and 6.8. This is because dBASE first compares the 'C' in the first position of the state field to the letter 'C'. These two are, of course, equal. When dBASE IV could not continue comparing (the value in the condition is only the single letter C), it evaluated the IF condition as true. If we only want *exact* matches, we include the SET EXACT ON command in our program (Figure 6.9). As you can see in the figure, no cities are displayed since none of the states is *exactly* equal to 'C'.

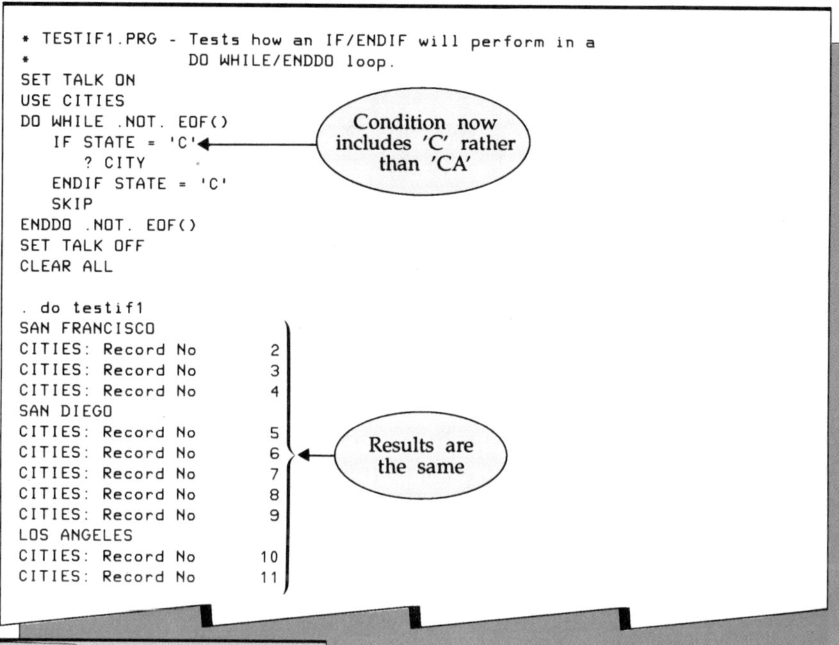

* TESTIF1.PRG - Tests how an IF/ENDIF will perform in a
* DO WHILE/ENDDO loop.
SET TALK ON
USE CITIES
DO WHILE .NOT. EOF()
IF STATE = 'C'
? CITY
ENDIF STATE = 'C'
SKIP
ENDDO .NOT. EOF()
SET TALK OFF
CLEAR ALL
. do testif1
SAN FRANCISCO
CITIES: Record No 2
CITIES: Record No 3
CITIES: Record No 4
SAN DIEGO
CITIES: Record No 5
CITIES: Record No 6
CITIES: Record No 7
CITIES: Record No 8
CITIES: Record No 9
LOS ANGELES
CITIES: Record No 10
CITIES: Record No 11
Condition now includes 'C' rather than 'CA'
Results are the same

Figure 6.8 MODIFYING THE IF STATEMENT

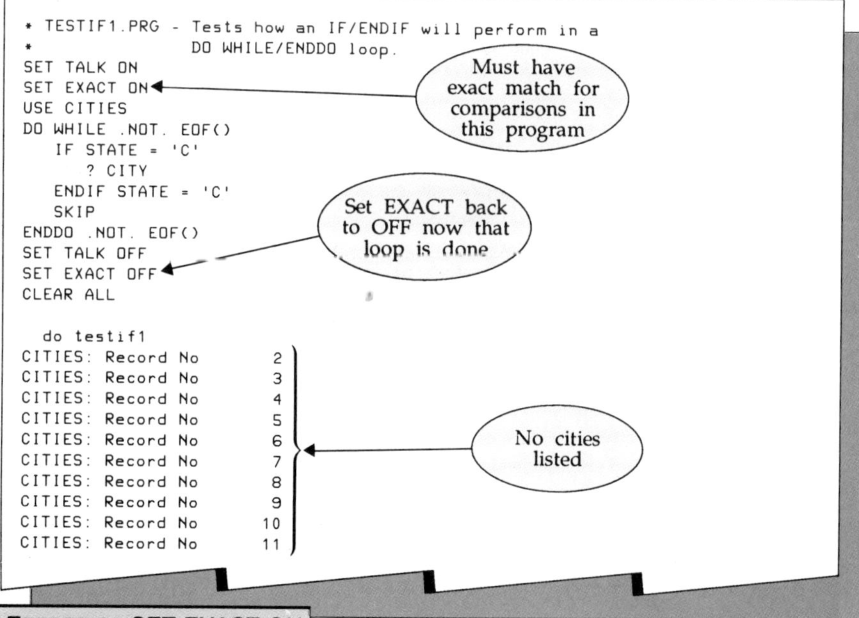

* TESTIF1.PRG - Tests how an IF/ENDIF will perform in a
* DO WHILE/ENDDO loop.
SET TALK ON
SET EXACT ON
USE CITIES
DO WHILE .NOT. EOF()
IF STATE = 'C'
? CITY
ENDIF STATE = 'C'
SKIP
ENDDO .NOT. EOF()
SET TALK OFF
SET EXACT OFF
CLEAR ALL
do testif1
CITIES: Record No 2
CITIES: Record No 3
CITIES: Record No 4
CITIES: Record No 5
CITIES: Record No 6
CITIES: Record No 7
CITIES: Record No 8
CITIES: Record No 9
CITIES: Record No 10
CITIES: Record No 11
Must have exact match for comparisons in this program
Set EXACT back to OFF now that loop is done
No cities listed

Figure 6.9 EFFECT OF SET EXACT ON

(**Note:** A properly written IF/ENDIF structure uses indentation for the statements within the structure and repeats the condition in the ENDIF statement. dBASE IV ignores any characters after the ENDIF because they are in the ENDDO, although it will display a warning message during compilation. As your programs become larger and more complicated, you will find that they are easier to read and easier to debug if you follow this convention.)

6.3 ELSE AND IIF()

When the IF statement is encountered, the comparison is evaluated as being either true or false. When the condition is true, the statements located between the IF and the ENDIF are executed. If the condition is false, program control skips to the first statement following the ENDIF. Note that in either case the statements following the ENDIF execute. This structure separates records into two groups: those that meet the condition and those that do not. However, only those records that produce a true condition are affected by the contents of the structure, whereas other records (false) are ignored.

USING ELSE

So far, we have examined the basic form of the IF statement:

```
IF condition
     dBASE command or commands
ENDIF
```

If the condition is true, the dBASE commands will be executed; if not, no special action will be taken. The IF statement has another form:

```
IF condition
   dBASE command or commands
ELSE
   dBASE command or commands
ENDIF
```

In this form, if the condition is true, the dBASE commands before the ELSE will be executed; if the condition is false, the dBASE commands after the ELSE will be executed.

Realize that when you use an ELSE, it means exactly what it says. Whenever the condition is false, the commands between the ELSE and the ENDIF will be executed. Be sure this is exactly what you want.

Consider the program shown in Figure 6.10, for example. This program works well as long as the value of the memnum variable is either greater than or less than 10, but it produces unintended and incorrect results when the value is exactly 10. The problem is that we actually have *three* possibilities—the number could be greater than 10, the number could be less than 10, or the number could be equal to 10. Simply knowing that `memnum > 10` is false does not give us enough information. Chapters 7 and 8 explain ways to program multiple possibilities.

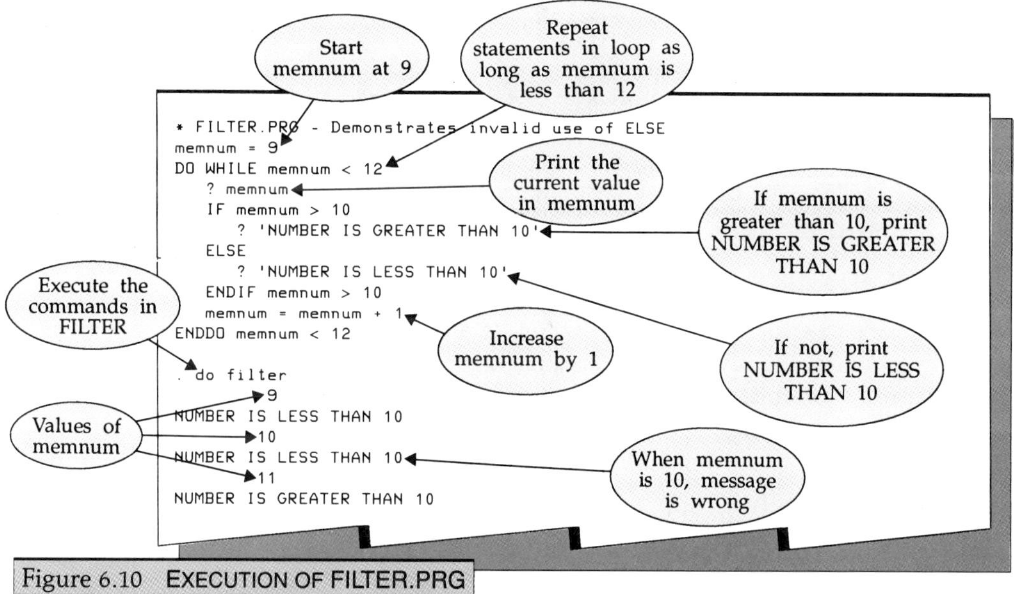

Figure 6.10 EXECUTION OF FILTER.PRG

USING IIF()

The IIF(), or immediate IF, command is similar to the IF/ELSE/ENDIF structure. A condition is placed after the left parenthesis, followed by a comma. Actions to be performed on both true and false conditions are then included before the right parenthesis, as in Figure 6.11 on the next page.

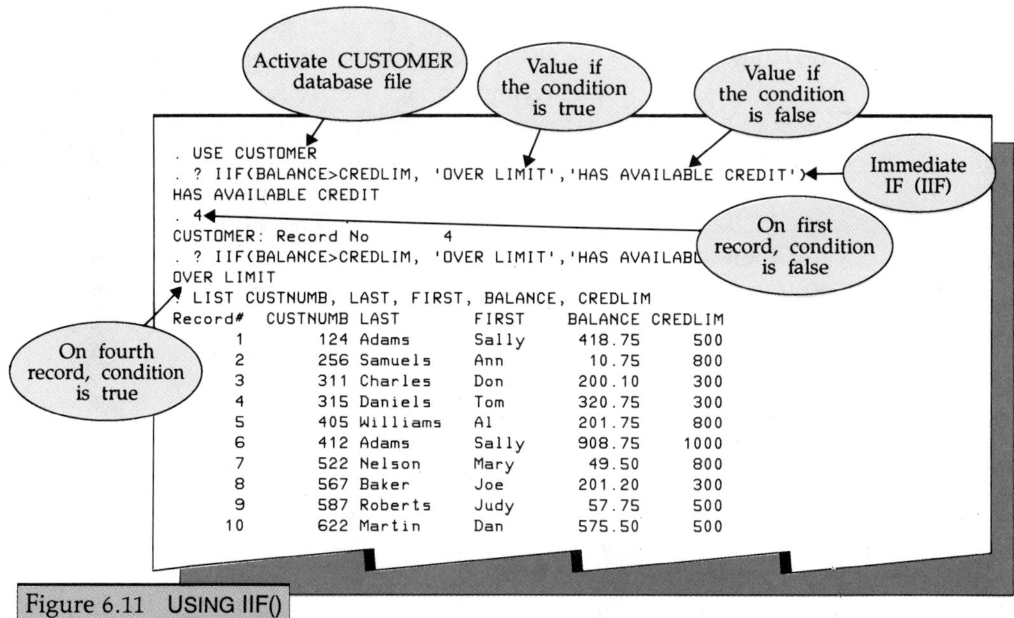

Figure 6.11 USING IIF()

The immediate IF command, IIF(), can be used from the dot prompt to perform the same function as an IF/ELSE/ENDIF unit on one line. This obviously gives the nonprogramming user of dBASE IV the opportunity to perform limited alternative tasks on the basis of a condition. It is also useful to the programmer in that he or she can observe how an IF/ENDIF structure will perform on certain data before placing it in a program. Another way to test an IF/ENDIF is to write the structure in a brief program and test it against records from the dot prompt.

6.4 WRITING A PROGRAM TO PRINT RECORDS SELECTIVELY

The processing loop used in Figure 6.12 prints the number, name (FIRST and LAST), and available credit (CREDLIM – BALANCE) for all customers in the CUSTOMER database file. Suppose, however, that we only want to print certain records. For example, suppose we only want to display the number, name, and amount of available credit for those customers whose balance is less than or equal to the credit limit. To do so, we could use the IF/ENDIF structure shown in Figure 6.13.

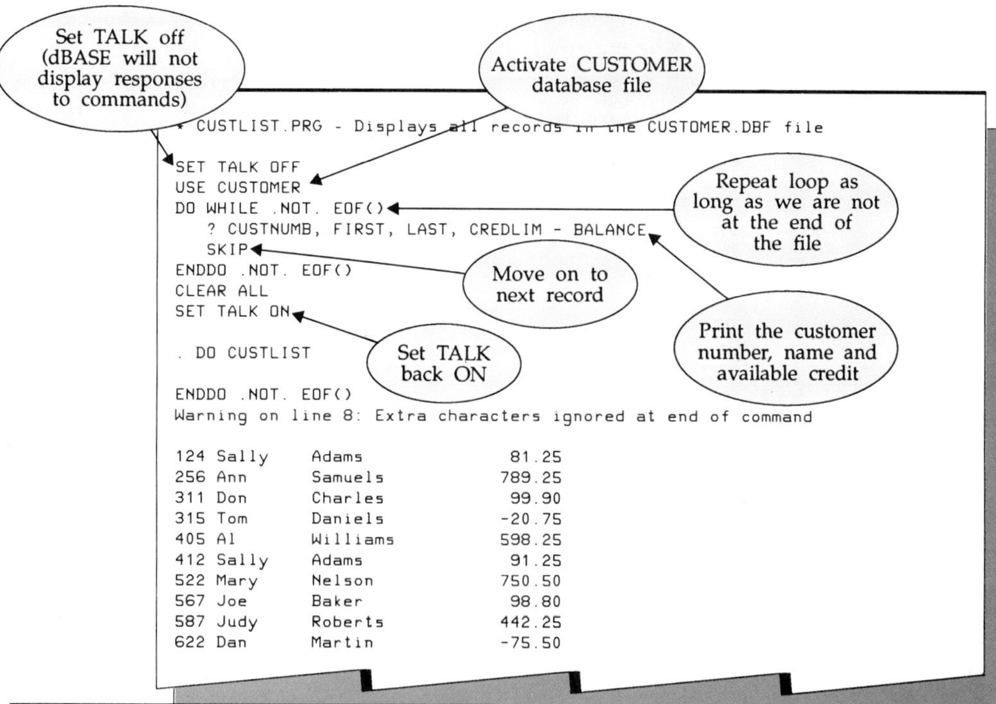

Figure 6.12 EXECUTION OF CUSTLIST.PRG

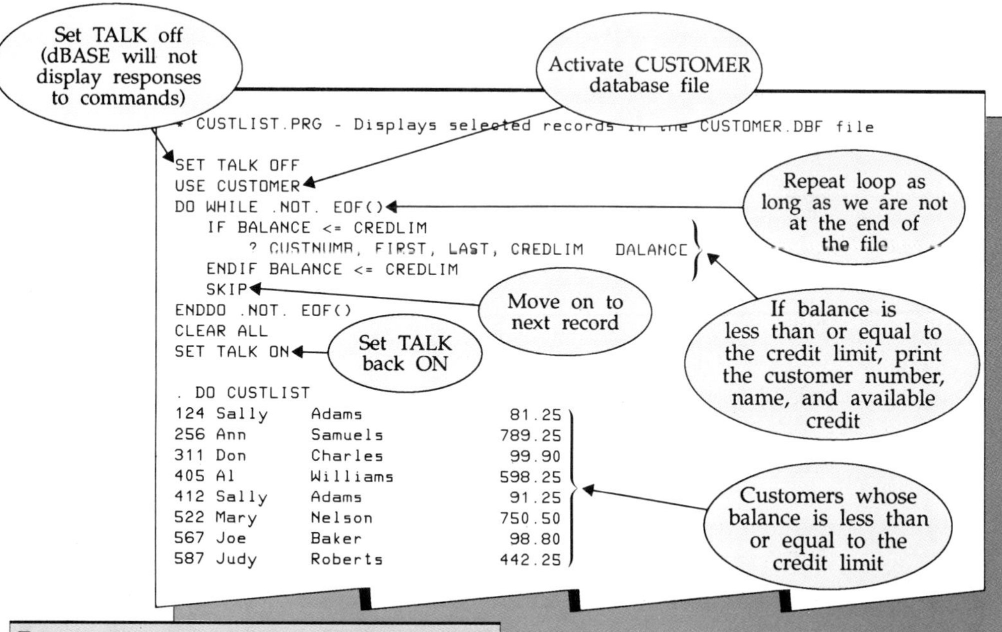

Figure 6.13 EXECUTION OF CUSTLIST.PRG

The program in Figure 6.13 accomplishes its purpose. Customers whose balance was over the credit limit are not included in the display. Of course, if you wanted to provide some action for the unselected records, you could use an ELSE. In the program in Figure 6.14, such customers are displayed along with a message.

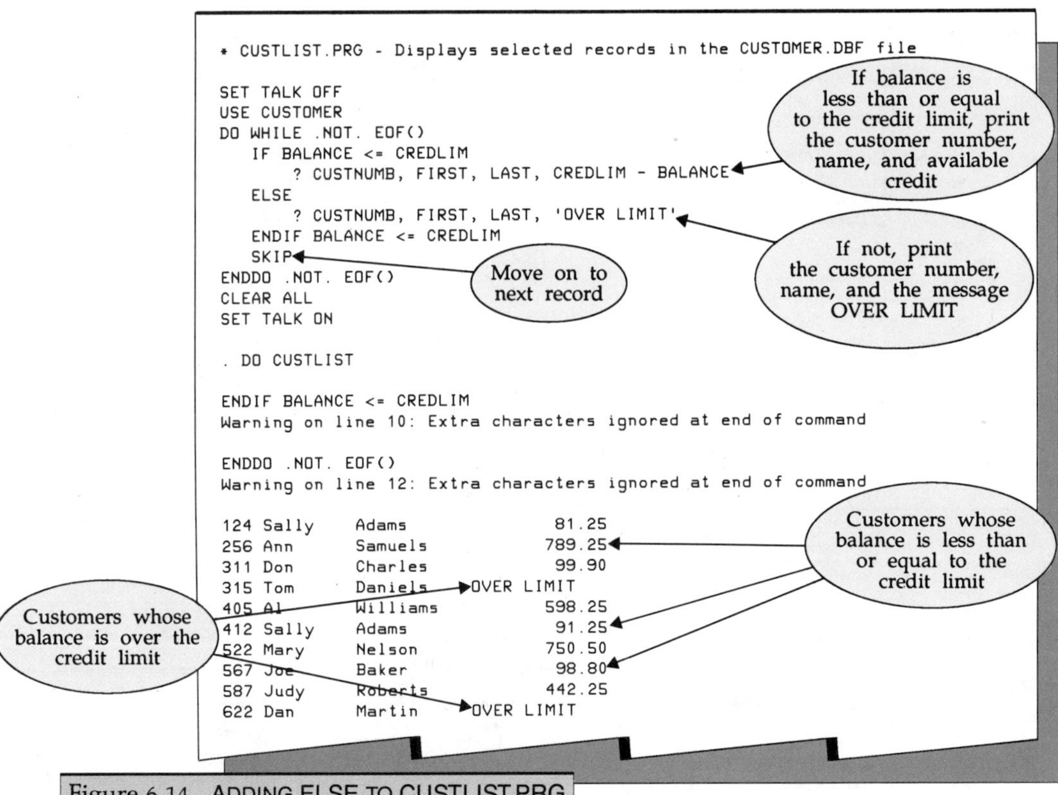

```
* CUSTLIST.PRG - Displays selected records in the CUSTOMER.DBF file

SET TALK OFF
USE CUSTOMER
DO WHILE .NOT. EOF()
   IF BALANCE <= CREDLIM
       ? CUSTNUMB, FIRST, LAST, CREDLIM - BALANCE
   ELSE
       ? CUSTNUMB, FIRST, LAST, 'OVER LIMIT'
   ENDIF BALANCE <= CREDLIM
   SKIP
ENDDO .NOT. EOF()
CLEAR ALL
SET TALK ON

. DO CUSTLIST

ENDIF BALANCE <= CREDLIM
Warning on line 10: Extra characters ignored at end of command

ENDDO .NOT. EOF()
Warning on line 12: Extra characters ignored at end of command

124 Sally     Adams            81.25
256 Ann       Samuels         789.25
311 Don       Charles          99.90
315 Tom       Daniels      OVER LIMIT
405 Al        Williams        598.25
412 Sally     Adams            91.25
522 Mary      Nelson          750.50
567 Joe       Baker            98.80
587 Judy      Roberts         442.25
622 Dan       Martin       OVER LIMIT
```


Figure 6.14 ADDING ELSE TO CUSTLIST.PRG

A common mistake when using IF/ENDIF is to include SKIP or some other command that doesn't belong in the structure. Suppose the SKIP command were placed in the position shown in Figure 6.15. The SKIP executes only on records not meeting the condition (after ELSE); the program goes into an endless loop on the first record that satisfies the condition (see Figure 6.16).

Sometimes records need to be selected on the basis of two criteria, or perhaps more. Suppose, for example, that we would like to print the number, name, and available credit of those customers whose balance is less than the credit limit *and* whose credit limit is 300. For other customers we want to print the number and name and the message 'NOT SELECTED'. We use the logical operator .AND. as shown in Figure 6.17.

```
* CUSTLIST.PRG - Displays selected records in the CUSTOMER.DBF file

SET TALK OFF
USE CUSTOMER
DO WHILE .NOT. EOF()
   IF BALANCE <= CREDLIM
       ? CUSTNUMB, FIRST, LAST, CREDLIM - BALANCE
   ELSE
       ? CUSTNUMB, FIRST, LAST, 'OVER LIMIT'
       SKIP
   ENDIF BALANCE <= CREDLIM
ENDDO .NOT. EOF()
CLEAR ALL
SET TALK ON
```

SKIP command is in the ELSE part of the IF

Figure 6.15 MISPLACED SKIP

```
. DO CUSTLIST

ENDIF BALANCE <= CREDLIM
Warning on line 11: Extra characters ignored at end of command

ENDDO .NOT. EOF()
Warning on line 12: Extra characters ignored at end of command

124 Sally    Adams                81.25
124 Sally    Adams                81.25
124 Sally    Adams                81.25
         .
         .
         .
```

Cut off execution by pressing the ESC key

Infinite loop

Figure 6.16 EFFECT OF MISPLACED SKIP

```
* CUSTLIST.PRG - Displays selected records in the CUSTOMER.DBF file

SET TALK OFF
USE CUSTOMER
DO WHILE .NOT. EOF()
   IF BALANCE <= CREDLIM .AND. CREDLIM = 300
       ? CUSTNUMB, FIRST, LAST, CREDLIM - BALANCE
   ELSE
       ? CUSTNUMB, FIRST, LAST, 'NOT SELECTED'
   ENDIF BALANCE <= CREDLIM .AND. CREDLIM = 300
   SKIP
ENDDO .NOT. EOF()
CLEAR ALL
SET TALK ON
```

Compound condition involving .AND.

Figure 6.17 COMBINING CONDITIONS WITH .AND.

The results of executing this program are shown in Figure 6.18. Notice that Don Charles and Joe Baker are the only customers who satisfy both conditions.

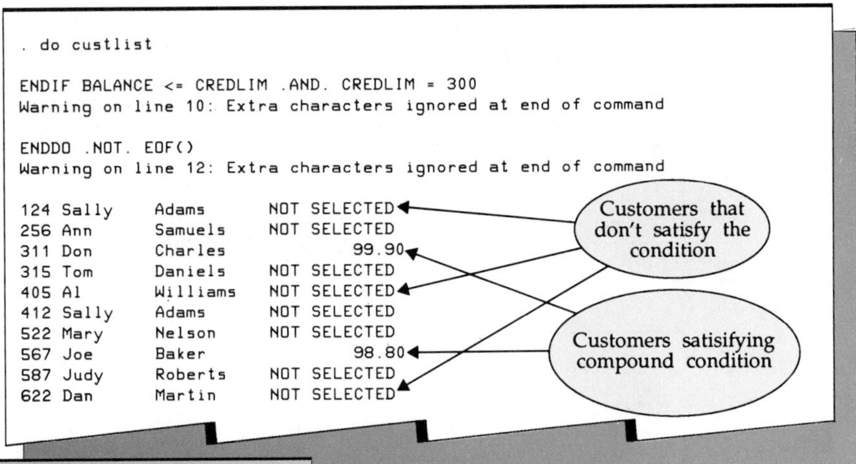

. do custlist
ENDIF BALANCE <= CREDLIM .AND. CREDLIM = 300
Warning on line 10: Extra characters ignored at end of command
ENDDO .NOT. EOF()
Warning on line 12: Extra characters ignored at end of command
124 Sally Adams NOT SELECTED
256 Ann Samuels NOT SELECTED
311 Don Charles 99.90
315 Tom Daniels NOT SELECTED
405 Al Williams NOT SELECTED
412 Sally Adams NOT SELECTED
522 Mary Nelson NOT SELECTED
567 Joe Baker 98.80
587 Judy Roberts NOT SELECTED
622 Dan Martin NOT SELECTED
Customers that don't satisfy the condition
Customers satisifying compound condition

Figure 6.18 OUTPUT OF CUSTLIST.PRG

Just as with conditions in a LIST statement, we can also use the logical operator .OR.. For a condition involving .OR. to be true, only one individual condition need be true. It is obviously much easier for a record to satisfy an .OR. operator than an .AND., as the chart in Table 6.1 shows.

TABLE 6.1 **Comparison of .AND. and .OR.**

RECORD	BALANCE < = CREDLIM	CREDLIM = 300	AND	OR
Adams, Sally	T	F	F	T
Samuels, Ann	T	F	F	T
Charles, Don	T	T	T	T
Daniels, Tom	F	T	F	T
Williams, Al	T	F	F	T
Adams, Sally	T	F	F	T
Nelson, Mary	T	F	F	T
Baker, Joe	T	T	T	T
Roberts, Judy	T	F	F	T
Martin, Dan	F	F	F	F

A word of caution is appropriate here. Be careful when you use logical operators. Not only do the conditions have to be correctly expressed, but the proper logical operator must also be chosen. Try to avoid using more than two conditions. Even if you properly state five linked conditions, others will have great difficulty sorting out the possibilities. If you must take such action, you should use parentheses to clarify your intentions. The alternatives to this arrangement include nesting (Chapter 8). In situations where several options are possible when a condition is tested, it is more convenient to use a DO CASE structure, which will be discussed in Chapter 7.

Effective IF/ENDIF structures provide power and flexibility in program control. Unfortunately, these commands can be a source of annoying errors. Some guidelines for writing IF/ENDIF structures follow.

1. Is the condition in the IF statement correct?
   - Same data type
   - Correct relational operator
   - Correct logical operator
   - No more than two conditions
2. Is the IF/ENDIF properly structured?
   - Indentation
   - Statements in correct order
   - All required statements present
   - All unwanted statements removed
3. Does it work?
   - Test it

CHAPTER SUMMARY

1. Comparing fields, variables, and expressions in order to determine relationships is critical to computer operations. Alternative actions may be performed as the result of a relationship being true or false. Numeric data is compared on the basis of value, as in algebra. Character data is compared character against character, according to the ASCII values. SET EXACT ON forces character comparisons to match exactly, including matches in length.
2. The IF/ENDIF structure consists of the IF statement with a condition, some statements that are to be executed conditionally, and the ENDIF. The condition is repeated after the ENDIF and interior statements are indented for clarity. The IF statement evaluates the condition under current circumstances as either true or false. If the condition is true, the interior statements are executed; if it is false, control branches to the statement following the ENDIF.

3. ELSE is an optional statement used in the IF/ENDIF structure to provide an alternative action if the condition is false. ELSE should be used with care since its effect is global. The IIF() function is useful for testing conditions before they are used in programs.
4. The placement of an IF/ENDIF unit within a DO WHILE/ENDDO structure permits the selective access of records. The IF selects certain records that satisfy the condition. The statements within the IF/ENDIF structure that print data are executed, whereas records that do not meet the criteria are branched around these statements. It is possible to combine two tests with the logical operators (.OR.; .AND.). An IF/ENDIF structure should be written carefully to ensure that it performs as expected and generates no errors.

KEY TERMS

selection
if-then-else
ASCII

COMMAND SUMMARY

Command Name	Use
IF	The first statement in the IF/ENDIF structure, which contains the condition.
ENDIF	The concluding statement in the IF/ENDIF structure.
SET EXACT ON	Requires data in conditions to match exactly.
ELSE	Provides an alternative action on a false condition.
IIF()	The immediate IF displays literals after evaluating a condition.

SELF-CHECK QUESTIONS

1. Why is a comparing operation useful in programming?
2. Why is it important to be able to compare names or other character fields?
3. What is ASCII? Why is it important to be familiar with it?
4. Why is the ENDIF needed in the IF/ENDIF structure?
5. Why are indentation and placing the condition after ENDIF useful?

6. Why must a programmer be cautious when including ELSE in a structure?
7. Could IIF() be included in a program?
8. Is it possible to write a single IF/ENDIF to handle three possibilities?
9. Is it better to include a selective condition in a DO WHILE loop, or to place an IF/ENDIF within the DO WHILE?
10. Why is the position of the SKIP command important?
11. Describe a situation in which tests could be combined with an .OR. logical operator. Do the same for the .AND. operator.

TRY IT YOURSELF

1. Indicate which relational operator would be used in the following tests:
   a. You must be 18 to vote.
   b. Balances over $500 are charged 15% interest.
   c. Businesses with fewer than five employees are eligible for a special loan.
2. Use the ? to test the following conditions. Indicate whether they are true or false.
   a. 'y' > 'az'
   b. .911 > .910
   c. 'a' > 'A'
   d. 'O Hara' = 'O HARA'
   e. 'ABC' = 'AB'
3. Write an IF/ENDIF structure for each of the following situations. Use your own field names, memory variables, or data where required.
   a. Print the Social Security number of all full-time students who have an F in a field called STATUS.
   b. Print the last name of all part-time students.
   c. Print the gross salary (the product of the rate and the hours) of all employees who worked less than 40 hours.
   d. Print all last names that begin with P.
   e. Print the phone number of clients living in Orlando (exactly as it appears).
4. Write an IIF() statement for each of the following situations:

	Condition	.T. Action	.F. Action
a.	Over 4 arrests	'Suspended'	'Warning'
b.	Age over 17	'Register'	'Under age'
c.	Income 5000 or less	'No tax'	'Pay tax'

5. Write a program that tests a name input with an ACCEPT. If the name is exactly 'Joe Piscioneri', print 'Valid user'. Any other name input should print 'Unauthorized'.
6. Modify the code in Exercise 5 to also allow the name 'Sally Sheets' as a valid user.
7. A credit card company charges 18% on balances under $500. All other balances are charged 21%. Write an IF/ENDIF structure to test the field BALANCE and print an appropriate message stating the correct rate.
8. Write an IF/ENDIF structure that prints 'Honors' for any grade point average that is 3.6 or higher. Other averages should print 'Next Semester?'
9. Create a database using the following data:

Invoice	Date	Amount	Terms
C495	10/13/92	1454.39	30
A982	8/23/92	556.89	10
C475	8/06/92	6500.00	30
B785	12/27/92	354.80	0
A292	5/10/92	12.54	10

   Write a program using a DO WHILE/ENDDO that accesses and displays each record.
10. Modify the program from Exercise 9 to include an IF/ENDIF unit that displays records having terms of 30 days.
11. Write a program using the invoice database that totals the invoices over $500.00. Display the total on the screen.
12. Write a program that displays on the printer all the fields of those invoices that were received on or after 10/1/92. Records received before the date should display the message 'Received before fourth quarter'. (**Note:** When you use dates in conditions, they must be enclosed between braces ({ }). Thus you should enter this date as {10/01/92}.)

PROGRAMMING PROJECT

Write a program that prints the part number, description, and price for those parts with prices over $100.00 but under $200.00.

- Print the part number, description, and then the message 'Price not in range' for any other parts.
- Print the title 'Parts within Quoted Price Range' at the top of the page and 'End of Report' at the bottom.
- Write pseudocode and test your comparison with IIF() before coding the program.

The following is the structure of the database file you will use for this project:

```
Structure for database: A:\PART.DBF
Field  Field Name  Type        Width    Dec    Index
    1  PARTNUMB    Character       4                Y
    2  PARTDESC    Character      10                N
    3  UNONHAND    Numeric         4                N
    4  ITEMCLSS    Character       2                N
    5  WREHSENM    Numeric         2                N
    6  UNITPRCE    Numeric         7      2         N
** Total **                       30
```

PARTNUMB is the part number, PARTDESC is the part description, and UNITPRCE is the price.

Learning Objectives

To learn the conditions under which DO CASE/ENDCASE should be used in place of a series of nested IF/ENDIFs. Also, to learn the use of CASE/ENDCASE and OTHERWISE to set conditions for DO CASE.

To learn the use of ACCEPT, WAIT, INPUT, and INKEY() for data entry.

To learn the value of menus and how to construct them using DO CASE/ENDCASE and DO WHILE/ENDDO.

To learn an efficient way to delete records by batching and PACKing them, using DO CASE/ENDCASE and DO WHILE.

7 Menus and Do Case/Endcase

Introduction

Imagine how difficult it would be if you went to a restaurant and the waiter asked you to just name whatever you wanted to eat. You and the waiter would be involved in a lengthy, frustrating conversation because he would know what items were available, but only you would know your personal preferences. The obvious solution to this problem is a menu. Because the choices are limited and clearly defined, patrons are able to place an order quickly and effectively.

You have learned a great deal about programming and dBASE IV in the last few chapters. As you develop more sophisticated techniques, you will want to begin to consider the needs of the user. People react best to a program that is convenient to use. Menus are an attractive and useful way of organizing a program.

7.1 THE DO CASE/ENDCASE STRUCTURE

Business decisions are not always neatly limited to two alternatives. Often a whole range of options and conditions must be evaluated before a single action can be performed. Income brackets are a good example. The Internal Revenue Service typically taxes individuals based on the income bracket into which their taxable income falls. You could construct an IF/ENDIF condition to evaluate the range of the first bracket and return the correct tax. However, there is another approach which we will illustrate using the tax table shown in Table 7.1.

TABLE 7.1 **Example of multiple options**

INCOME BRACKET	TAX
Under $32,450	15% of income
$32,450-$78,400	$4867.50 + 28% of excess over $32,450
$78,400-$185,730	$12,865.72 + 33% of excess over $78,400
Over $185,730	$18,017.67 + 28% of excess over $185,730

The IF/ENDIF structure is useful, provided that the number of options in a decision situation is no more than two. Sequential IF/ENDIF structures could be used to provide several alternative actions, but they are difficult to write and to understand. Chapter 8 will explore nesting, which can be used to handle several alternatives. However, nested IF/ENDIF structures can be clumsy and unclear. The DO CASE/ENDCASE structure offers the best means for handling a number of options with ease, clarity, and effectiveness.

The first statement in the structure is DO CASE, and the last is ENDCASE. Notice that there is a space in DO CASE and none in ENDCASE. CASE statements, which express each possible condition and its related commands, are placed between the DO CASE and the ENDCASE. The example in Figure 7.1 tests a memory variable, memstatus, to determine marital status.

In effect, dBASE IV is writing a series of IF/ENDIFs for you when you use DO CASE/ENDCASE. One difference is that DO CASE/ENDCASE does not evaluate the remaining options after a true condition is found, which makes DO CASE/ENDCASE more efficient than a series of IF/ENDIFs. Although the DO CASE/ENDCASE structure places no limit on the number of commands that can be included in a CASE, more than a single screenful of statements makes the program difficult to read. A large number of commands should be placed in another program and called when needed; this will be explained further in Chapter 8.

```
DO CASE
     CASE memstatus = 'S'
          ? 'Single'
     CASE memstatus = 'M'
          ? 'Married'
     CASE memstatus = 'D'
          ? 'Divorced'
     CASE memstatus = 'W'
          ? 'Widowed'
ENDCASE
```

Figure 7.1 STRUCTURE OF DO CASE/ENDCASE

Study the programs in Figures 7.2 through 7.4. (Figures 7.3 and 7.4 are on the next page.) They all perform the same task, but they vary in appearance. To get a feel for the way they work, you could type SET ECHO ON at the dot prompt and then execute each of the programs.

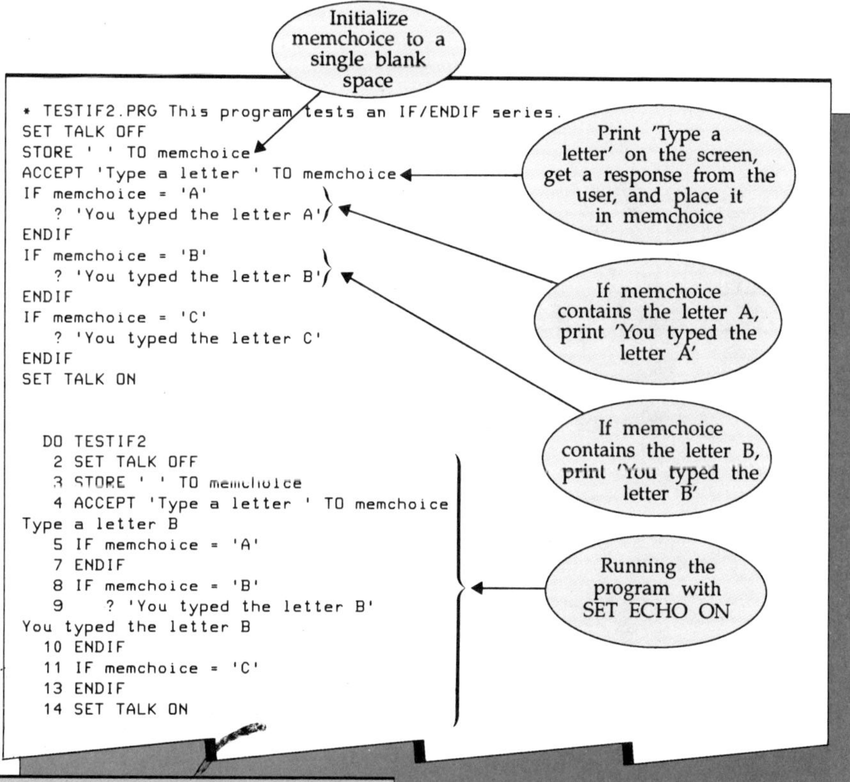
Initialize memchoice to a single blank space
Print 'Type a letter' on the screen, get a response from the user, and place it in memchoice
If memchoice contains the letter A, print 'You typed the letter A'
If memchoice contains the letter B, print 'You typed the letter B'
Running the program with SET ECHO ON

```
* TESTIF2.PRG This program tests an IF/ENDIF series.
SET TALK OFF
STORE ' ' TO memchoice
ACCEPT 'Type a letter ' TO memchoice
IF memchoice = 'A'
   ? 'You typed the letter A'
ENDIF
IF memchoice = 'B'
   ? 'You typed the letter B'
ENDIF
IF memchoice = 'C'
   ? 'You typed the letter C'
ENDIF
SET TALK ON

  DO TESTIF2
   2 SET TALK OFF
   3 STORE ' ' TO memchoice
   4 ACCEPT 'Type a letter ' TO memchoice
Type a letter B
   5 IF memchoice = 'A'
   7 ENDIF
   8 IF memchoice = 'B'
   9     ? 'You typed the letter B'
You typed the letter B
  10 ENDIF
  11 IF memchoice = 'C'
  13 ENDIF
  14 SET TALK ON
```

Figure 7.2 EXAMPLE OF SEQUENTIAL IF/ENDIFs

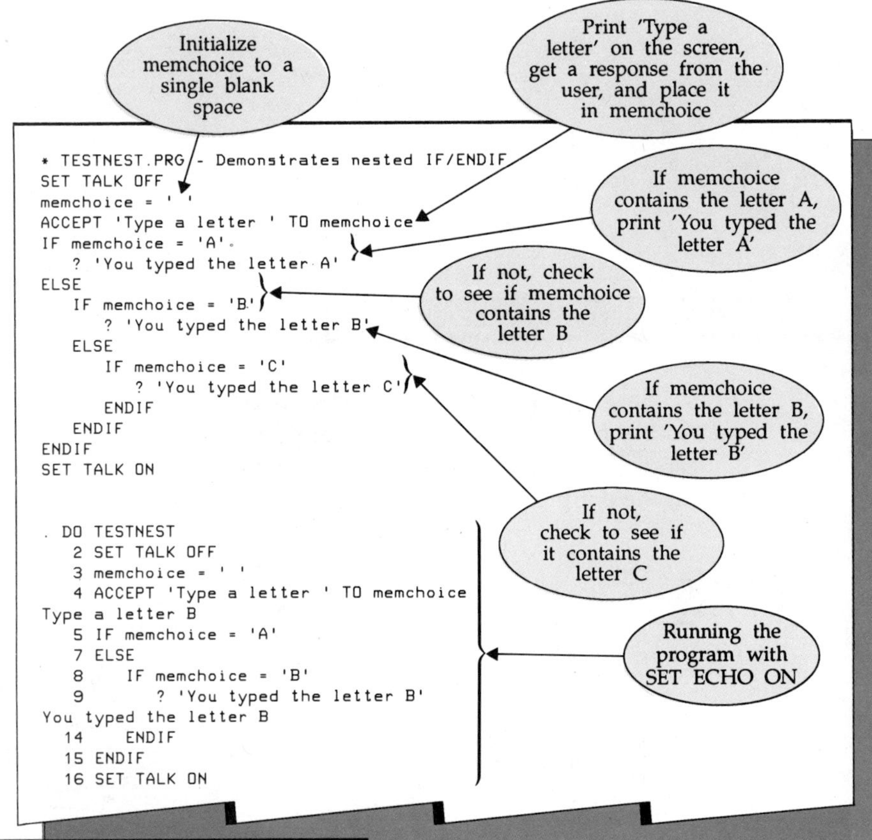
Initialize memchoice to a single blank space
Print 'Type a letter' on the screen, get a response from the user, and place it in memchoice
If memchoice contains the letter A, print 'You typed the letter A'
If not, check to see if memchoice contains the letter B
If memchoice contains the letter B, print 'You typed the letter B'
If not, check to see if it contains the letter C
Running the program with SET ECHO ON
* TESTNEST.PRG - Demonstrates nested IF/ENDIF
SET TALK OFF
memchoice = ' '
ACCEPT 'Type a letter ' TO memchoice
IF memchoice = 'A'
? 'You typed the letter A'
ELSE
IF memchoice = 'B'
? 'You typed the letter B'
ELSE
IF memchoice = 'C'
? 'You typed the letter C'
ENDIF
ENDIF
ENDIF
SET TALK ON
. DO TESTNEST
2 SET TALK OFF
3 memchoice = ' '
4 ACCEPT 'Type a letter ' TO memchoice
Type a letter B
5 IF memchoice = 'A'
7 ELSE
8 IF memchoice = 'B'
9 ? 'You typed the letter B'
You typed the letter B
14 ENDIF
15 ENDIF
16 SET TALK ON

Figure 7.3 EXAMPLE OF NESTED IF/ENDIFs

To conserve space, only three options are presented in Figures 7.2 through 7.4. The number of lines required to evaluate 26 options (the whole alphabet) for each of the structures follows:

STRUCTURE	NUMBER OF LINES
DO CASE	54
Nested IF/ENDIF	64
Series of IF/ENDIFs	78

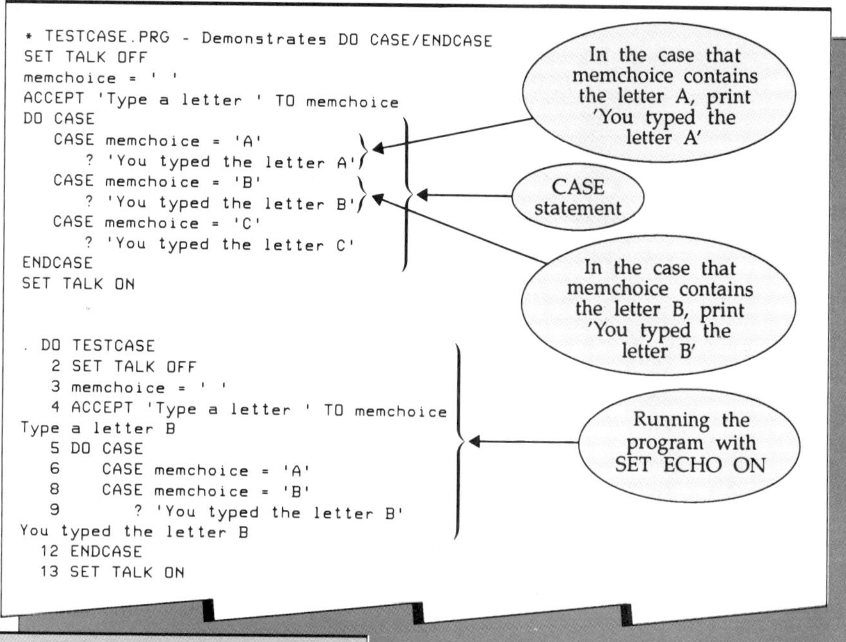
* TESTCASE.PRG - Demonstrates DO CASE/ENDCASE
SET TALK OFF
memchoice = ' '
ACCEPT 'Type a letter ' TO memchoice
DO CASE
CASE memchoice = 'A'
? 'You typed the letter A'
CASE memchoice = 'B'
? 'You typed the letter B'
CASE memchoice = 'C'
? 'You typed the letter C'
ENDCASE
SET TALK ON
. DO TESTCASE
2 SET TALK OFF
3 memchoice = ' '
4 ACCEPT 'Type a letter ' TO memchoice
Type a letter B
5 DO CASE
6 CASE memchoice = 'A'
8 CASE memchoice = 'B'
9 ? 'You typed the letter B'
You typed the letter B
12 ENDCASE
13 SET TALK ON
In the case that memchoice contains the letter A, print 'You typed the letter A'
CASE statement
In the case that memchoice contains the letter B, print 'You typed the letter B'
Running the program with SET ECHO ON

Figure 7.4 EXAMPLE OF DO CASE/ENDCASE

At the end of each program listing is a sample of the screen output, using SET ECHO ON in order to display the commands as they execute. The series of IF/ENDIF structures continues to evaluate all the remaining IF statements after the letter B was found, which is inefficient. Although the nested IF/ENDIF is exited after a true condition is found, it requires dBASE IV to deal with extra lines (ELSE and ENDIF). In comparison, the program in the DO CASE/ENDCASE example is much clearer.

There does not appear to be any significant difference in execution time among the preceding structures, although this is probably only the result of dBASE IV's good performance. All structures tested in one second the letters A through Z. Although there is no limit on the number of CASE statements, 26 options is an unrealistic number for most applications. Situations that require an unusually high number of options can be handled with the programming strategies presented in Chapter 11. In summary, DO CASE/ENDCASE is the structure of choice in situations where several options must be evaluated.

Make certain that all options are *mutually exclusive*; in other words, that only one option can be true in a given set of circumstances. The reason that this is important becomes clear when you understand how the DO CASE/ENDCASE structure operates. As the DO CASE is executed, each of the CASE statements is evaluated as it is encountered. The first time a true condition is found, dBASE IV executes the commands specified between that CASE and the next CASE statement, and then it branches out of the structure. Therefore, if it were possible for two options to be true, the first one encountered would be selected and the other would be ignored.

Figure 7.5 shows how Table 7.1 might be programmed using DO CASE. This example illustrates a way to provide an alternative action for all remaining possibilities outside the ones specified in the CASE statements. You have the option of placing an OTHERWISE clause after the final CASE statement for this purpose. This clause is introduced in this example to handle any income less than or equal to zero, in which case the tax would be zero.

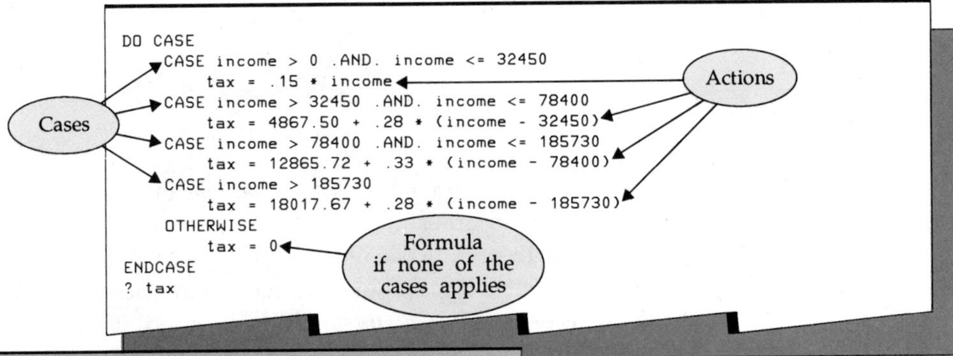

Figure 7.5 PROGRAMING WITH MULTIPLE OPTIONS

Although the DO CASE/ENDCASE structure is simple, you may on occasion omit or accidentally delete the ENDCASE statement. This prevents any of the statements within the structure from executing, but does not display an error message. If you find that the program ceases execution after one successful pass, the ENDCASE is probably missing.

7.2 USER INPUT

The five commands available in dBASE IV for user input are as follows:

```
INPUT
ACCEPT
WAIT
INKEY()
@..GET and READ
```

THE INPUT COMMAND

The INPUT statement has little practical programming value because it requires the user to place quotes around character data and to use special functions for dates. Since it is sometimes unclear what type of data is required by an INPUT, some risk to data integrity is incurred. However, since INPUT provides the only means for storing numeric data without using the @..GET and READ (which we will study later), we will use it in a program in this chapter. In the following example, a prompt message, which must be enclosed in quotes, is included to instruct the user. Notice the space after the word PRICE; without it, the area for the user's response would begin immediately after the E. Data entered is stored in the variable memprice after the TO.

```
STORE 0 to memprice
INPUT 'ENTER PRICE ' TO memprice
```

THE ACCEPT COMMAND

The ACCEPT command displays a prompt message and then obtains input from a user. It requires the user to press Enter. The user's input will then be stored in a memory variable. Since the programmer has no control over the data that may be entered by the user and stored in the memory variable, the ACCEPT command is typically used to solicit responses to general questions, such as

```
ACCEPT 'Would you like to continue? (Y/N) ' TO memanswer
```

THE WAIT COMMAND

The WAIT command allows the user to enter a single character without pressing Enter. This is useful for speeding up nonrisk operations such as moving from one menu to another. Users will appreciate the instant response of the program to the touch of one key. Should the wrong key be pressed, the data will not be damaged.

WAIT is often used in menu programs. Three examples of prompt messages are presented in Figure 7.6. A WAIT without a TO clause simply causes the program to pause until any key is pressed.

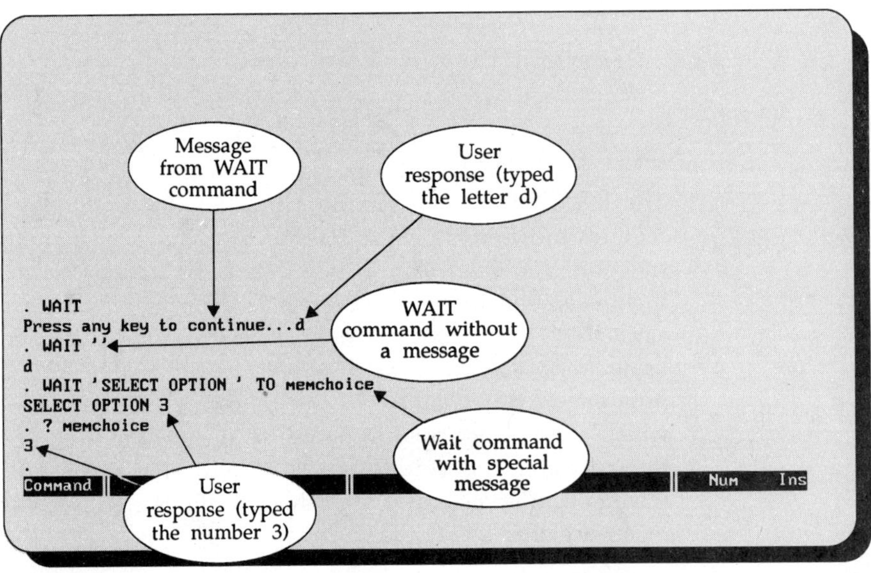

Figure 7.6 USING WAIT

In Figure 7.6, the first WAIT displays "Press any key to continue . . ." because no prompt was specified. The second contains a prompt (''), which is a *null string*, meaning that it contains no ASCII characters at all. Finally, the message SELECT OPTION is displayed and, since a memory variable is specified, the response is stored. In the figure, the `? memchoice` command demonstrates that the data typed by the user (3) has indeed been placed in memchoice.

THE INKEY FUNCTION

The INKEY() function is similar to WAIT in that it accepts a single keystroke from the user. However, it returns the ASCII code for the key pressed, which is usually not particularly helpful. It does have one important use, which is demonstrated in Figure 7.7.

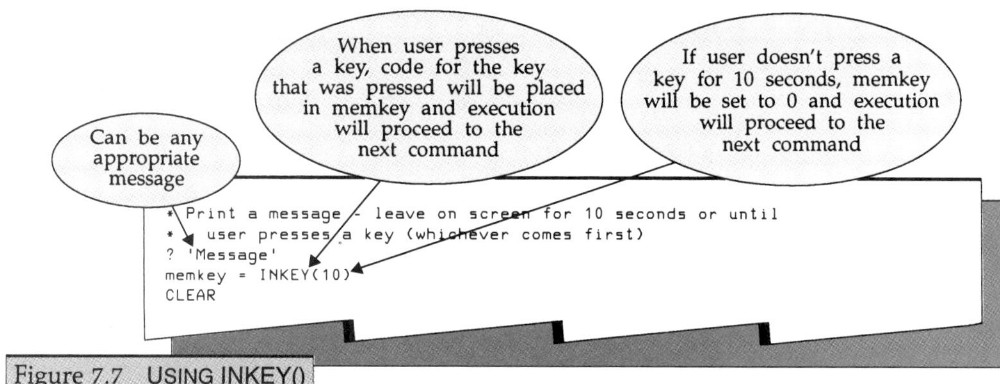

Figure 7.7 USING INKEY()

The command `memkey = INKEY(10)` will force the user to press a key and will place the ASCII value for the key in memkey. If the user does not press a key within 10 seconds, however, the command will terminate and place zero in memkey. Thus, we could place a message on the screen and then leave the message on the screen for 10 seconds or until the user presses a key, whichever comes first. (The number in parentheses does not have to be 10. We can use any number we want. This number indicates to dBASE how many seconds to wait before moving on to the next command.)

THE @..GET AND READ COMMANDS

The @..GET and READ commands, which will be presented in Chapter 10, provide the most useful means for accurate data entry. They allow *full-screen editing*, which means that the user can employ editing keys to enter data in attractive, formatted input blocks. Data can also be validated as it is entered. However, the ACCEPT and the WAIT commands are both useful for data entry on occasion.

7.3 CONSTRUCTING MENUS

Menus are important because users react very well to them and because they present options in a logical way. Users do not need a knowledge of dBASE IV to work effectively with a *menu-driven* program. Experienced users and programmers also appreciate the convenience of being able to preprogram lengthy command sequences so that they can be executed with the press of a key. The pseudocode for a menu portion of a program might look like Figure 7.8 on the next page.

Do these commands while the user does not wish to quit.
Display a screen containing instructions and listing options.
Pause the program until the user selects one of the options
Perform the commands required to complete the option chosen by the user.

Figure 7.8 PSEUDOCODE FOR A MENU PORTION OF A PROGRAM

A menu program might consist of a DO WHILE loop containing a screen display and a user input command such as WAIT. A DO CASE/ ENDCASE structure would provide the appropriate action as a reaction to the user's response. The DO WHILE loop should be either an endless loop (DO WHILE .T.) or a loop allowing all conditions except the exit option, as in the program shown in Figure 7.9 (pseudocode) and Figure 7.10 (dBASE code).

In the type of menu program shown in Figure 7.10, the test in the DO WHILE statement checks to see if the memory variable is not equal to the exit value. This strategy allows the screen to redisplay until the task is completed. Although the program in Figure 7.10 offers only five choices, the structure is in place to handle many more options by adding more CASE statements.

```
Set environment
Initialize variables
DO WHILE variable <> exit value
    Clear Screen
    Display choices
    Prompt user for choice
    DO CASE
        Menu choices and actions
    ENDCASE
ENDDO
```

Figure 7.9 PSEUDOCODE FOR A MENU PROGRAM

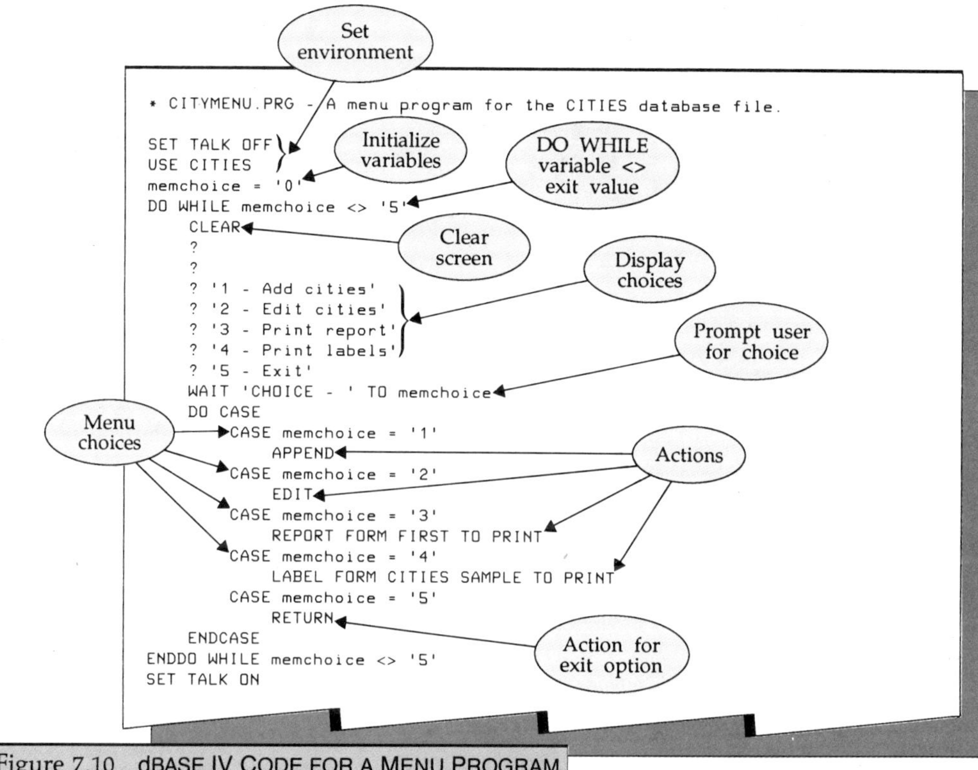

Figure 7.10 dBASE IV CODE FOR A MENU PROGRAM

Most studies indicate that users are comfortable with menus that contain between five and nine options. Chapter 8 will explain how, in more sophisticated applications, a menu often exits to another menu. Since you can create one menu to branch to other menus, you can limit each menu to nine or fewer options and still create all the options you need by branching. Either letters or numerals can be used to identify the options. Numeric values should be avoided since they are more error-prone and are difficult to handle. It is important to design the DO CASE and all other structures so that they have only one entrance and one exit. The last option in any menu should always be an exit from the program or a RETURN. The RETURN command will return you to the previous menu.

After you have completed Chapter 10, you will be able to construct sophisticated and attractive screen displays that will enhance your menu programs. However, the basic rules presented in Table 7.2 on the next page will still apply in creating user-friendly menus.

TABLE 7.2 Menu tips

1. Attempt to develop a consistent style and appearance for all menus.
2. Give each menu a title.
3. Use from five to nine options.
4. Use brief, meaningful labels for the options.
5. Include a single exit as the last option.

7.4 WRITING A PROGRAM TO DELETE RECORDS

In this section we will investigate a program to delete records. We will use the TEMP database file you created earlier in the sample program. If you followed along with the examples in the text, you previously removed (ZAPped) all the records in the file. To reconstruct the file, type the commands shown in Figure 7.11. When dBASE asks you if it is acceptable to overwrite the file, answer that it is (Y or y). You are now ready for the sample program.

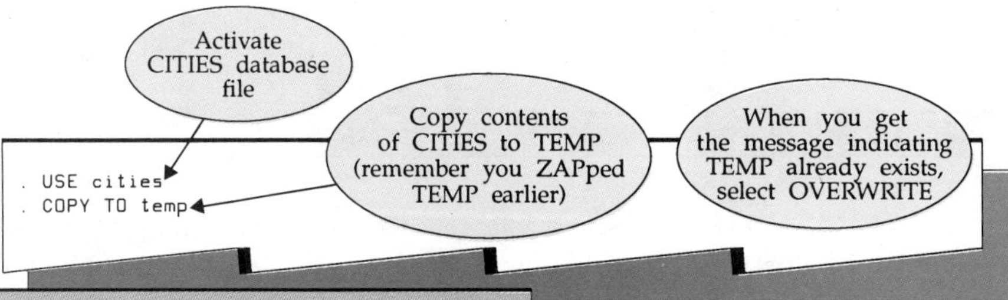

Figure 7.11 RECONSTRUCTING TEMP DATABASE FILE

Usually, a program to delete records should operate in a *batch mode* because it is more efficient to issue a PACK command once for a group of records than to issue one PACK per record. This simply means that the user will first identify all the records to be deleted. This will occur in a loop in which we will use the DELETE command. Once the user chooses to exit the loop, the program would execute a PACK command to complete the process.

(**Note:** This strategy assumes that this is an appropriate approach for the user. In certain situations, a user may prefer to have the records that are marked for deletion remain in the database for a period of time. Moreover, records sometimes must be placed in an *archive*, or historical file, before they are actually removed from the current database. Both of these situations require solutions other than the program outlined in this section.)

The physical removal of records is a drastic action for any organized file. This is especially true for a dBASE IV file because its relational basis requires that records be numbered sequentially and consecutively. Although you learned in Chapter 2 how this process operates, consider now the performance aspects of deleting records. Marking a record with the DELETE command, followed by a PACK statement, can be quite time-consuming, depending on the size of the database. This is because once the unwanted records are removed, the entire database must be rewritten in order for the records to be in proper order. Batching the deleted records and then issuing one PACK command obviously saves a great deal of time.

The user must have a way to indicate which records are to be deleted. This naturally leads to the idea of selecting records by searching through the file. In fact, this is the preferred method of selection. Chapter 9 will show how indexing can make this type of searching possible. In the program in this chapter, the record number is used to select records to be deleted. In reality, this method would not be very useful because the user would have to refer to a list of record numbers and select them manually. However, it can be used in the absence of an index.

The DEL_REC.PRG program (Figure 7.12 on the next page) combines WAIT, INPUT, and DO CASE in a menu program that automates the deletion process. This program could be called by another menu in addition to being executed with a DO command from the dot prompt.

After an identifying comment line, the program in Figure 7.12 begins by initializing the two memory variables, memchoice and memrec, to ' ' and 0, respectively. Since initialization provides good documentation and is required by some commands, it should be included at the start of every program.

The first section of a well-designed program establishes an environment. Useful commands include SET SAFETY OFF, which allows files to be overwritten without having to ask the user for permission to do so. SET TALK OFF must be used to prevent the display of system chatter, such as displaying the contents of memory variables during STORE commands. SET STATUS OFF removes the standard three-line display at the bottom of the screen; its removal allows for freedom in screen design. It is also a good idea to use SET DELETED ON. This excludes any deleted records from reports or displays.

The main body of the program is a DO WHILE loop that tests for the exit option, a '2' in memchoice. This permits the loop to continue to execute as long as the user wishes, since the menu inside will be redisplayed after each use. Sometimes a DO WHILE .T. is used for this purpose. We will see later how to make use of such a loop.

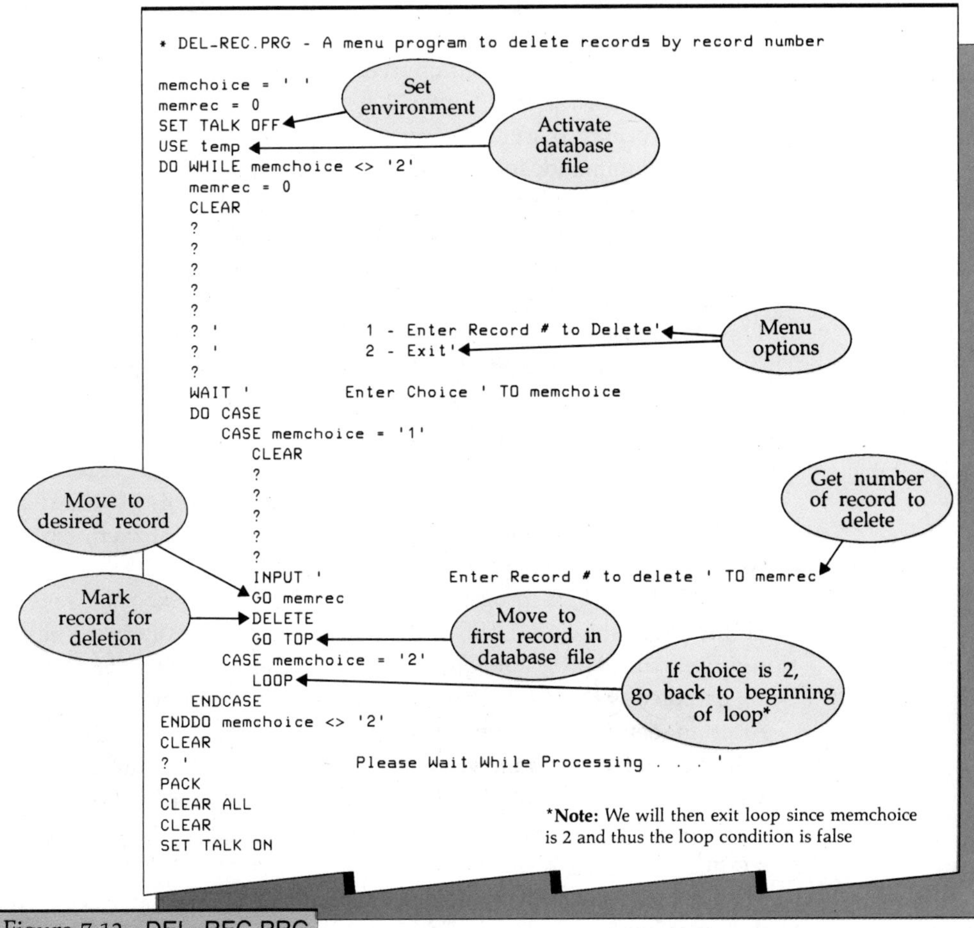

```
* DEL_REC.PRG - A menu program to delete records by record number

memchoice = ' '
memrec = 0
SET TALK OFF
USE temp
DO WHILE memchoice <> '2'
   memrec = 0
   CLEAR
   ?
   ?
   ?
   ?
   ?
   ? '           1 - Enter Record # to Delete'
   ? '           2 - Exit'
   ?
   WAIT '          Enter Choice ' TO memchoice
   DO CASE
      CASE memchoice = '1'
         CLEAR
         ?
         ?
         ?
         ?
         ?
         INPUT '           Enter Record # to delete ' TO memrec
         GO memrec
         DELETE
         GO TOP
      CASE memchoice = '2'
         LOOP
   ENDCASE
ENDDO memchoice <> '2'
CLEAR
? '             Please Wait While Processing . . . '
PACK
CLEAR ALL
CLEAR
SET TALK ON
```


Figure 7.12 DEL_REC.PRG

Because it will temporarily hold record numbers that have been chosen for deletion, memrec must be reset to 0 at the beginning of the loop. The screen must also be erased with the CLEAR command in order to display the menu. The eight ? commands that follow either print a blank line and move the cursor down the screen, or they display the options to the user. Once the options are visible, a WAIT command stores the user's choice in memchoice.

The DO CASE/ENDCASE structure provides the means to execute the appropriate commands, depending on the user's response. Either an opportunity will be provided to delete a record or the program will be terminated by LOOPing back to the DO WHILE command. (The LOOP command causes dBASE to move directly back to the DO WHILE.) In this case, '2' is currently stored in memchoice. Since this is the condition for exiting the DO WHILE loop, the program branches to the CLEAR that follows the ENDDO statement. One advantage of this strategy is that any characters other than '1' or '2' cause the screen to redisplay.

A '1' in memchoice requires the selection of a record number to delete. Record numbers are numeric, so we use an INPUT command to store the user's choice in memrec. The GO command positions the record pointer at the desired record before the DELETE command marks it for deletion. The record pointer is repositioned at the top of the file with GO TOP. Since the case is finished, the program branches to the statement after the ENDCASE, (`ENDDO memchoice <> '2'`). When the condition is evaluated at the DO WHILE, the body of the loop executes again. It is this looping that facilitates the batch processing of an unlimited number of records with rapid response.

The final section of the program is executed only after the user has decided to exit the loop. The screen is CLEARed and a message is displayed to reassure the user. The PACK command then physically removes the entire batch of records marked for deletion and rewrites the file. The files are closed, and memory variables are released with the CLEAR ALL command. Finally, the screen is CLEARed again and TALK is reset to ON.

DEL_REC.PRG is a good example of how useful procedures can be constructed by blending programming structures such as DO WHILE/ENDDO, DO CASE/ENDCASE, and IF/ENDIF. No magic formula is going to tell you how to write a program! However, clearly understanding how the structures will behave in a variety of conditions and examining the effect of several examples is an excellent beginning.

CHAPTER SUMMARY

1. Compared to a series of nested IF/ENDIFs, DO CASE/ENDCASE offers the advantages of speed and clarity when several mutually exclusive options must be evaluated. The structure must begin with a DO CASE and must finish with an ENDCASE. CASE statements and associated commands are placed between these statements. The CASE statements each contain a condition that will be evaluated until one is found to be true. The structure is then exited. An optional OTHERWISE can be included for any condition that is not specified in the CASE statements.

2. The @..GET/READ command combination is the best method for data entry. However, ACCEPT and WAIT are also useful in this regard. ACCEPT stores a character string in a variable and displays a prompt. WAIT pauses the program until a key is pressed, and stores input as well. INPUT and INKEY() are not as useful in programming.
3. Menus are valuable because they are an attractive and efficient way to direct program activity with user control. A menu displays options on a screen and accepts the user's choice. A DO CASE structure is used to select and execute the requested action. A DO WHILE/ENDDO loop is used to redisplay the menu. All menus should have one entry and one exit.
4. A program to delete records is more convenient to use if the records are marked for deletion as a batch and are then PACKed when the user employs the exit option in the menu. The record number is used to specify deletions. The program uses a menu with a DO CASE/ENDCASE unit contained within a DO WHILE loop.

KEY TERMS

mutually exclusive
menu-driven
null string
batch mode
full-screen editing
archive

COMMAND SUMMARY

Command Name	Use
DO CASE	The initial statement of the CASE structure.
ENDCASE	The final statement of the CASE structure.
CASE	The statement that contains the condition in a CASE structure.
OTHERWISE	A CASE command that identifies actions performed when all cases fail.
INPUT	A command sometimes employed for user input of numeric data.
WAIT	A command that accepts one character of user input.
ACCEPT	A command that accepts character input.
INKEY()	A function that captures a keystroke from the user.
SET SAFETY OFF	Overwriting of files is automatic.
SET STATUS OFF	The status line is not displayed.
SET DELETED ON	Deleted records are not displayed.

dBUG dBASE

- SET DEBUG ON sends all the ECHOed commands to the printer rather than the screen for documentation and more thorough study.
- Although it makes no difference in what order menu options are displayed on the screen, you should place the most frequently used option of DO CASE/ENDCASE as the first option in order to avoid having to scan the unused options frequently.
- Be as skeptical as possible about the new program until constant testing in a variety of circumstances validates the accuracy of the results. Use normal test data, and then varied and difficult data.
- When a program is first implemented, always operate in parallel; in other words, use the original program and the new one simultaneously. This is more time-consuming in the short run, but it can protect the users of the program from unforeseen disaster.

SELF-CHECK QUESTIONS

1. When is DO CASE/ENDCASE preferable to IF/ENDIF? Indicate whether IF/ENDIF or DO CASE/ENDCASE is best for programming each of the following situations:
   a. Individuals must be 16 years old to obtain a driver's license.
   b. Tennis players must be placed in ten tournament groups on the basis of their ranking.
   c. The dean's list requires a GPA of at least 3.6.
   d. Interest rates on certificates of deposit vary with the six terms (required time).
2. Is DO CASE/ENDCASE more efficient than several IF/ENDIFs? Why?
3. What are mutually exclusive options?
4. What does OTHERWISE do?
5. What is the difference between ACCEPT and WAIT?
6. What is full-screen editing?
7. Why is DO WHILE .T. useful in a menu program?
8. What is batch mode? When is it useful?
9. What are the disadvantages of using INPUT and INKEY()?
10. What is archiving?

TRY IT YOURSELF

1. Write an INPUT statement with a prompt to store a salary in the memory variable memsal.
2. Construct a DO CASE/ENDCASE structure to assign the appropriate tax rate to the variable memtax by evaluating the field STATE for the state code as follows:

   PA — 6%
   IL — 5%
   NE — 4.5%
   NM — 4.25%
   WY — 3%
3. Write DO CASE/ENDCASE structures for the situations you selected in Self-check Question 1.
4. Write CASE statements for the following conditions:
   a. Only full-time students (FT) may participate in athletics.
   b. A tolerance of 0.0002 must be attained before a part is passed by quality control.
   c. A youth club requires that its members be between the ages of 11 and 17.
   d. A car is considered an antique if it is more than 25 years old.
5. Decide whether INPUT, WAIT, or ACCEPT would be the best choice for each of the following tasks:
   a. Allow a user to move quickly through menus by pressing the indicated key.
   b. Enter test grades to compute an average.
   c. Display this message: "Press return when printer is ready."
   d. Ask the user's name and store it in a memory variable.
6. Write the appropriate statements for the previous exercise.
7. Write a command to enter the user's choice in Exercise 2.
8. Write a program that displays the following menu. Prompt the user and capture the response. In each case, write code that displays the user's choice and returns to the main menu.

```
KNERR MANUFACTURING
1. ACCOUNTS PAYABLE
2. ACCOUNTS RECEIVABLE
3. PAYROLL
4. INVENTORY
5. GENERAL LEDGER
6. EXIT

ENTER CHOICE -
```

9. Use the following pseudocode to write a program that performs all the functions specified. Use your own screen design. (You can make up any options you wish.)

```
Set environment
Continuously display main screen while user does not exit
Initialize variables
Clear screen
Display options
Accept user's response
Perform selected action
Redisplay on return
```

10. Write a program to accept the user's response when asked to enter a digit from 0 to 9. Display the message, "Your response was (one, two, etc.)."

PROGRAMMING PROJECT

Write a DO WHILE loop and DO CASE/ENDCASE structure to enclose the following portion of a menu program (use the variable memchoice). For option 1, the action should be APPEND. For option 2, the action should be DISPLAY. The action for option 3 should be EDIT and the action for option 4 should be PACK.

```
? '1 - Add a record'
? '2 - Display a record'
? '3 - Edit a record'
? '4 - Remove deleted records'
? '5 - Exit' ?
```

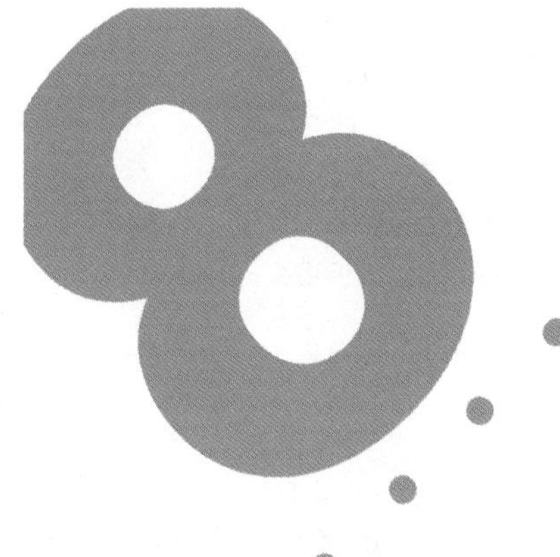

LEARNING OBJECTIVES

To examine the effect of nesting structures.

To use the modular concept to construct systems.

To compare the behavior of memory variable types in systems.

To incorporate data integrity within programs.

To reexamine structured programming.

8 ORGANIZING A SYSTEM

INTRODUCTION

A system may be defined as an interrelated group of elements working together for a common purpose. You have written several freestanding programs. In actual business practice, these programs would be grouped together in a system for ease of use and efficiency. This chapter presents several ways of organizing systems in a structured manner. Sophisticated business problems require this type of approach.

8.1 NESTING

You have studied the three control structures DO WHILE/ENDDO, IF/ENDIF, and DO CASE/ENDCASE in the previous three chapters. As you encounter more complex business problems, you will have to combine these structures within programs. Some of the program examples in earlier chapters occasionally placed an IF/ENDIF within a DO WHILE/ENDDO structure, using a strategy called *nesting*. A good analogy for nesting is a child's toy: a set of plastic barrels of different colors and sizes, each of which opens into two halves (see Figure 8.1). When the toy is assembled, the barrels are nested one inside the other. Think of structures being nested in this way. As with the toy, the halves must match in order for the program to work. Structures can be nested within one another in any combination as long as the arrangement is logically correct.

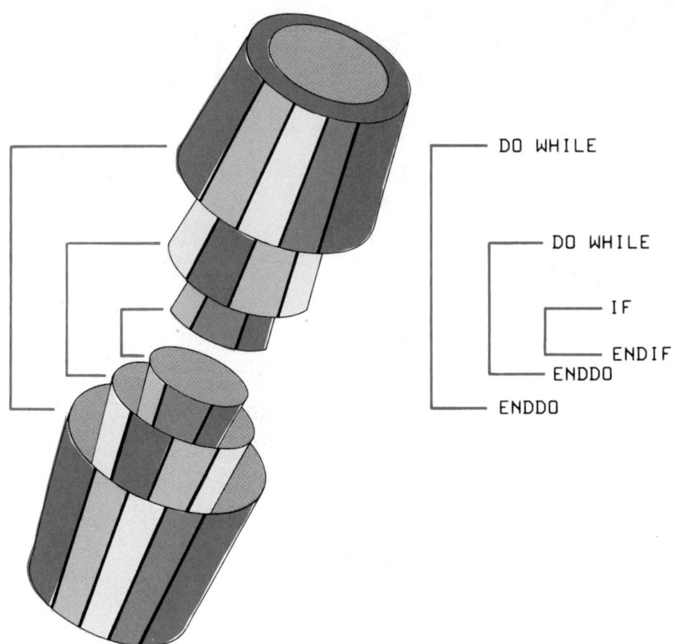

Figure 8.1 NESTED TOY BARRELS

The nesting arrangements in previous chapters are not complex because IF/ENDIF and DO CASE/ENDCASE are sequential structures, meaning that they do not loop or repeat. For this reason, they are relatively simple to understand when nested in a DO WHILE/ENDDO envelope. In the examples in Figure 8.2, the structures within the loop execute only once for each pass of the DO WHILE.

```
DO WHILE condition
    IF condition
         action
    ELSE
         action
    ENDIF
ENDDO
```

```
DO WHILE condition
    DO CASE
        CASE condition
             action
        CASE condition
             action
    ENDCASE
ENDDO
```

Figure 8.2 EXAMPLES OF NESTED STRUCTURES

When one DO WHILE/ENDDO loop is nested within another, as shown in Figure 8.3, it can be more difficult to predict or understand how the program will behave because the status of two loops must be monitored simultaneously. Naturally, the more levels of nesting that are added, the more involved the logic becomes.

DO WHILE condition
DO WHILE condition
action
ENDDO
ENDDO

Figure 8.3 NESTED DO WHILE/ENDDO LOOPS

An analogy might be a ride in an amusement park that takes you to the top of a tower in a car and spins you around three times as you descend. There would be three spins of the car for each trip down the tower. You might take many rides up and down the tower, but for each pass you would spin three times. In other words, three trips up and down the tower would yield nine spins of the car. (See Figure 8.4 on the next page.)

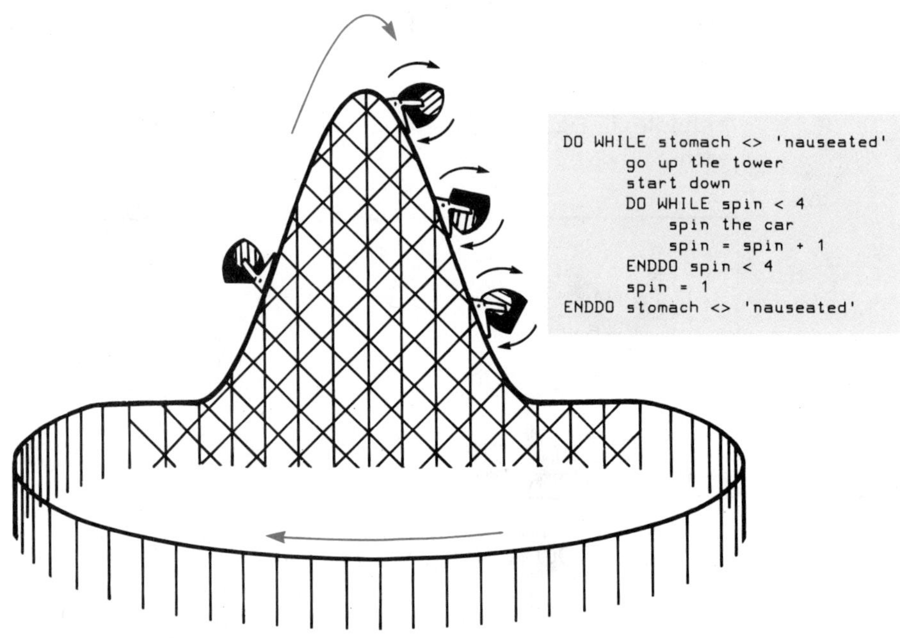

DO WHILE stomach <> 'nauseated'
go up the tower
start down
DO WHILE spin < 4
spin the car
spin = spin + 1
ENDDO spin < 4
spin = 1
ENDDO stomach <> 'nauseated'

Figure 8.4 A NESTED DO WHILE/ENDDO "RIDE"

You can see how both DO WHILE conditions must be monitored if you are to understand how the program is operating. If more loops were nested in this way, and perhaps other structures as well, it could be quite difficult to follow the logic. Although the previously explained structured programming conventions of indentation and documentation help, it is also useful to *bracket* structures for clarification. Figure 8.5 illustrates how the three control structures can be bracketed using *action diagrams*, a technique developed by James Martin.

Figure 8.5 DIAGRAMMING NESTED STRUCTURES

Figure 8.6 contains a program to display records on the screen in groups of fifteen. This is a good example of nested DO WHILE/ENDDO loops. One loop handles the menu, and another is required to access all the records in the file sequentially. When the necessary IF structures are included, the result is a structure like the one outlined in Figure 8.7.

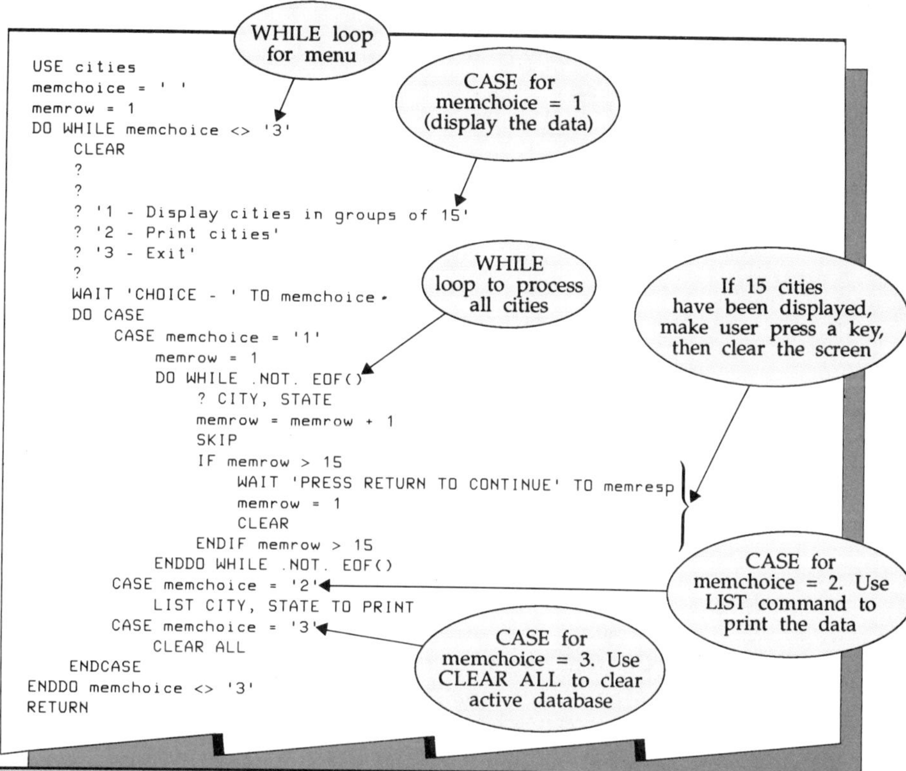

```
USE cities
memchoice = ' '
memrow = 1
DO WHILE memchoice <> '3'
     CLEAR
     ?
     ?
     ? '1 - Display cities in groups of 15'
     ? '2 - Print cities'
     ? '3 - Exit'
     ?
     WAIT 'CHOICE - ' TO memchoice
     DO CASE
          CASE memchoice = '1'
               memrow = 1
               DO WHILE .NOT. EOF()
                    ? CITY, STATE
                    memrow = memrow + 1
                    SKIP
                    IF memrow > 15
                         WAIT 'PRESS RETURN TO CONTINUE' TO memresp
                         memrow = 1
                         CLEAR
                    ENDIF memrow > 15
               ENDDO WHILE .NOT. EOF()
          CASE memchoice = '2'
               LIST CITY, STATE TO PRINT
          CASE memchoice = '3'
               CLEAR ALL
     ENDCASE
ENDDO memchoice <> '3'
RETURN
```

WHILE loop for menu
CASE for memchoice = 1 (display the data)
WHILE loop to process all cities
If 15 cities have been displayed, make user press a key, then clear the screen
CASE for memchoice = 2. Use LIST command to print the data
CASE for memchoice = 3. Use CLEAR ALL to clear active database

Figure 8.6 A PROGRAM ILLUSTRATING NESTED STRUCTURES

```
DO WHILE
   IF
      DO WHILE
         IF
         ENDIF
      ENDDO
   ELSE
      IF
      ENDIF
   ENDIF
ENDDO
```

Figure 8.7 OUTLINE OF NESTED STRUCTURES

The nested DO WHILE .NOT. EOF() in Figure 8.6 executes fifteen times for every execution of the outside loop, DO WHILE memchoice < > '2'. This allows you to browse the names in the file conveniently on the screen as often as you wish. It is rare to exceed two or three levels of nested DO WHILE loops, unless you are using more than one database file (as Chapter 11 will explain). Because they are so powerful, DO WHILE structures should be established only when they are clearly required to achieve repetition. You may be tempted to employ the condition testing of a DO WHILE command for selection, using a logical operator such as .AND.. This practice usually results in excessively complex structures that are difficult to construct and debug. You should use IF/ENDIF or DO CASE nested within a DO WHILE loop instead.

Unfortunately, there are no clear rules that apply to nesting. The problem at hand dictates how the structures must be organized to produce a solution. However, nested structures must be free from logical errors and they must perform the intended function efficiently. Although dBASE IV does not allow illogical structures to execute, you must use your knowledge and experience to ensure that the structures perform as expected.

8.2 THE MODULAR CONCEPT

By now, you have become accustomed to writing programs that accomplish a single task. While this is a useful, common approach to programming, many business situations require another strategy. When a project has a wide scope, it is often necessary to assign individual tasks to separate programs that are linked together in a system.

Modules are small programs that are sometimes referred to as *subroutines, subprograms, procedures,* or *called programs*. They are designed to perform one function, and they should be written as freestanding sections of code, meaning that they may be run alone or as part of a larger system. The concept of a set of individual modules linked together in a larger structure is an important principle of structured programming.

Modules are generally written as separate PRG files and are called from another program, called the *calling program*. Once developed and tested, the modules can be left as separate files or they can be combined into a single file. The issues we will discuss in this chapter apply in either case. (We will see how to combine them later.) The DO and RETURN commands are used for executing and then returning from modules. You have become accustomed to executing PRG files from the dot prompt, using the DO command. The DO command is also capable of executing or calling other PRG files from within a program.

In general, a module should begin by opening any required database or other files (if there are any) and initializing variables. At the conclusion of the module's operation these files are closed, and any memory variables are released. Writing modules in this fashion offers the following advantages:

1. Modules are independent; they do not depend on each other for data.
2. Each module can be tested and debugged individually.
3. Several programmers can conveniently work on the same system.
4. Modules can be modified for use in other applications.

The most obvious examples of module functions are appending, modifying, displaying, and deleting records. These functions could be placed together in a menu-driven system in order to allow a user who is unfamiliar with dBASE IV or programming to access them easily. The tasks are performed safely and efficiently because the critical commands are carefully written in PRG files. Other commonly used functions include displaying individual records, generating summary reports, and performing calculations.

It may be helpful to diagram the system structure in order to verify that the design is correct and effective. *Structure diagrams* aid in displaying the relationships among program modules. Other persons who become involved with the project will be more comfortable dealing with a structure diagram than with a listing of code.

The strategy of proceeding from the general goals of a system to more manageable task levels is called *functional decomposition*, or *top-down design*. Having too many modules on any one level is undesirable. A reasonable number is between two and six. The structure diagram shown in Figure 8.8 on the next page illustrates a well-balanced organization of a programming system.

The diagram in Figure 8.9, also on the next page, shows the X level calling ten modules in the Z level. Ten modules are too many. Inserting the Y level solves the problem, subgrouping the ten Z-level modules into the three Y-level modules. If this represented a menu structure, for example, the lowest level of the structure should be the individual task modules. Although it is certainly possible, it is unusual for systems to exceed three levels.

MAIN MENU
1 - Updates
2 - Reports
3 - Labels
4 - Utilities
5 - Exit

Main menu (first level)

Updates
1 - Add new customers
2 - Edit existing customers
3 - Delete customers
4 - Return to Main Menu

Reports
1 - Report 1
2 - Report 2
3 - Report 3
4 - Report 4
5 - Return to Main Menu

Labels
1 - Label 1
2 - Label 2
3 - Label 3
4 - Label 4
5 - Return to Main Menu

Utilities
1 - Utility 1
2 - Utility 2
3 - Utility 3
4 - Utility 4
5 - Return to Main Menu

Submenus (second level)

Add new customers

Edit existing customers

Delete customers

Actions (third level)

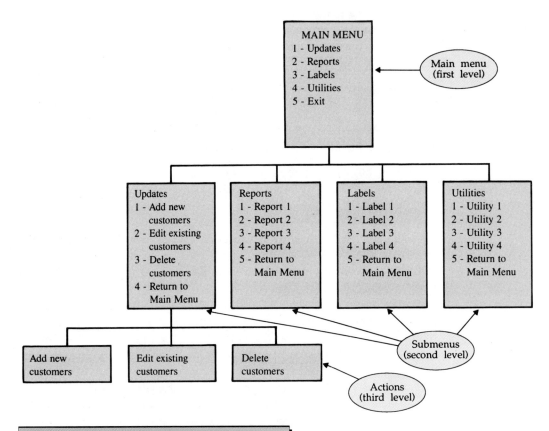

Figure 8.8 EXAMPLE OF A STRUCTURE DIAGRAM

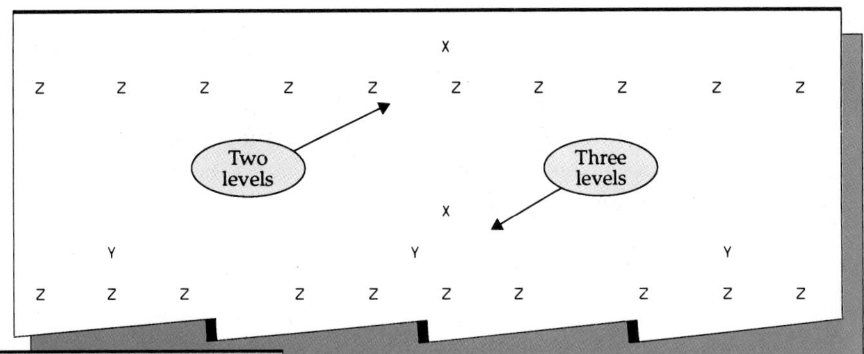

Figure 8.9 SUBGROUPING MODULES

In the example in Figure 8.9, the X module would allow the user to select any one of the three Y submenus or to leave the system. The Y modules would include the Z options or a return to the X module. The Z options would perform their individual tasks and return to the appropriate Y module.

Most business problems you will encounter will be of sufficient scope to require a system of modules rather than several loosely related but separate files. Solving problems in this way is effective, efficient, and responsible.

8.3 DEVELOPING PROGRAMS

USING STUBS

An important technique in developing modules is known as *stubbing*. Suppose, for example, that we wanted to develop the menu system illustrated in the structure chart shown in Figure 8.8. The first step is to develop the top module, that is, the main menu.

The difficulty is that when the users select options from the main menu, they will be taken to other menus. Thus, it would seem as though we have to develop all the modules simultaneously in order to be able to test any part of the system. Fortunately, we don't. Instead we use stubs for the lower modules.

Consider the two programs shown in Figure 8.10 on the next page. The CMENU.PRG program represents the main menu. (**Note:** We will be enhancing this menu program throughout the upcoming discussion. Only the final version is included on your disk.) All the options are included as well as all the references to other programs (DO updmenu, DO rptmenu, and so on).

The other program illustrated in the figure is UPDMENU.PRG. As you can see, this program (which will eventually contain the Updates menu) simply displays a message, uses the WAIT command to request that the user press a key, and then uses the RETURN command to return to the calling program. It is, in fact, what is often referred to as a *stub* or *nonfunctional test module*. The use of stubs is a convenient way to construct the skeleton of a program in order to ensure that the modules are called correctly. The individual modules can be finished later.

```
* CMENU.PRG - Customer menu

SET TALK OFF
memchoice1 = '0'
DO WHILE memchoice1 <> '5'
    CLEAR
    ? 'M A I N   M E N U'
    ?
    ? '1 - Updates'
    ? '2 - Reports'
    ? '3 - Labels'
    ? '4 - Utilities'
    ? '5 - Exit'
    ?
    WAIT 'CHOICE - ' TO memchoice1
    DO CASE
        CASE memchoice1 = '1'
            * Updates menu
            DO updmenu
        CASE memchoice1 = '2'
            * Reports menu
            DO rptmenu
        CASE memchoice1 = '3'
            * Labels menu
            DO lblmenu
        CASE memchoice1 = '4'
            * Utilities menu
            DO utlmenu
        CASE memchoice1 = '5'
            * Exit
            LOOP
        OTHERWISE
            WAIT 'INVALID CHOICE!  Press any key.'
    ENDCASE
ENDDO WHILE memchoice1 <> '5'
CLEAR
SET TALK ON
RETURN

* UPDMENU.PRG  Updates menu

CLEAR
? 'Updates menu stub'
WAIT
RETURN
```

UPDMENU is currently just a stub
Display a message
Wait for user to press a key
Return to calling program

Figure 8.10 CUSTOMER MENU WITH STUBS

If you were to execute CMENU (you can't since this is not the version on your data disk), you would first see the screen shown in Figure 8.11. If you selected option 1, the CMENU program would call UPDMENU. When UPDMENU is executed, your screen would look like the one shown in Figure 8.12. Once you pressed a key, you would be returned to CMENU and the original menu would be redisplayed.

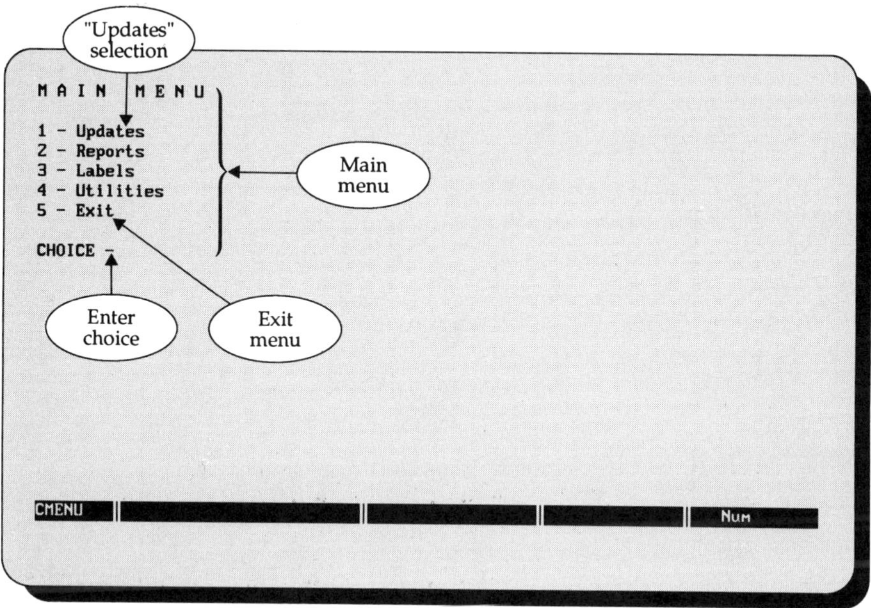

Figure 8.11 EXECUTING CMENU.PRG

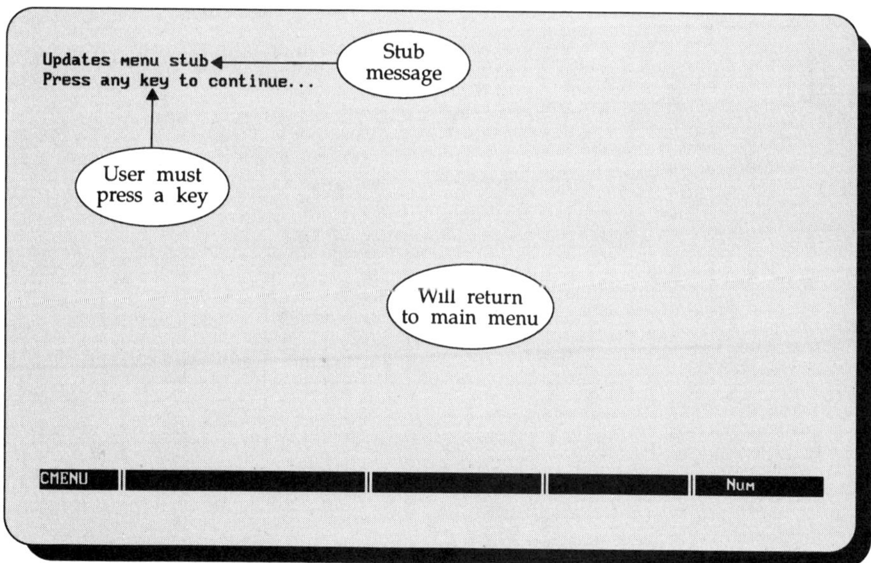

Figure 8.12 EXECUTING UPDMENU.PRG

Once we have tested the top-level module in this way, we can apply the same technique to the modules at the next level. Figure 8.13 shows the complete UPDMENU.PRG program. It also shows the ADD_CUST.PRG program, which represents one of the modules called by UPDMENU. Notice that it is simply a stub.

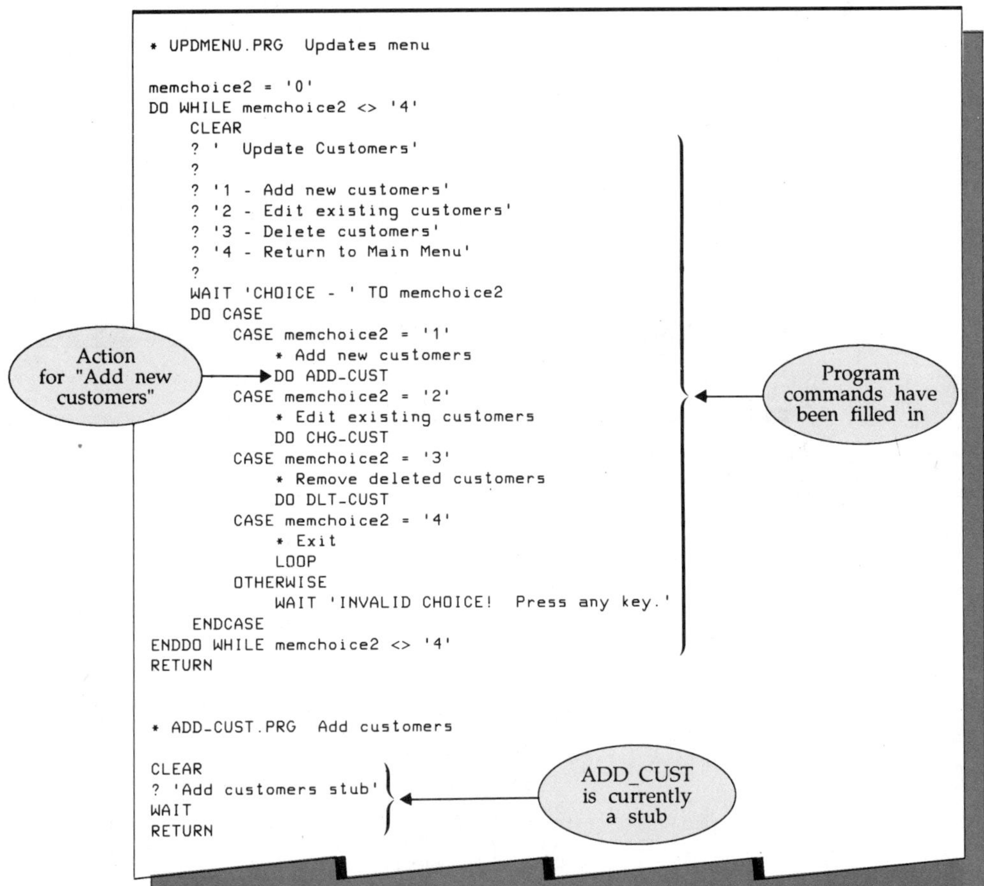

```
* UPDMENU.PRG  Updates menu

memchoice2 = '0'
DO WHILE memchoice2 <> '4'
    CLEAR
    ? '  Update Customers'
    ?
    ? '1 - Add new customers'
    ? '2 - Edit existing customers'
    ? '3 - Delete customers'
    ? '4 - Return to Main Menu'
    ?
    WAIT 'CHOICE - ' TO memchoice2
    DO CASE
        CASE memchoice2 = '1'
            * Add new customers
            DO ADD-CUST
        CASE memchoice2 = '2'
            * Edit existing customers
            DO CHG-CUST
        CASE memchoice2 = '3'
            * Remove deleted customers
            DO DLT-CUST
        CASE memchoice2 = '4'
            * Exit
            LOOP
        OTHERWISE
            WAIT 'INVALID CHOICE!  Press any key.'
    ENDCASE
ENDDO WHILE memchoice2 <> '4'
RETURN

* ADD-CUST.PRG  Add customers

CLEAR
? 'Add customers stub'
WAIT
RETURN
```

Action for "Add new customers"
Program commands have been filled in
ADD_CUST is currently a stub

Figure 8.13 UPDMENU.PRG PROGRAM AND ADD_CUST.PRG STUB

If you now execute CMENU and then select option 1, you will see the screen shown in Figure 8.14. If you select option 1 from this menu, the UPDMENU program will call ADD_CUST. When ADD_CUST is executed, your screen would look like the one shown in Figure 8.15. Once you press a key, you will be returned to UPDMENU.

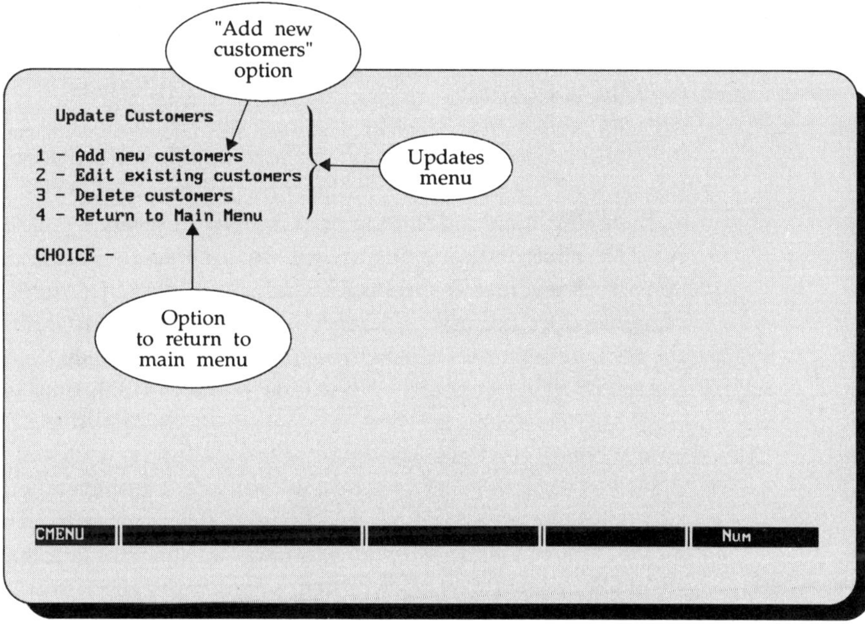

Figure 8.14 EXECUTION OF UPDCUST.PRG

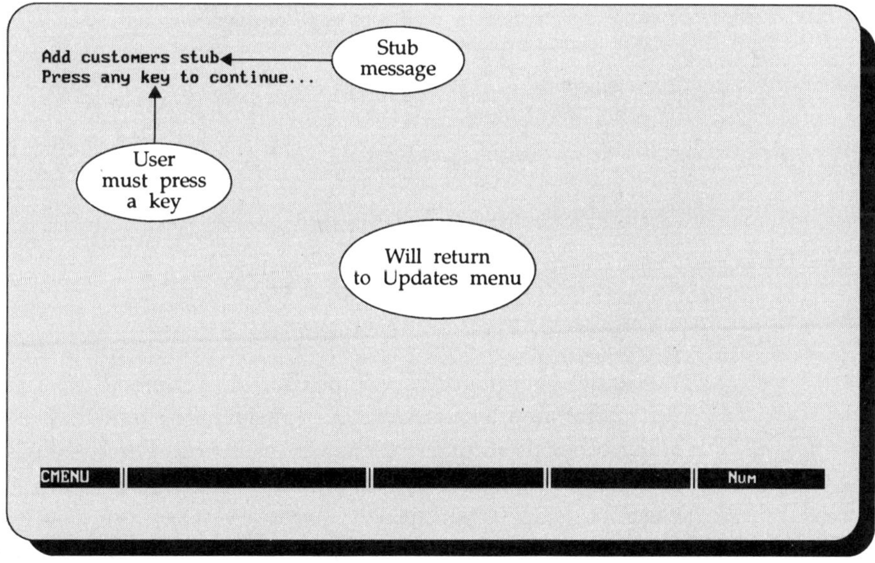

Figure 8.15 EXECUTION OF ADD_CUST.PRG

USING dBASE PROCEDURES

Once all the modules have been developed as separate PRG files, it is possible to combine them into a single PRG file. Figure 8.16 illustrates the inclusion of UPDMENU, RPTMENU, LBLMENU, and UTLMENU as *procedures* in CMENU.PRG. Notice that each begins with the word PROCEDURE followed by the name. The remainder of the procedure is exactly the same as the commands in the corresponding PRG file.

Including these modules in the CMENU program is a good idea for two reasons. First, without this ability, our one single "program" will usually consist of several separate command files scattered around the disk. This certainly does not give a very cohesive feel to the program. Second, if all the files are separate, dBASE has to open each file when it encounters a DO statement that refers to it. This adds to the running time of the program. Also, there is a limit on the total number of files that dBASE can have open at any one time. Thus, the more of these command files dBASE has open, the fewer database files, indexes, and so on it can have open.

You might wonder how far to take this approach. Should you also include the procedures for all the updates, reports, labels, and utilities in CMENU or should you keep them separate? While it would be more efficient to include them, it would produce a very large program, one that could be difficult to manage. The gain in efficiency would, in all probability, be offset by the difficulty in creating and maintaining such a program.

The best way to decide when to include a command file as a procedure is to do it by function. All the command files that have been included as procedures in CMENU, for example, deal with the process of obtaining a user's selection. Command files such as ADD_CUST and CHG_CUST, on the other hand, deal with taking specific actions. Thus, they would be kept separate. (If within ADD_CUST there is a DO statement calling on a command file to take some action related to adding a customer, this command file should ultimately be included as a procedure *within* ADD_CUST.)

8.4 PROGRAMMING WITH MEMORY VARIABLES

As in Pascal or C, two other widely used programming languages, dBASE IV includes commands to provide control over memory variables. The PRIVATE command localizes memory variables so that they are not available to any other programs that may be executed. The PUBLIC command, on the other hand, makes specified variables available to any program in the system. It is important to note that if a variable can be accessed, it can be changed. The programmer has control over PUBLIC variables. Variables are automatically declared PUBLIC when they are established at the dot prompt and declared PRIVATE when they are created within a program (unless they are declared PUBLIC by the programmer).

```
* CMENU.PRG - Customer menu

SET TALK OFF
memchoice1 = '0'
DO WHILE memchoice1 <> '5'
    CLEAR
    ? 'M A I N   M E N U'
    ?
    ? '1 - Updates'
    ? '2 - Reports'
    ? '3 - Labels'
    ? '4 - Utilities'
    ? '5 - Exit'
    ?
    WAIT 'CHOICE - ' TO memchoice1
    DO CASE
        CASE memchoice1 = '1'
            * Updates menu
            DO updmenu
        CASE memchoice1 = '2'
            * Reports menu
            DO rptmenu
        CASE memchoice1 = '3'
            * Labels menu
            DO lblmenu
        CASE memchoice1 = '4'
            * Utilities menu
            DO utlmenu
        CASE memchoice1 = '5'
            * Exit
            LOOP
        OTHERWISE
            WAIT 'INVALID CHOICE!  Press any key.'
    ENDCASE
ENDDO WHILE memchoice1 <> '5'
CLEAR
SET TALK ON
RETURN
```

Lower level programs included as procedures

```
PROCEDURE updmenu
memchoice2 = '0'
DO WHILE memchoice2 <> '4'
    CLEAR
    ? '  Update Customers'
    ?
    ? '1 - Add new customers'
    ? '2 - Edit existing customers'
    ? '3 - Delete customers'
    ? '4 - Return to Main Menu'
    ?
    WAIT 'CHOICE - ' TO memchoice2
    DO CASE
        CASE memchoice2 = '1'
            * Add new customers
            DO ADD-CUST
        CASE memchoice2 = '2'
            * Edit existing customers
            DO CHG-CUST
        CASE memchoice2 = '3'
            * Remove deleted customers
            DO DLT-CUST
        CASE memchoice2 = '4'
            * Exit
            LOOP
        OTHERWISE
            WAIT 'INVALID CHOICE!  Press any key.'
    ENDCASE
ENDDO WHILE memchoice2 <> '4'
RETURN
```

Procedure statement

Figure 8.16 CMENU PROGRAM

(continued)

```
PROCEDURE rptmenu
memchoice2 = '0'
DO WHILE memchoice2 <> '5'
    CLEAR
    ? '  Reports Menu'
    ?
    ? '1 - Report 1'
    ? '2 - Report 2'
    ? '3 - Report 3'
    ? '4 - Report 4'
    ? '5 - Return to Main Menu'
    ?
    WAIT 'CHOICE - ' TO memchoice2
    DO CASE
        CASE memchoice2 = '1'
            * Report 1 stub
            CLEAR
            ? 'Report 1 stub'
            WAIT
        CASE memchoice2 = '2'
            * Report 2 stub
            CLEAR
            ? 'Report 2 stub'
            WAIT
        CASE memchoice2 = '3'
            * Report 3 stub
            CLEAR
            ? 'Report 3 stub'
            WAIT
        CASE memchoice2 = '4'
            * Report 4 stub
            CLEAR
            ? 'Report 4 stub'
            WAIT
        CASE memchoice2 = '5'
            * Return to main menu
            LOOP
        OTHERWISE
            WAIT 'INVALID CHOICE!  Press any key.'
    ENDCASE
ENDDO WHILE memchoice2 <> '5'
RETURN
```

Options are stubbed within CMENU

```
PROCEDURE lblmenu
memchoice2 = '0'
DO WHILE memchoice2 <> '5'
    CLEAR
    ? '  Labels Menu'
    ?
    ? '1 - Label 1'
    ? '2 - Label 2'
    ? '3 - Label 3'
    ? '4 - Label 4'
    ? '5 - Return to Main Menu'
    ?
    WAIT 'CHOICE - ' TO memchoice2
    DO CASE
        CASE memchoice2 = '1'
            * Label 1 stub
            CLEAR
            ? 'Label 1 stub'
            WAIT
        CASE memchoice2 = '2'
            * Label 2 stub
            CLEAR
            ? 'Label 2 stub'
            WAIT
```

Figure 8.16 CMENU PROGRAM

```
        CASE memchoice2 = '3'
            * Label 3 stub
            CLEAR
            ? 'Label 3 stub'
            WAIT
        CASE memchoice2 = '4'
            * Label 4 stub
            CLEAR
            ? 'Label 4 stub'
            WAIT
        CASE memchoice2 = '5'
            * Return to main menu
            LOOP
        OTHERWISE
            WAIT 'INVALID CHOICE!  Press any key.'
    ENDCASE
ENDDO WHILE memchoice2 <> '5'
RETURN

PROCEDURE utlmenu
memchoice2 = '0'
DO WHILE memchoice2 <> '5'
    CLEAR
    ? '  Utilities Menu'
    ?
    ? '1 - Utility 1'
    ? '2 - Utility 2'
    ? '3 - Utility 3'
    ? '4 - Utility 4'
    ? '5 - Return to Main Menu'
    ?
    WAIT 'CHOICE - ' TO memchoice2
    DO CASE
        CASE memchoice2 = '1'
            * Utility 1 stub
            CLEAR
            ? 'Utility 1 stub'
            WAIT
        CASE memchoice2 = '2'
            * Utility 2 stub
            CLEAR
            ? 'Utility 2 stub'
            WAIT
        CASE memchoice2 = '3'
            * Utility 3 stub
            CLEAR
            ? 'Utility 3 stub'
            WAIT
        CASE memchoice2 = '4'
            * Utility 4 stub
            CLEAR
            ? 'Utility 4 stub'
            WAIT
        CASE memchoice2 = '5'
            * Return to main menu
            LOOP
        OTHERWISE
            WAIT 'INVALID CHOICE!  Press any key.'
    ENDCASE
ENDDO WHILE memchoice2 <> '5'
RETURN
```

Figure 8.16 CMENU PROGRAM

CALLING AND CALLED PROGRAMS

Variables that are created in a higher-level program, the *calling program*, are available in any lower-level program, the *called program*. For example, in the bottom of Figure 8.9, a variable created in level Y would be available in level Z but not in level X. Variables can be passed down the structure diagram, but they cannot move up because dBASE IV will RELEASE all PRIVATE variables when a RETURN command is executed.

Consider, for example, the portion of the CMENU.PRG file shown in Figure 8.17. Here we have included commands to clear the screen and display the contents of memchoicel and memchoice2 after the DO rptmenu command. Thus, the contents of these variables are to be displayed as soon as we return from RPTMENU.

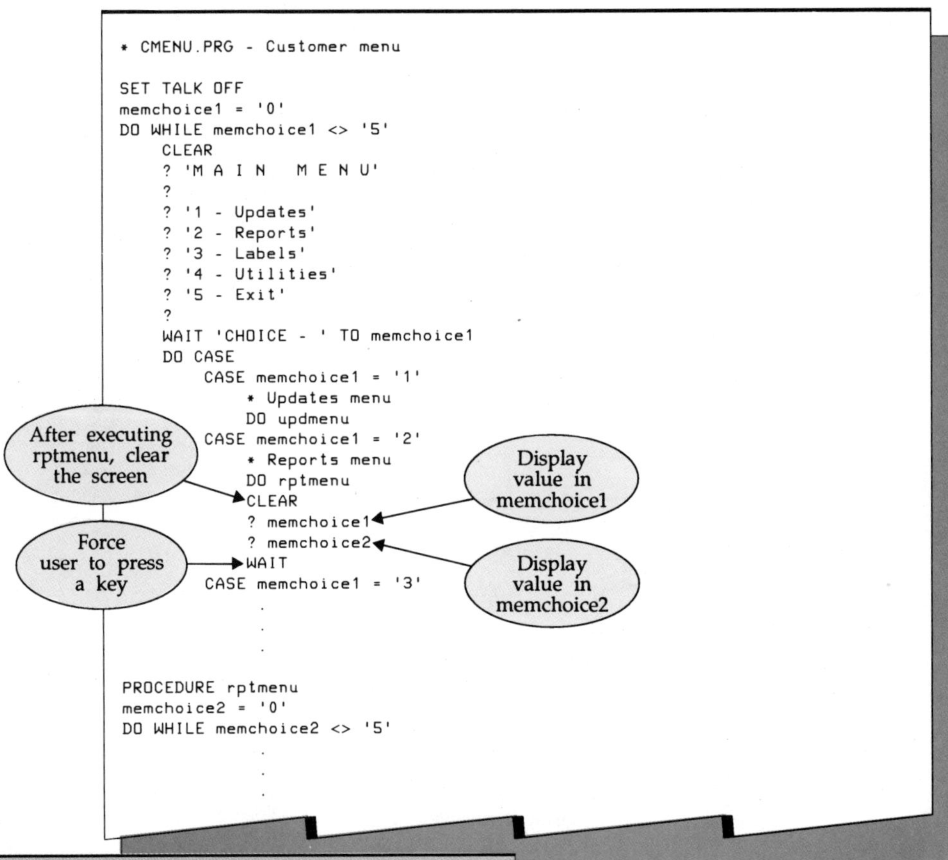

```
* CMENU.PRG - Customer menu

SET TALK OFF
memchoice1 = '0'
DO WHILE memchoice1 <> '5'
    CLEAR
    ? 'M A I N   M E N U'
    ?
    ? '1 - Updates'
    ? '2 - Reports'
    ? '3 - Labels'
    ? '4 - Utilities'
    ? '5 - Exit'
    ?
    WAIT 'CHOICE - ' TO memchoice1
    DO CASE
        CASE memchoice1 = '1'
            * Updates menu
            DO updmenu
        CASE memchoice1 = '2'
            * Reports menu
            DO rptmenu
            CLEAR
            ? memchoice1
            ? memchoice2
            WAIT
        CASE memchoice1 = '3'
            .
            .
            .

PROCEDURE rptmenu
memchoice2 = '0'
DO WHILE memchoice2 <> '5'
    .
    .
    .
```

After executing rptmenu, clear the screen
Force user to press a key
Display value in memchoicel
Display value in memchoice2

Figure 8.17 INTERACTION OF MEMORY VARIABLES

If we were to run this version of CMENU (DO cmenu), select "Reports" and then select "Return to main menu," our screen would look like the one shown in Figure 8.18. The problem is that memchoice2 is no longer available since it was automatically released when we returned from RPT-MENU.

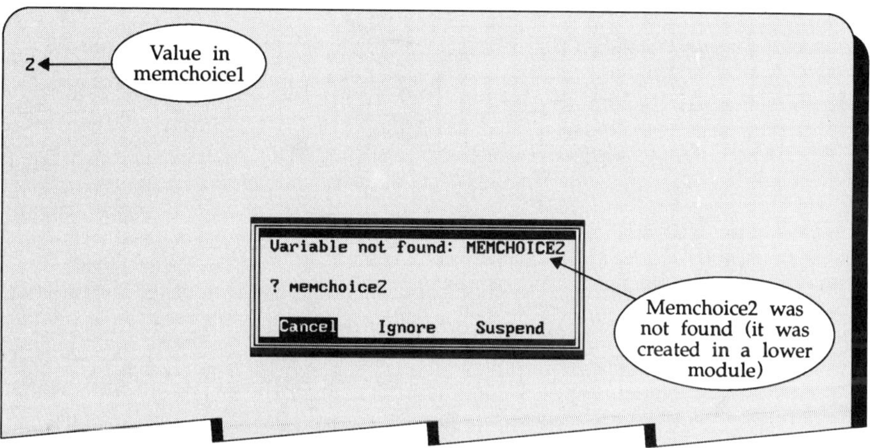

Figure 8.18 "VARIABLE NOT FOUND" ERROR

USING PUBLIC

When a variable is declared PUBLIC before it is assigned a value with a STORE command, it is available to programs at any level. In the RPT-MENU procedure shown in Figure 8.19, memchoice2 is declared as PUBLIC. This time if we follow the same steps as before, we will be able to display the value of memchoice2 (5) when we return to CMENU.

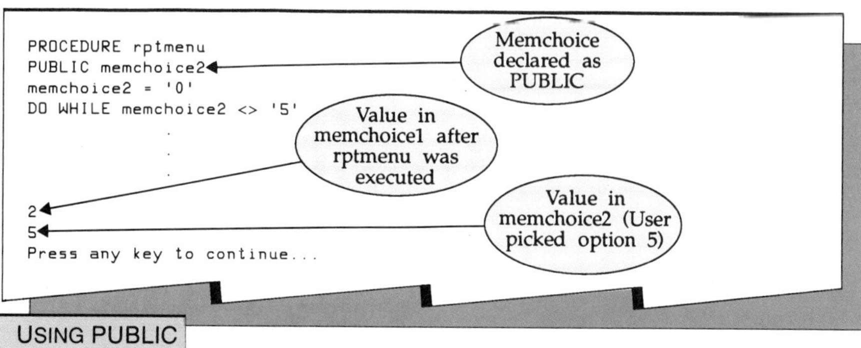

Figure 8.19 USING PUBLIC

It might be useful to declare a memory variable to hold the state sales tax PUBLIC in a program for retail merchants. The value would then be universally available for calculations throughout the system. Should the tax rate change, only one line of code, the STORE command, would need to be modified. Be cautious when declaring variables PUBLIC; you should always have a specific reason for doing so.

USING PRIVATE

To illustrate the fact that a variable declared in a calling program is available in the called program, consider Figure 8.20. In this example, memchoice1 is changed to 7 within RPTMENU. As the display at the end of the figure indicates, memchoice1 has this new value (7) even after we have returned from RPTMENU.

When a variable is declared as PRIVATE in a module, changes made to the variable in that module do not affect other modules. For example, in Figure 8.21, memchoice1 is declared as PRIVATE in RPTMENU. It is also changed to 7 within RPTMENU. Notice that the value displayed when we return to the main menu is still 2, the original value. Thus, the change to the value of memchoice1 within RPTMENU did not affect the value in other modules.

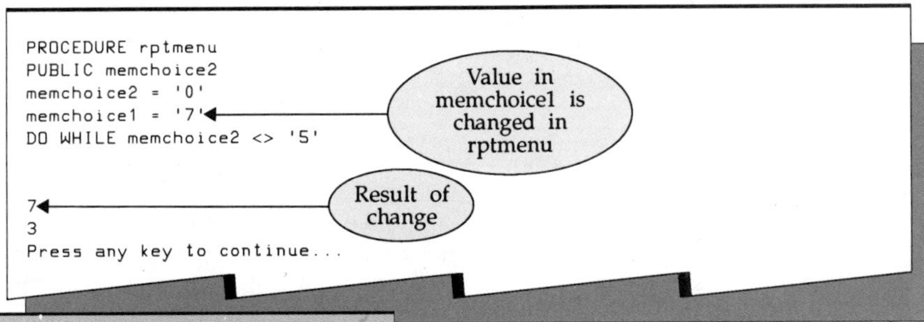

Figure 8.20 CHANGING A MEMORY VARIABLE

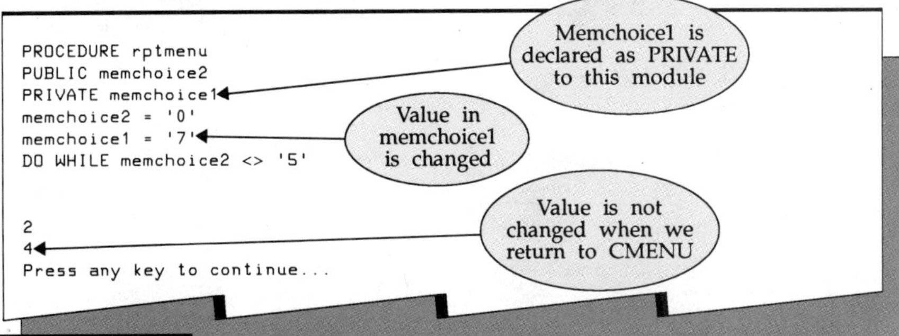

Figure 8.21 USING PRIVATE

USING DO WITH AND PARAMETER

The DO WITH and PARAMETER commands allow variables to be passed to other programs. PARAMETER must be the first executable command in the called program. In Figure 8.22, RPTMENU is called with memchoice1 as a parameter. Within RPTMENU, the PARAMETER statement identifies parm1 as the corresponding parameter. This means that memchoice1 has effectively been renamed parm1 for the duration of RPTMENU. In RPTMENU the value in parm1 is changed to 7. As the display indicates, this change is really made to the value in memchoice1.

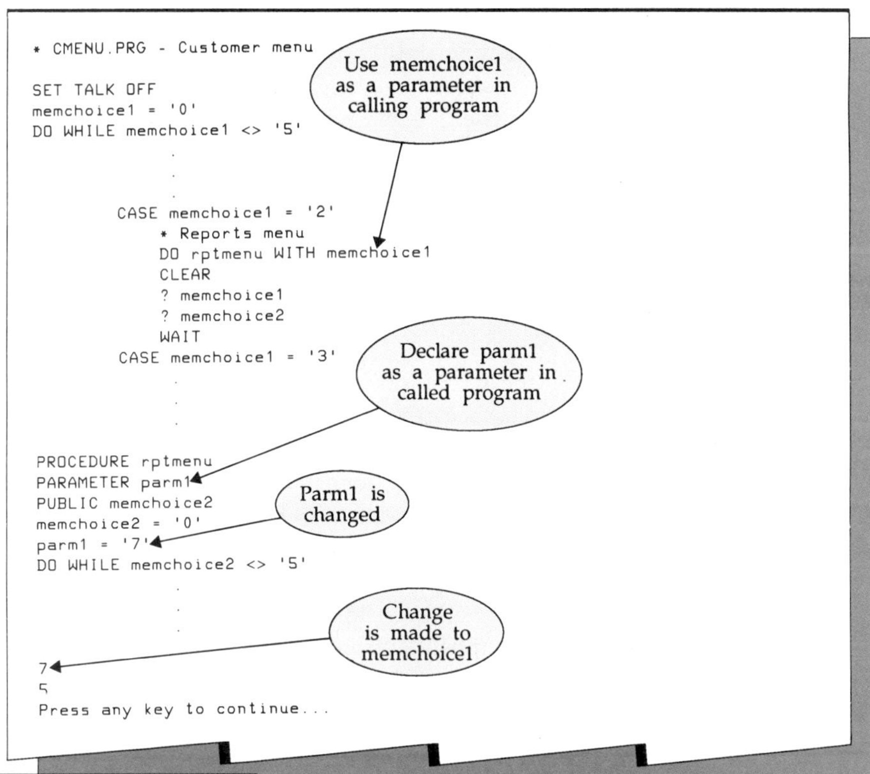

* CMENU.PRG - Customer menu
SET TALK OFF
memchoice1 = '0'
DO WHILE memchoice1 <> '5'
CASE memchoice1 = '2'
* Reports menu
DO rptmenu WITH memchoice1
CLEAR
? memchoice1
? memchoice2
WAIT
CASE memchoice1 = '3'
PROCEDURE rptmenu
PARAMETER parm1
PUBLIC memchoice2
memchoice2 = '0'
parm1 = '7'
DO WHILE memchoice2 <> '5'
7
5
Press any key to continue...
Use memchoice1 as a parameter in calling program
Declare parm1 as a parameter in called program
Parm1 is changed
Change is made to memchoice1

Figure 8.22 USING A PARAMETER

RELEASING VARIABLES

Once you no longer need a memory variable, you can recover the space in memory occupied by the variable by releasing it. You can release a single variable by typing RELEASE followed by the name of the variable. You can release all private memory variables by typing RELEASE ALL. You can release all public and private memory variables by typing CLEAR MEMORY.

It is important to understand the ways in which the public and private memory variables behave because you are likely to encounter them in advanced systems. In general, it is best not to declare variables PUBLIC unless it is absolutely necessary.

8.5 DATA INTEGRITY

Data integrity refers to the practice of controlling all access to the database through programming in order to ensure that the data is reliable and can be used with confidence. Of course, little can be done to prevent a well-meaning novice from tinkering with the data outside the system. However, the programmer can carefully prompt and monitor the user's activity. This helps provide a safe environment for appending, modifying, deleting, and displaying records efficiently within the system.

DBF files are fragile when they are open because any unexpected exit from dBASE IV, such as turning off the computer, will seriously damage the *header*, the portion of the file that contains the structure, the record count, and other information. Systems constantly pass control back and forth among individual programs. Since DBF files must be properly closed with the CLEAR ALL, CLOSE ALL/DATABASES, or QUIT command in order to ensure proper updating, you should always open the files that are required for the operation and be sure to close them at the end of the module. This is especially true for maintenance functions.

Whenever possible, include in each record a *key field* that contains some unique identifier such as a Social Security number, an account number, an employee number, or a part number. Names are usually a poor choice (Jim Smith?). Chapter 10 describes programming strategies for retrieving records quickly through the use of a *unique identifier*. Programs must insist on valid data in the key field before altering the file in any way. This is important when appending because of the danger of blank, duplicate, or invalid records. Table 8.1 lists points you should consider when writing modular programs.

TABLE 8.1 **Guidelines for data integrity**
1. Make certain that DBF files are opened and closed within the module.
2. Take extra precautions during maintenance operations such as appending, modifying, and deleting. Avoid duplicate or blank records.
3. Force the user to provide a vital piece of data as a unique identifier before performing any maintenance function.
4. Check data for reasonableness and proper form.
5. Ask users to verify their intentions with a Y or a Return key, or both.
6. Present users with verifying data to confirm their selection.

8.6 REEXAMINING STRUCTURED PROGRAMMING

When programming was introduced in Chapter 4, you were encouraged to apply structured principles to your work. Since many of the critical programming concepts have now been presented, it is appropriate to take a closer look at structured programming.

The inclusion of the three control structures DO WHILE/ENDDO, IF/ENDIF, and DO CASE/ENDCASE in dBASE IV relates to the ideas of Edsger W. Dijkstra. The concept that all programming can be accomplished by means of sequencing and nesting basic structures is central to structured programming. These fundamental control structures, or *Dijkstra structures* (if-then-else, while loop (iteration), and do case), must all be closed structures with a single entrance and exit. Further, the decision to enter or execute a structure should occur at the top. Programs in dBASE IV are forced to conform to structured principles through the restriction of branching to the limits of the control structures. The structures in Table 8.2 are sequenced in cascaded sections or nested, as Section 8.1 illustrated.

TABLE 8.2 Dijkstra structures in dBASE IV

DIJKSTRA STRUCTURES	dBASE IV
Basic Actions (printing, etc.)	? NAME
If-Then-Else	IF/ENDIF, DO CASE
Iteration	DO WHILE/ENDDO

As your programs become more complex, the need for documentation will increase. The points in Table 8.3 can help to make this process painless. Make them part of your programming style.

TABLE 8.3 Self-documentation tips

1. Spell out all dBASE IV commands fully in uppercase.
2. Enter memory variables in lowercase and precede them with mem or m.
3. Use enough comments to explain the purpose of all sections of code.
4. Place blank lines before and after sections of code.
5. Provide indentation for internal commands of DO WHILE/ENDDO, IF/ENDIF, and DO CASE/ENDCASE.
6. Repeat the condition as a comment following ENDDO and ENDIF.

A valuable piece of documentation can be generated with the STRUCTURE EXTENDED command. A database containing all the field names, types, and widths is produced with the COPY command by copying the structure (extended) to a database file. The structure contains the generic specifications, as shown in Figure 8.23. The LIST STRUCTURE command displays all the fields and their characteristics. If you use MODIFY STRUCTURE to add a description field, the data becomes more useful. A printed listing such as the one in Figure 8.24 becomes the *data dictionary,* or list of fields, in larger applications.

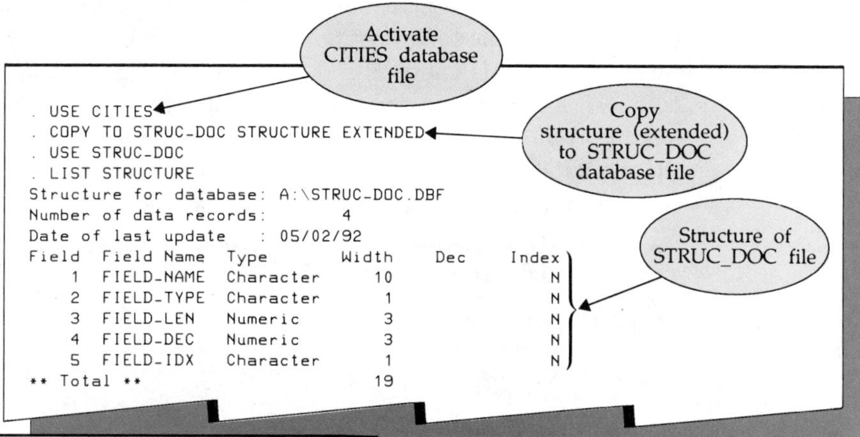

Figure 8.23 USING STRUCTURE EXTENDED

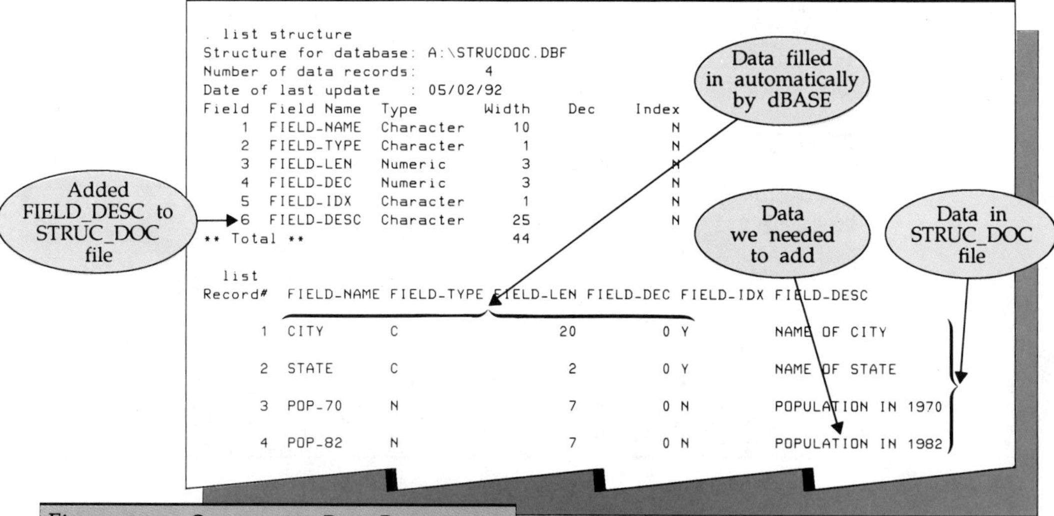

Figure 8.24 CREATING A DATA DICTIONARY

Chapters 4 through 8 have presented the basics of programming. You should now be capable of writing many useful programs and organizing them into systems. The remaining chapters of this text address ways in which you can make your programs more powerful and useful, and produce more attractive output.

CHAPTER SUMMARY

1. Nesting is placing one or more structures within one another. Structures can be nested in any pattern if they are logically correct. Bracketing can help show how nested DO WHILE loops will behave, since they can produce complex programs.
2. Arranging programs as modules in a system is a flexible and effective way of programming larger projects. Modules are called with the DO command from menu-driven main programs. The RETURN command reexecutes the calling program. Top-down design divides a project into manageable modules that can be called from submenus. Structure diagrams clarify the relationships in a system.
3. Memory variables are either PUBLIC (available to all programs) or PRIVATE (restricted to the source and all called programs). PARAMETER can be used to pass a variable to another program. Variables are usually PRIVATE, unless the situation requires a PUBLIC variable. Both types have specific behavior characteristics when used in systems.
4. Data integrity requires that programs that maintain data be carefully written in order to eliminate the possibility of blank, duplicate, or invalid fields. DBF files should be opened and closed within the module. All data should be verified.
5. In accordance with the principles of structured programming, dBASE IV nests and sequences control structures and basic actions. Self-documentation is another important concept of structured programming. STRUCTURE EXTENDED is useful in creating a data dictionary to document a DBF file.

KEY TERMS

top-down design
bracket
calling program
action diagrams
called program
modules
data integrity
subroutines
header
subprograms
key field
procedures
unique identifier
stub
nonfunctional test module
Dijkstra structures
procedure
structure diagram
iteration
functional decomposition
data dictionary

COMMAND SUMMARY

Command name	**Use**
PRIVATE ALL	Declare all memory variables private.
PUBLIC	Declare memory variables public.
RETURN	Pass program control to the next higher level.
PARAMETER	Specify variables to be passed.
DO WITH	Execute a program with passed variables.
STRUCTURE EXTENDED	Create a documentary DBF file.

dBUG dBASE

- SET STEP ON produces a pause after each command executes. You then have the option of executing the next command by pressing the space bar, S to suspend, or Esc to cancel. The Suspend option returns you to the dot prompt, where you can check the status of memory variables or record pointers. The program can be restarted at the next command with RESUME. By using SET STEP ON with SET ECHO ON, you can observe the execution of your program in precise detail. This is especially useful in diagnosing nesting problems.
- Declare all memory variables PUBLIC when you are debugging so that they will be available for inspection at any level, including the dot prompt. Of course, you must remember to reverse the action when debugging has been completed.

SELF-CHECK QUESTIONS

1. Would it be useful to include a direct branching statement such as GOTO in dBASE IV? Why?
2. What is nesting? Why is it useful?
3. What is a module? How are modules used?
4. Describe how DO and RETURN function with modules.
5. What is a stub?
6. What are some advantages of using modules?
7. Why is top-down design important?
8. What happens when a variable is declared PUBLIC?
9. How is a parameter used?
10. What is data integrity? Why is it important?
11. What is self-documentation?
12. What is a data dictionary? How can it be documented?

TRY IT YOURSELF

1. Using Figure 8.2 as an example, write the bare commands for the following structures.
   a. IF/ENDIF nested within a DO WHILE.
   b. DO WHILE containing a DO CASE.
   c. IF/ENDIF within a DO WHILE within another DO WHILE.
2. As in Exercise 1, write a structure for the following problem: Go through a student file. If the student is full-time, print five name labels.
3. Draw a structure diagram for a system with a main menu and two submenus. One submenu calls modules to append, modify and delete records; the other has functions for displaying a single record and printing a summary report.
4. Construct a STRUCTURE EXTENDED data dictionary as in Figure 8.24 for any DBF file on your disk.
5. Predict the outcome of this program and then test it.

```
x = 1
DO WHILE x <= 5
y = 1
DO WHILE y <= 3
   y = y + 1
   ? x, '  ', y
ENDDO WHILE y <= 3
x = x + 1
ENDDO WHILE x <= 5
```

6. Add a feature to CMENU that accepts a company name in the main menu and displays this company name at the top of each of the submenus.

PROGRAMMING PROJECTS

Construct a menu-driven system with the following options. Use stubs and test movement through the submenus.

```
MAIN MENU

1.  Maintenance
2.  Query
3.  Exit


MAINTENANCE MENU           QUERY MENU

1.  Add a record           1. Search by PO#
2.  Edit a record          2. Search by Dept.
3.  Delete a record        3. Search by Part
4.  Return to Main Menu    4. Return to Main Menu
```

LEARNING OBJECTIVES

To compare and use SORT and INDEX.

To apply INDEX in a variety of situations.

To understand the special uses for INDEX.

To use FIND and SEEK.

To become familiar with the functions used with INDEX.

9

INDEXING

INTRODUCTION

When you request a piece of information from a computer system, you expect an instantaneous response. When a report is prepared from the contents of a database, you expect the data to be in a useful order. In one report, you expect names should be in alphabetical order; in another, you expect account balances to be in descending order. Unfortunately, data that is stored in a database is very rarely arranged in any specific order. It is also difficult to locate individual items. The commands and techniques presented in this chapter will help you to solve these problems.

9.1 SORT AS AN ORDERING TOOL

dBASE IV provides two methods for ordering data: INDEXing and SORTing. INDEXing is usually superior to SORTing, as you will see.

The SORT command produces a copy of the original database file reordered on a selected field, called the *key field*. This method is initially satisfactory, but maintaining it is awkward for the following reasons:

1. You must re-SORT after any APPEND or EDIT that affects the order of records.
2. Only one order can be used for each SORT. (The file cannot be ordered by name and also ordered by balance at the same time.)
3. The powerful SEEK and FIND commands, for rapidly locating individual records, are not available when you use SORT.

Other more subtle reasons for choosing INDEX will become apparent as you gain the skills necessary to use it effectively.

If a database file is static (that is, the data rarely changes), SORT may be a more convenient ordering tool. In addition, new dBASE IV users may find that SORT is simpler to use.

Let's examine the manner in which we use SORT. We will use the PART database file, whose structure is shown in Figure 9.1. The records currently in the file are shown in Figure 9.2. Notice that they are currently sorted (ordered) by PARTNUMB. We will sort the records on PARTDESC. The sort process will create a new database file which we will call S_PART.

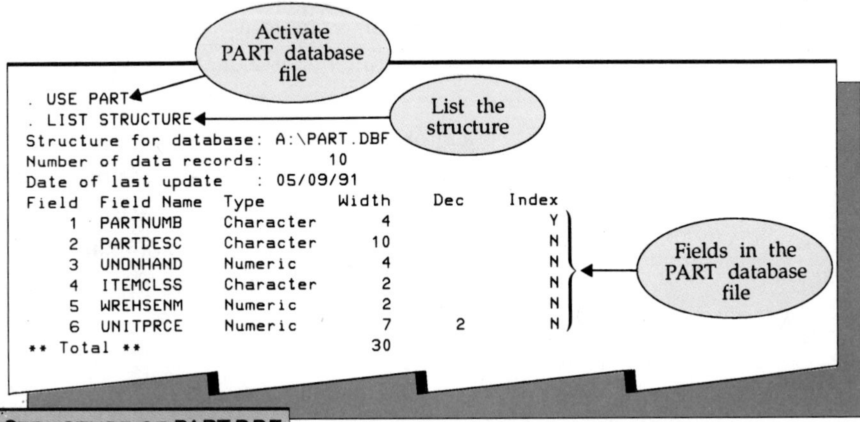

Figure 9.1 STRUCTURE OF PART.DBF

```
 LIST
Record#  PARTNUMB PARTDESC    UNONHAND ITEMCLSS WREHSENM UNITPRCE
      1  AX12     IRON             104 HW              3    17.95
      2  AZ52     SKATES            20 SG              2    24.95
      3  BA74     BASEBALL          40 SG              1     4.95
      4  BH22     TOASTER           95 HW              3    34.95
      5  BT04     STOVE             11 AP              2   402.99
      6  BZ66     WASHER            52 AP              3   311.95
      7  CA14     SKILLET            2 HW              3    19.95
      8  CB03     BIKE              44 SG              1   187.50
      9  CX11     MIXER            112 HW              3    57.95
     10  CZ81     WEIGHTS          208 SG              2   108.99
```

Records in the PART database file

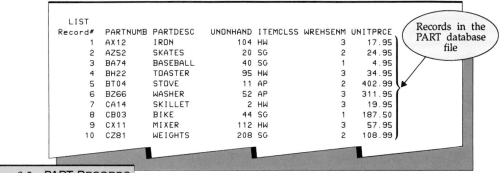

Figure 9.2 PART RECORDS

To perform this sort we use the first command in Figure 9.3. After the word ON we indicate the sort key (key field). After the word TO we indicate the name of the new file. Once the sort is complete, we need to activate the new file. As you can see in the figure, the records in this new file are indeed sorted by PARTDESC.

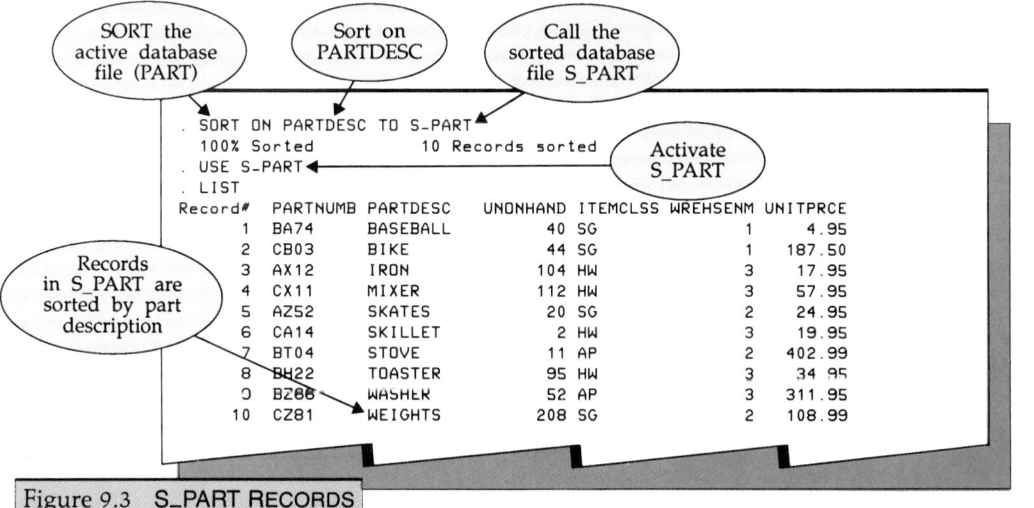

Figure 9.3 S_PART RECORDS

What would happen if we added a part to S_PART whose description was FOOTBALL? The file would then be out of order again. If we still wanted the records to be sorted by PARTDESC, we would have to re-sort. This fact alone limits the value of sorting for ordering data.

9.2 HOW TO USE AN INDEX

WHAT IS AN INDEX?

You are already familiar with the concept of an index. The index in the back of a book contains important words or phrases together with a list of pages on which the given words or phrases can be found. An *index* for a database file is similar. Figure 9.4, for example, shows the PART database file along with an index built on PARTDESC. The expression on which the index is built, in this case PARTDESC, is called the *index key*. When we use this index, the items of interest are part descriptions rather than key words or phrases.

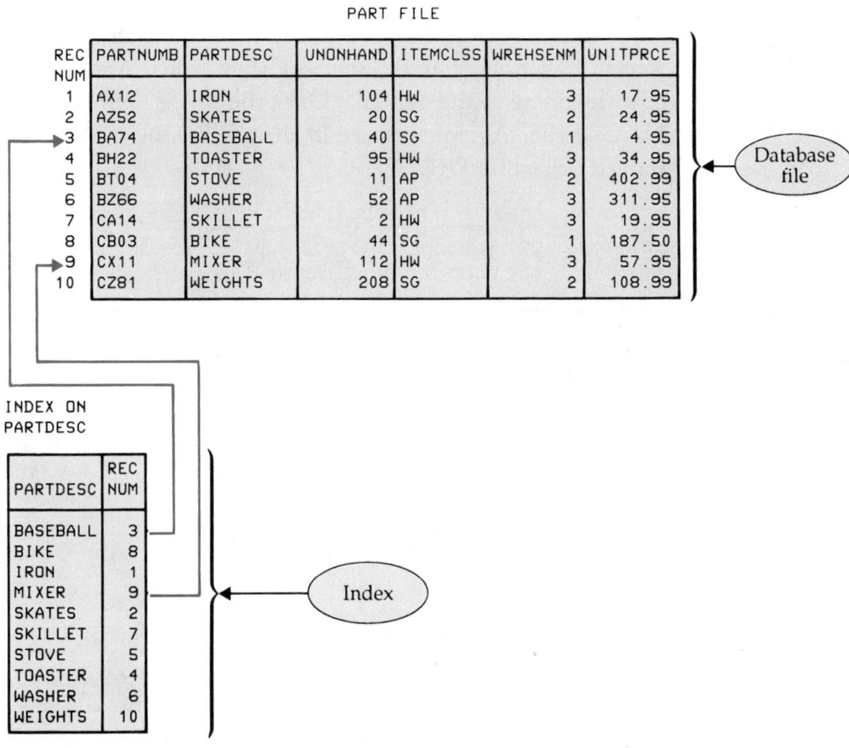

REC NUM	PARTNUMB	PARTDESC	UNONHAND	ITEMCLSS	WREHSENM	UNITPRCE
1	AX12	IRON	104	HW	3	17.95
2	AZ52	SKATES	20	SG	2	24.95
3	BA74	BASEBALL	40	SG	1	4.95
4	BH22	TOASTER	95	HW	3	34.95
5	BT04	STOVE	11	AP	2	402.99
6	BZ66	WASHER	52	AP	3	311.95
7	CA14	SKILLET	2	HW	3	19.95
8	CB03	BIKE	44	SG	1	187.50
9	CX11	MIXER	112	HW	3	57.95
10	CZ81	WEIGHTS	208	SG	2	108.99

PARTDESC	REC NUM
BASEBALL	3
BIKE	8
IRON	1
MIXER	9
SKATES	2
SKILLET	7
STOVE	5
TOASTER	4
WASHER	6
WEIGHTS	10

Figure 9.4 USE OF AN INDEX

Each part description occurs in the index along with the number of the record in which the part description is found. If you were to use this index to find MIXER, for example, you would find MIXER in the index, look at the corresponding record number (9), and then go immediately to record 9 in the PART file, thus finding this part much more rapidly than if you had to look at each part one at a time. This is precisely what dBASE does when using an index. Thus, indexes make the process of retrieving a record much more efficient.

Another benefit of indexes is that they provide an extremely efficient alternative to sorting. Look at the record numbers in the index in Figure 9.4 and suppose dBASE uses the index to list all parts. That is, dBASE simply follows down the record number column, listing the corresponding parts as it goes. In this example, dBASE would first list the part in record 3 (BASEBALL), then the part in record 8 (BIKE), then the part in record 1 (IRON), and so on. dBASE lists the parts ordered by part description *without sorting the file*.

CREATING AN INDEX

In dBASE IV, INDEXing is accomplished by creating an MDX file that is separate from, but related to, the DBF file. This file is called the *production index file*. For each index we create, the production index file contains the selected key field or fields from each record and the related record numbers. The file can hold up to 47 indexes. You are unable to LIST or examine the MDX file because it is designed specifically for use by the dBASE IV program.

There are two ways to create an index. When you are at the Database Design screen, you can simply place a Y in the Index column for any field for which you want an index created. You can also create indexes from the dot prompt by using the INDEX ON command. The INDEX ON command is followed by the field name(s) (which becomes the key), the word TO, and the name (dBASE calls it a *tag*) that you will assign to the index. The following command creates an index on the PARTDESC field and calls the index PARTDESC:

```
INDEX ON PARTDESC TAG PARTDESC
```

There is no redundancy in this example because the first PARTDESC is the name of the key field from the database file and the second PARTDESC becomes the name of the index. (**Note:** When indexes are created for individual fields, it's a good idea to give the index the same name as the field.)

Once we have created an index, dBASE will automatically maintain it. That is, when we make any changes to the database file that affect the index, dBASE will automatically update the index appropriately.

USING AN INDEX

Figure 9.5 illustrates the commands to create and use an index on the PARTDESC field. The INDEX ON command creates the index. The SET ORDER TO command instructs dBASE to use this index to order records. When we list the records, they are then ordered by the field on which the index was created, in this case PARTDESC. If you look at the record numbers in the figure, you will see that this is *not* the order in which these records actually occur in the file.

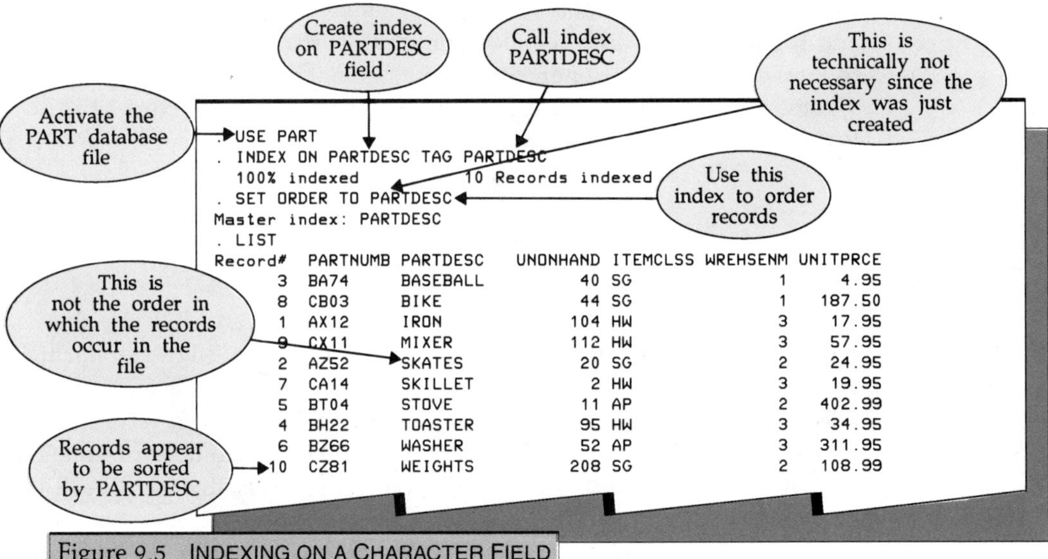

Figure 9.5 INDEXING ON A CHARACTER FIELD

(**Note:** If you have just created an index, the SET ORDER TO command is technically not necessary. Any time you want to use it in the future, however, you will need to use the SET ORDER TO command. For this reason, you should accustom yourself to activating it all the time, even when you first create the index.)

Although indexing is fast, the following three factors (other than hardware considerations) have an impact on indexing speed:

1. The number of indexes created for a database file.
2. The number of records in the database file.
3. The length of the key field.

You should create index files only if they are actually going to be used, because they do occupy disk space and also can slow down processing.

9.3 SPECIAL USES FOR INDEXES

INDEXING ON A NUMERIC FIELD

Character-, numeric-, or date-type fields can be key fields for index files. In Figure 9.6, the numeric field UNITPRCE is used to create an index that shows parts in order of unit price from lowest to highest.

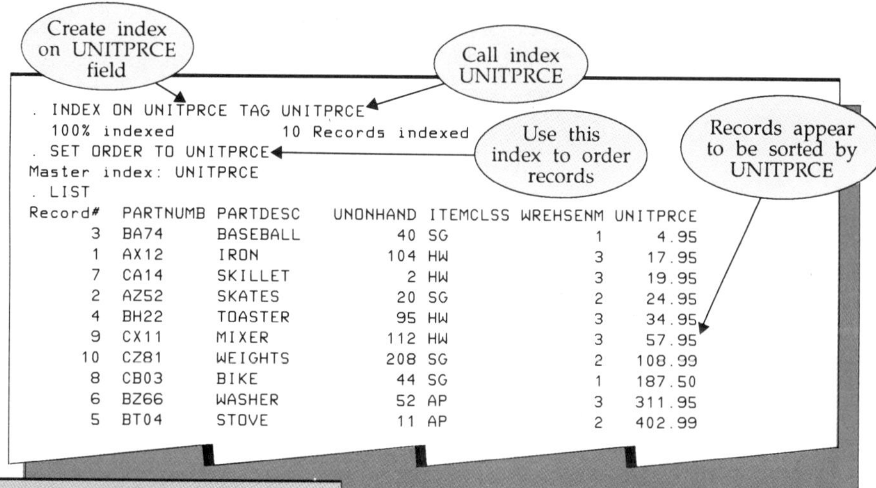

```
. INDEX ON UNITPRCE TAG UNITPRCE
  100% indexed          10 Records indexed
. SET ORDER TO UNITPRCE
Master index: UNITPRCE
. LIST
Record#  PARTNUMB PARTDESC    UNONHAND ITEMCLSS WREHSENM UNITPRCE
      3  BA74     BASEBALL          40 SG              1     4.95
      1  AX12     IRON             104 HW              3    17.95
      7  CA14     SKILLET            2 HW              3    19.95
      2  AZ52     SKATES            20 SG              2    24.95
      4  BH22     TOASTER           95 HW              3    34.95
      9  CX11     MIXER            112 HW              3    57.95
     10  CZ81     WEIGHTS          208 SG              2   108.99
      8  CB03     BIKE              44 SG              1   187.50
      6  BZ66     WASHER            52 AP              3   311.95
      5  BT04     STOVE             11 AP              2   402.99
```


Figure 9.6 INDEXING ON A NUMERIC FIELD

DESCENDING INDEXES

You can create an index that will order the records in descending order by simply including the word DESCENDING at the end of the INDEX statement. Figure 9.7 on the next page illustrates using this technique with the numeric field UNITPRCE. Here we have used D_UNITPRCE (for *D*escending *UNITPRCE*) as the tag for the index.

The technique applies equally well to character fields. Figure 9.8, also on the next page, illustrates its use in ordering the records by part description in descending order.

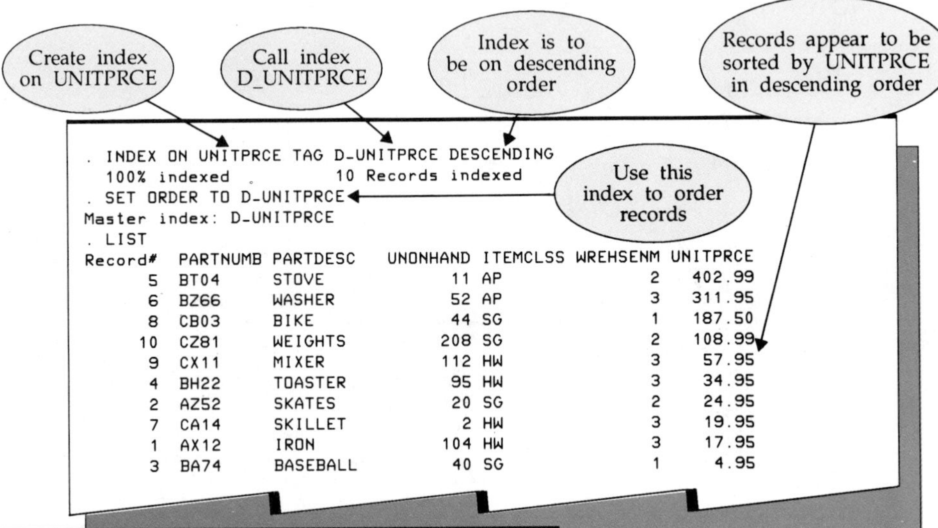


```
. INDEX ON UNITPRCE TAG D-UNITPRCE DESCENDING
  100% indexed          10 Records indexed
. SET ORDER TO D-UNITPRCE
Master index: D-UNITPRCE
. LIST
Record#  PARTNUMB PARTDESC      UNONHAND ITEMCLSS WREHSENM UNITPRCE
      5  BT04     STOVE               11 AP              2   402.99
      6  BZ66     WASHER              52 AP              3   311.95
      8  CB03     BIKE                44 SG              1   187.50
     10  CZ81     WEIGHTS            208 SG              2   108.99
      9  CX11     MIXER              112 HW              3    57.95
      4  BH22     TOASTER             95 HW              3    34.95
      2  AZ52     SKATES              20 SG              2    24.95
      7  CA14     SKILLET              2 HW              3    19.95
      1  AX12     IRON               104 HW              3    17.95
      3  BA74     BASEBALL            40 SG              1     4.95
```

Figure 9.7 INDEXING IN DESCENDING NUMERICAL ORDER

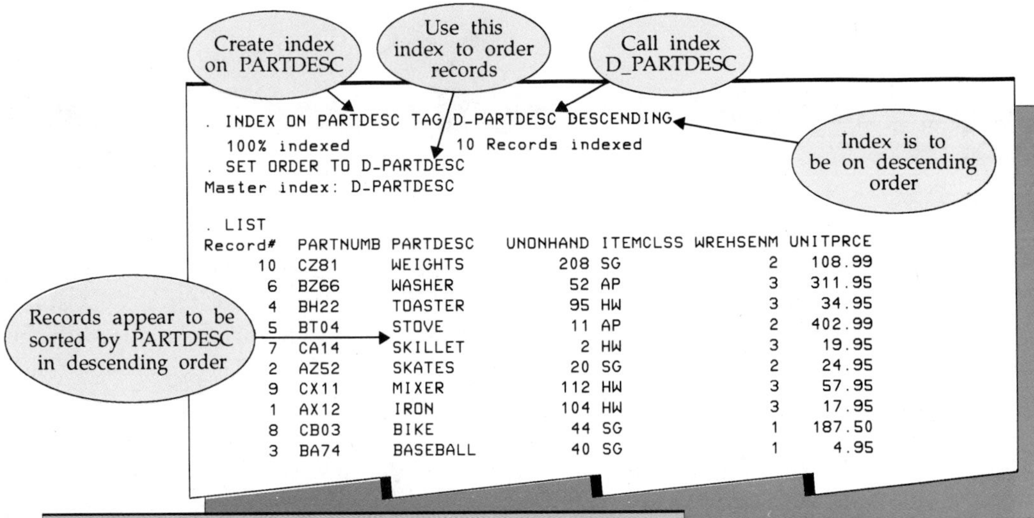


```
. INDEX ON PARTDESC TAG D-PARTDESC DESCENDING
  100% indexed          10 Records indexed
. SET ORDER TO D-PARTDESC
Master index: D-PARTDESC

. LIST
Record#  PARTNUMB PARTDESC      UNONHAND ITEMCLSS WREHSENM UNITPRCE
     10  CZ81     WEIGHTS            208 SG              2   108.99
      6  BZ66     WASHER              52 AP              3   311.95
      4  BH22     TOASTER             95 HW              3    34.95
      5  BT04     STOVE               11 AP              2   402.99
      7  CA14     SKILLET              2 HW              3    19.95
      2  AZ52     SKATES              20 SG              2    24.95
      9  CX11     MIXER              112 HW              3    57.95
      1  AX12     IRON               104 HW              3    17.95
      8  CB03     BIKE                44 SG              1   187.50
      3  BA74     BASEBALL            40 SG              1     4.95
```

Figure 9.8 INDEXING IN DESCENDING CHARACTER ORDER

INDEXING ON A COMBINATION OF FIELDS

Sometimes it is helpful to display records indexed on two keys instead of one. For example, you may wish to see parts in the database displayed in order of item class. You may also wish parts within each item class to be listed in order of part description.

This can be done through *concatenation,* which is the process of combining two character fields so that they will appear or operate as one. The field appearing first after INDEX ON is called the *major key,* and the next field, the field after the plus sign, is the *minor key*. In the example in Figure 9.9, ITEMCLSS is the major key and PARTDESC is the minor key. We have assigned this index the tag IC_PD, for ItemClss + PartDesc. (**Note:** When indexes are created on a combination of fields, it's a good idea to give the index a name that indicates the combination.)

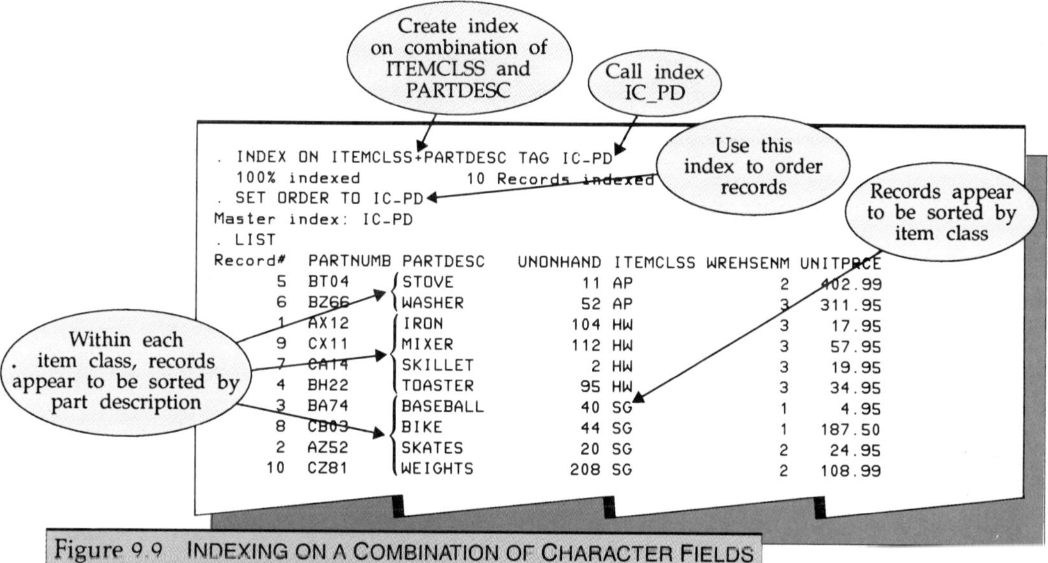

Figure 9.9 INDEXING ON A COMBINATION OF CHARACTER FIELDS

This technique can be used with character fields and numeric fields if you first convert the numeric field to a character string by means of the STR() function, as shown in Figure 9.10 on the next page. STR(UNITPRCE,7,2) indicates that UNITPRCE is to be converted to a string seven positions in length with the last two of those positions representing decimal places. Since STR() produces a character string there is no problem combining it with a character field. In this example, ITEMCLSS is the major key and UNITPRCE is the minor key.

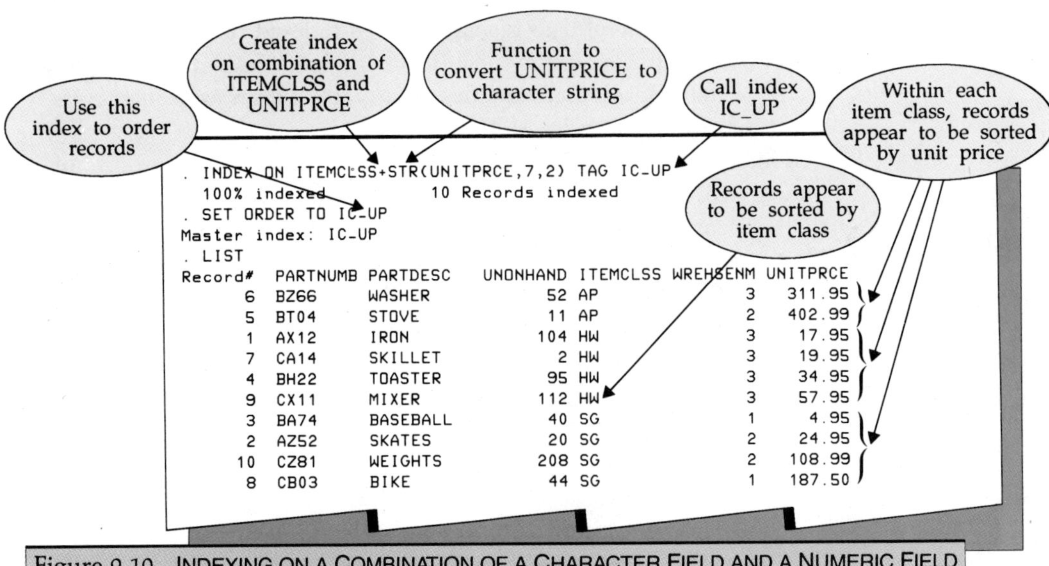

Figure 9.10 INDEXING ON A COMBINATION OF A CHARACTER FIELD AND A NUMERIC FIELD

(**Note:** Be careful when attempting to concatenate two numeric fields, because dBASE IV understands the plus sign (+) to mean addition, not concatenation, and you will end up with an index on the sum of the two numeric fields. The solution is to convert both numeric fields to character strings with the STR() function while concatenating.)

INDEXING ON A COMPUTATION

We can also index on a computation. For example, we might be interested in on-hand value, which is the product of units-on-hand (UNONHAND) and unit price (UNITPRCE). (Technically, on-hand value is the product of units-on-hand and unit *cost*, but we don't have a cost field in this database file.) In Figure 9.11, we are creating an index on this product and calling it ONHNDVAL. When we use it to order the records, they appear in order of on-hand value.

9.4 REMOVING UNWANTED INDEXES

Indexes occupy space on the disk. They also can slow down processing. Thus, if we decide we no longer need an index that we have created, we should remove it. The command to do so is DELETE TAG, as illustrated in Figure 9.12. In this figure we are removing the index called ONHNDVAL.

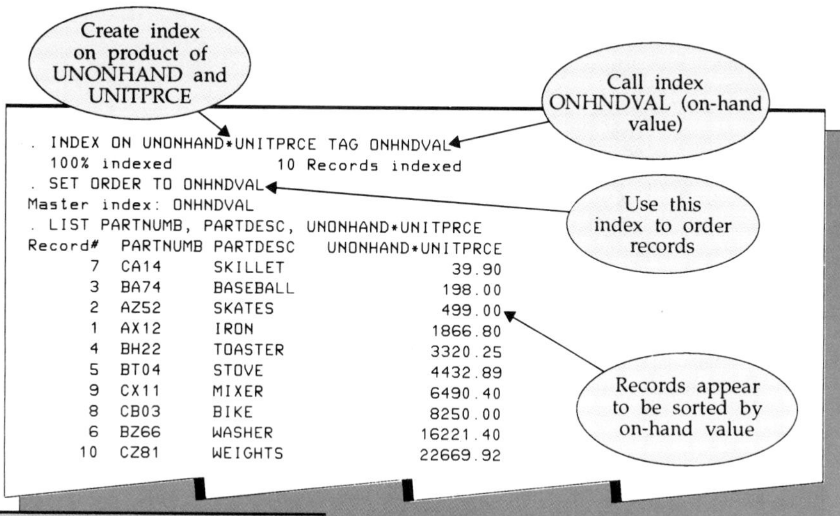

Figure 9.11 INDEXING ON A COMPUTATION

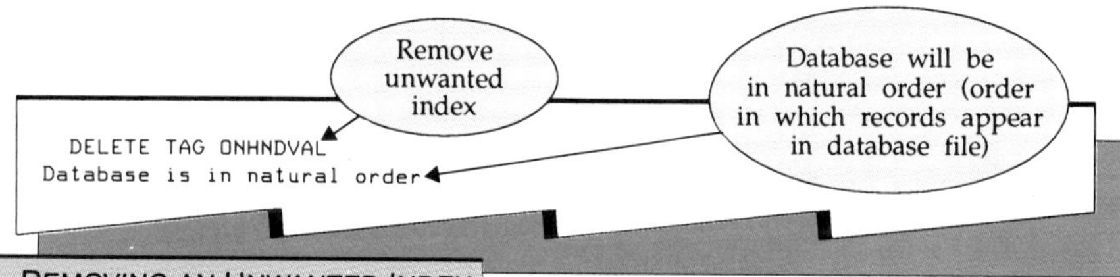

Figure 9.12 REMOVING AN UNWANTED INDEX

You might wonder what to do if you have forgotten the tag you gave to a particular index. Perhaps you remember the tag but aren't sure exactly what expression you used for the index. This could be a problem when you are deciding which indexes you might remove.

If you use DISPLAY STATUS or LIST STATUS, dBASE will indicate the tag for each index as well as the expression on which the index was created. Another approach is to type

```
MODIFY STRUCTURE
```

to move to the Database Design screen (the same screen you used when you created the database file). Select the "Remove unwanted index tag" option of the Organize menu (Figure 9.13 on the next page). You will then see a list of tags. The expression for the index will be displayed when you move the highlight to its tag. Once you have an index you want to remove highlighted, press Enter.

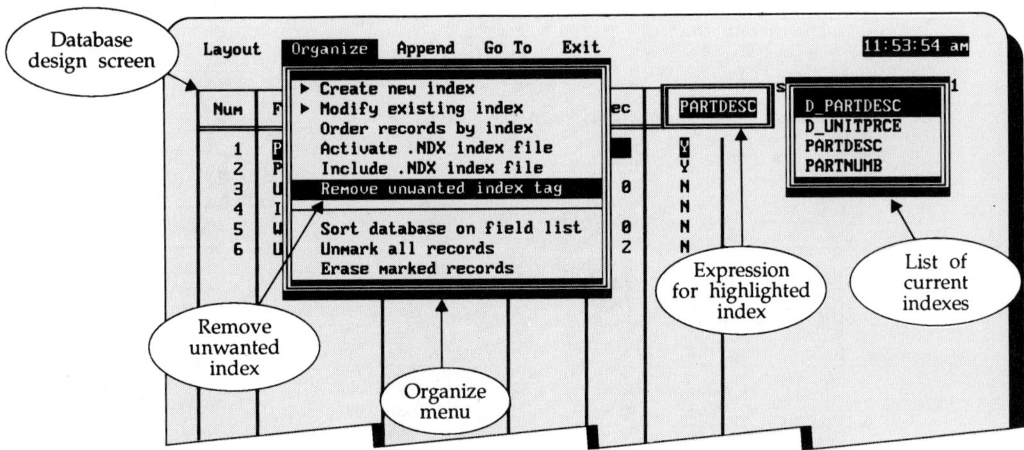

Figure 9.13 USING MODIFY STRUCTURE TO REMOVE AN UNWANTED INDEX

If you have created all the indexes shown in the figure, use this technique to remove D_PARTDESC and D_UNITPRCE. Don't remove PARTDESC or PARTNUMB.

9.5 FIND AND SEEK

The FIND and the SEEK commands are critical to the programmer. They allow rapid access to specific records in the database file on the basis of values for the key field. Users type in some information (such as a name or an account number) in order to retrieve additional relevant information. This is what most people envision when they think of a database, or, for that matter, a computer.

The FIND and SEEK commands both use indexes to achieve this goal. The principal advantage of the FIND and SEEK commands is that they provide the fastest access to specific records available to the programmer. They work by taking a piece of information, such as a name, and through the use of a rapid-search algorithm, matching the piece of data with an identical or nearly identical field in the index. Remember, the index contains the key field and the associated record number in the database file. If dBASE finds a match, the record pointer is positioned at the proper record number in the database file. It is then up to the programmer to present the other data contained in the record to the user or to perform some other function with the record. When we use this technique, we will need to address the following possible situations.

1. The matching field may not be found.
2. Other fields in the index may also match the criteria provided.

These possibilities are addressed in Chapter 11.

USING FIND

The FIND command works only with string (character) data. Figure 9.14 illustrates its use. The first command in the figure activates the index on PARTDESC. Notice that it is exactly the same command we used when we were using indexes to order records. The second command locates the record in which the description is STOVE. The single quotation marks around STOVE are essential.

Figure 9.15 illustrates the use of the FIND command with a memory variable. Notice the ampersand (&) in front of MEMDESC. The & is called the *macro expansion function*. It indicates that MEMDESC is to be replaced by its contents in the command. That is, the command

```
FIND &MEMDESC
```

is, in effect, the same as

```
FIND 'STOVE'
```

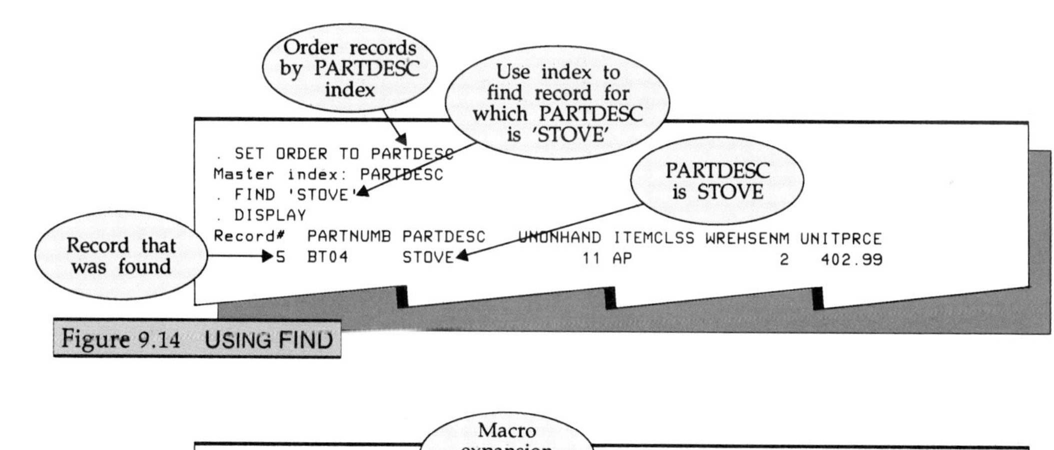

Figure 9.14 USING FIND

Macro expansion function

FIND command produces same results as in the previous example

```
. MEMDESC = 'STOVE'
STOVE
. FIND &MEMDESC
. DISPLAY
Record#  PARTNUMB PARTDESC   UNONHAND ITEMCLSS WREHSENM UNITPRCE
      5  BT04     STOVE            11 AP              2   402.99
```

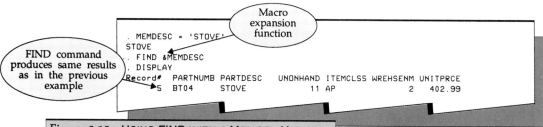

Figure 9.15 USING FIND WITH A MEMORY VARIABLE

As you can see we get the same results as before. If we forget the &, dBASE searches for MEMDESC as a value in the index. In other words, it searches for a part whose description is MEMDESC. Naturally, dBASE fails to find such a record, so it displays a "Find not successful" error message, as shown in Figure 9.16.

Figure 9.16 USING FIND INCORRECTLY

USING SEEK

The SEEK command is more useful than FIND because you can use numeric expressions. You can also use character data as shown in Figure 9.17. In addition, the macro expansion function (&) is not required when we use SEEK with memory variables (see Figure 9.18). The SEEK command automatically uses the *contents* of the memory variable.

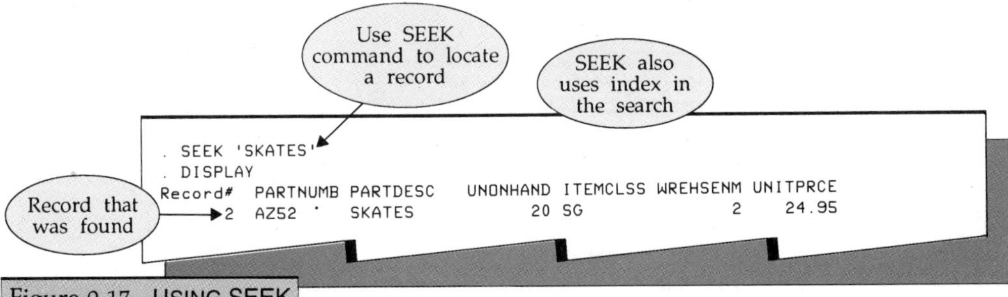

Figure 9.17 USING SEEK

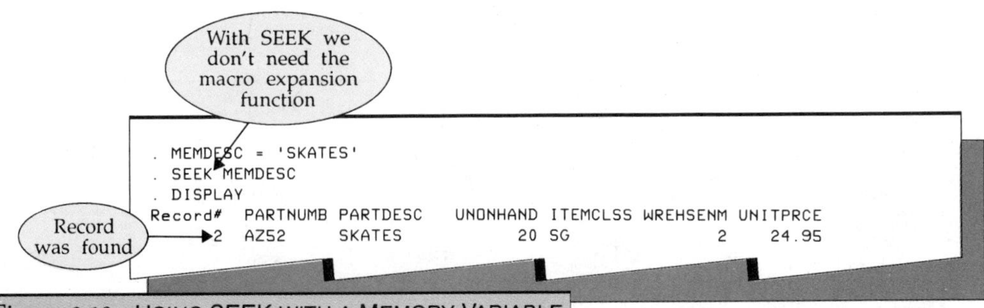

Figure 9.18 USING SEEK WITH A MEMORY VARIABLE

9.6 USING INDEXES IN PROGRAMS

USING FOUND()

We are going to write a program that uses an index to find records. Before we do, we need to look at a special dBASE function, FOUND(). We use this function to determine whether a FIND or SEEK command is successful. We will also look at a way to make sure our indexes are current.

The FOUND() function is illustrated in Figure 9.19. In this figure, we first activated the PART file and then used a SET ORDER TO command to order the records by PARTNUMB. At this point, FOUND() is false, since we have not yet attempted to find any records. We next used a SEEK command to try to locate part XZ34. FOUND() is still false since there is no such part. Finally, we used a SEEK command to try to locate part BT04. Since there is such a part, FOUND() is true. In addition, we will be positioned on the record for part BT04.

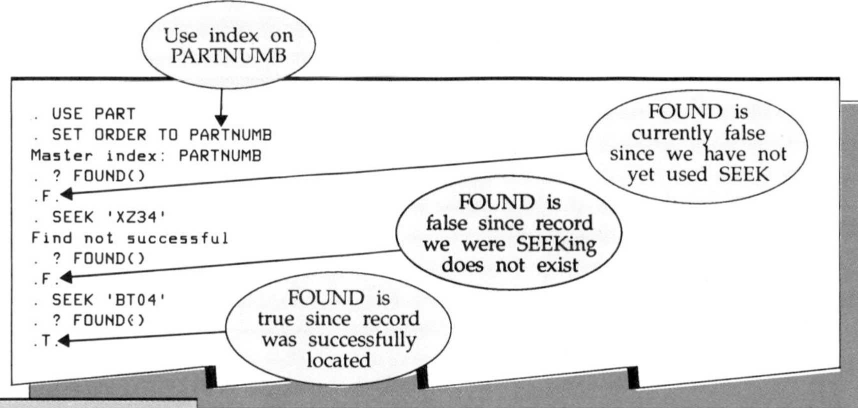

Figure 9.19 USING FOUND()

USING REINDEX

Should you have a power failure or other problem while a database file is being updated, it is possible that the indexes for the file may be *corrupted*. This means that they may no longer match the actual data in the database file. This usually manifests itself in errors during operations that use the corrupt indexes. Fortunately, it is easy to correct this problem. Make sure the database file is active and then type REINDEX as shown in Figure 9.20 on the next page. All indexes currently associated with this file will be rebuilt. As you see in the figure, dBASE will display messages to confirm that this is happening.

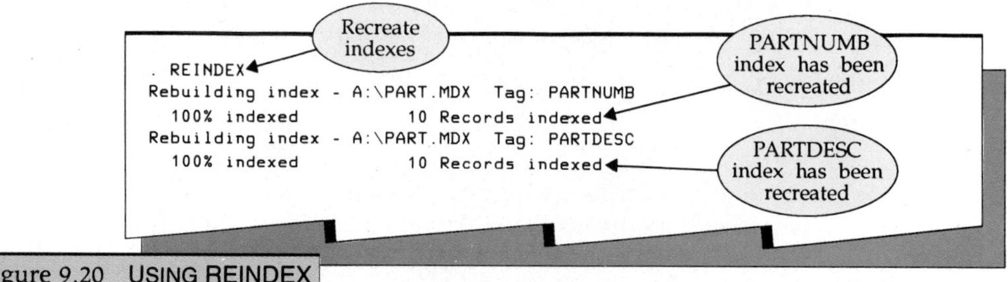

Figure 9.20 USING REINDEX

A PROGRAM TO FIND RECORDS

Now let's turn to a program to find records. The program we will examine is called SHW_PART and is on your data disk. When you run it you first see the screen shown in Figure 9.21. You can now select whether you wish to find a part by using its number or its description.

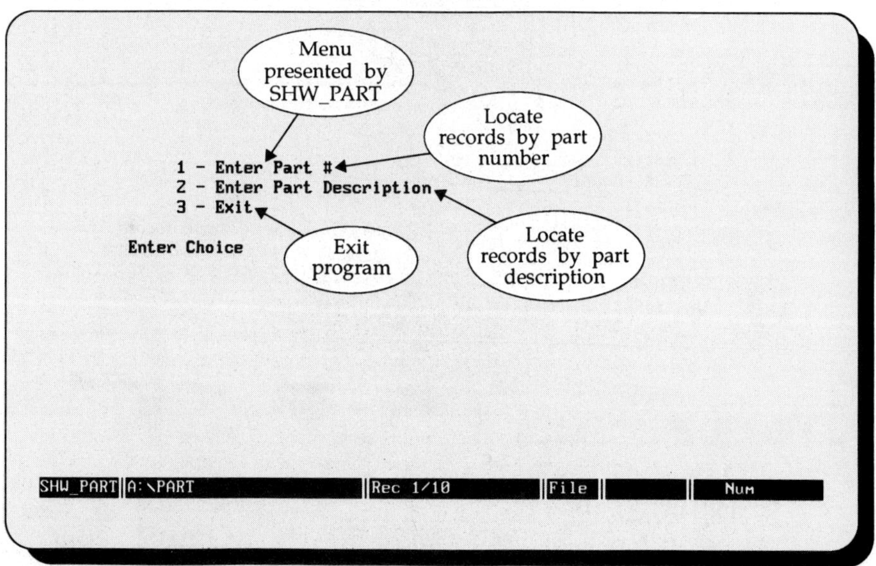

Figure 9.21 PROGRAM SHW_PART (MENU SCREEN)

If you select option 1 (Part #), you will see the screen shown in Figure 9.22. Here you enter the number of the part you want to find. If you enter BT04, for example, you will then see all the details concerning part BT04 (Figure 9.23). If you enter an invalid part number, you will simply be returned to the menu.

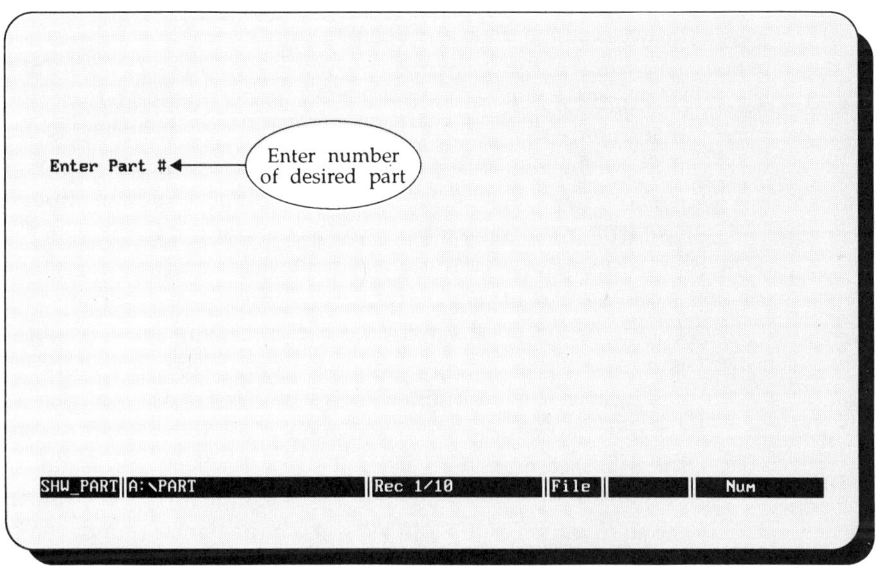

Figure 9.22 PROGRAM SHW_PART (PART NUMBER SELECTION SCREEN)

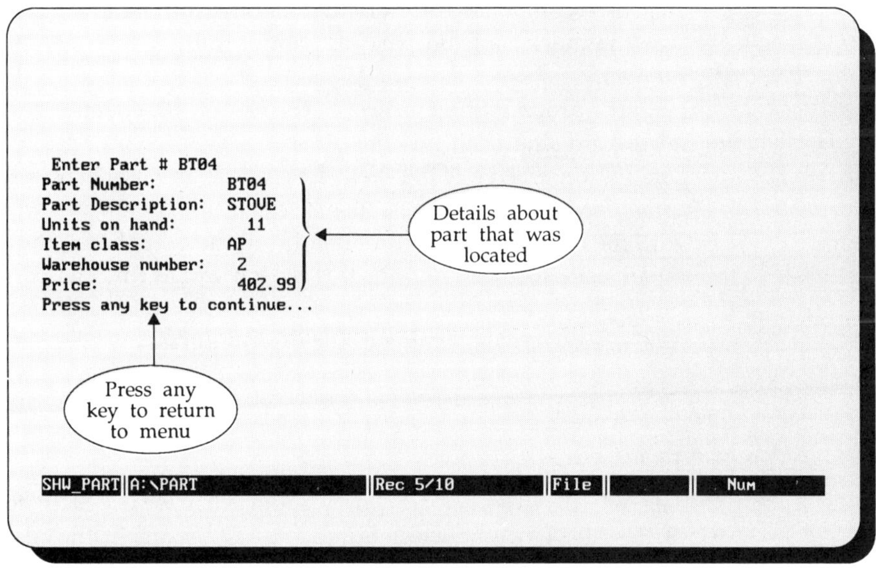

Figure 9.23 SHW_PART PROGRAM (RESULT OF PART SELECTION)

Option 2 (Part Description) works in much the same fashion. The only difference is that you will enter a part description rather than a number. As you will see if you try this program, you can enter a partial part number or description. You could find STOVE, for example, by selecting option 2 and then typing ST.

Now that we have seen the program at work, let's look at it in detail. It is shown in Figure 9.24. The general loop structure should be familiar to you from previous examples. Let's look at the CASE statement.

If memchoice is 1, we begin by getting a part number from the user. Since the part number is a character field, we cannot use the INPUT command. Since it has a length more than 1 character, we cannot use the WAIT command. The command that is appropriate here is ACCEPT.

Once we have obtained a part number from the user, we use the SET ORDER TO command to activate the index on PARTNUMB. We then use the SEEK command to attempt to find a part whose number matches the one entered by the user. If the part is not found, we use the LOOP command to return to the DO WHILE. If the part is found, the commands after the ENDCASE will display all details concerning the part.

If you examine the commands for the case memchoice = '2', you will see that they are almost identical. There are two differences. We are dealing with part descriptions rather than part numbers, so the message in the ACCEPT command is different. The other difference is that we must activate the index built on part description rather than the one built on part number.

In the programming project at the end of this chapter, you will construct a program similar to this one. It will have an extra option in it, however. The option will be "Find Next Record." If the user had just found a part using the part number and then selected this option, we would find a part with the next higher part number. If, on the other hand, the user had found a part using the description, this option would find the part with the next higher description.

The appropriate command for this option is

```
SKIP
```

USING EOF()

The only thing we need to worry about when we use SKIP concerns the end of the file. If we had just found the last record in the file, executing the SKIP command would not produce another record. Instead the special end-of-file function, EOF(), would be set to true. We would test for this the same way we would test for the existence of a record after a SEEK command. The only difference is we would have `IF EOF()` rather than `IF FOUND()` in the IF statement.

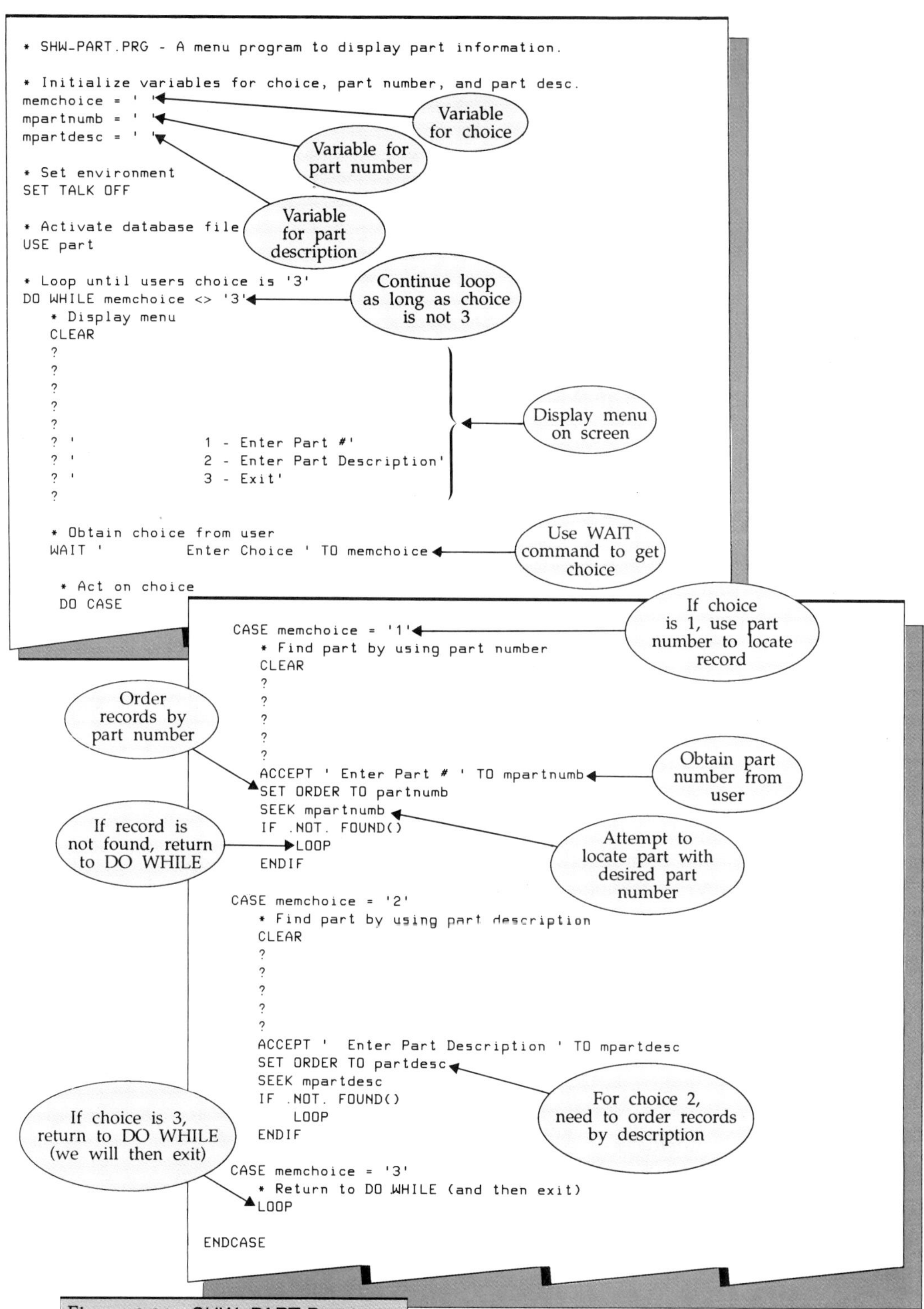
Variable for choice
Variable for part number
Variable for part description
Continue loop as long as choice is not 3
Display menu on screen
Use WAIT command to get choice
If choice is 1, use part number to locate record
Order records by part number
Obtain part number from user
If record is not found, return to DO WHILE
Attempt to locate part with desired part number
For choice 2, need to order records by description
If choice is 3, return to DO WHILE (we will then exit)

```
* SHW_PART.PRG - A menu program to display part information.

* Initialize variables for choice, part number, and part desc.
memchoice = ' '
mpartnumb = ' '
mpartdesc = ' '

* Set environment
SET TALK OFF

* Activate database file
USE part

* Loop until users choice is '3'
DO WHILE memchoice <> '3'
   * Display menu
   CLEAR
   ?
   ?
   ?
   ?
   ?
   ? '              1 - Enter Part #'
   ? '              2 - Enter Part Description'
   ? '              3 - Exit'
   ?

   * Obtain choice from user
   WAIT '         Enter Choice ' TO memchoice

    * Act on choice
    DO CASE
      CASE memchoice = '1'
         * Find part by using part number
         CLEAR
         ?
         ?
         ?
         ?
         ?
         ACCEPT ' Enter Part # ' TO mpartnumb
         SET ORDER TO partnumb
         SEEK mpartnumb
         IF .NOT. FOUND()
            LOOP
         ENDIF
      CASE memchoice = '2'
         * Find part by using part description
         CLEAR
         ?
         ?
         ?
         ?
         ?
         ACCEPT '  Enter Part Description ' TO mpartdesc
         SET ORDER TO partdesc
         SEEK mpartdesc
         IF .NOT. FOUND()
            LOOP
         ENDIF
      CASE memchoice = '3'
         * Return to DO WHILE (and then exit)
         LOOP

    ENDCASE
```

Figure 9.24 SHW_PART PROGRAM

(continued)

```
    * Print part info
    ? "Part Number:         ", partnumb
    ? "Part Description:    ", partdesc
    ? "Units on hand:       ", unonhand
    ? "Item class:          ", itemclss
    ? "Warehouse number:    ", wrehsenm
    ? "Price:               ", unitprce
    WAIT

ENDDO memchoice <> '3'

* Close databases, clear screen, and restore environment.
CLEAR ALL
CLEAR
SET TALK ON
RETURN
```

Display information for part that was found

Figure 9.24 SHW_PART PROGRAM

CHAPTER SUMMARY

1. SORT produces a copy of the DBF file sorted on a specified field or combination of fields, but is of limited use since it requires too much maintenance and provides slow access to records.
2. INDEX creates an index that allows data to be viewed in a variety of orders. It is easy to maintain and allows rapid access to records through the FIND and SEEK commands. Once created, indexes are maintained automatically by dBASE.
3. Records can be displayed in many ways by establishing indexes creatively. By using combinations of fields, functions, and arithmetic operations, relationships among the records can be examined.
4. FIND positions the record pointer on a record that matches the expression after the command. Criteria that are stored in memory variables must use the macro expansion function (&). SEEK operates with numeric fields and does not require the ampersand.
5. Other functions and commands, such as SET ORDER TO, FOUND(), REINDEX, and EOF(), are useful in working with index files.

KEY TERMS

key field
production index file
index key
tag
major key
minor key
concatenation
corrupted

COMMAND SUMMARY

Command Name	Use
SORT	Sort records on a key field and write to a new file.
INDEX	Create an index.
SET ORDER TO	Activate index.
STR()	Convert a numeric value to a character string.
FIND	Point to a record using an indexed search on a character field.
SEEK	Point to a record using an indexed search on either a numeric or a character field.
&	The macro expansion function.
FOUND()	Indicates success or failure of an indexed search.
EOF()	Indicates whether the end of the file has been reached.
REINDEX	Rebuild all indexes.

dBUG dBASE

- The status of indexes is a constant concern in programs. Records may appear to be missing, or a "Record out of range" error may occur as the result of an index that is not synchronized with the database file. The solution to this problem is to regenerate the index.
- Avoid using dBASE IV commands as memory variable names. For example, if you use COUNT = 9 in a program, dBASE IV assumes a COUNT command and issues an error message.

SELF-CHECK QUESTIONS

1. Name three disadvantages of using SORT as opposed to INDEX.
2. What happens when you issue an INDEX ON command?
3. What do you need to do to make sure indexes are updated along with a database file?
4. Are indexes created every time they must be used?
5. Will an index change the physical order of the records in the DBF file?
6. How many indexes can be contained in an MDX file?
7. Is it possible to index on numeric- or date-type fields?
8. What is concatenation?
9. Why is the STR() function sometimes useful during indexing?

10. What does the SEEK command do?
11. What are some disadvantages of the FIND command?
12. What does the REINDEX command do?

TRY IT YOURSELF

1. On your data disk there is a database file called DIARY.DBF. Activate it and examine its structure. APPEND at least ten events and dates from your own life. SORT by date and LIST the new file. APPEND your date of birth to the new file and LIST.
2. APPEND two cities of your choice to CITIES.DBF. INDEX on the state and LIST the file.
3. APPEND DENVER, CO with a 1982 population of 505,563 and a 1970 population of 514,678 to the file. LIST and note the position of the record.
4. INDEX on the 1982 population and LIST the file. Making certain that this index is active, EDIT the JACKSONVILLE record. Change the 1982 population to 4 million and LIST the file.
5. INDEX the CITIES database by descending 1970 population and LIST.
6. Activate the index on city name. STORE 'DALLAS' to a memory variable, and use FIND to position the record pointer to combine the city field name with a literal to place the following message on the screen:

   ```
   DALLAS is close to FT. WORTH
   ```

   (Hint: Use the ? and the &)
7. Activate the index by 1982 population. Use SEEK to position the record pointer at the record containing a 1982 population of 915,956. DISPLAY the record, and check the status of the FOUND() function.
8. Rebuild all the indexes in the CITIES database.
9. Open the DIARY database and LIST the records. INDEX by date and LIST. INDEX by event and LIST.

PROGRAMMING PROJECT

Make sure that you have indexes on both the CITY and STATE fields in the CITIES database file. Then write a program that is similar to the SHW_PART program we examined in this chapter. There should be four choices:

```
1.  Find city using city name.
2.  Find city using state name.
3.  Find next city.
4.  Exit.
```

The first choice should allow the user to enter all or part of a city name and find the city. The second should allow the user to enter a state and find the first city in that state. The third choice should allow the user to find the next city.

Test your program by selecting option 2 and then entering CA as the state. Which city did you find? Select option 3. Which city did you find? Select option 3 again. Which city did you find this time?

LEARNING OBJECTIVES

To design and code input screen modules.

To use the screen painter to create both general and specific designs.

To validate input data.

To write a program to append records.

10 CONSTRUCTING SCREENS

INTRODUCTION

Most people agree that first impressions are important. An attractive report cover and title page, for instance, are likely to please the reader. On the other hand, he or she may dismiss material that is disorganized and unattractive, regardless of its content. The same is true of programs. Satisfied users are the best measure of a program's success, and attractive screens are critical in user satisfaction. dBASE IV has many screen-creation features that will greatly contribute to the success of your programs.

10.1 INPUT SCREENS

DESIGNING INPUT SCREENS

As a programmer you are naturally concerned with the internal operation of your programs. Tasks such as opening and closing files, repeating procedures, and using indexes demand a great deal of your attention and energy. Yet, this internal operation, the elegance and efficiency of your work—or its ungainliness—will not be visible to the user. Although quick operation and reliable performance are unquestionably desirable, users are more greatly affected by the physical appearance of your program.

Users are going to spend most of their time viewing the screens and reports that your system produces. Therefore, user satisfaction always depends, to some degree, on the appearance and convenience of these aspects. This chapter focuses on designing custom input screens. A program to append records through the use of a custom screen is also discussed.

You have already used APPEND to add new records to a database file and EDIT to change existing records. When you did, you used a form on the screen to enter data (Figure 10.1). Although the form helped, it was not particularly pleasing. The fields were merely stacked on top of each other. The names shown on the screen were the names of the fields, which are not as descriptive as we might like.

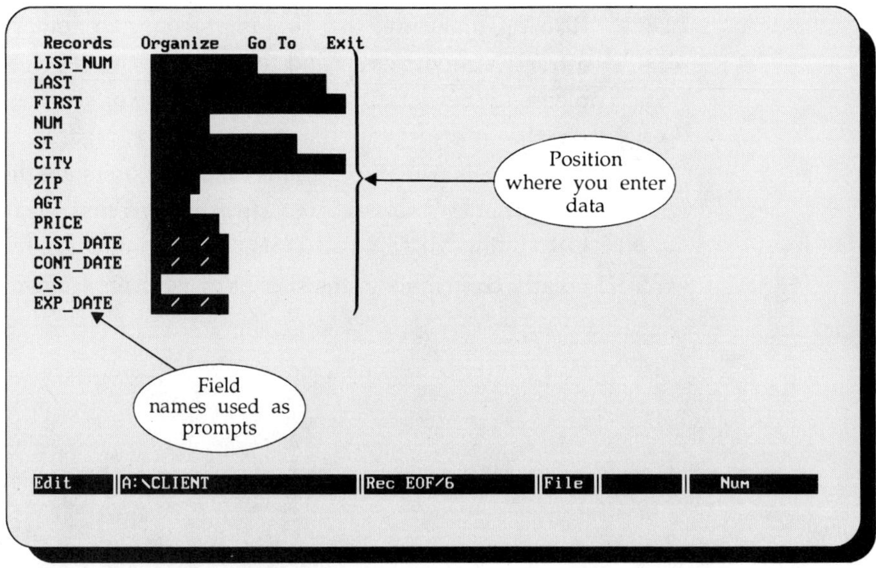

Figure 10.1 THE DEFAULT APPEND SCREEN

In this section, you will create custom forms like the one shown in Figure 10.2 to use in place of the ones dBASE normally supplies. You will then include these custom forms in update programs.

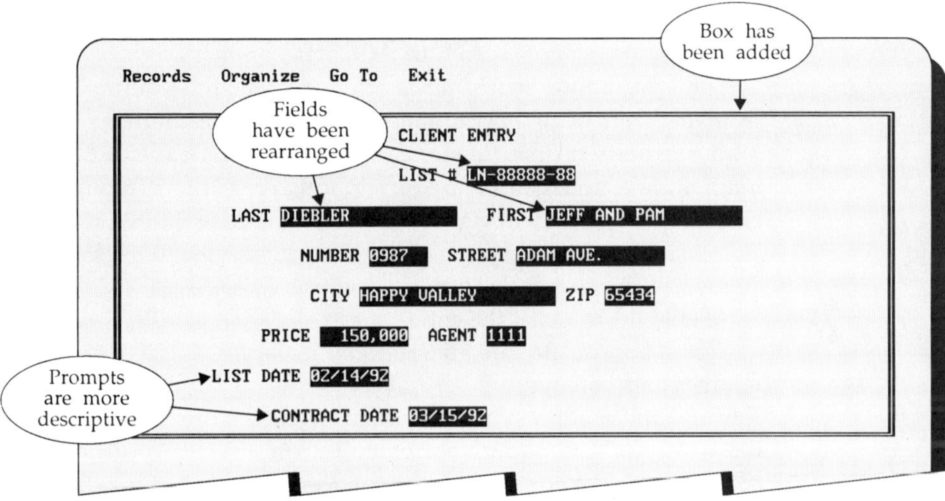

Figure 10.2 A CUSTOM DATA-ENTRY FORM

Ten programmers could design ten screens very different in appearance and operation, yet which accomplish the same task. Consequently, you need to have a clear idea of what will best serve the user's interests. To do this, you may have to observe office operations or interview those persons who will be using the programs you design, or both. It is the needs of users that drive the design specifications. Always, but especially when you are designing input screens, you must think first of the user. Table 10.1 lists some issues to consider when you are designing screens.

TABLE 10.1 Screen design considerations

- Determine the level of computer experience.
- Find out whether the screen is replacing a paper form.
- Ascertain whether the speed of data entry is a consideration.
- Find out how much help or "hand-holding" will be required.
- Use a consistent screen design throughout the system.
- Make screens attractive and easy to understand and to change.
- Display titles and borders in a uniform way from screen to screen.
- Use color, boxes, and lines to produce a pleasant design.

USING @..SAY AND @..GET

Custom screens are produced with a series of @..SAY and @..GET commands. These commands display data and allow data entry at specific locations on the screen. A system of coordinates enables the @..SAY and @..GET commands to use the entire screen more conveniently and more accurately than the ?, WAIT, or ACCEPT commands.

The screen coordinates range from 0 through 24 vertically (rows) and from 0 through 79 horizontally (columns). The number of the row is always expressed first. Row 6, column 10 would be coded 6,10. The maximum number that can be used in printing for either coordinate is 255, but exceeding 24 or 79 will generate an error message in a screen display. Line 22 usually contains the scoreboard display, and line 0 usually contains the status line. These can be removed with SET SCOREBOARD OFF and SET STATUS OFF to make the entire screen available for displays.

Screen coordinates are addressed by including in the @ command a row number and column number indicating the cursor position. Following the row and column numbers we usually have the word SAY to display data or the word GET to allow data entry by the user. SAY displays variables, constants, or the contents of fields in the current record. Figure 10.3 (a and b) shows the syntax and results of @..SAY.

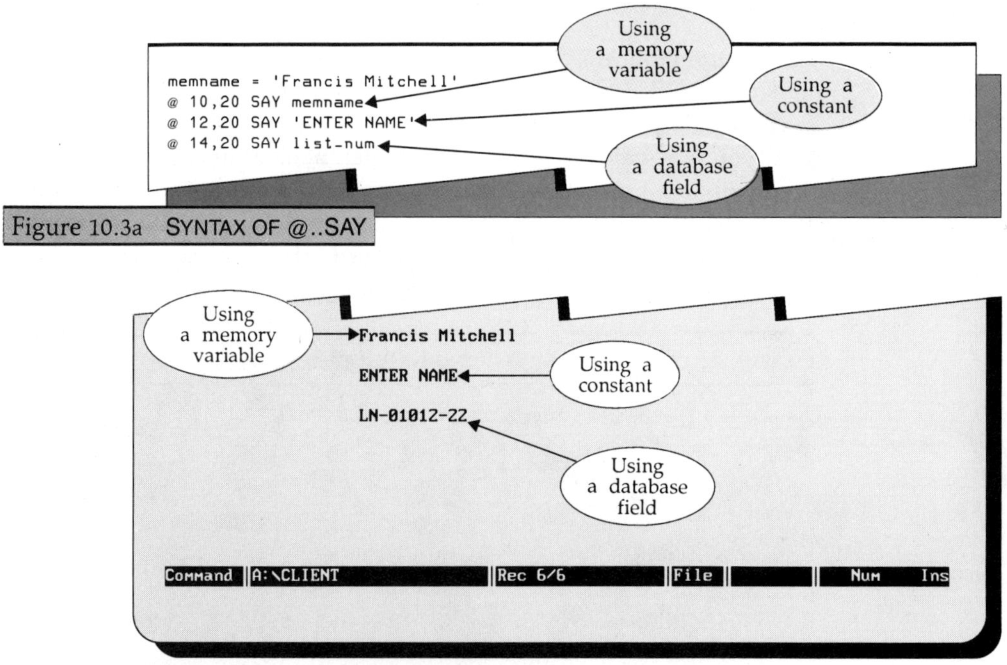

Figure 10.3a SYNTAX OF @..SAY

Figure 10.3b RESULTS OF @..SAY COMMANDS

USING RELATIVE ADDRESSING

If the distance between two rows or columns must remain static, you can use *relative addressing* to specify a location a certain distance away from the present position of the cursor. The ROW() and COL() functions return the current numeric value of that position, and they can be used in arithmetic expressions (see Figure 10.4 a and b).

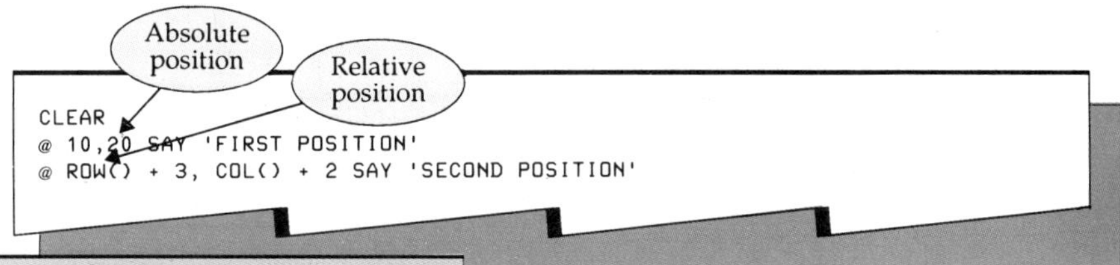

Figure 10.4a USING RELATIVE POSITIONING

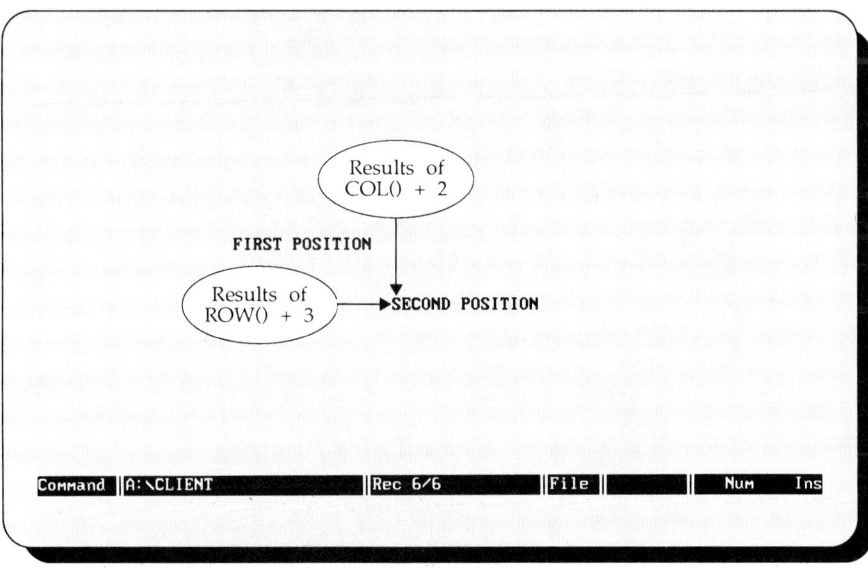

Figure 10.4b RESULTS OF USING RELATIVE POSITIONING

USING VARIABLES FOR TABS AND TITLES

You can use memory variables to act as tab functions by initializing them at the start of the program, and then including them in @..SAY/GET commands (see Figure 10.5 a and b on the next page). You can store frequently used titles or prompts to variables in order to reduce coding in programs (see Figure 10.6, also on the next page).

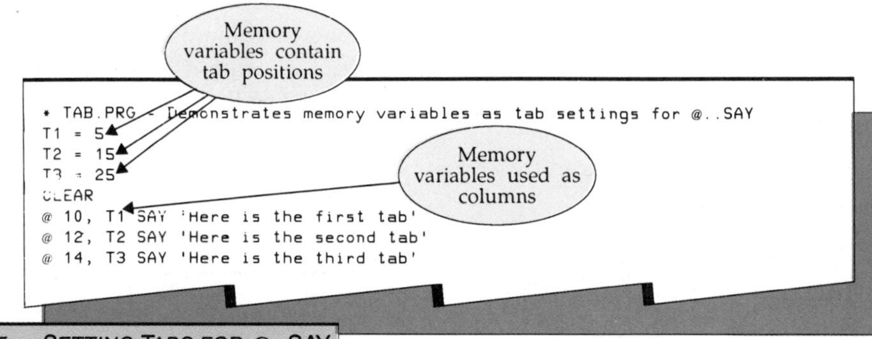


```
* TAB.PRG - Demonstrates memory variables as tab settings for @..SAY
T1 = 5
T2 = 15
T3 = 25
CLEAR
@ 10, T1 SAY 'Here is the first tab'
@ 12, T2 SAY 'Here is the second tab'
@ 14, T3 SAY 'Here is the third tab'
```

Figure 10.5a SETTING TABS FOR @..SAY

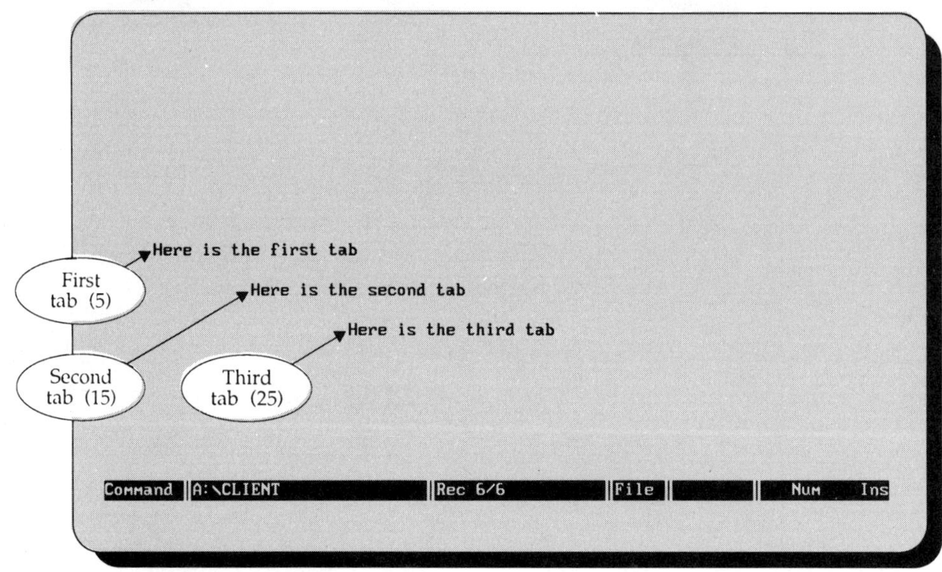

Figure 10.5b RESULTS OF USING TABS

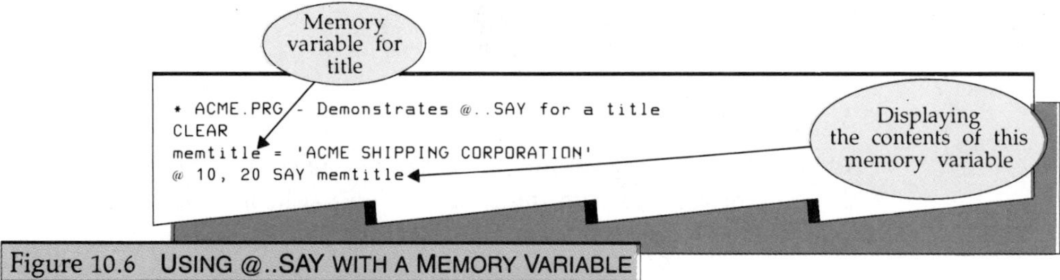


```
* ACME.PRG - Demonstrates @..SAY for a title
CLEAR
memtitle = 'ACME SHIPPING CORPORATION'
@ 10, 20 SAY memtitle
```

Figure 10.6 USING @..SAY WITH A MEMORY VARIABLE

CLEARING PORTIONS OF THE SCREEN

Individual rows are cleared simply by specifying the row and column with the @ sign. For instance, @ 15,0 clears row 15. You can also clear a portion of a row. Typing @ 2,10, for example, clears row 2 from column 10 to the end. Another effective way to clear a portion of a row is to fill the portion with spaces, as in @ 15,10 SAY SPACE(35).

DRAWING LINES AND BOXES

A useful option in screen design is the capability to draw lines and boxes (see Figure 10.7). This feature can be used to frame entry areas and to replicate paper forms.

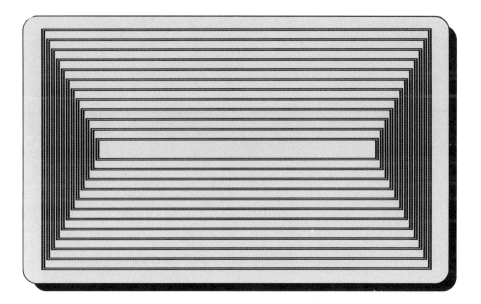

Figure 10.7 PATTERN OF LINES AND BOXES

All that is required to draw a line or a box is an @ symbol and the proper coordinates. Placing the DOUBLE option after the last coordinate produces a double line or box. Consider the following examples.

```
@ 5,1 TO 5,79            && Draw a line across the fifth row.
@ 5,1 CLEAR TO 5,79      && Erase it.
@ 5,5 TO 15,60           && Draw a box.
@ 5,5 CLEAR TO 15,60     && Erase the box and its contents.
@ 10,10 TO 20,70 DOUBLE  && Draw a box with double lines.
@ 11,11 CLEAR TO 19,69   && Erase the contents but leave the box.
```

You can easily test these commands from the dot prompt. (Whenever the screen seems too cluttered, simply type CLEAR. The current contents of the screen will be erased.) The program in Figure 10.8 produces the screen shown in Figure 10.7 and illustrates the scope of the boxes that can be specified.

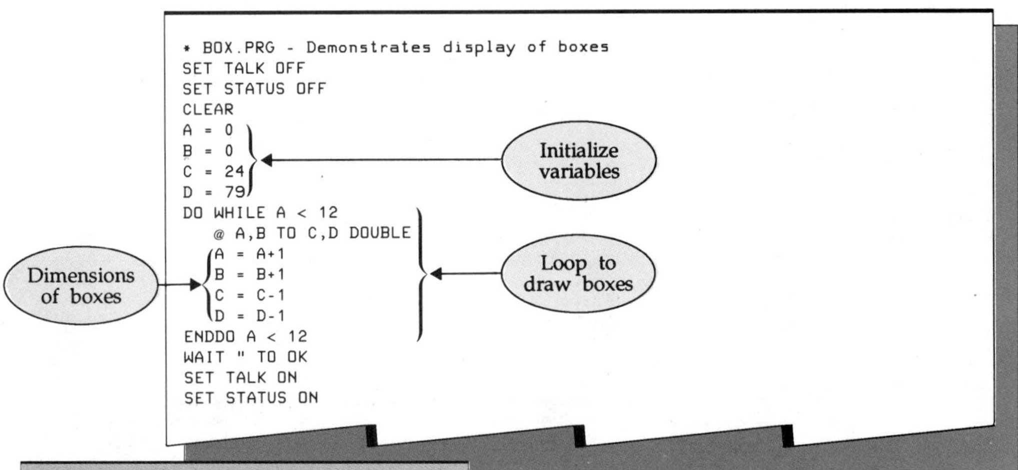

Figure 10.8 A BOX DRAWING PROGRAM

DISPLAYING BLOCKS OF TEXT

On occasion, it may be useful to display large blocks of text on the screen. In such cases, it is often easier to use TEXT/ENDTEXT than a collection of @..SAY commands. (See Figure 10.9 a and b.)

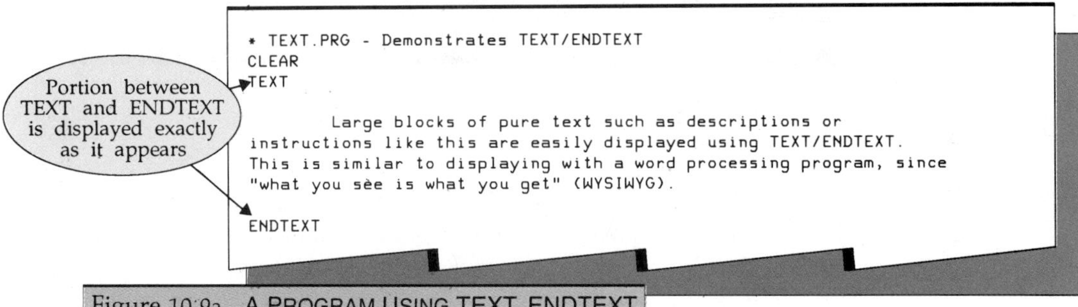

* TEXT.PRG - Demonstrates TEXT/ENDTEXT
CLEAR
TEXT
Large blocks of pure text such as descriptions or
instructions like this are easily displayed using TEXT/ENDTEXT.
This is similar to displaying with a word processing program, since
"what you sèe is what you get" (WYSIWYG).
ENDTEXT
Portion between TEXT and ENDTEXT is displayed exactly as it appears

Figure 10.9a A PROGRAM USING TEXT..ENDTEXT

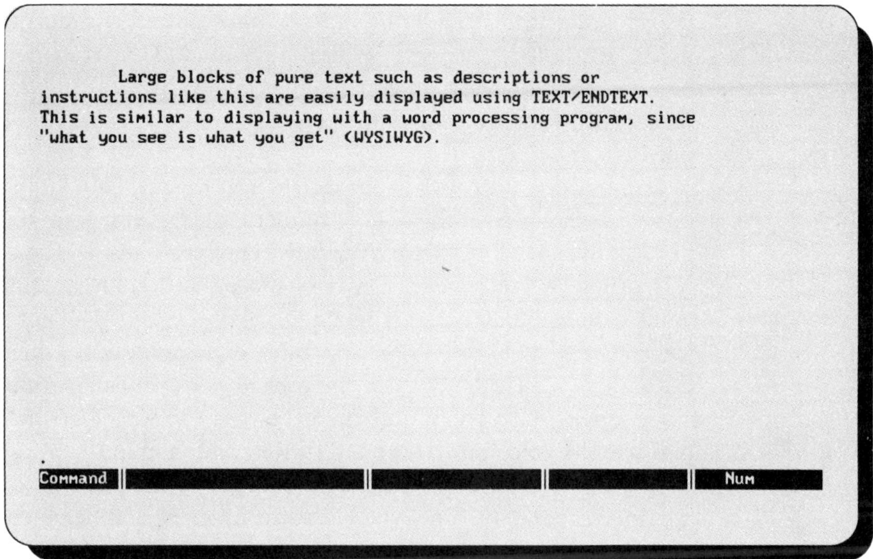
Large blocks of pure text such as descriptions or
instructions like this are easily displayed using TEXT/ENDTEXT.
This is similar to displaying with a word processing program, since
"what you see is what you get" (WYSIWYG).
Command
Num

Figure 10.9b USING TEXT/ENDTEXT

OBTAINING USER INPUT

The @..SAY command is frequently used as a prompt for GET commands to produce custom data entry screens. Using @..SAY/GET is called *full-screen editing* because users can roam over the screen at will, making changes as if they were completing a paper form. This is preferable to single-command responses at the dot prompt, such as responding to ACCEPT commands.

The command to get user input is @..GET. It is similar to @..SAY. Consider the following sample @..GET command:

```
@ 9,34 GET balance
```

This command does two things. First, it displays the current value of BALANCE at the indicated position on the screen in reverse video. (We must make sure it already has some value prior to executing this command; otherwise, we will get an error message.) Second, when a READ command is encountered later, dBASE moves the cursor to this spot on the screen, allows the user to enter a value, and then places whatever value the user has entered in the indicated variable. If the user does not type a value but simply presses Enter, the current value of BALANCE remains.

It is important to remember that a READ statement is required later in the program in order for the input to take place. Without it, the user will not be requested to enter any data. Several @..GET statements can appear before a single READ statement, however. When this happens, the user is prompted to enter all the data specified in the various @..GET statements, one after the other.

If you have too many characters for the available space, truncation occurs. It is worse in the case of numeric fields. Numbers that are too large to display cause a numeric overflow. They are then displayed in exponential format. If you use REPLACE to place that data in a database field, the value cannot be edited and retained. Make certain that numeric fields are large enough to hold the greatest value expected. Also, whenever possible, do not include fields that ask the user to perform calculations because this slows down data entry and increases the chance of error. It is better to perform the calculation with a STORE command in the program.

A GET can be combined with a SAY on the same line, or it can be specified separately. Since the block for memacc will be placed immediately after the prompt in the first statement in Figure 10.10 (a), a space must be provided as the last character in the prompt to separate it from the user's response.

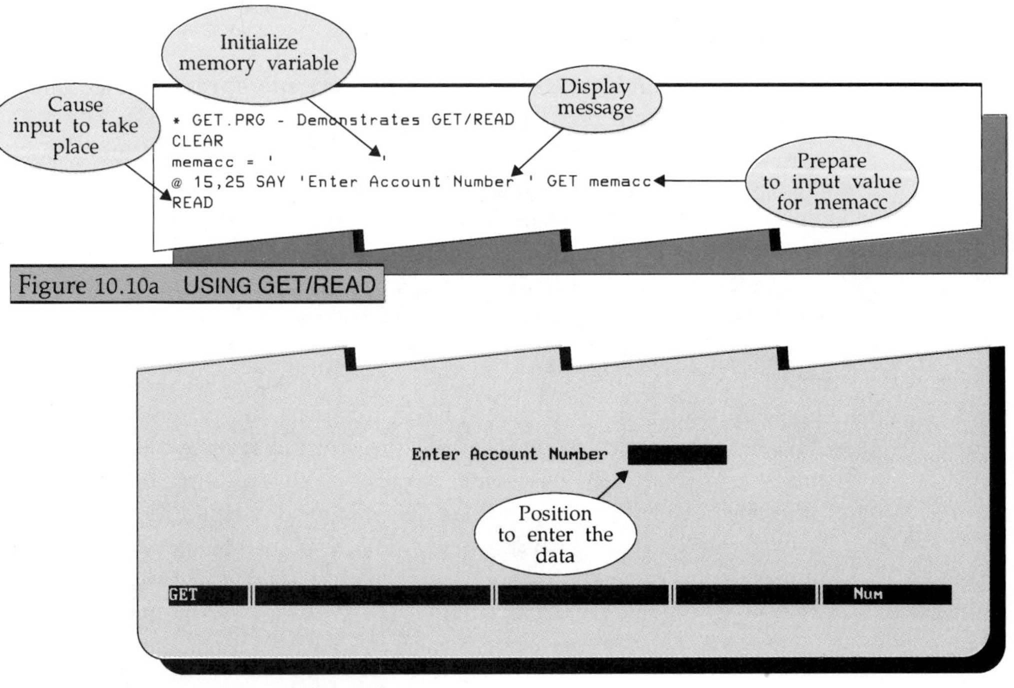

Figure 10.10a USING GET/READ

Figure 10.10b RESULTS OF GET.PRG

10.2 USING THE SCREEN PAINTER

We will now use a special dBASE tool, the *screen painter*, to create the custom form shown in Figure 10.2. Later we will see how to incorporate the form created by this tool into our programs. Since the form involves the CLIENT database file, this file must be active before we begin the process. Once it is, we invoke the screen generator by typing CREATE SCREEN followed by the name we want to assign to our custom form. Assuming we would like the form to also be called CLIENT, the command would be

```
CREATE SCREEN CLIENT
```

At this point, your screen should look like the one in Figure 10.11. Although you can create a form totally from scratch, it is usually simpler to let dBASE get you started. To do so, select "Quick layout" (remember that you have a similar choice when you create reports).

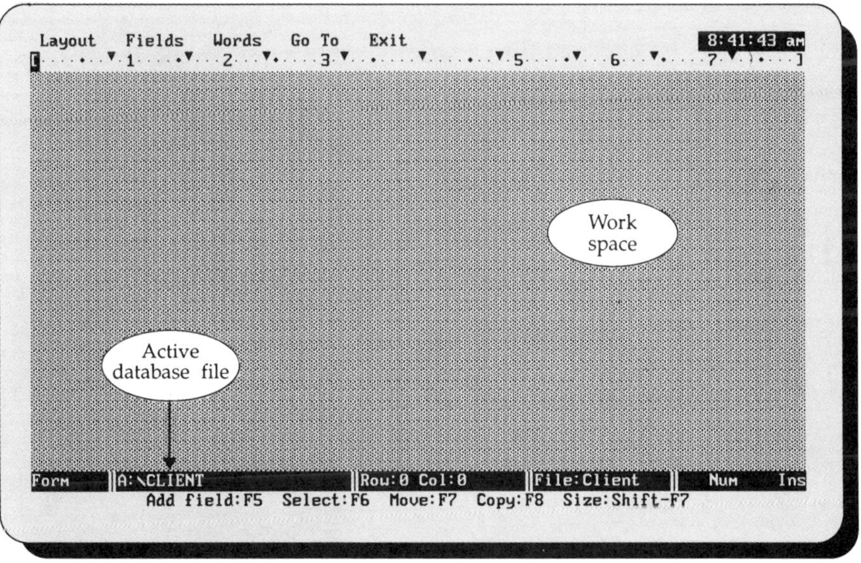

Figure 10.11 INITIAL FORM DESIGN SCREEN

At this point, dBASE creates the form shown in Figure 10.12 on the next page. (Does it look familiar? It is precisely the form you normally see on the Edit screen. Just as with reports and labels, the 9s and Xs represent the fields.) We now modify this form, gradually turning it into precisely what we want. In creating forms, you can use the keys shown in Table 10.2, also on the next page.

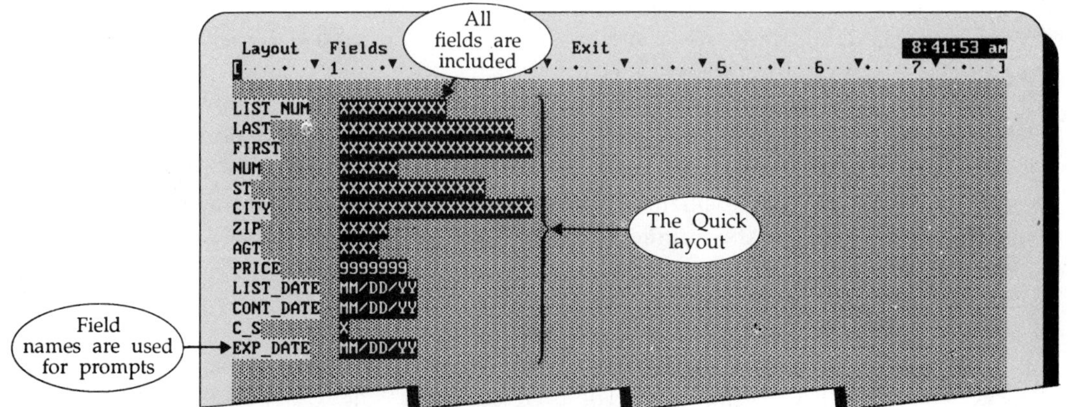

Figure 10.12 FORM DESIGN SCREEN QUICK LAYOUT

TABLE 10.2 Special keys used when creating screens

KEY	PURPOSE
↑	Moves the cursor up one row
↓	Moves the cursor down one row
→	Moves the cursor one position to the right
←	Moves the cursor one position to the left
[Tab]	Moves to the next tab setting
[Shift-Tab]	Moves to the previous tab setting
[Page Down]	Moves to bottom of screen
[Page Up]	Moves to top of screen
[Home]	Moves to beginning of line
[End]	Moves to end of line
[Backspace]	Moves cursor one position to the left and erases character that was in that position
[Insert]	Switches between Insert mode and Replace mode
[Enter]	In Insert mode, moves down one line and inserts a new line. Otherwise, simply moves down one line
[Ctrl-Y]	Deletes the line the cursor is on
[Ctrl-N]	Inserts a new line at the cursor
[F5]	Adds a new field at the current cursor position
[F6]	Selects field or block for subsequent work
[F7]	Moves selected field or block
[F8]	Copies selected field or block
[Delete]	Deletes selected field or block. If none selected, deletes character at current cursor position

MOVING FIELDS AND CHARACTERS

Let's begin by adding four blank lines. To insert a blank line, move the cursor to the beginning of the line and type Ctrl-N. Most of our work in completing the transformation of the form involves the following operations:

1. **Move a field.** To move a field, first move the cursor into the field. Next select the field by pressing F6 ("Select") and then pressing Enter. Once you have selected the field, press F7 ("Move"), move the cursor to the new position, and press Enter. There will be a faint strip, exactly the size of the field, that moves right along with the cursor. This helps you judge exactly where you should position the cursor to complete the move.
2. **Change text.** To delete a character, move the cursor to it and press delete. To add a character, move the cursor to the desired location and type the character.
3. **Move text.** To move a string of characters, first select the string you want to move by placing the cursor at the first character, pressing F6, then moving the cursor to the last character, and pressing Enter. Next press F7, move the cursor to the new location, and press Enter. As in moving fields, there will be a faint strip, exactly the size of the selected portion, that moves with the cursor. (If the move would result in covering existing fields or text, you will be asked if this is acceptable. If you answer that it is, the move will take place and the covered fields or text will be deleted.)
4. **Delete a field.** To delete a field, first move the cursor into the field. Next select the field by pressing F6 and then pressing Enter. Once you have selected the field, press the Delete key.
5. **Add a field.** To add a field, move the cursor to the position where you want the field to be placed, then select the "Add field" option of the Fields menu. Choose the desired field from the list and press Ctrl-End.

To begin, use these techniques to move the LIST_NUM field into the position shown in Figure 10.13 on the next page. Change the prompt from "LIST_NUM" to "LIST #" and move it to the position shown in the figure.

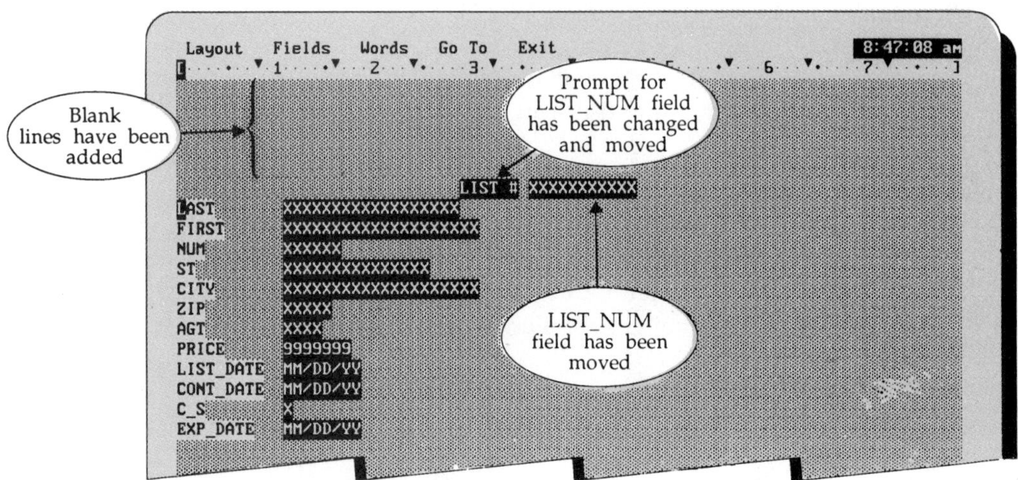

Figure 10.13 FORM DESIGN SCREEN EDIT (1)

Next add a blank line between the line that begins FIRST and the line that begins NUM. This will give you room to move the fields. Move the LAST and FIRST fields and prompts into the positions shown in Figure 10.14. Move the NUMBER and STREET fields to the positions shown in Figure 10.15.

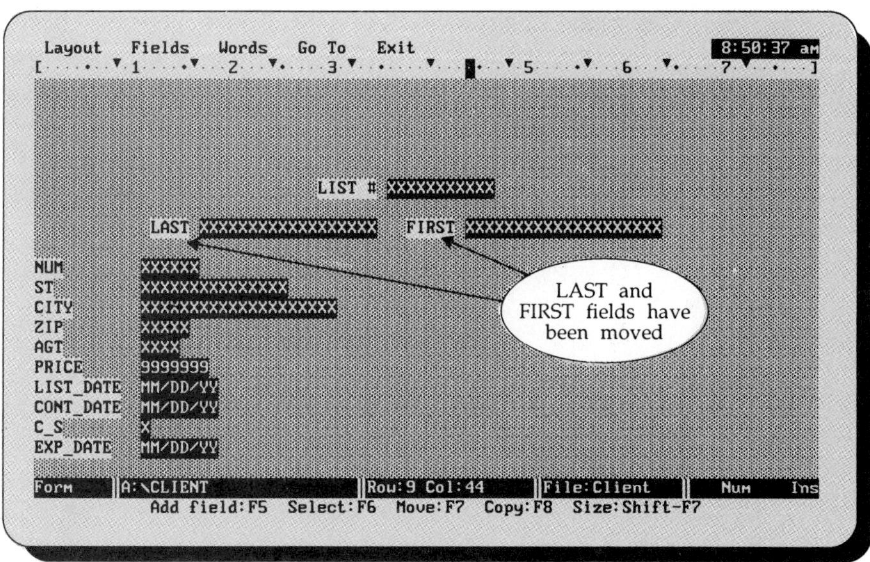

Figure 10.14 FORM DESIGN SCREEN EDIT (2)

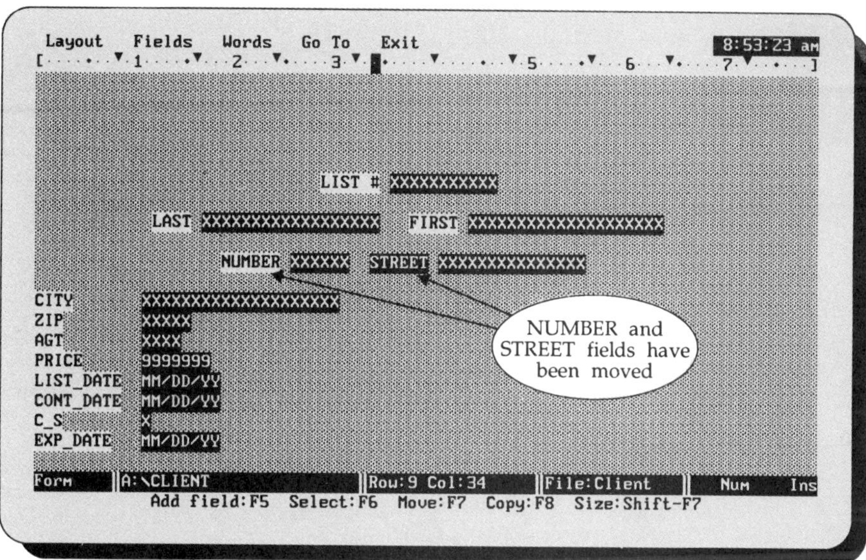

Figure 10.15 FORM DESIGN SCREEN EDIT (3)

Next move the remaining fields and prompts into the positions shown in Figure 10.16. Notice that the C_S and EXP_DATE fields have not been moved. They will not appear on the final form.

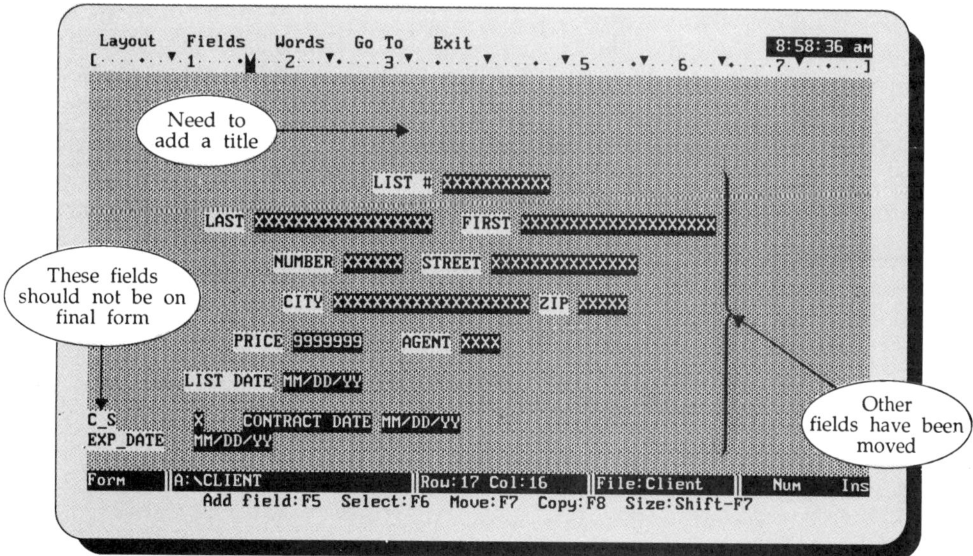

Figure 10.16 FORM DESIGN SCREEN EDIT (4)

Delete the fields C_S and EXP_DATE, and type the title CLIENT ENTRY in the position shown in Figure 10.17.

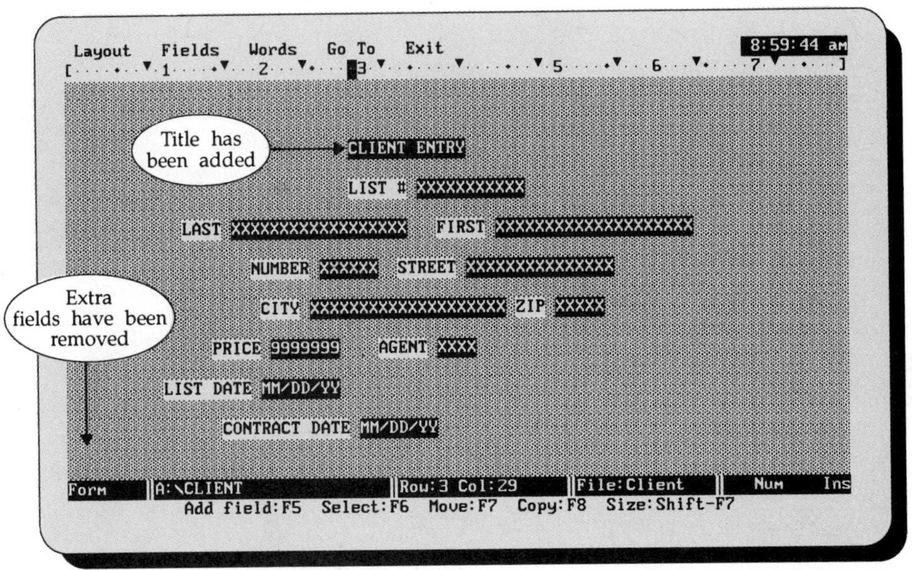

Figure 10.17 FORM DESIGN SCREEN EDIT (5)

We can improve the look of a form by adding boxes. In this form, we will place a double box around the entire form. To do so, select the "Box" option of the Layout menu. You are then asked if you want to use a single line, a double line, or some special character. Choose double line. You are then instructed to move the cursor to the upper left corner of the box and press Enter. In our case, the upper left corner is at the beginning of the line above the line containing the title. Move to this position and press Enter. You are then instructed to "Stretch box with cursor keys, complete with Enter." Move the cursor to the end of the line below the line that contains the contract date. Press Enter and the box is in place (Figure 10.18).

The form is now complete, so we should save it. To do so, select "Save changes and exit" from the Exit menu.

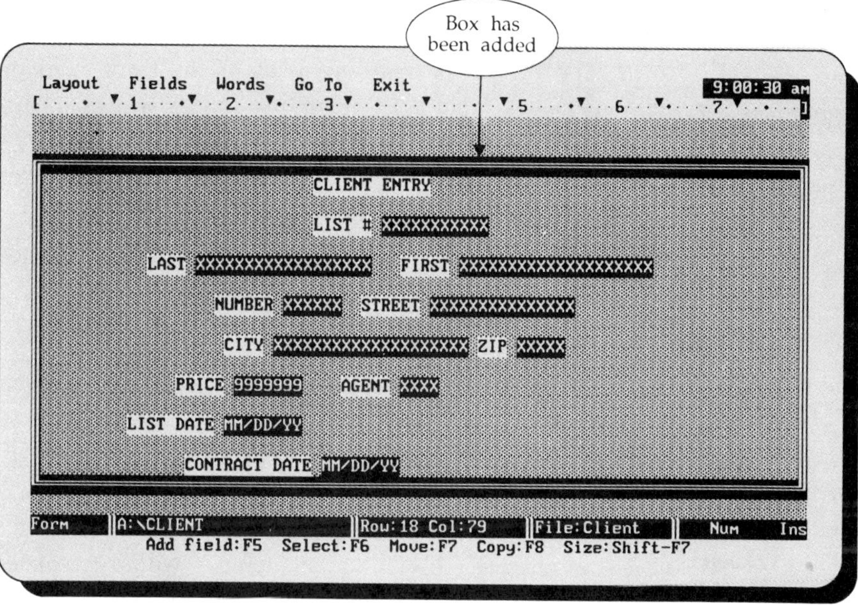

Figure 10.18 FORM DESIGN SCREEN EDIT (6)

USING THE FORM

When we first create a form, the form is active. Activating a different database file, activating a different form, or leaving dBASE deactivates the form. To reactivate it later, we first need to activate the corresponding database file. Then we type SET FORMAT TO followed by the name of the form. In this case, we would type

```
SET FORMAT TO CLIENT
```

Now if you type either APPEND or EDIT, the normal dBASE form is replaced with your own custom form. Even with a new form, you use the Edit screen exactly as you learned before. You can still use it to add records and to make changes exactly as you did before. You can still move to the next record by pressing Page Down. You can still use the Go To menu to find records. You will just see a different form on the screen, one that looks much nicer.

10.3 VALIDATING USER INPUT

With what we have accomplished so far, we have made a more pleasing form. The boxes, the rearrangement of the fields, and more descriptive prompts make a form more interesting and pleasant. We have done nothing, however, to make sure that users enter data correctly. That is what we will tackle next. To do so, be sure the CLIENT database file is active and type

```
MODIFY SCREEN CLIENT
```

You will return to the Form Design Screen and your form is displayed.

At this point, you could choose to further move fields on your screen. You could delete fields, add new fields, add additional boxes, or type additional characters on the screen. You do all these things as you have done before. But what we're going to focus on is changing characteristics of existing fields to enhance the data-entry process. We can use three features to do this: templates, picture functions, and edit options.

USING TEMPLATES

One way to govern how data is entered is with a template. To see how a template is used, move the cursor to the LIST_NUM field (labeled LIST # on your form) and select the "Modify field" option of the Fields menu. In the lower half of the box, you see the word "Template" followed by XXXX-XXXXXXX in brackets (Figure 10.19). This is the field's current template.

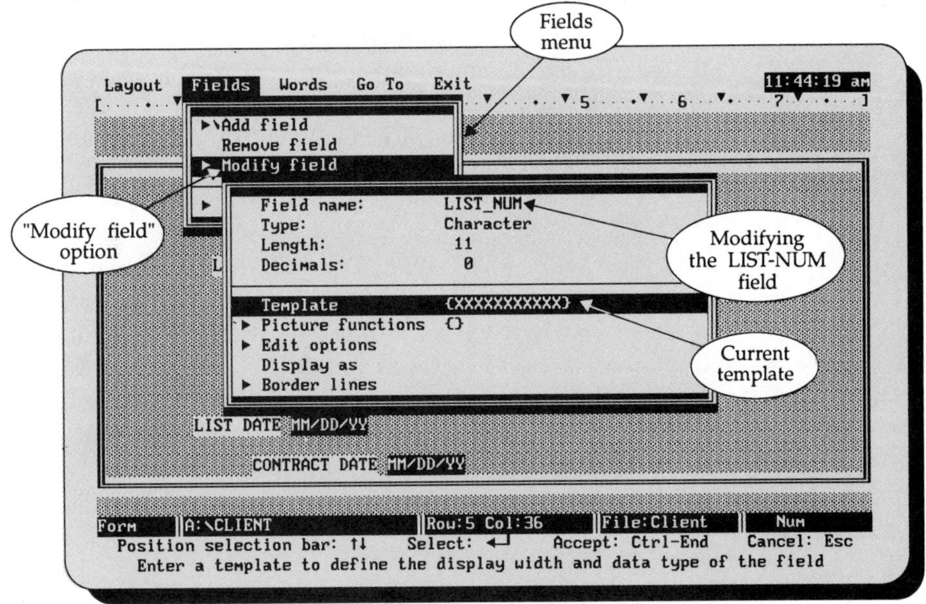

Figure 10.19 FORM DESIGN SCREEN: MODIFY FIELD OPTION

A *template* is a series of characters, one for each position in the field, that indicate how data is to be entered into the field. To see the possibilities, move the highlight to the Template line and press Enter. The brackets disappear, and you can type a different template. To help you select the appropriate symbols, dBASE displays them on the screen (see Figure 10.20).

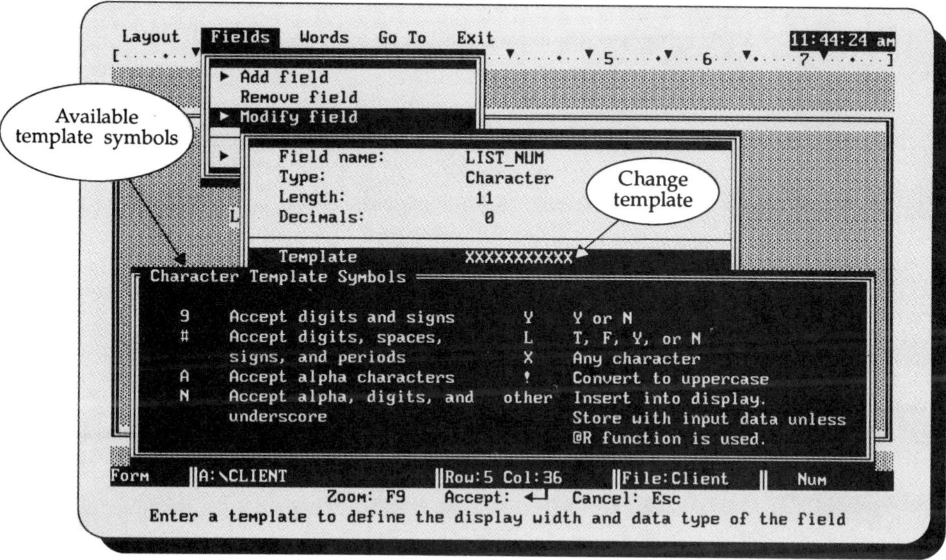

Figure 10.20 FORM DESIGN SCREEN: CURRENT TEMPLATE

As you can see, the symbol "X" indicates that dBASE will accept any character. The symbol "A" indicates that dBASE will accept only alpha characters (letters). Thus, a template of AAAAAAAAA would prevent the user from entering numbers or special characters, such as a semicolon, in the field. The symbol "!" indicates that letters are to be converted to uppercase. A template of !!!!!!!!! would cause any lowercase letter entered by the user to automatically be converted to uppercase letters. The symbol "other" simply indicates that other characters besides the ones shown are inserted into the display and stored as part of the field. A template of !!-99999-99, for example, would force the user to enter numbers in the positions indicated by the 9s. The exclamation points would cause letters entered in those positions to be converted to uppercase. The hyphens would be displayed on the screen in the correct positions (the user would not have to type them) and would be automatically included as part of the field. Before any data is entered in the field, it would look like

When the cursor moves in this field, it will automatically skip the positions already filled. If the user types AA1111111, for example, the screen would show

```
AA-11111-11
```

This entire value, including both the hyphens, would then be stored in the database file.

At this point, let's suppose we have decided that !!-99999-99 is an appropriate template for LIST_NUM. Type this template and then press Enter. Press Ctrl-End to indicate to dBASE that the modification is complete.

(**Note:** The list of available template symbols for numeric fields is different than the list for character fields. If you move the cursor to the PRICE field, for example, and then select "Template" you will see the list of templates available for numeric fields.) (See Figure 10.21).

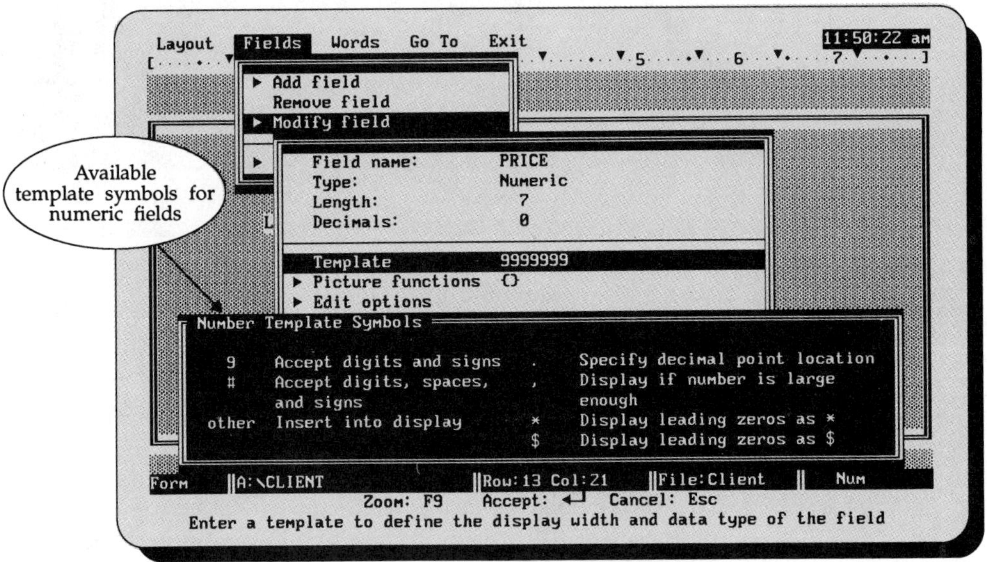

Figure 10.21 FORM DESIGN SCREEN: NUMERIC TEMPLATE SYMBOLS

USING PICTURE FUNCTIONS

A second way to govern how data is entered is to use a *picture function.* To see how picture functions are used, move the cursor to the LAST field and select the "Modify field" option of the Fields menu. In the lower half of the box, you see "Picture functions."

Whereas each template symbol that you entered in a template affected only a single position, a picture function affects the entire field. The possible picture functions vary from one field to another, depending on the type of data that can be stored in the field. The list for numeric fields, for example, is different from the list for character fields. Fortunately, we don't have to remember which picture functions are available because dBASE always shows us the correct list.

Move the highlight to the "Picture functions" line and press Enter. Your screen should now look like the one in Figure 10.22. The box contains the various picture functions that are possible for this field. If the word "OFF" appears next to the picture function, the picture function is not in effect. As you can see, there are currently no picture functions in effect for this field. To select any of these picture functions, move the highlight to it and press Enter. The word "OFF" changes to "ON." (If you change your mind or select one incorrectly, simply repeat the process. The word "ON" changes back to "OFF.") At this point, select "Upper-case conversion." This option automatically converts all lowercase letters to uppercase (just as you did on the *LIST_NUM* field with a template).

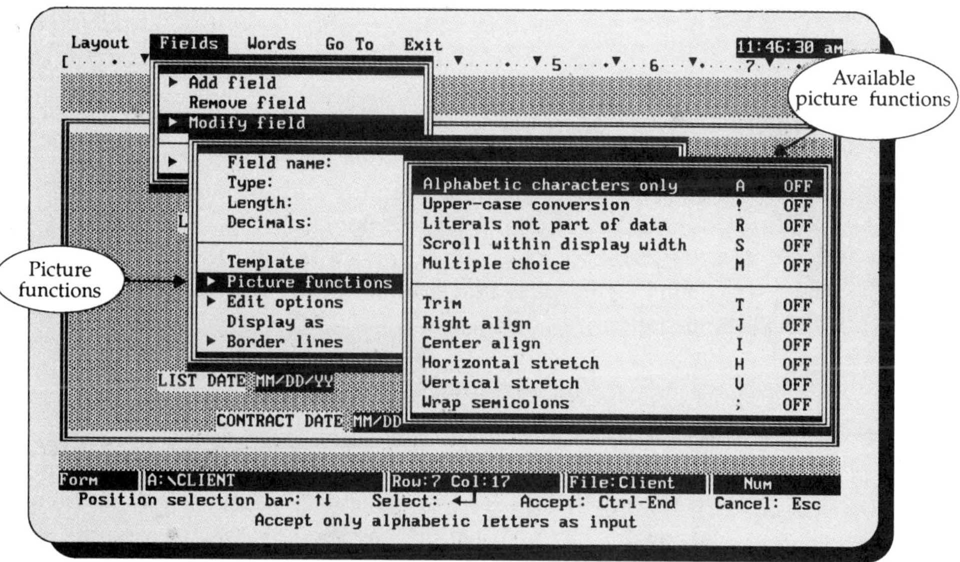

Figure 10.22 FORM DESIGN SCREEN: PICTURE FUNCTIONS

You can get help on the meaning of these picture functions by pressing F1. The following three picture functions are just a little bit more involved, so they deserve some explanation here.

"Literals not part of data." If this function is ON, any of the "other" characters in a template (added by the template itself) will be displayed on the form, but not stored in the database. In the example we looked at earlier, !!-99999-99, if the user typed AA1111111, it would appear on the screen as

```
AA-11111-11
```

If this function is OFF, AA-11111-11 (including hyphens) would be stored. If this function is ON, only AA1111111 would actually be stored in the database.

"Scroll within display width." This option allows the user to enter more data into the field than will actually fit on the screen. Once the user has filled the field, the contents move to the left to allow further entry. If you choose this option, you are asked for the width of the portion of the screen to be used for scrolling. Type the width you desire and press Enter. To turn this option OFF, select it again and change the width to zero.

"Multiple choice." When you selected a field type on the Database Design screen, you cycled through the various possible values by repeatedly pressing the Spacebar. When you had the one you wanted on the screen, you pressed Enter. This is called "multiple choice," and you can create such a field in your own form by using this picture function. If you select it, you are asked for the choices. Enter all the choices you want, separated by commas. If you decide you don't want to use multiple choice after all, select the option again and delete the choices.

The list of picture functions available for numeric fields is shown in Figure 10.23. Again, you can press F1 to obtain help on the specific meaning of the option in case it is not clear to you from the brief description on the screen. Change the template for the PRICE field to 9,999,999. This template indicates that commas are to be displayed in appropriate places in the field.

TEMPLATES VS. PICTURE FUNCTIONS

We have seen that we could turn lowercase letters to uppercase with an appropriate template or by using an appropriate picture function. You may wonder which to use. In general, if you can accomplish what you want through a picture function, you should do it that way. It's simpler to make a single choice and know that it applies to the whole field. If you cannot accomplish what you want through a picture function, use a template. This is particularly appropriate if you need to use different symbols within your template, as in !!-99999-99. When you are done, use Ctrl-End to leave this menu (you'll need to press it twice).

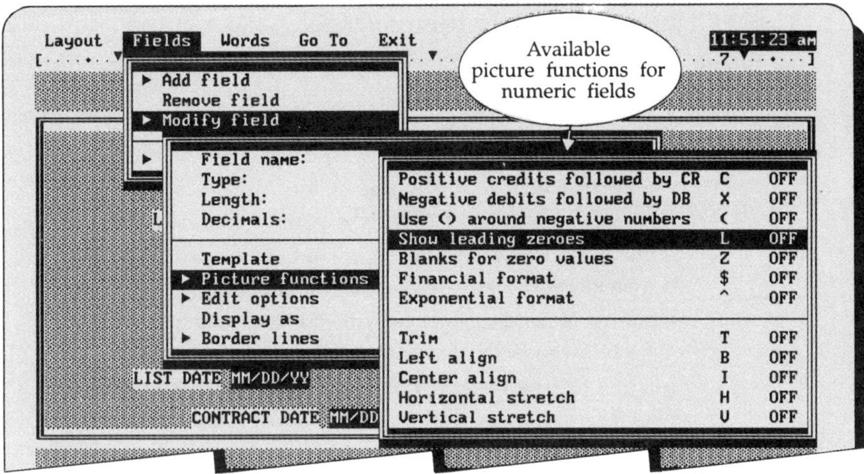

Figure 10.23 PICTURE FUNCTIONS FOR NUMERIC FIELDS

USING EDIT OPTIONS

Another way to control input is with edit options. To see how we use these, move the cursor to the PRICE field and select the "Modify field" option of the Fields menu. In the lower half of the box, you see "Edit options." Move the cursor to this line and press Enter. Your screen is then similar to the one in Figure 10.24. (It will not yet be identical because some of the entries that we will now discuss have already been made in the figure.) Let's look at the options.

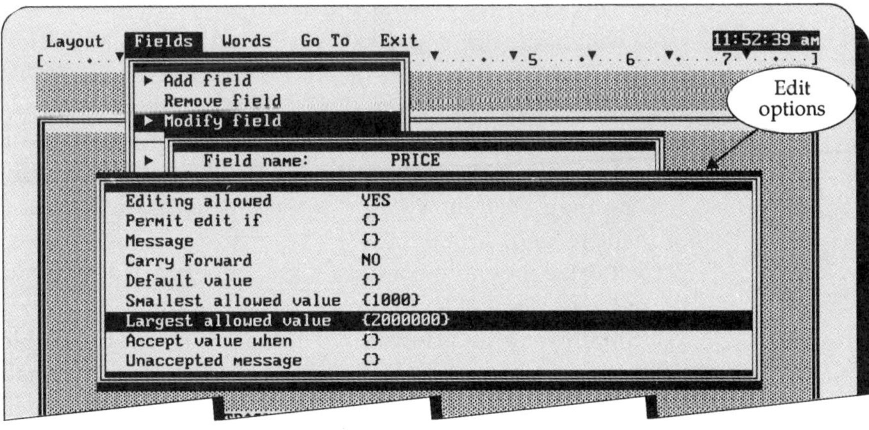

Figure 10.24 FORM DESIGN SCREEN: EDIT OPTIONS

"Editing allowed." If this option is YES, the user is permitted to change the contents of the field. If it is NO, the user cannot make changes. If you were creating a form for a user who could see prices but could not change them, for example, you would change this value to NO. To do so, make sure the highlight is on this line and press Enter. You will probably not use this very often, and you may find that you never need it.

"Permit edit if." You use this option to enter a condition concerning a prior field. Editing of this field is only allowed if the condition is met. You might have some special code that is entered in a prior field, and the current field can be edited only if the code entered previously is "Y," for example. This is another option you will not use often, if ever.

"Message." If you wish to have a special message displayed when the user moves the cursor into this field, use this option. Press Enter, type the message, and press Enter again. You typically use this option if you have something special you want to tell a user about a field. For example, in our FIRST field, the user can enter two names. We might modify the FIRST field and then use this option to enter a message of

```
You may enter two first names separated by the word AND
```

Whenever the cursor moves to the FIRST field, this message would automatically be displayed at the bottom of the screen.

"Carry Forward." When you are adding records, the contents of all the fields for one record are normally erased before you begin entering data for the next record. If you would rather have the value in a particular field remain on the screen, change the value for "Carry Forward" to YES. To do so, make sure the highlight is on this line and press Enter.

"Default value." This option also applies specifically to adding new records. If you would like data entry to start with a particular value in this field, you enter the value as a default. If you think, for example, that the most common price is 200000, you could make it the default value. That way, if a user is entering a record on which the price is 200000, the right value will already be on the screen. The user does not need to type it, but instead can simply press Enter when the cursor gets to the PRICE field. If the price is anything other than 200000, the user must type it, but he will type no more than he would without a default value. Thus a default value often helps and, in any case, will not hurt. Prices vary so greatly that a default value probably does not make sense here. In certain cases, however, it can be very valuable.

"Smallest value allowed." If there is a smallest possible value for the field, you can enter it here. dBASE then prohibits any smaller value from being entered. Enter a smallest value of 1000 by moving the highlight to this line, pressing Enter, typing 1000, and pressing Enter again (in the figure, this has already been done).

"Largest value allowed." If there is a largest possible value for the field, you can enter it here. Enter a largest value of 2000000 (this has also been done in the figure). (**Note:** The screen painter automatically combines the smallest value allowed and largest value allowed into a special RANGE clause. This clause is simply the word RANGE followed by the two values. In this case, for example, the clause would be `RANGE 1000,2000000`.)

"Accept value when." This is a very useful option. It allows us to impose our own special conditions on the data. Suppose that a PART database file contains a field called itemclss (item class). Suppose further that the only legal values for itemclss are AP, HW, and SG. We can make sure that no user enters any other value by entering the condition

```
itemclss="AP" .OR. itemclss="HW" .OR. itemclss="SG"
```

on this line. We first press Enter, then type the condition, and then press Enter again.

"Unaccepted message." dBASE does not allow the user to add to the database any data that violates our conditions. This option allows us to enter a message that is displayed in the event the user attempts to violate the condition. For the PART database file, for example, we might enter the message

```
Item classes must be AP, HW, or SG
```

Once you have finished making your modifications, press Ctrl-End twice to complete the process, once to leave the Edit Options screen and then once again to leave the Modify Field screen.

When you have made all your changes, choose "Save changes and exit" from the Exit menu. To test the changes you have made, start adding a record with your form. Remember that both your database file and your form must be active in order to do so. On the Edit screen, select the "Add new records" option from the Records menu. Since we do not want to actually change the contents of CLIENT at this time, press Esc when you are on the last field (contract date). This brings you out of this screen without saving the new record you are adding.

10.4 WRITING A PROGRAM TO ADD RECORDS

There are two basic strategies for a program to add records. You can use either GET commands alone or a combination of GET and REPLACE commands to load the data into the fields for the new record. The use of the GET alone requires that the actual field names be used, which is how the screen painter feature works. The actual field names from the database file are loaded to the screen, which defines their type and length. Any additional validation must be coded later. However, the preferred method is to use a set of memory variables, which must first be initialized, and then to use the REPLACE command to transfer the data from the memory variables to the actual field names. This allows the user to change the data before it is written to the file and, more importantly, allows the program to validate the data. (See Table 10.3.)

TABLE 10.3 Append module program steps

1. Define all memory variables.
2. Use @..GET to input data to variables.
3. Validate the contents of the variables.
4. Have the user decide whether or not to append.
5. APPEND BLANK and REPLACE to add record.
6. Loop.

Memory variables should be carefully initialized with a STORE command at the start of the program. Attempts to reference an uninitialized variable will generate a syntax error, which will interrupt the program. Table 10.4 provides some guidance for this process.

TABLE 10.4 Initialization of memory variables

mstate = ' '	Initialization of character fields establishes the length of the field.
mprice = 0.00	Numeric fields should be initialized to a value that contains the expected number of decimal places. dBASE IV permits only valid numeric characters in the field.
mdob = {03/02/92}	Dates must be enclosed in braces (curly brackets). Only allowable date values are accepted as input. The month must be a number between 1 and 12; the day must be within the range for that month. Even leap years are taken into account for February. Years are assumed to be in the twentieth century, but they can be adjusted with the SET CENTURY command. (Chapter 12 will explain date arithmetic and the use of the SET CENTURY command.)
ok = .T.	Logical variables accept only T,F,Y,N in uppercase or lowercase. The value must be enclosed between periods.

A helpful strategy is to allow the user to edit entries before the data is actually written to the file in an APPEND or a modification. All the data entry operations must be nested within a DO WHILE loop that will execute as long as the user wants to continue editing. The user responds to a prompt at the bottom of the loop, indicating the intention to edit or to move on to the next activity (see Table 10.5 and Figure 10.25).

TABLE 10.5 Steps to accept a user's response

1. Initialize a logical variable to 'Y'.
2. Include a DO WHILE with the logical variable.
3. Place a GET/READ before the ENDDO to accept the user's intentions.

```
mname='
ok = .Y.
DO WHILE ok
   CLEAR
   @ 10, 12 SAY 'NAME:'
   @ 10, 18 GET mname PICTURE '!!!!!!!!!!'
   READ
   @ 15, 20 SAY 'Any Changes? (Y/N)' GET ok
   READ
ENDDO WHILE ok
```

Figure 10.25 USER TERMINATION OF A LOOP

The program section in Figure 10.25 allows the user to input and edit until the information is correct. Although only a name field is requested here, a whole screenful of fields could be nested in the DO WHILE loop. When the user types "n" (or any character other than "y" or "t"), control passes to the command after the ENDDO ok. Once the user has indicated that the data is correct, REPLACE commands can be used to begin the critical operations of appending or modifying.

Let's examine a complete program to append records to the CLIENT.DBF file. The structure is listed in Figure 10.26 on the next page for your reference. Most of the ideas presented in this chapter are included in the pseudocode in Table 10.6, also on the next page. The program itself appears in Figure 10.27 on page 263.

```
. list structure
Structure for database: A:\CLIENT.DBF
Number of data records:        6
Date of last update   : 10/28/92
Field  Field Name  Type       Width    Dec    Index
    1  LIST-NUM    Character     11               Y
    2  LAST        Character     18               N
    3  FIRST       Character     20               N
    4  NUM         Character      6               N
    5  ST          Character     15               N
    6  CITY        Character     20               N
    7  ZIP         Character      5               N
    8  AGT         Character      4               N
    9  PRICE       Numeric        7               N
   10  LIST-DATE   Date           8               N
   11  CONT-DATE   Date           8               N
   12  C-S         Character      1               N
   13  EXP-DATE    Date           8               N
** Total **                     132

. list
Record#  LIST-NUM     LAST                FIRST                NUM    ST
    CITY                ZIP   AGT   PRICE LIST-DATE CONT-DATE C-S EXP-DATE
      1  LN-88888-88 DIEBLER           JEFF AND PAM            0987   ADAM AVE.
    HAPPY VALLEY        65434 1111  150000 02/14/92  03/15/92         /  /
      2  LN-99999-99 SCHILLING         WILLIAM                 265    BUENA VISTA
WAY UPLAND CA           19178 4444  234000 02/02/92  04/24/92         /  /
      3  LN-77777-77 CAROLINE          ELIZABETH               75     DERBY WAY
    COVINGTON           40693 1234  115000 01/15/92  08/23/92         /  /
      4  LN-33333-33 JORDAN            AARON & ELIZABETH       127    NORTH 27TH S
T.  CAMP HILL           17011 1234  275000 10/13/92    /  /           /  /
      5  LN-11111-11 SHUGART           KIM & JERRY             8399   JASON CIRCLE
    JARED               11023 2222   50000 09/01/92  09/16/92         /  /
      6  LN-01012-22 SCHEFFEY          DAVE & TISH             0344   SIERRA WAY
    SANTA BARBARA       09543 2222  230000 08/06/92    /  /           /  /
```

Figure 10.26 STRUCTURE FOR CLIENT.DBF

TABLE 10.6 **Pseudocode for an append module**
Set environment
Initialize memory variables and open files
Display screen
Input Listing Number
Exit if number is blank
Loop if number exists
GET to memory variables
Append blank when user is done
Replace

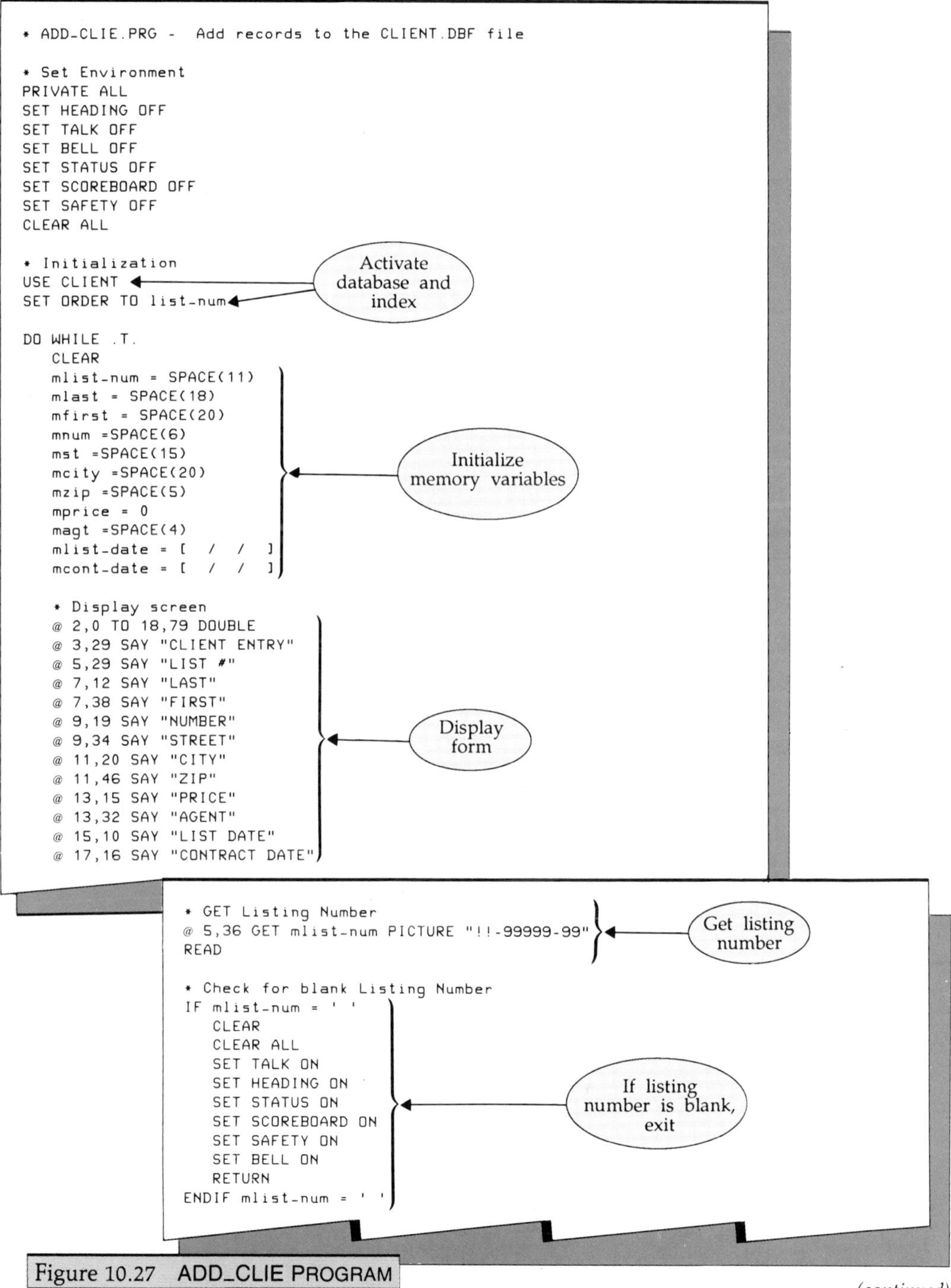

```
* ADD-CLIE.PRG -  Add records to the CLIENT.DBF file

* Set Environment
PRIVATE ALL
SET HEADING OFF
SET TALK OFF
SET BELL OFF
SET STATUS OFF
SET SCOREBOARD OFF
SET SAFETY OFF
CLEAR ALL

* Initialization
USE CLIENT
SET ORDER TO list-num

DO WHILE .T.
   CLEAR
   mlist-num = SPACE(11)
   mlast = SPACE(18)
   mfirst = SPACE(20)
   mnum =SPACE(6)
   mst =SPACE(15)
   mcity =SPACE(20)
   mzip =SPACE(5)
   mprice = 0
   magt =SPACE(4)
   mlist-date = [  /  /  ]
   mcont-date = [  /  /  ]

   * Display screen
   @ 2,0 TO 18,79 DOUBLE
   @ 3,29 SAY "CLIENT ENTRY"
   @ 5,29 SAY "LIST #"
   @ 7,12 SAY "LAST"
   @ 7,38 SAY "FIRST"
   @ 9,19 SAY "NUMBER"
   @ 9,34 SAY "STREET"
   @ 11,20 SAY "CITY"
   @ 11,46 SAY "ZIP"
   @ 13,15 SAY "PRICE"
   @ 13,32 SAY "AGENT"
   @ 15,10 SAY "LIST DATE"
   @ 17,16 SAY "CONTRACT DATE"
```

```
* GET Listing Number
@ 5,36 GET mlist-num PICTURE "!!-99999-99"
READ

* Check for blank Listing Number
IF mlist-num = ' '
   CLEAR
   CLEAR ALL
   SET TALK ON
   SET HEADING ON
   SET STATUS ON
   SET SCOREBOARD ON
   SET SAFETY ON
   SET BELL ON
   RETURN
ENDIF mlist-num = ' '
```

Activate database and index
Initialize memory variables
Display form
Get listing number
If listing number is blank, exit

Figure 10.27 ADD_CLIE PROGRAM

(continued)

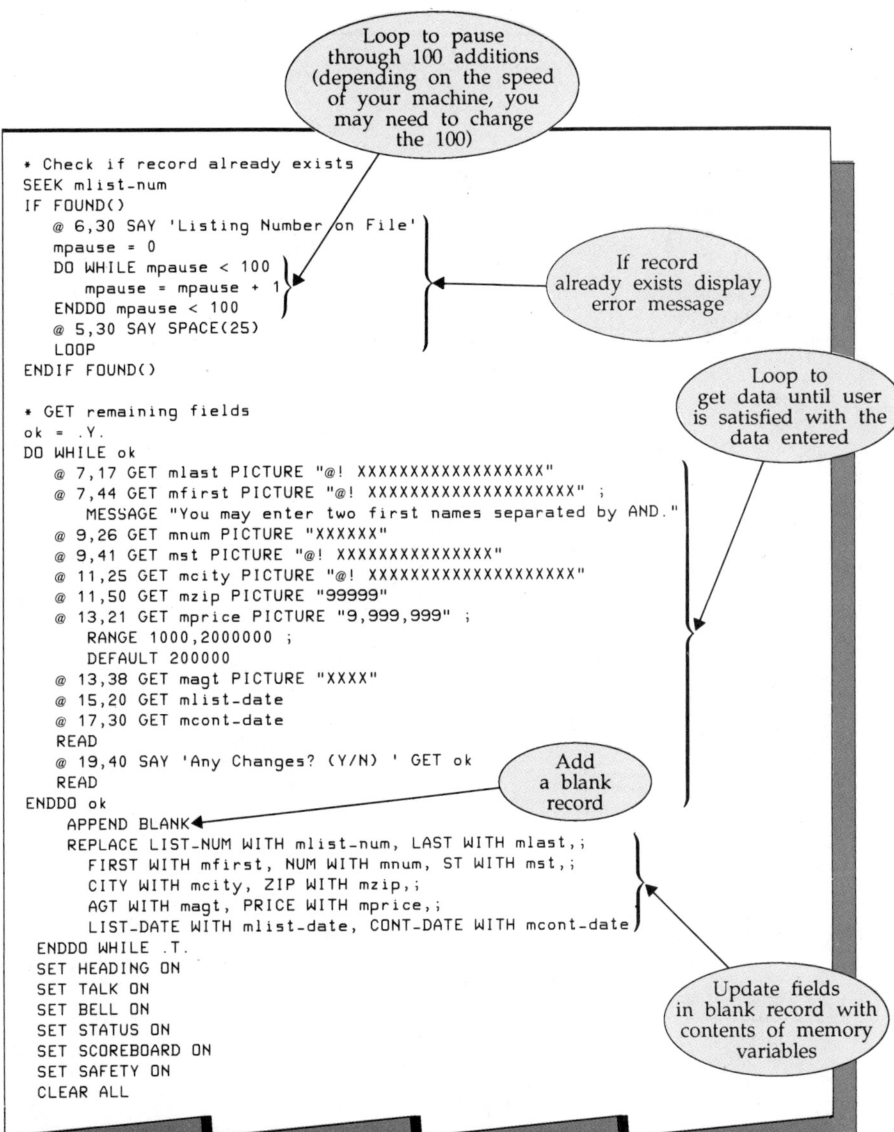
```
* Check if record already exists
SEEK mlist-num
IF FOUND()
   @ 6,30 SAY 'Listing Number on File'
   mpause = 0
   DO WHILE mpause < 100
      mpause = mpause + 1
   ENDDO mpause < 100
   @ 5,30 SAY SPACE(25)
   LOOP
ENDIF FOUND()

* GET remaining fields
ok = .Y.
DO WHILE ok
   @ 7,17 GET mlast PICTURE "@! XXXXXXXXXXXXXXXXXX"
   @ 7,44 GET mfirst PICTURE "@! XXXXXXXXXXXXXXXXXXXX" ;
      MESSAGE "You may enter two first names separated by AND."
   @ 9,26 GET mnum PICTURE "XXXXXX"
   @ 9,41 GET mst PICTURE "@! XXXXXXXXXXXXXXX"
   @ 11,25 GET mcity PICTURE "@! XXXXXXXXXXXXXXXXXXXX"
   @ 11,50 GET mzip PICTURE "99999"
   @ 13,21 GET mprice PICTURE "9,999,999" ;
      RANGE 1000,2000000 ;
      DEFAULT 200000
   @ 13,38 GET magt PICTURE "XXXX"
   @ 15,20 GET mlist-date
   @ 17,30 GET mcont-date
   READ
   @ 19,40 SAY 'Any Changes? (Y/N) ' GET ok
   READ
ENDDO ok
    APPEND BLANK
    REPLACE LIST-NUM WITH mlist-num, LAST WITH mlast,;
      FIRST WITH mfirst, NUM WITH mnum, ST WITH mst,;
      CITY WITH mcity, ZIP WITH mzip,;
      AGT WITH magt, PRICE WITH mprice,;
      LIST-DATE WITH mlist-date, CONT-DATE WITH mcont-date
 ENDDO WHILE .T.
 SET HEADING ON
 SET TALK ON
 SET BELL ON
 SET STATUS ON
 SET SCOREBOARD ON
 SET SAFETY ON
 CLEAR ALL
```
Loop to pause through 100 additions (depending on the speed of your machine, you may need to change the 100)
If record already exists display error message
Loop to get data until user is satisfied with the data entered
Add a blank record
Update fields in blank record with contents of memory variables

Figure 10.27 ADD_CLIE PROGRAM

The first section of the program establishes settings to provide a good working environment. The database is opened with an index for the listing number, which is a unique identifier. Eleven memory variables are initialized to match the database fields. This is done within a DO WHILE .T. to clear the fields at the beginning of each entry cycle. Title and prompt lines for each field are displayed on the screen with @..SAY commands framed by a double-line box. A GET with a PICTURE clause to match the expected form for the listing number is placed at the appropriate location. The READ stores the user's response in mlist_num.

The value stored in mlist_num must be carefully validated. The PICTURE clause ensures the proper form, which includes two letters and seven numbers separated by two hyphens. If the user simply presses Enter, the field is filled with blanks because of the initialization. An IF/ENDIF structure is used to avoid unusable blanks in the unique identifier. It provides a convenient exit from the module. In addition, there cannot be two records with the same listing number in the database. The fastest means for this validation is to use a SEEK command with the index and test to determine whether the record can be found. Success in this case is undesirable, so an error message is displayed. After a delay to give the user time to view the message, the LOOP command returns control back to the DO WHILE.

A nested DO WHILE is used to GET the remaining data fields, which are validated with PICTURE and RANGE clauses. The DO WHILE ok command allows the user to edit the data on the screen by responding with a Y when asked if he or she wishes to make "Any changes?" When the user eventually responds to this question with an N, the update will take place. The APPEND BLANK will add a new, totally blank record at the end of the file. The REPLACE command replaces the fields in this blank record with the contents of the appropriate memory variables. Notice that several variables were addressed with one REPLACE.

Circumstances may dictate a modification of the strategy in ADD_CLIE.PRG. For example, there may be no unique identifier. More stringent data validation may be required in some cases. However, the basis of this program is a good one to emulate. Studying examples and writing modules yourself are excellent ways to develop your ability to construct effective programs.

10.5 USING THE OUTPUT FROM THE SCREEN PAINTER

Once you have become comfortable with the basic structure of the ADD_CLIE program, you should be able to use it as a model to write add programs for other database files. The only portion of such a program that would require any significant work would be the @..SAY and @..GET commands. You can certainly type these commands into your program. Visualizing what the form would look like from simply looking at the numbers in the commands, however, can be difficult. In addition, entering the PICTURE clauses can also be tedious and prone to error. A solution is to first use the screen painter to create the form you want. You then use a special file created by the screen painter that contains the @..GET and SAY statements for that form.

To illustrate the process, let's use the CLIENT form we created earlier. The screen painter created two files for this form, CLIENT.SCR and CLIENT.FMT. The CLIENT.SCR file is used by dBASE for its own purposes. The CLIENT.FMT file, on the other hand, contains normal dBASE commands. This is the file that we will use.

The contents of the file are shown in Figure 10.28. This is actually a dBASE program. The only portion of this program that is useful to us is the portion containing the @..SAY and @..GET commands. Our first step is to delete all the other commands, producing the file shown in Figure 10.29 on page 266.

```
****************************************************************************
*-- Name....... CLIENT.FMT
*-- Date....... 5-21-92
*-- Version.... dBASE IV, Format 1.1
*-- Notes...... Format files use "" as delimiters!
****************************************************************************

*-- Format file initialization code -----------------------------------------

*-- Some of these PRIVATE variables are created based on CodeGen and may not
*-- be used by your particular .fmt file
PRIVATE lc-talk, lc-cursor, lc-display, lc-status, lc-carry, lc-proc,;
        ln-typeahd, gc-cut

IF SET("TALK") = "ON"
   SET TALK OFF
   lc-talk = "ON"
ELSE
   lc-talk = "OFF"
ENDIF
lc-cursor = SET("CURSOR")
SET CURSOR ON

lc-status = SET("STATUS")
*-- SET STATUS was ON when you went into the Forms Designer.
IF lc-status = "OFF"
   SET STATUS ON
ENDIF
```

Initialization code (not needed for our program)

```
*-- @ SAY GETS Processing. ------------------------------------------------------

*--  Format Page: 1
@ 2,0 TO 18,79 DOUBLE
@ 3,29 SAY "CLIENT ENTRY"
@ 5,29 SAY "LIST #"
@ 5,36 GET List-num PICTURE "!!-99999-99"
@ 7,12 SAY "LAST"
@ 7,17 GET Last PICTURE "@! XXXXXXXXXXXXXXXXX"
@ 7,38 SAY "FIRST"
@ 7,44 GET First PICTURE "@! XXXXXXXXXXXXXXXXXXXX" ;
   MESSAGE "You may enter two first names separated by AND."
@ 9,19 SAY "NUMBER"
@ 9,26 GET Num PICTURE "XXXXXX"
@ 9,34 SAY "STREET"
@ 9,41 GET St PICTURE "@! XXXXXXXXXXXXXXX"
@ 11,20 SAY "CITY"
@ 11,25 GET City PICTURE "@! XXXXXXXXXXXXXXXXXXXX"
@ 11,46 SAY "ZIP"
@ 11,50 GET Zip PICTURE "99999"
@ 13,15 SAY "PRICE"
@ 13,21 GET Price PICTURE "9,999,999" ;
   RANGE 1000,2000000
@ 13,32 SAY "AGENT"
@ 13,38 GET Agt PICTURE "XXXX"
@ 15,10 SAY "LIST DATE"
@ 15,20 GET List-date
@ 17,16 SAY "CONTRACT DATE"
@ 17,30 GET Cont-date
*-- Format file exit code -----------------------------------------------------

*-- SET STATUS was ON when you went into the Forms Designer
IF lc-status = "OFF"  && Entered form with status off
   SET STATUS OFF     && Turn STATUS "OFF" on the way out
ENDIF
SET CURSOR &lc-cursor.
SET TALK &lc-talk.

RELEASE lc-talk,lc-fields,lc-status
*-- EOP: CLIENT.FMT
```

@..SAYs and @..GETs

Exit code (not needed for our program)

Figure 10.28 FMT FILE PRODUCED BY SCREEN PAINTER

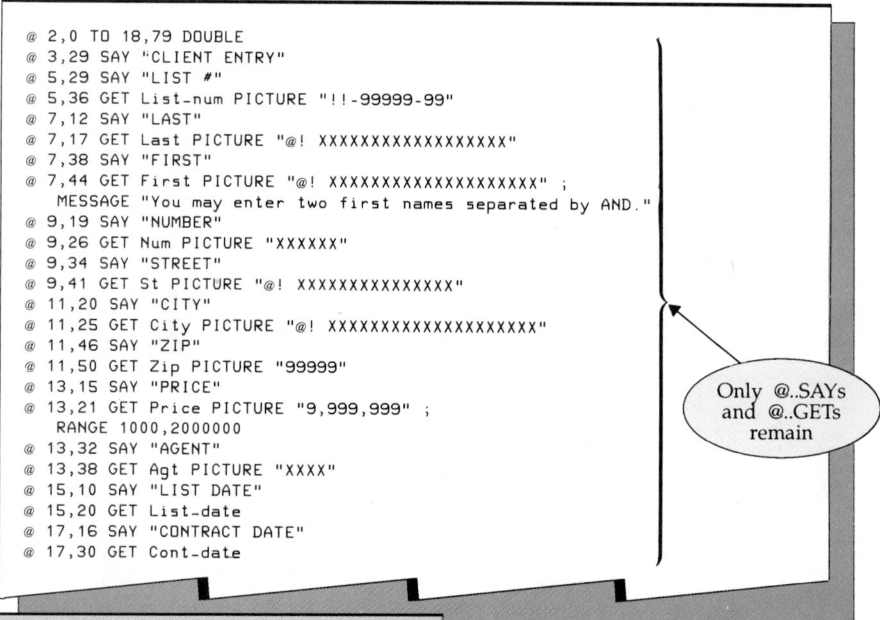

```
@ 2,0 TO 18,79 DOUBLE
@ 3,29 SAY "CLIENT ENTRY"
@ 5,29 SAY "LIST #"
@ 5,36 GET List-num PICTURE "!!-99999-99"
@ 7,12 SAY "LAST"
@ 7,17 GET Last PICTURE "@! XXXXXXXXXXXXXXXXXX"
@ 7,38 SAY "FIRST"
@ 7,44 GET First PICTURE "@! XXXXXXXXXXXXXXXXXXXX" ;
   MESSAGE "You may enter two first names separated by AND."
@ 9,19 SAY "NUMBER"
@ 9,26 GET Num PICTURE "XXXXXX"
@ 9,34 SAY "STREET"
@ 9,41 GET St PICTURE "@! XXXXXXXXXXXXXXX"
@ 11,20 SAY "CITY"
@ 11,25 GET City PICTURE "@! XXXXXXXXXXXXXXXXXXXX"
@ 11,46 SAY "ZIP"
@ 11,50 GET Zip PICTURE "99999"
@ 13,15 SAY "PRICE"
@ 13,21 GET Price PICTURE "9,999,999" ;
   RANGE 1000,2000000
@ 13,32 SAY "AGENT"
@ 13,38 GET Agt PICTURE "XXXX"
@ 15,10 SAY "LIST DATE"
@ 15,20 GET List-date
@ 17,16 SAY "CONTRACT DATE"
@ 17,30 GET Cont-date
```

Only @..SAYs
and @..GETs
remain

Figure 10.29 FMT FILE WITH EXTRA CODE REMOVED

In the style of program illustrated in the previous section, the @..SAY commands are separate from the @..GET commands. Our next step is to separate them (Figure 10.30). The simplest way to do this is to use a block copy to make two copies of the lines shown in this program. To copy a block of text, do the following:

1. Move the cursor to the beginning of the block and press F6 (Select).
2. Move the cursor to the end of the block and press Enter.
3. Move the cursor to the new location and press F8 (Copy).

(We use a similar procedure to move a block of text. The only difference is we press F7 rather than F8).

Once you have copied the block, delete all the @..GET statements from the first block of lines and all the @..SAY statements from the second block. When you delete an @..GET command that takes more than one line, be sure to delete all the lines that make up the command.

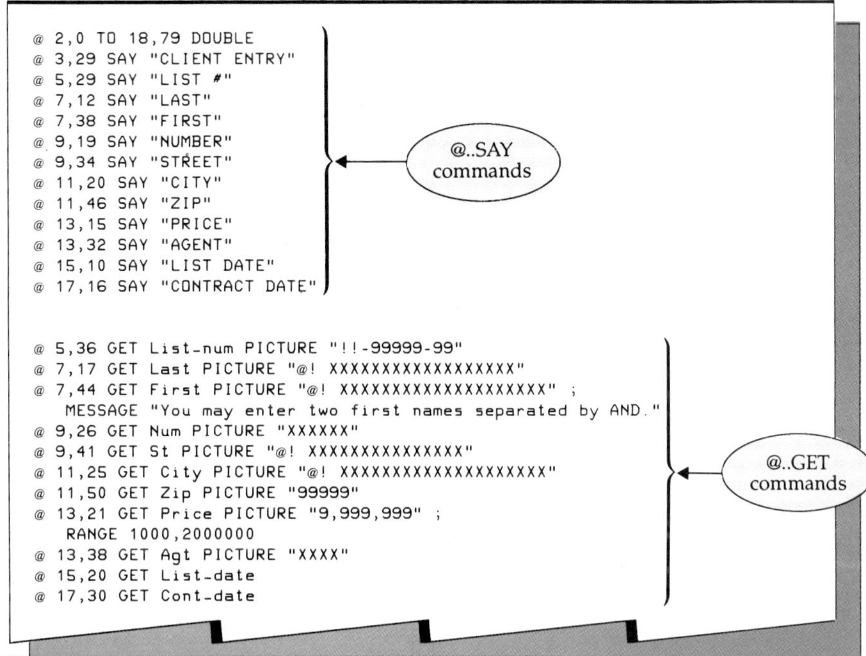

```
@ 2,0 TO 18,79 DOUBLE
@ 3,29 SAY "CLIENT ENTRY"
@ 5,29 SAY "LIST #"
@ 7,12 SAY "LAST"
@ 7,38 SAY "FIRST"
@ 9,19 SAY "NUMBER"
@ 9,34 SAY "STREET"
@ 11,20 SAY "CITY"
@ 11,46 SAY "ZIP"
@ 13,15 SAY "PRICE"
@ 13,32 SAY "AGENT"
@ 15,10 SAY "LIST DATE"
@ 17,16 SAY "CONTRACT DATE"

@ 5,36 GET List-num PICTURE "!!-99999-99"
@ 7,17 GET Last PICTURE "@! XXXXXXXXXXXXXXXXXX"
@ 7,44 GET First PICTURE "@! XXXXXXXXXXXXXXXXXXXX" ;
   MESSAGE "You may enter two first names separated by AND."
@ 9,26 GET Num PICTURE "XXXXXX"
@ 9,41 GET St PICTURE "@! XXXXXXXXXXXXXXX"
@ 11,25 GET City PICTURE "@! XXXXXXXXXXXXXXXXXXXX"
@ 11,50 GET Zip PICTURE "99999"
@ 13,21 GET Price PICTURE "9,999,999" ;
   RANGE 1000,2000000
@ 13,38 GET Agt PICTURE "XXXX"
@ 15,20 GET List-date
@ 17,30 GET Cont-date
```


Figure 10.30 FMT FILE WITH @..SAYS AND @..GETS SEPARATED

Finally, we use memory variables rather than database fields in the @..GET commands, so you need to replace the field names with the names of corresponding memory variables. The simplest way to do this is to just precede each field name with the letter "m" (Figure 10.31 on the next page). (If you have a field name that is ten characters long, adding an m would create a name with eleven characters. This is too long for the name of a memory variable, so you will need to make some kind of modification to the name. Usually our field names are less than ten characters long, however, so this is typically not a problem.)

Once we have modified this FMT file, we can incorporate it into our program. If you are using MODIFY COMMAND, for example, to edit your program, you would use the "Read/write text file" option to read the contents of the FMT file. You could then move portions of this file to the appropriate locations by selecting them (F6) and then moving them (F7). If you compare the ADD_CLIE program shown in Figure 10.27 with the commands shown in Figure 10.31, you can see where these lines will be positioned.

```
@ 2,0 TO 18,79 DOUBLE
@ 3,29 SAY "CLIENT ENTRY"
@ 5,29 SAY "LIST #"
@ 7,12 SAY "LAST"
@ 7,38 SAY "FIRST"
@ 9,19 SAY "NUMBER"
@ 9,34 SAY "STREET"
@ 11,20 SAY "CITY"
@ 11,46 SAY "ZIP"
@ 13,15 SAY "PRICE"
@ 13,32 SAY "AGENT"
@ 15,10 SAY "LIST DATE"
@ 17,16 SAY "CONTRACT DATE"


@ 5,36 GET mlist-num PICTURE "!!-99999-99"
@ 7,17 GET mlast PICTURE "@! XXXXXXXXXXXXXXXXXX"
@ 7,44 GET mfirst PICTURE "@! XXXXXXXXXXXXXXXXXXXX" ;
   MESSAGE "You may enter two first names separated by AND."
@ 9,26 GET mnum PICTURE "XXXXXX"
@ 9,41 GET mst PICTURE "@! XXXXXXXXXXXXXXX"
@ 11,25 GET mcity PICTURE "@! XXXXXXXXXXXXXXXXXXXX"
@ 11,50 GET mzip PICTURE "99999"
@ 13,21 GET mprice PICTURE "9,999,999" ;
   RANGE 1000,2000000
@ 13,38 GET magt PICTURE "XXXX"
@ 15,20 GET mlist-date
@ 17,30 GET mcont-date
```

Field names replaced by memory variables

Figure 10.31 FMT FILE WITH MEMORY VARIABLES

If you need to modify the form at some point in the future, you will usually find it simplest just to modify the appropriate commands within ADD_CLIE rather than using the screen painter. You should be aware that if you modify the form with the screen painter, the process will create a *new* FMT file. dBASE will then destroy the contents of the current one.

CHAPTER SUMMARY

1. Custom screens can be produced by plotting the specific locations of titles, prompts, data entry blocks, lines, and boxes on a grid of coordinates. Literals, variables, and field names are displayed by @..SAY commands in any desired arrangement, using tabbing, ROW(), and COL(). Areas can be cleared, and single or double lines and boxes can be drawn with the CLEAR and @ commands. Large blocks of text can be displayed with TEXT/ENDTEXT. The @..GET command displays an enhanced block to accept input data to variables or field names with the READ statement.
2. The screen painter is a menu-driven feature that produces an FMT file containing @..SAY and @..GET commands that may be edited and used in a PRG file. It enables you to add, delete, and move fields, titles, and boxes on a work screen easily.
3. The validation of user-entered data is critical to data integrity. The initialization of variables by means of PICTURE and RANGE clauses and programming checks is used for this purpose. The PICTURE clause is an option of GET, which uses templates consisting of functions and symbols to restrict the user's response to acceptable characters. The RANGE option permits only values that fall between two limits in a numeric or date field.
4. An effective strategy for an APPEND module is to accept data to initialized variables through a custom screen, validate the data, and use APPEND BLANK to write the record when the user is finished editing. Nested DO WHILE and IF/ENDIF structures are required as well as an indexed search using SEEK to check for blank or duplicate records.
5. One way to create the @..SAY and @..GET commands for an update program is to use the screen painter to design the form and then edit the FMT file it produces.

KEY TERMS

relative addressing
screen painter
template symbols
full-screen editing
template functions
picture functions

COMMAND SUMMARY

Command Name	**Use**
@..SAY	Display data at a screen location.
@..GET	Input data at a screen location.
SET SCOREBOARD OFF	Suppress scoreboard display.
SET STATUS OFF	Turns off the status line.
ROW()	Return the row position.
COL()	Return the column position.
SPACE()	Display a number of spaces.
DOUBLE	Draw a double line or box.
CLEAR	Clear entire screen.
CLEAR TO	Remove a line or box.
TEXT	Display a block of text.
ENDTEXT	End of TEXT/ENDTEXT structure.
CREATE SCREEN	Use the screen painter to create a screen.
MODIFY SCREEN	Use the screen painter to modify a screen.
SCR	An internal file used by CREATE SCREEN.
FMT	A file containing @..SAY and GET commands.
SET FORMAT TO	Activate a custom form.
PICTURE	Control data input with GET.
RANGE	Set limits for numeric data input with GET.

SELF-CHECK QUESTIONS

1. Why are custom-designed screens preferable to those provided with dBASE IV?
2. What does the APPEND BLANK command do?
3. What are some important considerations to bear in mind when designing screens?
4. Why is @..SAY/GET more desirable than other input commands for custom screens?
5. How can you clear one row of a screen display?
6. What does TEXT/ENDTEXT do?
7. What is the end product of the proper use of the screen painter?
8. What does the READ command do?
9. Why is it advantageous to use memory variables as opposed to field names in custom screens?
10. Name three potential uses for a PICTURE clause.
11. What does a RANGE clause do?
12. What is the importance of data validation?
13. How are date-type fields initialized?

TRY IT YOURSELF

1. Working from the dot prompt, STORE your name and address to variables, CLEAR the screen, and place the data with titles at any preselected location on the screen.
2. Do Exercise 1 again, using variable tab settings as coordinates and storing a title to a variable before displaying it.
3. Produce a facsimile of an organization chart, using literals, boxes, and lines. Use TEXT/ENDTEXT for the description. Erase the top box and its contents.
4. Write a module that uses GETs to input the data in Exercise 1. Test the results with ? from the dot prompt.
5. Use the screen painter to design an input screen for the CITIES database. Include a box and titles. Test the screen by using the EDIT command.
6. Modify the FMT file in Exercise 5 to include PICTURE clauses on all fields. Convert the field names to memory variables, and specify RANGEs for the populations in order to reject values that are less than 50,000 or greater than 10,000,000.

Write program modules to accept data to memory variables on custom screens using the following parameters:

7. Accept a yearly income of at least $10,000 but no more than $50,000 at row 12, column 25. Include an appropriate prompt.
8. Accept an account balance of any amount at row 10, column 40. Display the balance at row 15, column 40 with CR or DB after positive or negative amounts. Place a single-line box around the result. Precede the result in the box with the message, "Current balance is:".
9. Prompt the user to input a part number at row 16, column 20 in the format, 2-9742138-1. The dashes must automatically appear and only digits should be accepted. Display the number at row 20, column 20.
10. Place a double-line box from row 3, column 10 to row 5, column 50. Accept a price of less than $1,000 and display with an appropriate label.

PROGRAMMING PROJECTS

1. Write a program to append records, using the CITIES database file. Exit the procedure if a blank is placed in the CITY field.
2. This programming project uses the following database file:

```
Structure for database: A:\CUSTOMER.DBF
Number of data records:       10
Date of last update   : 05/14/92
Field  Field Name  Type       Width    Dec     Index
    1  CUSTNUMB    Numeric        3                Y
    2  LAST        Character     10                N
    3  FIRST       Character      8                N
    4  ADDRESS     Character     20                N
    5  BALANCE     Numeric        7      2         N
    6  CREDLIM     Numeric        4                N
    7  SLSRNUMB    Numeric        2                N
** Total **                      55

 CUSTNUMB LAST       FIRST   ADDRESS                BALANCE CREDLIM SLSRNUMB
      124 Adams      Sally   481 Oak,Lansing,MI      418.75     500        3
      256 Samuels    Ann     215 Pete,Grant,MI        10.75     800        6
      311 Charles    Don     48 College,Ira,MI       200.10     300       12
      315 Daniels    Tom     914 Cherry,Kent,MI      320.75     300        6
      405 Williams   Al      519 Watson,Grant,MI     201.75     800       12
      412 Adams      Sally   16 Elm,Lansing,MI       908.75    1000        3
      522 Nelson     Mary    108 Pine,Ada,MI          49.50     800       12
      567 Baker      Joe     808 Ridge,Harper,MI     201.20     300        6
      587 Roberts    Judy    512 Pine,Ada,MI          57.75     500        6
      622 Martin     Dan     419 Chip,Grant,MI       575.50     500        3
```

Write a program that is similar to ADD_CLIE to update the CUSTOMER database file, using a custom screen. In particular, your program should do the following:

- Terminate when the user enters a customer number of zero.
- If the user enters a customer number that matches that of an existing customer, the program should print an error message and force the user to reenter the customer number.
- Make sure the balance is between 0 and 2000. Use 500 as a default value for CREDLIM. When the cursor is in the SLSRNUMB field, the message "Enter the number of a valid sales rep" should appear on the screen.
- Test the program by updating several records and then LISTing from the dot prompt.

LEARNING OBJECTIVES

To organize a system and its data.

To manipulate files with SELECT and ALIAS.

To chain multiple files using SET RELATION TO.

To write a program to display records.

11 System Design Using Multiple Files

Introduction

When applications are developed in mainframe installations, the work is traditionally shared by system analysts and programmers. The system analysts study needs and requirements, and develop specifications for the proposed system. The programmers then write the code to produce the final product. In a microcomputer environment, all these tasks are often performed by one person. You will need more tools than you have already acquired if you are to work with complicated sets of data. This chapter presents some advanced methods and commands that should help you design a system that uses more than one database.

11.1 SYSTEM PLANNING

NEED FOR PLANNING

The previous chapters have prepared you to approach business problems with a set of tools for managing, retrieving, and reporting data. All of the examples in these chapters have involved a single database, which is often sufficient to meet a user's needs. However, the complexity of the data and the tasks to be performed often requires the use of more than one database. This chapter presents ways to plan systems effectively for more complicated business problems.

Obviously, a system *should* be planned, but it is surprising how often a dBASE IV system grows "organically," without plans. This is the result when problems are addressed as they come up. This short-term planning is directed only toward solving one immediate crisis after another. The end result of such haphazard development is that the system is eventually unable to perform necessary functions and is impossible to use because it contains so many errors.

Besides the inevitable downfall of a haphazard design, there are other reasons to plan a database system. Planning uncovers opportunities to use the features and power of dBASE IV. It directs programming toward accurate modeling, which helps achieve the objective or purpose of the program and meet the needs of the user. Moreover, planning often uncovers error-generating or inefficient procedures before they are implemented.

USING I-P-O CHARTS

One tool that is useful for system planning is the *I-P-O chart*. The acronym stands for input, processing, and output. Input consists of all the stored-data fields, but it might also include data input by the user for calculations. Processing is the functions and procedures to be performed on the data. Finally, output is any reports or query screens. The advantage of this approach is that you can get a concise image of the essential parts of the system. Each area can be expanded in further detail as necessary. The I-P-O chart is an implementation of top-down design. For example, the processing section can become the basis for the pseudocode, and the output section can evolve into screen or report designs. Table 11.1 is an I-P-O chart for a proposed system to track employee training activity.

TABLE 11.1 **I-P-O chart to track employee training**

INPUT	PROCESSING	OUTPUT
Org. Code	Add Records	Display Record
Emp. #	Modify Records	Print Yearly Report
Emp. Name	Delete Records	Print Rosters
Supervisor	Calculate Attendance	
Mail Stop	Calculate Frequency Using Course Date	
Job Code		
Job Title		
Date of Hire		
Course		
Course Date		

DETERMINING DATA FIELDS AND RECORDS

The goal of planning is to develop a system in which data is easy to maintain and access. The key to achieving the goal is the data itself. You need to examine data in terms of its interrelationships in order to make certain that it is limited to essential dependencies. This may involve assigning data fields to multiple database files according to their function. Fortunately, established methods are available to achieve integrity of purpose among the data fields.

The processing and output aspects of the system have been examined in previous chapters. They are both dependent on the *data dictionary,* meaning a listing of the system's characteristics and the complete set of all data used by the system. The data dictionary that is included in the system will eventually contain the field names in whatever databases are established. Attempt at first to identify as many data items as possible; they can be organized and reduced later if necessary. Eventually you will maintain or include only the data that is needed to satisfy user needs.

Often, you will be gathering the data items from an existing manual system. Specify each field's type and length to prepare to establish the structure of the databases. Then examine the fields to determine the relationships that may exist.

Before establishing a field, be sure that it is unique in the set. Two fields should not contain the same information under different names. For example, including the fields NAME and EMP_NAME would be redundant.

Although dBASE IV does not allow duplicate field names, you should also avoid names that are too similar, for example, NUMBER_PH and NUMBER_PO. In this case, the names PHONE and PURCH_ORD might be better.

Another common problem is handling mutually exclusive fields. This term was used to describe the options of a menu in Chapter 7. When mutually exclusive fields occur among data, they should be handled by one category field. Since it is impossible to be both a full-time and a part-time student, for instance, placing an F or a P in one field called STATUS is preferable to maintaining two logical fields named PART_TIME and FULL_TIME.

It is often better to calculate a field than to store it. Dates frequently provide a good example of this. You might store the first date of registration for a student and subtract it from the system date (the current date stored in the computer) in order to yield the number of days the student has been enrolled. This is more efficient than attempting to maintain a second date field in the database for this purpose. (Chapter 12 will explain how to calculate dates.) Table 11.2 lists the steps to be taken in the initial phase of system design.

TABLE 11.2 Initial system design

1. Design the input from the manual system.
2. Place the data elements in a data dictionary.
3. Design the output with paper and pencil.
4. Define the functions that are to be performed.
5. Design the files so as to avoid redundancy.
6. Revise as needed.

NORMALIZATION

Structured data design uses *normalization* to lower the incidence of redundancy in the database. The benefits of normalization include clarity, optimum grouping, and reduced need for future maintenance. E. F. Codd is responsible for the mathematical basis for normalization, which he proposed in the early 1970s. The five forms of normalization, referred to as the first through fifth normal forms, form a progression. A relation (record) in first normal form is better than one that is not in first normal form. A relation in second normal form is better yet, and so on. By working through the normal forms, we gradually eliminate redundancy. In practice, we rarely use the fourth and fifth forms, so we will really be concerned only with first, second, and third normal forms.

PRIMARY KEYS

In order to understand the normal forms, you have to be familiar with the concept of a key. The *key* (technically the *primary key*) is the field or combination of fields used to uniquely identify a record. For example, a Social Security number is a unique identifier for an individual's name, city, and other data.

FIRST NORMAL FORM

Consider the example shown in Table 11.3. (The dots in many of the entries simply indicate that only a portion of the entry is shown in the table to conserve space.) The notation at the top of the table is a convenient shorthand for describing the structure of a record. The shorthand in this table describes a record called EMP. The entries inside the parentheses are the fields of EMP. The primary key is underlined. The key is a combination of an organization code and an employee number. The organization code refers to the department in which the employee works. (You might be wondering why the key is not just the employee number. In this company, the same employee number can be used in more than one department. Thus, both the organization code and the employee number are required).

TABLE 11.3 **Unnormalized record (contains repeating group)**

```
EMP (ORG_CODE, EMP_NO, EMP_NAME, SUPERVISOR, MAIL,
     JOB_CODE, JOB_TITLE, HIRE_DATE, COURSE, CRSE_DATE)
```

EMP

ORG_ CODE	EMP_ NO	EMP_NAME	SUPERVISOR	MAIL	JOB_ CODE	JOB_TITLE	HIRE_ DATE	COURSE	CRSE_ DATE
0544	28573	ZUCCO...	POLLARD...	92-33	11	Manage...	05/10/72		
0365	84771	LINTN,..	MILLER,...	77-11	45	Secret...	01/15/83	T198	04/09/91
								T184	03/11/91
0194	10447	PISCI...	ROGERS,...	03-55	19	Micro ...	10/13/77	T198	01/30/91
0365	64995	DEVER...	MILLER,...	77-11	28	Progra...	08/23/79	T201	03/04/91
								T184	03/14/91
0544	83551	ALLEN...	POLLARD...	92-33	73	Data E...	08/06/83	T201	05/10/91
								T184	02/02/91
0354	20266	ANN, ...	PARRISH...	83-44	62	Execut...	12/27/75	T198	04/11/91
0365	20266	BRONI...	MILLER,...	77-11	19	Micro ...	07/08/90		

The bar above COURSE and CRSE_DATE indicates that this combination is what is termed a *repeating group* or *repeating field*. Consider, for example, the sample data shown in the table for the employee whose ORG_CODE is 0365 and whose EMP_NO is 84771. Look at the COURSE and CRSE_DATE fields. You will see two entries in each field. This indicates that this employee has taken two courses. Repeating fields pose severe problems.

How many entries do we allow in these repeating fields? If we allow room for five entries, for example, what about the records that only have one or two? On these records there is wasted space. What do we do when we encounter the first record that would require six entries? No matter what number we choose we will have problems. Another major problem is that many database management systems, including dBASE IV, do not have any way of supporting repeating fields within records.

This leads to the definition of first normal form. A record is in *first normal form* if it does not contain repeating fields. As far as the shorthand is concerned, converting to first normal form is easy; we simply remove the repeating field symbol (see Table 11.4). The effect of doing this is that the first eight fields would have to be included every time the employee completed a training course. This would be a highly redundant data situation. Fortunately, we will fix this problem when we convert to second normal form.

The primary key has changed in Table 11.4. If you examine the sample data, you'll see that the combination of ORG_CODE and EMP_NO no longer is sufficient to uniquely identify a record. We also need the COURSE. Thus, the key is now the combination of ORG_CODE, EMP_NO, and COURSE.

SECOND NORMAL FORM

Although the key for the record shown in Table 11.4 has three parts, not every field in the record requires all three. The supervisor's name and the mail stop, for example, really only depend on ORG_CODE. Likewise, the employee's name, job code, job title, and hire data only depend on ORG_CODE and EMP_NO. The dependency of a field on only a portion of the key is called a *partial dependency*.

We can now define second normal form. A record is in *second normal form* if it is in first normal form and if it does not contain any partial dependencies. To convert to second normal form, we split the record into two or more records. In the process, we place each field with the minimum key on which it depends.

TABLE 11.4 **First normal form (no repeating groups)**

```
EMP (ORG_CODE, EMP_NO, EMP_NAME, SUPERVISOR, MAIL,
    JOB_CODE, JOB_TITLE, HIRE_DATE, COURSE, CRSE_DATE)
```

EMP

ORG_ CODE	EMP_ NO	EMP_NAME	SUPERVISOR	MAIL	JOB_ CODE	JOB_TITLE	HIRE_ DATE	COURSE	CRSE_ DATE
0365	84771	LINTN...	MILLER,...	77-11	45	Secret...	01/15/83	T198	04/09/91
0365	84771	LINTN...	MILLER,...	77-11	45	Secret...	01/15/83	T184	03/11/91
0194	10447	PISCI...	ROGERS,...	03-55	19	Micro ...	10/13/77	T198	01/30/91
0365	64995	DEVER...	MILLER,...	77-11	28	Progra...	08/23/79	T201	03/04/91
0365	64995	DEVER...	MILLER,...	77-11	28	Progra...	08/23/79	T184	03/14/91
0544	83551	ALLEN...	POLLARD...	92-33	73	Data E...	08/06/83	T201	05/10/91
0544	83551	ALLEN...	POLLARD...	92-33	73	Data E...	08/06/83	T184	02/02/91
0354	20266	ANN, ...	PARRISH...	83-44	62	Execut...	12/27/75	T198	04/11/91

This has been done in Table 11.5 on the next page. Since SUPERVISOR and MAIL only depend on ORG_CODE, they are placed in the record that has ORG_CODE as the primary key. Since EMP_NAME, JOB_CODE, JOB_TITLE, and HIRE_DATE depend on the combination of ORG_CODE and EMP_NO, they are placed in the record with this combination as the primary key. Finally, since CRSE_DATE depends on all three, it is placed in the record that has ORG_CODE, EMP_NO, and COURSE as the primary key. Notice how this approach has eliminated the redundancy we discussed earlier.

TABLE 11.5 Second normal form (no partial dependencies)

EMP (ORG_CODE, EMP_NO, EMP_NAME, JOB_CODE, JOB_TITLE, HIRE_DATE)

EMP

ORG_ CODE	EMP_ NO	EMP_NAME	JOB_ CODE	JOB_TITLE	HIRE_ DATE
0544	28573	ZUCCO, DANIEL	11	Manager	05/10/72
0365	84771	LINTNER, NANCY	45	Secretary	01/15/83
0194	10447	PISCIONERI, ANTHONY	19	Micro Support Spec	10/13/77
0365	64995	DEVERE, LENORE	28	Programmer/Analyst	08/23/79
0544	83551	ALLEN, MARY ANN	73	Data Entry/Reception	08/06/83
0354	20266	ANN, JENNA	62	Executive	12/27/75
0365	20266	BRONITSKY, CARL	19	Micro Support Spec	07/08/90

ORG (ORG_CODE, SUPERVISOR, MAIL)

ORG

ORG_ CODE	SUPERVISOR	MAIL
0194	ROGERS, ART	03-55
0354	PARRISH, DON	83-44
0365	MILLER, PAM	77-11
0544	POLLARD, DON	92-33

COURSE (ORG_CODE, EMP_NO, COURSE, CRSE_DATE)

COURSE

ORG_ CODE	EMP_ NO	COURSE	CRSE_ DATE
0365	84771	T198	04/09/91
0365	84771	T184	03/11/91
0544	83551	T201	05/10/91
0544	83551	T184	02/02/91
0354	20266	T198	04/11/91
0194	10447	T198	01/30/91
0194	10477	T201	06/23/91
0365	64995	T201	03/04/91
0365	64995	T184	03/14/91

THIRD NORMAL FORM

Sometimes fields in a record are redundant but not because of their relationship with the primary key. In this case, a field is dependent on a nonkey field. This situation is called a *transitive dependency*. An example is the job title in the EMP record, which is directly related to the job code, a nonkey field.

A record is in *third normal form* if it is in second normal form and if it does not contain any transitive dependencies. To convert to third normal form, we move the transitive dependency to a separate record (see Table 11.6). Notice that we have removed JOB_TITLE title from the EMP record, but we have left JOB_CODE. By doing so, we can use JOB_CODE to retrieve JOB_TITLE whenever we need it.

TABLE 11.6 **Third normal form (no transitive dependencies)**

```
EMP (ORG_CODE, EMP_NO, EMP_NAME, JOB_CODE, HIRE_DATE)
```

EMP

ORG_ CODE	EMP_ NO	EMP_NAME	JOB_ CODE	HIRE_ DATE
0544	28573	ZUCCO, DANIEL	11	05/10/72
0365	84771	LINTNER, NANCY	45	01/15/83
0194	10447	PISCIONERI, ANTHONY	19	10/13/77
0365	64995	DEVERE, LENORE	28	08/23/79
0544	83551	ALLEN, MARY ANN	73	08/06/83
0354	20266	ANN, JENNA	62	12/27/75
0365	20266	BRONITSKY, CARL	19	07/08/90

```
JOB (JOB_CODE, JOB_TITLE)
```

JOB

JOB_ CODE	JOB_TITLE
19	Micro Support Spec
11	Manager
45	Secretary
28	Programmer/Analyst
73	Data Entry/Reception
62	Executive

Table 11.7 summarizes the results of the normalization process for this example. Table 11.8 explains the requirements of the three normal forms.

TABLE 11.7 **Summary of the results of normalization**

```
EMP (ORG_CODE, EMP_NO, EMP_NAME, SUPERVISOR, MAIL,
    JOB_CODE, JOB_TITLE, HIRE_DATE, COURSE, CRSE_DATE)
```

is replaced by

```
EMP (ORG_CODE, EMP_NO, EMP_NAME, JOB_CODE, HIRE_DATE)

ORG (ORG_CODE, SUPERVISOR, MAIL)

COURSE (ORG_CODE, EMP_NO, COURSE, CRSE_DATE)

JOB (JOB_CODE, JOB_TITLE)
```

TABLE 11.8 **Normal form requirements**

NORMAL FORM	REQUIREMENT (DEFINITION)
First	Has no repeating fields
Second	In first normal form and has no partial dependencies
Third	In second normal form and has no transitive dependencies

DATA ANALYSIS

Larger systems require a careful analysis of the data dictionary to remove repeating fields, partial dependencies, and transitive dependencies. Each time such elements are removed, they are moved to another file. Obviously, this produces several databases that must work together to provide the user with the necessary data. The benefits of multiple files are considerable. To have virtually no redundancy dramatically reduces storage requirements. (However, the key fields will still be redundant among the databases.) Data entry and maintenance, and their associated errors, are kept to a minimum. Also, we can make major changes much more easily than in a single database. In the example in Table 11.9 (the final collection of files), only one record has to be updated in order to change a job title for all employees. In the previous structures, every employee bearing a given title would require a record modification.

TABLE 11.9 **Third normal form collection of records**

EMP

ORG_ CODE	EMP_ NO	EMP_NAME	JOB_ CODE	HIRE_ DATE
0544	28573	ZUCCO, DANIEL	11	05/10/72
0365	84771	LINTNER, NANCY	45	01/15/83
0194	10447	PISCIONERI, ANTHONY	19	10/13/77
0365	64995	DEVERE, LENORE	28	08/23/79
0544	83551	ALLEN, MARY ANN	73	08/06/83
0354	20266	ANN, JENNA	62	12/27/75
0365	20266	BRONITSKY, CARL	19	07/08/90

COURSE

ORG_ CODE	EMP_ NO	COURSE	CRSE_ DATE
0365	84771	T198	04/09/91
0365	84771	T184	03/11/91
0544	83551	T201	05/10/91
0544	83551	T184	02/02/91
0354	20266	T198	04/11/91
0194	10447	T198	01/30/91
0194	10477	T201	06/23/91
0365	64995	T201	03/04/91
0365	64995	T184	03/14/91

ORG

ORG_ CODE	SUPERVISOR	MAIL
0194	ROGERS, ART	03-55
0354	PARRISH, DON	83-44
0365	MILLER, PAM	77-11
0544	POLLARD, DON	92-33

JOB

JOB_ CODE	JOB_TITLE
19	Micro Support Spec
11	Manager
45	Secretary
28	Programmer/Analyst
73	Data Entry/Reception
62	Executive

Table 11.10 on the next page gives some tips for analyzing data.

TABLE 11.10 Procedure for analyzing data

1. Identify the fields.
2. Identify how each field will be used for access, interactive query, reports, or archiving.
3. Identify the keys (unique identifiers).
4. Identify the relationships among the fields and files (indexes, common fields in each database).
5. Arrange the data in third normal form.

11.2 SELECT, ALIAS, AND MULTIPLE FILES

The process of normalization usually results in two or more separate database files. You need to know the commands and programming strategies used with multiple files to perform such basic functions as appending or reporting in these situations.

USING AREAS

With dBASE IV, you can assign each database file to a separate *work area.* Ten work areas are available and it is possible to access database files in separate areas simultaneously. The areas can be referred to by number (1 through 10), letter (A through J), or by the database file that is currently active in the area. At any given point in time, only one area is considered active. We use the SELECT command to activate an area. The command is simply SELECT followed by the area to activate. (See Figure 11.1.)

After these commands have been issued, the data in any database can be accessed through the appropriate work area. This is accomplished by using the work area name with a hyphen (-) and a greater than sign (>) to form an "arrow" as a prefix to a field name. For example, A->EMP_NAME identifies the field EMP_NAME of the database file active in area A. The major benefit is that all field names in all SELECTed work areas can be referenced for display simply by including the prefix.

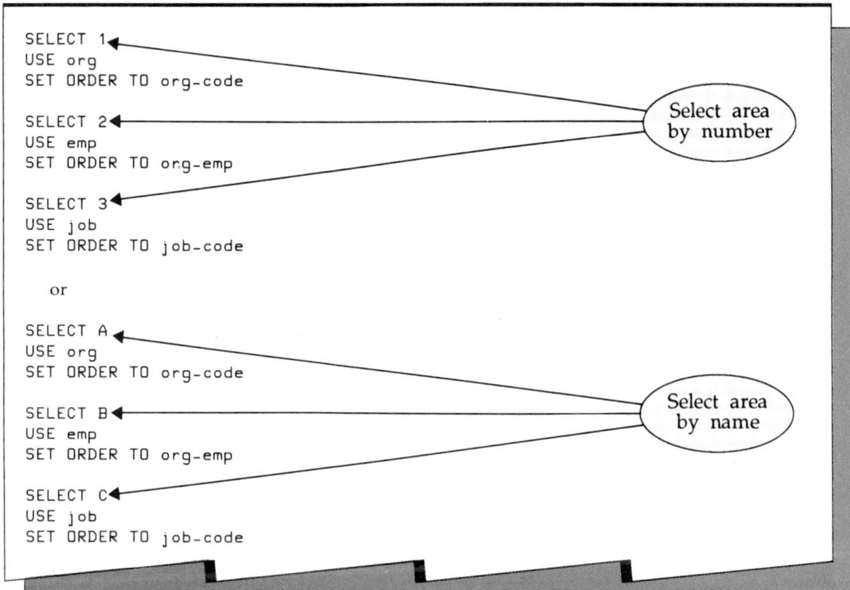

Figure 11.1 USING THE SELECT STATEMENT

USING AN ALIAS

We can also identify a field by the name of the database file, for example EMP->EMP_NAME. As a convenience, you can also use an alias (Figure 11.2). By indicating an alias (alternative database filename) in the USE statement, we can then use the alias to identify fields, for example EMPLOYEE->EMP_NAME. If we have used an alias, however, we can no longer use the database filename; that is, EMP->EMP_NAME would no longer be valid. An ALIAS command may make it more evident what database is being used. (The program example at the end of this chapter uses both conventions for comparison.) Figure 11.3 on the next page shows how you can use aliases and field names in a program.

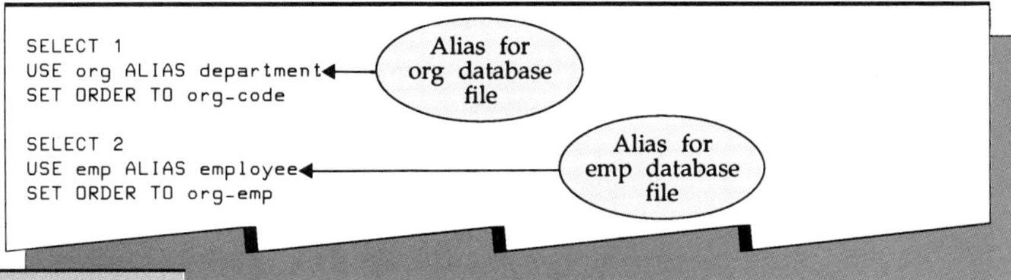

Figure 11.2 USING ALIAS

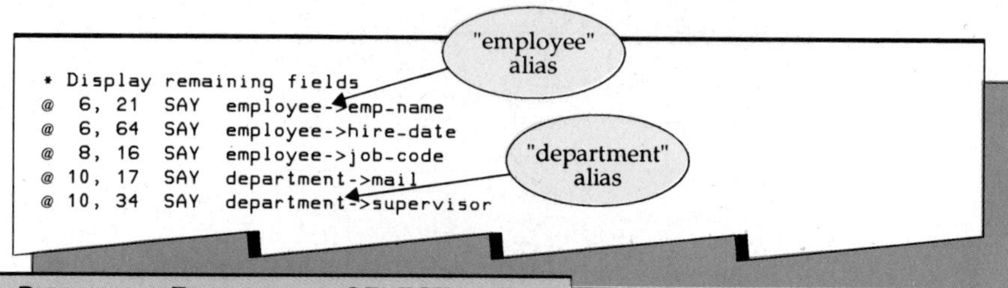

"employee" alias
* Display remaining fields
@ 6, 21 SAY employee->emp-name
@ 6, 64 SAY employee->hire-date
@ 8, 16 SAY employee->job-code
@ 10, 17 SAY department->mail
@ 10, 34 SAY department->supervisor
Seek will use org_code from employee to find matching department
"department" alias

Figure 11.3 DISPLAYING FIELDS FROM SELECTED FILES

USING SELECT STATEMENTS

Figure 11.4 demonstrates that when any operation other than displaying the data must be performed using a certain file without an alias or prefix, you must include a SELECT statement first to activate the area containing the database file. Here the SELECT statement activates the area containing the ORG database file (which has the alias department). The SEEK command will then apply to this area and this file.

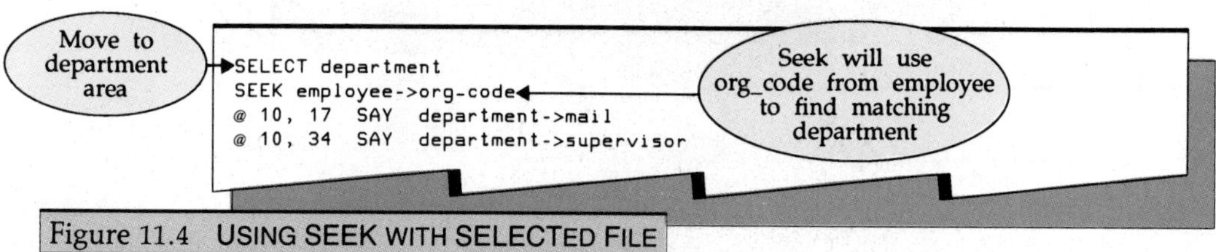

Figure 11.4 USING SEEK WITH SELECTED FILE

11.3 CHAINING FILES WITH SET RELATION TO

The SET RELATION TO command is used to link database files on a common field. It can be a convenient replacement for the SEEK command in a programming strategy with related database files. Both methods perform well, but SET RELATION TO greatly simplifies the code in our program.

Figure 11.5 shows the way SET RELATION TO is used. Both of the database files to be related must be active. The area containing the main database file must be the active area. The other database file must have an index active on the matching field.

We will process the main database file. Every time we access a record in the main database file, dBASE will automatically locate the *single* matching records in the other database file. (**Note:** Since dBASE will only locate a single record in the other database file, this technique is only appropriate if each record in the main file is only related to a single record in the other database file.)

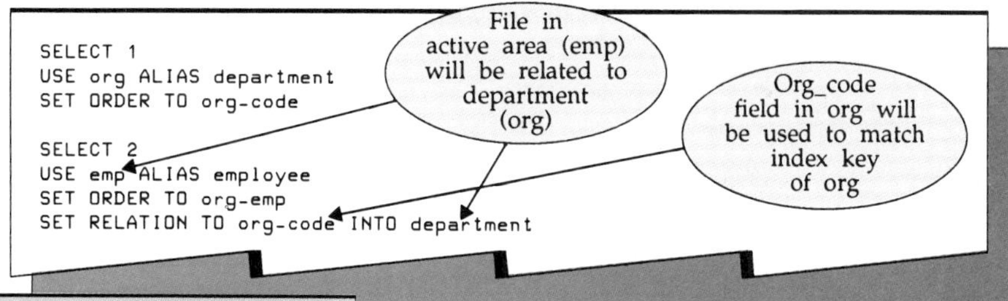
SELECT 1
USE org ALIAS department
SET ORDER TO org-code
SELECT 2
USE emp ALIAS employee
SET ORDER TO org-emp
SET RELATION TO org-code INTO department
File in active area (emp) will be related to department (org)
Org_code field in org will be used to match index key of org

Figure 11.5 USING SET RELATION TO

To see how it works, consider the two database files shown in Figure 11.6, the EMP file and the ORG file. Since each record in EMP is related to a single record in ORG, SET RELATION TO is appropriate. In this example, if record 1 (employee Daniel Zucco) is the current active record in EMP, dBASE knows that the related record in ORG is record 4 (department 0544, supervisor Don Pollard) since the ORG_CODEs match (see the arrows in Figure 11.6). dBASE will allow you to use not only fields in the EMP file but also any fields in the ORG file. Thus, if you list the supervisor for Daniel Zucco, you will get Don Pollard, since it is the name on the related record in the ORG file.

EMP

ORG_ CODE	EMP_ NO	EMP_NAME	JOB_ CODE	HIRE_ DATE
0544	28573	ZUCCO, DANIEL	11	05/10/72
0365	84771	LINTNER, NANCY	45	01/15/83
0194	10447	PISCIONERI, ANTHONY	19	10/13/77
0365	64995	DEVERE, LENORE	28	08/23/79
0544	83551	ALLEN, MARY ANN	73	08/06/83
0354	20266	ANN, JENNA	62	12/27/75
0365	20266	BRONITSKY, CARL	19	07/08/90

ORG

ORG_ CODE	SUPERVISOR	MAIL
0194	ROGERS, ART	03-55
0354	PARRISH, DON	83-44
0365	MILLER, PAM	77-11
0544	POLLARD, DON	92-33

Matching values for ORG_ CODE

Figure 11.6 RELATION BETWEEN EMP AND ORG

Suppose you make record 2 (employee Nancy Lintner) of the EMP file the current active record (Figure 11.7). Then the corresponding record in the ORG file is record 3 (department 0365, supervisor Pam Miller). If you list the supervisor for this employee, you will get Pam Miller. If you list the mail stop for the employee's department, you will get 77-11.

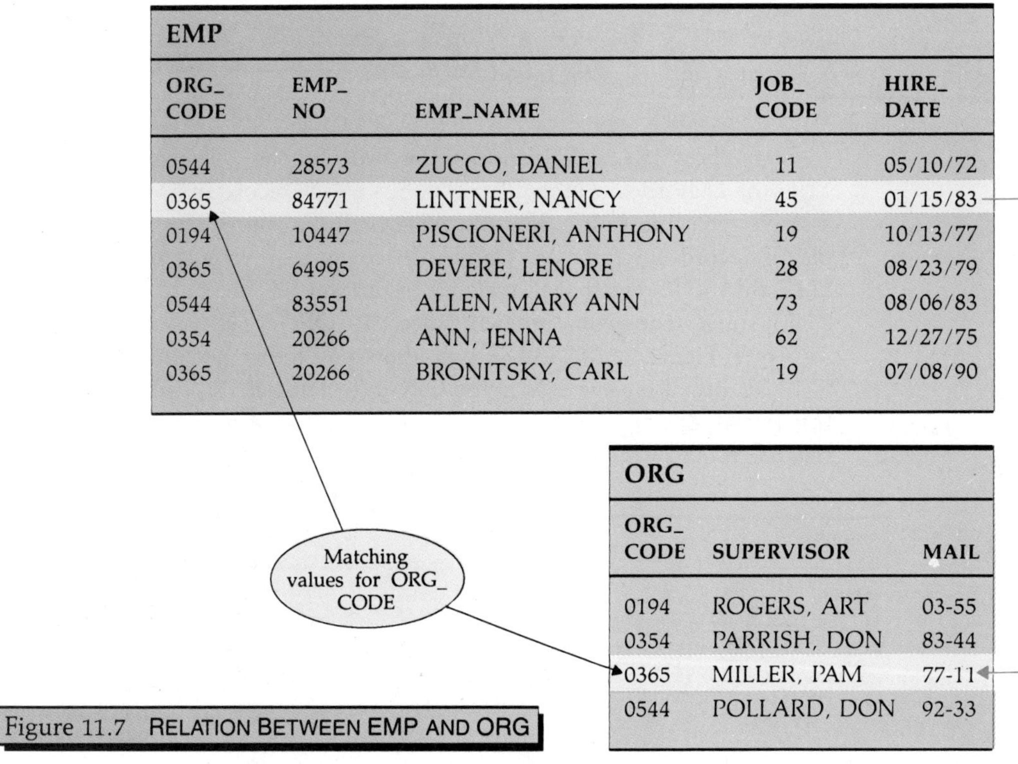

EMP

ORG_ CODE	EMP_ NO	EMP_NAME	JOB_ CODE	HIRE_ DATE
0544	28573	ZUCCO, DANIEL	11	05/10/72
0365	84771	LINTNER, NANCY	45	01/15/83
0194	10447	PISCIONERI, ANTHONY	19	10/13/77
0365	64995	DEVERE, LENORE	28	08/23/79
0544	83551	ALLEN, MARY ANN	73	08/06/83
0354	20266	ANN, JENNA	62	12/27/75
0365	20266	BRONITSKY, CARL	19	07/08/90

ORG

ORG_ CODE	SUPERVISOR	MAIL
0194	ROGERS, ART	03-55
0354	PARRISH, DON	83-44
0365	MILLER, PAM	77-11
0544	POLLARD, DON	92-33

Figure 11.7 RELATION BETWEEN EMP AND ORG

When you use SET RELATION TO, you don't have to be aware of these details. They will be handled for you automatically by dBASE. The following are some of the crucial points to bear in mind when using SET RELATION TO.

1. Each record in the main database file must be related to a single record in the other database file.
2. The other database file must have an index active on the field that is used for the relationship.

3. The area containing the main database file must be the currently selected area when the SET RELATION TO command is executed.
4. We only need to process the main database file. Records in the other file are located automatically.

The first part of Figure 11.8 shows the code we would need to use to find details about a matching department in the event we were not using SET RELATION TO. The second part of the figure shows the corresponding code in the event we are using SET RELATION TO. Notice that we do not need the SELECT or SEEK commands.

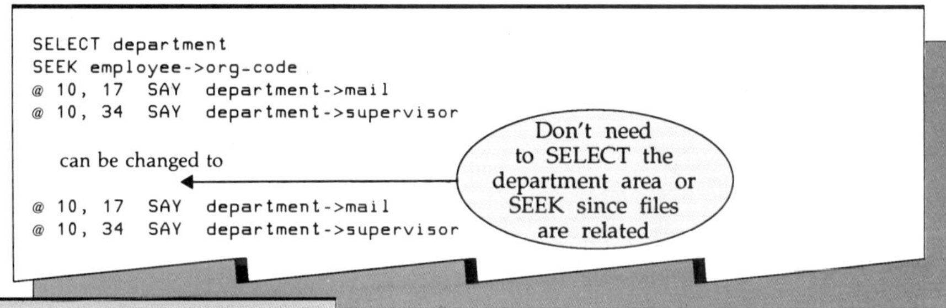

SELECT department
SEEK employee->org-code
@ 10, 17 SAY department->mail
@ 10, 34 SAY department->supervisor
can be changed to
@ 10, 17 SAY department->mail
@ 10, 34 SAY department->supervisor
Don't need to SELECT the department area or SEEK since files are related

Figure 11.8 USING SET RELATION TO

We can use more than one relation in a SET RELATION TO command. In this way we can relate multiple database files. Each relation must follow the rules outlined above. In the next section we will encounter an example that uses two relations in a SET RELATION TO command.

11.4 WRITING A PROGRAM TO DISPLAY RECORDS

The rapid retrieval and display of data is an essential function of a system. Users expect accurate and informative responses to their inquiries. The program that is presented in this section is an example of how you can plan carefully to achieve effective results.

The four databases that resulted from the normalization in Section 11.1 are shown in Figures 11.9 through 11.12 on the following pages. The figures also include the sample data that is on your data disk in these files. The purpose of the program is to retrieve all the relevant data about an employee. The data is based on the organization code and employee number, which the user supplies. Clearly, this involves working with all the databases simultaneously.

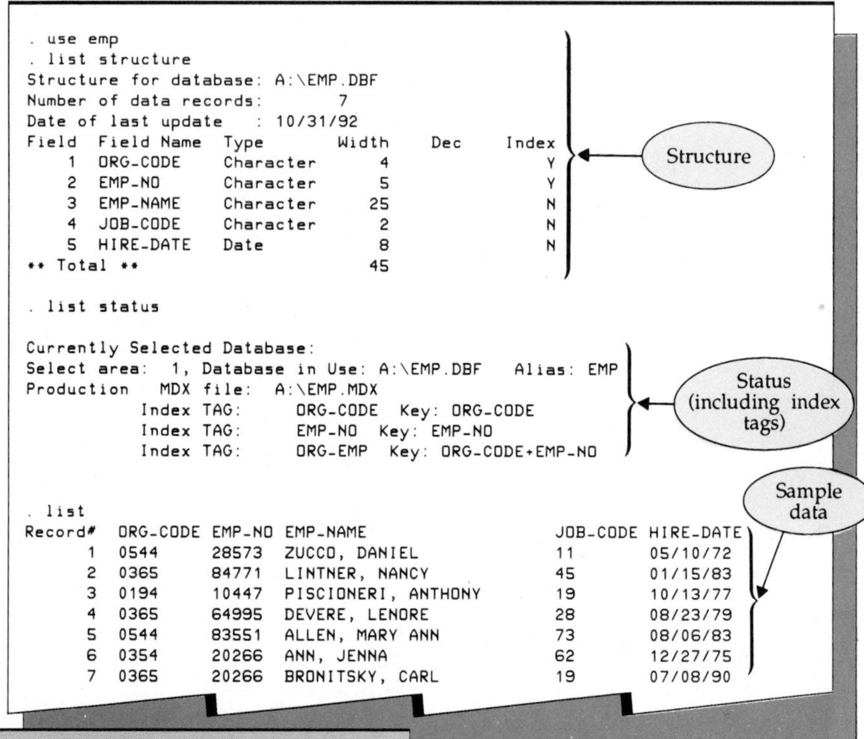

```
. use emp
. list structure
Structure for database: A:\EMP.DBF
Number of data records:        7
Date of last update   : 10/31/92
Field  Field Name  Type       Width    Dec    Index
    1  ORG-CODE    Character      4               Y
    2  EMP-NO      Character      5               Y
    3  EMP-NAME    Character     25               N
    4  JOB-CODE    Character      2               N
    5  HIRE-DATE   Date           8               N
** Total **                      45

. list status

Currently Selected Database:
Select area:  1, Database in Use: A:\EMP.DBF    Alias: EMP
Production   MDX file:  A:\EMP.MDX
           Index TAG:     ORG-CODE  Key: ORG-CODE
           Index TAG:     EMP-NO  Key: EMP-NO
           Index TAG:     ORG-EMP   Key: ORG-CODE+EMP-NO


. list
Record#  ORG-CODE EMP-NO EMP-NAME                   JOB-CODE HIRE-DATE
      1  0544     28573  ZUCCO, DANIEL              11        05/10/72
      2  0365     84771  LINTNER, NANCY             45        01/15/83
      3  0194     10447  PISCIONERI, ANTHONY        19        10/13/77
      4  0365     64995  DEVERE, LENORE             28        08/23/79
      5  0544     83551  ALLEN, MARY ANN            73        08/06/83
      6  0354     20266  ANN, JENNA                 62        12/27/75
      7  0365     20266  BRONITSKY, CARL            19        07/08/90
```


Figure 11.9 STRUCTURE AND DATA FOR EMP.DBF

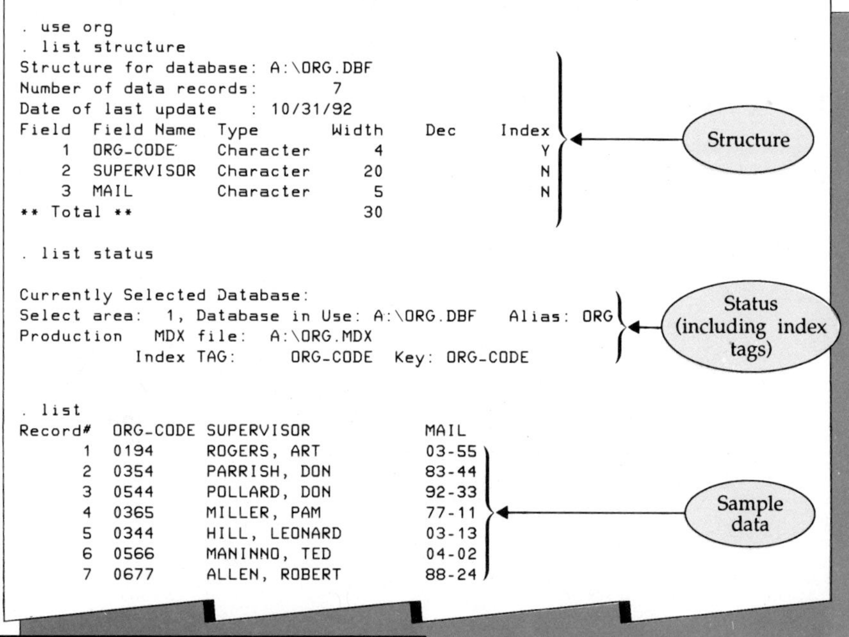

```
. use org
. list structure
Structure for database: A:\ORG.DBF
Number of data records:        7
Date of last update   : 10/31/92
Field  Field Name  Type       Width    Dec    Index
    1  ORG-CODE    Character      4               Y
    2  SUPERVISOR  Character     20               N
    3  MAIL        Character      5               N
** Total **                      30

. list status

Currently Selected Database:
Select area:  1, Database in Use: A:\ORG.DBF    Alias: ORG
Production   MDX file:  A:\ORG.MDX
           Index TAG:     ORG-CODE  Key: ORG-CODE

. list
Record#  ORG-CODE SUPERVISOR          MAIL
      1  0194     ROGERS, ART         03-55
      2  0354     PARRISH, DON        83-44
      3  0544     POLLARD, DON        92-33
      4  0365     MILLER, PAM         77-11
      5  0344     HILL, LEONARD       03-13
      6  0566     MANINNO, TED        04-02
      7  0677     ALLEN, ROBERT       88-24
```


Figure 11.10 STRUCTURE AND DATA FOR ORG.DBF

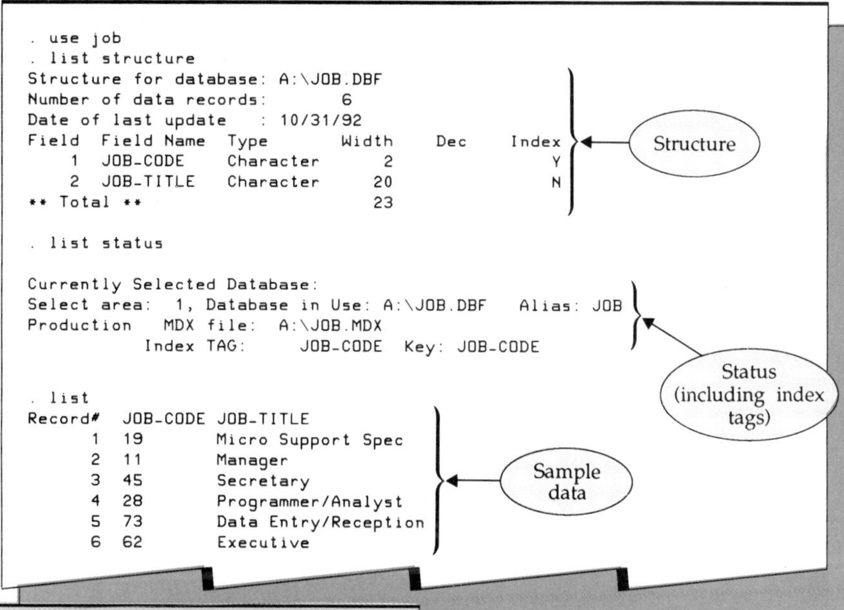

```
. use job
. list structure
Structure for database: A:\JOB.DBF
Number of data records:       6
Date of last update   : 10/31/92
Field  Field Name  Type       Width    Dec    Index
    1  JOB-CODE    Character      2               Y
    2  JOB-TITLE   Character     20               N
** Total **                      23

. list status

Currently Selected Database:
Select area:  1, Database in Use: A:\JOB.DBF    Alias: JOB
Production   MDX file:  A:\JOB.MDX
          Index TAG:     JOB-CODE  Key: JOB-CODE


. list
Record#  JOB-CODE JOB-TITLE
      1  19       Micro Support Spec
      2  11       Manager
      3  45       Secretary
      4  28       Programmer/Analyst
      5  73       Data Entry/Reception
      6  62       Executive
```


Figure 11.11 STRUCTURE AND DATA FOR JOB.DBF

```
. use course
. list structure
Structure for database: A:\COURSE.DBF
Number of data records:       9
Date of last update   : 10/31/92
Field  Field Name  Type       Width    Dec    Index
    1  ORG-CODE    Character      4               Y
    2  EMP-NO      Character      5               Y
    3  COURSE      Character      4               N
    4  CRSE-DATE   Date           8               N
** Total **                      22

. list status

Currently Selected Database:
Select area:  1, Database in Use: A:\COURSE.DBF   Alias: COURSE
Production   MDX file:  A:\COURSE.MDX
           Index TAG:     ORG-CODE  Key: ORG-CODE
           Index TAG:     EMP-NO  Key: EMP-NO
           Index TAG:     ORG-EMP  Key: ORG-CODE+EMP-NO


. list
Record#  ORG-CODE EMP-NO COURSE CRSE-DATE
      1  0365     84771  T198   04/09/91
      2  0365     84771  T184   03/11/91
      3  0544     83551  T201   05/10/91
      4  0544     83551  T184   02/02/91
      5  0354     20266  T198   04/11/91
      6  0194     10447  T198   01/30/91
      7  0194     10477  T201   06/23/91
      8  0365     64995  T201   03/04/91
      9  0365     64995  T184   03/14/91
```

Status (including index tags)

Structure

Sample data

Figure 11.12 STRUCTURE AND DATA FOR COURSE.DBF

Examine the pseudocode in Figure 11.13. In terms of the structure, there is a nested DO WHILE loop to deal with the access of the course data. Several nested IF/ENDIFs are also required for error checking and for responding to user requests.

```
Pseudocode for EMP_DISP.PRG

Open files and set relations
Do while the user does not want to exit
        Get a key from user
        If key is blank - exit
        Find matching record in Employee file
        If key is not found - try again
        Use key to access Organization file
        Use key to access Job Code file
        Display employee data
        Use key to access Course Transaction File
        Do while key matches
                Retrieve transactions
                Display course data
                Adjust screen rows
        End of transaction routine
End of the user does not want to exit routine
Close files
```

Figure 11.13 PSEUDOCODE FOR EMP_LIST.PRG

When you run this program (EMP_DSP1), you will first see the screen shown in Figure 11.14. You now need to enter an organization code and an employee number. Once you have done so, the remaining data for this employee will be displayed (Figure 11.15). Notice that this employee has taken two different courses.

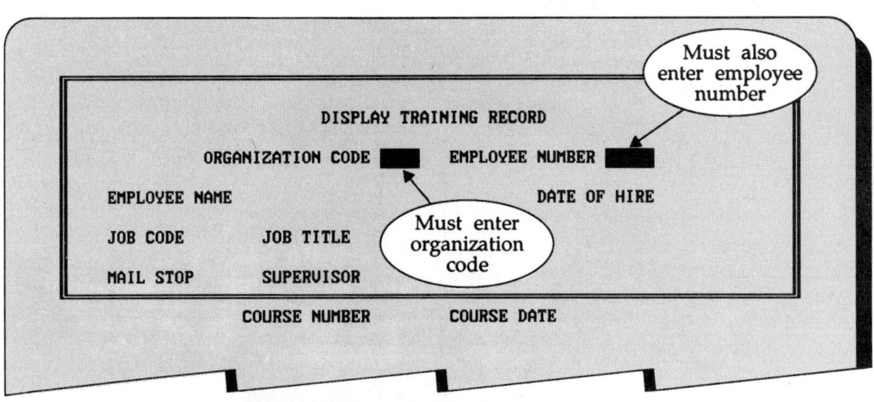

Figure 11.14 DISPLAYING EMPLOYEE RECORDS—INITIAL SCREEN

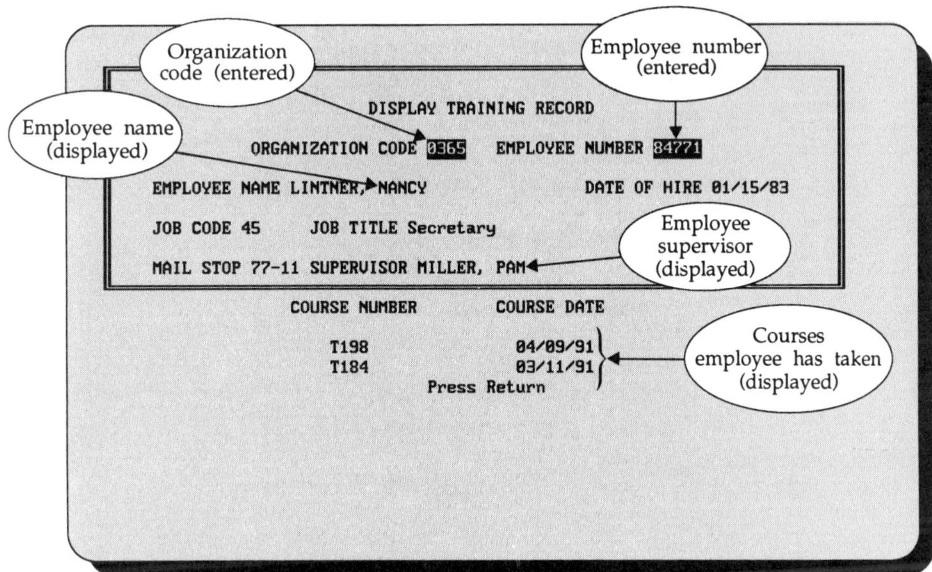

Figure 11.15 DISPLAYING DATA FOR ONE EMPLOYEE

The EMP_DSP1.PRG file in Figure 11.16 on the following pages begins typically by setting an environment and initializing some variables that will be used to accept the user's request. Each of the four databases is assigned to a work area with a SELECT statement. The ORG file, indexed on ORG_CODE, is placed in work area 1 using the alias DEPARTMENT. Work area 2 contains the EMP.DBF file indexed on ORG_EMP (the combination of ORG_CODE and EMP_NO). It's alias is EMPLOYEE. The SET RELATION TO command establishes a relationship with the ORG.DBF file. The JOB database and its index on JOBCODE occupy work area 3, and the COURSE database and its index are in work area 4. Neither has an alias.

The DO WHILE .T. loop permits as many inquiries as the user desires. The user can exit the routine by entering blanks in both the organization code and the employee number. The routine begins by making the area containing EMPLOYEE the active area. A custom screen displays all the titles and GET blocks to accept the user's request. After the READ command executes, storing the values found in the GET blocks to the variables, the two variables are concatenated into memkey for the sake of convenience. A SEEK is issued against the index in the employee area. If no such record exists, the IF/ENDIF structure that follows gives the user another chance by LOOPing back to the DO WHILE .T..

```
* EMP-DSP1.PRG -  Display records from course databases.

* Set Environment
PRIVATE ALL
SET HEADING OFF
SET TALK OFF
SET BELL OFF
SET STATUS OFF
SET SCOREBOARD OFF
SET SAFETY OFF
CLEAR ALL

* Initialization

SELECT 1
USE org ALIAS department
SET ORDER TO org-code

SELECT 2
USE emp ALIAS employee
SET ORDER TO org-emp
SET RELATION TO org-code INTO department

SELECT 3
USE job
SET ORDER TO job-code

SELECT 4
USE course
SET ORDER TO org-emp

* Processing Loop
DO WHILE .T.
```

```
SELECT employee
morgcode = '     '
mempno = '     '
* GET Org. Code and Emp. # and display screen
@  2, 29  SAY "DISPLAY TRAINING RECORD"
@  4, 17  SAY "ORGANIZATION CODE"
@  4, 35  GET  morg-code
@  4, 42  SAY "EMPLOYEE NUMBER"
@  4, 58  GET  memp-no
@  6,  7  SAY "EMPLOYEE NAME"
@  6, 51  SAY "DATE OF HIRE"
@  8,  7  SAY "JOB CODE"
@  8, 23  SAY "JOB TITLE"
@ 10,  7  SAY "MAIL STOP        SUPERVISOR"
@ 12, 21  SAY "COURSE NUMBER          COURSE DATE"
@  0,  2  TO 11, 77    DOUBLE
READ
* Check for blank Org. Code or Emp. #
IF morg-code = '     ' .OR. memp-no = '     '
   CLEAR
   CLEAR ALL
   SET HEADING ON
   SET TALK ON
   SET BELL ON
   SET STATUS ON
   SET SCOREBOARD ON
   SET SAFETY ON
   RETURN
ENDIF morg-code
```

Make employee area the active area

Exit if either org_code or emp_no is blank

Figure 11.16 LISTING FOR EMP_DSP1.PRG

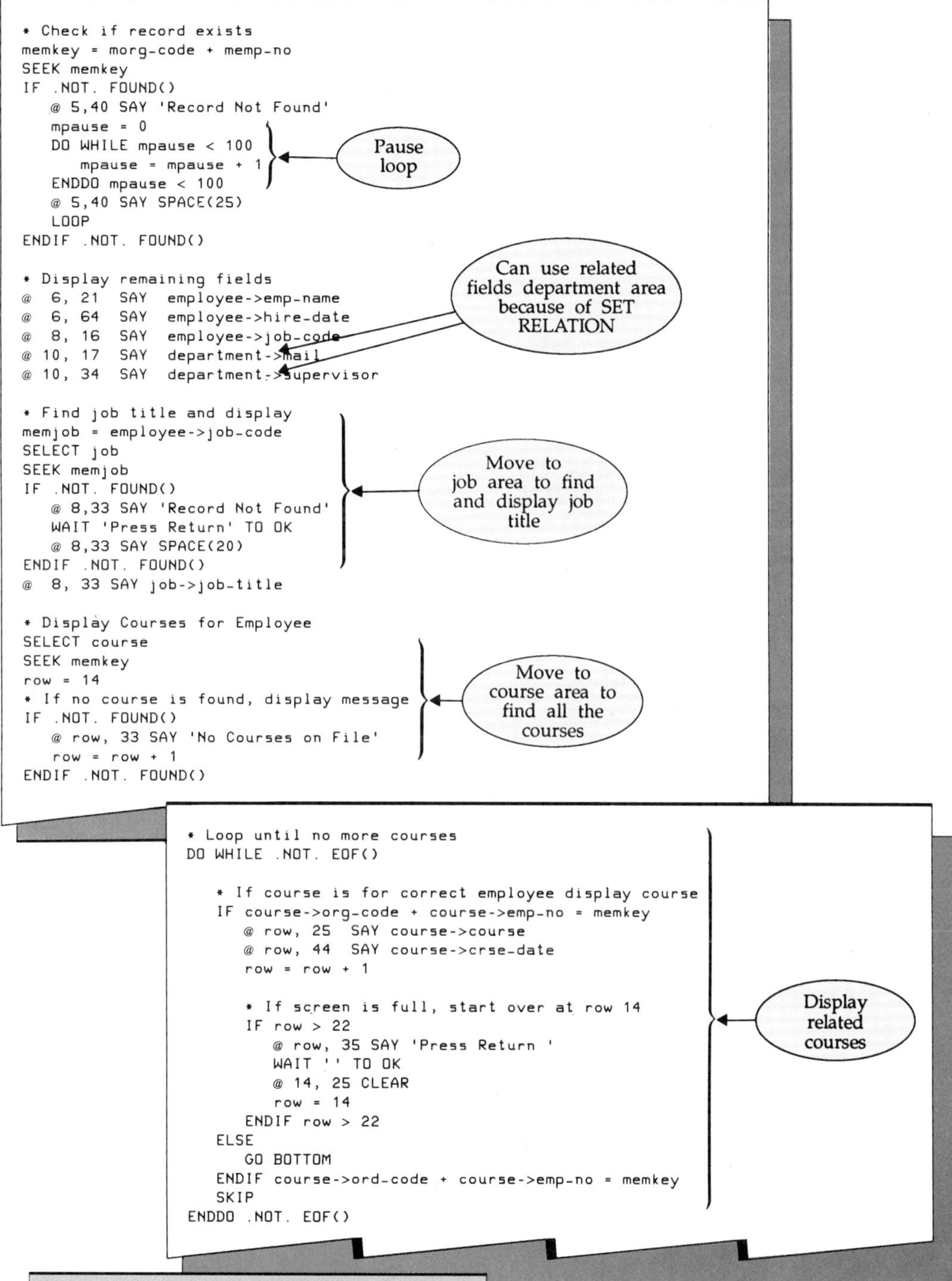

Pause loop
Can use related fields department area because of SET RELATION
Move to job area to find and display job title
Move to course area to find all the courses
Display related courses

```
* Check if record exists
memkey = morg-code + memp-no
SEEK memkey
IF .NOT. FOUND()
   @ 5,40 SAY 'Record Not Found'
   mpause = 0
   DO WHILE mpause < 100
      mpause = mpause + 1
   ENDDO mpause < 100
   @ 5,40 SAY SPACE(25)
   LOOP
ENDIF .NOT. FOUND()

* Display remaining fields
@  6, 21  SAY  employee->emp-name
@  6, 64  SAY  employee->hire-date
@  8, 16  SAY  employee->job-code
@ 10, 17  SAY  department->mail
@ 10, 34  SAY  department->supervisor

* Find job title and display
memjob = employee->job-code
SELECT job
SEEK memjob
IF .NOT. FOUND()
   @ 8,33 SAY 'Record Not Found'
   WAIT 'Press Return' TO OK
   @ 8,33 SAY SPACE(20)
ENDIF .NOT. FOUND()
@  8, 33 SAY job->job-title

* Display Courses for Employee
SELECT course
SEEK memkey
row = 14
* If no course is found, display message
IF .NOT. FOUND()
   @ row, 33 SAY 'No Courses on File'
   row = row + 1
ENDIF .NOT. FOUND()
```

```
* Loop until no more courses
DO WHILE .NOT. EOF()

   * If course is for correct employee display course
   IF course->org-code + course->emp-no = memkey
      @ row, 25  SAY course->course
      @ row, 44  SAY course->crse-date
      row = row + 1

      * If screen is full, start over at row 14
      IF row > 22
         @ row, 35 SAY 'Press Return '
         WAIT '' TO OK
         @ 14, 25 CLEAR
         row = 14
      ENDIF row > 22
   ELSE
      GO BOTTOM
   ENDIF course->ord-code + course->emp-no = memkey
   SKIP
ENDDO .NOT. EOF()
```

Figure 11.16 LISTING FOR EMP_DSP1.PRG

(continued)

```
   @ row, 35 SAY 'Press Return'
   WAIT ''
   CLEAR
ENDDO WHILE .T.

CLEAR ALL
CLEAR
SET HEADING ON
SET TALK ON
SET BELL ON
SET STATUS ON
SET SCOREBOARD ON
SET SAFETY ON
RETURN
```

Figure 11.16 LISTING FOR EMP_DSP1.PRG

When a valid record is found, @..SAYs using the ALIAS prefixes display the data from both the EMP database and the ORG database. (No special action for the ORG database file is required since we related the files with SET RELATION TO.) Next, the value in JOBCODE is stored in memjob; the JOB work area is SELECTed; and a SEEK locates the appropriate record. This search was necessary because no relation was set. Should the EMPLOYEE->JOB_CODE field contain an error, the screen simply prints an error message and the program continues.

The next section of the program begins by selecting the area containing the COURSE database file. The SEEK memkey statement deserves some special mention. The index for COURSE was created on the combination of ORG_CODE, EMP_NO, and COURSE. The variable memkey, on the other hand, contains only an ORG_CODE and an EMP_NO. The SEEK will find the first record in COURSE matching this combination (assuming one exists, of course). That is, it will find the first course for the employee identified by the ORG_CODE and EMP_NO just entered by the user. The program addresses the possibility that the employee has not had any courses.

Assuming the employee has had courses, the DO WHILE .NOT. EOF() accesses the remaining records. An IF/ENDIF is nested in the DO WHILE loop to display any consequent valid records, that is, records with the correct ORG_CODE and EMP_NO. Once the ORG_CODE and EMP_NO no longer match the correct employee, the ELSE portion of the IF advances the record pointer to the last record in the file (GO BOTTOM). The SKIP will then make EOF() true and the loop will terminate.

Since the top portion of the screen contains the previously displayed data, the course data must be scrolled underneath, between rows 14 and 22 if needed. This is accomplished by using the variable row in the SAY and incrementing it each time a new record must be displayed. Should the list of courses approach the bottom of the screen, an IF/ENDIF pauses, resets the row counter, and CLEARs the bottom half of the screen when the user presses a key. When a record that does not satisfy the matching condition or the end-of-file condition is eventually encountered, the entire screen clears. The user then has another opportunity to display an employee record.

The EMP_DSP2.PRG program shown in Figure 11.17 on the following pages is almost identical to the EMP_DSP1.PRG program we just examined, with two differences. First, after the USE for the EMP database file, there is a SET RELATION TO that contains *two* relations. The second relation relates EMP to the JOB database file. (This also requires that the USE for JOB be moved before the USE for EMP so that the JOB database file is active when the SET RELATION TO command is executed.)

The other difference concerns displaying the job title (just after the @..SAYs for emp_name, hire_date, and so on). In the first version of the program, this process required several commands (see the commands following the comment "Find job title and display"). In this program, it only requires a single command.

This chapter combined some elements of system planning and dBASE IV multiple-file handling features that are essential for addressing more complex business needs. These concepts can be applied to other system functions besides the screen display program you have just studied. Consider what strategy would be required to append records, for example. It would be necessary to append to both the EMP and the COURSE files after checking the validity of the data in the JOB_CODE and ORG_CODE fields, among other things. If a system (including the data dictionary) is thoughtfully designed, these tasks will be much more manageable, and your system will serve the users well.

```
* EMP-DSP2.PRG -  Display records from course databases.

* Set Environment
PRIVATE ALL
SET HEADING OFF
SET TALK OFF
SET BELL OFF
SET STATUS OFF
SET SCOREBOARD OFF
SET SAFETY OFF
CLEAR ALL

* Initialization

SELECT 1
USE org ALIAS department
SET ORDER TO org-code

SELECT 2
USE job
SET ORDER TO job-code

SELECT 3
USE emp ALIAS employee
SET ORDER TO org-emp
SET RELATION TO org-code INTO department, job-code INTO job

SELECT 4
USE course
SET ORDER TO org-emp
```

```
* Processing Loop
DO WHILE .T.

   SELECT employee
   morg-code = '     '
   memp-no = '     '
   * GET Org. Code and Emp. # and display screen
   @  2, 29  SAY "DISPLAY TRAINING RECORD"
   @  4, 17  SAY "ORGANIZATION CODE"
   @  4, 35  GET  morg-code
   @  4, 42  SAY "EMPLOYEE NUMBER"
   @  4, 58  GET  memp-no
   @  6,  7  SAY "EMPLOYEE NAME"
   @  6, 51  SAY "DATE OF HIRE"
   @  8,  7  SAY "JOB CODE"
   @  8, 23  SAY "JOB TITLE"
   @ 10,  7  SAY "MAIL STOP       SUPERVISOR"
   @ 12, 21  SAY "COURSE NUMBER         COURSE DATE"
   @  0,  2  TO 11, 77    DOUBLE
   READ

* Check for blank Org. Code or Emp. #
IF morg-code = '     ' .OR. memp-no = '     '
   CLEAR
   CLEAR ALL
   SET HEADING ON
   SET TALK ON
   SET BELL ON
   SET STATUS ON
   SET SCOREBOARD ON
   SET SAFETY ON
   RETURN
ENDIF morg-code
```

Make employee area the active area
Exit if either org_code or emp_no is blank

Figure 11.17 LISTING FOR EMP_DSP1.PRG

```
* Check if record exists
memkey = morg-code + memp-no
SEEK memkey
IF .NOT. FOUND()
   @ 5,40 SAY 'Record Not Found'
   mpause = 0
   DO WHILE mpause < 100
      mpause = mpause + 1
   ENDDO mpause < 100
   @ 5,40 SAY SPACE(25)
   LOOP
ENDIF .NOT. FOUND()

* Display remaining fields
@  6, 21  SAY  employee->emp-name
@  6, 64  SAY  employee->hire-date
@  8, 16  SAY  employee->job-code
@ 10, 17  SAY  department->mail
@ 10, 34  SAY  department->supervisor

@  8, 33 SAY job->job-title

* Display Courses for Employee
SELECT course
SEEK memkey
row = 14
* If no course is found, display message
IF .NOT. FOUND()
   @ row, 33 SAY 'No Courses on File'
   row = row + 1
ENDIF .NOT. FOUND()
```

Pause loop
Can use related fields from job area because of SET RELATION
Can use related fields department area because of SET RELATION
Move to course area to find all the courses

```
   * Loop until no more courses
   DO WHILE .NOT. EOF()

      * If course is for correct employee display course
      IF course->org-code + course->emp-no = memkey
         @ row, 25  SAY course->course
         @ row, 44  SAY course->crse-date
         row = row + 1

         * If screen is full, start over at row 14
         IF row > 22
            @ row, 35 SAY 'Press Return '
            WAIT '' TO OK
            @ 14, 25 CLEAR
            row = 14
         ENDIF row > 22
      ELSE
         GO BOTTOM
      ENDIF course->ord-code + course->emp-no = memkey
      SKIP
   ENDDO .NOT. EOF()
   @ row, 35 SAY 'Press Return'
   WAIT ''
   CLEAR
ENDDO WHILE .T.

CLEAR ALL
CLEAR
SET HEADING ON
SET TALK ON
SET BELL ON
SET STATUS ON
SET SCOREBOARD ON
SET SAFETY ON
RETURN
```

Figure 11.17 LISTING FOR EMP_DSP1.PRG

CHAPTER SUMMARY

1. System planning is essential in larger applications because design errors and inefficiency are magnified in them. I-P-O charts help the programmer assemble the elements of the system and develop them further. The data dictionary shows all the fields used within the system. Redundant and mutually exclusive fields should be eliminated. Normalization is a process whereby data is organized on the basis of function and relationship in order to reduce redundancy. The target in the normalization process is third normal form.
2. The SELECT statement is used to access multiple work areas. Ten work areas are available and each may have a database file active in it. All fields in the work areas are available for display, using either a prefix containing the filename or alias with the -> symbol. Other operations, such as an indexed search, require a SELECT statement.
3. The SET RELATION TO command is a convenient way to synchronize the record pointers in two files that are indexed on the same key. It is a substitute for programming a search with SEEK and a DO WHILE loop.
4. A program to display records using multiple files typically includes several nested control structures. SELECT statements must be issued to activate each database file. Files can be related using SET RELATION TO provided each record in the main file is only related to one record in the other file. When the record pointer is positioned at the queried record, all related fields can be displayed using @..SAY.

KEY TERMS

I-P-O chart
second normal form
data dictionary
repeating group
repeating field
partial dependency
transitive dependency
normalization
third normal form
primary key
work area
first normal form
alias
->

COMMAND SUMMARY

Command Name	Use
SELECT	Open a work area for a DBF file.
ALIAS	Specify an alias name for a DBF file.
SET RELATION TO	Link two DBF files through an index.

dBUG dBASE

- Using the same column number and PICTURE clause in @..SAY commands for two or more numbers causes these numbers to be displayed in an aligned column.
- When names of memory variables and field names are identical, dBASE IV assumes that a name refers to a memory variable first in a STORE, but a field name first in a GET. It is safer to make sure the names are different so there is no confusion.

SELF-CHECK QUESTIONS

1. List three reasons why system planning is important.
2. Why is redundancy undesirable?
3. Name three criteria for determining whether a field should be placed in a separate DBF file.
4. What does the SELECT command do?
5. What is the function of the -> prefix?
6. What is the advantage of using the SET RELATION TO command?
7. Under what circumstances would an alias be useful?
8. Is the normalization of data always appropriate? Why?

TRY IT YOURSELF

1. Develop an I-P-O chart and a data dictionary for any application presented in Chapters 5 through 10.
2. Place the following in third normal form. (The primary key is the Social Security number.)

```
Social Security number
Name
Address
City
Zip
Department
Supervisor
Local Tax Code
Local Municipality Name
Gross Pay (Repeats)
```

3. Write SELECT statements, USE statements, and SET ORDER TO statements to activate the following database files. Include an alias for each.

```
TAXMSTR.DBF (indexed on field called TAXNO)
TAXTRANS.DBF (indexed on field called TAXNUM)
```

4. Chain the TAXTRANS file to the TAXMSTR file with an appropriate SET RELATION TO statement. The matching fields are both called TAXNO.

PROGRAMMING PROJECTS

Using the data in Exercise 2, write a program to display records keyed on the Social Security number. CREATE three databases: one for the basic employee fields, one for the gross pay keyed on the Social Security number, and one containing the local municipality name keyed on the local tax code. Design a screen to input the employee's Social Security number and to exit if the field is blank or the number is not found. Display the employee's data, including the local municipality name and all gross pay entries, on an attractive screen.

LEARNING OBJECTIVES

To use functions to manipulate strings.

To perform arithmetic operations with functions.

To calculate and display dates with functions.

To use utility functions.

To write a program to update files.

To develop and use user-defined functions (UDFs).

12 FUNCTIONS—THE PROGRAMMER'S TOOLKIT

INTRODUCTION

There is much more to dBASE IV than the programming and the interactive commands you have learned. Every good programming language also contains a programmer's toolkit. The tools, called *functions*, are small internal programs that are always available to perform very useful and interesting tasks.

Would you like to know on what day of the week you were born or how many days you have been alive? Perhaps you need to find the square root or logarithm of a number. If a user had entered names in a file with the first name followed by the last name, and you wanted to index by last name, what could you do about it? In this chapter, you will learn the functions that exist to deal with all of these tasks and many more. The user's needs can best be served by functions that help expand the form and usage of existing data. Also, you will learn how to create your own functions and add them to the vast collection already available in dBASE.

12.1 HANDLING STRINGS

Functions are preset routines that are available in dBASE IV to solve a wide variety of programming problems. They are most often used to look at data in different and useful ways. The operation of a function produces a value. We say that the function *returns* this value. We can use this value in a variety of ways. We can display it on the screen, we can print it in a report, we can use it to replace the contents of a memory variable or field, we can combine it with other values in some expression, and so on.

All functions include the name of the function followed by a set of parentheses. Many functions require *arguments,* that is, the values on which the function will operate. These arguments are placed within the parentheses. Functions can be sensitive to improper syntax, especially concerning the arguments.

Experiment first with the function in the interactive mode to be sure it will perform as expected. Type the examples given throughout the chapter (such as those in Figure 12.1), or others of your choosing, at the dot prompt as you study the behavior and usage of the functions presented in the rest of this chapter.

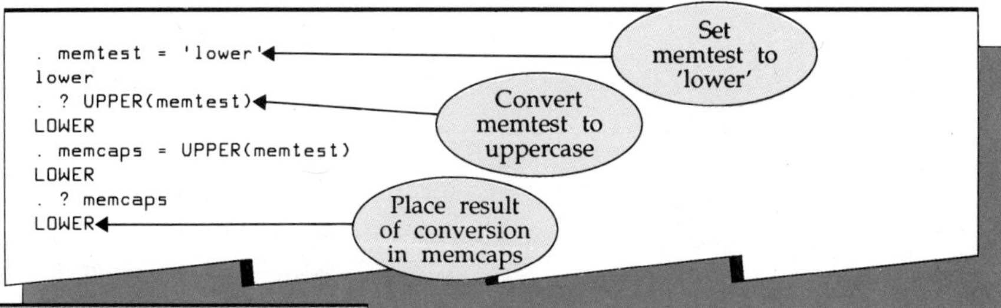

Figure 12.1 TESTING FUNCTIONS WITH ?

Figure 12.1 illustrates the UPPER() function. In the figure, the argument is the memory variable memtest, which currently contains 'lower'. This function returns the value that is the result of converting all lowercase letters to uppercase. In this example, it returns 'LOWER'. The first use of the function in the figure simply displays the value. The second example sets the memory variable memcaps to the value returned by UPPER(). As you can see, memcaps will then contain 'LOWER'.

The rich collection of functions that are available in dBASE IV for manipulating strings makes it difficult to imagine a task that cannot be performed. Through the use of functions, you can cut and paste strings and change their appearance in many ways, as the examples in this section demonstrate. For example, LOWER(), the inverse of UPPER(), converts all characters in the argument to lowercase. (See Figure 12.2.)

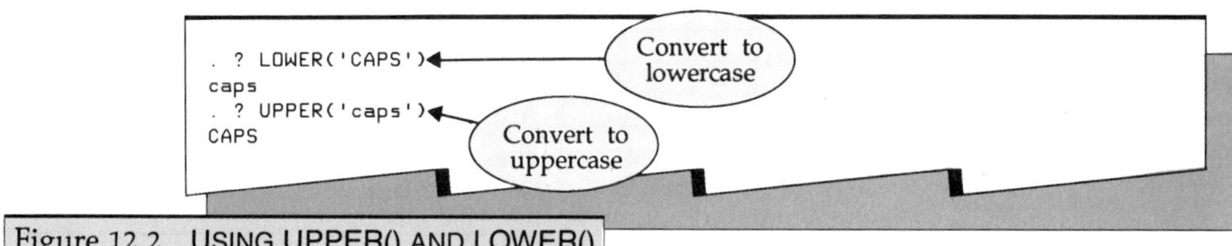

Figure 12.2 USING UPPER() AND LOWER()

The dollar sign ($) function returns a logical T or F (True or False), depending on the presence or absence of the object of the search in the specified string. The function operates on string expressions that are delimited with quotation marks or brackets, variables, or field names. The $ function is most useful when the data being searched is in an uncertain condition. Suppose you had to find an important name or term in a comment field of a DBF file. A LIST command or a DO WHILE loop could be used with the $ function to display any fields containing the term in question. (Technically the $ is called an *operator* rather than a function.) (See Figure 12.3.)

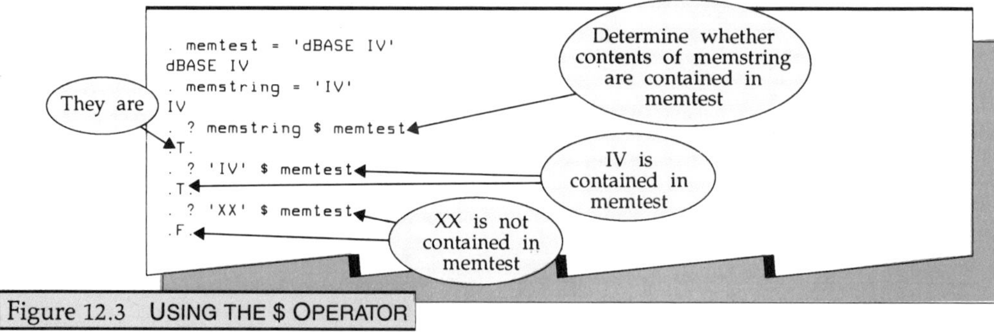

Figure 12.3 USING THE $ OPERATOR

ASC() returns the ASCII decimal equivalent of the leftmost character of the string argument. (Refer to Chapter 6 for an explanation of the hierarchy of the ASCII code.) This function may be useful in situations where you need to determine how characters will be evaluated in an IF/ENDIF condition, for example. Note that the function operates on only the leftmost character. (See Figure 12.4.)

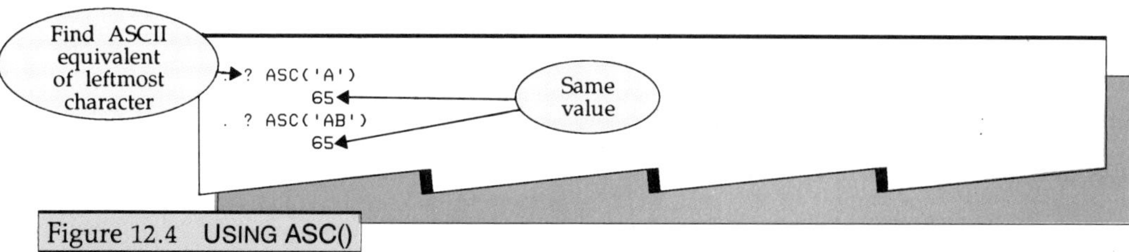

Figure 12.4 USING ASC()

CHR() is the inverse of ASC(). If you use a value between 0 and 255 as the argument, the function returns the symbol assigned to that value in the ASCII code. Appendix D contains a complete listing of the ASCII code. Not all values display a symbol on the screen or printer. For example, CHR(7) causes the computer's speaker to beep. (See Figure 12.5.)

Figure 12.5 USING CHR()

The SPACE() function has appeared in other chapters as a means of initializing character variables to a specified number of blanks. The ISALPHA(), ISLOWER(), and ISUPPER() functions all evaluate the first character of a string expression and return a logical T if the character is alphabetic, lowercase, or uppercase, respectively. (See Figure 12.6.)

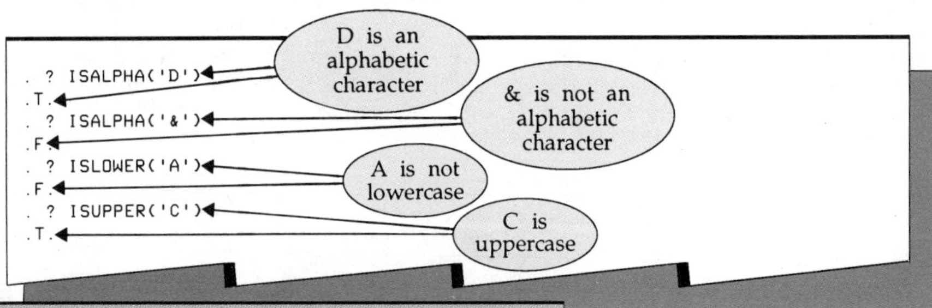

Figure 12.6 USING ISALPHA(), ISLOWER(), AND ISUPPER()

When a string expression or variable and an integer are used as arguments in LEFT(), the leftmost number of characters specified is returned; you specify how many characters will be included. The RIGHT() function operates identically, except that it counts from the right. LEN() simply counts the number of characters in the string and returns the value. (See Figure 12.7.)

Unwanted blanks are easily trimmed from the left or right of a string through the use of LTRIM() or RTRIM(). TRIM() is identical to RTRIM(). (See Figure 12.8.)

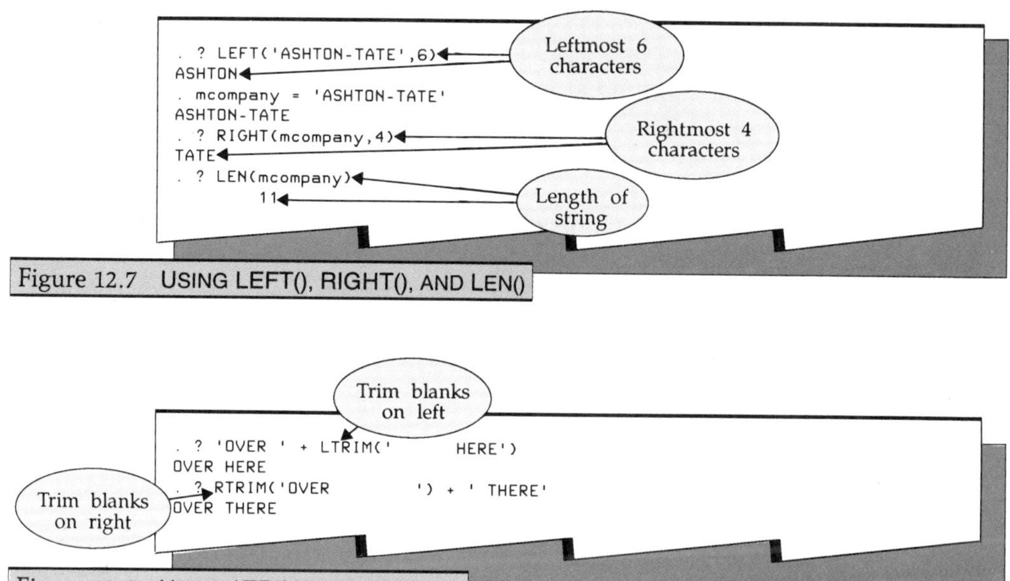

Figure 12.7 USING LEFT(), RIGHT(), AND LEN()

Figure 12.8 USING LTRIM() AND RTRIM()

STUFF() inserts one string into another at any specified location. SUBSTR() is the inverse of STUFF(). It removes a substring from another string. The AT() function returns the starting location of one string within another if you would prefer to have the computer do your counting for you. The value returned could then be used in the LEFT(), RIGHT(), STUFF(), or SUBSTR() function. If the string is not found, AT() returns 0. (See Figure 12.9.)

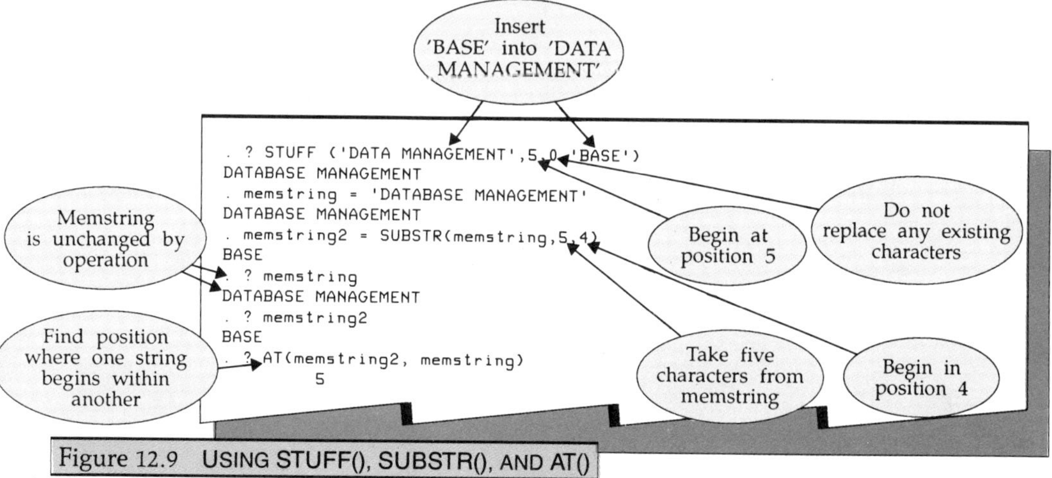

Figure 12.9 USING STUFF(), SUBSTR(), AND AT()

The first example in Figure 12.9 inserts the string 'BASE', beginning at the fifth position of 'DATA MANAGEMENT', without replacing any characters. The second example sets memstring2 equal to four characters of memstring, starting at position 5. Notice that memstring is unchanged in the process. The AT() returns the first location where memstring2 occurs within memstring.

The SWITCH.PRG program that appears in Figure 12.10 makes liberal use of several string-handling functions. It accepts a person's first and last name in either order and in either case, and then it reverses the order and displays the names in uppercase. A DO WHILE .T. is used so that the program can be repeated as often as the user wishes. Pressing Enter at the GET block causes the program to exit because blanks are stored in memname. The RTRIM() function is used to remove any trailing blanks from the string that might interfere with searches. Also, since the program will not operate properly if there is no blank between the two names, the $ operator is used in an IF/ENDIF to force the user to include one. (A sample of the program's execution is shown in Figure 12.11 on page 316.)

SWITCH.PRG uses several functions that base their actions on the location of the blank as a delimiter between the two names. The AT() function determines the location and stores it as a numeric value in mblank. The front part of the memname is extracted with the LEFT() function by specifying the location of the blank less one as the length to store in mfront. Although RIGHT() could have been used to extract the back part of the string, SUBSTR() was used to demonstrate the nesting of functions. In this case, the length of the string LEN() less the location of the blank is used to specify the length of the second name. The two parts of the name are then reassembled, separated by a blank as the argument of the UPPER() function, and then displayed. The switching algorithm in SWITCH.PRG could be used with REPLACE to reverse the order of names previously stored in a DBF file.

```
* SWITCH.PRG - exchanges the positions of two names in a string
*              based on a search for a blank.

SET TALK OFF
SET SCOREBOARD OFF
SET STATUS OFF

DO WHILE .T.
   CLEAR
   memname = SPACE(30)
   mblank = 0
   mfront = ''
   mback = ''
   memrev = ''

   @ 10,10 SAY 'Type your name in any order '
   @ 10,38 GET memname
   READ

   * Exit if all blanks
   IF memname = SPACE(30)
      SET TALK ON
      SET SCOREBOARD ON
      SET STATUS ON
      RETURN
      CLEAR
   ENDIF

   * Trim trailing blanks
   memname = RTRIM(memname)

   * Check for no blank in name
   IF .NOT. ' ' $ memname
      @ 12,15 SAY 'Please include a blank'
      delay = 1
      DO WHILE delay < 25
         delay = delay + 1
      ENDDO delay < 25
      LOOP
   ENDIF .NOT. ' ' $ memname

   * Look for a blank
   mblank = AT(' ',memname)

    * Extract first section
    mfront = LEFT(memname, mblank-1)

    * Extract the second section
    mback = SUBSTR(memname, mblank+1, LEN(memname) - mblank)

    * Assemble the reversed name and print it upper case
    memrev = UPPER(mback + ' ' + mfront)

    @ 12,1 SAY 'Here is your name reversed in Caps * * '
    @ 12,42 SAY memrev
    @ 14,15 SAY 'Press any key to continue'
    WAIT ''

 ENDDO WHILE .T.

 SET TALK ON
 SET STATUS ON
 SET SCOREBOARD ON
```

Initialize memory variables
Is a blank contained within memname?
"Delay" loop will leave message on screen for a brief period
Find position of first blank
Set mfront to portion of memname up to position just before blank
Numbers of characters to include in mback
Set mback up to portion of name beginning just after blank
Use mfront and mback to create memrev

Figure 12.10 THE SWITCH.PRG PROGRAM

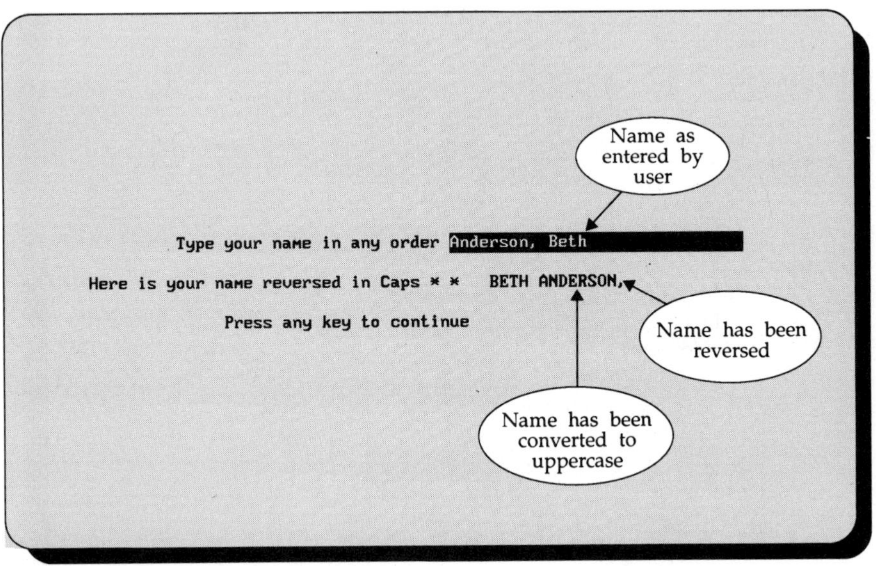

Figure 12.11 RUNNING SWITCH.PRG

12.2 ARITHMETIC FUNCTIONS

The arithmetic functions included in dBASE IV are certainly sufficient for dealing with typical business problems, although they are not designed to handle sophisticated mathematical applications such as those found in engineering. You should experiment with these functions at the dot prompt, as you did with the string functions. Before we look at the functions, let's indicate the number of decimal places that we would like to see displayed when appropriate. To do so, we use the SET DECIMAL TO command. Let's request five decimal places by executing the command:

```
SET DECIMAL TO 5
```

Now that we have done so, let's turn to the functions.

ABS() returns the absolute value of a numeric expression. This means that the number will be expressed as positive regardless of the stated sign of the value. (See Figure 12.12.)

Figure 12.12 USING ABS()

EXP() returns the natural, or Napierian, exponent of the numeric argument. It is based on the approximate value of *e*, 2.718282, rather than 2, which is used in binary arithmetic. (See Figure 12.13. Notice that precisely five decimal places are displayed.)

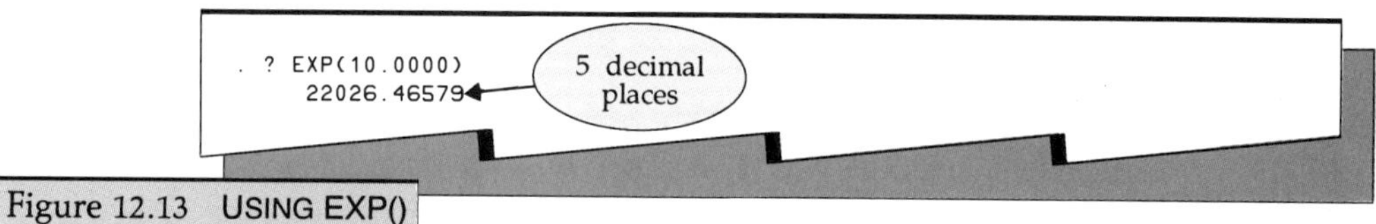

Figure 12.13 USING EXP()

INT() truncates any value to the right of the decimal point, producing an integer, or whole number. (See Figure 12.14.)

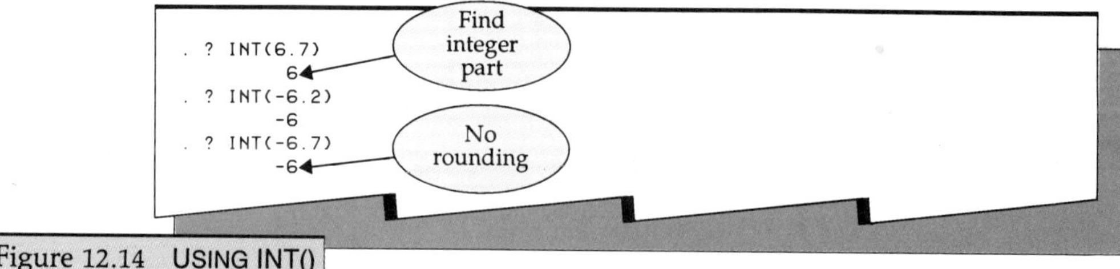

Figure 12.14 USING INT()

LOG() returns the natural logarithm of the numeric argument on the basis of the value of *e*, as in the EXP() function. The base 10 log can be calculated as in Figure 12.15.

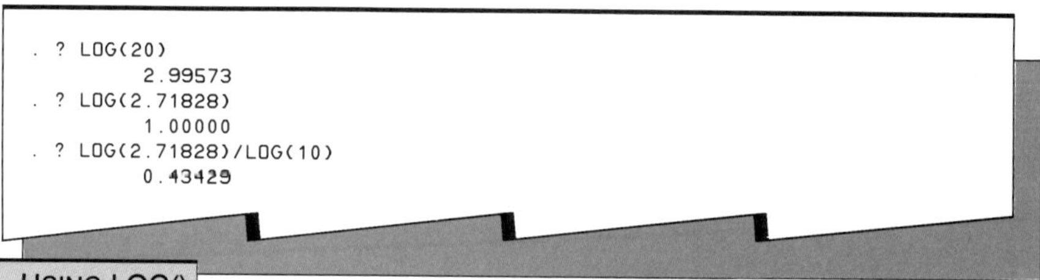

Figure 12.15 USING LOG()

MAX() returns the highest of two values included in the argument. MIN() returns the lowest of any two values. (See Figure 12.16 on the next page.)

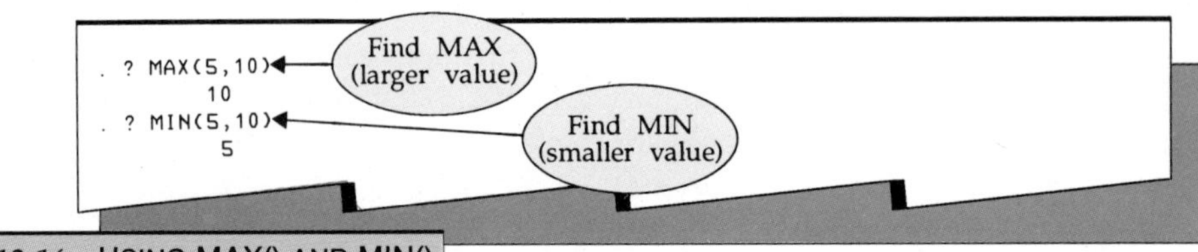

Figure 12.16 USING MAX() AND MIN()

MOD() returns the remainder of a division operation expressed as a whole number. It is used in modulo arithmetic. (See Figure 12.17.)

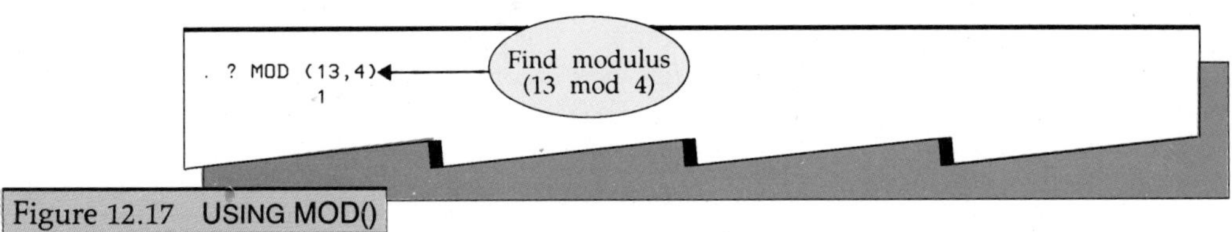

Figure 12.17 USING MOD()

ROUND() establishes the number of decimal places to be recognized in an operation and rounds to that value. (See Figure 12.18.)

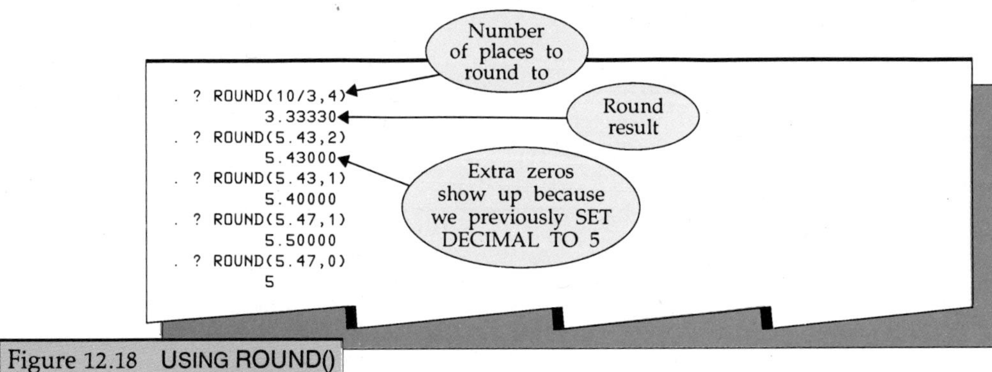

Figure 12.18 USING ROUND()

SQRT() returns the square root of the argument. (See Figure 12.19.)

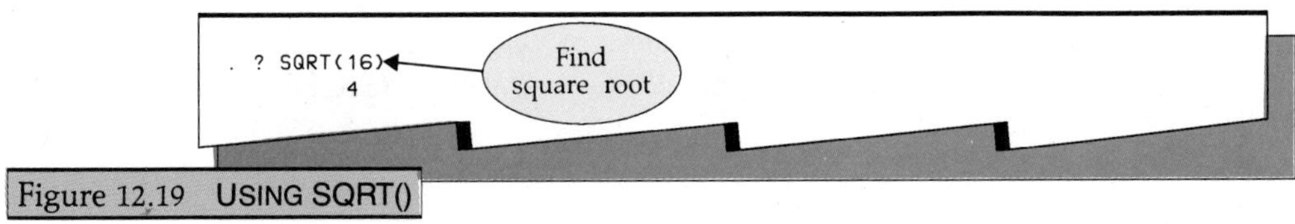

Figure 12.19 USING SQRT()

VAL() converts an alphanumeric number to a numeric value. STR() converts numeric values to strings. You must include the number of digits and the number of decimal places in the argument. The STR() function can be used to produce a single dollar sign in a screen or printer display. Combining VAL() with @..SAY allows the user to determine the position of a display, as shown in Figure 12.20.

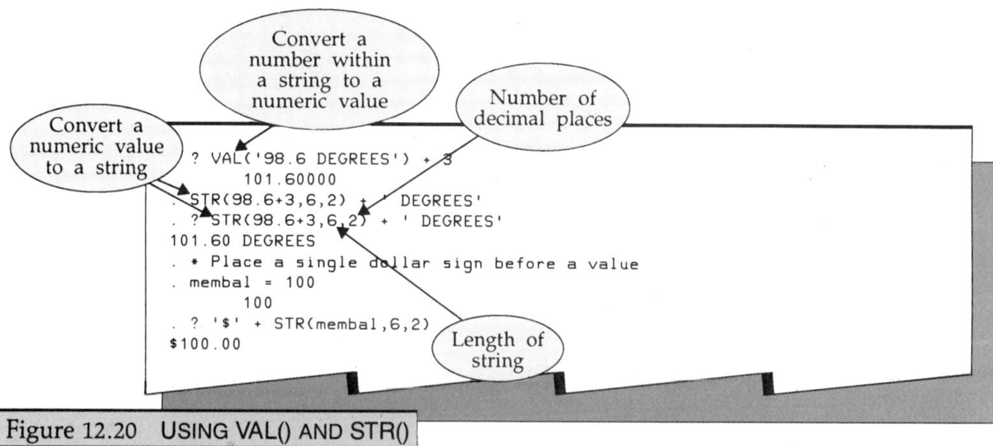

Figure 12.20 USING VAL() AND STR()

12.3 DATE FUNCTIONS AND OPERATIONS

Dates are stored in a special format that allows the maximum use of the data in comparisons, ordering operations, and date calculations. You can compare dates and sort by dates. You can subtract one date from another to find out how many days are between the two dates.

Dates are assumed to be in the twentieth century (19XX) unless the command SET CENTURY ON is activated. (See Figure 12.21.) This requires the user to include the full four digits of the year instead of just the last two. Therefore, when the century changes in a few short years, dBASE IV programs will not be obsolete. YEAR() displays the full year, which indicates the correct century.

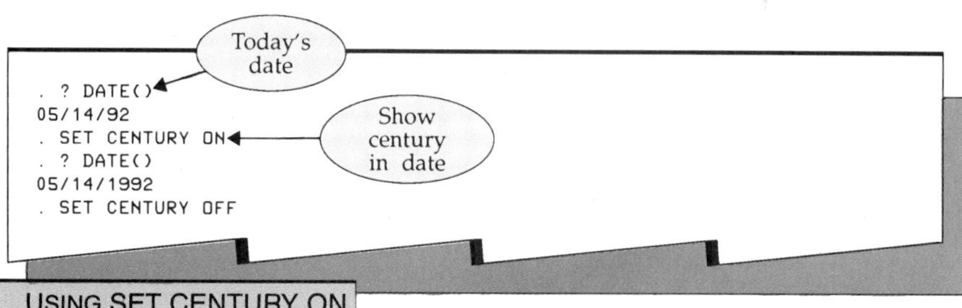

Figure 12.21 USING SET CENTURY ON

You can find the day of the week by using the DOW or CDOW functions as shown in Figure 12.22. DOW gives the numeric day of the week and CDOW gives the character version. In the figure, we first set BIRTHDATE to 6/26/74. Notice that we did so by enclosing the date in braces (curly brackets). Then using DOW and CDOW, we see that 6/26/74 occurred on the fourth day of the week, which is Wednesday. CMONTH gives the character version of the month in which that date occurred (June).

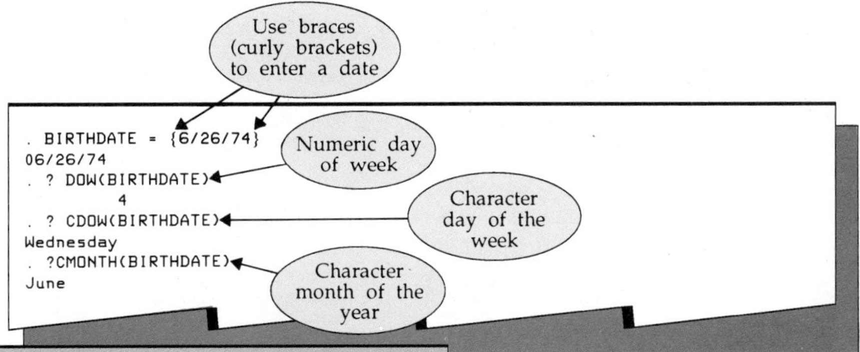

Figure 12.22 USING DOW(), CDOW() AND CMONTH()

DTOC() converts date-type fields to character strings (Figure 12.23). The second expression in the figure, BIRTHDATE + " is Tammy's birthday.", will produce a "Data type mismatch" error. The problem is we are trying to combine a date and a character string. The solution is to use the DTOC function to convert the date to a character string as you can see in the third expression in the figure.

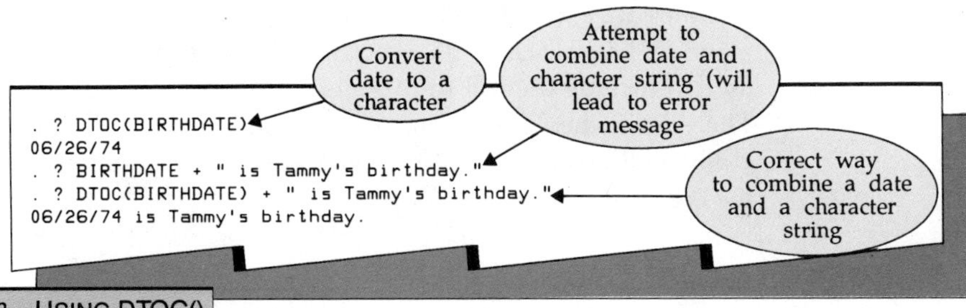

Figure 12.23 USING DTOC()

DATE() is useful because it contains the system date as set by DOS. This function is convenient for reports and date calculations. Figure 12.24 illustrates the use of dates in arithmetic expressions. Here we are subtracting today's date from a due date. The result will be the number of days inbetween the two dates.

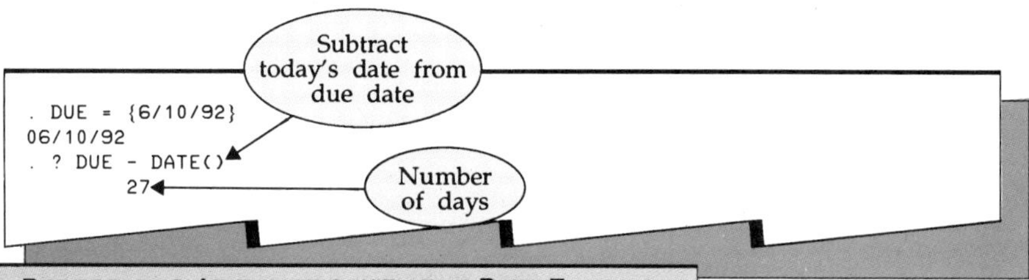

Figure 12.24 PERFORMING ARITHMETIC WITH THE DATE FUNCTIONS

To convert the DATE() display from the typical format to a form more appropriate for correspondence, you could use the command shown in Figure 12.25. In this figure DUE is a date variable containing 06/10/92. For this date, the command produces June 10, 1992.

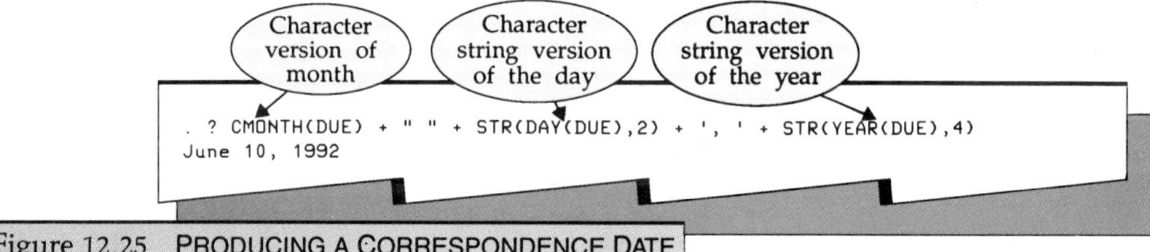

Figure 12.25 PRODUCING A CORRESPONDENCE DATE

Table 12.1 summarizes the functions that can be used for converting from one type of data to another.

TABLE 12.1 Conversion functions

TO CONVERT FROM:	TO:	USE THIS FUNCTION:
Character	Date	CTOD()
Date	Character	DTOC()
Numeric	String	STR()
String	Numeric	VAL()
Character	Ascii code	ASC()
ASCII code	Character	CHR()

12.4 UTILITY FUNCTIONS

Chapter 9 introduced the & function, which is the macro expansion or substitution function. It was used there with the FIND command and variables to extract the actual value stored in the variable rather than the name of the variable itself. It may be convenient to store lengthy command lines in a variable and execute them with the &. No space is permitted after the &. Also, the macro expansion character should not be used in a DO WHILE condition because it does not evaluate properly. (See Figure 12.26.)

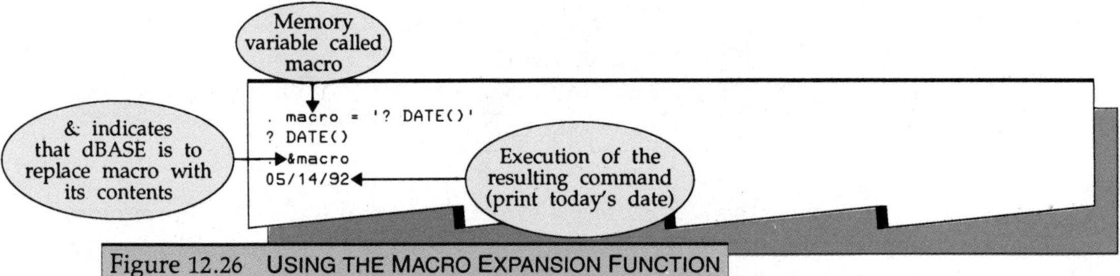

Figure 12.26 USING THE MACRO EXPANSION FUNCTION

COL() and ROW() return the current position of the cursor on the screen. (See Figure 12.27.)

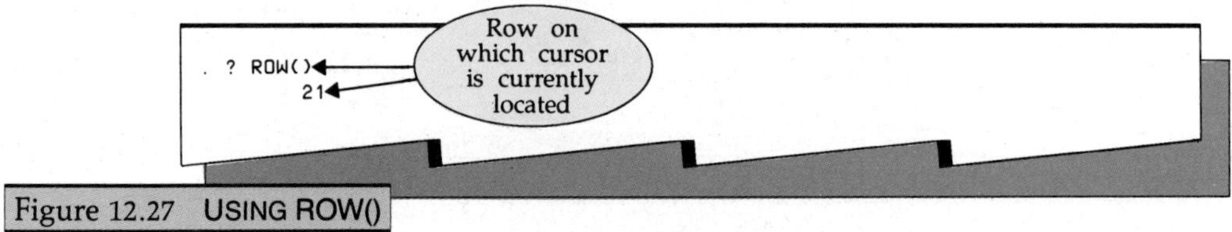

Figure 12.27 USING ROW()

Several functions are valuable because they provide useful information that may not be immediately evident while you are working with a database. Some of this information can also be obtained with the DISPLAY STATUS command. The functions and the returned results are listed in Table 12.2. Figure 12.28 provides examples of the functions described in Table 12.2.

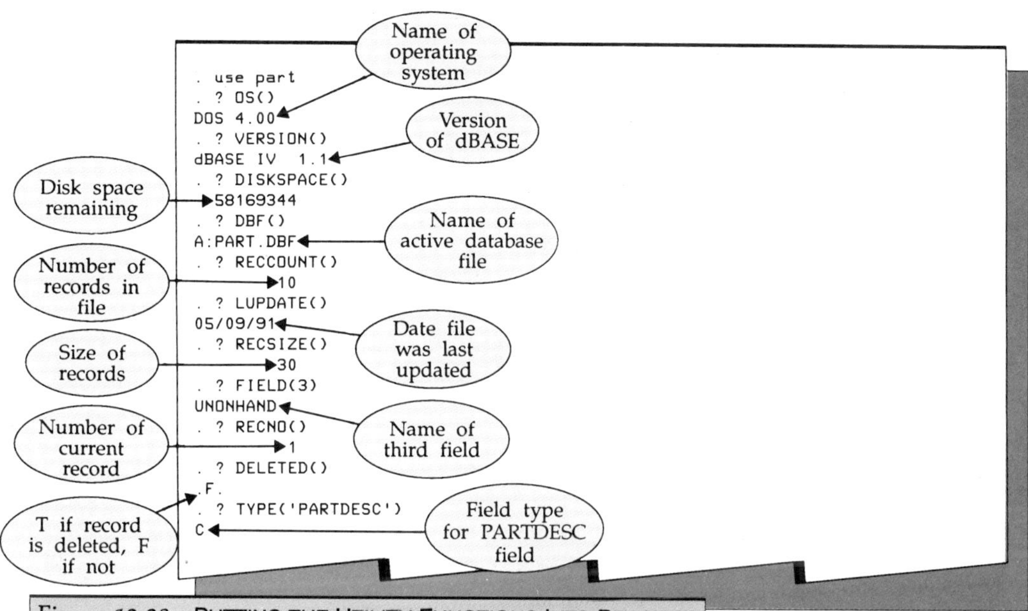

Figure 12.28 PUTTING THE UTILITY FUNCTIONS INTO PRACTICE

TABLE 12.2 Utility functions

FUNCTION	RESULT RETURNED
OS()	Name of the current operating system.
VERSION()	Version of dBASE IV in use.
DISKSPACE()	The number of bytes that are free on the currently active disk.
FILE()	A logical .T. or .F, depending on whether or not the file specified as an argument exists.
DBF()	The name of the DBF currently in use.
RECCOUNT()	The number of records listed in the structure in the currently active DBF file.
LUPDATE()	A date-type field stored as the last date on which the active DBF file was updated in any way.
RECSIZE()	The record size in the current DBF file.
FIELD()	The name of the field based on a number from 1 through 128 as an argument.
RECNO()	The record number relating to the current position of the record pointer.
DELETED()	A logical .T. or .F., depending on whether or not the current record was deleted.
TYPE()	The data type C,N,L,M.

REPLICATE() permits any ASCII character to be displayed on the screen or dot matrix printer. Creative use of these symbols can be quite attractive. The first argument in the REPLICATE function is the character and the second argument indicates how many times the character is to be replicated. (Figure 12.29.)

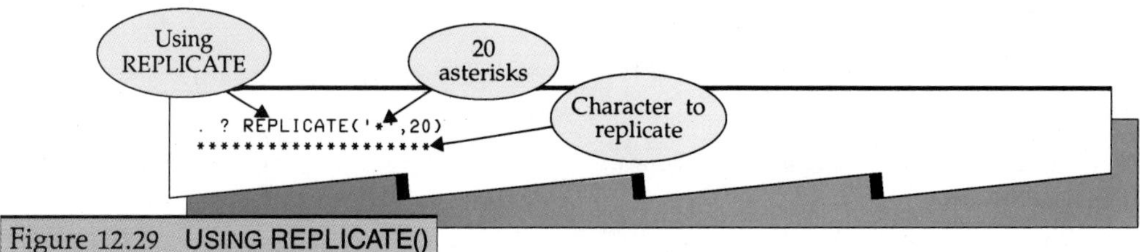

Figure 12.29 USING REPLICATE()

SOUNDEX() produces a "sounds-like" code for a character string. The details of the steps used to produce the code are not important. The critical feature of this function is that if two character strings would sound alike or similar, the code produced should be the same. As you can see in Figure 12.30, SOUNDEX() returns the code A350 for both ADAM and ATOM. A typical use for such a function is shown in Figure 12.30. We first create an index using SOUNDEX(), then we can use this index whenever we know the sound of a name but not the exact spelling.

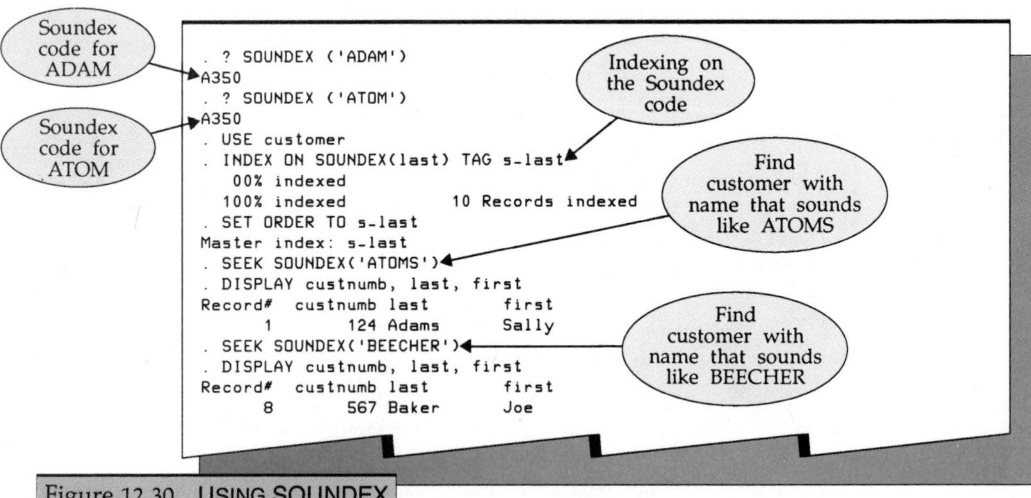

Figure 12.30 USING SOUNDEX

LOOKUP() allows us to use a value from the database file in the active area to find a matching record in a database file that is active in another area. In Figure 12.31, for example, we have a CLIENT database file active in area 1. The CLIENT database file contains a field called AGT which is the number of the client's agent. The AGENT database file, which is active in area 2, contains a field called AGT_NUMB. This is the field we will use to look up an agent. To make the lookup operation more efficient, we have activated the index that was created on this field. The SELECT 1 command makes area 1 once again the active area. Thus the active area is 1, the CLIENT database file is active in area 1, and the AGENT database file is active in area 2.

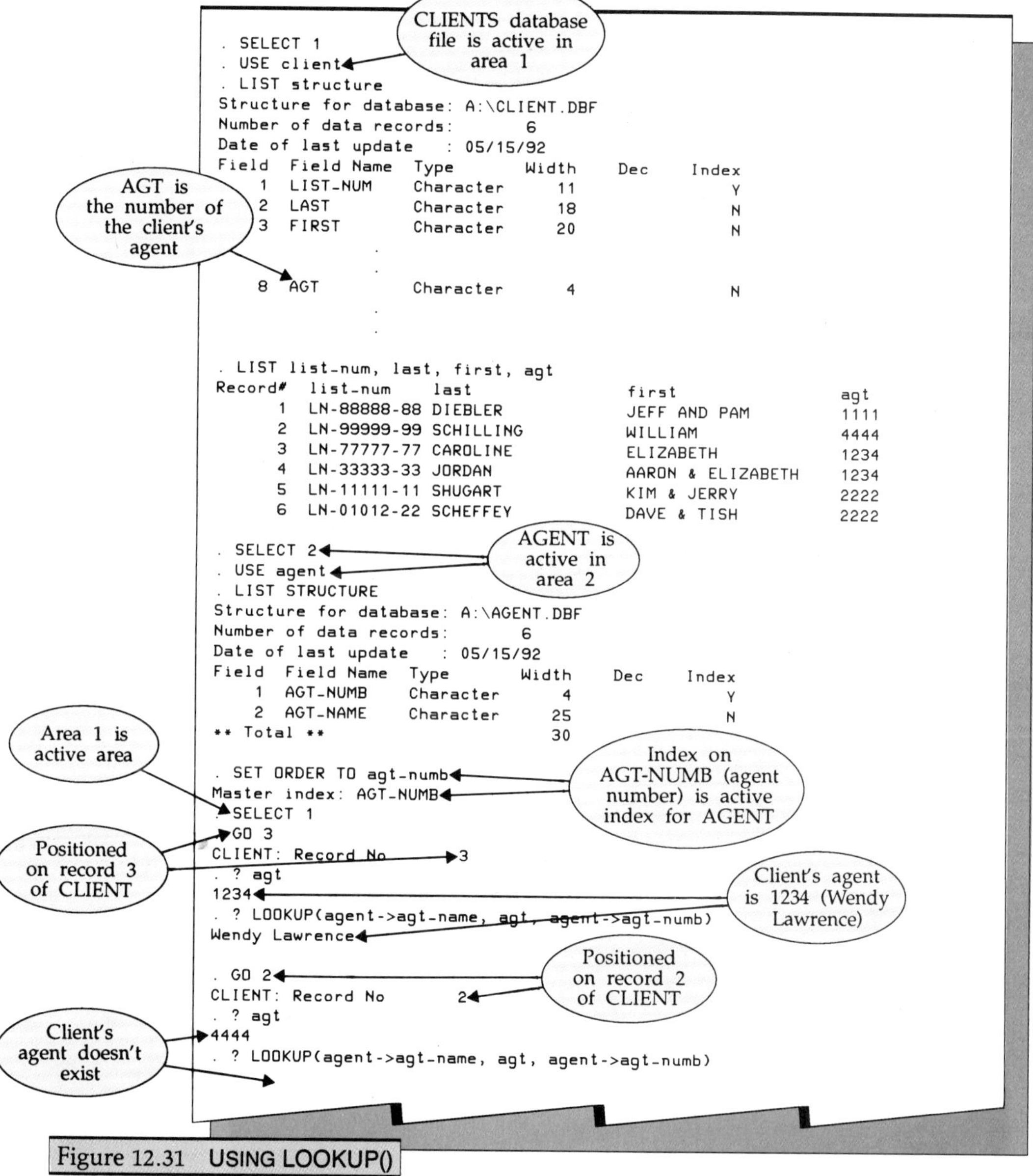

```
. SELECT 1
. USE client
. LIST structure
Structure for database: A:\CLIENT.DBF
Number of data records:        6
Date of last update   : 05/15/92
Field  Field Name  Type        Width    Dec     Index
    1  LIST-NUM    Character      11                Y
    2  LAST        Character      18                N
    3  FIRST       Character      20                N
                     .
                     .
    8  AGT         Character       4                N
                     .
                     .

. LIST list-num, last, first, agt
Record#  list-num      last               first                agt
      1  LN-88888-88 DIEBLER              JEFF AND PAM         1111
      2  LN-99999-99 SCHILLING            WILLIAM              4444
      3  LN-77777-77 CAROLINE             ELIZABETH            1234
      4  LN-33333-33 JORDAN               AARON & ELIZABETH    1234
      5  LN-11111-11 SHUGART              KIM & JERRY          2222
      6  LN-01012-22 SCHEFFEY             DAVE & TISH          2222

. SELECT 2
. USE agent
. LIST STRUCTURE
Structure for database: A:\AGENT.DBF
Number of data records:        6
Date of last update   : 05/15/92
Field  Field Name  Type        Width    Dec     Index
    1  AGT-NUMB    Character       4                Y
    2  AGT-NAME    Character      25                N
** Total **                       30

. SET ORDER TO agt-numb
Master index: AGT-NUMB
. SELECT 1
. GO 3
CLIENT: Record No        3
. ? agt
1234
. ? LOOKUP(agent->agt-name, agt, agent->agt-numb)
Wendy Lawrence

. GO 2
CLIENT: Record No        2
. ? agt
4444
. ? LOOKUP(agent->agt-name, agt, agent->agt-numb)
```


Figure 12.31 USING LOOKUP()

If you examine the use of the LOOKUP() function in the figure, you'll see that it has three arguments. The first gives the name of the field we wish to find, in this case AGT_NAME (the agent's name). Since this is a field in AGENT and AGENT is not in the active area, we must qualify it (AGENT->AGT_NAME). The second argument gives the field containing the value used to look for a match. Here it is the AGT field from the CLIENT database file. The final one gives the field in the other database file that must match AGT. In this case it is AGT_NUMB and, like AGT_NAME, it must be qualified.

Just prior to the first LOOKUP() in the figure, we positioned ourselves on the third record in the CLIENT file. The value for AGT on this record is 1234. The LOOKUP() function indicates that the name of the agent whose number is 1234 is Wendy Lawrence. We then positioned ourselves on record 2. On this record, the value for AGT is 4444 and it turns out that there is no agent 4444. In this case, LOOKUP() will not be able to locate a matching record in AGENT and so will position the pointer for AGENT at the end of the file. It will not be able to give us a name. We will see how to treat this case in the next section.

12.5 USER-DEFINED FUNCTIONS (UDFs)

As you have seen, dBASE contains a rich collection of functions. Using these functions we can accomplish a variety of tasks, quickly and easily. But what if we would like to use a function for some special purpose and dBASE doesn't contain a function that would do the job? Fortunately, dBASE gives us the facility for creating and using our own functions. Such functions are called User-Defined Functions (UDFs).

Let's examine the structure of a UDF. Consider the function called longdate in Figure 12.32. Its purpose is to return the longer version of a date. (For example, the long form of 6/26/74 would be June 26, 1974.)

The first command in a UDF, FUNCTION, identifies the name of the UDF. The second command, PARAMETERS, identifies the arguments for the function. In this case, there is only one, m_date. When the user invokes (uses) this function, he or she will need to specify a single argument, that is, a single value or variable between the parentheses. For purposes of the UDF, this value or the contents of this variable is placed in m_date. The commands in the UDF will then use m_date.

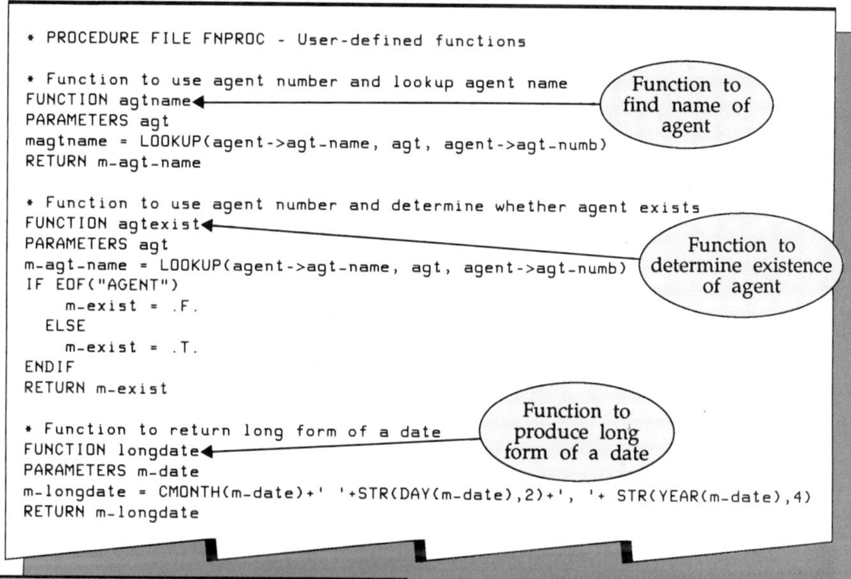

* PROCEDURE FILE FNPROC - User-defined functions
* Function to use agent number and lookup agent name
FUNCTION agtname
PARAMETERS agt
magtname = LOOKUP(agent->agt-name, agt, agent->agt-numb)
RETURN m-agt-name
* Function to use agent number and determine whether agent exists
FUNCTION agtexist
PARAMETERS agt
m-agt-name = LOOKUP(agent->agt-name, agt, agent->agt-numb)
IF EOF("AGENT")
m-exist = .F.
ELSE
m-exist = .T.
ENDIF
RETURN m-exist
* Function to return long form of a date
FUNCTION longdate
PARAMETERS m-date
m-longdate = CMONTH(m-date)+' '+STR(DAY(m-date),2)+', '+ STR(YEAR(m-date),4)
RETURN m-longdate
Function to find name of agent
Function to determine existence of agent
Function to produce long form of a date

Figure 12.32 FILE OF USER-DEFINED FUNCTIONS

The last command, RETURN, is always followed by a single variable. In this example the variable is m_longdate. The value returned by the function will be the value in this variable. Between PARAMETERS and RETURN will be the command or commands necessary to correctly fill in the value in this variable. In this example, it is a single command that uses m_date (the only parameter) and some built-in dBASE functions to calculate the value for m_longdate.

The other two UDFs in Figure 12.32 are agtname and agtexist. The first, agtname, is designed to use the LOOKUP() function to find the name of the agent whose number is passed to the function. In the agtname function, this means that the number will be stored in the variable called agt.

The second, agtexist, uses the same LOOKUP() function, but is intended merely to determine whether a record exists with the given agent number. After the LOOKUP() command, however, there is an IF statement to determine whether the record was found. If the record was not found, the pointer will be positioned at the end of the file, so we use EOF() in the test. When this function is invoked, the active area will be the area containing CLIENT rather than the area containing AGENT. Thus, we need to use EOF("AGENT") rather than simply EOF(). If it is the end of the file, we set m_exist to false, otherwise we set it to true. We then return the value of m_exist.

A typical method of using UDFs is to combine all the UDFs you will need into a single file, called a *procedure file*. This file will have a PRG extension, just like command files. In Figure 12.32, for example, the agtname, agtexist, and longdate UDFs have been combined into the procedure file called FNPROC.

Once you have created such a procedure file you can activate it by using the SET PROCEDURE TO command followed by the name of the procedure file. (SET PROCEDURE TO without a filename closes the active procedure file.)

The first command after activating the database files in Figure 12.33 activates the procedure file. From that point on, we can use any of the UDFs in it. You'll see in the figure that we were able to use agtname, agtexist, and longdate without taking any other special action. (**Note:** If TALK is ON when you execute the commands in the figure, the results will appear twice, once as a result of TALK and once as a result of the ? command. If you would rather not see the duplication, execute a SET TALK OFF command before executing the commands in the figure.)

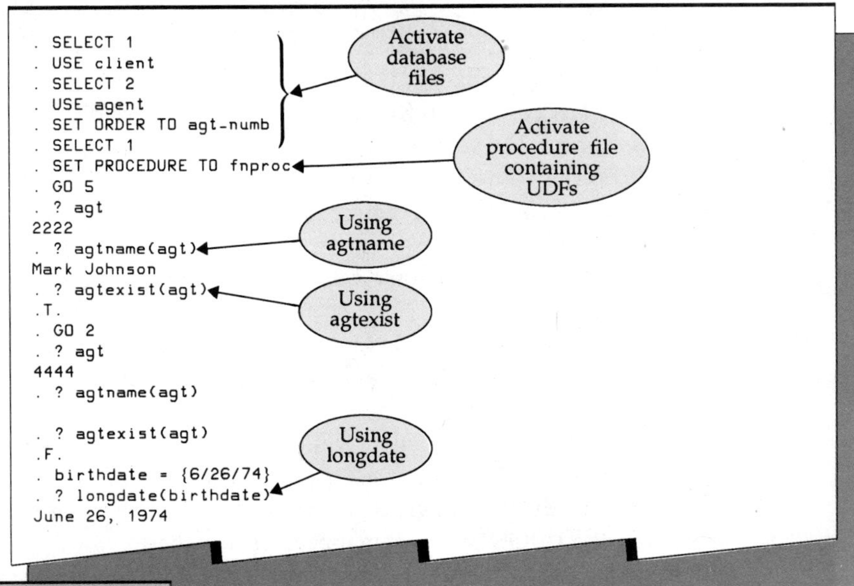

Figure 12.33 USING UDFS

The ability to create and use our own functions can be a major time-saver. For example, once we have created the longdate function, we can use it whenever we need to convert to the long format of a date. We no longer have to write that lengthy expression involving CMONTH, STR, DAY, and YEAR. If, for example, we have a field called startdate that is stored in the typical form (MM/DD/YY) and we wish to display the long form version of it, all we would need to do is use longdate(startdate).

12.6 WRITING A PROGRAM TO UPDATE FILES

Updating or modifying records is very similar to appending because user input data must be written to the file. The difference is that the data must be retrieved from a specific record and displayed both to verify that the correct record has been found and to show the user the current contents. Figure 12.34 shows the structure of CLIENT.DBF, the file that will be updated by this program, and AGENT.DBF, a file that contains the numbers and names of the agents. This second file will be used to verify that only legitimate agent numbers (the AGT field) will be entered. We will also use this file to display the name of the client's agent on the screen.

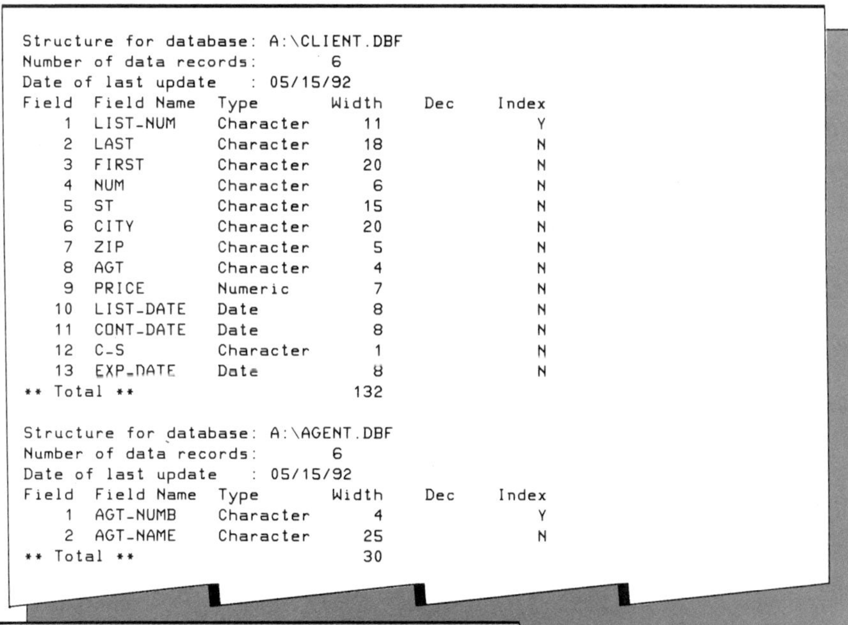

```
Structure for database: A:\CLIENT.DBF
Number of data records:       6
Date of last update   : 05/15/92
Field  Field Name  Type       Width    Dec    Index
    1  LIST-NUM    Character     11               Y
    2  LAST        Character     18               N
    3  FIRST       Character     20               N
    4  NUM         Character      6               N
    5  ST          Character     15               N
    6  CITY        Character     20               N
    7  ZIP         Character      5               N
    8  AGT         Character      4               N
    9  PRICE       Numeric        7               N
   10  LIST-DATE   Date           8               N
   11  CONT-DATE   Date           8               N
   12  C-S         Character      1               N
   13  EXP-DATE    Date           8               N
** Total **                     132

Structure for database: A:\AGENT.DBF
Number of data records:       6
Date of last update   : 05/15/92
Field  Field Name  Type       Width    Dec    Index
    1  AGT-NUMB    Character      4               Y
    2  AGT-NAME    Character     25               N
** Total **                      30
```

Figure 12.34 STRUCTURE OF CLIENT.DBF AND AGENT.DBF

Figure 12.35 presents the pseudocode for the CHG_CLIE.PRG program, and the program itself appears in Figure 12.36 on the following pages. CHG_CLIE.PRG uses a DO WHILE .T. loop to allow users to update records until they press Enter without entering a value for mlist_num. The program will then exit the loop as a result of the IF/ENDIF testing for blanks in that field.

```
Set environment
Open files
Do while user wants to continue
    Initialize memory variables
    Display screen
    Input listing number
    Exit if number is blank
    Loop if number does not exist
    Move present data to memory variables on screen
    Do while user wants to change data
        Get and validate new data from user
        Ask if user wants to Update database, change data, or abort
        If user wants to update database or abort, exit loop
    End of change data routine
    If user wants to update database
        Replace fields with updated memory variables
    End if
End of outer loop
```

Figure 12.35 PSEUDOCODE FOR CHG_CLIE.PRG

The routine begins by clearing the screen and initializing all memory variables in preparation for accepting changes to the existing data in each field. A series of @..SAYs displays the input screen titles, and one @..GET block is provided for mlist_num. Notice that one of the entries on the screen uses our UDF called longdate to display a long version of today's date.

The test to exit the program follows a READ. The next task is to use an indexed search to locate the record that matches the contents of mlist_num. An error routine allows the user to reenter the number if the search fails. When an existing record is located, the current data is STOREd to the memory variables on the screen.

Once the screen has been filled with the current data, the user can scan the screen and employ full-screen editing to change any field except the listing number. The changes are made in a DO WHILE loop, which can be exited by entering an action of U (update the database) or A (abort the transaction). If the user enters C (change screen data) the program will execute the loop again. Finally, if the user types U to exit the loop, the contents of the fields are REPLACEd with the updated memory variables.

```
* CHG-CLIE.PRG -  Update records in the CLIENT.DBF file

* Set Environment
PRIVATE ALL
SET HEADING OFF
SET TALK OFF
SET BELL OFF
SET STATUS OFF
SET SCOREBOARD OFF
SET SAFETY OFF
CLEAR ALL

* Initialization
SELECT 1
USE client
SET ORDER TO list-num
SELECT 2
USE AGENT
SET ORDER TO agt-numb
SELECT 1

* Make UDF library available to program
SET PROCEDURE TO FNPROC

DO WHILE .T.
   CLEAR
   mlist-num = SPACE(11)
   mlast = SPACE(18)
   mfirst = SPACE(20)
   mnum =SPACE(6)
   mst =SPACE(15)
   mcity =SPACE(20)
   mzip =SPACE(5)
   mprice = 0
   magt =SPACE(4)
   mlist-date = {  /  /  }
   mcont-date = {  /  /  }
```

Activate database files

```
   * Display screen
   @ 2,0 TO 18,79 DOUBLE
   @ 3,29 SAY "CLIENT ENTRY"
   @ 3,60  SAY longdate(DATE())
   @ 5,29 SAY "LIST #"
   @ 7,12 SAY "LAST"
   @ 7,38 SAY "FIRST"
   @ 9,19 SAY "NUMBER"
   @ 9,34 SAY "STREET"
   @ 11,20 SAY "CITY"
   @ 11,46 SAY "ZIP"
   @ 13,15 SAY "PRICE"
   @ 13,32 SAY "AGENT"
   @ 15,10 SAY "LIST DATE"
   @ 17,16 SAY "CONTRACT DATE"
* GET Listing Number
@ 5,36 GET mlist-num PICTURE "!!-99999-99"
READ
```

Using longdate UDF in a @..SAY command
Display background of form and get mlist_num

```
* Check for blank Listing Number
IF mlist-num = ' '
   CLEAR
   CLEAR ALL
   SET HEADING ON
   SET TALK ON
   SET BELL ON
   SET STATUS ON
   SET SCOREBOARD ON
   SET SAFETY ON
   RETURN
 ENDIF mlist-num = ' '
```

If mlist_num is left blank, exit loop

Figure 12.36 A PROGRAM TO UPDATE RECORDS

(continued)

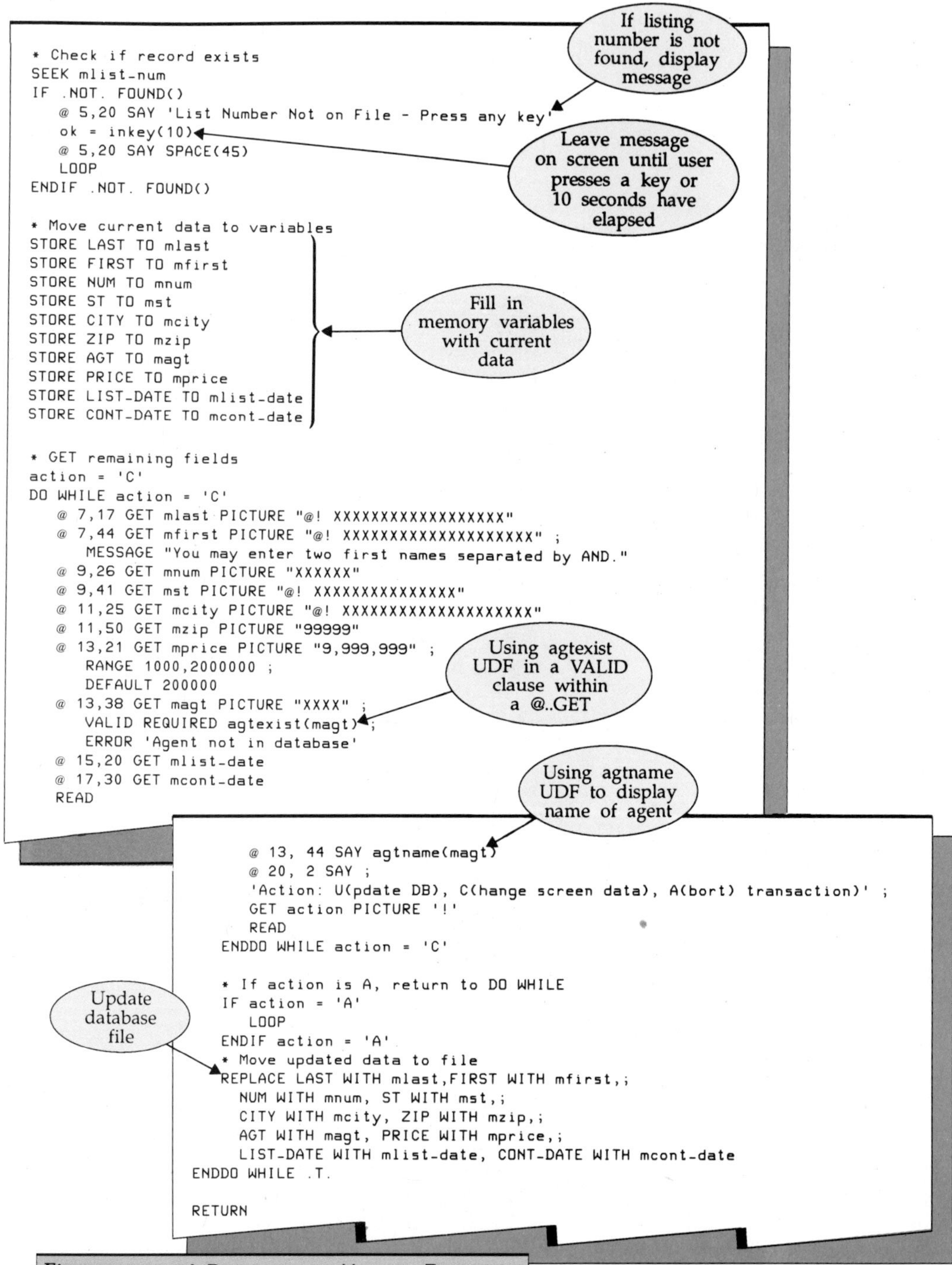

```
* Check if record exists
SEEK mlist-num
IF .NOT. FOUND()
   @ 5,20 SAY 'List Number Not on File - Press any key'
   ok = inkey(10)
   @ 5,20 SAY SPACE(45)
   LOOP
ENDIF .NOT. FOUND()

* Move current data to variables
STORE LAST TO mlast
STORE FIRST TO mfirst
STORE NUM TO mnum
STORE ST TO mst
STORE CITY TO mcity
STORE ZIP TO mzip
STORE AGT TO magt
STORE PRICE TO mprice
STORE LIST-DATE TO mlist-date
STORE CONT-DATE TO mcont-date

* GET remaining fields
action = 'C'
DO WHILE action = 'C'
   @ 7,17 GET mlast PICTURE "@! XXXXXXXXXXXXXXXXXX"
   @ 7,44 GET mfirst PICTURE "@! XXXXXXXXXXXXXXXXXXXX" ;
      MESSAGE "You may enter two first names separated by AND."
   @ 9,26 GET mnum PICTURE "XXXXXX"
   @ 9,41 GET mst PICTURE "@! XXXXXXXXXXXXXXX"
   @ 11,25 GET mcity PICTURE "@! XXXXXXXXXXXXXXXXXXXX"
   @ 11,50 GET mzip PICTURE "99999"
   @ 13,21 GET mprice PICTURE "9,999,999" ;
      RANGE 1000,2000000 ;
      DEFAULT 200000
   @ 13,38 GET magt PICTURE "XXXX" ;
      VALID REQUIRED agtexist(magt) ;
      ERROR 'Agent not in database'
   @ 15,20 GET mlist-date
   @ 17,30 GET mcont-date
   READ
      @ 13, 44 SAY agtname(magt)
      @ 20, 2 SAY ;
      'Action: U(pdate DB), C(hange screen data), A(bort) transaction)' ;
      GET action PICTURE '!'
      READ
   ENDDO WHILE action = 'C'

   * If action is A, return to DO WHILE
   IF action = 'A'
      LOOP
   ENDIF action = 'A'
   * Move updated data to file
   REPLACE LAST WITH mlast,FIRST WITH mfirst,;
     NUM WITH mnum, ST WITH mst,;
     CITY WITH mcity, ZIP WITH mzip,;
     AGT WITH magt, PRICE WITH mprice,;
     LIST-DATE WITH mlist-date, CONT-DATE WITH mcont-date
ENDDO WHILE .T.

RETURN
```

If listing number is not found, display message
Leave message on screen until user presses a key or 10 seconds have elapsed
Fill in memory variables with current data
Using agtexist UDF in a VALID clause within a @..GET
Using agtname UDF to display name of agent
Update database file

Figure 12.36 A PROGRAM TO UPDATE RECORDS

The strategy for updating must attempt to maintain data integrity as much as possible by providing PICTURE clauses and protecting the key field. Notice the use of the agtexist UDF in the VALID clause for the magt field. This guarantees that only agent numbers that correspond to agents in the AGENT database file will be accepted. The agtname UDF is used to display the name of the agent. This helps users make sure they have entered the correct agent number.

Figures 12.37 and 12.38 on the next page illustrate the execution of this program. The user first sees a form like the one in Figure 12.37, but without this data. The user must then fill in the listing number. As soon as this has been done, current data appears as shown in Figure 12.37. The user can then make changes to this data. If a change to the agent field would result in an invalid agent, the program will display an error message and force the user to make a correction. Once the user has finished entering data correctly, the program will display the corresponding agent and ask the user to indicate the type of action to be taken (Figure 12.38). The user can choose U to update the database with the data on the screen, C to change the data on the screen, or A to abort the transaction without making any changes to the database.

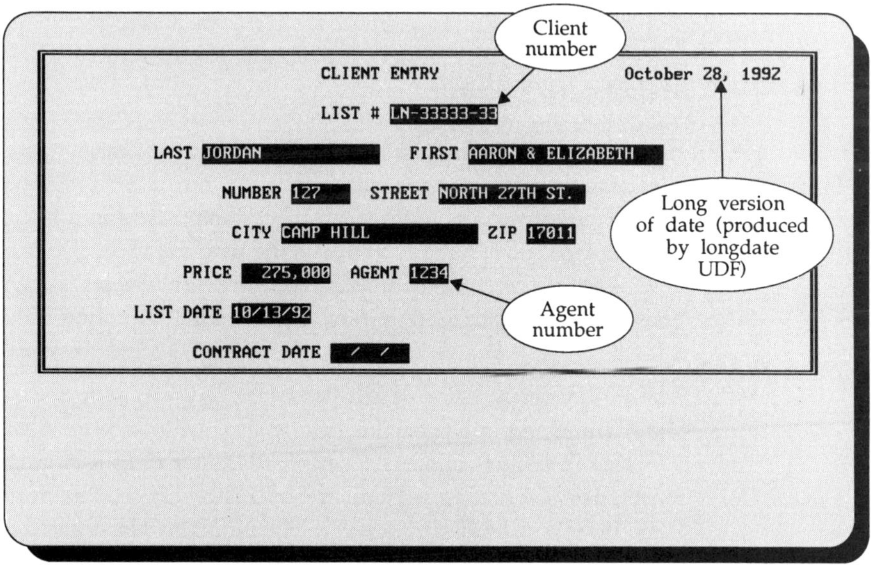

Figure 12.37 USING CHG_CLIE TO CHANGE CLIENT DATA

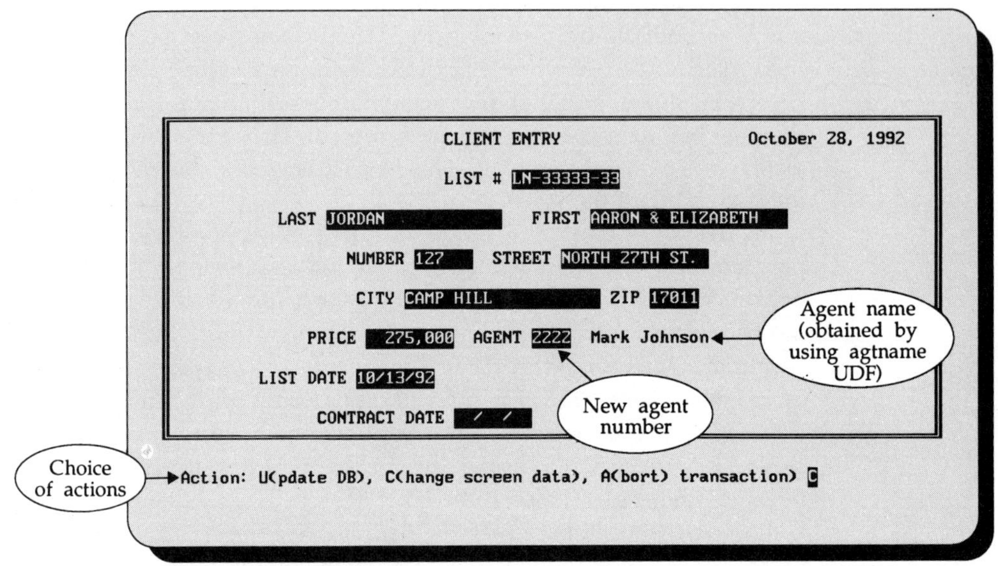

Figure 12.38 DATA HAS BEEN CHANGED

CHAPTER SUMMARY

1. Functions are internal algorithms that produce a variety of effects on data. The results of a function can be displayed or STOREd. Arguments, the data to be affected and other specifications, are placed in parentheses after the name of the function. Some of the available functions operate on character data or strings. Some string function effects shown as examples include changing case, trimming blanks, and extracting substrings.
2. Arithmetic functions include ABS(), INT(), MAX(), ROUND(), VAL(), and STR().
3. Dates are stored in a special format that permits arithmetic operations. The DTOC() function converts dates to character data for the sake of convenience. All aspects of a date are accessible with date functions such as CMONTH(), CDOW(), DOW(), DAY(), MONTH(), and YEAR().
4. A number of convenient utility functions report on the status of the operating system, active disk, and DBF file. These include OS(), DISKSPACE(), RECCOUNT(), and TYPE(). These functions are normally used in the interactive mode.

5. Two special functions are SOUNDEX(), which returns a "sounds-like" code, and LOOKUP(), which allows using a value in one database file for searching for a matching record in another.
6. Users can supplement the collection of built-in functions in dBASE by creating and using User-Defined Functions (UDFs).
7. A program to update records is similar to appending. The record must be retrieved and displayed in a custom entry screen. The user can then edit the data, which is stored in memory variables. When the operation has been completed, the updated data is REPLACEd to the DBF file.

KEY TERMS

function
operator
algorithm
argument
User-Defined Functions (UDFs)
procedure file

COMMAND SUMMARY

Command Name	**Use**
UPPER()	Convert letters to uppercase.
LOWER()	Convert letters to lowercase.
ASC()	ASCII code of character.
CHR()	Display ASCII character.
SPACE()	Fill with spaces.
ISALPHA()	Determine if character is alphabetic.
ISLOWER()	Determine if letter is lowercase.
ISUPPER()	Determine if letter is uppercase.
LEFT()	Extract leftmost characters of string.
RIGHT()	Extract rightmost characters of string.
LEN()	Length of string.
LTRIM()	Remove leading blanks.
RTRIM()	Remove trailing blanks.
TRIM()	Remove trailing blanks.
STUFF()	Insert substring into another string.

AT()	Determine position of substring.
SET DECIMAL TO	Set number of decimal positions.
ABS()	Absolute value.
EXP()	Exponential value.
INT()	Integer of value.
LOG()	Logarithm of value.
MAX()	Greater of two values.
MIN()	Lesser of two values.
MOD()	Modulus of value.
ROUND()	Round value.
SQRT()	Square root of value.
STR()	Convert numeric value to string.
SET CENTURY ON	Display four digits of year.
YEAR()	Numeric value of year in date.
CDOW()	Display character day of week.
CMONTH()	Display character month of date.
CTOD()	Convert character string to date.
DTOC()	Convert date to character string.
DATE()	System date.
DOW()	Day of week as numeric value.
DAY()	Numeric day of month.
MONTH()	Numeric value of month.
$	Evaluate presence of substring.
&	Macro expansion function.
COL()	Cursor column position.
ROW()	Position of cursor row.
OS()	Name of operating system.

VERSION()	Display version of dBASE IV.
DISKSPACE()	Amount of free disk space.
FILE()	Indicate existence of file.
DBF()	Name of current DBF file.
RECCOUNT()	Number of records in file.
LUPDATE()	Date of last file update.
RECSIZE()	Size of current record.
FIELD()	Field name of specified field.
RECNO()	Number of current record.
DELETED()	Deletion status of record.
TYPE()	Display type of field.
REPLICATE()	Repeat character.
SOUNDEX()	Finds "sounds-like" code.
LOOKUP()	Uses value from one database file to find match in another.
FUNCTION	Names user-defined function (UDF).
PARAMETERS	Used in UDFs to specify list of parameters.
RETURN	Used in UDFs to specify return value.
SET PROCEDURE TO	Activates procedure file.

dBUG dBASE

- Avoid making your system case-sensitive by using uppercase as a standard and converting everything automatically so the user does not have to worry about Shift keys or the Caps Lock. For the sake of consistency, you can convert the contents of memory variables to uppercase, using the following UPPER function:

```
memchoice = UPPER(memchoice)
```

- MESSAGE() displays the dBASE IV error message of the most recently issued error code that can be displayed with ERROR().

SELF-CHECK QUESTIONS

1. What is a function?
2. How can the result of a function be preserved for later use in a program?
3. What is an algorithm? What is an argument?
4. Why is it important to consider the case of character data?
5. Name a use for the $ operator.
6. What part does the ASCII code play in the use of functions?
7. What results do the ISALPHA(), ISLOWER(), and ISUPPER() functions produce?
8. Suggest a function to perform each of the following tasks:
   a. Extract the first six characters of a string.
   b. Extract a person's middle name from his or her full name.
   c. Extract the last five characters of a string.
9. What happens if a calculation produces too large a result?
10. What does the INT() function do?
11. How do you specify the number of decimal places to round in the ROUND() function?
12. What is the purpose of the two numeric arguments in STR()?
13. What does SET CENTURY ON do?
14. In what form are dates actually stored?
15. How can you determine the day of the week from a date field?
16. What function displays the record size of the active DBF file?
17. What function can we use to find names if we only know the sound of the names?
18. With what function can we use a value in one table to look up a value in another?
19. What is a UDF? How do we construct and use one?

TRY IT YOURSELF

1. Write a function to determine whether or not the letter "z" is in a string.
2. Select a graphic character with an ASCII value above 128 and write a brief program to fill one line with the character.
3. Write three commands to extract each of the following three names from msailor.

   ```
   msailor = 'John Paul Jones'
   ```

4. Insert ' Fitzgerald ' in mpres as the middle name.

   ```
   mpres = 'John Kennedy'
   ```

5. Display the length of the result of Exercise 4.
6. Display the location of the letter F in Exercise 4.
7. Display the integer parts of -7.8 and 9.25.
8. Round 5.677 to two decimal places.
9. Convert the numbers in mstreet to a numeric value, add 2, and display 125 Main St. (Hint: Two functions needed.)

   ```
   mstreet = '123 Main St.'
   ```

10. Store your birthday to a date-type variable.
11. Determine the day of the week on which you were born.
12. How many days have you been alive as of today?
13. Display the number of days until your next birthday.
14. Display the system date in correspondence format.
15. What version of DOS are you using?
16. Display the type of mcheck. `mcheck = 161`
17. Make up a name that sounds like yours and then determine whether the SOUNDEX function indicates that they sound alike.
18. Create and use a User-Defined Function that will reverse words. For example, if the argument to the function is "good baked," the function would return "baked good."

PROGRAMMING PROJECTS

The programming project uses the following database files:

```
Structure for database: A:\CUSTOMER.DBF
Field Field Name  Type        Width     Dec     Index
    1 CUSTNUMB    Numeric         3                 Y
    2 LAST        Character      10                 N
    3 FIRST       Character       8                 N
    4 ADDRESS     Character      20                 N
    5 BALANCE     Numeric         7       2         N
    6 CREDLIM     Numeric         4                 N
    7 SLSRNUMB    Numeric         2                 N
** Total **                      55
```

CUSTNUMB	LAST	FIRST	ADDRESS	BALANCE	CREDLIM	SLSRNUMB
124	Adams	Sally	481 Oak,Lansing,MI	418.75	500	3
256	Samuels	Ann	215 Pete,Grant,MI	10.75	800	6
311	Charles	Don	48 College,Ira,MI	200.10	300	12
315	Daniels	Tom	914 Cherry,Kent,MI	320.75	300	6
405	Williams	Al	519 Watson,Grant,MI	201.75	800	12
412	Adams	Sally	16 Elm,Lansing,MI	908.75	1000	3
522	Nelson	Mary	108 Pine,Ada,MI	49.50	800	12
567	Baker	Joe	808 Ridge,Harper,MI	201.20	300	6
587	Roberts	Judy	512 Pine,Ada,MI	57.75	500	6
622	Martin	Dan	419 Chip,Grant,MI	575.50	500	3

```
Structure for database: A:\SLSREP.DBF
Field Field Name  Type        Width     Dec     Index
    1 SLSRNUMB    Numeric         2                 Y
    2 SLSRNAME    Character      15                 N
    3 SLSRADDR    Character      22                 N
    4 TOTCOMM     Numeric         8       2         N
    5 COMMRATE    Numeric         4       2         N
** Total **                      52
```

SLSRNUMB	SLSRNAME	SLSRADDR	TOTCOMM	COMMRATE
3	Jones, Mary	123 Main,Grant,MI	2150.00	0.05
6	Smith, William	102 Raymond,Ada,MI	4912.50	0.07
12	Brown, Sam	419 Harper,Lansing,MI	2150.00	0.05

Write a program that is similar to CHG_CLIE to update the CUSTOMER.DBF file, using a custom screen. In particular, your program should do the following:

1. The program will terminate when the user enters a customer number of zero.
2. If the user enters a customer number that doesn't match an existing customer, the program should print an error message and force the user to reenter the customer number.
3. Make sure the user enters valid data. Legitimate values for credit limit (CREDLIM) are 300, 500, 800, or 1000. The sales rep number (SLSRNUMB), must match the number of a sales rep currently in the sales rep file.
4. After the user has entered all the data, display the name of the corresponding sales rep.
5. Give the user the option of updating the database with the data on the screen, changing the data on the screen, or aborting the transaction.
6. Test the program by updating several records and then LISTing from the dot prompt.
7. Use User-Defined Functions for validation and also for displaying the long version of today's date.

LEARNING OBJECTIVES

To learn special techniques at the dot prompt.

To learn how to use arrays.

To learn how to use formatted output for a report.

To learn how to use streaming output for a report.

13 Special Techniques

Introduction

dBASE offers a number of special techniques to make working with the dot prompt easier and/or more efficient. We begin this chapter by examining these techniques. Next, the chapter covers the construction and use of arrays in dBASE programs. Finally we will examine two approaches to report programs. One uses @..SAY commands to produce what is termed formatted output. The other uses ? and ?? commands. This type of output is called streaming output. We will also examine the advantages and disadvantages of each of these types.

13.1 SPECIAL TECHNIQUES AT THE DOT PROMPT

On occasion, working with data from the dot prompt may be more convenient than writing a program. This would be the case, for example, if a piece of information was needed only once. Suppose a sales manager needed to know how many of her firm's clients lived in Texas in order to establish sales territories. To provide the answer, it would clearly be more efficient to issue two or three well-designed commands at the dot prompt than to write and debug a program. This section illustrates interactive commands which will increase your power to manipulate data.

USING A WHILE CLAUSE

A WHILE clause can be used with interactive dedicated commands such as LIST, DISPLAY, SUM, COUNT, and REPORT. WHILE is more efficient than FOR because it only accesses records as long as the WHILE comparative expression is true. The execution ceases as soon as the expression is no longer true. This eliminates unnecessary executions. The advantages of this technique are amplified when it is employed with an index.

Figure 13.1 illustrates the use of LIST..WHILE. The first two commands in the figure activate the CUSTOMER database file as well as the index on the SLSRNUMB field. Next there is a typical LIST..FOR with the condition `slsrnumb = 6`.

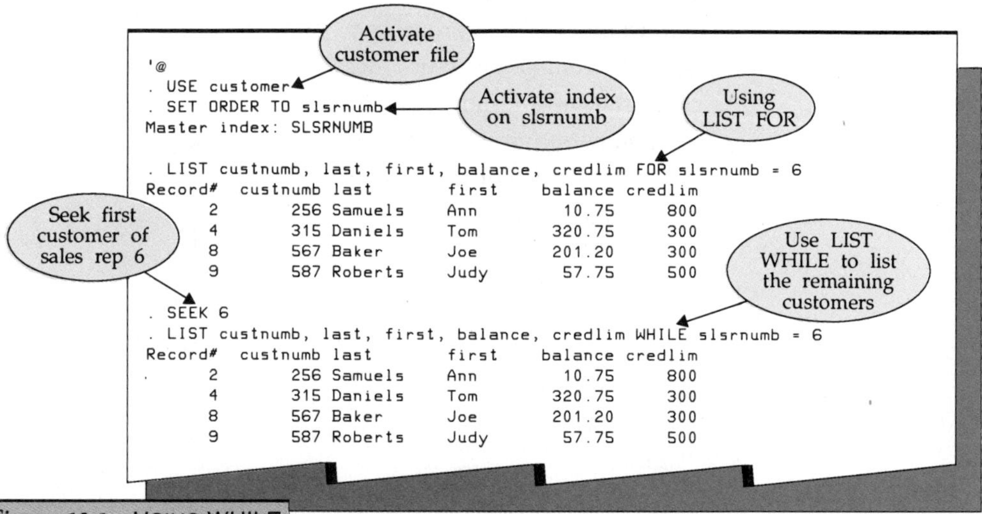

Figure 13.1 USING WHILE

As you can see from the output, the next two commands accomplish the same thing as the LIST..FOR. The SEEK command locates the first record on which SLSRNUMB is equal to 6. The LIST..WHILE command will then list records as long as SLSRNUMB is equal to 6. (Since the records are currently ordered by SLSRNUMB, all the other customers of sales rep 6 will immediately follow this first one.) Once a customer represented by someone other than sales rep 6 is encountered, the LIST..WHILE will terminate.

You might wonder why the SEEK and LIST..WHILE combination is so much better than a corresponding LIST..FOR. After all, there is an extra command to type (SEEK) and the results seem to be the same. With the small database files on your disk, you probably didn't notice any difference in the time it took to produce the two listings.

With large database files, however, the difference in time can be striking. Suppose, for example, that CUSTOMER contained 10,000 records, 100 of which represented customers of sales rep 6. The LIST..FOR command would access each of the 10,000 records. The LIST..WHILE command would access only 101 records, the 100 records on which SLSRNUMB is 6 as well as the first record on which SLSRNUMB is not 6. It would then terminate. In this case, the difference in the time it takes the two commands to display the records would be dramatic.

USING A REST CLAUSE

On occasion it may become necessary to display all the records from the current location of the record pointer to the end of the file. The clause to accomplish this is REST, as shown in Figure 13.2.

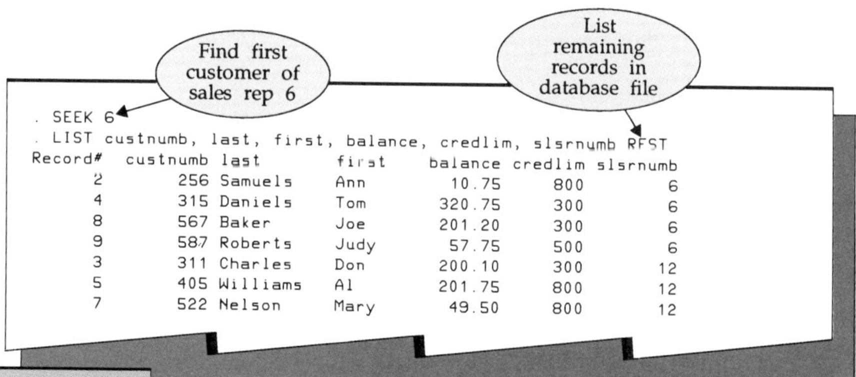

Figure 13.2 USING REST

CHECKING FOR AN EMPTY DATABASE FILE

You can test to see if a file has no records by opening the file and seeing if EOF() is true. The ZAP command removes all the records while retaining the structure. (See Figure 13.3.)

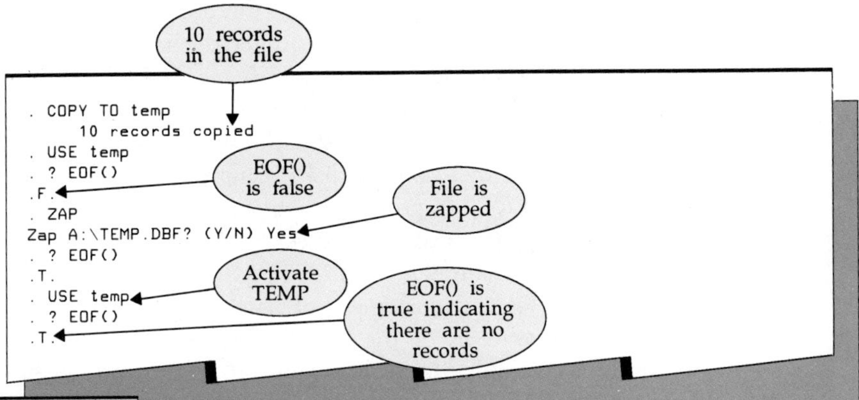

Figure 13.3 USING ZAP

USING A TRANSFORM() CLAUSE

TRANSFORM() enables you to use the template functions and picture symbols from Chapter 10 with LIST, DISPLAY, LABEL, and REPORT. Figure 13.4 gives several examples of the use of this clause. Notice that the templates must be enclosed in quotation marks. If the template begins with an @ sign, the symbol immediately following is a picture function. There must be a space following the picture function. The remainder is the template. (Chapter 10 gave details concerning templates and picture functions.)

```
. USE customer
. LIST last, first, balance
Record#  last        first     balance
      1  Adams       Sally      418.75
      2  Samuels     Ann         10.75
      3  Charles     Don        200.10
      4  Daniels     Tom        320.75
      5  Williams    Al         201.75
      6  Adams       Sally      908.75
      7  Nelson      Mary        49.50
      8  Baker       Joe        201.20
      9  Roberts     Judy        57.75
     10  Martin      Dan        575.50

. LIST last, first, TRANSFORM(balance,'@$ 9,999.99')
Record#  last        first     TRANSFORM(balance,'@$ 9,999.99')
      1  Adams       Sally      $418.75
      2  Samuels     Ann         $10.75
      3  Charles     Don        $200.10
      4  Daniels     Tom        $320.75
      5  Williams    Al         $201.75
      6  Adams       Sally      $908.75
      7  Nelson      Mary        $49.50
      8  Baker       Joe        $201.20
      9  Roberts     Judy        $57.75
     10  Martin      Dan        $575.50

. LIST last, first, credlim - balance
Record#  last        first     credlim - balance
      1  Adams       Sally                 81.25
      2  Samuels     Ann                  789.25
      3  Charles     Don                   99.90
      4  Daniels     Tom                  -20.75
      5  Williams    Al                   598.25
      6  Adams       Sally                 91.25
      7  Nelson      Mary                 750.50
      8  Baker       Joe                   98.80
      9  Roberts     Judy                 442.25
     10  Martin      Dan                  -75.50
```

Include dollar sign

Transform balance

Transform credlim - balance

Include dollar sign

```
. LIST last, first, TRANSFORM(credlim - balance, '@$')
Record#  last        first     TRANSFORM(credlim - balance, '@$')
      1  Adams       Sally             $81.25
      2  Samuels     Ann              $789.25
      3  Charles     Don               $99.90
      4  Daniels     Tom              $-20.75
      5  Williams    Al               $598.25
      6  Adams       Sally             $91.25
      7  Nelson      Mary             $750.50
      8  Baker       Joe               $98.80
      9  Roberts     Judy             $442.25
     10  Martin      Dan              $-75.50

. LIST last, first, TRANSFORM(credlim-balance,'@( 999.99')
Record#  last        first     TRANSFORM(credlim-balance,'@( 999.99')
      1  Adams       Sally       81.25
      2  Samuels     Ann        789.25
      3  Charles     Don         99.90
      4  Daniels     Tom        ( 20.75)
      5  Williams    Al         598.25
      6  Adams       Sally       91.25
      7  Nelson      Mary       750.50
      8  Baker       Joe         98.80
      9  Roberts     Judy       442.25
     10  Martin      Dan        ( 75.50)
```

Display negative numbers in parentheses

Figure 13.4 USING TRANSFORM()

USING SET FILTER AND SET FIELDS

SET FILTER TO stores a FOR condition so that it can be assumed during interactive processing. After the command in Figure 13.5 is issued, LIST recognizes only those records that contain 6 in the SLSRNUMB field. To turn the filter off, use SET FILTER TO with no condition.

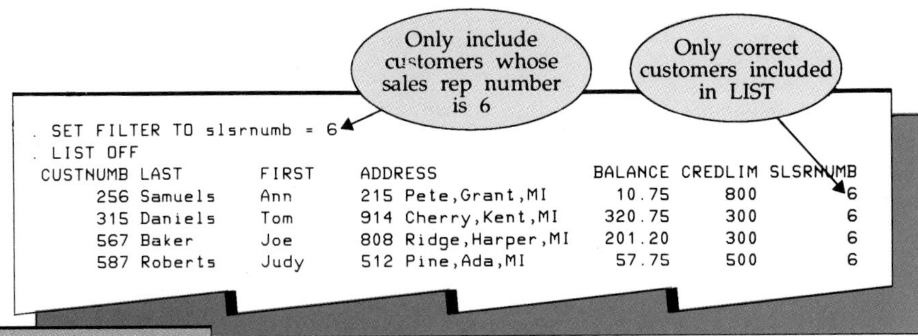

Figure 13.5 USING A FILTER

SET FIELDS TO performs the same function for a list of fields. Only last name, first name, address, and balance are referenced with the command shown in Figure 13.6. The selected fields are listed after the command, separated by commas. To include all fields, use SET FIELDS TO ALL.

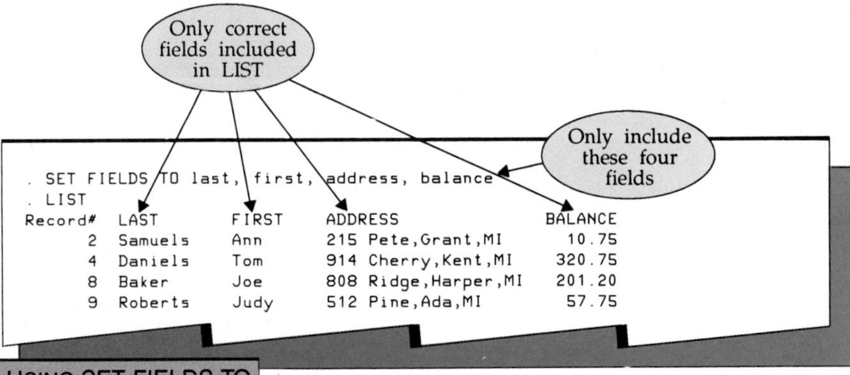

Figure 13.6 USING SET FIELDS TO

USING HISTORY

You are already aware of the convenience of using the Up Arrow key to retrieve previously issued commands from the HISTORY buffer. It is possible to edit a command line at the dot prompt by retrieving them in this way and using the keys shown in Table 13.1. You can save many keystrokes and errors by retrieving commands and modifying them instead of retyping.

TABLE 13.1 **Command line editing keys**

KEY	FUNCTION
Insert	Set Insert on or off.
Home	Move to start of previous word.
^Y (Ctrl-Y)	Delete rest of line.
Delete	Delete current character.
^T (Ctrl-T)	Delete current word.
End	Move to start of next word.
Esc	Delete current line.

USING SET ALTERNATE

SET ALTERNATE TO establishes a text file that can be opened with SET ALTERNATE ON. (See Figure 13.7 on the next page.) Any screen displays that do not use full-screen editing will echo to the file to produce a transcription of the work session on disk. The file can be viewed with TYPE, MODIFY COMMAND, or an external word processor. If a printer is not currently available, processed data can be saved to a file for printing at a later time. The examples in this text were reproduced with the SET ALTERNATE TO command.

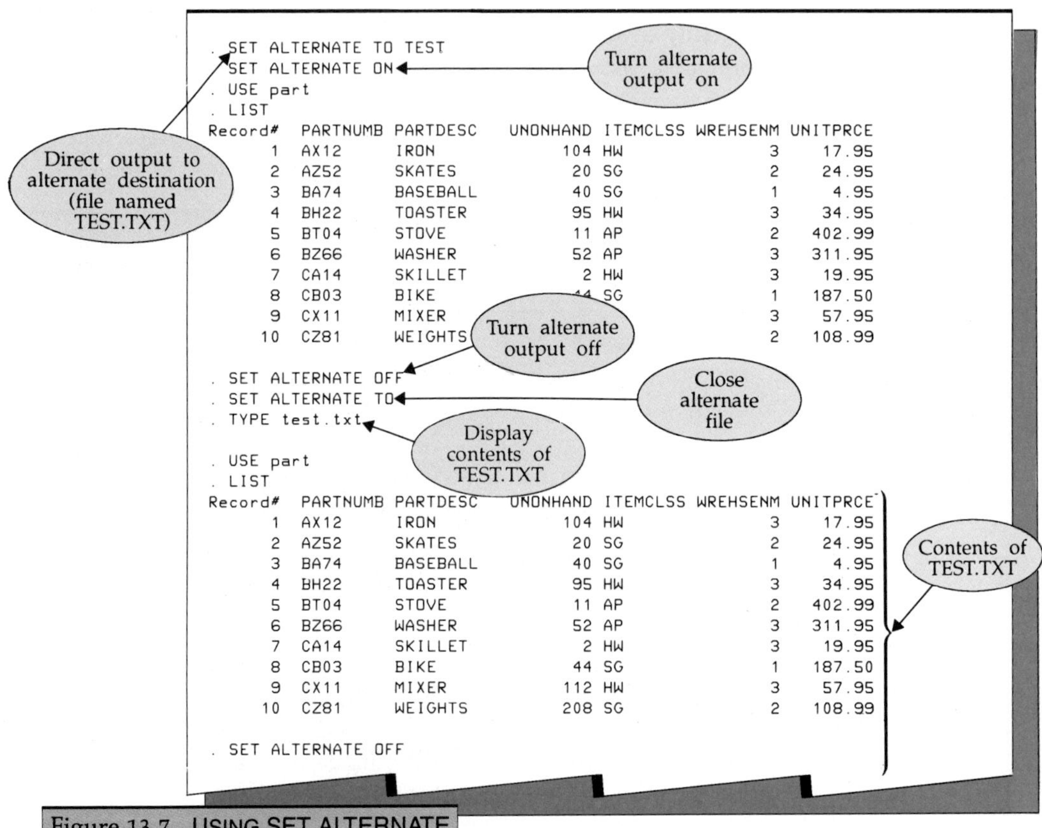

Figure 13.7 USING SET ALTERNATE

Experimentation and testing are the best tools for increasing your skills with these special techniques at the dot prompt. Journals and books that recommend timesaving procedures and strategies for dBASE are also widely available.

13.2 USING ARRAYS

DECLARING AND USING ARRAYS

Like many other programming languages, dBASE IV supports arrays. Whereas a memory variable is a name for a single element, an *array* is a name for a set of elements. Arrays are created with the DECLARE statement. To declare marray as an array containing ten elements, for example, the command would be

```
DECLARE marray [10]
```

The name of the array is marray. The 10 between the square brackets indicates that this array contains ten elements. We can picture this array as a list (see Figure 13.8). To refer to an individual entry in the array, we use a *subscript*. The subscript is also enclosed between square brackets. The third element in the array, for example, would be referred to as

```
marray[3]
```

The subscript can also be a memory variable. If mrow is a variable that currently contains the number 3,

```
marray[mrow]
```

would also refer to the third element in marray.

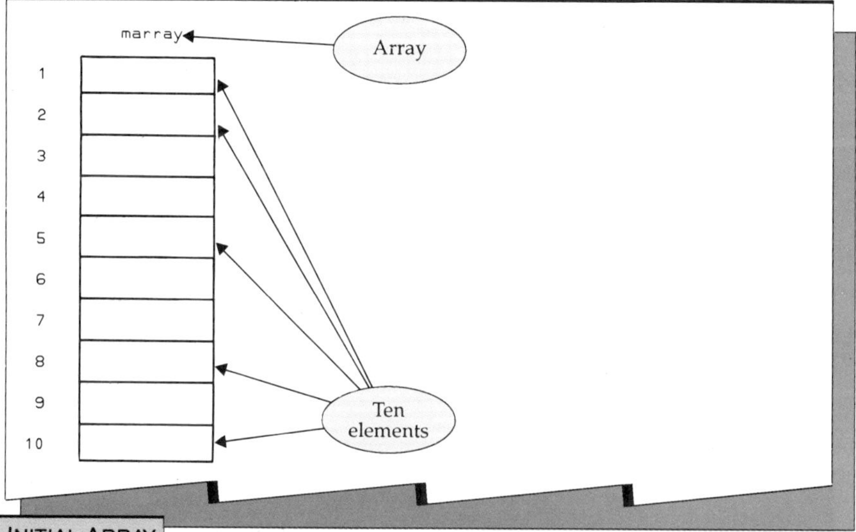

Figure 13.8 INITIAL ARRAY

The program shown in Figure 13.9 on the next page illustrates the process of declaring an array with ten elements, filling the first five elements (see Figure 13.10, also on the next page), and then displaying all ten. Notice that, unlike other programming languages, in dBASE the various entries in the array can be of different types. The first and second entries are numbers, the third is true (.T.), the fourth is a character string, and the fifth is a date. Notice also the loop used to display the entries in the array. It is very typical of loops to process elements in arrays. Finally, notice that the values for the elements not yet filled in are displayed as false (.F.).

```
* ARRAY1.PRG - Tests features of using arrays.

SET TALK OFF

DECLARE marray[10]

* Initialize elements in array
marray[1] = 12
marray[2] = 5.7
marray[3] = .T.
marray[4] = 'Jones, Mary'
marray[5] = {06/15/92}

* Display the entries in marray
mrow = 1
DO WHILE mrow <= 10
    ? marray[mrow]
    mrow = mrow + 1
ENDDO WHILE mrow <= 10

SET TALK ON

RETURN

. do array1

        12
      5.70
.T.
Jones, Mary
06/15/92
.F.
.F.
.F.
.F.
.F.
```

Declare marray

Notice that the data types of the values are all different

Fill first five locations of marray

Loop to display the contents of marray

Five values we placed in the array

We have not filled positions six through ten

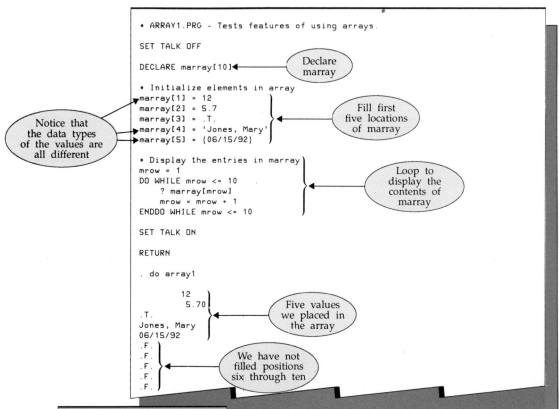

Figure 13.9 USING AN ARRAY

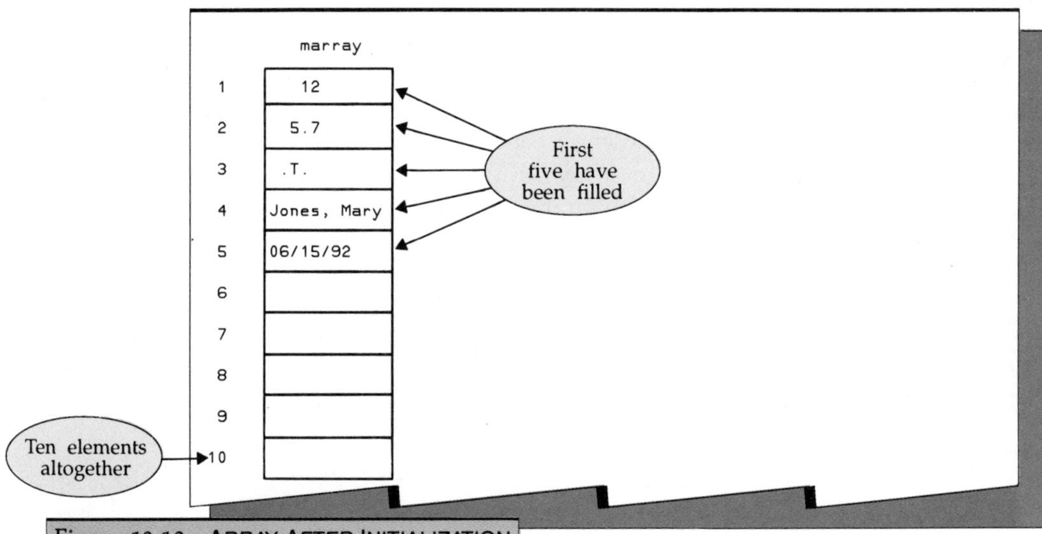

Figure 13.10 ARRAY AFTER INITIALIZATION

VARIABLE-LENGTH ARRAYS

In many cases, you won't know exactly how many elements you will need in an array. In other words, what you really need is a *variable-length array*. One time you run the program, you may use five elements; later, eight. Still another time you may need 25 elements.

Unfortunately, when we declare an array we must enter a specific number. We don't have to use the entire array in our program, however. Thus, we declare the array to be large enough to hold the largest number of entries we expect. We will then fill only the portion required. We will also set a memory variable equal to the number of elements we have actually used.

The program in Figure 13.11 on the next page illustrates the process. The DECLARE statement creates an array called marray with ten elements. The DO WHILE loop that follows obtains values from the user of the program and places them in marray. Once the user enters a value of zero, the process terminates. The number of entries actually entered by the user (that is, not counting the zero) will be placed in mnumrows. This is accomplished by subtracting one from mrow. Note that if the user enters ten nonzero numbers, the process will also terminate. In this case mrow would be 11, so mnumrows will be set to 10.

The next DO WHILE loop displays the entries in the array. Notice that it terminates once the value in mrow exceeds the value in mnumrows. If, for example, the user had entered six entries, this would ensure that only six entries were displayed.

The next loop displays the same entries. The difference is that mrow starts at mnumrows rather than one. Each time through the loop, the value in mrow is decreased, rather than increased, by one. The effect is that the entries are displayed in reverse order.

The final loop illustrates the process of adding all the entries in the array. To do so, we initialize the variable that will contain the total (mtotal) to zero. Each time through the loop we will add the corresponding entry in the array to mtotal. Once we exit the loop, mtotal will contain the total of all the entries.

```
* ARRAY2.PRG - Illustrates filling and using arrays.

SET TALK OFF

DECLARE marray[10]

* Accept values from user and place them in an array.
*    Process will terminate when user enters a value of
*    zero.  Set mnumrows to number of elements entered
*    by user.
mrow = 1
DO WHILE mrow <= 10
    marray[mrow] = 0
    INPUT 'Enter a value (0 to exit) ' to marray[mrow]
    IF marray[mrow] = 0
        EXIT
    ELSE
        mrow = mrow + 1
    ENDIF marray[mrow] = 0
ENDDO WHILE mrow <= 10
* Don't count entry of zero as legitimate entry
mnumrows = mrow - 1

* Display entries in marray.
? 'Entries in marray.'
mrow = 1
DO WHILE mrow <= mnumrows
    ? marray[mrow]
    mrow = mrow + 1
ENDDO WHILE mrow <= mnumrows
?

* Display entries in reverse order.
? 'Entries in reverse order.'
mrow = mnumrows
DO WHILE mrow > 0
    ? marray[mrow]
    mrow = mrow - 1
ENDDO WHILE mrow > 0
?

* Calculate and display total of elements in marray

mrow = 1
mtotal = 0
DO WHILE mrow <= mnumrows
    mtotal = mtotal + marray[mrow]
    mrow = mrow + 1
ENDDO WHILE mrow <= mnumrows
? 'The total is: ', mtotal

SET TALK ON

RETURN
```

Get value from user

If value is zero exit, otherwise place in array

Calculate number of entries actually entered (don't count the zero)

Loop to display entries

Loop to display entries in reverse order

Loop to calculate total of entries

Figure 13.11 MANIPULATING AN ARRAY

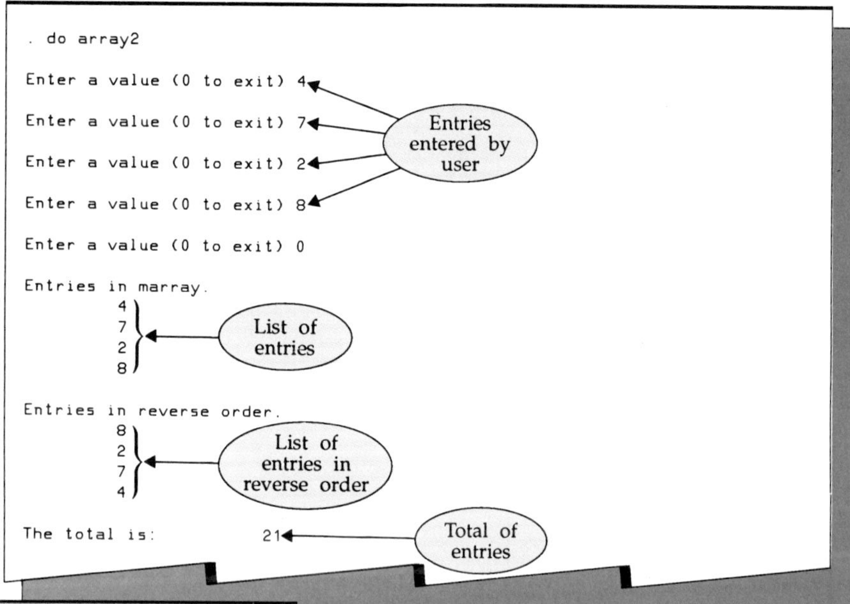
. do array2
Enter a value (0 to exit) 4
Enter a value (0 to exit) 7
Enter a value (0 to exit) 2
Enter a value (0 to exit) 8
Enter a value (0 to exit) 0
Entries entered by user
Entries in marray.
4
7
2
8
List of entries
Entries in reverse order.
8
2
7
4
List of entries in reverse order
The total is: 21
Total of entries

Figure 13.11 MANIPULATING AN ARRAY

USING ARRAYS FOR SEARCHING

In scientific applications, it is common to use arrays in a wide variety of ways. In business-type applications, which represent the bulk of the programming done in dBASE, arrays are used in much more limited ways. By far the most common is for searching. To use an array for searching, we begin by filling the array with appropriate values. Later in the program, we examine the contents of an array to determine whether a particular value is contained in the array or not.

The program shown in Figure 13.12 on the next page illustrates this process. The array magt_numb is the array used for searching. The DO WHILE loop fills this array as well as the magt_name array with agent numbers and names from the AGENT database file.

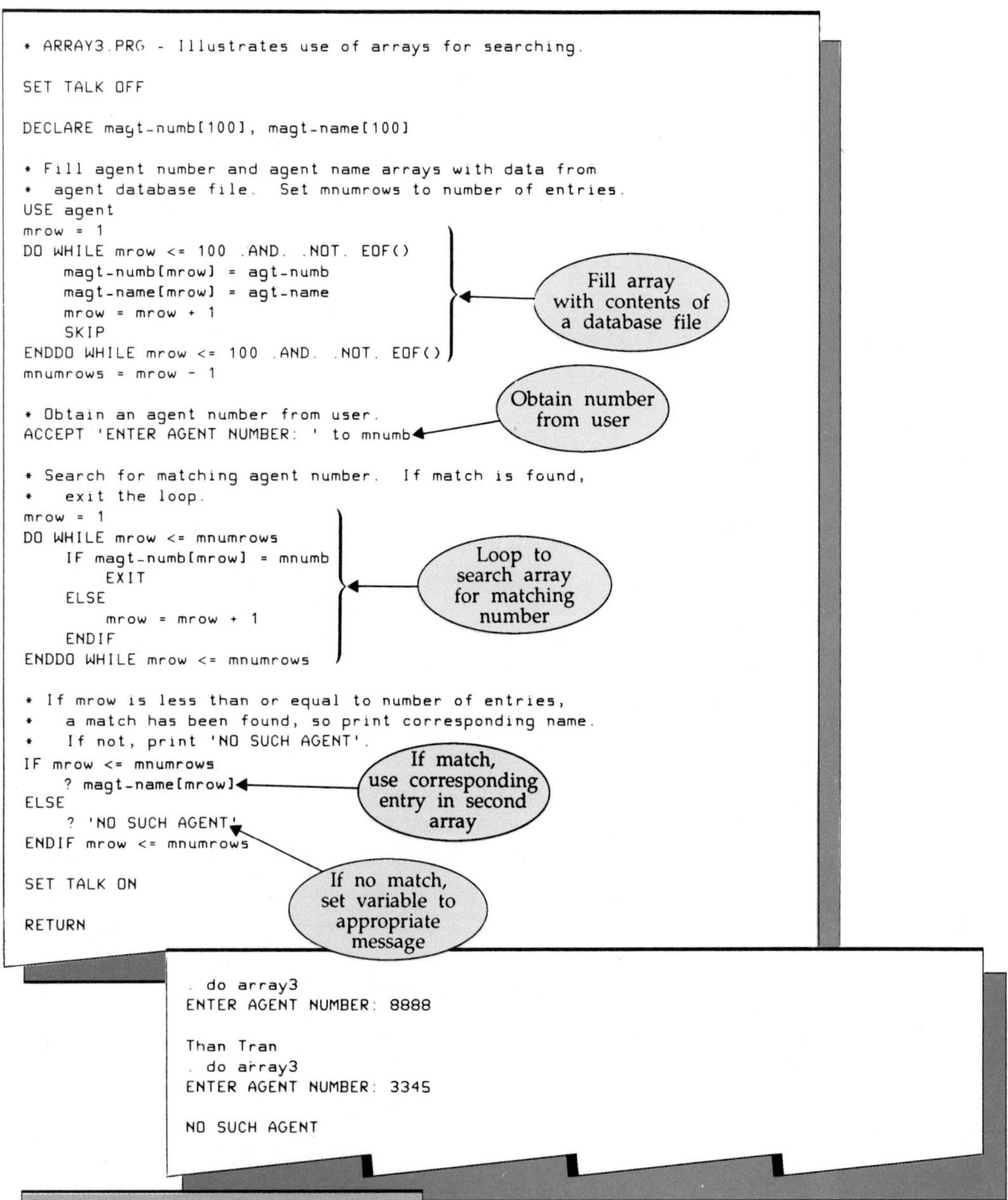
```
* ARRAY3.PRG - Illustrates use of arrays for searching.

SET TALK OFF

DECLARE magt-numb[100], magt-name[100]

* Fill agent number and agent name arrays with data from
*  agent database file.  Set mnumrows to number of entries.
USE agent
mrow = 1
DO WHILE mrow <= 100 .AND. .NOT. EOF()
    magt-numb[mrow] = agt-numb
    magt-name[mrow] = agt-name
    mrow = mrow + 1
    SKIP
ENDDO WHILE mrow <= 100 .AND. .NOT. EOF()
mnumrows = mrow - 1

* Obtain an agent number from user.
ACCEPT 'ENTER AGENT NUMBER: ' to mnumb

* Search for matching agent number.  If match is found,
*   exit the loop.
mrow = 1
DO WHILE mrow <= mnumrows
    IF magt-numb[mrow] = mnumb
        EXIT
    ELSE
        mrow = mrow + 1
    ENDIF
ENDDO WHILE mrow <= mnumrows

* If mrow is less than or equal to number of entries,
*   a match has been found, so print corresponding name.
*   If not, print 'NO SUCH AGENT'.
IF mrow <= mnumrows
    ? magt-name[mrow]
ELSE
    ? 'NO SUCH AGENT'
ENDIF mrow <= mnumrows

SET TALK ON

RETURN
```

Fill array with contents of a database file
Obtain number from user
Loop to search array for matching number
If match, use corresponding entry in second array
If no match, set variable to appropriate message

```
. do array3
ENTER AGENT NUMBER: 8888

Than Tran
. do array3
ENTER AGENT NUMBER: 3345

NO SUCH AGENT
```

Figure 13.12 SEARCHING AN ARRAY

Once this has been done (Figure 13.13), we are ready to use the array for searching. In this example, we will obtain a number from the user by using the ACCEPT command. The search is accomplished in the next DO WHILE loop in Figure 13.12. Before the loop the subscript mrow is set to 1. In the loop the value in magt_numb[mrow] is compared to the value entered by the user. If the two are equal, the loop will be exited. If not, the value in mrow will be incremented by one. The process will continue until we have found a match and consequently exited the loop, or when mrow exceeds the number of entries in the array.

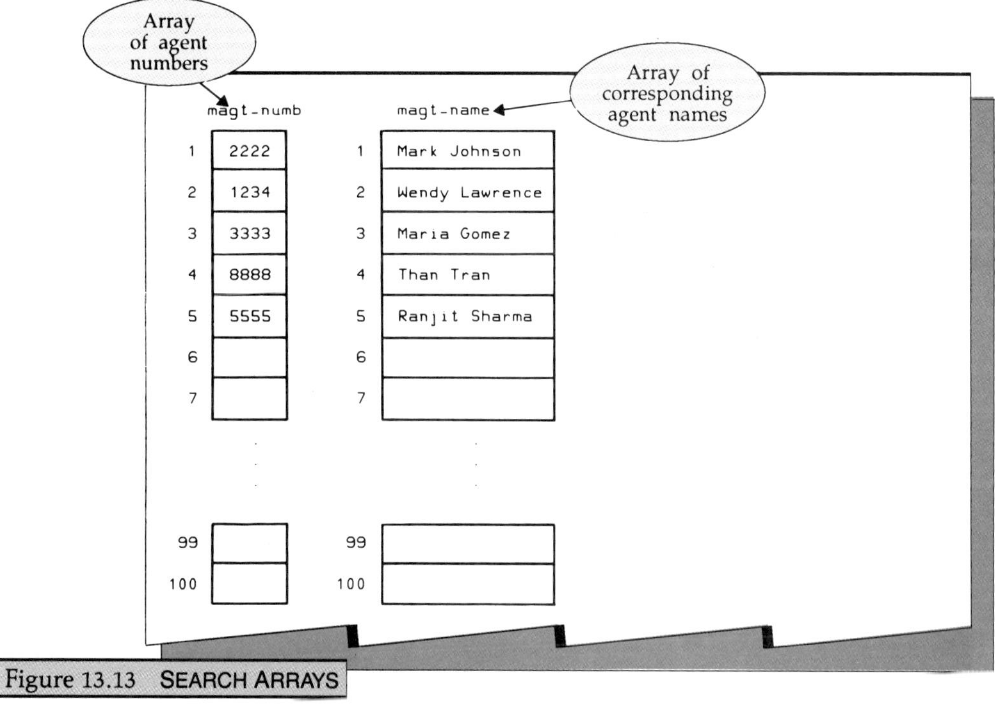

Figure 13.13 SEARCH ARRAYS

The next portion checks to see whether a match was actually found. If mrow does not exceed mnumrows, then we must have left the loop early and consequently a match must have been found. In this particular example, we will then display the corresponding entry in magt_name, that is, the name of the agent whose number was entered by the user. If not, the program will display an error message.

Figure 13.12 also shows the results of executing this program. It is worthwhile for you to run through the logic of the program yourself to see how the program produces the indicated results.

You may wonder why we would do this type of search. After all, you accomplished the same thing with a SEEK in UDFs in the last chapter. The answer is that a SEEK involves disk accesses and also requires the corresponding database file to be active. By using the technique shown in the ARRAY3 program, we could fill the arrays once at the beginning of a program and then close the database file. Thus, neither this database file nor its index will need to be active during the main body of the program. Since we do have limits on the number of files that can be active at any one time, this can be important. Further, it is more efficient to search an array in memory than to access data on a disk. Thus, each search may very well take less time than a corresponding SEEK command.

If the database file is very large, we probably will not be able to create arrays large enough to contain the entire file. In such cases, this technique is not appropriate. Often, however, it comes in quite handy.

TWO-DIMENSIONAL ARRAYS

The types of arrays we have been discussing so far are called *one-dimensional arrays*. They represent a single string of entries. In some cases, it would be more convenient to use a grid of entries such as the one shown in Figure 13.14. This is called a *two-dimensional array*.

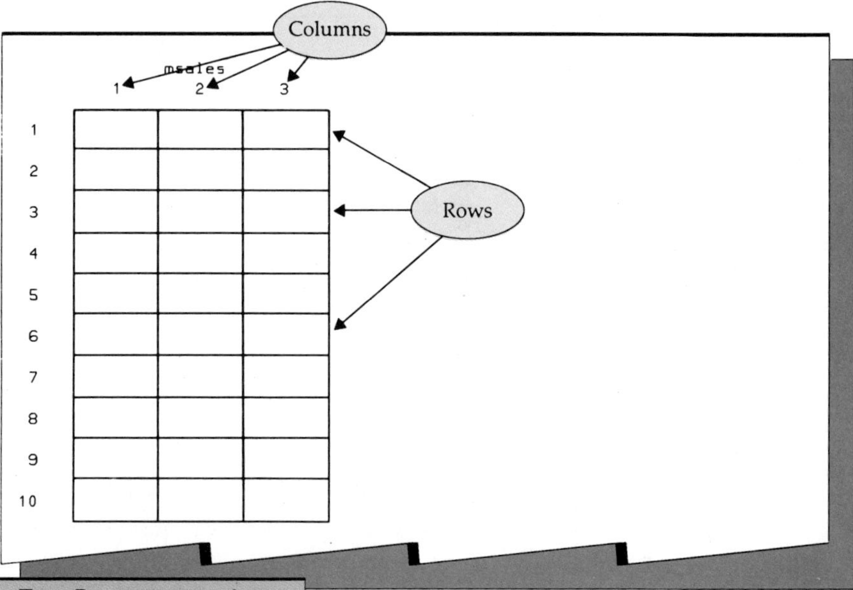

Figure 13.14 TWO-DIMENSIONAL ARRAY

To declare a two-dimensional array, we indicate the number of rows and columns in the array. For example, if the array msales is to contain ten rows and three columns, the DECLARE statement would be

```
DECLARE msales[10,3]
```

To refer to a specific entry in such an array, we need to specify both a row and a column. The entry in the second column of the fourth row, for example, would be

```
msales[4,2]
```

To illustrate the use of such an array, consider the program ARRAY4 shown in Figure 13.15 on the next page. This program uses the msales array. The rows represent departments and the columns represent months. The entries represent sales figures. For example, the entry in msales[4,2] would be the amount of sales for department 4 in month 2. There are two one-dimensional arrays. The array mdeptsls will contain the total sales for each department over the entire three-month period. The array mmonsls will contain the total sales for all departments for a given month.

The program begins with a pair of nested DO WHILE loops to fill the entire msales array with zeros (Figure 13.16 on page 362). The DO WHILE .T. loop that follows the nested loop in Figure 13.15 will first obtain a department number from the user. If the user enters a department number of zero, the loop is exited. Assuming the number is not zero, we next obtain a month from the user.

```
* ARRAY4.PRG - Illustrates use of two dimensional arrays.

SET TALK OFF

* Declare arrays
DECLARE msales[10,3], mdeptsls[10], mmonsls[3]

CLEAR

* Initialize msales array to zero.
mdept = 1
DO WHILE mdept <= 10
    mmonth = 1
    DO WHILE mmonth <= 3
        msales[mdept,mmonth] = 0
        mmonth = mmonth + 1
    ENDDO WHILE mmonth <= 3
    mdept = mdept + 1
ENDDO WHILE mdept <= 10
```

Nested loop to set all entries in two-dimensional array to zero

```
* Obtain sales entries from user.
DO WHILE .T.
    mdept = 0
    INPUT 'Enter dept # (0 to exit) ' TO mdept
    IF mdept = 0
        EXIT
    ENDIF
    mmonth = 0
    INPUT 'Enter month ' TO mmonth
    IF mdept < 1 .OR. mdept > 10 .OR. mmonth < 1 .OR. mmonth > 3
        LOOP
    ENDIF
    INPUT 'Enter sales amount ' TO msales[mdept,mmonth]
ENDDO WHILE .T.
```

If department is zero, exit the loop

Obtain department number and month from user (will use these as subscripts)

Obtain sales amount

```
* Calculate department totals.
mdept = 1
DO WHILE mdept <= 10
    mmonth = 1
    mdeptsls[mdept] = 0
    DO WHILE mmonth <= 3
        mdeptsls[mdept] = mdeptsls[mdept] + msales[mdept,mmonth]
        mmonth = mmonth + 1
    ENDDO WHILE mmonth <= 3
    mdept = mdept + 1
ENDDO WHILE mdept <= 10
```

Nested loops to calculate totals by department

```
* Calculate month totals.
mmonth = 1
DO WHILE mmonth <= 3
    mdept = 1
    mmonsls[mmonth] = 0
    DO WHILE mdept <= 10
        mmonsls[mmonth] = mmonsls[mmonth] + msales[mdept,mmonth]
        mdept = mdept + 1
    ENDDO WHILE mdept <= 10
    mmonth = mmonth + 1
ENDDO WHILE mmonth <= 3
```

Nested loops to calculate totals by month

```
* Display sales values by department and department totals.
mdept = 1
DO WHILE mdept <= 10
    ? mdept, msales[mdept,1], msales[mdept,2],msales[mdept,3], ;
        mdeptsls[mdept]
    mdept = mdept + 1
ENDDO
```

Nested loops to display sales by department

Figure 13.15 USING A TWO-DIMENSIONAL ARRAY

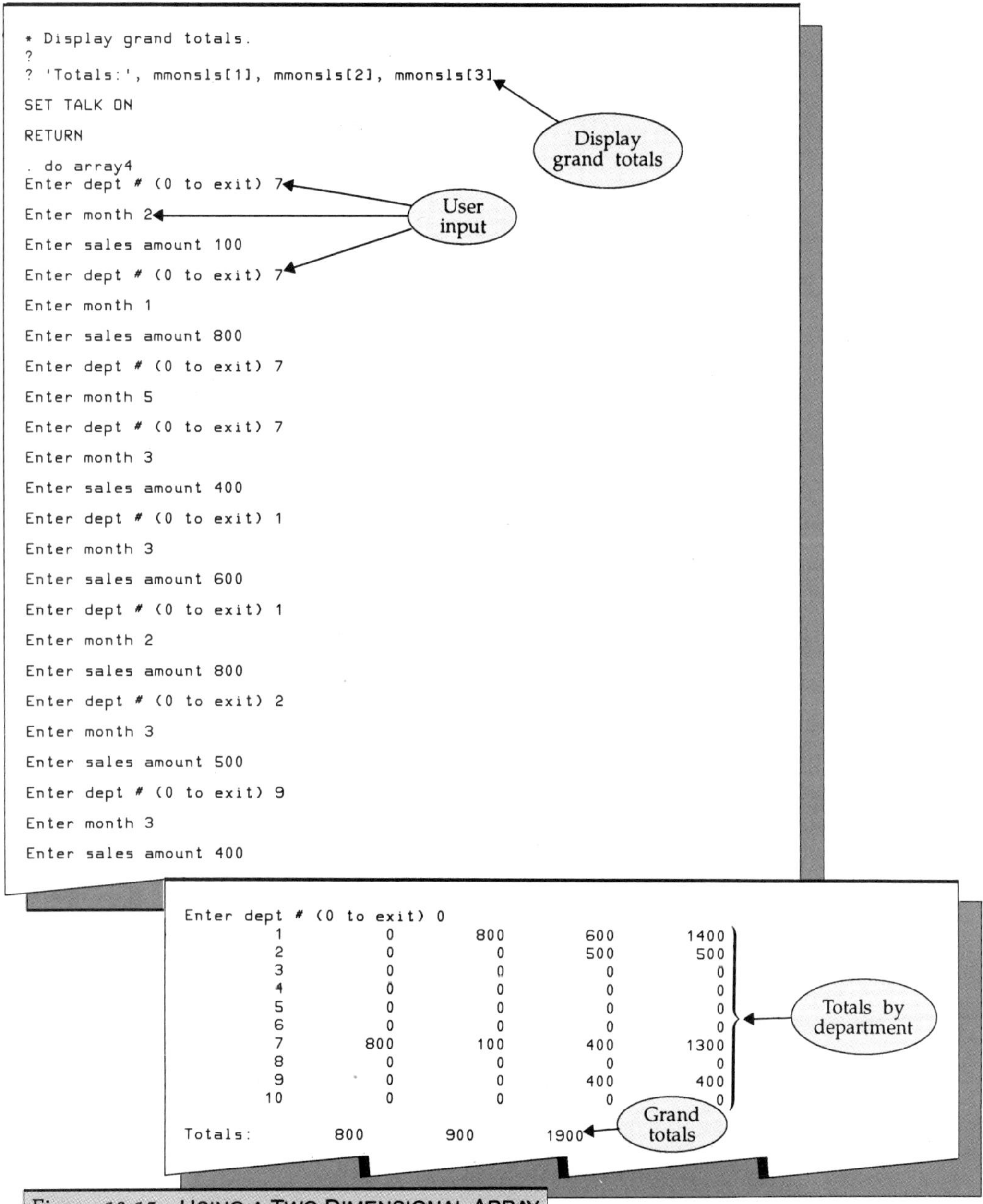

```
* Display grand totals.
?
? 'Totals:', mmonsls[1], mmonsls[2], mmonsls[3]
SET TALK ON
RETURN
. do array4
Enter dept # (0 to exit) 7
Enter month 2
Enter sales amount 100
Enter dept # (0 to exit) 7
Enter month 1
Enter sales amount 800
Enter dept # (0 to exit) 7
Enter month 5
Enter dept # (0 to exit) 7
Enter month 3
Enter sales amount 400
Enter dept # (0 to exit) 1
Enter month 3
Enter sales amount 600
Enter dept # (0 to exit) 1
Enter month 2
Enter sales amount 800
Enter dept # (0 to exit) 2
Enter month 3
Enter sales amount 500
Enter dept # (0 to exit) 9
Enter month 3
Enter sales amount 400
```

```
Enter dept # (0 to exit) 0
        1         0       800       600      1400
        2         0         0       500       500
        3         0         0         0         0
        4         0         0         0         0
        5         0         0         0         0
        6         0         0         0         0
        7       800       100       400      1300
        8         0         0         0         0
        9         0         0       400       400
       10         0         0         0         0
Totals:         800       900      1900
```


Figure 13.15 USING A TWO-DIMENSIONAL ARRAY

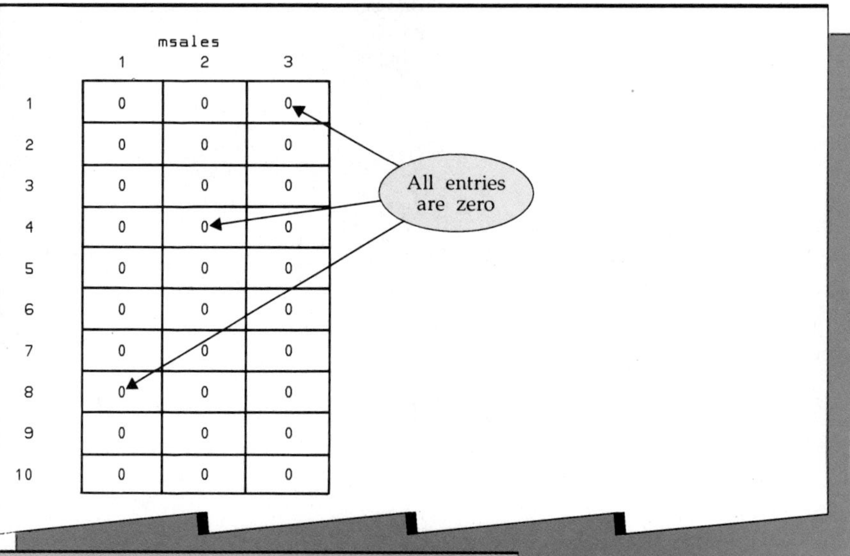

Figure 13.16 TWO-DIMENSIONAL ARRAY FILLED WITH ZEROS

If the department number is outside of the range 1 through 10, or the month is outside the range 1 to 3, the LOOP command returns control to the beginning of the loop where the process will begin again. Assuming both the department number and month are in the correct ranges, we obtain a sales amount from the user and place it in the appropriate entry in msales. Notice that the department number serves as the row number, and the month serves as the column. For example, Figure 13.17 shows the results of the user entering 7 as the department number, 2 as the month, and 100 as the sales amount.

Next in the ARRAY4 program there are two sets of nested DO WHILE loops. The first set calculates the department totals, and the second set calculates the monthly totals. The final DO WHILE loop displays, for each department, the sales figures for the three months followed by the total sales. Following these figures, the grand totals will be displayed.

The last part of the figure shows the execution of this program. Notice the place where the user entered 5 as a month. Instead of being asked for a sales figure, the user was immediately asked for another department. Figure 13.18 shows the final status of the msales array after all the data was entered.

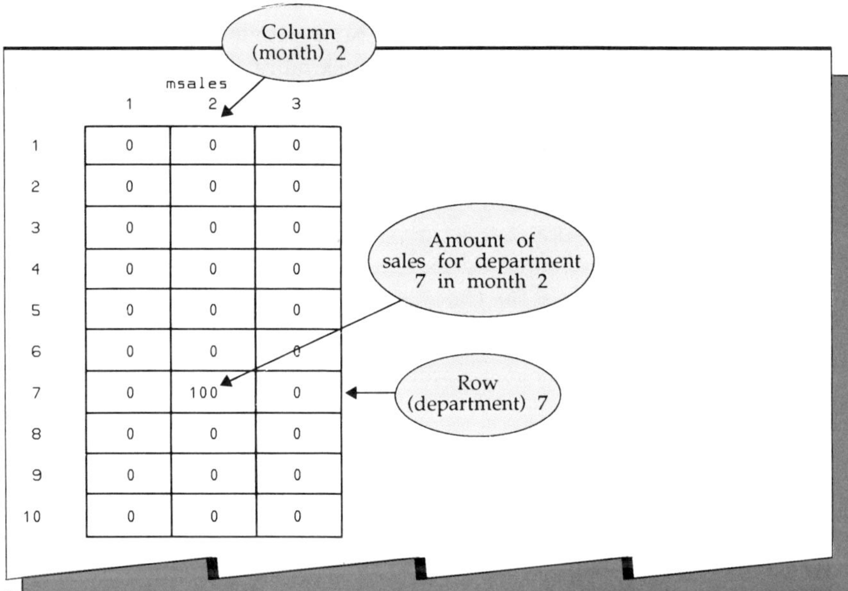

Figure 13.17 TWO-DIMENSIONAL ARRAY AFTER USER'S FIRST ENTRY

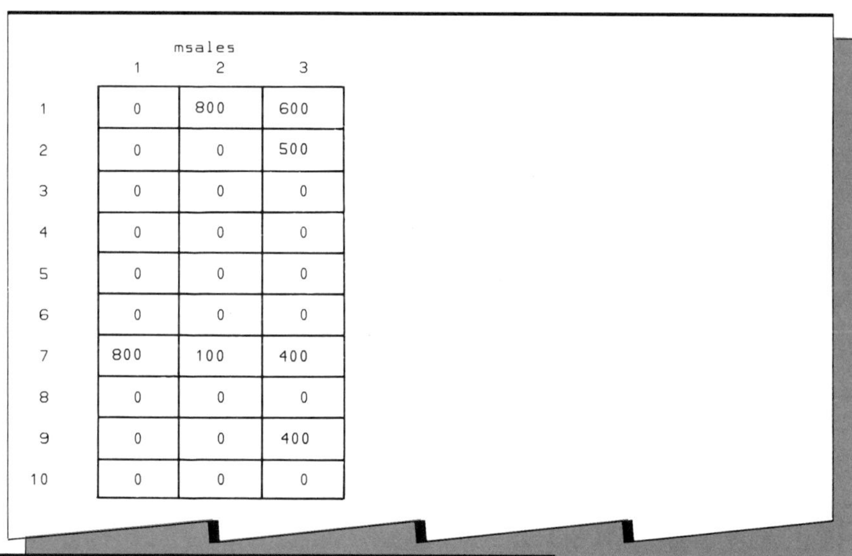

Figure 13.18 TWO-DIMENSIONAL ARRAY WITH USER'S ENTRIES

13.3 USING FORMATTED OUTPUT IN REPORT PROGRAMS

The dBASE REPORT generator provides us with a convenient and quick way to create reports. Occasionally, though, a particular report will be beyond the capabilities of the facility. In such cases, our only alternative would be to write a complete program to produce the report.

In this section, we will examine report programs in more detail. In particular, we will write a program to produce the report shown in Figure 13.19. Note that it involves data from both the customer file (customer number, name, address, balance, credit limit, and sales rep number) *and* the sales rep file (sales rep name).

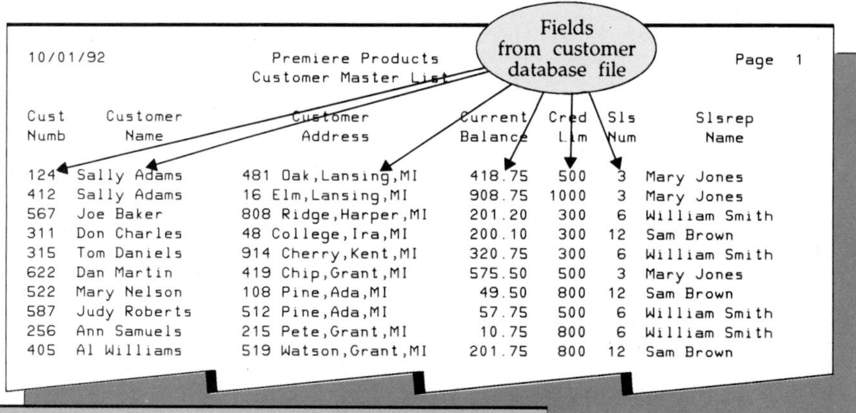

10/01/92 Premiere Products Page 1
Customer Master List

Cust Numb	Customer Name	Customer Address	Current Balance	Cred Lim	Sls Num	Slsrep Name
124	Sally Adams	481 Oak,Lansing,MI	418.75	500	3	Mary Jones
412	Sally Adams	16 Elm,Lansing,MI	908.75	1000	3	Mary Jones
567	Joe Baker	808 Ridge,Harper,MI	201.20	300	6	William Smith
311	Don Charles	48 College,Ira,MI	200.10	300	12	Sam Brown
315	Tom Daniels	914 Cherry,Kent,MI	320.75	300	6	William Smith
622	Dan Martin	419 Chip,Grant,MI	575.50	500	3	Mary Jones
522	Mary Nelson	108 Pine,Ada,MI	49.50	800	12	Sam Brown
587	Judy Roberts	512 Pine,Ada,MI	57.75	500	6	William Smith
256	Ann Samuels	215 Pete,Grant,MI	10.75	800	6	William Smith
405	Al Williams	519 Watson,Grant,MI	201.75	800	12	Sam Brown

Figure 13.19 CUSTOMER MASTER LIST WITH SALES REP NAME

There are two different approaches available in dBASE for report programs. The one we will study in this section involves the same @..SAY commands we have used for data-entry screens. This type of report is called *formatted output*. In the next section we will study the alternative, which is called streaming output.

REPORT USING A SINGLE DATABASE FILE

Rather than face the problem of retrieving data from two files right away, let's first try to produce the report as shown but without any reference to the name of the sales rep, that is, the report shown in Figure 13.20. In this case, only data from the customer file is used to produce the report.

```
10/01/92                   Premiere Products                    Pag
                          Customer Master List

Cust     Customer            Customer            Current  Cred  Sls
Numb       Name               Address            Balance   Lim  Num

124  Sally Adams      481 Oak,Lansing,MI         418.75    500   3
412  Sally Adams      16 Elm,Lansing,MI          908.75   1000   3
567  Joe Baker        808 Ridge,Harper,MI        201.20    300   6
311  Don Charles      48 College,Ira,MI          200.10    300  12
315  Tom Daniels      914 Cherry,Kent,MI         320.75    300   6
622  Dan Martin       419 Chip,Grant,MI          575.50    500   3
522  Mary Nelson      108 Pine,Ada,MI             49.50    800  12
587  Judy Roberts     512 Pine,Ada,MI             57.75    500   6
256  Ann Samuels      215 Pete,Grant,MI           10.75    800   6
405  Al Williams      519 Watson,Grant,MI        201.75    800  12
```

Sales rep name
is not included
in this version

Figure 13.20 CUSTOMER MASTER LIST WITHOUT SALES REP NAME

A program to produce this report is shown in Figure 13.21 on the next page. The program begins by clearing the screen and activating the customer file, ordered by the index called NAME. Next, the memory variable pagenum, which is used to hold the number of the current page of the report, is initialized to 1.

Before discussing the way in which the memory variable linenum is initialized, let's discuss its use in the program. In the loop, you will see statements like the following:

```
@ linenum, 0 SAY customer->custnumb
```

This statement indicates that the value in custnumb is to be displayed in column 0 on the line that is indicated by the value currently stored in linenum. Collectively, the statements starting with

```
@ linenum, 0 SAY customer->custnumb
```

and ending with

```
@ linenum, 59 SAY customer->slsrnumb
```

cause a single line of the report to be printed on the line that is indicated by the value in linenum. This line is called a *detail line,* since it contains the main detail of the report.

Once a detail line has been printed, linenum is incremented by 1 (linenum = linenum + 1) in preparation for printing the next detail line. Then the next record of the database file is read (SKIP). This process continues until we reach the end of the file. At this point, the condition EOF() becomes true, and the loop will terminate.

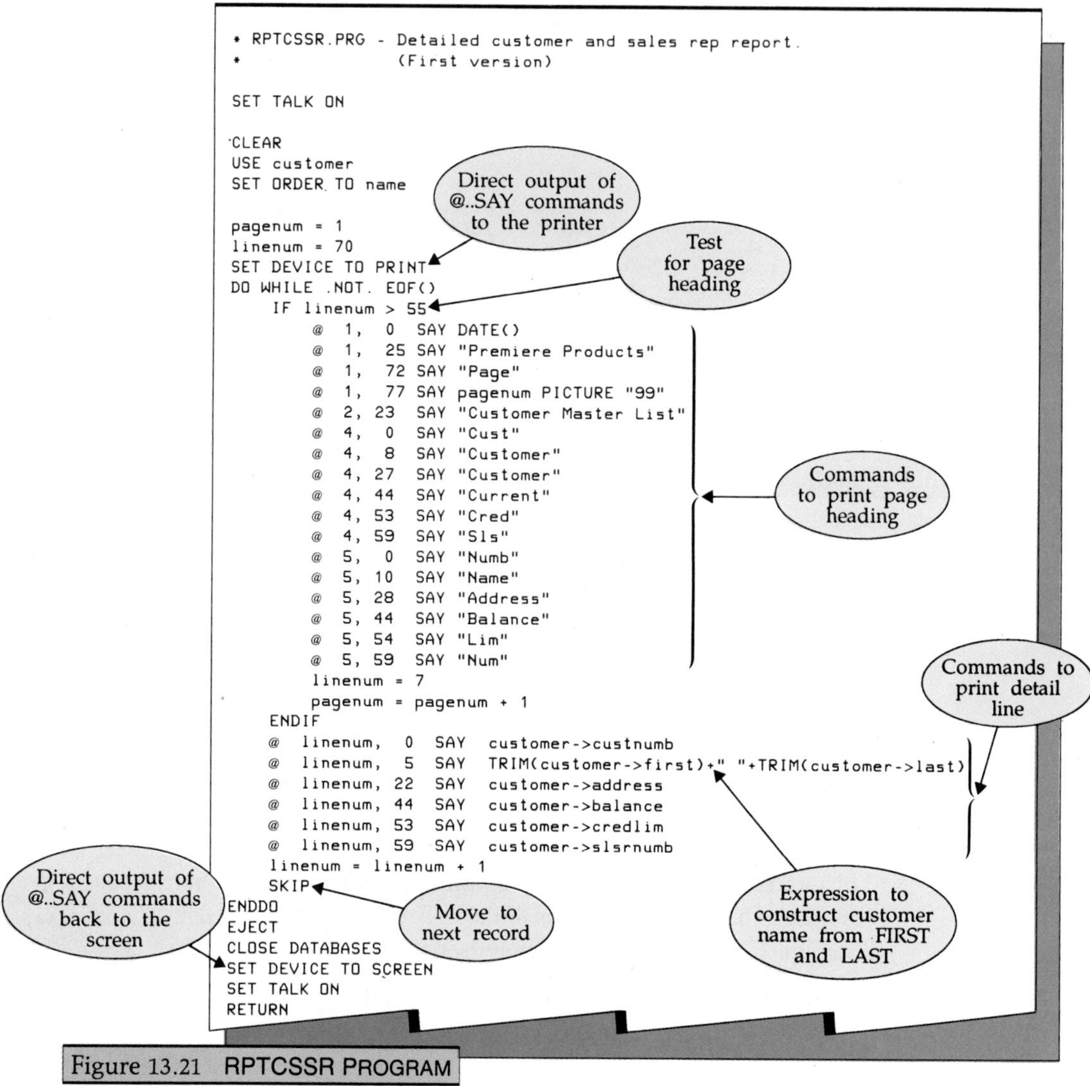

```
* RPTCSSR.PRG - Detailed customer and sales rep report.
*               (First version)

SET TALK ON

CLEAR
USE customer
SET ORDER TO name

pagenum = 1
linenum = 70
SET DEVICE TO PRINT
DO WHILE .NOT. EOF()
    IF linenum > 55
        @  1,  0  SAY DATE()
        @  1, 25  SAY "Premiere Products"
        @  1, 72  SAY "Page"
        @  1, 77  SAY pagenum PICTURE "99"
        @  2, 23  SAY "Customer Master List"
        @  4,  0  SAY "Cust"
        @  4,  8  SAY "Customer"
        @  4, 27  SAY "Customer"
        @  4, 44  SAY "Current"
        @  4, 53  SAY "Cred"
        @  4, 59  SAY "Sls"
        @  5,  0  SAY "Numb"
        @  5, 10  SAY "Name"
        @  5, 28  SAY "Address"
        @  5, 44  SAY "Balance"
        @  5, 54  SAY "Lim"
        @  5, 59  SAY "Num"
        linenum = 7
        pagenum = pagenum + 1
    ENDIF
    @ linenum,  0  SAY  customer->custnumb
    @ linenum,  5  SAY  TRIM(customer->first)+" "+TRIM(customer->last)
    @ linenum, 22  SAY  customer->address
    @ linenum, 44  SAY  customer->balance
    @ linenum, 53  SAY  customer->credlim
    @ linenum, 59  SAY  customer->slsrnumb
    linenum = linenum + 1
    SKIP
ENDDO
EJECT
CLOSE DATABASES
SET DEVICE TO SCREEN
SET TALK ON
RETURN
```


Figure 13.21 RPTCSSR PROGRAM

There is a condition under which we do not simply want to print a detail line, however. If the next detail line to be printed is too far down the page, we want to go to a new page and print a page heading before printing the detail line. This is accomplished by the IF statement at the top of the loop. This is the condition in the IF statement:

```
linenum > 55
```

If this condition is true, the indicated action is to first print today's date, which is obtained by the dBASE function DATE() starting in column 2 of line 1, then the words "Premiere Products" starting in column 25 of line 1, and so on. Information will thus be printed on lines 1, 2, 4, and 5.

At this point, we set linenum to 7 (which leaves line 6 blank) and add 1 to the page number, in preparation for the next page. We are now ready to print the detail line.

How does dBASE know it must go to the start of a new page to print this information? In many languages, if we want information to be printed on the top of a new page, we must issue some special command, like EJECT, to ensure that the printing will take place there. But in dBASE, if a report is being produced with @..SAY commands, and a command refers to a line number that is lower than that of the last line printed, an automatic EJECT command will be issued. Therefore, we do not need to code such a command in our loop.

Now let's return to the manner in which linenum was initialized. We must ensure that a page heading is printed on the very first page; and since one is printed if the value of linenum is greater than 55, we can force a page heading to be printed on the first page simply by initializing linenum to some value greater than 55. The choice of 70 was purely arbitrary; any number over 55 would have worked just as well.

The command following the initialization of linenum is

```
SET DEVICE TO PRINT
```

which is used to indicate that the output from the @..SAY commands should be directed to the printer, *not* to the screen, as is usually the case. (Table 13.2 lists some commands used to direct output to various devices.)

TABLE 13.2 Printer usage commands

COMMAND	MEANING
SET PRINT ON	Output of ?, ??, TALK, LIST, and so on are directed to the printer.
SET PRINT OFF	Output of ?, ??, TALK, LIST, and so on are not directed to the printer.
SET CONSOLE ON	Output of ?, ??, TALK, LIST, and so on are directed to the console.
SET CONSOLE OFF	Output of ?, ??, TALK, LIST, and so on are not directed to the console.
SET DEVICE TO SCREEN	All @..SAY and @..GET statements go to the screen only.
SET DEVICE TO PRINT	All @..SAY statements go only to the printer (@..GET will not work).
SET DEVICE TO FILE filename	All @..SAY statements go only to the indicated file (@..GET will not work).

Once the loop has been completed, we need to take care of only a few details. Since the report has ended in the middle of a page, using an EJECT command to bring the printer to the start of a new page adds a nice touch. We close all databases that were in use and set the device back to the screen (@..SAY commands will once more direct output to the screen). We can then return to the program that called this one.

REPORT USING TWO DATABASE FILES

It is now time to tackle the problem of including the name of the sales rep on each line of the report. A fully documented version of the program to do this is shown in Figure 13.22.

In order to accomplish the task, we need to access both the customer file and the sales rep file. In our case, since only two database files need to be active, we will use areas 1 and 2: area 1 for the customer file and area 2 for the sales rep file. Since we will need to find sales reps by using the sales rep number, we order the record in SLSREP by SLSRNUMB. Once we have done this, we once again make area 1, the area containing the CUSTOMER database file, the active area with the command

```
SELECT customer
```

The only other new part of the program is located near the bottom of the loop. The new commands are

```
SELECT slsrep
SEEK customer->slsrnumb
IF FOUND()
    m_slsrname = slsrep->slsrname
ELSE
    m_slsrname = "*** NO SLSREP ***"
ENDIF
SELECT customer
```

The first designates the area that contains the sales rep file as the active area. The SEEK command will thus apply to the sales rep file. SEEK is a command that attempts to locate a record in a database file by means of the master index. It will use this index to look for a record whose key value matches the value that follows the word SEEK. In this example, it will look for a record whose sales rep number matches the value stored in customer ->slsrnumb; that is, the sales rep number from the current customer record. If the SEEK is successful, the dBASE function FOUND() will be set to true. If not, it will be set to false.

```
* RPTCSSR2.PRG - Detailed customer and sales rep report.
*                (Second version)

SET TALK OFF

CLEAR

* Activate customer table in area 1.  Order by last name, first
*    name by using index called "name."  Activate sales rep
*    table in area 2.  Order by index built on slsrnumb.
*    Make area containing customer table the active area.
SELECT 1
USE customer
SET ORDER TO name
SELECT 2
USE slsrep
SET ORDER TO slsrnumb
SELECT customer

* Initialize page number to 1.  Initialize line number to a
*   large number to force a page header immediately.
pagenum = 1
linenum = 70

* Direct output to printer.
SET DEVICE TO PRINT

* Loop until end of file.
DO WHILE .NOT. EOF()
```

Activate both database files

```
    * If more then 55 lines have been printed, put out page
    *    heading, set line number to 7, and increment page
    *    number.
    IF linenum > 55
        @  1,  0  SAY DATE()
        @  1,  25 SAY "Premiere Products"
        @  1,  72 SAY "Page"
        @  1,  77 SAY pagenum PICTURE "99"
        @  2, 23  SAY "Customer Master List"
        @  4,  0  SAY "Cust"
        @  4,  8  SAY "Customer"
        @  4, 27  SAY "Customer"
        @  4, 44  SAY "Current"
        @  4, 53  SAY "Cred"
        @  4, 59  SAY "Sls"
        @  4, 68  SAY "Slsrep"
        @  5,  0  SAY "Numb"
        @  5, 10  SAY "Name"
        @  5, 28  SAY "Address"
        @  5, 44  SAY "Balance"
        @  5, 54  SAY "Lim"
        @  5, 59  SAY "Num"
        @  5, 69  SAY "Name"
        linenum = 7
        pagenum = pagenum + 1
    ENDIF
* Make the area containing the sales rep file the active
*   area.  Try to find matching sales rep.  If one exists,
*   set m-slsrname to slsrname.  If not, set slsrname to
*   "*** NO SLSREP ***".  Make the area containing the
*   customer file the active area once again.
SELECT slsrep
SEEK customer->slsrnumb
```

Find matching sales rep

Figure 13.22 RPTCSSR2 PROGRAM

(continued)

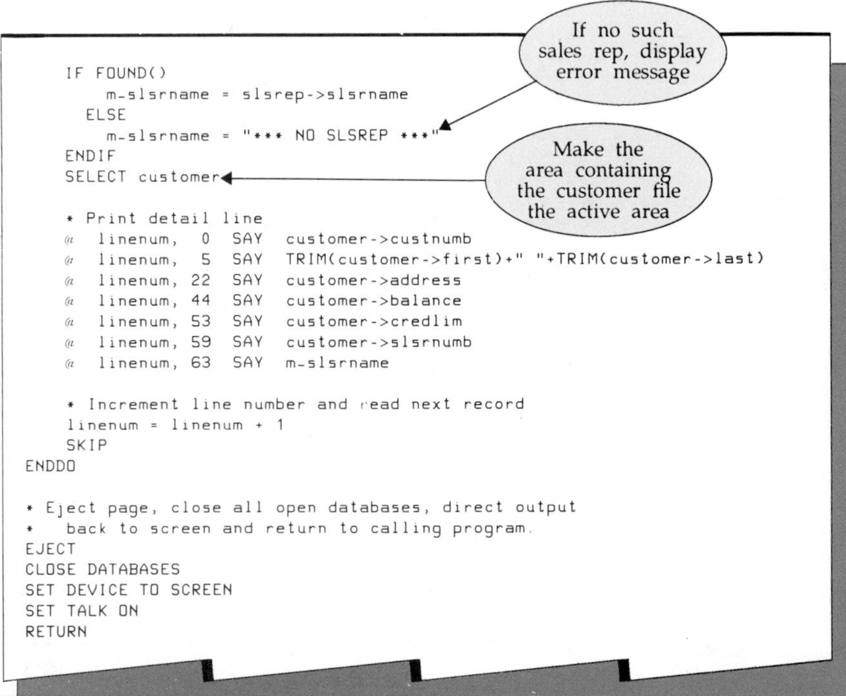
If no such sales rep, display error message
Make the area containing the customer file the active area

```
    IF FOUND()
       m-slsrname = slsrep->slsrname
     ELSE
       m-slsrname = "*** NO SLSREP ***"
    ENDIF
    SELECT customer

    * Print detail line
    @  linenum,  0  SAY  customer->custnumb
    @  linenum,  5  SAY  TRIM(customer->first)+" "+TRIM(customer->last)
    @  linenum, 22  SAY  customer->address
    @  linenum, 44  SAY  customer->balance
    @  linenum, 53  SAY  customer->credlim
    @  linenum, 59  SAY  customer->slsrnumb
    @  linenum, 63  SAY  m-slsrname

    * Increment line number and read next record
    linenum = linenum + 1
    SKIP
ENDDO

* Eject page, close all open databases, direct output
*   back to screen and return to calling program.
EJECT
CLOSE DATABASES
SET DEVICE TO SCREEN
SET TALK ON
RETURN
```

Figure 13.22 RPTCSSR2 PROGRAM

The IF statement will fill in a value for the memory variable m_slsrname appropriately. If a match is found, m_slsrname will be set to the value of slsrname on the record that was found. Otherwise, m_slsrname will be set to the value *** NO SLSREP ***. In either case, the value of m_slsrname will be displayed, starting in column 63 of the line being printed (the line indicated by linenum). (**Note:** If we knew we would always find a sales rep to match a customer, we could have just displayed slsrep->slsrname rather than the memory variable m_slsrname. The possibility that a customer may have a sales rep number that does not match the number of a sales rep who is already in the database is what leads us to the approach taken in this program.)

The only other thing that needs to be done is to once again designate the area that contains CUSTOMER as the active area. The SELECT statement after the ENDIF accomplishes this.

These commands will accurately fill in m_slsrname. In addition, we must, of course, add the command

```
@ linenum, 63 SAY m-slsrname
```

to the lines that print a detail line in order to get the value in m_slsrname to appear on the report.

Finally, it is necessary to qualify a field name; in other words, to precede the field name with the name of the database file to which it corresponds, *only* if the field is not in the currently selected area. It is never wrong to qualify fields, however.

If you want to check the special message for sales rep name, add customer 111, (name: Jan Baker, address: 123 Mill,Grant,MI, balance: 0.00, credit limit: 500, sales rep number: 9). If you run the program with this additional data it should look like the one shown in Figure 13.23. Notice the message in place of the sales rep name for Jan Baker.

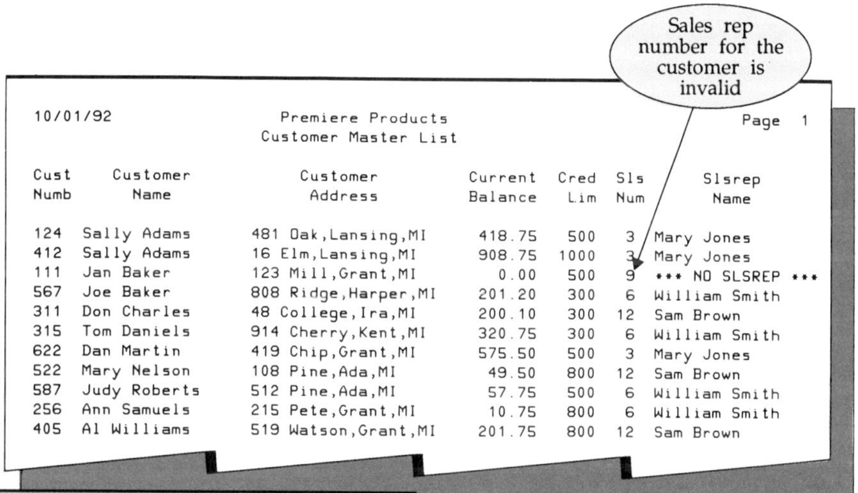

Sales rep number for the customer is invalid

```
10/01/92                     Premiere Products                                Page  1
                           Customer Master List

Cust     Customer             Customer            Current  Cred  Sls      Slsrep
Numb       Name                Address            Balance   Lim  Num       Name

124  Sally Adams      481 Oak,Lansing,MI          418.75   500    3  Mary Jones
412  Sally Adams      16 Elm,Lansing,MI           908.75  1000    3  Mary Jones
111  Jan Baker        123 Mill,Grant,MI             0.00   500    9  *** NO SLSREP ***
567  Joe Baker        808 Ridge,Harper,MI         201.20   300    6  William Smith
311  Don Charles      48 College,Ira,MI           200.10   300   12  Sam Brown
315  Tom Daniels      914 Cherry,Kent,MI          320.75   300    6  William Smith
622  Dan Martin       419 Chip,Grant,MI           575.50   500    3  Mary Jones
522  Mary Nelson      108 Pine,Ada,MI              49.50   800   12  Sam Brown
587  Judy Roberts     512 Pine,Ada,MI              57.75   500    6  William Smith
256  Ann Samuels      215 Pete,Grant,MI            10.75   800    6  William Smith
405  Al Williams      519 Watson,Grant,MI         201.75   800   12  Sam Brown
```

Figure 13.23 CUSTOMER AND SALES REP REPORT

REPORT USING SEVERAL DATABASE FILES

In this section we will examine a program to produce a detailed order report. Figure 13.24 on the next page contains the first portion of the report. For each order, the order number, order date, customer number, customer name, and customer address are listed as well as the number, name, and address of the sales rep who represents the customer. Also, for each order line within the order, the report shows the part number, part description, number ordered, quoted price, and extension (the product of number ordered and quoted price). Finally, there is a total of all the extensions for all the order lines for the given order. The report is sorted by order number. The program to produce this report is called RPTORDS and is shown in Figure 13.25 on pages 373–375.

Since data from all five database files is required in this report, the program begins by activating all five files and appropriate indexes. After the database files have been activated, the area that contains the orders file is selected, since this is the file that drives the whole program.

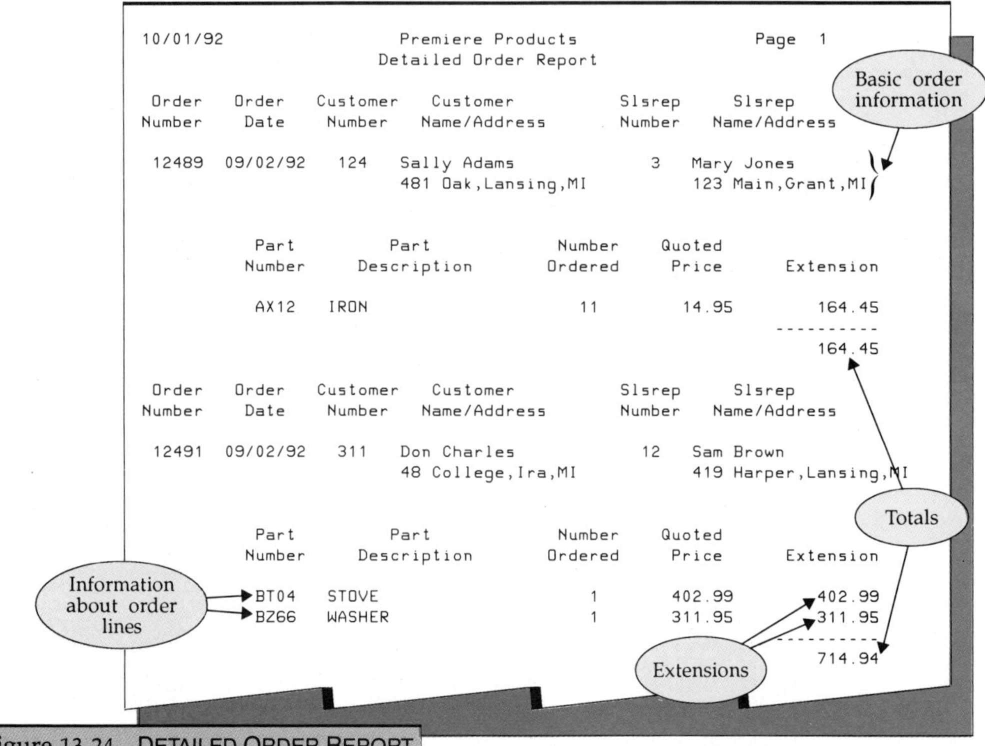

```
10/01/92                  Premiere Products                   Page  1
                        Detailed Order Report

 Order   Order   Customer   Customer          Slsrep    Slsrep
Number    Date    Number   Name/Address       Number   Name/Address

 12489  09/02/92   124    Sally Adams            3   Mary Jones
                          481 Oak,Lansing,MI         123 Main,Grant,MI

          Part         Part           Number   Quoted
         Number     Description      Ordered    Price      Extension

          AX12    IRON                  11       14.95        164.45
                                                            ----------
                                                              164.45

 Order   Order   Customer   Customer          Slsrep    Slsrep
Number    Date    Number   Name/Address       Number   Name/Address

 12491  09/02/92   311    Don Charles           12   Sam Brown
                          48 College,Ira,MI          419 Harper,Lansing,MI

          Part         Part           Number   Quoted
         Number     Description      Ordered    Price      Extension

          BT04    STOVE                  1      402.99        402.99
          BZ66    WASHER                 1      311.95        311.95
                                                            ----------
                                                              714.94
```


Figure 13.24 DETAILED ORDER REPORT

The basic structure of the program is the same as the previous report programs. Both pagenum and linenum are initialized in the same manner and serve the same function as they did before. The same loop structure is used, along with the same initial test, to determine whether a page heading should be printed.

The loop is executed once for each order. The loop begins with an IF statement that determines whether or not a page heading should be printed and, if so, prints the heading. Next, m_totext, a memory variable that will be used to calculate the total extension for the order, is initialized to 0.

From the order file, we have the order number, order date, and customer number. We also need the customer's name and address. The next part of the loop is devoted to this task. The area that contains the customer file is selected and a SEEK statement is used to look for the customer whose number matches the customer number from the order file record. We still need more information, however, if the numbers match. We need to find the sales rep who represents this customer. This is done by selecting the area that contains the sales rep file and using an appropriate SEEK statement. After all of this has been done, we once again make the area that contains the orders file the selected area.

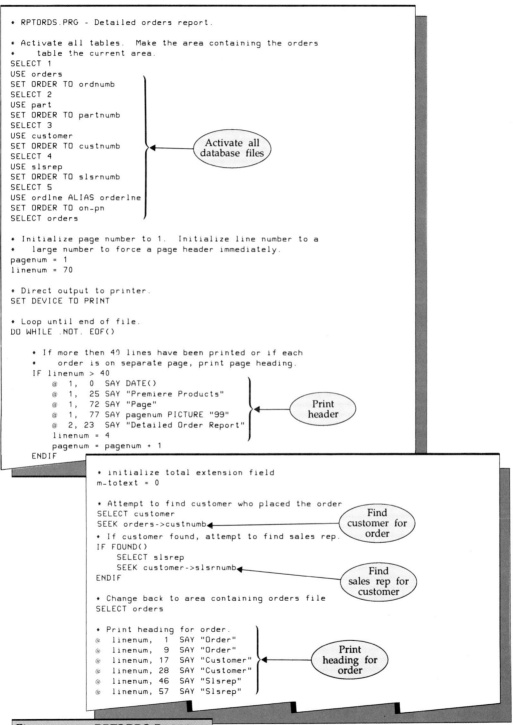

```
* RPTORDS.PRG - Detailed orders report.

* Activate all tables.  Make the area containing the orders
*     table the current area.
SELECT 1
USE orders
SET ORDER TO ordnumb
SELECT 2
USE part
SET ORDER TO partnumb
SELECT 3
USE customer
SET ORDER TO custnumb
SELECT 4
USE slsrep
SET ORDER TO slsrnumb
SELECT 5
USE ordlne ALIAS orderlne
SET ORDER TO on-pn
SELECT orders

* Initialize page number to 1.  Initialize line number to a
*    large number to force a page header immediately.
pagenum = 1
linenum = 70

* Direct output to printer.
SET DEVICE TO PRINT

* Loop until end of file.
DO WHILE .NOT. EOF()

    * If more then 40 lines have been printed or if each
    *     order is on separate page, print page heading.
    IF linenum > 40
        @  1,   0  SAY DATE()
        @  1,  25  SAY "Premiere Products"
        @  1,  72  SAY "Page"
        @  1,  77  SAY pagenum PICTURE "99"
        @  2, 23   SAY "Detailed Order Report"
        linenum = 4
        pagenum = pagenum + 1
    ENDIF
```



```
* initialize total extension field
m-totext = 0

* Attempt to find customer who placed the order
SELECT customer
SEEK orders->custnumb
* If customer found, attempt to find sales rep.
IF FOUND()
    SELECT slsrep
    SEEK customer->slsrnumb
ENDIF

* Change back to area containing orders file
SELECT orders

* Print heading for order.
@  linenum,  1  SAY "Order"
@  linenum,  9  SAY "Order"
@  linenum, 17  SAY "Customer"
@  linenum, 28  SAY "Customer"
@  linenum, 46  SAY "Slsrep"
@  linenum, 57  SAY "Slsrep"
```


Figure 13.25 RPTORDS PROGRAM

(continued)

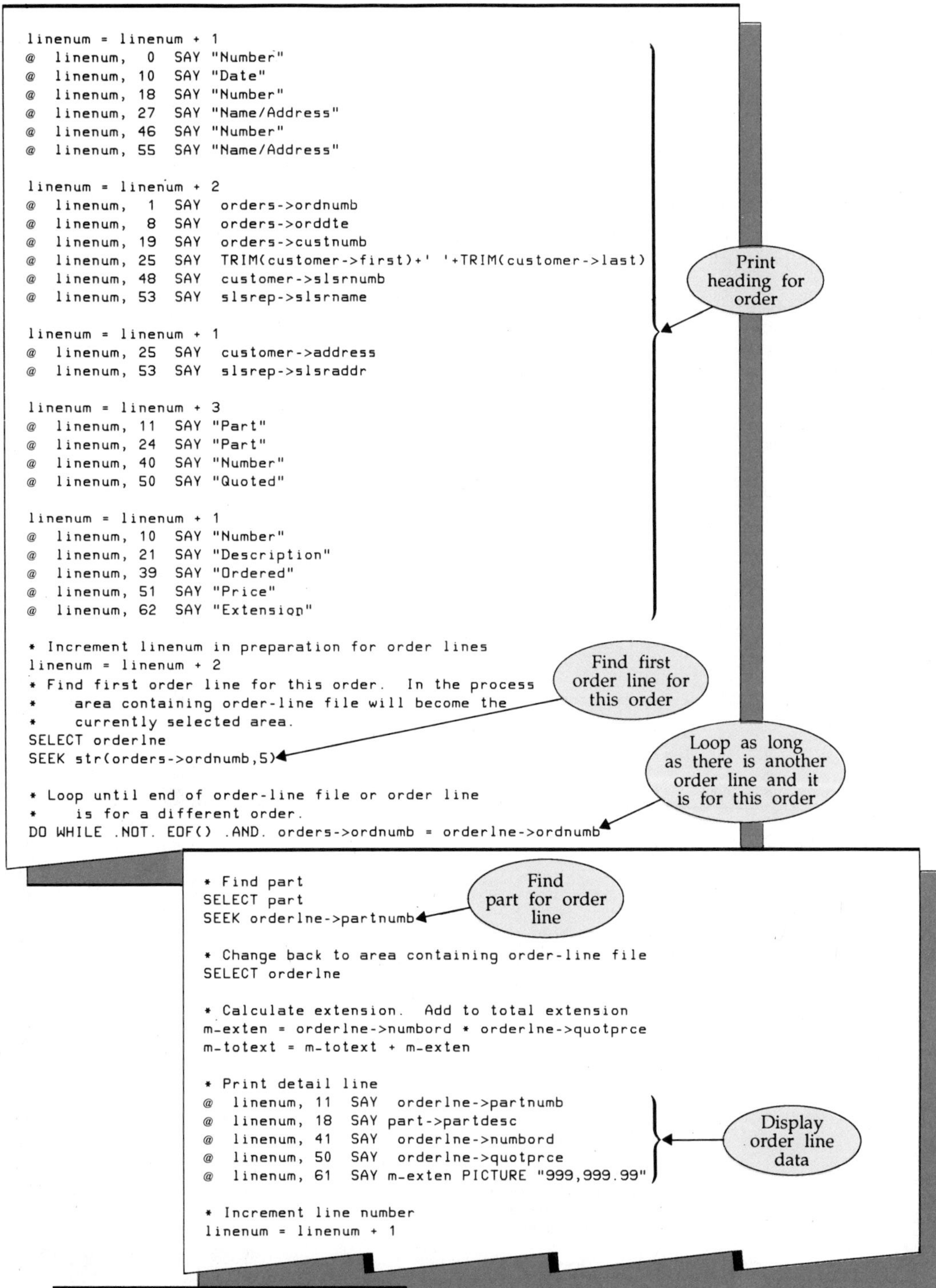

```
linenum = linenum + 1
@  linenum,  0  SAY "Number"
@  linenum, 10  SAY "Date"
@  linenum, 18  SAY "Number"
@  linenum, 27  SAY "Name/Address"
@  linenum, 46  SAY "Number"
@  linenum, 55  SAY "Name/Address"

linenum = linenum + 2
@  linenum,  1  SAY  orders->ordnumb
@  linenum,  8  SAY  orders->orddte
@  linenum, 19  SAY  orders->custnumb
@  linenum, 25  SAY  TRIM(customer->first)+' '+TRIM(customer->last)
@  linenum, 48  SAY  customer->slsrnumb
@  linenum, 53  SAY  slsrep->slsrname

linenum = linenum + 1
@  linenum, 25  SAY  customer->address
@  linenum, 53  SAY  slsrep->slsraddr

linenum = linenum + 3
@  linenum, 11  SAY "Part"
@  linenum, 24  SAY "Part"
@  linenum, 40  SAY "Number"
@  linenum, 50  SAY "Quoted"

linenum = linenum + 1
@  linenum, 10  SAY "Number"
@  linenum, 21  SAY "Description"
@  linenum, 39  SAY "Ordered"
@  linenum, 51  SAY "Price"
@  linenum, 62  SAY "Extension"

* Increment linenum in preparation for order lines
linenum = linenum + 2
* Find first order line for this order.  In the process
*    area containing order-line file will become the
*    currently selected area.
SELECT orderlne
SEEK str(orders->ordnumb,5)

* Loop until end of order-line file or order line
*    is for a different order.
DO WHILE .NOT. EOF() .AND. orders->ordnumb = orderlne->ordnumb

* Find part
SELECT part
SEEK orderlne->partnumb

* Change back to area containing order-line file
SELECT orderlne

* Calculate extension.  Add to total extension
m-exten = orderlne->numbord * orderlne->quotprce
m-totext = m-totext + m-exten

* Print detail line
@  linenum, 11  SAY  orderlne->partnumb
@  linenum, 18  SAY part->partdesc
@  linenum, 41  SAY  orderlne->numbord
@  linenum, 50  SAY  orderlne->quotprce
@  linenum, 61  SAY m-exten PICTURE "999,999.99"

* Increment line number
linenum = linenum + 1
```

Print heading for order
Find first order line for this order
Loop as long as there is another order line and it is for this order
Find part for order line
Display order line data

Figure 13.25 RPTORDS PROGRAM

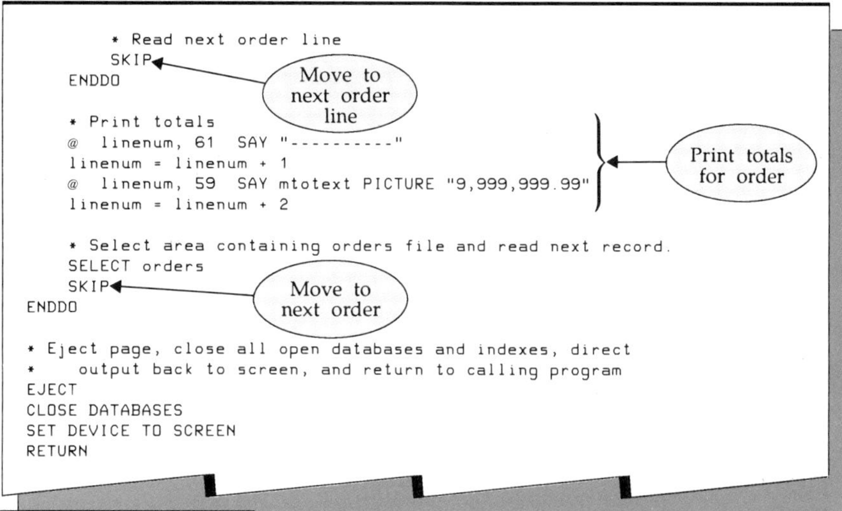
```
        * Read next order line
        SKIP
    ENDDO

    * Print totals
    @  linenum, 61  SAY "----------"
    linenum = linenum + 1
    @  linenum, 59  SAY mtotext PICTURE "9,999,999.99"
    linenum = linenum + 2

    * Select area containing orders file and read next record.
    SELECT orders
    SKIP
ENDDO

* Eject page, close all open databases and indexes, direct
*     output back to screen, and return to calling program
EJECT
CLOSE DATABASES
SET DEVICE TO SCREEN
RETURN
```


Figure 13.25 RPTORDS PROGRAM

At this point, we are ready to print the heading for an order. The next several lines accomplish this task. In the process, linenum is repeatedly incremented. After the last heading line is printed, linenum is once more incremented, this time by 2. This is in preparation for the order lines that we will now print.

In order to print the order lines, we first make the area that contains the order line file the selected area. Then we use a SEEK command. The master index on the order line file was built on the concatenation (combination) of ordnumb and partnumb. When we build an index on the concatenation of two fields, the fields must be combined as a string, so the index was really built on

```
STR(orderlne->ordnumb,5)+partnumb
```

It is possible to SEEK on just a portion of such an index, and that's what we are doing here. The command

```
SEEK STR(orders->ordnumb,5)
```

is really a request to find the *first* record in the order line file where the first part of the key matches the order number that we are currently processing. (Note that in the SEEK command it is the order number from ORDERS that we are attempting to match.)

After this SEEK command is executed, the record pointer will be positioned at the first such record, assuming that one exists. If not, it will be positioned at the end of the file. If such a record does exist, we would like to process it and all following records in the order line file until we either hit the end of the file or encounter an order line that is for a different order. Thus, the loop to accomplish this task will execute as long as the condition

```
.NOT. EOF() .AND. orders->ordnumb = orderlne->ordnumb
```

remains true.

Within the loop, we begin by finding the corresponding part. The reason this is necessary is that the part description is to be included in the report. We do this by selecting the area that contains the part file and then seeking orderlne->partnumb. Then we again select the area containing the order line file. It is not absolutely necessary that we do so at this point, but we *must* make this the primary area before we get to the SKIP statement at the end of this loop, since it is the next order line that we want to obtain. If the area containing PART were still the primary area at that point, we would obtain the next part record instead.

Next, the product of numbord and quotprce is calculated and placed in the memory variable m_exten. This value is added to m_totext. We now print a detail line that includes a number of database fields and the memory variable m_exten. Note that we did not use a picture clause with any of the database fields since dBASE already knows their characteristics. We only needed one with the memory variable.

At this point, the line number is incremented and the next record in the order line file is obtained. This ends the loop to process all of the order lines for the order.

When this loop is done, we print the total of the extensions, which is stored in the memory variable m_totext, and increment the line counter by two in preparation for the next order. The area containing orders is made the primary area and a SKIP command is used to obtain the next order. This is the end of the loop to process all of the orders. It will terminate when the end of the orders file is reached, at which time we eject a page, close all open databases, SET DEVICE back to the screen, and RETURN to the calling program.

13.4 USING STREAMING OUTPUT IN REPORT PROGRAMS

The other approach to report programs uses what is termed *streaming output*. Streaming output simply refers to any output that is sent to the printer or screen one line at a time. In dBASE IV, there are special system variables that control many aspects of the way streaming output will be formatted. These variables are shown in Table 13.3.

TABLE 13.3 **System variables for printing reports**

SYSTEM VARIABLE	VALUES	USAGE
_alignment	"LEFT", "RIGHT", "CENTER"	Indicates alignment for expressions displayed by ? or ?? commands.
_box	TRUE or FALSE	If TRUE, displays contents of DEFINE BOX command.
_indent	between 0 and 254	Number of positions indented for the first line of new paragraph. (_wrap variable must be TRUE or this does not take effect.)
_lmargin	between 0 and 254	Left margin (_wrap variable must be TRUE).
_padvance	"FORMFEED", "LINEFEEDS"	Determines how printer advances paper (line or form).
_pageno	between 1 and 32767	Current page number.
_pbpage	between 1 and 32767	Beginning page for PRINTJOB.
_pcolno	between 0 and 255	Starting column for output stream.
_pcopies	between 1 and 32767	Number of copies printed by PRINTJOB.
_pdriver	a valid DOS filename	Name of printer driver to be used by PRINTJOB.
_pecode	string less than 255 char	Ending control codes for a PRINTJOB
_peject	"BEFORE","AFTER", "BOTH", "NONE"	Determines whether EJECT occurs before PRINTJOB; after PRINTJOB; both before and after; or neither.
_pepage	between 1 and 32767	Ending page for PRINTJOB.
_pform	a valid DOS filename	Name of current print form file.
_plength	between 1 and 32767	Length of output page (standard 8-1/2 × 11 should be 66).
_plineno	between 0 and (_plength-1)	Line number.
_ploffset	between 0 and 254	Left page offset (left margin).
_ppitch	"PICA", "ELITE", "CONDENSED", "DEFAULT"	Printer pitch.
_pquality	TRUE or FALSE	Letter quality (TRUE) or draft (FALSE).
_pscode	string less than 255 char	Starting printer code (sent to printer when PRINTJOB is executed).
_pspacing	integers 1, 2, or 3	Line spacing (single, double, or triple).
_pwait	TRUE or FALSE	If TRUE, printer will pause after each page. If FALSE, printing will be continuous.
_rmargin	between 1 and 255	Specifies right margin for ? commands. (_wrap variable must be TRUE or this does not take effect.)
_tabs	string of numbers separated by commas in ascending order	Defines list of tab stops for output. Also sets tab stops for dBASE editor.
_wrap	TRUE or FALSE	If TRUE, word wrap is on. If FALSE, it is not.

Figure 13.26 illustrates the use of streaming output to produce the same customer and sales rep report produced by the RPTCSSR2.PRG program we examined earlier. The program could begin by setting the special system variables to appropriate values. This approach would change the values in these variables for *the entire dBASE session*. It's safer to change them only for the duration of the program. To do so, we must save the original values. Thus, the first step is to store the original values in memory variables. Once this has been done, the next group of commands in the program makes the actual changes.

(**Note:** The values shown in this program are fairly typical. You should examine them to see the effect of each of the changes. Refer to Table 13.3 for the specific function of each of the variables.)

The ON PAGE command indicates that the header procedure is to be performed (DO header) whenever the line number reaches 55 (AT LINE 55). By changing the 55, we can easily adjust how far down the page we wish the report to extend. The SET PRINTER ON command directs output of ? and ?? commands to the printer.

The next new command in the program is PRINTJOB. The characteristics of the variables we have specified will apply to the report produced between the PRINTJOB command and an ENDPRINTJOB command. Thus, the PRINTJOB command indicates the beginning of the report. Following the PRINTJOB command is a command to print the header on the first page (DO header). From this point on the ON PAGE command will ensure that the page header is printed automatically.

Rather than a DO WHILE loop, this program uses the SCAN/ENDSCAN structure. When you use this structure, you don't need to include a SKIP command since moving to the next record happens automatically at the ENDSCAN. (You can also include a FOR or WHILE clause in the SCAN command rather than the word ALL to limit the records that will be accessed.)

The detail lines are printed within the SCAN/ENDSCAN, and the header is printed within the procedure called header. In both cases, we use ? and ?? statements to produce the output. The ?? command prints the output on the same line as we are already positioned. The ? produces output on the next line. A ? command without an expression simply moves to the next line. The patterns of ? and ?? statements illustrated in this program are very common—a collection of ?? statements to print a single line of output and then a single ? statement to advance to the next line.

```
* RPTCSSR3.PRG - Detailed customer and sales rep report.
*                (Third version - uses streaming output)

SET TALK OFF

CLEAR

* Store current settings of system variables
mplength  = _plength
mploffset = _ploffset
mlmargin  = _lmargin
mrmargin  = _rmargin
mppitch   = _ppitch
mwrap     = _wrap
mpeject   = _peject

* Modify system variables for report
_plength  = 66
_ploffset = 0
_lmargin  = 0
_rmargin  = 80
_ppitch   = "PICA"
_plineno  =  1
_wrap     = .F.
_peject   = "AFTER"
_pageno   = 1

* Set up line number for page break procedure
ON PAGE AT LINE 55 DO header

SET PRINTER ON
```

Save current settings so we can restore them later

Change settings to the ones we need for this report

Identify number of lines for page header as well as prodedure to be performed

Turn on output to the printer

```
* Activate customer table in area 1.  Order by last name, first
*    name by using index called "name."  Activate sales rep
*    table in area 2.  Order by index built on slsrnumb.
*    Make area containing customer table the active area.
SELECT 1
USE customer
SET ORDER TO name
SELECT 2
USE slsrep
SET ORDER TO slsrnumb
SELECT customer

* Start print job
PRINTJOB

* Print header for first page.  The remaining page headings will be
*     automatic.
DO header

* Loop until end of file.
SCAN ALL

    * Make the area containing the sales rep file the active
    *   area.  Try to find matching sales rep.  If one exists,
    *   set m_slsrname to slsrname.  If not, set slsrname to
    *   "*** NO SLSREP ***".  Make the area containing the
    *   customer file the active area once again.
    SELECT slsrep
    SEEK customer->slsrnumb
    IF FOUND()
        m_slsrname = slsrep->slsrname
      ELSE
        m_slsrname = "*** NO SLSREP ***"
    ENDIF
    SELECT customer
```

Beginning of print job

Print header for first page

Use SCAN..ENDSCAN to process records

Figure 13.26 PRTCSSR3 PROGRAM

(continued)

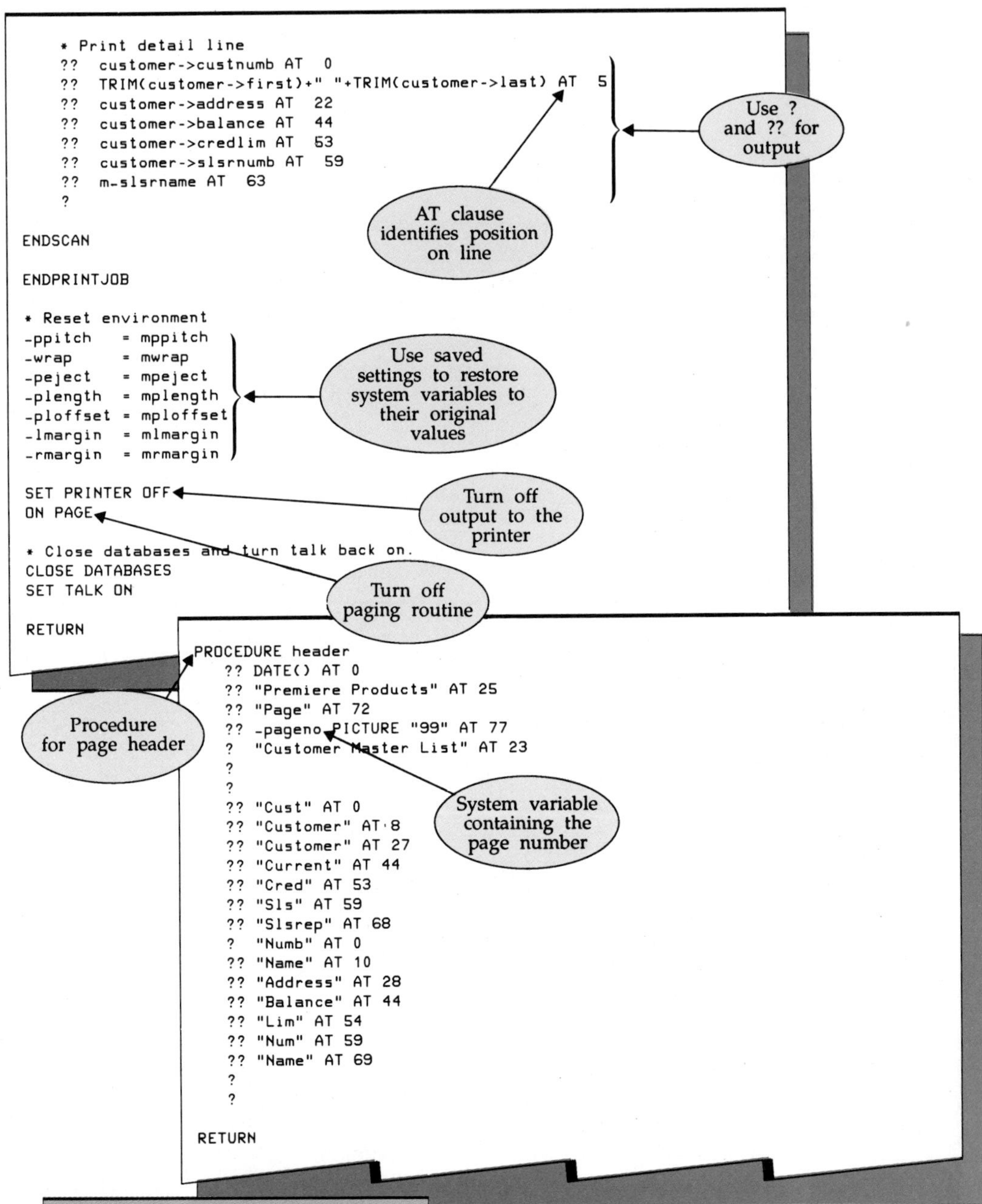

* Print detail line
?? customer->custnumb AT 0
?? TRIM(customer->first)+" "+TRIM(customer->last) AT 5
?? customer->address AT 22
?? customer->balance AT 44
?? customer->credlim AT 53
?? customer->slsrnumb AT 59
?? m-slsrname AT 63
?
ENDSCAN
ENDPRINTJOB
* Reset environment
-ppitch = mppitch
-wrap = mwrap
-peject = mpeject
-plength = mplength
-ploffset = mploffset
-lmargin = mlmargin
-rmargin = mrmargin
SET PRINTER OFF
ON PAGE
* Close databases and turn talk back on.
CLOSE DATABASES
SET TALK ON
RETURN
PROCEDURE header
?? DATE() AT 0
?? "Premiere Products" AT 25
?? "Page" AT 72
?? _pageno PICTURE "99" AT 77
? "Customer Master List" AT 23
?
?
?? "Cust" AT 0
?? "Customer" AT 8
?? "Customer" AT 27
?? "Current" AT 44
?? "Cred" AT 53
?? "Sls" AT 59
?? "Slsrep" AT 68
? "Numb" AT 0
?? "Name" AT 10
?? "Address" AT 28
?? "Balance" AT 44
?? "Lim" AT 54
?? "Num" AT 59
?? "Name" AT 69
?
?
RETURN
Use ? and ?? for output
AT clause identifies position on line
Use saved settings to restore system variables to their original values
Turn off output to the printer
Turn off paging routine
Procedure for page header
System variable containing the page number

Figure 13.26 PRTCSSR3 PROGRAM

Notice that the ? and ?? statements include both an expression and an AT clause. The AT clause indicates the position on the line at which the output is to be produced. These statements can also include PICTURE clauses to indicate special format characteristics and STYLE clauses to indicate special effects. Special effects available in STYLE clauses are B (boldface), U (underline), I (italics), R (superscript, also referred to as raised), and L (subscript, also referred to as lowered). The following command, for example,

```
?? "Name" AT 69 STYLE "UB"
```

would print "Name" at position 69 underlined and boldfaced. The command

```
?? customer->balance AT 44 PICTURE "@$ 9,999.99"
```

would print the contents of the balance field at position 44 formatted as indicated by the picture (that is, with a dollar sign.)

Once the SCAN/ENDSCAN has been completed, the contents of the memory variables created at the beginning of the program are used to reset the values in the system variables to their original settings. Output to the printer is then turned off (SET PRINTER OFF). The ON PAGE command without any other clauses then removes the provision for paging.

Other than the use of ? and ?? commands, the only new feature in the header procedure is the use of the system variable _pageno. This variable automatically contains the correct page number.

One of the advantages of streaming output is that we can easily adjust certain characteristics of a report by changing the values of the system variables. It is easy, for example, to adjust margins, number of copies, page length, where page ejects will occur, and so on. Another advantage is that it is possible to send the output to more than one destination at the same time. By including both SET PRINTER ON and SET CONSOLE ON, for example, the output will go to both the printer and the screen. The final advantage is that we can include special effects, such as boldfacing and underlining, that are not available with @..SAY commands.

The chief advantage of formatted output is that we have total control over the placement of all the items on a report. We also have total control over paging. In reports with several different types of lines, for example, we might want to allow detail lines to begin as far down the page as line 56. On the other hand, we may not want a heading such as the one for orders in RPTORDS to begin any further down the page than line 40.

CHAPTER SUMMARY

1. There are a variety of special techniques available at the dot prompt. Using a SEEK and an index with the LIST..WHILE command provides rapid access of data. TRANSFORM() permits the use of template functions with LIST. SET FIELDS and SET FILTER conveniently store specifications with the LIST command as well. Interactive commands respond to editing keys. SET ALTERNATE TO/ON stores all screen displays to a TXT file.
2. An array is a name for a set of elements. Arrays are created with a DECLARE statement. Individual elements in an array are referenced by using a subscript. Arrays can be one-dimensional or two-dimensional. A very common use for arrays in business programming is for searching.
3. One approach used in programs for printing reports is formatted output. Programs using formatted output use @..SAY commands to display data at desired positions. The SET DEVICE TO PRINT command causes the output of these commands to be printed. An @..SAY command referencing a row that is less than the row currently being printed causes a page eject to occur.
4. Another approach used to print reports is streaming output. Streaming output uses ? and ?? commands to produce the output. Control over such details as page length, margins, number of copies, and so on is accomplished by setting appropriate system variables to the necessary values. Details concerning paging are contained in a routine that is referenced in the ON PAGE command. The portion of the program that actually prints the report is preceded by a PRINTJOB command and followed by an ENDPRINTJOB command.

KEY TERMS

array
subscript
variable-length array
one-dimensional array
two-dimensional array
formatted output
streaming output
detail line

COMMAND SUMMARY

Command Name	Use
TRANSFORM()	Use template functions in a command line.
SET FILTER TO	Establish a condition.
SET FIELDS TO	Limit display to specified fields.
SET ALTERNATE TO	Open an alternate file.
SET DEVICE TO PRINT	Direct @..SAY commands to printer.
EJECT	Advance a page on the printer.
SET PRINT ON	Direct output of ?, ??, TALK, LIST, and so on, to printer.
PRINTJOB	Marks beginning of report portion of program using streaming output.
ENDPRINTJOB	Marks end of report portion of program using streaming output.

dBUG dBASE

- Be careful when you work with arrays that you do not exceed the array's dimension. For example, if you have declared that an array consists of ten elements, make sure your subscript is never greater than ten. A subscript that is out of the appropriate range causes your program to abort with the error message "Bad array dimensions." If you are reading array entries from a database file, or obtaining entries from a user, make sure to include a test to ensure that you don't attempt to fill more entries than exist in the array.
- If you are only filling a portion of an array, make sure that the remainder of your program only manipulates the portion that you actually filled. If, for example, you attempt to calculate a total of *all* the entries in the array, you will get a meaningless answer.
- The flexibility of the commands SET PRINT, SET DEVICE, and SET ALTERNATE in directing output to various devices can be useful during debugging. For example, suppose you are debugging a program using formatted output in which the output of @..SAY commands are directed to the printer with SET DEVICE TO PRINT. You could insert ? commands into the program for debugging purposes and then direct the output of these commands to the screen (SET CONSOLE ON) or to a file (SET ALTERNATE ON). The output of these commands can then be examined separately from the report itself. Without this flexibility, the output of these commands would be interspersed with lines of the report, greatly complicating the debugging process.

SELF-CHECK QUESTIONS

1. What is an array? Why are arrays useful?
2. Why is WHILE more efficient than FOR?
3. For what purpose could a file generated by SET ALTERNATE TO be used?
4. What is the purpose of the DECLARE statement?
5. What is the difference between a one-dimensional array and a two-dimensional array? How is each created?
6. How can we use an array for searching?
7. How can we direct the output from @..SAY commands to the printer?
8. Let's assume that the output from @..SAY commands is being directed to the printer and that the last such command caused a value to be printed on line 30. If the next @..SAY command caused data to be printed on line 20, what would happen?
9. Discuss why the program for producing a detailed order report used the indexes that it did.
10. Discuss each of the SELECT statements in the program that produces a detailed order report. Indicate why each SELECT statement is necessary. Also indicate whether any of these SELECT statements could be placed elsewhere in the program.
11. The condition for the loop to process order lines is

    ```
    .NOT. EOF() .AND. orders->ordnumb = orderlne->ordnumb
    ```

    Are both parts of this condition really necessary? Why or why not?
12. How do you direct the output of ? and ?? commands to the printer? What is the difference between these two commands?
13. Near the beginning of the program in Figure 13.26, some of the special system variables are assigned values. Describe the effect of assigning each of these variables the values shown in the program.
14. What is the purpose of the ON PAGE command?

TRY IT YOURSELF

1. Use an index on the ITEMCLSS field in the PART database file along with a SEEK and a LIST..WHILE to list all parts in item class HW.
2. Use the TRANSFORM() function to list the last and first names of all customers in the CUSTOMER database file in uppercase.

3. Use SET FILTER TO, SET FIELDS TO, and LIST to list the part number and description for all records in the PART database file that are located in warehouse 3.
4. Open an alternate file; SET ALTERNATE ON; display some data on the screen; close the file; and view the contents with the TYPE command.
5. Create an array of sales rep numbers and an array of sales rep names. Allow 10 elements each. Write a program which will load these two arrays with data from the SLSREP database file and then display the contents of the two arrays.
6. Add a search routine to the program you created in Exercise 5. The routine should accept a sales rep number from the user. If the sales rep is present, the name of the sales rep should be displayed. If not, the program should print an error message.
7. Write a report program using formatted output to create a report. The report is to include all the fields from the PART database file except the warehouse number. There should be two lines of column headings. The report title should have a date, PREMIERE PRODUCTS, and a page number on the first line. It should have PART MASTER LIST on the second line.
8. Write a report program using streaming output to produce the report described in Exercise 7.

PROGRAMMING PROJECTS

1. Modify RPTCSSR2 and RPTCSSR3 to include the arrays specified in Try It Yourself Exercise 5. The data from the SLSREP database file should be used to load the arrays. Once the arrays have been loaded, the SLSREP file should be closed. Modify the portion of the program whose function is to find a sales rep name. Rather than a SEEK command, the program should use an array search similar to the one you created in Try It Yourself Exercise 6.
2. Write a program using formatted output to produce a report of parts on order. For each part the report should list the part number, description, number of units on hand, and price. In addition, for each order on which the part is present, the report should list the order number, date, customer number, customer name, quantity ordered, and quoted price.
3. Write a report program using streaming output to produce the report described in Programming Project 2.

Learning Objectives

To examine the use of bar menus, pull-down and pop-up menus, and windows.

To create and use procedure files.

To include features in a system of programs to make it as error-proof as possible.

To examine the use of color in dBASE IV programs.

To discuss the use of locking when dBASE IV is used on a local area network (LAN).

To use BEGIN TRANSACTION and END TRANSACTION commands.

To examine the security features of dBASE IV.

14 Advanced Topics

Introduction

In this chapter, we will examine some advanced dBASE IV features. We will see how bar, pull-down, and pop-up menus can be used in programs and how windows are used. We will examine the use of procedure files to create libraries of readily available user-defined functions (UDFs) and procedures.

Any system we create should be as error-free and as untroubled by bugs as possible, and should include features to prevent users from taking action that would compromise the integrity of the system. We discuss the issues involved as well as programming strategies that help achieve this goal.

Local area networks (LANs) are allowing people to work together in a powerful new environment. Special issues arise, however, when dBASE IV is installed on a LAN because several users can access the same database at the same time. To protect data integrity, a user accessing a portion of the database must be able to lock it, so no other user can interfere with the update process. We also need special security features to protect the database from unauthorized access.

14.1 MENUS AND WINDOWS

In this section, we will explore some special features that can improve the appearance of the screens our programs present to users: bar menus, pop-up menus, and windows. To illustrate the concepts, we will implement the menu system we created back in Chapter 8 using these features.

HORIZONTAL BAR, PULL-DOWN, AND POP-UP MENUS

The main menu is shown in Figure 14.1. It consists of the choices in the horizontal bar across the top of the screen. Menus with choices arranged in a horizontal bar are called *horizontal bar menus*. When any of the first four options in the menu are highlighted, the corresponding submenu appears automatically.

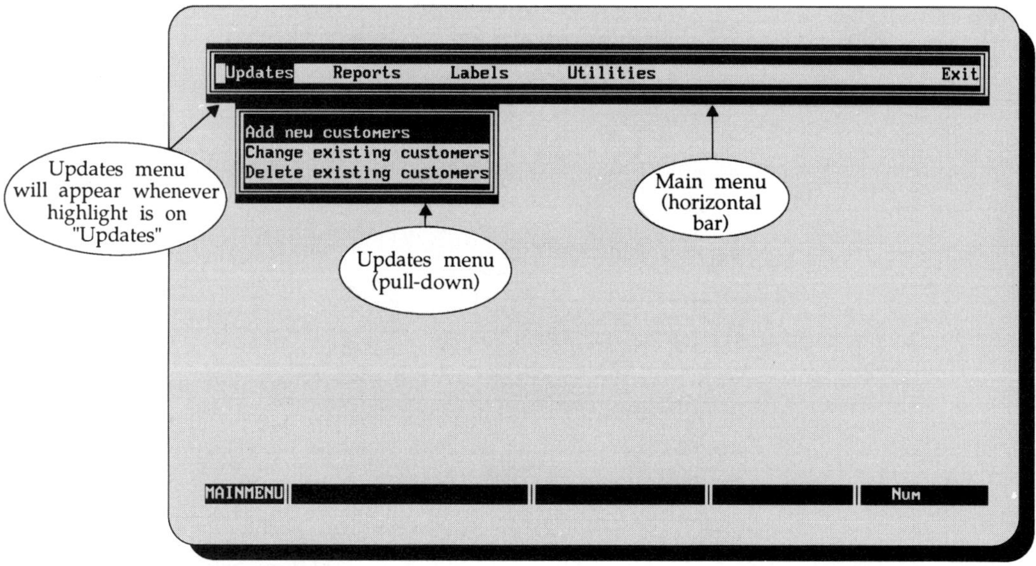

Figure 14.1 UPDATES MENU

In the figure, "Updates" is highlighted, so the Updates menu automatically appears on the screen. If the user presses the Right Arrow key, the highlight moves to "Reports," the Updates menu disappears, and the Report menu appears (see Figure 14.2). Menus that appear automatically in this way are called *pull-down menus*. If we would have to press Enter before the menus became visible, they would be called *pop-up menus*.

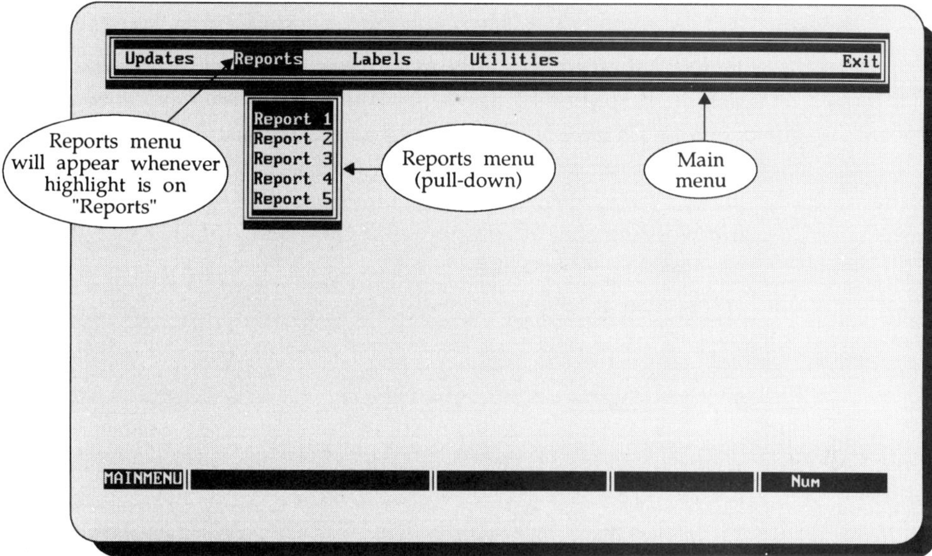

Figure 14.2 REPORTS MENU

To make a selection from any submenu, first use the Left or Right arrows to bring the desired submenu to the screen. Once you have done so, use the Up or Down arrows to move the highlight to the desired option. Finally, press Enter.

The only exception in this example is "Exit." If you move the highlight to "Exit," there is no pull-down menu (Figure 14.3). To leave the system, simply move the highlight to Exit and press Enter.

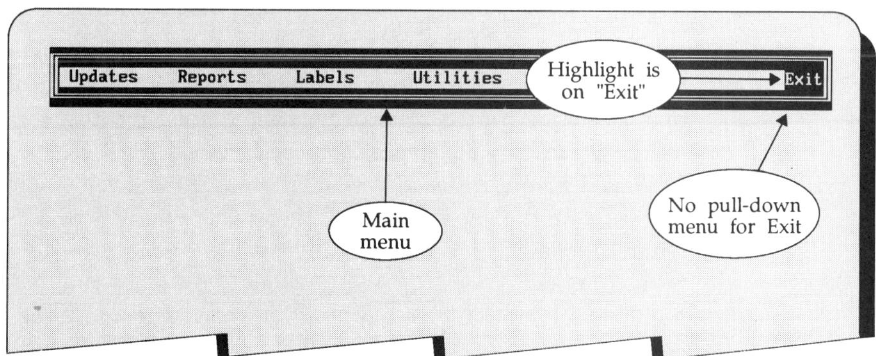

Figure 14.3 "EXIT" OPTION

DEFINING BAR MENUS

Figure 14.4 illustrates the process of defining a horizontal bar menu. The DEFINE MENU command begins the process and assigns the menu a name. Each of the options within a bar menu is technically called a "pad" and is defined with a DEFINE PAD command. Each pad must be assigned a name. The figure takes a very common approach to naming pads, calling them simply PAD_1, PAD_2, and so on. The PROMPT clause indicates the specific wording that is to appear on the menu for this pad. The AT clause then indicates the position.

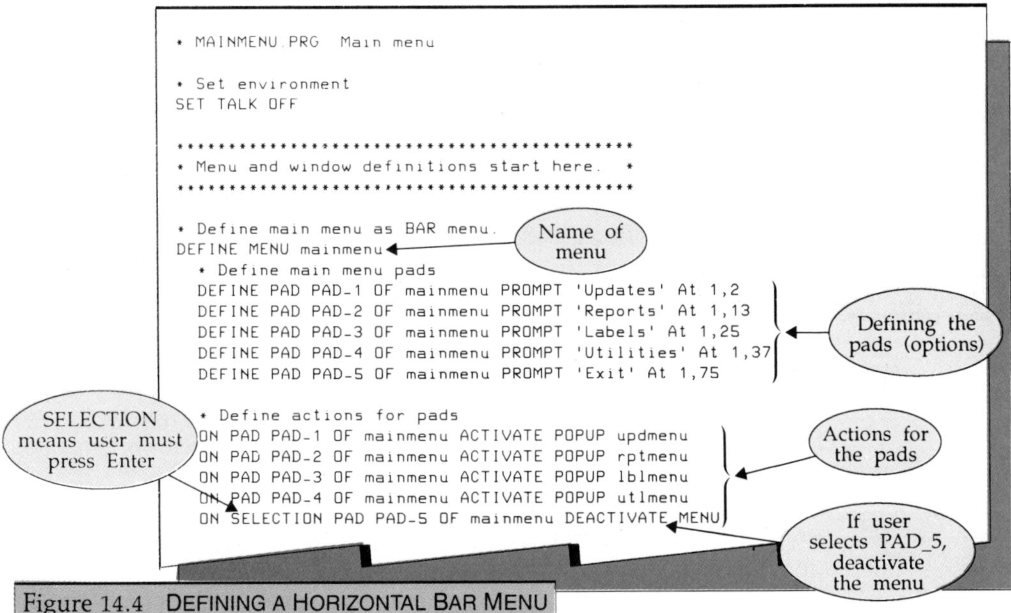

```
* MAINMENU.PRG  Main menu

* Set environment
SET TALK OFF

********************************************
* Menu and window definitions start here.  *
********************************************

* Define main menu as BAR menu.
DEFINE MENU mainmenu
  * Define main menu pads
  DEFINE PAD PAD-1 OF mainmenu PROMPT 'Updates' At 1,2
  DEFINE PAD PAD-2 OF mainmenu PROMPT 'Reports' At 1,13
  DEFINE PAD PAD-3 OF mainmenu PROMPT 'Labels' At 1,25
  DEFINE PAD PAD-4 OF mainmenu PROMPT 'Utilities' At 1,37
  DEFINE PAD PAD-5 OF mainmenu PROMPT 'Exit' At 1,75

  * Define actions for pads
  ON PAD PAD-1 OF mainmenu ACTIVATE POPUP updmenu
  ON PAD PAD-2 OF mainmenu ACTIVATE POPUP rptmenu
  ON PAD PAD-3 OF mainmenu ACTIVATE POPUP lblmenu
  ON PAD PAD-4 OF mainmenu ACTIVATE POPUP utlmenu
  ON SELECTION PAD PAD-5 OF mainmenu DEACTIVATE MENU
```


Figure 14.4 DEFINING A HORIZONTAL BAR MENU

The next portion of the definition uses ON PAD commands to indicate the action to be taken when the highlight is on the particular pad. Notice that the action for the first four pads is simply to activate another menu.

There are two differences for the last pad. First, not only does it not activate a menu, it deactivates the current menu (mainmenu). This means that if the user picks this option, the main menu will no longer be active. It will disappear from the screen and the user will not be able to make selections from it. Second, the action will not take place automatically when the highlight moves to the pad. Instead, the user must move the highlight to the pad *and press Enter*. If we used this option for the first pad, for example, the Updates menu would not appear until the highlight was on Updates and the user pressed Enter. It would be a *pop-up* rather than a *pull-down* menu.

All we have done so far is to define the menu. It will not yet be on the screen. As we will see shortly, special action is required to make use of the menu.

DEFINING POP-UP AND PULL-DOWN MENUS

Figure 14.5 illustrates the process of defining pop-up or pull-down menus. We define both types of menus as pop-up menus. The difference comes in the way they are used by the horizontal bar menu (whether we use the word SELECTION or not).

Before defining a menu, we can use the SET BORDER TO command to specify the type of border the menu will have. A very common style is SET BORDER TO DOUBLE which will produce a double-line border around the menu. (You can also use SET BORDER TO SINGLE for a single-line border, or SET BORDER TO NONE to omit a border.)

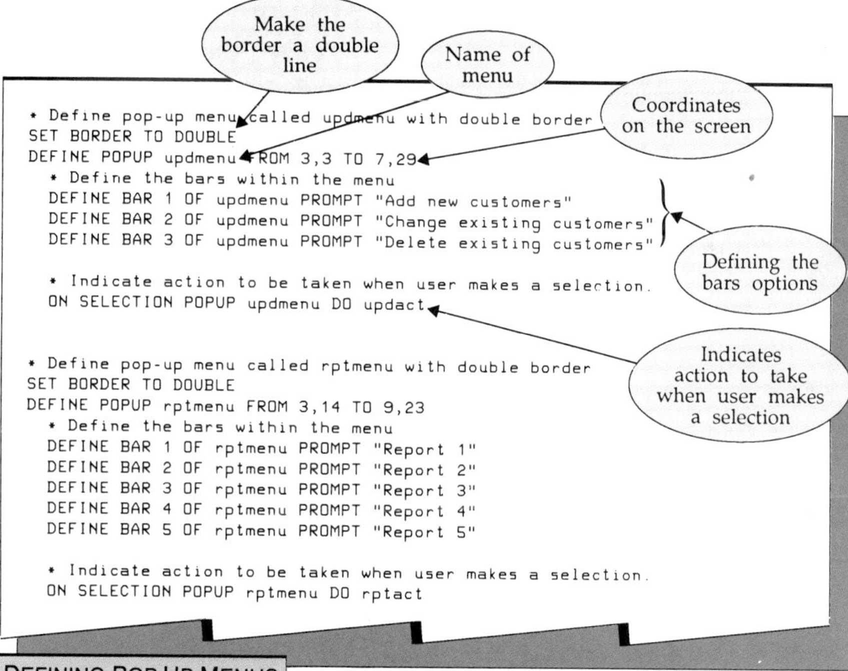

```
* Define pop-up menu called updmenu with double border
SET BORDER TO DOUBLE
DEFINE POPUP updmenu FROM 3,3 TO 7,29
  * Define the bars within the menu
  DEFINE BAR 1 OF updmenu PROMPT "Add new customers"
  DEFINE BAR 2 OF updmenu PROMPT "Change existing customers"
  DEFINE BAR 3 OF updmenu PROMPT "Delete existing customers"

  * Indicate action to be taken when user makes a selection.
  ON SELECTION POPUP updmenu DO updact

* Define pop-up menu called rptmenu with double border
SET BORDER TO DOUBLE
DEFINE POPUP rptmenu FROM 3,14 TO 9,23
  * Define the bars within the menu
  DEFINE BAR 1 OF rptmenu PROMPT "Report 1"
  DEFINE BAR 2 OF rptmenu PROMPT "Report 2"
  DEFINE BAR 3 OF rptmenu PROMPT "Report 3"
  DEFINE BAR 4 OF rptmenu PROMPT "Report 4"
  DEFINE BAR 5 OF rptmenu PROMPT "Report 5"

  * Indicate action to be taken when user makes a selection.
  ON SELECTION POPUP rptmenu DO rptact
```


Figure 14.5 DEFINING POP-UP MENUS

The actual definition process begins with the DEFINE POPUP command which specifies the name of the menu and its location on the screen. The options within a pop-up or pull-down menu are called bars and are defined with the DEFINE BAR command. Finally, the action to be taken when the user makes a selection from the menu is indicated with the ON SELECTION POPUP command. The action is typically to execute some procedure. In the indicated procedure will be commands which will determine the option the user selected and then take appropriate action. Again, all we have done is to define the menu. It will not yet be on the screen.

DEFINING WINDOWS

You already know how to draw boxes on the screen, place data and messages in these boxes, and erase the contents of boxes. dBASE IV includes another option that is similar to boxes but is much more flexible and powerful. You can define any rectangular portion of the screen as a *window*.

You define a window with the DEFINE WINDOW command as illustrated in Figure 14.6. The command specifies the name of the window, along with the coordinates of the window.

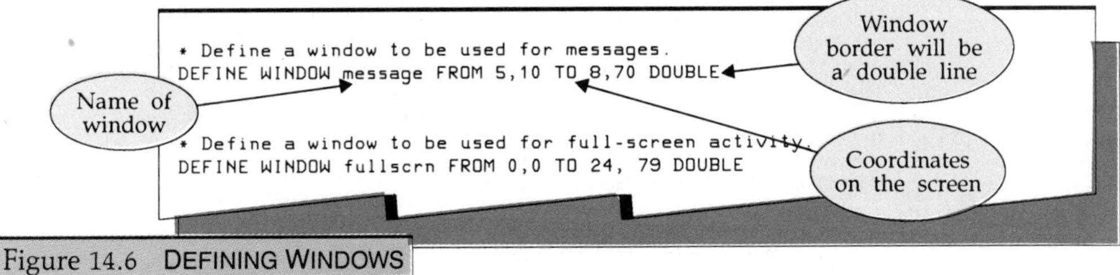

Figure 14.6 DEFINING WINDOWS

Optionally, the DEFINE WINDOW command can include a specification for the window border. In the examples in the figure, the border will be a double line.

Once we have defined a window, we can use it in the remainder of the program. The big advantage of using a window as opposed to a box is that when we remove the window, the portion of the screen that was underneath the window is restored to its original state. When we remove a box, the portion of the screen under the box is blank.

USING THE DEFINED MENUS AND WINDOWS

Figure 14.7 shows the way we use the main menu we have defined. We simply activate the menu with an ACTIVATE MENU command. There is a special action you might wish to take first, however. Unlike pop-up menus, bar menus cannot be automatically assigned a border with the SET BORDER TO command. If we want such a border, we need to include a command to specifically place it on the screen. The @ command in the figure places a double border around the area where the bar menu will appear. The COLOR clause creates a color scheme for the border that is consistent with the colors dBASE will use for other borders.

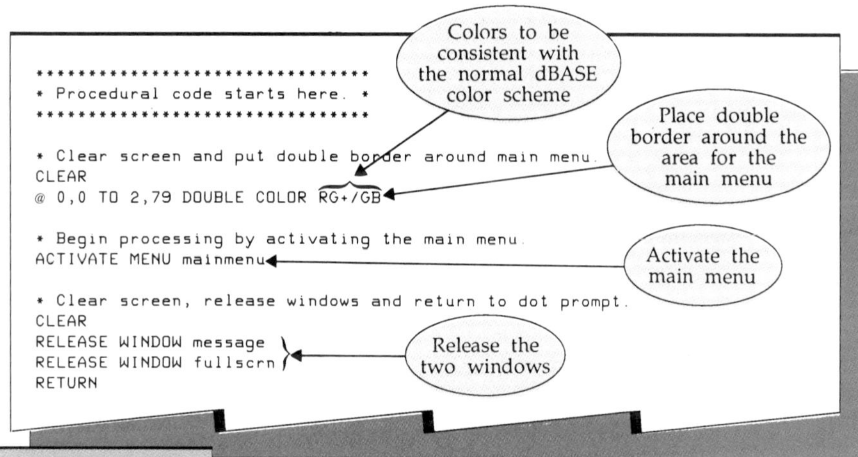

Figure 14.7 USING THE MENU

Once the ACTIVATE MENU command is executed, the main menu will appear on the screen. The highlight will be positioned on the first pad, and the menu activated by that pad will appear on the screen. From this point on, the menu will control the processing that occurs. When the user selects "Exit," the menu will be deactivated and the program clears the screen. Although, as you will see, the windows will not be on the screen at this point, they still occupy space in main memory. The RELEASE WINDOW command removes them from main memory; they will no longer be available for use. In general, it is a good idea to release windows when they are no longer needed. Once the program has released the windows, it ends with a RETURN command.

PROCEDURES FOR PULL-DOWN MENU ACTIONS

When the user selects an option from a pop-up or pull-down menu, the action indicated in the ON SELECTION POPUP will take place. The action is usually to execute a procedure. Figure 14.8 shows a typical form for such a procedure.

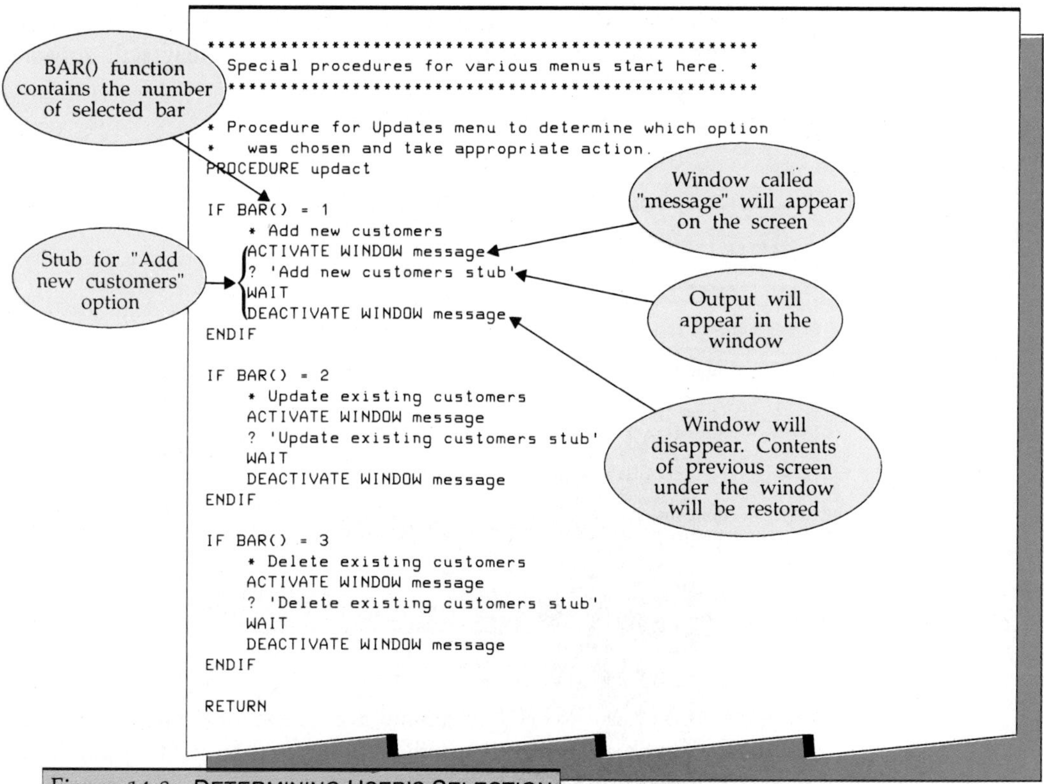


```
**************************************************
Special procedures for various menus start here.  *
**************************************************

* Procedure for Updates menu to determine which option
*   was chosen and take appropriate action.
PROCEDURE updact

IF BAR() = 1
    * Add new customers
    ACTIVATE WINDOW message
    ? 'Add new customers stub'
    WAIT
    DEACTIVATE WINDOW message
ENDIF

IF BAR() = 2
    * Update existing customers
    ACTIVATE WINDOW message
    ? 'Update existing customers stub'
    WAIT
    DEACTIVATE WINDOW message
ENDIF

IF BAR() = 3
    * Delete existing customers
    ACTIVATE WINDOW message
    ? 'Delete existing customers stub'
    WAIT
    DEACTIVATE WINDOW message
ENDIF

RETURN
```

Figure 14.8 DETERMINING USER'S SELECTION

The procedure uses the BAR() function. This function will contain the number of the bar selected by the user. Thus, the procedure simply checks the value currently contained in BAR() and takes appropriate action accordingly.

At present, all actions within this procedure are stubs. The stubs use the window called "message" that was defined earlier in the program. The ACTIVATE WINDOW command places the window on the screen. At this point, any output produced by the program will be placed in the window. In this case, the message "Add new customers stub" along with the instructions displayed by the WAIT command will appear in this window.

Once the user presses a key in response to the WAIT command's message, the DEACTIVATE WINDOW command will be executed. This command removes the window from the screen. It also restores the portion of the screen that was underneath the window to the state it was in when the window was placed on the screen. Finally, the RETURN command at the end of this procedure returns control to the main menu. (**Note:** The procedures for the other menus are similar to the one shown in Figure 14.8.)

RUNNING THE MENU PROGRAM

When we run the program we will first see the main menu and the Updates submenu. We can now try the various options from all the different menus. If we select the "Add new customers" option of the Updates submenu, our screen would look like the one shown in Figure 14.9. Notice how the message from the stub appears in a window that overlays a portion of the Updates submenu. Once we press a key, this window will be removed from the screen and the Updates submenu will be restored in its entirety.

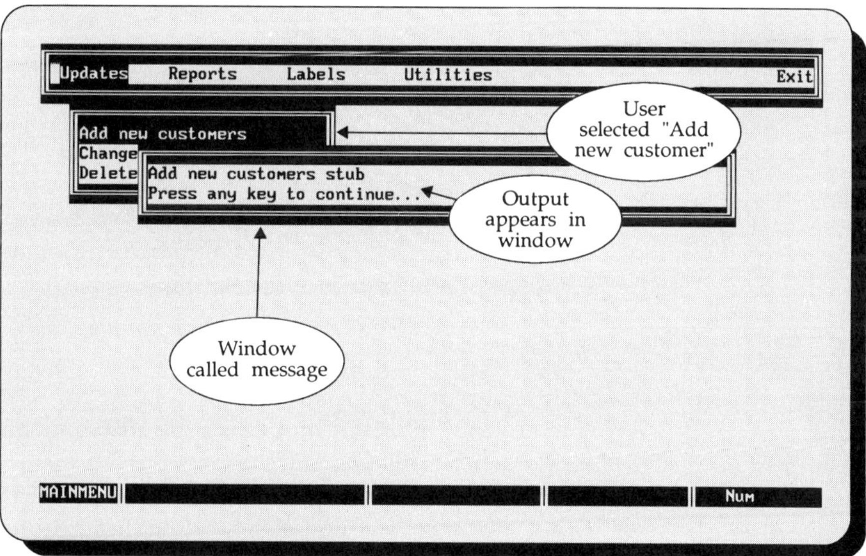

Figure 14.9 "ADD NEW CUSTOMERS" STUB

MORE ON WINDOWS

To further explore the use of windows, let's suppose we change the portion of the procedure for the Reports submenu to the commands shown in Figure 14.10. Notice that the stub for option 2 uses the menu called "fullscrn," which encompasses the entire screen, rather than the window called "message." The stubs for options 3 and 4 don't use a menu. The only difference between them is that the stub for option 4 clears the screen before displaying the message.

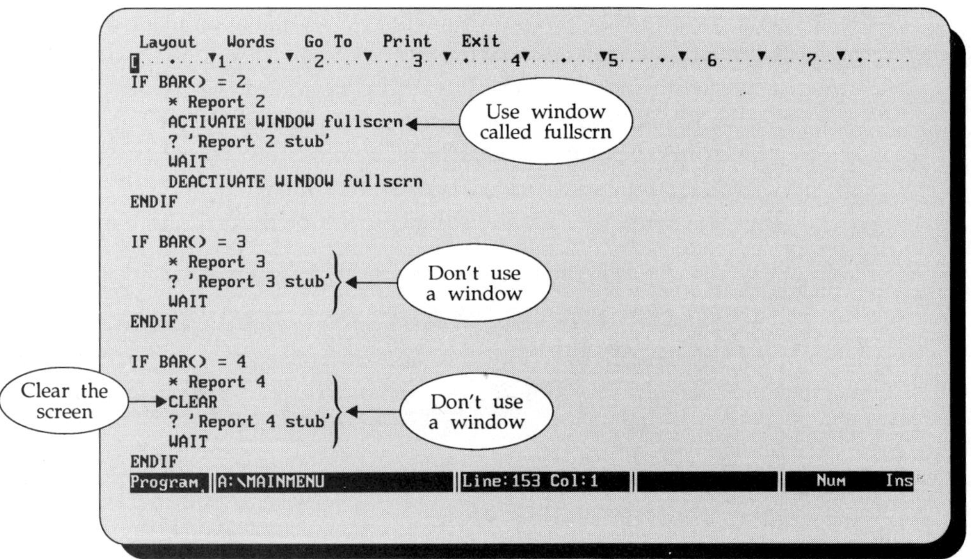

Figure 14.10 STUB VARIATION

When we run the program and select the first option of the Reports submenu, the stub would appear in the same fashion we saw earlier (Figure 14.11). If we select the second option, the window would occupy the whole screen (Figure 14.12) so that no portion of the menus is visible. When we press a key, however, the menus will be correctly restored to the screen.

The approaches in options 3 and 4 pose problems, however. When we select the third option, the screen will look like the one shown in Figure 14.13. Notice that the message from the WAIT command has written over a portion of the submenu. While pressing a key restores the Reports submenu, it still leaves a portion of the output from the stub on the screen (Figure 14.14 on page 398).

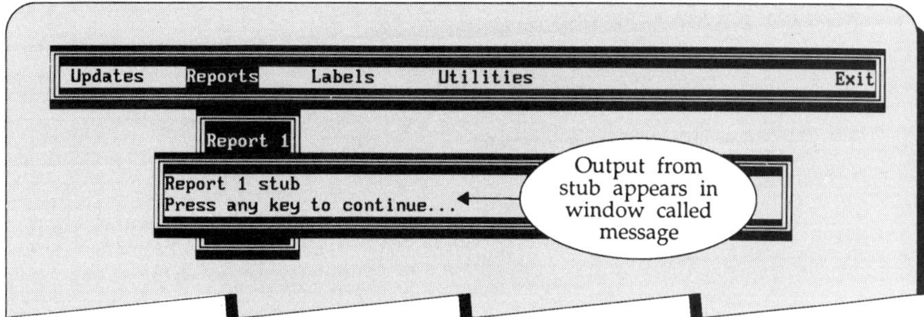

Figure 14.11 STUB USING "MESSAGE" WINDOW

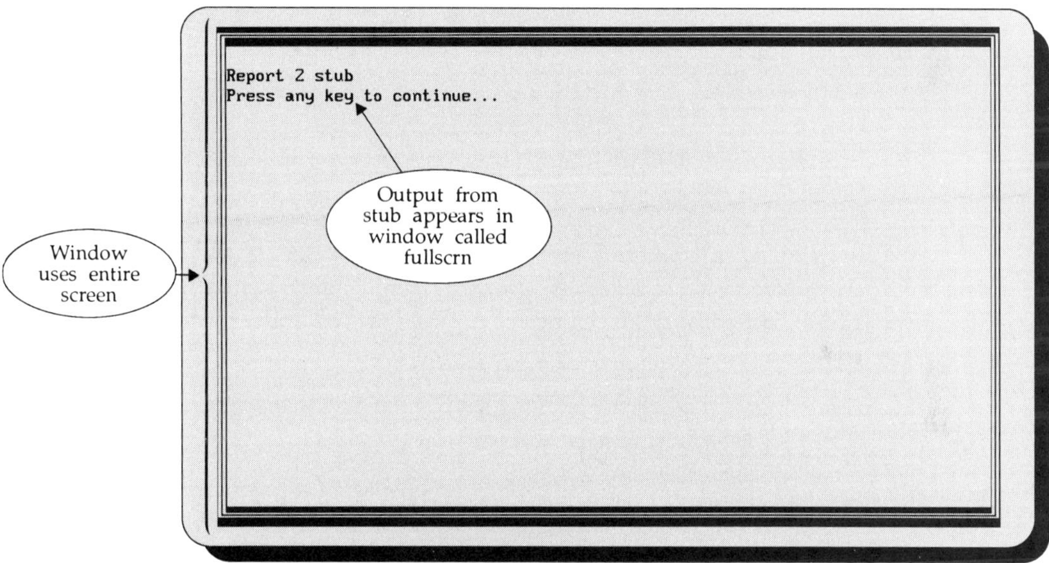

Figure 14.12 STUB USING "FULLSCRN" WINDOW

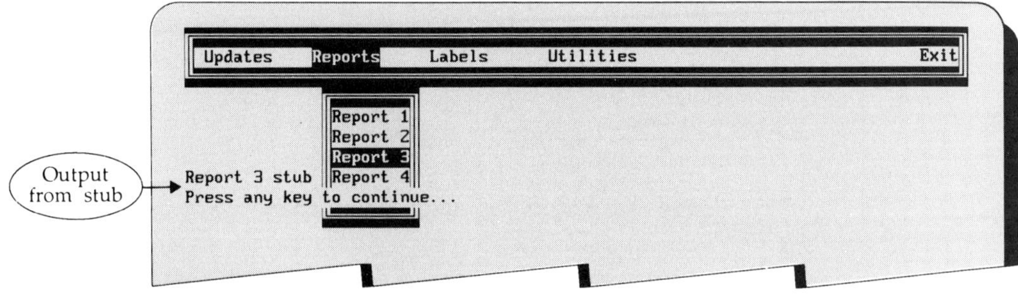

Figure 14.13 STUB WITHOUT A WINDOW

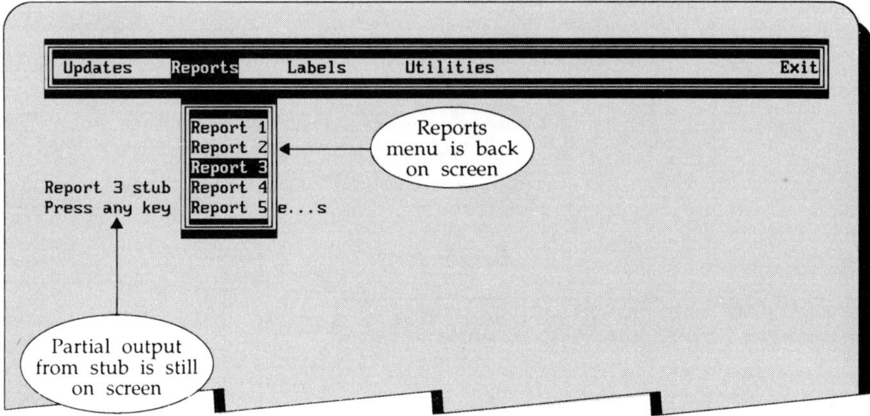

Figure 14.14 REPORTS MENU

Initially, the approach taken for option 4 seems to work. When we select the option, we see the stub message as shown in Figure 14.15. Pressing a key, however, produces the result shown in Figure 14.16. The output from the stub is still present, but the main menu is not. If we press the Right Arrow to move on to Labels, the main menu is once again displayed (Figure 14.17). Unfortunately, the box is not redisplayed and a portion of the output from the stub is still visible.

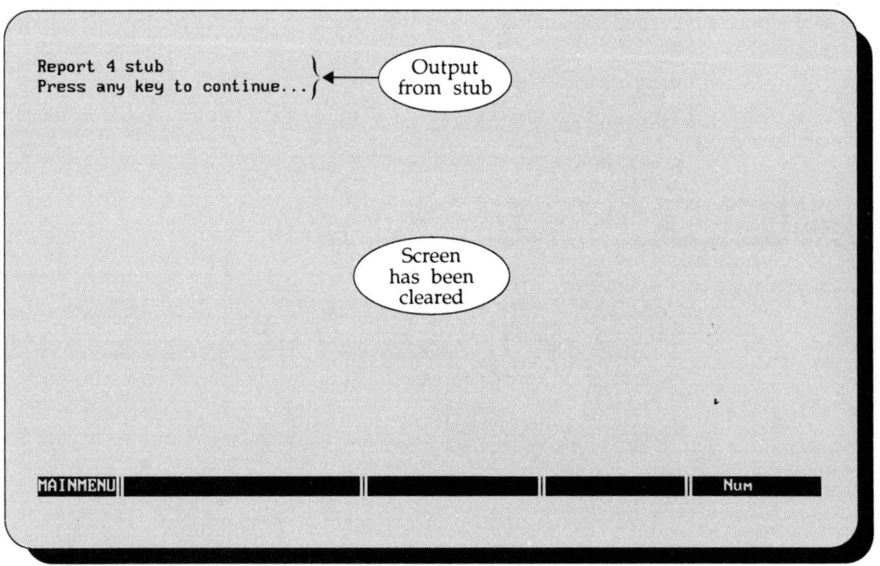

Figure 14.15 STUB USING CLEAR

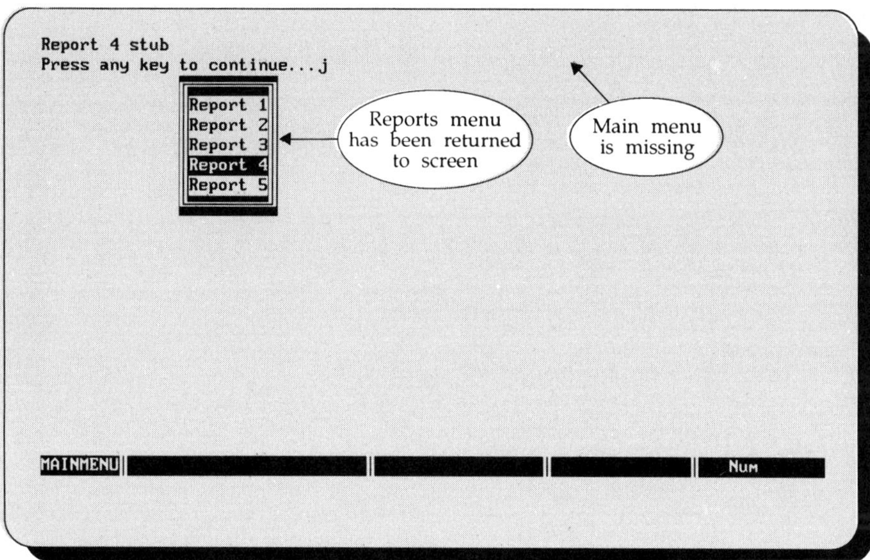

Figure 14.16 REPORTS MENU BUT NO MAIN MENU

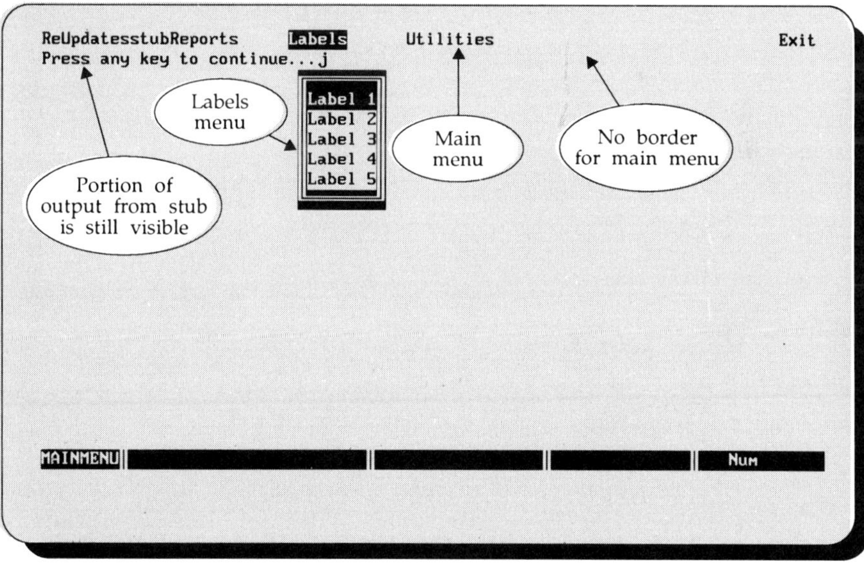

Figure 14.17 LABELS MENU

Figure 14.18 on the next page shows the entire MAINMENU.PRG program, which we have discussed in this chapter; it is also on your data disk.

```
* MAINMENU.PRG  Main menu

* Set environment
SET TALK OFF

*******************************************
* Menu and window definitions start here.  *
*******************************************

* Define main menu as BAR menu.
DEFINE MENU mainmenu
  * Define main menu pads
  DEFINE PAD PAD-1 OF mainmenu PROMPT 'Updates' At 1,2
  DEFINE PAD PAD-2 OF mainmenu PROMPT 'Reports' At 1,13
  DEFINE PAD PAD-3 OF mainmenu PROMPT 'Labels' At 1,25
  DEFINE PAD PAD-4 OF mainmenu PROMPT 'Utilities' At 1,37
  DEFINE PAD PAD-5 OF mainmenu PROMPT 'Exit' At 1,75

  * Define actions for pads
  ON PAD PAD-1 OF mainmenu ACTIVATE POPUP updmenu
  ON PAD PAD-2 OF mainmenu ACTIVATE POPUP rptmenu
  ON PAD PAD-3 OF mainmenu ACTIVATE POPUP lblmenu
  ON PAD PAD-4 OF mainmenu ACTIVATE POPUP utlmenu
  ON SELECTION PAD PAD-5 OF mainmenu DEACTIVATE MENU

* Define pop-up menu called updmenu with double border
SET BORDER TO DOUBLE
DEFINE POPUP updmenu FROM 3,3 TO 7,29
  * Define the bars within the menu
  DEFINE BAR 1 OF updmenu PROMPT "Add new customers"
  DEFINE BAR 2 OF updmenu PROMPT "Change existing customers"
  DEFINE BAR 3 OF updmenu PROMPT "Delete existing customers"

  * Indicate action to be taken when user makes a selection.
  ON SELECTION POPUP updmenu DO updact

* Define pop-up menu called rptmenu with double border
SET BORDER TO DOUBLE
DEFINE POPUP rptmenu FROM 3,14 TO 9,23
  * Define the bars within the menu
  DEFINE BAR 1 OF rptmenu PROMPT "Report 1"
  DEFINE BAR 2 OF rptmenu PROMPT "Report 2"
  DEFINE BAR 3 OF rptmenu PROMPT "Report 3"
  DEFINE BAR 4 OF rptmenu PROMPT "Report 4"
  DEFINE BAR 5 OF rptmenu PROMPT "Report 5"
```

```
  * Indicate action to be taken when user makes a selection.
  ON SELECTION POPUP rptmenu DO rptact


* Define pop-up menu called lblmenu with double border
SET BORDER TO DOUBLE
DEFINE POPUP lblmenu FROM 3,26 TO 9,34
  * Define the bars within the menu
  DEFINE BAR 1 OF lblmenu PROMPT "Label 1"
  DEFINE BAR 2 OF lblmenu PROMPT "Label 2"
  DEFINE BAR 3 OF lblmenu PROMPT "Label 3"
  DEFINE BAR 4 OF lblmenu PROMPT "Label 4"
  DEFINE BAR 5 OF lblmenu PROMPT "Label 5"

  * Indicate action to be taken when user makes a selection.
  ON SELECTION POPUP lblmenu DO lblact
```

Figure 14.18 MAINMENU.PRG PROGRAM

```
* Define pop-up menu called utlmenu with double border
SET BORDER TO DOUBLE
DEFINE POPUP utlmenu FROM 3,38 TO 9,48
  * Define the bars within the menu
  DEFINE BAR 1 OF utlmenu PROMPT "Utility 1"
  DEFINE BAR 2 OF utlmenu PROMPT "Utility 2"
  DEFINE BAR 3 OF utlmenu PROMPT "Utility 3"
  DEFINE BAR 4 OF utlmenu PROMPT "Utility 4"
  DEFINE BAR 5 OF utlmenu PROMPT "Utility 5"

  * Indicate action to be taken when user makes a selection.
  ON SELECTION POPUP utlmenu DO utlact


* Define a window to be used for messages.
DEFINE WINDOW message FROM 5,10 TO 8,70 DOUBLE


* Define a window to be used for full-screen activity.
DEFINE WINDOW fullscrn FROM 0,0 TO 24, 79 DOUBLE
********************************
* Procedural code starts here. *
********************************

* Clear screen and put double border around main menu.
CLEAR
@ 0,0 TO 2,79 DOUBLE COLOR RG+/GB

* Begin processing by activating the main menu.
ACTIVATE MENU mainmenu

* Clear screen, release windows and return to dot prompt.
CLEAR
RELEASE WINDOW message
RELEASE WINDOW fullscrn
RETURN


*****************************************************
* Special procedures for various menus start here.  *
*****************************************************

* Procedure for Updates menu to determine which option
*   was chosen and take appropriate action.
PROCEDURE updact
    IF BAR() = 1
        * Add new customers
        ACTIVATE WINDOW message
        ? 'Add new customers stub'
        WAIT
        DEACTIVATE WINDOW message
    ENDIF

    IF BAR() = 2
        * Update existing customers
        ACTIVATE WINDOW message
        ? 'Update existing customers stub'
        WAIT
        DEACTIVATE WINDOW message
    ENDIF
```

Figure 14.18 MAINMENU.PRG PROGRAM

(continued)

```
IF BAR() = 3
    * Delete existing customers
    ACTIVATE WINDOW message
    ? 'Delete existing customers stub'
    WAIT
    DEACTIVATE WINDOW message
ENDIF

RETURN

* Procedure for Reports menu to determine which option
*   was chosen and take appropriate action.
PROCEDURE rptact

IF BAR() = 1
    * Report 1
    ACTIVATE WINDOW message
    ? 'Report 1 stub'
    WAIT
    DEACTIVATE WINDOW message
ENDIF

IF BAR() = 2
    * Report 2
    ACTIVATE WINDOW message
    ? 'Report 2 stub'
    WAIT
    DEACTIVATE WINDOW message
ENDIF

IF BAR() = 3
    * Report 3
    ACTIVATE WINDOW message
    ? 'Report 3 stub'
    WAIT
    DEACTIVATE WINDOW message
ENDIF

IF BAR() = 4
    * Report 4
    ACTIVATE WINDOW message
    ? 'Report 4 stub'
    WAIT
    DEACTIVATE WINDOW message
ENDIF
```

```
IF BAR() = 5
    * Report 5
    ACTIVATE WINDOW message
    ? 'Report 5 stub'
    WAIT
    DEACTIVATE WINDOW message
ENDIF

RETURN
* Procedure for Labels menu to determine which option
*   was chosen and take appropriate action.
PROCEDURE lblact

IF BAR() = 1
    * Label 1
    ACTIVATE WINDOW message
    ? 'Label 1 stub'
    WAIT
    DEACTIVATE WINDOW message
ENDIF
```

Figure 14.18 MAINMENU.PRG PROGRAM

```
IF BAR() = 2
    * Label 2
    ACTIVATE WINDOW message
    ? 'Label 2 stub'
    WAIT
    DEACTIVATE WINDOW message
ENDIF

IF BAR() = 3
    * Label 3
    ACTIVATE WINDOW message
    ? 'Label 3 stub'
    WAIT
    DEACTIVATE WINDOW message
ENDIF

IF BAR() = 4
    * Label 4
    ACTIVATE WINDOW message
    ? 'Label 4 stub'
    WAIT
    DEACTIVATE WINDOW message
ENDIF

IF BAR() = 5
    * Label 5
    ACTIVATE WINDOW message
    ? 'Label 5 stub'
    WAIT
    DEACTIVATE WINDOW message
ENDIF

RETURN

* Procedure for Utilities menu to determine which option
*   was chosen and take appropriate action.

IF BAR() = 1
    * Utility 1
    ACTIVATE WINDOW message
    ? 'Utility 1 stub'
    WAIT
    DEACTIVATE WINDOW message
ENDIF
```

```
IF BAR() = 2
    * Utility 2
    ACTIVATE WINDOW message
    ? 'Utility 2 stub'
    WAIT
    DEACTIVATE WINDOW message
ENDIF

IF BAR() = 3
    * Utility 3
    ACTIVATE WINDOW message
    ? 'Utility 3 stub'
    WAIT
    DEACTIVATE WINDOW message
ENDIF

IF BAR() = 4
    * Utility 4
    ACTIVATE WINDOW message
    ? 'Utility 4 stub'
    WAIT
    DEACTIVATE WINDOW message
ENDIF
```

Figure 14.18 MAINMENU.PRG PROGRAM

(continued)

```
IF BAR() = 5
    * Utility 5
    ACTIVATE WINDOW message
    ? 'Utility 5 stub'
    WAIT
    DEACTIVATE WINDOW message
ENDIF

RETURN
```

Figure 14.18 MAINMENU.PRG PROGRAM

14.2 PROCEDURE FILES

You have already seen a procedure file, FNPROC.PRG, in Chapter 12. This file happened to contain only User-Defined Functions, but it could have contained procedures as well. A *procedure file* is a file that contains procedures and User-Defined Functions. (A procedure file can actually contain up to 973 User-Defined Functions and/or procedures. This should be more than sufficient for any situation.)

ACTIVATING A PROCEDURE FILE

A procedure file is activated from within a program or at the dot prompt by the SET PROCEDURE TO command. The command is simply SET PROCEDURE TO followed by the name of the procedure file. (If no name follows the word TO, the command will close the active procedure file.)

Once a procedure file has been activated, all the User-Defined Functions and procedures in it are available to the program, *just as though they were part of the program itself*. The program can use any UDF or perform any procedure in the procedure file. The same rules for use of variables and parameters that would apply to procedures or UDFs within a program apply to procedures and UDFs within the procedure file.

WHAT TO INDLUDE IN A PROCEDURE FILE

A natural question is, "Should a particular User-Defined Function or procedure be incorporated into the program or should it be placed in a separate procedure file?" The best way to make this determination is to ask yourself if the function or procedure serves some *specific* need for the program on which you are working or if it is something that many programs could use. If it is specific to the program, it should be placed in the program. If not, placing it in a separate procedure file would make it readily available to other programs.

Using this guideline, the agtname and agtexist procedures in FNPROC should probably have been placed in the program that used them. They served that program, but chances are they would not serve many others. The longdate UDF, on the other hand, which converted a date to the long form of a date, is something many programs could use.

If we follow this approach in deciding where to place UDFs and procedures, we end up creating a procedure file that contains a number of general-purpose routines, available to any program that needs them. We sometimes call this a *procedure library*.

SAMPLE PROCEDURE FILE

Figure 14.19 offers a sample of such a procedure file. The procedure file is called PROCLIB (for PROCedure LIBrary). It contains the longdate UDF you saw in Chapter 12. It also contains a UDF to combine city, state, and zip into a single address. Notice that this UDF will convert the state to uppercase. In addition, it uses the TRANSFORM() function on the zip. The @L picture function in this example will make sure that leading zeros appear (2110 will appear as 02110), which is appropriate for a zip code.

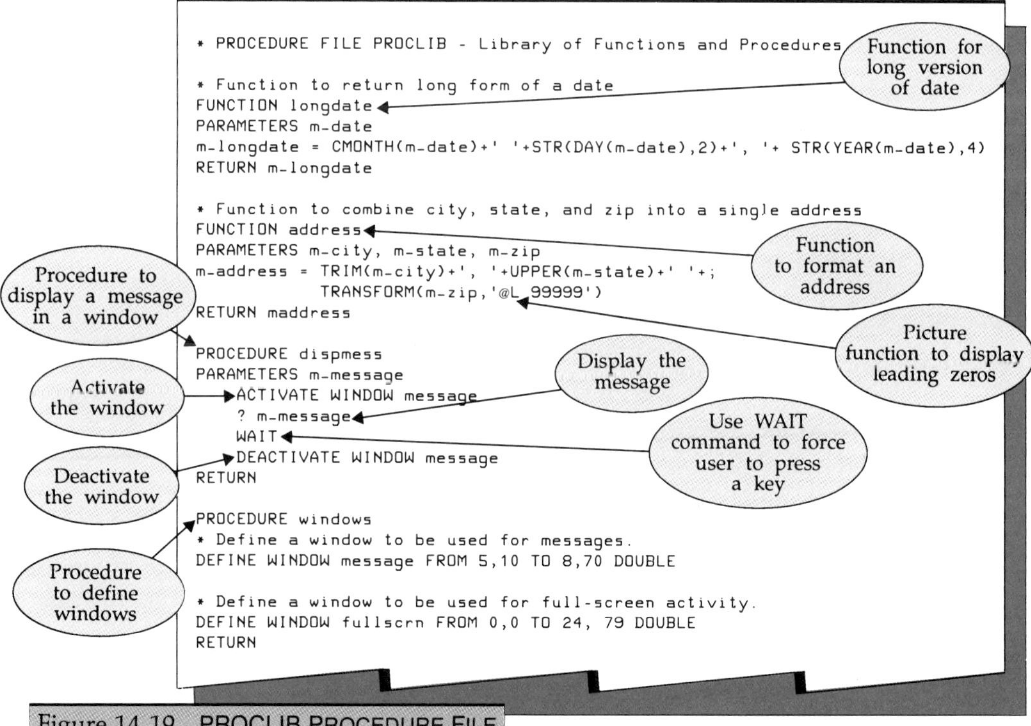

```
* PROCEDURE FILE PROCLIB - Library of Functions and Procedures

* Function to return long form of a date
FUNCTION longdate
PARAMETERS m-date
m-longdate = CMONTH(m-date)+' '+STR(DAY(m-date),2)+', '+ STR(YEAR(m-date),4)
RETURN m-longdate

* Function to combine city, state, and zip into a single address
FUNCTION address
PARAMETERS m-city, m-state, m-zip
m-address = TRIM(m-city)+', '+UPPER(m-state)+' '+;
         TRANSFORM(m-zip,'@L 99999')
RETURN maddress

PROCEDURE dispmess
PARAMETERS m-message
   ACTIVATE WINDOW message
   ? m-message
   WAIT
   DEACTIVATE WINDOW message
RETURN

PROCEDURE windows
* Define a window to be used for messages.
DEFINE WINDOW message FROM 5,10 TO 8,70 DOUBLE

* Define a window to be used for full-screen activity.
DEFINE WINDOW fullscrn FROM 0,0 TO 24, 79 DOUBLE
RETURN
```


Figure 14.19 PROCLIB PROCEDURE FILE

The procedure file also contains a procedure, "dispmess," which uses a window, "message," to display a message and then prompt the user to press a key. The final procedure, "windows," defines two windows, "message" and "fullscrn." With this procedure in place, any program can define both windows by simply executing the command DO windows.

USING A PROCEDURE FILE

We will examine the use of the procedure file from the dot prompt. It would be used in programs in exactly the same fashion.

Figure 14.20 illustrates the use of the address UDF in this procedure file. The SET PROCEDURE TO proclib command activates this procedure file, making all its functions and procedures available. The address function is used in a ? command. Its arguments are city (Boston), state (Ma), and zip (2110). The function combines these to create an address of

```
Boston, MA 02110
```

In the process, it converted the state to uppercase and displayed the zip as **02110 rather than** 2110 as the number would normally appear.

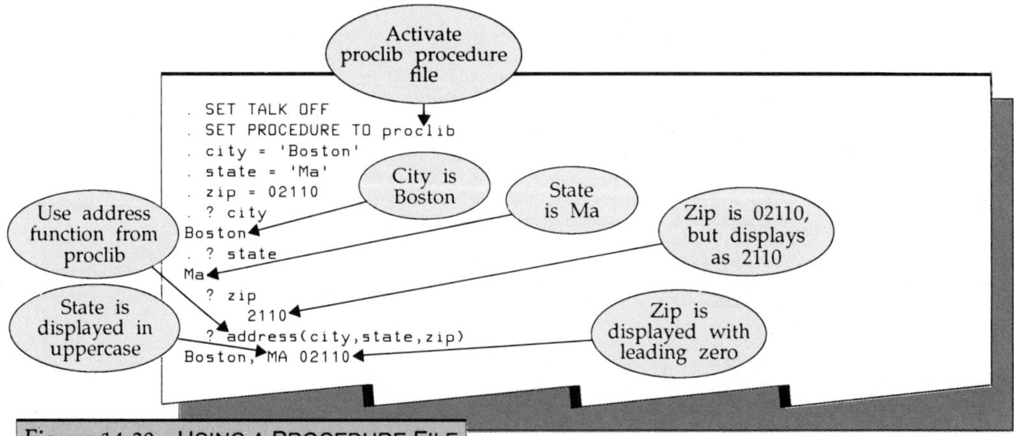

Figure 14.20 USING A PROCEDURE FILE

With this procedure file active, we can define the message and fullscrn window by simply typing DO windows. This will execute the commands in the procedure called windows to define the message and fullscrn windows. We can then uses these windows in the same ways we saw earlier. Since we have the dispmess procedure, however, we can use it to display text in the message window. For example, to display "Add customers stub" in the window we only need type

```
DO dispmess WITH 'Add customers stub'
```

The window will appear with this message on the first line and the WAIT command message on the second (Figure 14.21). When we press a key, the window will be removed from the screen. Thus, this single command could replace a collection of commands we saw in the MAINMENU program.

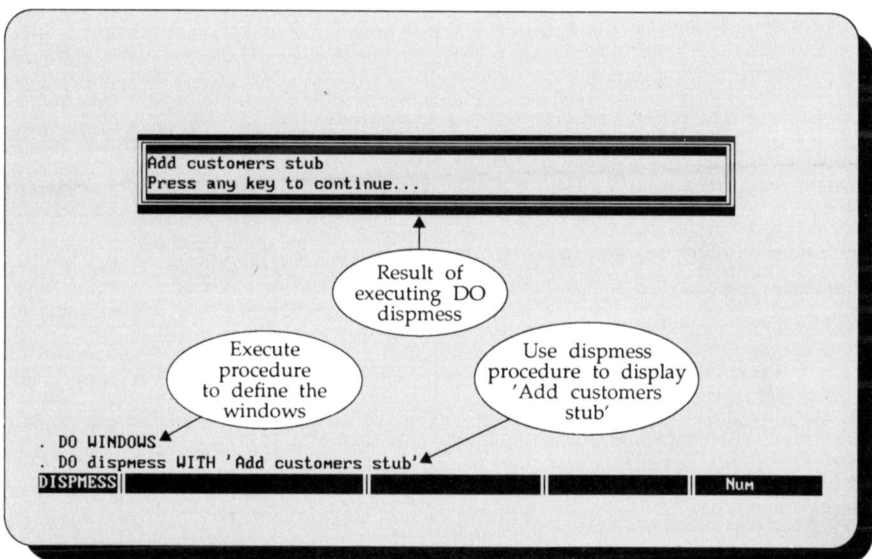

Figure 14.21 RESULT OF DISPMESS

In another program, we may need to display the message "Invalid list number." To do so, we could type

```
DO dispmess WITH 'Invalid list number'
```

This would produce the display shown in the middle of the screen in Figure 14.22.

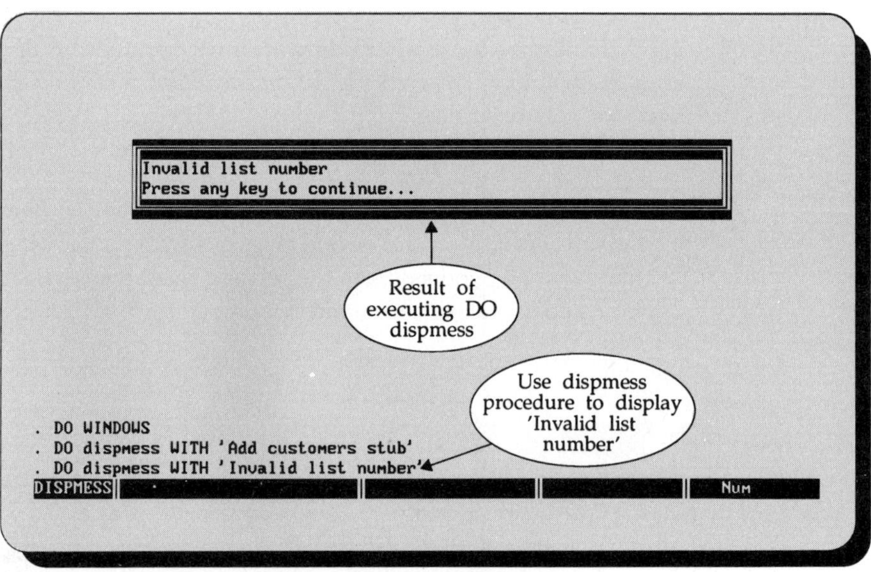

Figure 14.22 RESULT OF DISPMESS WITH DIFFERENT MESSAGE

14.3 ERROR-PROOFING A SYSTEM

When you create a system of programs for some user, you would naturally like the system to be as *error-proof* as possible. You don't want to compromise the integrity of your system by allowing its users to unwittingly take some destructive action. The most obvious aspect of error-proofing a system is to thoroughly test it, making sure it is as free of bugs as possible. This is not the only consideration, however.

DATA INTEGRITY

Your programs should ensure that your database files contain only valid data. You have already done this in your update programs. Your program made sure, for example, that the agent number entered for a client was valid; that is, that it matched the number of an agent in the AGENT database file.

Even though your programs prevent the user from entering invalid data, it is still possible that such data finds its way into the database. Some program might contain a bug that allows this to happen. Even if the programs are totally correct, some user may bypass your whole system and use the dBASE EDIT command, in which case no error-checking would be taking place.

To guard against this, it is a good idea to include a utility program in your system that checks the data currently in the database, looking for errors. The program segment in Figure 14.23, for example, examines each client record, looking for those clients whose agent number is invalid.

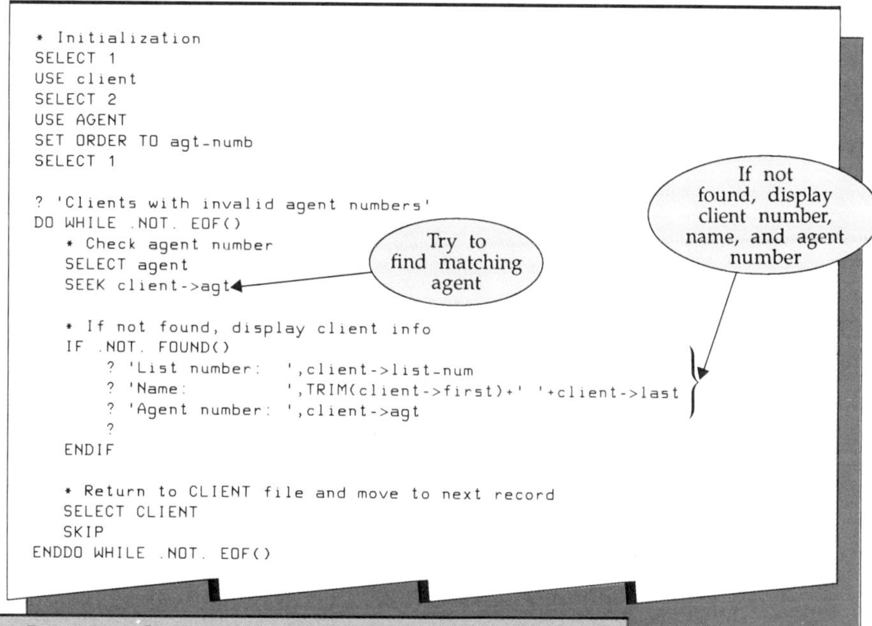

```
* Initialization
SELECT 1
USE client
SELECT 2
USE AGENT
SET ORDER TO agt-numb
SELECT 1

? 'Clients with invalid agent numbers'
DO WHILE .NOT. EOF()
   * Check agent number
   SELECT agent
   SEEK client->agt

   * If not found, display client info
   IF .NOT. FOUND()
       ? 'List number:   ',client->list-num
       ? 'Name:          ',TRIM(client->first)+' '+client->last
       ? 'Agent number:  ',client->agt
       ?
   ENDIF

   * Return to CLIENT file and move to next record
   SELECT CLIENT
   SKIP
ENDDO WHILE .NOT. EOF()
```

Try to find matching agent
If not found, display client number, name, and agent number

Figure 14.23 PROGRAM SEGMENT TO FIND INVALID AGENT NUMBERS

The other important aspect of data integrity is to include options in our Utilities menu for backing up and restoring a database. The database files that are being used on a day-to-day basis are called the *live* versions, or live copies, of the files. To back up these files, we copy each live version over another file, called a *backup* or *save* file. Should any of the live files be damaged in some way, we could use these backup copies to *recover* the files simply by copying the backup versions over the live versions.

Remember, a special index file, called the *production index file,* is associated with each database file. This file has the same name as the corresponding database file, but it has an extension of MDX rather than DBF. We want to back up these files as well.

The program to back up the database files in the Premiere Products database is shown in Figure 14.24. An example of the statements that back up the database files would be

```
COPY FILE d_custom.dbf TO custback.dbf
```

which copies the customer database file (d_custom.dbf) over the customer database backup (custback.dbf). The statements that include references to files with MDX extensions are the ones that back up the production index files.

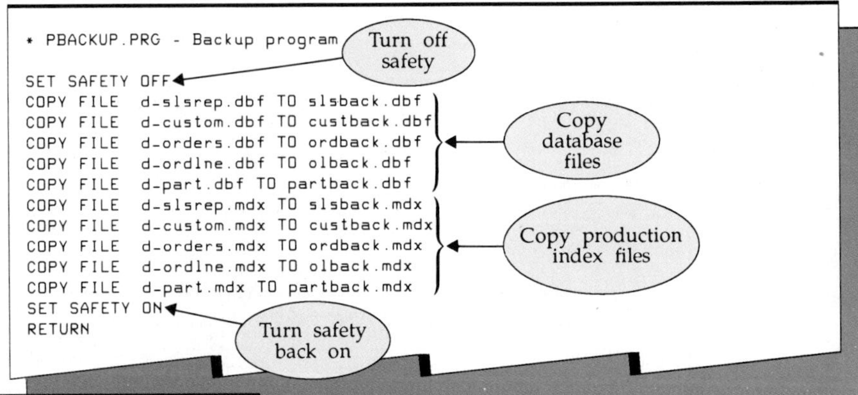

Figure 14.24 PROGRAM PBACKUP

Two other new statements in the program are as follows:

```
SET SAFETY OFF
```

and

```
SET SAFETY ON
```

The normal setting for SAFETY is ON. This means that whenever an operation would overwrite an existing file, dBASE asks the user if this is acceptable. However, since the backup procedure intentionally overwrites the old backup file with the new one, this safety feature is unnecessary. If we set SAFETY to OFF, dBASE does not interact with the user but proceeds to overwrite the file. In general, setting SAFETY to ON is a desirable feature; it prevents the accidental erasure of crucial files. We should always be sure to turn it back on before we leave the program.

A program to recover the database files would be very similar. The only difference is that the COPY statements are reversed; for example, custback.dbf would be copied over d_custom.dbf.

PROVIDING FOR ERRORS

The other aspect of making your system as error-proof as possible is to make provision for errors. If there is special action a user must take, like turning on a printer, inform the user of this fact. To provide for the possibility of a user choosing the wrong option, we should include some escape mechanism.

If there are errors that can be caused by a problem the user can correct, give the user a chance to make the correction. Finally, if an error occurs that a user cannot correct, display an appropriate message and then cleanly shut down your system. If you don't do this, users will see the normal dBASE message and might very well not know how to respond. They may decide to simply shut the machine off, a potentially damaging act.

(We will illustrate all these features by including them in the first version of the customer and sales rep report. The version including these features is called RPTCSSR4.PRG and is on your data disk.)

To provide for an escape mechanism, we use the ON ESCAPE command as shown in Figure 14.25. The command is simply ON ESCAPE followed by the action to be taken if the user presses the Escape key. Usually the action will be DO followed by a procedure name. In this example, if the user should ever press Escape, dBASE would immediately execute the procedure called "stoprtn." This procedure closes all active databases and then returns control to RPTCSSR4. As we will see when we examine the complete RPTCSSR4 program, the program will then terminate.

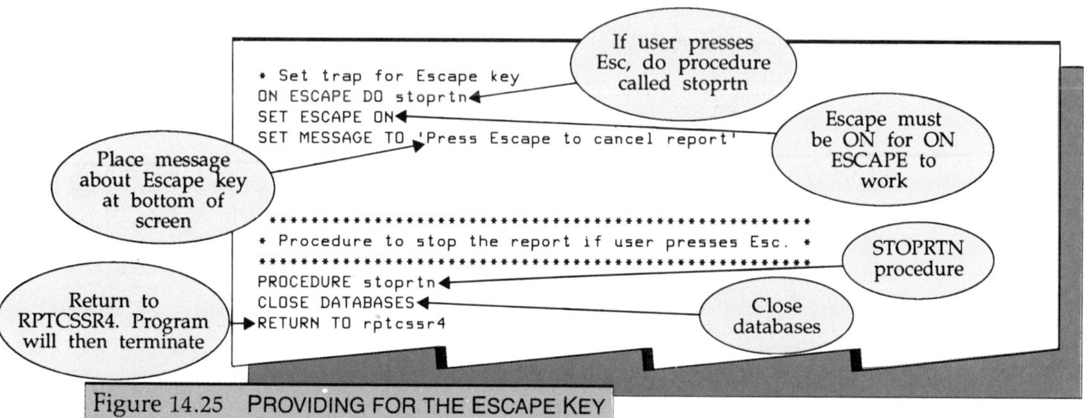

Figure 14.25 PROVIDING FOR THE ESCAPE KEY

In order for the ON ESCAPE command to function, ESCAPE must be ON. It normally is, so this usually wouldn't pose a problem. To guard against the possibility that another program might have turned it off, however, it is a good idea to include the SET ESCAPE ON command in the program. It is also a good idea to include a SET MESSAGE TO command as shown in the figure. This command will display the indicated message at the bottom of the screen. In this case, the message will inform the user of the fact that pressing Escape will cancel the report.

Note: You might want to use a function key, rather than Escape, for terminating the report or for some other purpose. The idea is exactly the same. In that case, you would use the ON KEY LABEL command in place of the ON ESCAPE command. To use F5 for terminating the report, for example, the command would be

```
ON KEY LABEL F5 DO stoprtn
```

Figure 14.26 shows how to trap for errors. The command is ON ERROR. Just as with ON ESCAPE or ON KEY LABEL, the ON ERROR command is followed by an action, typically a DO statement. In this case, if any error is encountered as the program is running, dBASE will immediately execute the procedure called "trapper".

The trapper procedure begins by testing for the special errors that a user might be able to correct, namely a problem with the printer. These are represented by error codes 125 and 126 (a complete list of error codes and meanings are given in Appendix E). If one of these is encountered, the program uses the window called message to inform the user of the problem and determine whether the user wants to correct the problem. If the user does not select Y, the program will be shut down. The SET PROCEDURE TO, ON ESCAPE, ON ERROR, and SET MESSAGE TO commands cancel the effect of previous commands. The CANCEL command cancels the whole program and returns the user to the dot prompt.

If dBASE makes it to the next portion of the code in the trapper procedure, there is an error, but the code is not 125 or 126. In this case, we use the window called fullscrn to display a message to the user describing the error. (The MESSAGE() function contains the description of the error that occurred.) We also use the WAIT command to force the user to press a key. Once the user has seen the message and pressed a key, the program is shut down.

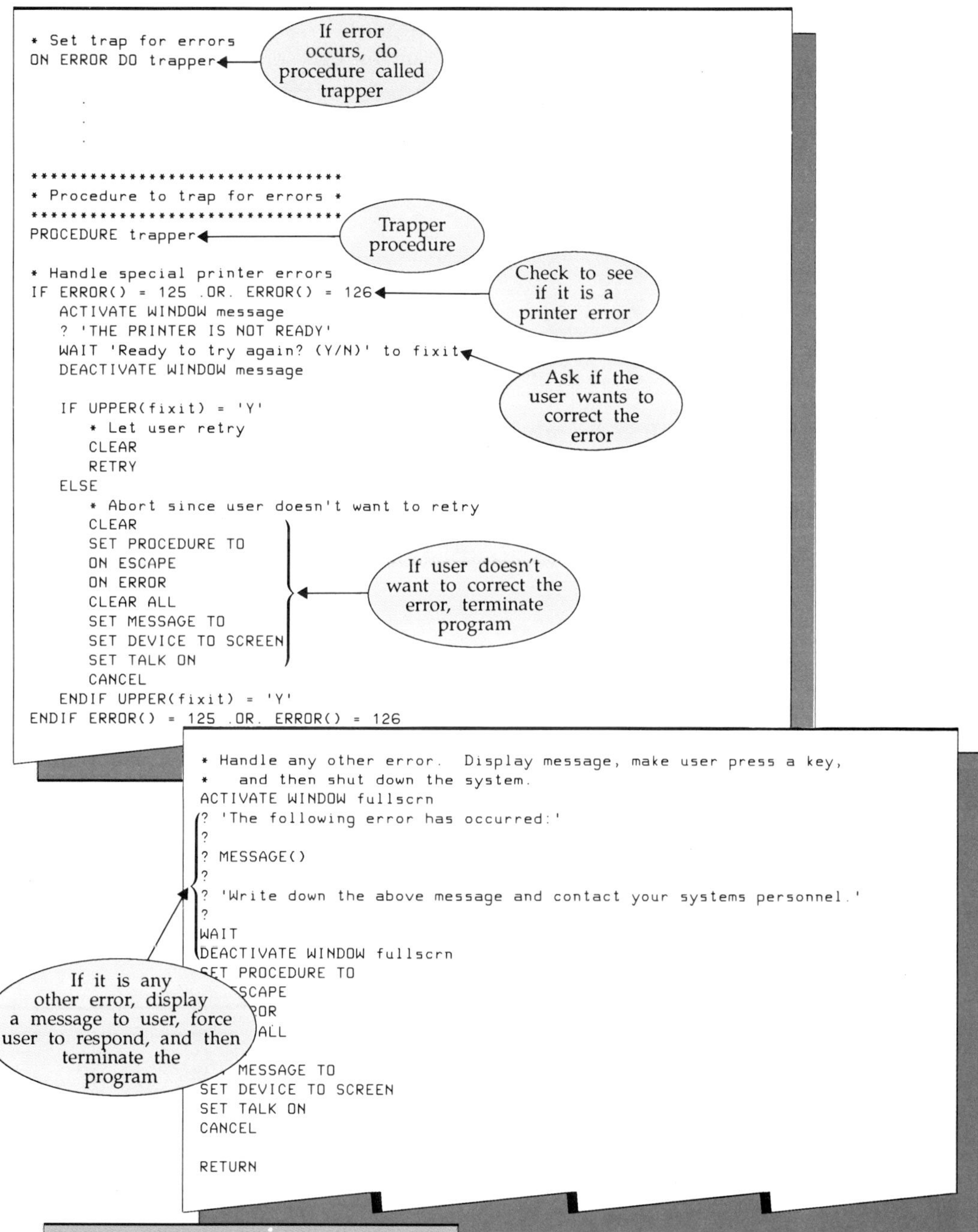

* Set trap for errors
ON ERROR DO trapper
If error occurs, do procedure called trapper
.
.
.
****
* Procedure to trap for errors *
****
PROCEDURE trapper
Trapper procedure
* Handle special printer errors
IF ERROR() = 125 .OR. ERROR() = 126
Check to see if it is a printer error
ACTIVATE WINDOW message
? 'THE PRINTER IS NOT READY'
WAIT 'Ready to try again? (Y/N)' to fixit
Ask if the user wants to correct the error
DEACTIVATE WINDOW message
IF UPPER(fixit) = 'Y'
* Let user retry
CLEAR
RETRY
ELSE
* Abort since user doesn't want to retry
CLEAR
SET PROCEDURE TO
ON ESCAPE
ON ERROR
CLEAR ALL
SET MESSAGE TO
SET DEVICE TO SCREEN
SET TALK ON
If user doesn't want to correct the error, terminate program
CANCEL
ENDIF UPPER(fixit) = 'Y'
ENDIF ERROR() = 125 .OR. ERROR() = 126
* Handle any other error. Display message, make user press a key,
* and then shut down the system.
ACTIVATE WINDOW fullscrn
? 'The following error has occurred:'
?
? MESSAGE()
?
? 'Write down the above message and contact your systems personnel.'
?
WAIT
DEACTIVATE WINDOW fullscrn
SET PROCEDURE TO
SCAPE
OR
ALL
MESSAGE TO
SET DEVICE TO SCREEN
SET TALK ON
CANCEL
RETURN
If it is any other error, display a message to user, force user to respond, and then terminate the program

Figure 14.26 PROVIDING FOR ERRORS

Figure 14.27 shows the complete program. Notice that the logic from the earlier report program is now contained within the procedure called "prtrpt." Notice also that the program uses the dispmess procedure from PROCLIB to display a message indicating that the user should make sure the printer is ready. Finally, notice how the procedures for using Escape and handling errors have been incorporated into this program.

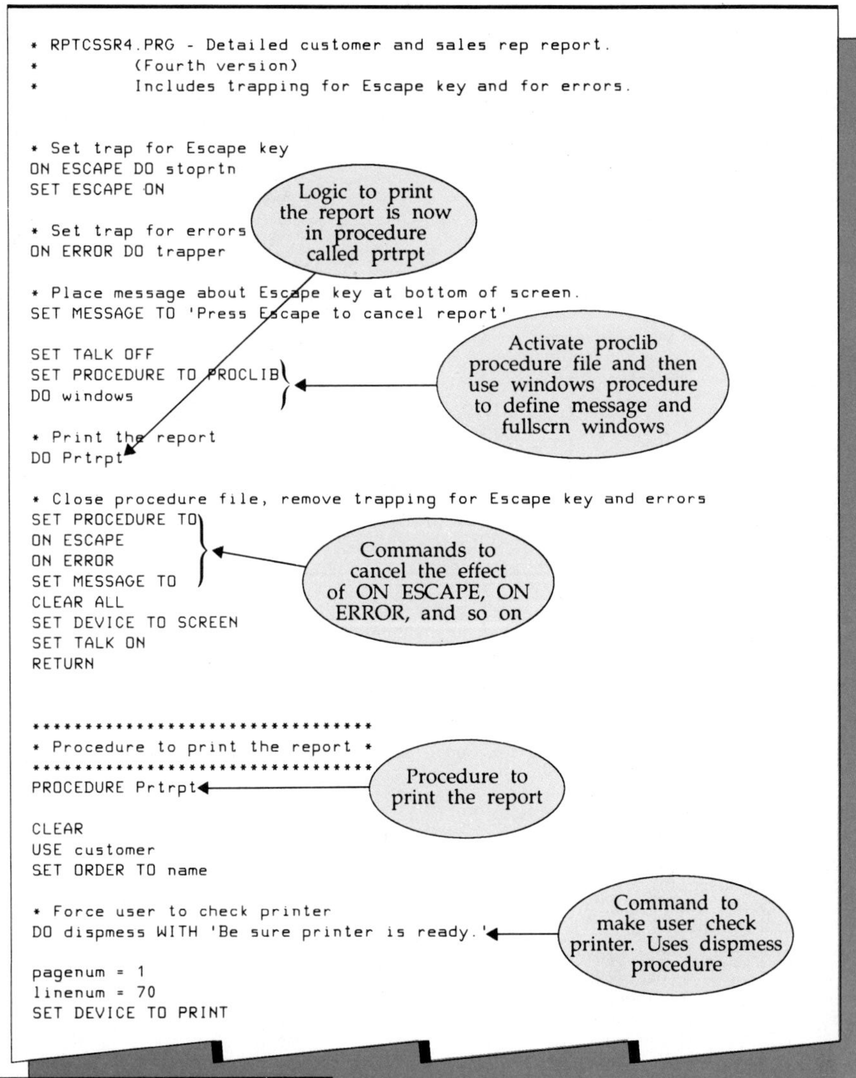

```
* RPTCSSR4.PRG - Detailed customer and sales rep report.
*         (Fourth version)
*         Includes trapping for Escape key and for errors.

* Set trap for Escape key
ON ESCAPE DO stoprtn
SET ESCAPE ON

* Set trap for errors
ON ERROR DO trapper

* Place message about Escape key at bottom of screen.
SET MESSAGE TO 'Press Escape to cancel report'

SET TALK OFF
SET PROCEDURE TO PROCLIB
DO windows

* Print the report
DO Prtrpt

* Close procedure file, remove trapping for Escape key and errors
SET PROCEDURE TO
ON ESCAPE
ON ERROR
SET MESSAGE TO
CLEAR ALL
SET DEVICE TO SCREEN
SET TALK ON
RETURN


*********************************
* Procedure to print the report *
*********************************
PROCEDURE Prtrpt

CLEAR
USE customer
SET ORDER TO name

* Force user to check printer
DO dispmess WITH 'Be sure printer is ready.'

pagenum = 1
linenum = 70
SET DEVICE TO PRINT
```


Figure 14.27 RPTCSSR4.PRG PROGRAM

```
DO WHILE .NOT. EOF()
   IF linenum > 20
       @  1,   0  SAY DATE()
       @  1,  25  SAY "Premiere Products"
       @  1,  72  SAY "Page"
       @  1,  77  SAY pagenum PICTURE "99"
       @  2, 23   SAY "Customer Master List"
       @  4,   0  SAY "Cust"
       @  4,   8  SAY "Customer"
       @  4, 27   SAY "Customer"
       @  4, 44   SAY "Current"
       @  4, 53   SAY "Cred"
       @  4, 59   SAY "Sls"
       @  5,   0  SAY "Numb"
       @  5, 10   SAY "Name"
       @  5, 28   SAY "Address"
       @  5, 44   SAY "Balance"
       @  5, 54   SAY "Lim"
       @  5, 59   SAY "Num"
       linenum = 7
       pagenum = pagenum + 1
   ENDIF
   @  linenum,  0  SAY  customer->custnumb
   @  linenum,  5  SAY  TRIM(customer->first)+" "+TRIM(customer->last)
   @  linenum, 22  SAY  customer->address
   @  linenum, 44  SAY  customer->balance
   @  linenum, 53  SAY  customer->credlim
   @  linenum, 59  SAY  customer->slsrnumb
   linenum = linenum + 1
   SKIP
ENDDO
EJECT
CLOSE DATABASES

RETURN
```

```
*****************************************************
* Procedure to stop the report if user presses Esc. *
*****************************************************
PROCEDURE stoprtn
CLOSE DATABASES
RETURN TO rptcssr4

********************************
* Procedure to trap for errors *
********************************
PROCEDURE trapper

* Handle special printer errors
IF ERROR() = 125 .OR. ERROR() = 126
   ACTIVATE WINDOW message
   ? 'THE PRINTER IS NOT READY'
   WAIT 'Ready to try again? (Y/N)' to fixit
   DEACTIVATE WINDOW message
   IF UPPER(fixit) = 'Y'
      * Let user retry
      CLEAR
      RETRY
   ELSE
      * Abort since user doesn't want to retry
      CLEAR
      SET PROCEDURE TO
      ON ESCAPE
      ON ERROR
      CLEAR ALL
      SET MESSAGE TO
      SET DEVICE TO SCREEN
      SET TALK ON
      CANCEL
   ENDIF UPPER(fixit) = 'Y'
ENDIF ERROR() = 125 .OR. ERROR() = 126
```

Stoprtn procedure

Trapper procedure

Figure 14.27 RPTCSSR4.PRG PROGRAM

(continued)

```
* Handle any other error.  Display message, make user press a key,
*   and then shut down the system.
ACTIVATE WINDOW fullscrn
? 'The following error has occurred:'
?
? MESSAGE()
?
? 'Write down the above message and contact your systems personnel.'
?
WAIT
DEACTIVATE WINDOW fullscrn
SET PROCEDURE TO
ON ESCAPE
ON ERROR
CLEAR ALL
CLEAR
SET MESSAGE TO
SET DEVICE TO SCREEN
SET TALK ON
CANCEL

RETURN
```

Figure 14.27 RPTCSSR4.PRG PROGRAM

(You might be wondering why we need to check for printer errors, since we told the user to make sure the printer is ready. We do this since the user may indeed turn on the printer, but there could still be a printer problem. Perhaps the printer is unplugged or has malfunctioned; the paper may be jammed. Thus, to be safe we still need to check for printer errors.)

14.4 USING COLOR

In previous versions of dBASE, the normal display mode was white letters on a black background. In order to make their programs more appealing visually, programmers would include commands to change the colors of various portions of the screen. Since many users of dBASE IV find its built-in color scheme quite appealing, dBASE IV programmers do not normally include such commands in their programs.

If you decide that you would like to customize your color scheme, you will find the information in Tables 4.1 and 4.2 helpful. Table 4.1 gives the codes for the various possible colors. To specify a particular combination, you write the code for the foreground, a slash, and then the code for the background. For example, to specify red letters on a black background, the code would be R/N.

TABLE 14.1 dBASE IV color codes

COLOR	LOW INTENSITY	HIGH INTENSITY
Black	N	
Blue	B	B+
Green	G	G+
Cyan	BG (or GB)	BG+ (or GB+)
Gray	N+	
Red	R	R+
Magenta	RB (or BR)	RB+ (or BR+)
Brown	GR (or RG)	
Yellow	GR+ (or RG+)	
White	W	W+
ATTRIBUTE (MONOCHROME)		
Bold	W+	
Underlined	U	
Reverse video	I	

Note: Following any attribute with an asterisk will make the appropriate screen portion blink.

TABLE 14.2 Screen groups

GROUP	DEFAULT	DESCRIPTION OF GROUP
NORMAL	W+/B	Messages and text. Background of work surface in many of the design screens. Prompts on Edit screen.
MESSAGES	W/N	Menu options. Message and navigation line. Messages in error boxes.
TITLES	W/B	Column headings (LIST, DISPLAY, Browse), borders of boxes on Browse screen.
HIGHLIGHT	GR+/BG	Menu highlights.
BOX	GR+/BG	Borders of various types of boxes.
INFORMATION	B/W	Status bar, border of error and help boxes.
FIELDS	N/BG	Entered data.

Table 4.2 shows and describes the various portions of the screen to which you can assign color schemes. It also indicates the *default* color scheme, that is, the scheme dBASE will use if you don't change it. To change the color scheme for any portion, use the SET COLOR OF command. For example, to change the color scheme for the highlight to cyan on blue, the command would be

```
SET COLOR OF HIGHLIGHT TO BG/B
```

In addition to being able to change these portions of the screen, there are a number of commands, such as @..SAY and DEFINE WINDOW, that allow you to specify colors. (If you are unsure whether a particular command supports color or not, get help on the command and see if there is a COLOR clause included as one of the possible clauses.) For commands that support color, all you need to do is end the command with the word COLOR followed by the color scheme you want.

14.5 LOCKING

A *local area network* (*LAN*) is a group of two or more personal computers, with or without printers and other peripheral devices, that are connected with cable, twisted wire, or fiber optics. Each computer, or workstation, has a circuit board installed and has access to software that allows the transfer of data throughout the network. One computer is designated as the file server. It is usually a powerful PC with a high-capacity hard disk that is shared by others on the network. The file server processes requests for the use of shared files and peripherals. In most networks, the file server can still function as a normal PC while the network is in operation. Other workstations have the option of working on the network or functioning as freestanding PCs as well. The file server is a critical node because all network operations are dependent on its status. If it should "crash," network operations would cease. Figure 14.28 is diagram of a LAN.

The hard disk of the file server is partitioned into private directories and one shared directory that contains all the shared files accessible by the other workstations. The users who have signed on to the network can work with the shared files as if they were stored on their own disks. Programs that are installed on the file server are available to all network users.

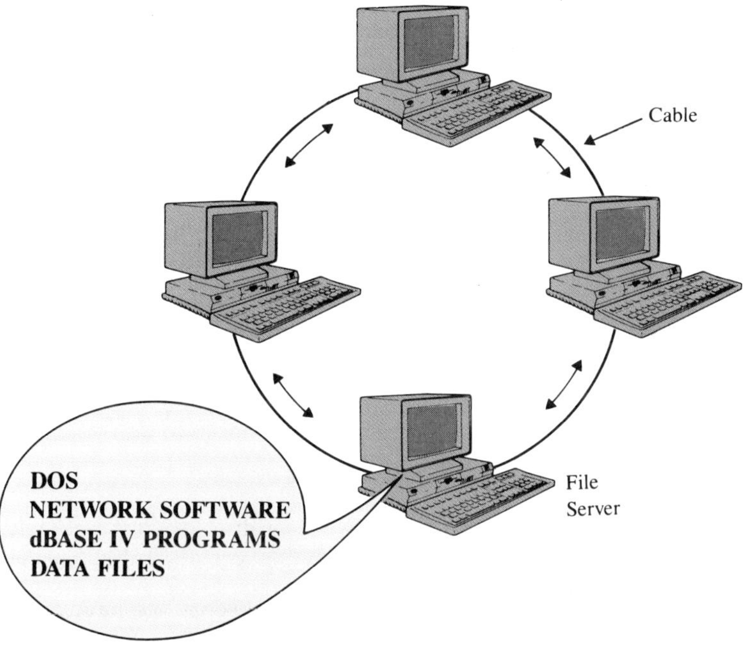

Figure 14.28 DIAGRAM OF A LOCAL AREA NETWORK, OR LAN

When the special network version of dBASE IV is installed, two or more users can access the same database at the same time. Normally, when database files are activated, they are opened in an *exclusive mode*; that is, the user who activates the database file has exclusive use of the file. If another user tries to activate the file, he or she gets an error message. By executing the command

```
SET EXCLUSIVE OFF
```

either at the dot prompt or within a program, database files can be activated in a *shared mode*, which allows many users to access the file simultaneously. Fortunately, dBASE contains facilities to manage such shared usage.

There are actually two ways of working in a shared environment in dBASE: automatic locking and program locking. With automatic locking, dBASE automatically locks and unlocks records. Locked records are beyond other users' reach. The user who attempts to access a locked record receives a message indicating that the record is locked. (A command called SET REPROCESS can be used to force dBASE to try to access the record a specified number of times before sending the user the message.) A user can even determine which other user has the record locked.

Although automatic locking is desirable in many ways and is very easy to implement in a program, sometimes it is not appropriate. If transactions are particularly complex, requiring many updates that involve many database files, it is often better for programmers to build appropriate locking into the program. It gives them much better control and can, if done correctly, improve overall performance. To do this, the statement

```
SET LOCK OFF
```

must be executed at the dot prompt or contained within the program. Programming our own locking gives us the following capabilities:

1. We can determine whether the record we have attempted to access is currently locked by examining the value of the error code. If the value is 109, the record is locked. Thus, we might include an IF statement such as

   ```
   IF ERROR() = 109
   ```

   It is up to us to determine the appropriate action at this point. A typical response would be to try repeatedly to access the record. The process would continue until either the user successfully accessed the record or some preset number of tries was reached. In the latter case, the user would have to move on to some other transaction and return later to try this one again.

2. We can lock an entire file. This is done in a somewhat unusual way through the FLOCK() function, which is typically used in an IF statement such as

   ```
   IF FLOCK()
   ```

   There is a lot more to the preceding IF statement than meets the eye. From the way FLOCK() is used in the statement, we would guess that it must either be true or false, and this is indeed the case. It will be true if the database file in question can be locked, and false if it cannot; that is, if some other user already has a lock on all or part of the file.

   Moreover, if it is true, *it will also give us a lock on the file*. This is *not* a typical function, which would merely give us a value. As you can see, this function might also take some action on our behalf. As long as we have a lock on the file, no other user can access the file in any way.

3. We can lock a single record, namely, the current record for the database file. The method for doing this is similar to the method for file locking, but we use the RLOCK() function (for Record LOCK) rather than FLOCK(). (It is legitimate to simply use LOCK() rather than RLOCK(), but most dBASE programmers prefer RLOCK() because it is more descriptive.) Like FLOCK(), RLOCK() is typically used in an IF statement such as

   ```
   IF RLOCK()
   ```

   This function returns a value of true if the record in question can be locked, and false if it cannot; that is, if some other user already has a lock on it. If it returns the value of true, *it will also give us a lock on the record.* As long as we have a lock on the record, no other user can access it.

4. We can unlock a record or a database file with the UNLOCK command. The syntax of this command is simply

   ```
   UNLOCK
   ```

   When this command is executed, any record lock or file lock that we held on the database file is released. The record or file is then available to other users.

14.6 BEGIN AND END TRANSACTION

Sometimes we encounter situations where a particular set of updates, for example, all the updates necessary for entering an order, must be done together. Either all must be made or none of them must be made. If our database is left in a state where some of the updates have been made and others haven't, we have real problems.

Fortunately, dBASE IV contains useful facilities for such situations. To use these facilities, a program should execute the statement

```
BEGIN TRANSACTION
```

before making such a set of updates. At this point, dBASE begins keeping a journal of all updates made to the database file. Once the updates have all been made, the program should execute the statement

```
END TRANSACTION
```

at which point, dBASE deletes the journal. (The whole process can then begin again, if necessary.)

If everything goes smoothly, there is no need to use the journal. If there is a problem, such as an abnormal program termination or a power failure, we have the situation we wanted to avoid. Some, but not all, of the updates have been made to the database, and there is no practical way to make the rest. To rectify this, we execute the command

```
ROLLBACK
```

either directly or within a program. This command uses the data in the journal to restore the database to the state it was in immediately prior to the last BEGIN TRANSACTION.

14.7 SECURITY

When dBASE IV is installed on a network, a utility called PROTECT is available to make password assignments. There are several types of privileges (permitted actions) that may be associated with these passwords. Some of the privileges pertain to a whole file. These *file-access privileges* are:

1. Add new records to a file.
2. Delete records from a file.
3. Read records from a file.
4. Change records in a file.

Others pertain to individual fields. These *field-access privileges* are:

1. Read and write the field (user can see and change the data in the field).
2. Read but not write the field (user can see but cannot change the data in the field).
3. Neither read nor write the field (user cannot even see the data in the field).

When this type of protection is used, a user must fill in information that is required on a log-in screen before accessing dBASE. This information includes a group name, an individual name, and a password. The user can proceed only if all three of these match a legitimate combination that has been predetermined by the system administrator. If the combination that has been entered is valid, dBASE determines which privileges are associated with this combination and then prevents the user from taking any action that is not permitted.

CHAPTER SUMMARY

1. A horizontal bar menu is one in which the options are arranged horizontally. It is typically used for a main menu. Menus in which the options are arranged vertically are either pop-up or pull-down menus. They are pop-up menus if the user must press Enter before the menu is displayed. They are pull-down menus if they appear automatically whenever the corresponding option in the bar menu is highlighted.
2. A window is a rectangular portion of the screen. Once a window is activated, displays occur only within the window. When a window is deactivated, it is removed from the screen and the portion of the screen under the window is restored to its former condition.
3. A procedure file is a single file that can contain up to 973 User-Defined Functions and/or procedures. A procedure file is activated with the SET PROCEDURE TO command. Once it is active, programs can use any of the UDFs or procedures within it, just as though they were contained within the program.
4. One facet of error-proofing a system is ensuring that the data in the database files is valid. Data-entry programs should contain logic to prevent invalid data from being entered into any database file. In addition, programs should be included in the system that make it easy for the user to backup and restore the data in the database files.
5. Another important facet of error-proofing is to include logic in programs that checks for errors and reacts appropriately to them. Programs should inform users if the users need take any special action, such as making sure the printer is on. Programs should also include escape mechanisms.
6. The colors of various portions of the screen can be changed with the SET COLOR OF command. In addition, certain commands, such as @..SAY and DEFINE WINDOW can include COLOR specifications.
7. A local area network (LAN) links computers together to share files and peripherals. The file server stores the files and programs which the workstations access and update. Collisions are avoided by locking files and records.
8. The BEGIN TRANSACTION, END TRANSACTION, and ROLLBACK commands provide support for situations where a collection of updates must occur together (all must occur or none must occur).
9. dBASE IV provides security features through passwords. Each password can be associated with a collection of file- and field-access privileges.

KEY TERMS

horizontal bar menu	error-proof	local area network (LAN)
pull-down menu	live file	exclusive mode
pop-up menu	backup file	shared mode
window	save file	file-access privilege
procedure file	recover	field-access privilege
procedure library		

COMMAND SUMMARY

Command Name	**Use**
DEFINE MENU	Defines a horizontal bar menu.
DEFINE PAD	Defines pad (option) within horizontal bar menu.
ON PAD	Indicates action to take when a pad is highlighted.
SET BORDER TO	Indicates border style for pop-up menu.
DEFINE POPUP	Defines pop-up or pull-down menu. (Whether menu is pop-up or pull-down depends on how it is treated in the horizontal bar menu.)
ON SELECTION POPUP	Defines action to take when an option is selected from a pop-up menu.
DEFINE WINDOW	Creates a window.
ACTIVATE MENU	Activates a menu.
ACTIVATE WINDOW	Places a window on screen and makes it active.
DEACTIVATE WINDOW	Removes window from screen and restores screen to original state.
SET PROCEDURE TO	Activates procedure file.
COPY FILE..TO	Makes a copy of file.
SET SAFETY OFF	Users won't be told if their action would overwrite existing file.
SET SAFETY ON	Users will be told if their action would overwrite existing file.
ON ESCAPE	Sets up action to be taken if user presses Escape.
SET MESSAGE TO	Indicates a message to be displayed at the bottom of the screen.
ON KEY LABEL	Sets up action to be taken if user presses the indicated function key.
ON ERROR	Sets up action to be taken if error occurs.

ERROR()	Function giving error code.
MESSAGE()	Function giving message corresponding to error code.
SET COLOR OF	Changes color scheme for indicated portion of the screen.
SET EXCLUSIVE OFF	Open files to all network users.
SET LOCK OFF	Turns off automatic locking.
SET REPROCESS TO	Forces dBASE to try to access record specified number of times.
FLOCK()	File locking function
UNLOCK	Unlock a network record or file.
RLOCK()	Record locking function.
BEGIN TRANSACTION	Marks beginning of set of updates that must be accomplished together.
END TRANSACTION	Makes all updates since last BEGIN TRANSACTION permanent.
ROLLBACK	Reverses all updates since last BEGIN TRANSACTION.

dBUG dBASE

- Be sure to deactivate windows before you exit your program. Otherwise, the user will be left in the window. If, for example, your program returned a user to the dot prompt, the dot prompt would appear in the window. **Note:** The CLEAR ALL command deactivates all active windows.
- Test the procedures you plan to put in your procedure library thoroughly before placing them in the library. That way all programmers can be sure they are accessing routines that have been thoroughly debugged. If they have a problem using one of these procedures, they know the problem is in their own code, not the procedure from the library that they are using.
- Placing extensive error-checking routines in programs can be tedious and time-consuming. It pays off dramatically, however, when users run your programs. It's much easier to prevent errors right away than have to track them down later.
- If you plan to alter the dBASE color scheme, create a procedure whose specific function is to restore the color scheme to the original colors. Place the procedure in your procedure library and be sure to execute this procedure before terminating your system (that is, before the RETURN that takes the user back to the dot prompt). This way you won't inadvertently leave the users with puzzling colors on the screen.

- You need to be careful when displaying messages in report programs. If you are using @..SAY commands and these have been directed to the printer, use ? commands to display the messages so they appear on the screen. Likewise, if you are using ? commands to produce the report and have directed these to the printer, use @..SAY commands for the messages.

SELF-CHECK QUESTIONS

1. What is a horizontal bar menu? How do you create one? What is a pop-up menu? How do you create one? What is a pull-down menu? How do you turn a pop-up menu into a pull-down menu?
2. What is the function of the ON PAD and ON SELECTION POPUP commands? What is the difference between them?
3. How do you create a double-line border for a pop-up menu? How do you create one for a horizontal bar menu?
4. What is a window? How do you create one? How do you use one? What advantage is there to using a window rather than a box?
5. What is a procedure file? How do you create one? How do you use one? How do you determine whether a particular procedure should be placed in a procedure file or in a program?
6. What steps should you take in your programs to guarantee that your database files have integrity?
7. How can you provide an escape mechanism for a user? What commands do you use for this purpose?
8. How can you trap errors in your programs? Why should you trap for errors? What commands do you use for this purpose?
9. How can you change the color scheme used by dBASE?
10. When is locking important? What commands are provided by dBASE to support locking?
11. What is the purpose of the BEGIN TRANSACTION, END TRANSACTION, and ROLLBACK commands? Why are they important and when would you use them?
12. What types of privileges may be associated with passwords in dBASE?

TRY IT YOURSELF

1. Create a menu system for the charity database you first created in Chapter 2. The system should use horizontal bar and pull-down menus and be similar to the one we examined in this chapter.
2. Create menus and options that are as similar as possible to the menus and options of the main Control Center screen. You can stub all the options except the options on the Exit menu. The Exit menu options should function as they do on the Control Center screen.
3. Modify the customer update programs you created in earlier chapters so that they use windows. The main update screen should be in a window that encompasses the entire screen. Any messages should be displayed in appropriately sized windows.
4. Take any procedure you have created in any program and include it in PROCLIB. Modify the program that contained the procedure so that it uses the version in PROCLIB.
5. Pick any color scheme you wish and modify a previous update program to use this scheme. Reset the colors back to the normal dBASE scheme when the program is finished.
6. Put error-trapping and escape-handling routines into any report program you have created. Test the modified programs to make sure these routines are working correctly.

PROGRAMMING PROJECTS

1. Complete the menu system for the CUSTOMER database file. The choices on the Updates menu should lead to appropriate programs. The Reports menu should contain reference to specific reports (not Report 1, Report 2, and so on), and the choices should all lead to appropriate programs. The Labels menu should contain reference to at least one specific set of labels. (Create the labels with the labels utility and use the LABEL FORM command in the program.) The Utilities menu should contain a backup option and a restore option.

   All options should use windows. Each option should contain some type of escape mechanism. All options should be fully error-trapped.

   If you wish, vary the color scheme.
2. Develop a similar menu-driven system for the PART database file.

The On-Line Debugger

Introduction

One of the best approaches to debugging is to use an *on-line debugger*. This tool allows you to step through your program, pause whenever you like, and look at the current values in your variables at any time. Many other features are included in a good debugger, but this should give you the idea.

dBASE contains an excellent debugger. A thorough examination of all its features is beyond the scope of this text. We'll look at its basic use, however, through an example.

The example we will use is the RPTCSSR2 program from Chapter 13, a program to produce a report of customers and sales reps. We will introduce a bug into the program by removing an important command. To do so, use the editor to remove the line that reads `SELECT customer` after the last IF statement in the program.

If you remember the logic of the program, you realize that the SKIP statement that comes a little later will now refer to the sales rep file rather than to the customer file. Thus, we will never move on to the second customer. (If you run this modified version of the program, you will see the record for the first customer repeated over and over. You can get out of the program by pressing Esc. Since the program did not complete successfully, you must then type CLOSE DATABASES and press Enter to close any databases that the program left open. You must also type SET DEVICE TO SCREEN and press Enter. This will return the output of @..SAY commands to the screen.)

We may spot this error without needing to resort to any special debugging techniques, but let's suppose we don't. We want to use the debugger to help us find the problem. To begin, type `debug rptcssr2` and press Enter.

You will then see the screen in Figure A.1 This is the debugger screen. In the upper lefthand corner, you see the first portion of your program. In the upper right you see a list of available debugger commands. We will use some of these commands shortly. You can remove this list from the screen by pressing F1. If it is not on the screen, you can bring it back by pressing F1. Usually, we do not want it on the screen, so press F1. If we ever need to look up a command, we can press F1, look up the desired information, and then press F1 again to remove it from the screen.

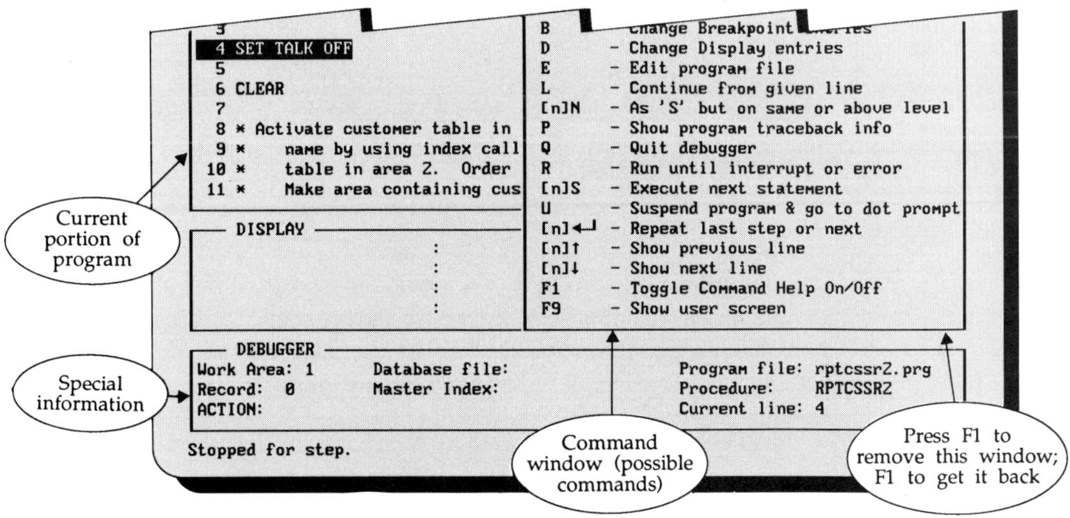

Figure A.1 DEBUGGER (PART 1 OF 11)

The next box down on the lefthand side of the screen is the Display window. The box next to it is called the Breakpoints window, which is not visible in the figure. (We will see the uses of these windows shortly.) The box at the bottom gives special information such as the currently selected area, the currently active database file, the master index in use, the program being run, and the line in the program that we are about to execute. In this case, we are about to execute line 4.

We can now take a number of possible actions. One of the most common is to simply step to the next command in the program. To do so, type the letter S. Line 4 is executed and we move to line 6. Type S again and we move to line 12 (Figure A.2). The lines between 4 and 12 are all either blank lines or comments. The debugger skips right over such lines.

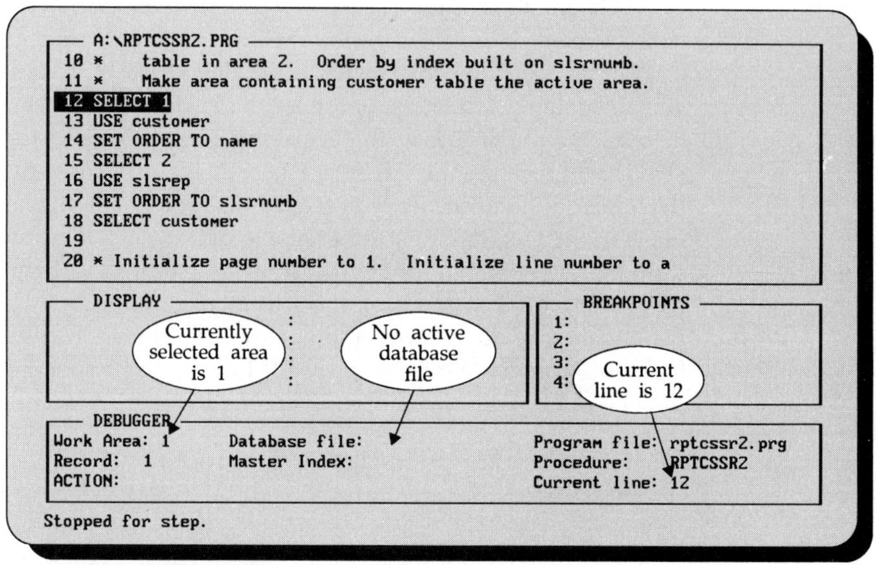

Figure A.2 DEBUGGER (PART 2 OF 11)

If we keep typing the letter S, we move through the lines that activate the database files. In Figure A.3, we are about to execute line 17. Note that the currently selected area is 2, the active database file in this area is SLSREP, and there is no master index because we have not yet executed the SET ORDER TO command. Repeatedly type S until you are about to execute line 23 (Figure A.4).

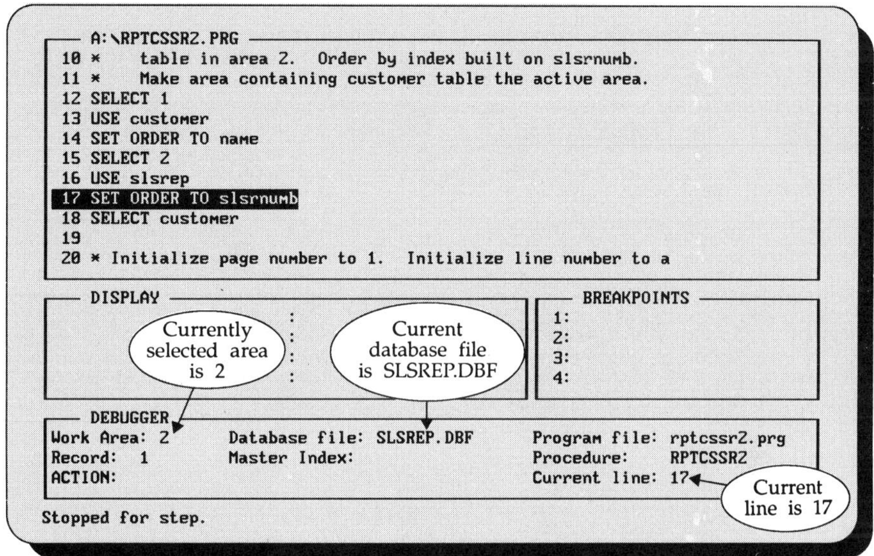

Figure A.3 DEBUGGER (PART 3 OF 11)

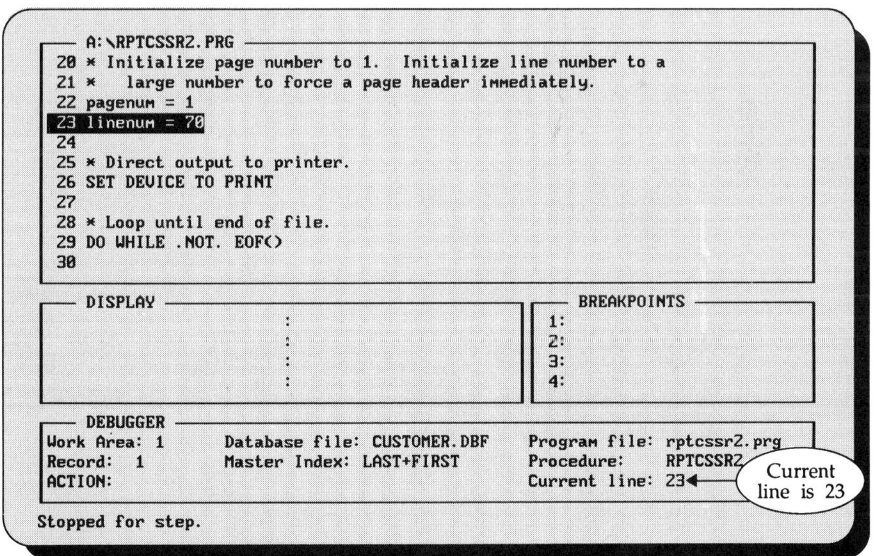

Figure A.4 DEBUGGER (PART 4 OF 11)

Let's look at the current value in linenum at this point. Type D (for display). Type `linenum` in the display window (Figure A.5) and press Enter.

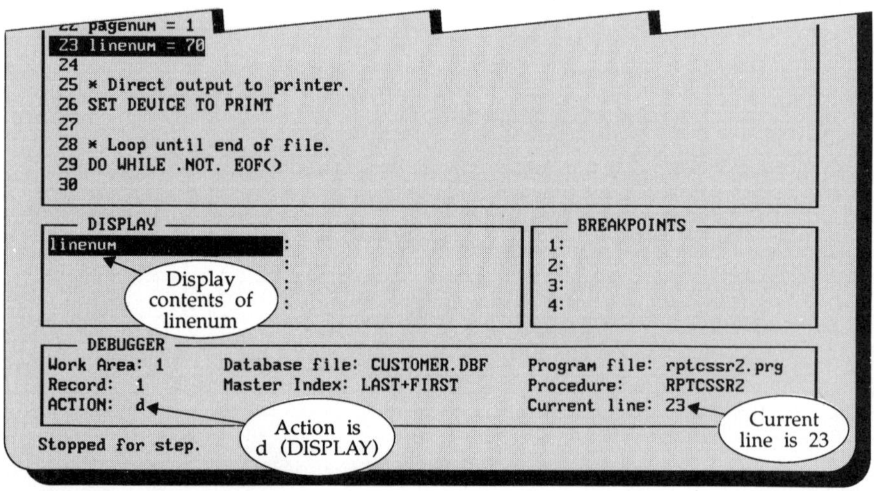

Figure A.5 DEBUGGER (PART 5 OF 11)

You then see the current contents of the variable (Figure A.6). In this case, linenum has not yet been assigned a value. This is indicated by the message "Variable not found" in the position where we would expect to see a value. Press Ctrl-End to leave the Display window and the type S to step.

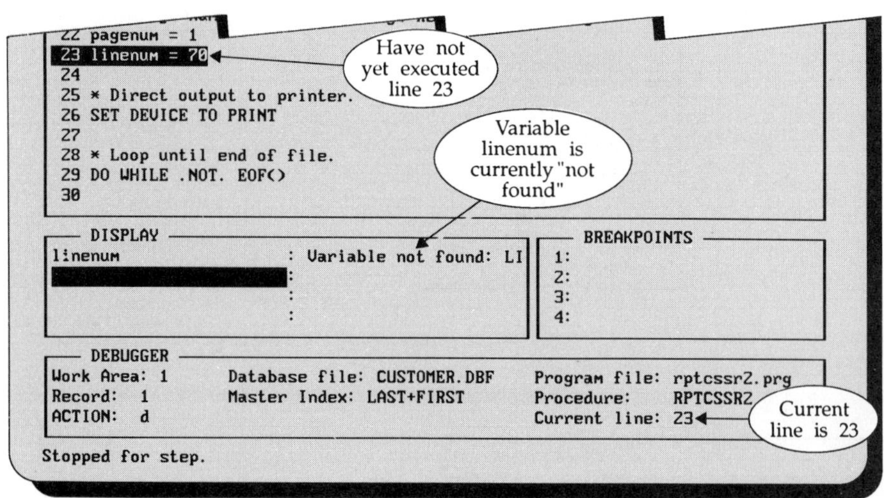

Figure A.6 DEBUGGER (PART 6 OF 11)

We executed line 23 so linenum now has a value (Figure A.7). No further action was required to display this value. It was automatically displayed when we stepped through a line that made a change to the value in linenum.

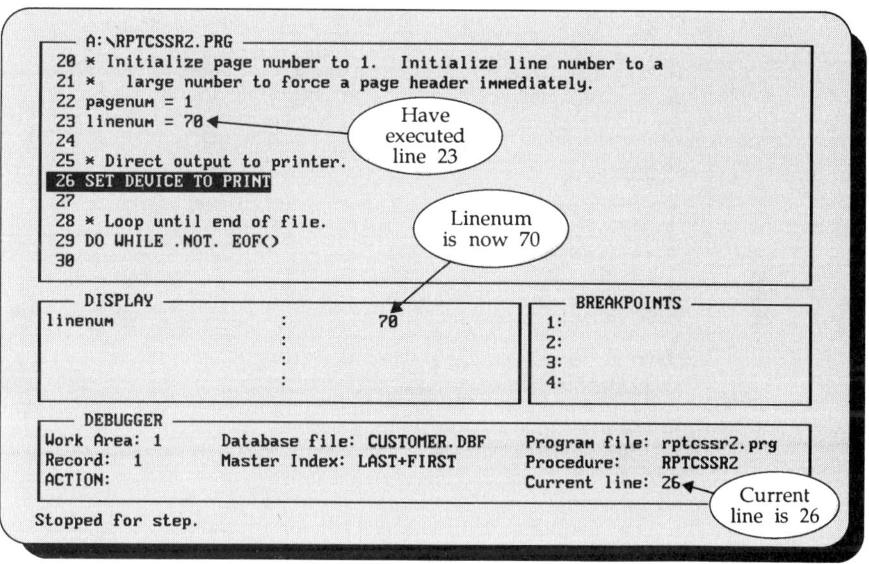

Figure A.7 DEBUGGER (PART 7 OF 11)

(**Note:** You can step several lines at a time by typing a number in front of the letter S. Typing 5S, for example, would cause dBASE to step through five commands rather than just one.)

Step until you are about to execute line 66. Add FOUND() to the Display window.

Your screen should now look like the one shown in Figure A.8 on the next page. Notice that the current value in FOUND() is T (true). Step until you are about to execute line 73. Add the custnumb field in the CUSTOMER database file to the Display window.

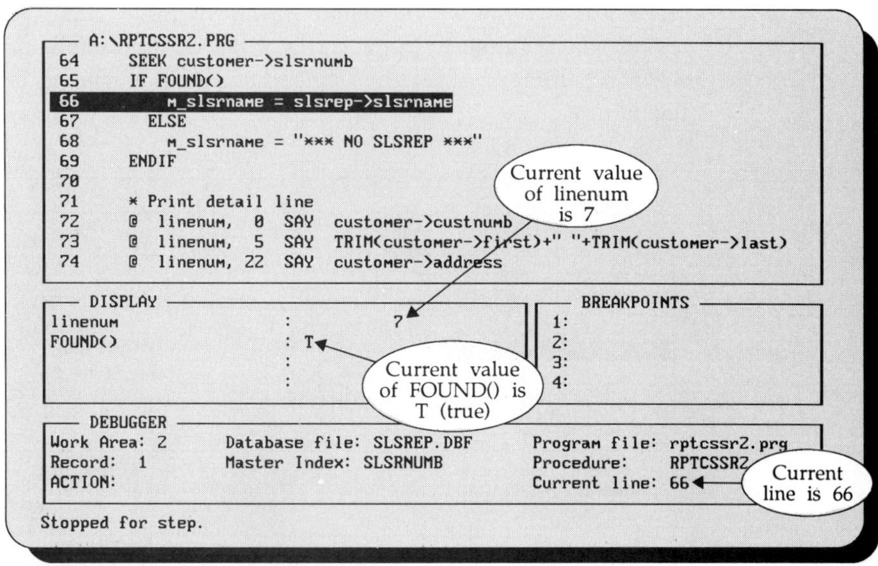

Figure A.8 DEBUGGER (PART 8 OF 11)

Your screen should now look like Figure A.9. In this case, the value of custnumb is 124, which is exactly what we would expect because it is the first customer's number.

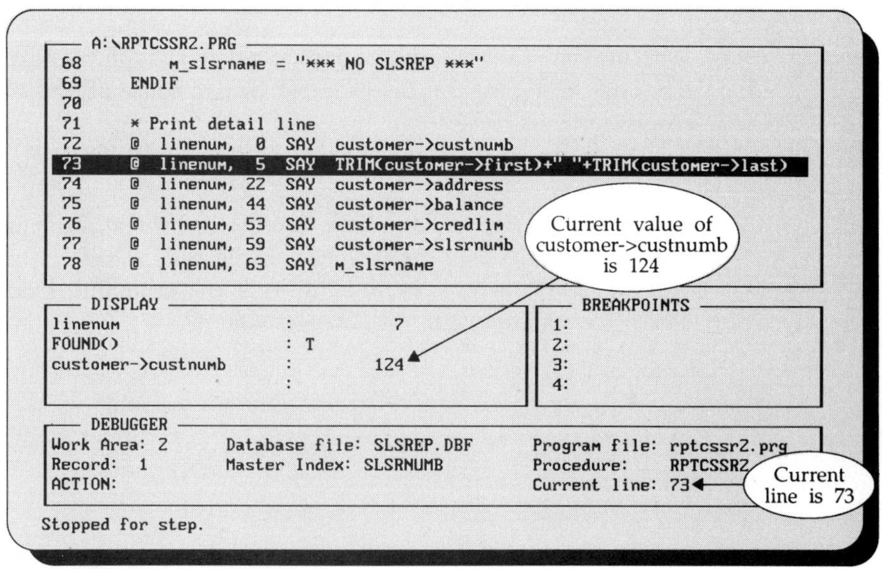

Figure A.9 DEBUGGER (PART 9 OF 11)

Let's suppose we now decide to have the program run for a while and then pause so we can look at the contents of these variables. The simplest way to do this is to set what is called a *breakpoint,* which is a point at which the program pauses. Let's say we have decided to have the program pause as soon as linenum reaches 15 because this will take us through a few more customers. Type B (for Breakpoint window).

We then need to type in the condition that determines the breakpoint. Type `linenum=15` (Figure A.10). Press Ctrl-End to exit the Breakpoint window and type R (for run).

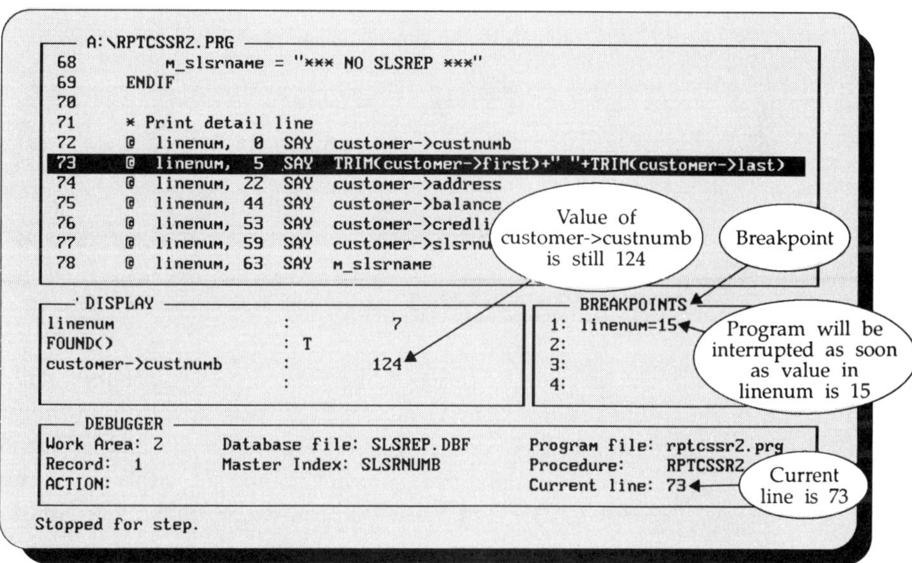

Figure A.10 DEBUGGER (PART 10 OF 11)

The program runs until interrupted at this breakpoint (Figure A.11 on the next page). Notice that the value in linenum is now 15, as we expected, and that the value in custnumb is still 124. It has not changed at all.

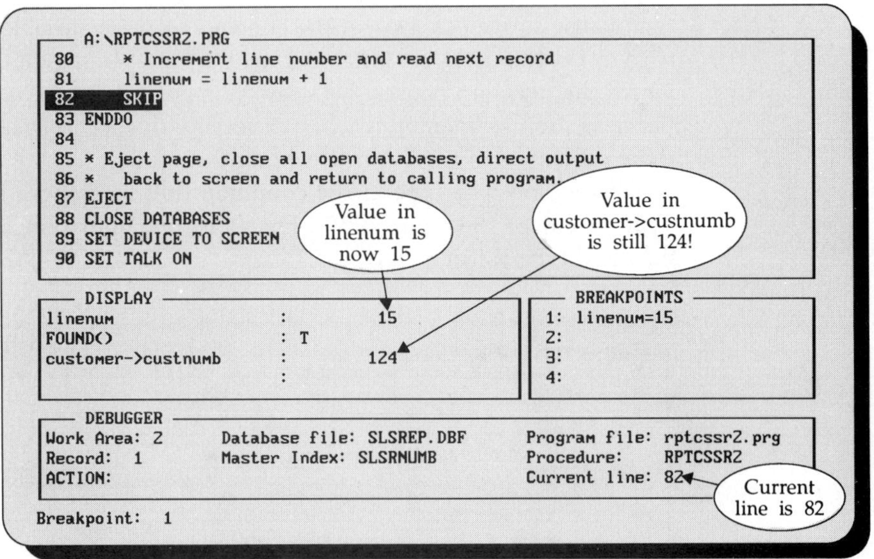

Figure A.11 DEBUGGER (PART 11 OF 11)

At this point, we would be very suspicious of the SKIP command. We would probably spot that the SKIP was occurring in the wrong file. This would lead us to realize that we were missing a SELECT statement to make the area containing the customer database file the active area.

(**Note:** If we still hadn't spotted the problem, we could again step one line at a time. We would pay especially close attention to the database file listed on the screen. In particular, we would see that the sales rep file was the active file when we were about to execute the SKIP command. This would certainly identify the problem.)

Type Q (to quit the debugger). Type CLOSE DATABASES and press Enter. Type SET DEVICE TO SCREEN and press Enter. (This command will return the output of @..SAY commands to the screen.) Finally, use the editor to correct the program by inserting the SELECT customer command that you removed earlier.

This quick tour through a very powerful facility should give you the flavor of using the debugger. If you want to experiment further, remember that you can always obtain help by pressing F1. In addition, Table A.1 gives more complete explanations of the available commands than those shown on the help screen.

TABLE A.1 **Commands in the Debugger**

COMMAND	MEANING
B	Use Breakpoint window to create or change up to ten breakpoint conditions.
D	Use Display window to create or change up to ten entries whose values will be displayed in the window.
E	Move to the editor to edit the program (PRG) file.
L	Run the program starting from the specified line.
[n]N	Same as 'S' but will not step through procedures called by current procedure.
P	Show program traceback information (programs and procedures that called the current procedure).
Q	Quit debugger.
R	Run until interrupted by pressing Esc, by an error occurring, or by encountering a breakpoint.
[n]S	Execute next statement. If a number precedes the S, it will execute that many statements. If a procedure calls another procedure, it will execute steps within the called procedure.
U	Suspend program and go to dot prompt.
[n][ENTER]	Repeat last step (or number of steps specified).
[n][UP]	Show previous line (or number of lines specified).
[n][DOWN]	Show next line (or number of lines specified).
F1	Remove help screen if it is currently displayed. Display help screen if it is not currently displayed.
F9	Display screen as it would normally appear to the user if currently in the debugger. Return to the debugger if currently displaying user screen.

THE REPORT FACILITY

INTRODUCTION

This section covers the dBASE IV Report Generator and should give you a good feel for the ways in which you can use this important tool.

B.1 WORKING WITH THE REPORT DESIGN SCREEN

Before we start working on our report, let's look at a few tips concerning working with the Report Design screen.

CORRECTING MISTAKES

The more you work with the Report Design screen, the easier you will find it to correct mistakes. Until you get comfortable with the various correction techniques, you can follow a few simple tips. You can insert and delete lines using the following:

1. Use Ctrl-Y to delete the cursor line (the line on which the cursor is located).
2. Use Ctrl-N to insert a blank line before the cursor line.
3. Use the "Add line" option from the Words menu to insert a blank line after the cursor line.

If you have an extra line you don't want, delete it with Ctrl-Y. If you need an additional line, insert one. If you have made mistakes on a particular line that you don't know how to correct, use Ctrl-Y to delete the line and then insert a new line. This combination erases the contents of the line and you can now reconstruct it the way it should be. If you need to insert a field, move the cursor to the position for the field, select the "Add field" option from the Fields menu, select the desired field, press Enter, and then press Ctrl-End (as you did with labels). If you need to insert a string of characters, move the cursor to the position for these characters and simply type them.

Occasionally you might decide that it would be simpler to start over rather than to make a number of individual corrections. If so, select "Abandon changes and exit" from the Exit menu. dBASE then asks you if you are sure you want to abandon the operation. You do, so select "Yes." At this point, you are returned to the dot prompt without any of your work being saved. You can now start the process from scratch.

SELECTING FIELDS AND TEXT

dBASE allows you to easily move, delete, or resize fields on the screen. You can also move and delete text. In any case, before you take any of these actions, you must *select* the portion of the screen with which you want to work.

To select a single field, first move the cursor into it, then press F6 (which is one of the special keys shown on the screen). A message will indicate that you can complete the selection process by pressing Enter. If you want to select only this single field, press Enter. If you want to select a larger portion of the screen, first use the arrows to move the cursor to the other end of the portion you want to select and then press Enter. In either case, once you press Enter, the selection is made.

REMOVING FIELDS OR TEXT

To remove a field or text from a report, first select the field or text (F6 and Enter). Once you have done so, press the Delete key.

RESIZING FIELDS

To resize a field on a report, select it and then press Shift-F7. Use the arrow keys to change the size and then press Enter.

MOVING FIELDS OR TEXT

To move a field or text, select the field or text (F6 and Enter) and press F7. Use the arrow keys to move the field or text to the new location and then press Enter. If a portion of an existing field would be covered, you will be asked if it is acceptable to delete the covered field. dBASE is warning you that the movement you are requesting would require deletion of an existing field. If you want to complete the move, type Y. The move will take place and the covered field will be deleted. If not, type N and the move will *not* take place. (A move to a new position that does not cover an existing field will take place immediately.)

MODIFYING A REPORT DESIGN

To change the design of an existing report, activate the database file for the report. Then at the dot prompt type MODIFY REPORT followed by the name of the report and press Enter. At this point, you are returned to the Report Design screen, where the current design appears. You can now make changes to this design in exactly the same manner you did when you first created it. When you have finished, select "Save changes and exit" from the Exit menu.

B.2 CREATING A REPORT

In Chapter 3 you constructed a report that contained totals at the end. The report we construct in this appendix also contains subtotals (intermediate totals). In particular, the report groups customers by sales rep. At the end of the group of customers for a particular sales rep, there will be subtotals for two of the fields.

ACTIVATING THE DATABASE FILE

The report we are going to produce uses data from the CUSTOMER database file. Since the records are to be grouped by sales rep, the records must be ordered by sales rep number. To do so, use the following commands:

```
USE customer
SET ORDER TO slsrnumb
```

USING QUICK LAYOUT

Let's call the report CREDRPT. To begin constructing CREDRPT, use the following command

```
CREATE REPORT credrpt
```

Next choose the "Quick layout" option from the Layout menu. (Remember that this gets you started with the dBASE Quick Report layout.) Choose "Column layout" from the list presented. Your screen should now contain this quick layout (see Figure B.1). All the fields from the view are included, although the last field is not completely visible because part of it is off the righthand edge of the screen.

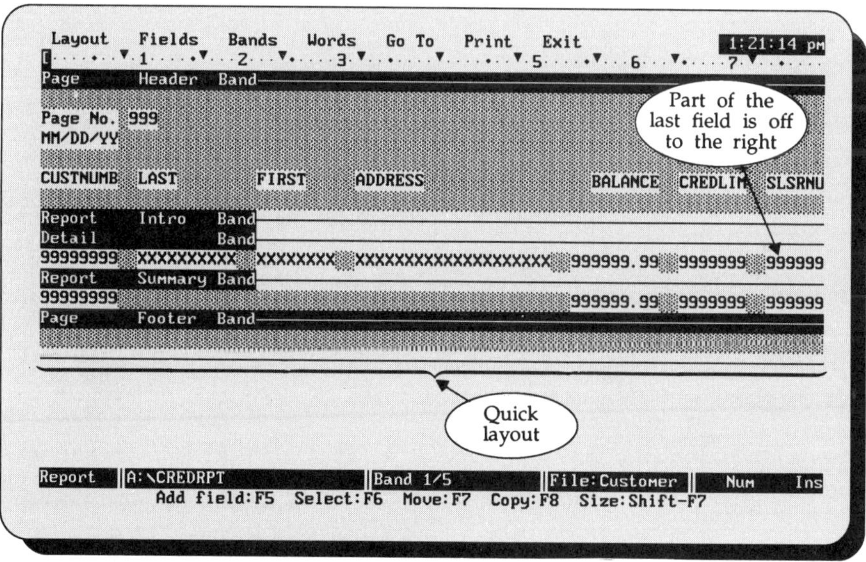

Figure B.1 REPORT DESIGN SCREEN: QUICK LAYOUT

FIXING THE DETAIL BAND

Currently the fields on the Detail band are CUSTNUMB, LAST, FIRST, ADDRESS, BALANCE, CREDLIM, and SLSRNUMB. We need to change the band so that the fields are CUSTNUMB, FIRST, LAST, ADDRESS, BALANCE, and CREDLIM. In addition, we want to add a field that will represent the available credit (credit limit – balance). Thus, we need to interchange LAST and FIRST, remove SLSRNUMB, and add AVAILCRD. In addition, we need to change the size of some of the fields.

Now that we have reviewed the steps, let's get started. Reduce the size of the CUSTNUMB field to four digits. Then move FIRST so that it follows CUSTNUMB with three spaces between them. In the process, you have covered LAST, which consequently is deleted.

The LAST field, which is no longer in the report, should follow the FIRST field with one space between them. Move the cursor to this position. Since LAST is no longer part of the Detail band, you need to reinstate it. Select the "Add field" option of the Fields menu. You then see the list of possible fields (see Figure B.2). Move the cursor to LAST and press Enter. You then see a second screen where you could, if you desired, change the field's template and picture functions. Since we do not need to do so at this time, press Ctrl-End.

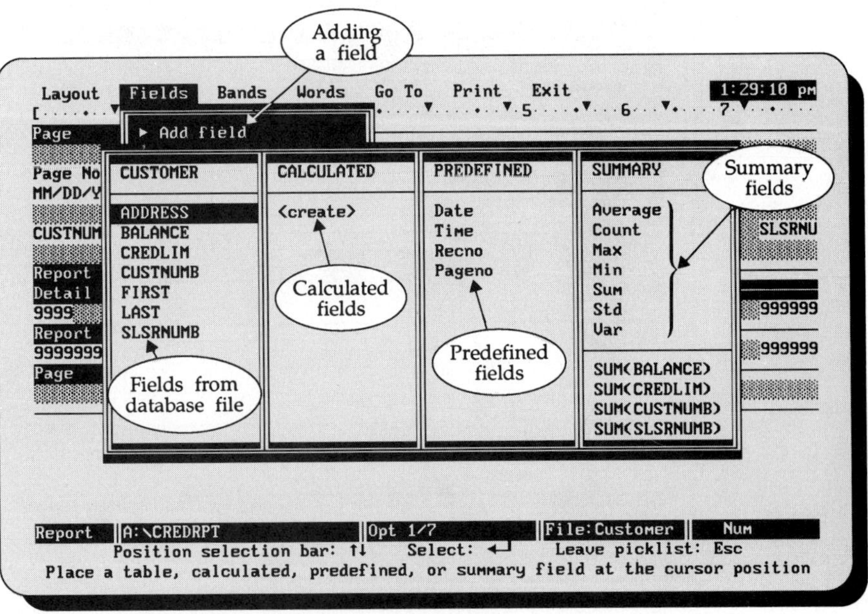

Figure B.2 REPORT DESIGN SCREEN: ADD FIELDS OPTION

Next resize the CREDLIM field, delete the SLSRNUMB field, and move the remaining fields in the Detail band into the positions shown in Figure B.3. To add available credit to the Detail band, move the cursor so that it follows CREDLIM with two spaces between them. Select the "Add field" option of the Fields menu (Figure B.4) and select `<create>` in the CALCULATED column.

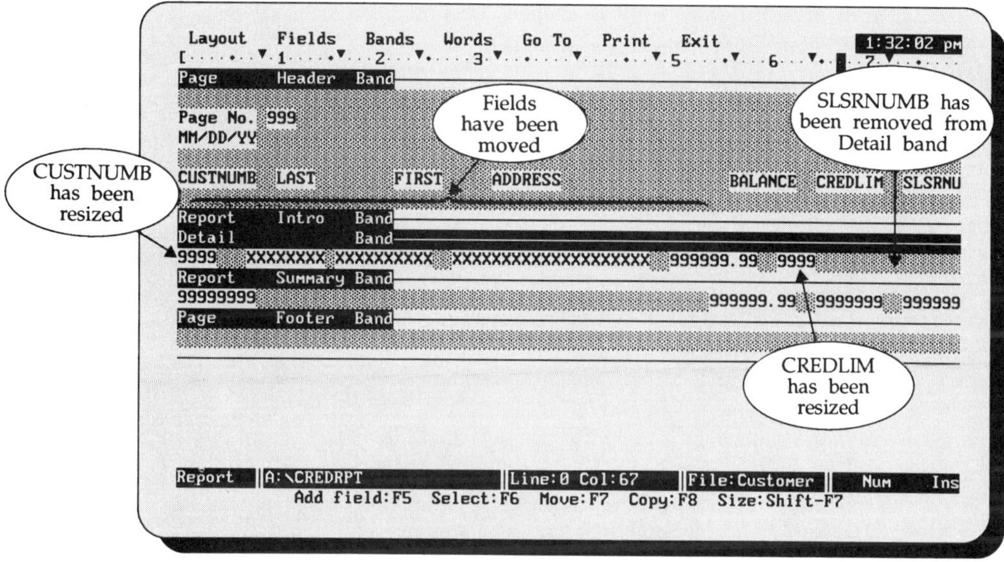

Figure B.3 REPORT DESIGN SCREEN: RESIZING AND MOVING FIELDS

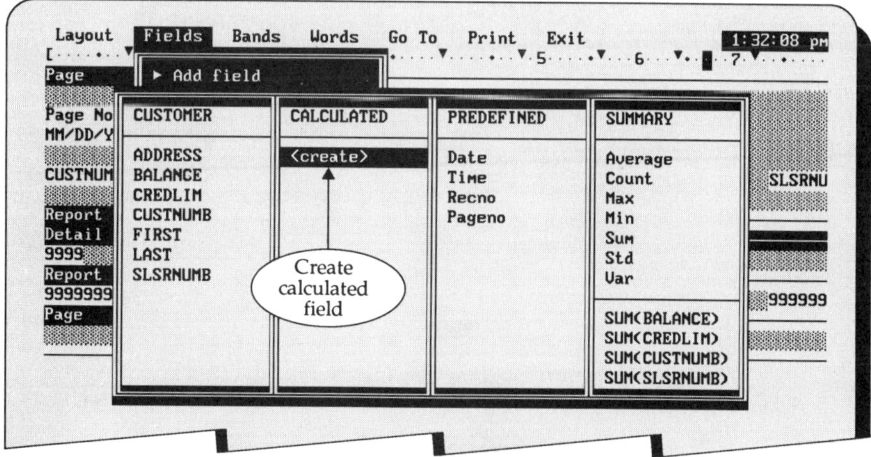

Figure B.4 REPORT DESIGN SCREEN: CREATING A CALCULATED FIELD

To enter the name AVAILCRD for the field, make sure the highlight is on "Name," press Enter, type `AVAILCRD`, and press Enter again. You don't need to enter a description. To enter the expression, move the highlight to "Expression," press Enter, type

```
CREDLIM - BALANCE
```

and press Enter again. Your screen should now look like the one shown in Figure B.5. To finish, press Ctrl-End. You have now added AVAILCRD to your Detail band (Figure B.6).

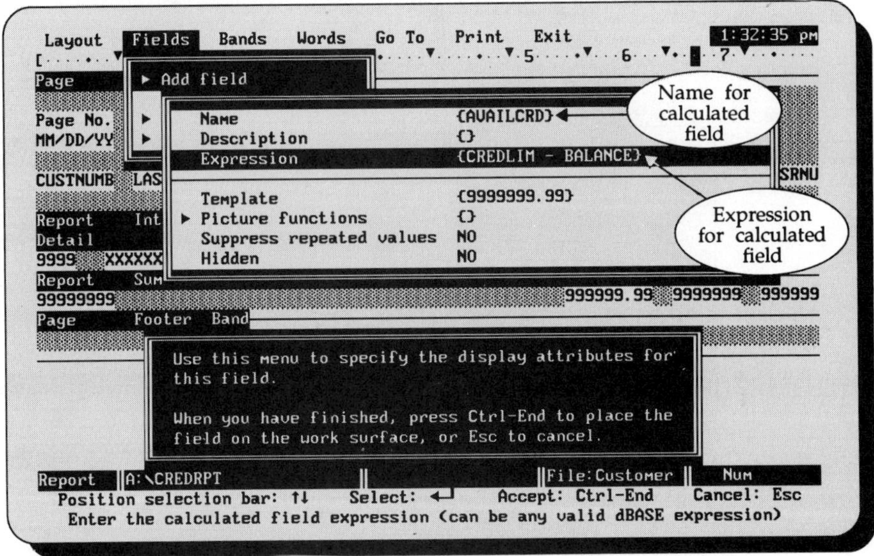

Figure B.5 REPORT DESIGN SCREEN: DEFINING A CALCULATED FIELD

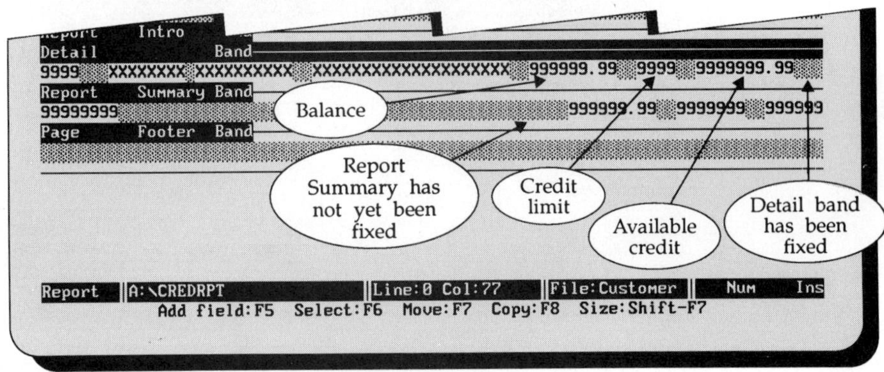

Figure B.6 REPORT DESIGN SCREEN: DETAIL BAND FIXED

FIXING THE REPORT SUMMARY BAND

Next, let's fix the Report Summary band. Delete the sum of customer numbers, the sum of credit limits, and the sum of sales rep numbers. Move the field for the sum of balances so that it lines up with the BALANCE field in the Detail band (Figure B.7). Next, we need to add the sum of available credits to the Report Summary band. Move the cursor so that is in the Report Summary band directly under the first position of the AVAILCRD field. Select the "Add field" option of the Fields menu (Figure B.8).

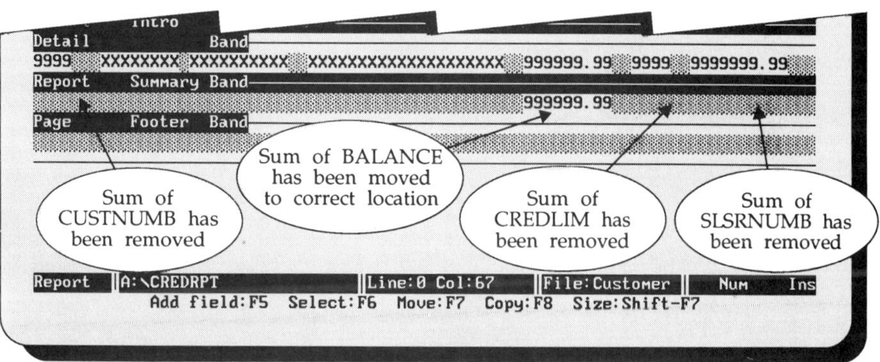

Figure B.7 REPORT DESIGN SCREEN: REMOVING SUMMARY FIELDS

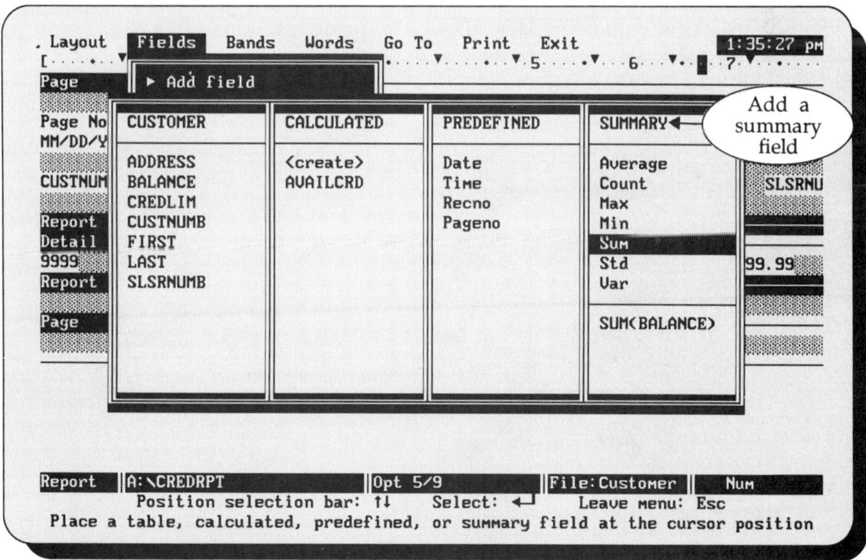

Figure B.8 REPORT DESIGN SCREEN: ADDING SUMMARY FIELD

Since you want to calculate a sum, select "Sum" in the SUMMARY column. On the next screen enter TOTCRED as the name and select AVAILCRD as the field on which to summarize (Figure B.9). Press Ctrl-End when you have done so. Your Report Summary band is now complete (Figure B.10).

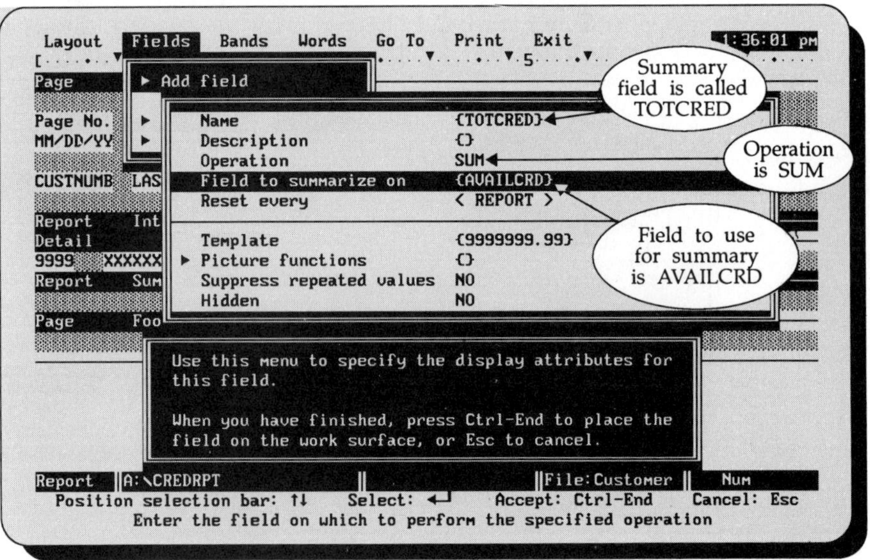

Figure B.9 REPORT DESIGN SCREEN: DEFINING SUMMARY FIELD

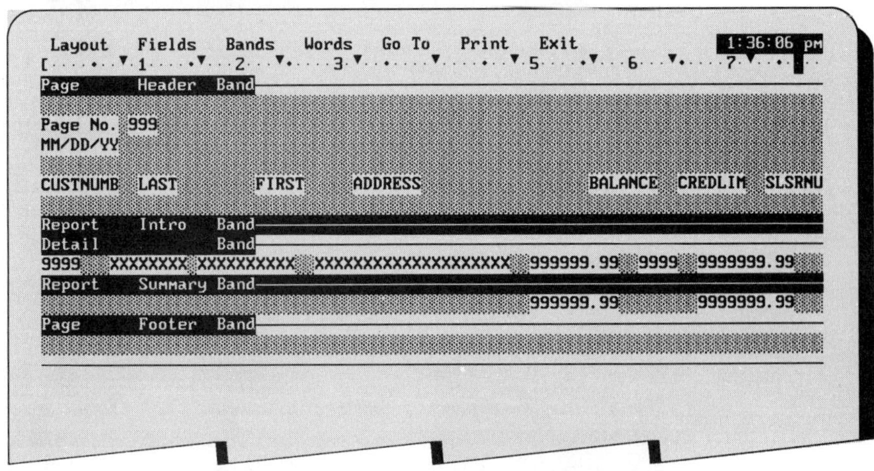

Figure B.10 REPORT DESIGN SCREEN: REPORT SUMMARY BAND FIXED

FIXING THE PAGE HEADER BAND

Change your page header to the one shown in Figure B.11. Remember that you can delete an existing line by pressing Ctrl-Y and insert a new one by pressing Ctrl-N. Note that you need one extra line.

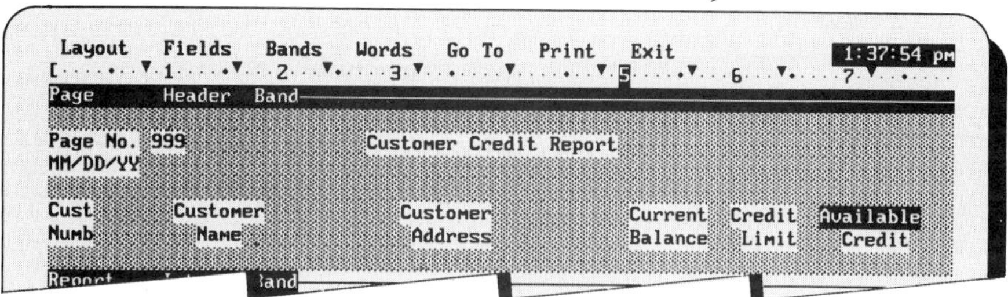

Figure B.11 REPORT DESIGN SCREEN: PAGE HEADER CHANGES

(**Note:** If you delete the original line of column headers, you should not have a problem. If you simply replaced these with new headers, you might still have the portion of the SLSRNUMB column header that is off the righthand edge of the screen. You should move the cursor to this header and delete it by repeatedly pressing the Delete key.)

VIEWING THE REPORT

At this point, let's see what the report looks like. Select "View report on screen" from the Print menu. Your screen should show a report that looks like the one in Figure B.12. If it doesn't, make the necessary corrections and view it again.

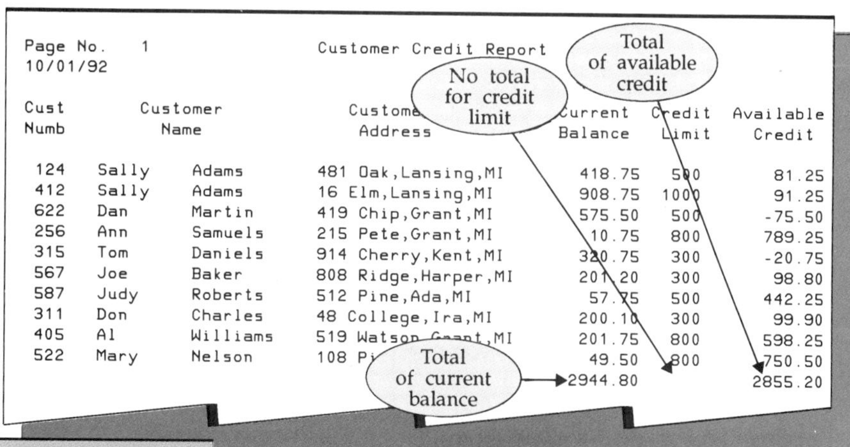

Page No. 1 Customer Credit Report
10/01/92

Cust Numb	Customer Name		Customer Address	Current Balance	Credit Limit	Available Credit
124	Sally	Adams	481 Oak,Lansing,MI	418.75	500	81.25
412	Sally	Adams	16 Elm,Lansing,MI	908.75	1000	91.25
622	Dan	Martin	419 Chip,Grant,MI	575.50	500	-75.50
256	Ann	Samuels	215 Pete,Grant,MI	10.75	800	789.25
315	Tom	Daniels	914 Cherry,Kent,MI	320.75	300	-20.75
567	Joe	Baker	808 Ridge,Harper,MI	201.20	300	98.80
587	Judy	Roberts	512 Pine,Ada,MI	57.75	500	442.25
311	Don	Charles	48 College,Ira,MI	200.10	300	99.90
405	Al	Williams	519 Watson,Grant,MI	201.75	800	598.25
522	Mary	Nelson	108 Pine,Harper,MI	49.50	800	750.50
				2944.80		2855.20

Figure B.12 SAMPLE REPORT I

SAVING THE REPORT

Now let's save our report. Select the "Save changes and exit" option of the Exit menu.

ADDING SUBTOTALS

We are now ready to tackle the process of calculating and displaying subtotals. For each sales rep we would like to display the total of the balances and available credits for all the customers of that sales rep. To do so, the records must, of course, be sorted by sales rep number. Since we have already ordered the records by SLSRNUMB, this is not a problem. Thus, we are ready to return to our report. To do so, type

```
MODIFY REPORT credrpt
```

ADDING A GROUP BAND

To calculate and display subtotals, we need to *group* records by sales rep number. This involves the use of a new kind of band, called a *Group band.*

To add the necessary Group band to the report, first place your cursor on the Report Intro band since, as we will see, the Group band will follow the Report Intro band. Next, select the "Add a group band" option of the Bands menu (see Figure B.13).

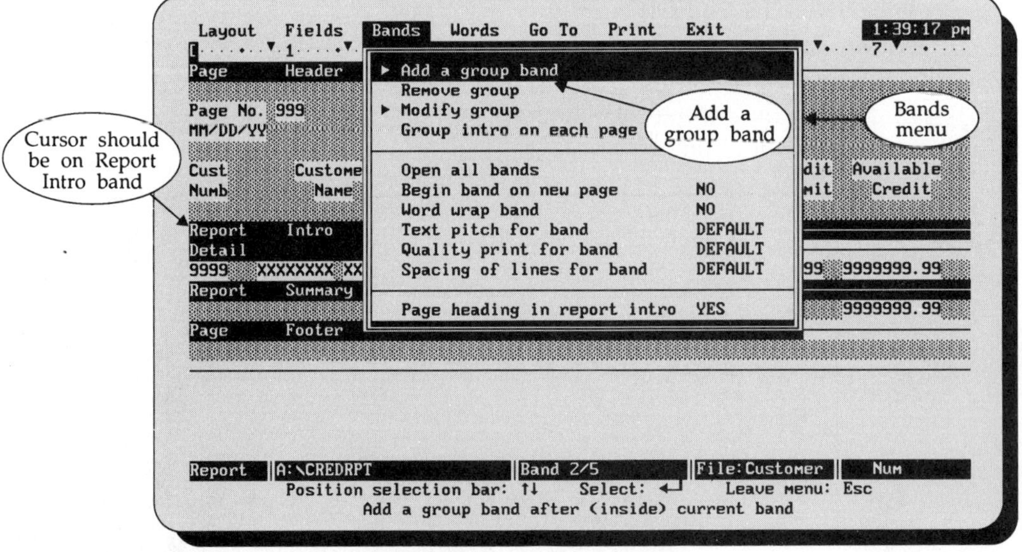

Figure B.13 REPORT DESIGN SCREEN: ADDING A GROUP BAND

At this point, you are asked to enter the value on which grouping takes place. You can enter a field value, an expression value, or a record count; but almost always you will use a field value. Make sure the highlight is on "Field value" and press Enter. A list of all the fields appears. Select SLSRNUMB since this is the field on which the grouping takes place.

Your screen should now look like the one in Figure B.14. Note that two new bands have appeared, one labeled "Group 1 Intro Band" and the other labeled "Group 1 Summary Band." The collection of all customers with the same sales rep number is called a *group*. Whatever we specify in the Group 1 Intro band is displayed immediately before each group (it *intro*duces the group). Whatever we specify in the Group 1 Summary band is displayed immediately after each group (it provides a *summary* for the group). We now need to lay out these two bands. Before we do, however, we need to look briefly at another topic: opened and closed bands.

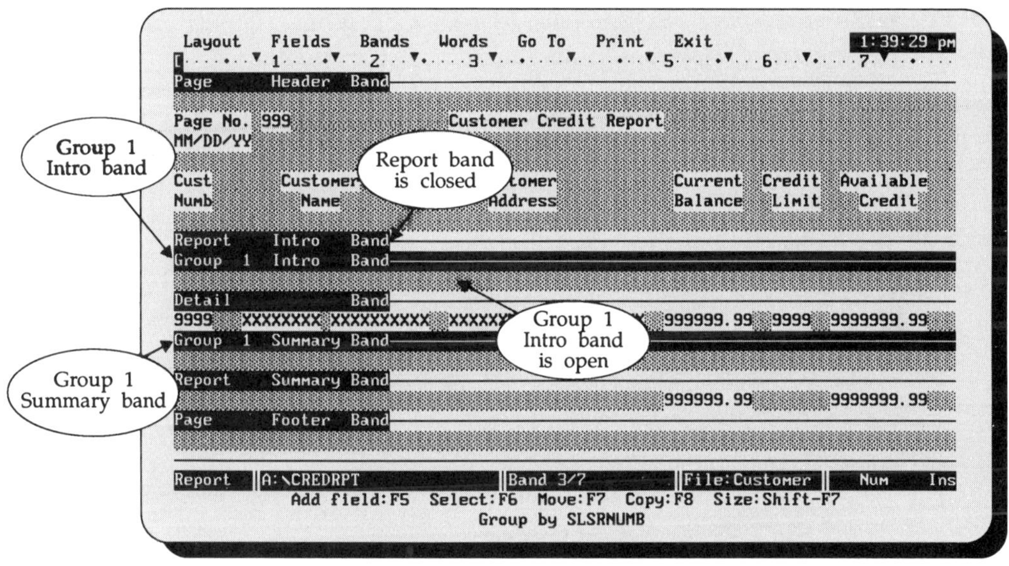

Figure B.14 REPORT DESIGN SCREEN: OPEN AND CLOSED BANDS

OPENED AND CLOSED BANDS

Look at the Report Intro band and the Group 1 Intro band in Figure B.14. Do you notice a difference? A blank line follows the Group 1 Intro band, but none follows the Report Intro band. Any band that does not have at least one line following it is *closed* and the contents of the band, whatever they may be, are not printed on the report. The other bands are *open* and their contents will print. Currently the Group 1 Intro band consists of just a single blank line. This still appears on the report, however. The group of customers of any given sales rep are preceded (introduced) by a single blank line.

To close a band that is currently open or to open a band that is currently closed, move the cursor to the line that gives the name of the band and press Enter. Try closing the Group 1 Intro band and you should see the blank line disappear.

FIXING THE GROUP BANDS

Let's now add totals to the Group Summary band. Move the cursor to the blank line in the band and place it under the first 9 of the BALANCE field on the Detail band. Now select the "Add field" option of the Fields menu. Since we want the sum of BALANCE, and that is already an option on your screen, we could simply select it. Let's pretend it's not there, however, so we can see exactly what we need to do if the combination we want is not listed. Select "Sum" from the SUMMARY column.

Your screen should now look like the one shown in Figure B.15. You don't need to name this field, but it's a good idea. Make sure the highlight is on the Name line, press Enter, type TOTBAL as the name, and press Enter again. This assigns the name TOTBAL at this point. In the same fashion you could, if you wished, assign a description. We will skip this step.

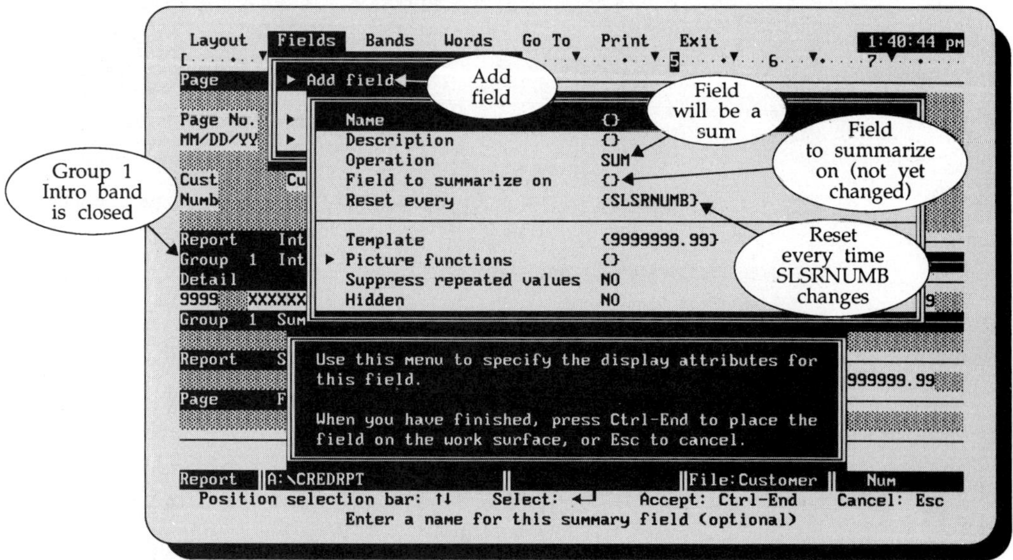

Figure B.15 REPORT DESIGN SCREEN: ADDING TOTALS TO GROUP SUMMARY BAND

The operation we want is SUM, and that is already on the screen. Thus we can skip to "Field to summarize on." This is the field that will be used in the calculation. Press Enter, move the highlight to BALANCE, and press Enter again. The final option is "Reset every." This is already filled in with SLSRNUMB, which is correct. This simply means that this total is reset (returned to zero) every time we move on to a new sales rep. The "Reset every" option almost always contains the correct field. If, by some chance, you need something different, move the highlight to this line, press Enter, type the correct name, and press Enter again. We are now done with this menu, so press Ctrl-End.

Next, fill in the sum of available credits in exactly the same way. Name the field TOTAVL. If either field is in the wrong position or has the wrong size, make the necessary modifications as you have done before. If you view your report, it should look like the one in Figure B.16.

```
Page No.   1                 Customer Credit Report
10/01/92

Cust        Customer            Customer            Current  Credit  Available
Numb          Name               Address            Balance   Limit    Credit

 124  Sally    Adams     481 Oak,Lansing,MI           418.75    500      81.25
 412  Sally    Adams     16 Elm,Lansing,MI            908.75   1000      91.25
 622  Dan      Martin    419 Chip,Grant,MI            575.50    500     -75.50
                                                     1903.00              97.00
 256  Ann      Samuels   215 Pete,Grant,MI             10.75    800     789.25
 315  Tom      Daniels   914 Cherry,Kent,MI           320.75    300     -20.75
 567  Joe      Baker     808 Ridge,Harper,MI          201.20    300      98.80
 587  Judy     Roberts   512 Pine,Ada,MI               57.75    500     442.25
                                                      590.45            1309.55
 311  Don      Charles   48 College,Ira,MI            200.10    300      99.90
 405  Al       Williams  519 Watson,Grant,MI          201.75    800     598.25
 522  Mary     Nelson    108 Pine,Ada,MI               49.50    800     750.50
                                                      451.35            1448.65
                                                     2944.80            2855.20

           Cancel viewing: ESC,  Continue viewing: SPACEBAR
```

Sum of available credit for first sales rep
Sum of current balance for first sales rep
Sum of all current balances
Sum of all available credits

Figure B.16 SAMPLE REPORT II

Let's now expand the Group 1 Summary band to look like the one in Figure B.17. Add a new first line by placing the cursor at the beginning of the line and pressing Enter. Then type the hyphens in the positions shown. We also need to add a new last line. Unfortunately the technique of pressing Ctrl-N does not work here. If you move the cursor to the Report Summary band and press Ctrl-N to add a new line to the Group 1 Summary band, you hear a beep and nothing changes. To add a line at the end of a band, move the cursor to the last line in the band and select the "Add line" option from the Words menu.

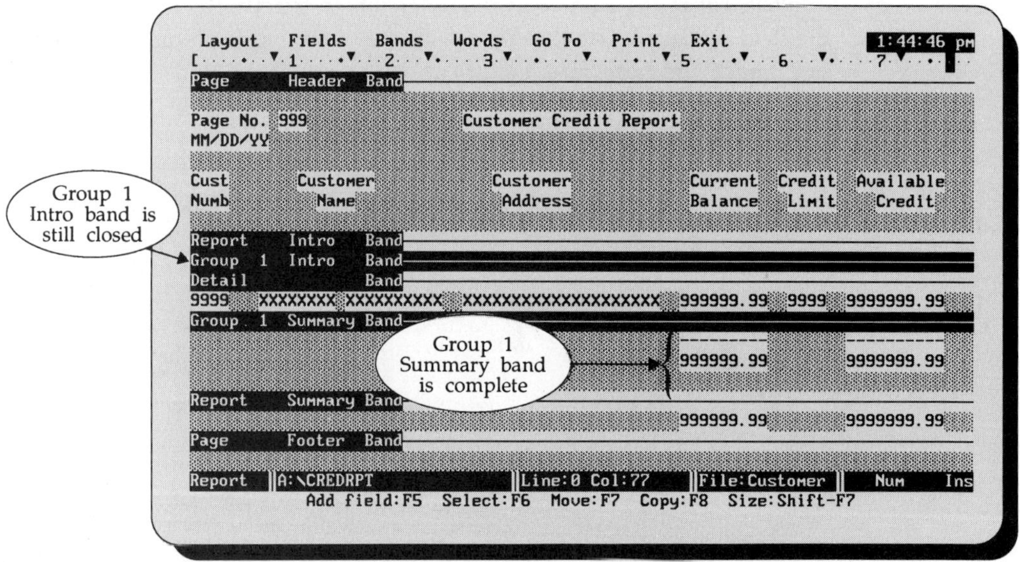

Figure B.17 REPORT DESIGN SCREEN: EXPANDING THE SUMMARY BAND

Complete the process by changing the Group 1 Intro band and the Report Summary band to those shown in Figure B.18. To change the Group 1 Intro band, you first need to open it. Then add the words "Sales rep: ", followed by the SLSRNUMB field. Make sure these are positioned as shown in the figure. When you have finished, your report should look like the one in Figure B.19. Again, if yours is different, make the corrections before you save the report. When you are satisfied that it is correct, select "Save changes and exit" from the Exit menu.

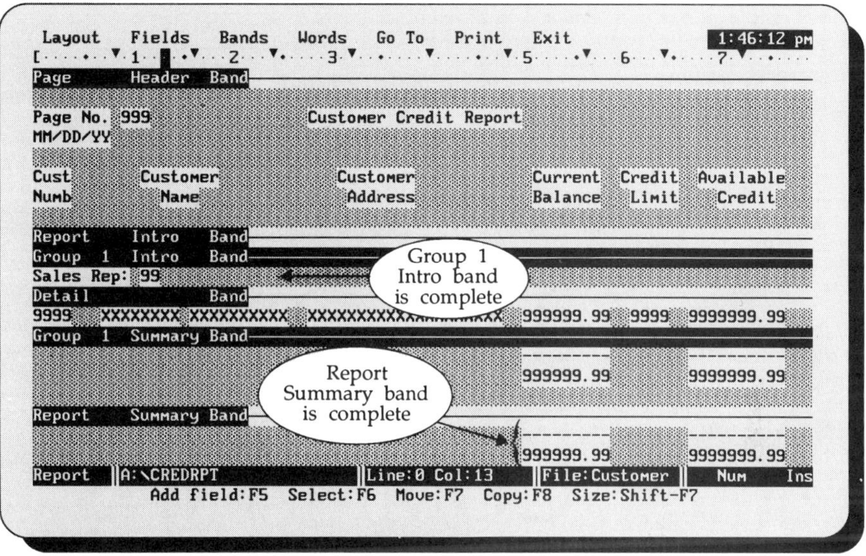

Figure B.18 REPORT DESIGN SCREEN: FINAL CHANGES

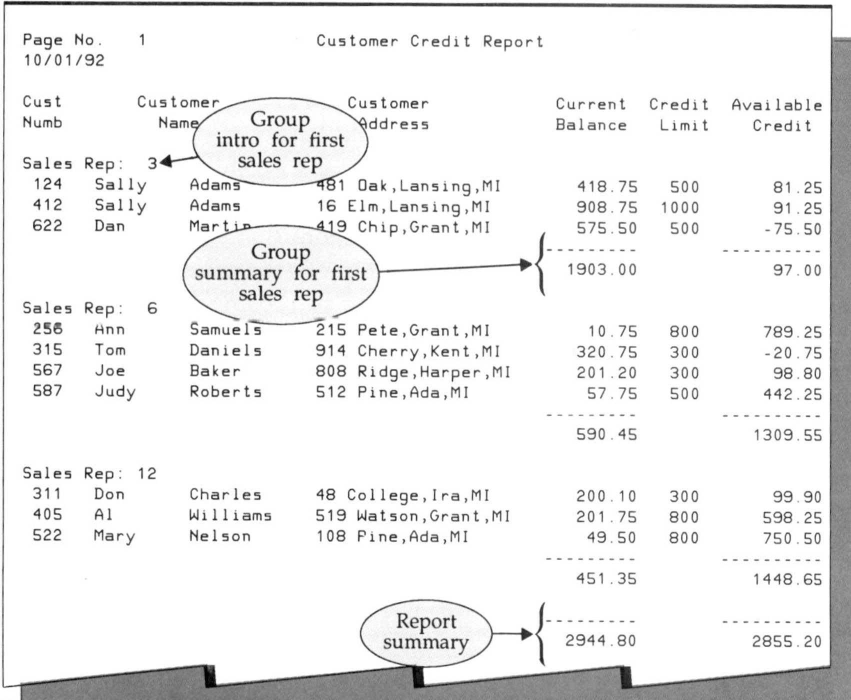
Page No. 1 Customer Credit Report
10/01/92

Cust Numb	Customer Name		Customer Address	Current Balance	Credit Limit	Available Credit
Sales Rep: 3						
124	Sally	Adams	481 Oak,Lansing,MI	418.75	500	81.25
412	Sally	Adams	16 Elm,Lansing,MI	908.75	1000	91.25
622	Dan	Martin	419 Chip,Grant,MI	575.50	500	-75.50
				---------		----------
				1903.00		97.00
Sales Rep: 6						
256	Ann	Samuels	215 Pete,Grant,MI	10.75	800	789.25
315	Tom	Daniels	914 Cherry,Kent,MI	320.75	300	-20.75
567	Joe	Baker	808 Ridge,Harper,MI	201.20	300	98.80
587	Judy	Roberts	512 Pine,Ada,MI	57.75	500	442.25
				---------		----------
				590.45		1309.55
Sales Rep: 12						
311	Don	Charles	48 College,Ira,MI	200.10	300	99.90
405	Al	Williams	519 Watson,Grant,MI	201.75	800	598.25
522	Mary	Nelson	108 Pine,Ada,MI	49.50	800	750.50
				---------		----------
				451.35		1448.65
				---------		----------
				2944.80		2855.20

Figure B.19 FINISHED SAMPLE REPORT

dBASE IV COMMANDS

INTRODUCTION

The dBASE language is one of the largest of any offered with a microcomputer DBMS. This appendix contains both dBASE syntax and descriptions of a highly useful subset of the dBASE programming language. For simplicity, we have omitted some of the commands and functions that you will probably not need, as we have some of the options for certain commands. A great deal of productive work can be accomplished with the commands and functions that are listed in this appendix. If you decide to move even further into dBASE programming, you can look in the dBASE manual for details on the commands and functions that are omitted here.

C.1 dBASE COMMANDS

Command syntax is described here the same way as it is in the dBASE manuals. Items enclosed in square brackets ([ ]) are optional; items enclosed within angle brackets (< >) are to be selected by the user. (For example, <filename> means that the user is to enter some legitimate filename at this point in the command.) Items in capital letters are to be entered exactly as they appear. The abbreviation "exp" represents any expression. The abbreviation "expN" represents an expression that must be numeric. The abbreviation "memvar" stands for a memory variable. The list of dBASE command syntax follows.

?/?? [<exp list>] [PICTURE<picture>] [AT <expN>] [STYLE <style>] — Prints the expressions in expression list. The output will be sent to the printer if SET PRINT is ON. ? prints on next line. ?? prints on same line.

@ <row>,<column> GET <exp> [PICTURE<picture>] [RANGE<exp>,<exp>] [VALID <condition>] [ERROR <exp>] [DEFAULT <exp>] [MESSAGE <exp>] [COLOR <standard>, <enhanced>] — Displays the expression at the position on the screen which is determined by row and column in reverse video (or is ignored if you have SET DEVICE TO PRINT). If a PICTURE clause is included, it will determine format characteristics.

When a READ statement is executed, users will be prompted to edit the fields specified by all GET statements that have been executed since the last READ statement. PICTURE clauses will be used to format and validate data that is entered by the user. RANGE clauses specify the range of permissible values. Any value outside the range causes dBASE to generate an error message and force the user to reenter values.

@ <row>,<column> SAY <exp> [PICTURE<picture>] — Displays the expression at the position on the screen which is determined by row and column in standard video (or on the printer if you have SET DEVICE TO PRINT). If a PICTURE clause is included, it will determine format characteristics.

@ <row1>,<column1> TO <row2>,<column2> [DOUBLE] [COLOR <color>] — Draws a line or box whose upper lefthand corner is determined by row1,column1 and whose lower righthand corner is given by row2,column2. If the word DOUBLE is included, the line or box is drawn with a double line.

ACCEPT [<prompt>] to <memvar> — Stores character string entered by user into indicated memory variable.

ACTIVATE MENU <menu> — Activates indicated bar menu.

ACTIVATE POPUP <pop-up> — Makes indicated pop-up menu active.

ACTIVATE WINDOW <window> — Calls up indicated window. Window will appear on screen and all screen output will appear in window.

APPEND BLANK — Adds one blank record to the currently selected database file.

ASSIST — Moves to the Control Center.

AVERAGE [<expN list>] [FOR <condition>] [TO <memvar list>] — Calculates the average value for each expression in the list. If a condition is included, only values from those records which satisfy it are considered in the computation. If a memory variable list is included, the average of the first expression in the expression list is stored in the first memory variable; the average of the second expression in the second memory variable; and so on. If no memory variable list is included, the results are simply displayed (provided SET TALK is ON).

BEGIN TRANSACTION — Starts transaction. Changes to the database file are recorded so they can be undone in the event of a ROLLBACK.

BROWSE — Enters the Browse mode. Editing will take place in a list-type format on the currently selected database file.

CALCULATE <computation> [FOR condition] [TO <memvar list>] [TO ARRAY <array name>] — Makes indicated computation (AVG, CNT, MAX, MIN, STD, SUM, VAR). Optionally stores results to variables in memvar list or to entries in indicated array.

CLEAR — Clears the screen.

CLEAR ALL — Closes database files, menus, windows, and releases memory variables.

CLOSE [ALL/ALTERNATE/DATABASES] — Closes indicated types of files.

CONTINUE — Moves to the next record satisfying the condition in the most recent LOCATE command.

COPY FILE <file1> TO <file2> — Creates a copy of file1 that has the name specified by file2. Since any type of file may be copied, file extensions must by given for both file1 and file2. If file2 already exists and SET SAFETY is ON, dBASE will ask the user whether it may overwrite file2 with the new data. If SET SAFETY is OFF, file2 will be overwritten automatically.

COPY STRUCTURE TO <filename> — Copies the structure, but not the data, from the active database.

COPY TO <filename> [FIELDS <field list>] [FOR <condition>] — Copies records from the database file in the currently selected area to a database file with the indicated filename. If a list of fields is included, only those fields which are in the list are copied. If a condition is included, only those records which meet the condition are copied.

COUNT [FOR <condition>] [TO <memvar>] — Counts the number of records in the database file in the currently selected area. If a condition is included, only those records which satisfy the condition are counted. If a memory variable is included, the count is stored in the memory. If no memory variable is included, the result is simply displayed (provided SET TALK is ON).

CREATE <filename>/LABEL <filename>/REPORT <filename>/ SCREEN <filename> — Creates database file/label file/report file/ screen file.

CREATE VIEW <view filename> FROM ENVIRONMENT — Creates a view using all the relations that are currently active, as well as any filter or format. The view will be stored in a file with the indicated name and an extension of VUE.

DEACTIVATE MENU — Deactivates the active bar menu and erases it from screen.

DEACTIVATE POPUP <pop-up> — Shuts down the active pop-up menu and erases it from screen.

DEACTIVATE WINDOW <window> — Deactivates indicated window and erases it from screen.

DEBUG <program name> — Begins session with on-line debugger.

DECLARE <array[dimensions]> — Creates a one- or two-dimensional array.

DEFINE BAR <bar number> OF <pop-up name> PROMPT <expC> [MESSAGE <expC>] — Defines option in a pop-up menu.

DEFINE MENU <menu name> — Defines a horizontal bar menu.

DEFINE PAD <pad name> of <menu name> PROMPT <expC> [AT <row>,<column>] — Defines option in horizontal bar menu.

DEFINE POPUP <pop-up name> FROM <row1>,<col1> TO <row2>,<col2> — Defines pop-up menu.

DEFINE WINDOW <window name> FROM <row1>,<col1> TO <row2>,<col2> [DOUBLE/PANEL/NONE] [COLOR <color>] — Defines window. **Note:** This command simply defines a window. It does *not* display it on the screen.

DELETE — Marks the current record for deletion.

DELETE ALL FOR <condition> — Marks all records that match the condition for deletion.

DELETE TAG <tag name> — Deletes index with indicated tag.

DISPLAY ALL [<exp list>] [FOR <condition>] [TO PRINT] [OFF] — Displays the fields in the expression list for all records that satisfy the given condition. If no expression list is included, all fields are displayed. If no condition is given, all records are displayed. If the user specifies TO PRINT, the output is directed to the printer. If OFF is included, record numbers are not displayed.

DISPLAY HISTORY [TO PRINT] — Displays the contents of history with a pause between screens. If TO PRINT is included, the display is also sent to the printer.

DISPLAY STATUS [TO PRINT] — Displays the status of the environment with a pause between screens. For each active database file, the display includes the area, the database name, the index name and key expression for all indexes, the name of any format file, any filter condition, and any relation. The display also includes such things as all current SET options. If TO PRINT is included, the display is also sent to the printer.

DISPLAY STRUCTURE [TO PRINT] — Displays the structure of the database file in the currently selected area with a pause between screens. For each field, the display includes the name, type, length, and number of decimal places (for numeric fields). If TO PRINT is included, the display is also sent to the printer.

DO <program or procedure name> WITH <parameter list> — Runs the specified program or procedure. If a procedure file is open and the name listed is one of the procedures in the procedure file, this command runs the specified procedure.

DO CASE..ENDCASE — Selects one possible course of action from among several alternatives. The general form of the statement is

```
DO CASE
     CASE <condition 1>
          <program statements>
     CASE <condition 2>
          <program statements>
          .
          .
          .
     [OTHERWISE
          <program statements>]
ENDCASE
```

The conditions are evaluated in the listed order. When one of the conditions is found to be true, the program statements following the condition are executed, and then control passes to the statement that follows ENDCASE; in other words, no further conditions are examined. If none of the conditions are true and the optional OTHERWISE clause is included, the statements that follow the OTHERWISE are executed. If none of the conditions are true and no OTHERWISE clause is present, control simply passes to the statement that follows the ENDCASE, with no action being taken.

DO WHILE..ENDDO — Repeats a series of commands as long as a specified condition is true. The general form of the statement is

```
DO WHILE <condition>
     <program statements>
ENDDO
```

As long as the condition is true, the statements between DO WHILE and ENDDO will be executed. The EXIT statement may be used to force an immediate exit from the structure. When either the condition is false or an EXIT statement is executed, control passes to the command that immediately follows ENDDO.

EDIT — Enters the Edit mode. Editing will take place on the database file that is active in the currently selected area.

EJECT — Causes the printer to advance to the top of the next page (a page eject).

ERASE <filename> — Erases the specified file from the disk. The filename must include the extension.

EXIT — Immediately exits from the currently running DO WHILE loop. Execution resumes with the command that immediately follows the ENDDO.

FUNCTION <function> — Identifies a User-Defined Function (UDF).

GOTO <expN>/BOTTOM/TOP — Positions the currently-selected database file at the specified record. GOTO expN positions the database file at the record whose record number is expN, GOTO BOTTOM positions it at the last record in the file, and GOTO TOP positions it at the first record in the file. The word GO may be used in place of GOTO.

HELP [<keyword>] — Displays help text for the specified keyword; if no keyword is included, displays a Help menu.

IF..ELSE..ENDIF — Selects one course of action from two alternatives. The general form of the statement is

```
IF <condition>
     <program statements>
  [ELSE
     <program statements>]
ENDIF
```

If the condition is true, the program statements between the condition and the ELSE are executed. If the condition is false, the program statements between the ELSE and the ENDIF are executed. Once the appropriate statements have been executed, control passes to the statement that follows ENDIF. If the optional ELSE clause is omitted and the condition is false, control simply passes to the statement that follows the ENDIF, with no action taken.

INDEX ON <key expression> TAG <tag> — Builds an index for the database file in the currently selected area. Index is built on the key expression and is given the indicated tag. If the key consists of two or more fields, they must be converted to a character expression.

INPUT [<prompt>] TO <memvar> — Prompts user for entry and stores it in the indicated memory variable.

JOIN WITH <alias> TO <filename> FOR <condition> [FIELDS <field list>] — Obeying the condition, creates a new database file with the indicated name by matching records in the selected database file with records in the one identified by the alias. If the optional FIELDS clause is included, only those fields which are in the list will appear in the new database file. Otherwise, all fields from both database files will appear.

Note 1: The database file that has been created is not open. Thus, before it is processed, it must be activated with an appropriate USE statement.

Note 2: This is a very inefficient operation. Before using JOIN, consider whether the problem can be handled in some other way. The obvious alternative: use a relation.

LABEL FORM <label format file> [FOR <condition>] [TO PRINT] — Produces labels from the data in the currently selected database file according to the layout specified in the Label Format file. If a condition is included, labels are printed only for those records which satisfy the condition. If the TO PRINT clause is included, labels will be printed; otherwise, they will appear on the screen.

LIST ALL [<exp list>] [FOR <condition>] [TO PRINT] [OFF] — Lists the fields in the expression list for all records that satisfy the given condition. If no expression list is included, all fields are displayed. With no condition included, all records are displayed. If you order TO PRINT, the output is directed to the printer. IF OFF is included, record numbers are not displayed.

LIST HISTORY [TO PRINT] — Same as DISPLAY HISTORY except that there is no pause between screens.

LIST STATUS [TO PRINT] — Same as DISPLAY STATUS except that there is no screen pause.

LIST STRUCTURE [TO PRINT] — Same as DISPLAY STRUCTURE except that there is no pause between screens.

LOCATE FOR <condition> — Finds the next record satisfying the condition.

MODIFY <filename>/LABEL <filename>/REPORT <filename>/SCREEN <filename> — Modifies structure of database file/label file/report file/screen file.

MODIFY COMMAND <filename> — Invokes the dBASE text editor to edit or create a file. If no file extension is given, assumes an extension of PRG (program).

ON [ERROR/ESCAPE/KEY LABEL <key>] <command> — On (error/pressing of Escape key/pressing of indicated function key) execute the indicated command. **Note:** The command is usually a DO command to execute the commands in a specified procedure.

ON PAD <pad name> OF <menu name> ACTIVATE POPUP <pop-up name> — Associates pop-up menu with pad of bar menu.

ON PAGE AT LINE <expN> <command> — Used with streaming output. When output reaches indicated line, will execute the indicated command.

ON SELECTION PAD <pad name> OF <menu name> <command> — Associates action (command) with pad of bar menu.

ON SELECTION POPUP <pop-up name> <command> — Indicates command to be executed according to selection from indicated pop-up.

PACK — Removes deleted records from the database file that is active in the currently selected area and rebuilds all active indexes.

PARAMETERS <parameter list> — Indicates list of variables that will use values passed from calling program with DO..WITH command.

PRINTJOB..ENDPRINTJOB — Commands that control a print job.

PRIVATE <memvar list> — Indicates variables as being local to the procedure.

PROCEDURE <procedure name> — Used to identify procedures within a procedure file. Each procedure must begin with a PROCEDURE statement and must end with a RETURN.

PROTECT — Utility that furnishes security features in the LAN version of dBASE.

PUBLIC <memvar list> — Indicates memory variables are available to all other programs and procedures.

QUIT — Deactivates all active files and exits to DOS.

READ — Allows user to enter/edit values in those variables identified by all the @..GET commands that have been executed since the last READ statement.

RECALL [FOR <condition>] — Unmarks any marked records that satisfy the condition. If no condition is included, only applies to current active record.

REINDEX — Rebuilds all active indexes for the database file in the currently selected area.

RELEASE <memvar list>/MENUS <menu list>/POPUPS <pop-up list>/SCREENS <screen list>/WINDOWS <window list> — Removes the indicated items from memory.

REPLACE [ALL] <field> WITH <exp> [FOR <condition>] — Replaces the contents of the named field with the value in exp for the database file in the currently selected area. If a condition is included, replacement will take place only if the condition is satisfied. If ALL is included, all records will be affected by the REPLACE command; otherwise, only the current record is affected.

REPORT FORM <report form file> [FOR <condition>] [TO PRINT] — Produces a report from the data in the database file in the currently selected area according to the layout specified in the Report Form file. If a condition is included, only those records which satisfy the condition will appear on the report. If the TO PRINT clause is included, labels will be printed; otherwise, they will appear on the screen. More than one database file can be used, provided that all database files are active and are linked with SET RELATION commands.

RESUME — Resumes execution of a currently suspended program.

RETRY — Reexecute command that caused an error.

RETURN — Causes dBASE to return control to the calling program or to the dot prompt, depending on the place from which the program was invoked (the place where the DO command was executed).

ROLLBACK — Undoes updates since last BEGIN TRANSACTION.

SCAN [FOR condition] ..ENDSCAN — Selects records from the database file meeting the condition and applies commands between SCAN and ENDSCAN to selected records.

SEEK <exp> — Searches the master index for the database file in the currently selected area to find a record whose index key matches the specified expression. If the search is successful, FOUND() is set to true and EOF() is set to false. If the search is not successful, FOUND() is set to false and EOF() is set to true.

SELECT <area number/alias> — Changes the currently selected area (also called the active area or primary area) to your area number specification (1-10) or by the alias of the database file that is active in the area.

SET ALTERNATE on/OFF, SET ALTERNATE TO <filename> — Provided SET ALTERNATE is ON, sends all output other than fullscreen commands to the indicated file. The default choice is OFF.

SET BELL ON/off — Determines whether dBASE sounds the bell (beeper) when an entry completely fills a field. If ON, the bell will sound; if OFF, it will not. The default choice is ON.

SET BORDER TO [SINGLE/DOUBLE/PANEL/NONE] — Indicates border style for pop-up menus and windows.

SET CATALOG TO [<catalog filename>] — If a name is given, activates a catalog with that name. If no such catalog exists, dBASE creates one. If no name is given, closes the active catalog.

SET CENTURY on/OFF — Indicates whether or not century is to be included in dates. The default choice is OFF.

SET COLOR OF NORMAL/MESSAGES/TITLES/BOX/HIGHLIGHT/INFORMATION/FIELDS TO <color> — Sets color for indicated portion of screen.

SET COLOR ON/OFF — Switches between color and monochrome monitors.

SET COLOR TO [<standard>] [,[<enhanced>], [,[<perimeter>] [,[<background>]]]]] — Sets colors for foreground, highlighted areas, borders, and background of screen.

SET CONFIRM on/OFF — Determines whether user must press Enter before proceeding to next GET even if a field has been completely filled. If ON, the user must press Enter to proceed to the next item, even with a completely filled field. If OFF, the cursor will advance automatically when a field is filled. The default choice is OFF.

SET CONSOLE ON/off — Turns screen display on and off. The default choice is ON.

SET DEBUG on/OFF — Determines whether commands printed by the SET ECHO ON command are displayed on the screen or the printer. If ON, the output is sent to the printer. If OFF, the output is sent to the screen. The default choice is OFF.

SET DEFAULT TO <drive> — Changes the default drive to the indicated drive.

SET DELETED on/OFF — Determines whether dBASE ignores deleted records during processing. If ON, deleted records are ignored. If OFF, they are not ignored, although there is usually an indication of some sort that they have been deleted. The default choice is OFF.

SET DEVICE TO printer/SCREEN/FILE <filename> — Determines whether the output of @..SAY commands is displayed on the printer, the screen, or sent to a file. The default choice is SCREEN.

SET DOHISTORY on/OFF — Determines whether commands executed from within dBASE programs are stored in history. If ON, these commands are stored in history along with any commands typed at the dot prompt. If OFF, only those commands which have been typed at the dot prompt are stored in history. The default choice is OFF.

SET ECHO on/OFF — Determines whether commands in programs are displayed on the screen as they are executed. If ON, they are displayed; if OFF, they are not. The default choice is OFF.

SET ESCAPE ON/off — If ON, user can interrupt a program by pressing Escape key. If off, pressing Escape key has no effect. The default choice is ON.

SET FIELDS TO [<field list>/ALL] — Determines whether or not fields from active database files are available without qualification. By executing a SET FIELDS TO command, the fields in the list (or all fields if ALL is chosen) in the database file in the currently selected area will be available without qualification even after another area is selected; that is, the name does not need to be preceded by the name of the database file and an arrow.

SET FILTER TO <condition> — Limits processing to only those records that satisfy the condition.

SET FORMAT TO [<format filename>] — Activates a Format file with the indicated name.

SET HISTORY TO <expN> — Changes the size of history so that it will accommodate the indicated number of commands.

SET MESSAGE TO <expC> — Displays expC at the bottom of the screen.

SET ORDER TO <tag> — Uses index with indicated tag to order records.

SET PRINT on/OFF — Determines whether output that is sent to the screen (other than through @..SAY and @..GET commands) is also sent to the printer. The default choice is OFF.

SET PRINTER TO <destination> — Changes destination of @..SAY commands. Can be a device or a filename.

SET PROCEDURE TO [<procedure filename>] — Activates a procedure file of the indicated name if a name is given; closes currently active procedure file if no name is given.

SET RELATION TO [<key expression>] INTO <alias> — Creates a relationship between the database file that is in the currently selected area and the database file that is identified by the alias. The key expression is a field or concatenation of fields (as a character string) from the first database file. The second database file (the one identified by the alias) must have a master index that has been activated on a similar key expression. Each record from the first database file will be associated with the single record in the second database file for which there is a value in the index that matches the key expression. For example, let's suppose that the customer database file is active in the selected area, and the sales rep file is active in another area. The master index for the sales rep file has been built on the sales rep number and the sales rep file has the alias *slsrep*.

```
SET RELATION slsrnumb INTO slsrep
```

The field *slsrnumb* in the SET RELATION command refers to the *slsrnumb* field in the customer file, since the customer file is in the currently selected area. This field will have to match values in the master index for the sales rep file. Thus, this statement creates a relation between the customer file and the sales rep file, in which each customer is related to the sales rep with a matching number.

SET SAFETY ON/off — Determines whether dBASE displays a warning message before file is to be overwritten with new data. If ON, a warning message will be displayed and dBASE will not overwrite the file without confirmation from the user. If OFF, the file will be overwritten without any notification to the user. The default choice is ON.

SET SQL on/OFF — Activates SQL mode. When ON, only SQL commands and those dBASE commands that are compatible with SQL are allowed. The default choice is OFF.

SET STATUS ON/off — If ON, status bar displays at the bottom of the screen. If OFF, it does not. The default choice is ON.

SET STEP on/OFF — Determines whether dBASE will execute programs in single-step mode. If ON, dBASE pauses after every command. User can choose to cancel by pressing Esc, to suspend by pressing the letter S, or to execute the next command by pressing the space bar. If OFF, execution proceeds normally. The default choice is OFF.

SET TALK ON/off — Determines whether the results of certain commands are displayed on the screen. If ON, they are displayed; if OFF, they are not. The default choice is ON.

SET VIEW TO <view filename> — Activates a view file with the indicated name. This automatically activates all database files, indexes, and relations that make up the view.

SKIP [<expN>] — Moves the record pointer for the database file in the currently selected area by the number of records identified by expN. If expN is omitted, it is assumed to be 1. If expN is negative, the pointer will move backward. If a SKIP moves the pointer past the end of the file, EOF() is set to true.

SORT TO <new filename> ON <field list> [FOR <condition>] — Creates a new database file with the indicated name from all those records in the database file which are in the currently selected area. If a condition is included, only those records which satisfy the condition will be placed in the new file. Records in the new file are sorted on the field or fields that are indicated in the field list. Fields are listed in order of importance; thus, the first field is the major sort key. The sort will be made in ascending order unless a field name is followed with /D which indicates descending order. **Note:** SORT is not particularly efficient. It is usually better to use an appropriate index than to sort a file.

STORE <exp> to <memvar> <memvar> = <exp> — Stores the value of the expression in the memory variable. Assigns the memory variable the same data type as the expression.

SUM [<expN list>] [FOR <condition>] [TO <memvar list>] — Calculates the sum for each expression in the list. If a condition is included, only values from those records which satisfy the condition are considered in the computation. If a memory variable list is included, the sum of the first expression in the expression list is stored in the first memory variable; the sum of the second expression is stored in the second memory variable; and so on. If no memory variable list is included, the results are simply displayed (provided SET TALK is ON).

TEXT..ENDTEXT — Block of characters between TEXT and ENDTEXT will be sent to the screen or printer exactly as they appear.

TYPE <filename> [TO PRINT] — Displays the contents of the file on the screen; if TO PRINT is included, also prints the contents of the file. The filename must include its extension.

UNLOCK [ALL] — Releases the most recent file or record lock placed on the database file in the currently selected area. ALL releases all locks placed on this file.

USE <filename> [ORDER <tag name>] [ALIAS <alias>] — Activates the database with the specified filename in the currently selected area. ORDER will order records by indicated index. If the ALIAS clause is used, the indicated name can be used in place of the filename to identify the database file for purposes of qualification and area selection.

WAIT — Causes dBASE to display the message "Press any key to continue..." and then waits until the user presses a key before proceeding to the next command in the program.

ZAP — Removes all records from active database file.

C.2 dBASE FUNCTIONS

When a function is referenced in a program, it will be set equal to some value. Technically, we say that the function *returns* this value. In the description of the dBASE functions, the value to which the function will be set is described after the word "returns."

ABS(<expN>) — Returns: Absolute value of expression.

ASC(<expC>) — Returns: ASCII code for first character in expC.

AT(<expC>,<expC>) — Returns: Starting position of first string within second.

BAR() — Returns: Number of most recently selected option in pop-up menu.

CDOW (<date>) — Returns: Character day of week.

CHR(<number>) — Returns: The character that is the ASCII equivalent of the number.

CMONTH(<date>) — Returns: Character month of year.

COL() — Returns: Column for current cursor position.

COS(<expN>) — Returns: Cosine of angle.

CTOD(<character expression>) — Returns: The date that is equivalent to the character expression.

DATE() — Returns: The system date.

DELETED() — Returns: True (.T.) if the current record has been deleted; false (.F.) if not.

DOW(<date>) — Returns: Numeric day of week.

DTOC(<date>) — Returns: The character-string equivalent of date.

EOF([alias]) — Returns: True if the record pointer is beyond the last record in the file in the currently selected area; otherwise, false.

ERROR() — Returns: The number that corresponds to the error that has just occurred.

EXP(<expN>) — Returns: *e* raised to the power of the expression.

FLOCK() — Returns: True if it is possible to lock the file in the currently selected area; otherwise false. If true, it will also lock the file.

FOUND() — Returns: True if a record was found with a matching value during a SEEK command; otherwise false.

IIF (<condition>, <exp1>, <exp2>) — Returns: Exp1 if condition is true and exp2 if condition is false.

INKEY ([integer]) — Returns: Integer representing key pressed. Optional integer represents number of seconds to wait for user. If no key is pressed in that amount of time, command terminates and returns a value of zero.

INT(<expN>) — Returns: Integer part of expression.

ISALPHA(<expC>) — Returns: True if expC begins with a letter. False otherwise.

ISLOWER(<expC>) — Returns: True if expC begins with a lowercase letter. For any other case, false.

ISUPPER(<expC>) — Returns: True if expC begins with an uppercase letter. False otherwise.

LOCK() — Returns: True if it is possible to lock the current record in the database file in the currently selected area; otherwise false. If true, it will also lock the record. Same as RLOCK().

LOG(<expN>) — Returns: Log to the base *e* of expression.

LOG10(<expN>) — Returns: Log to the base 10 of expression.

LOOKUP (<field1>,<exp>,<field2>) — Returns: Search for record on which field2 matches exp. If it finds such a record, returns value in field1.

LOWER(<character string>) — Returns: The lowercase equivalent of the character string.

MAX (<exp1>,<exp2>) — Returns: The larger of exp1 and exp2.

MESSAGE() — Returns: Message for current error code.

MIN (<exp1>,<exp2>) — Returns: The smaller of exp1 and exp2.

MOD (<integer1>,<integer2>) — Returns: The remainder when integer1 is divided by integer2.

PAD() — Returns: Name of most recently selected pad.

PI() — Returns: Value of *pi*.

PRINTSTATUS() — Returns: True if printer is ready to receive output. False otherwise.

READKEY() — Returns: ASCII code of key that was pressed to exit Edit mode.

RECNO() — Returns: The number of the current record in the database file in the currently selected area.

RLOCK() — Returns: True if it is possible to lock the current record in the database file in the currently selected area; otherwise false. If true, it will also lock the record. Same as LOCK().

ROUND(<number>,<decimals>) — Returns: The numeric result of rounding the number to the indicated number of decimal places.

ROW() — Returns: Row number for cursor.

SIN(<expN>) — Returns: Sine of angle expN.

SOUNDEX(<expC>) — Returns: Soundex code of expC.

SPACE(<number>) — Returns: A character string that consists entirely of blanks (spaces) and whose length is equal to the indicated number.

SQRT(<expN>) — Returns: Square root of expN.

STR(<number>[,<length>][,<decimals>]) — Returns: The character equivalent of the number. Has length indicated by the length argument and optionally by the number of decimal places indicated by the decimals argument.

STUFF (<expC1>, <expN1>, <expN2>, <expC2>) — Returns: String obtained by inserting expC2 into expC1, starting at position expN1 and replacing expN2 characters.

SUBSTR (<expC>, <expN1>, <expN2>) — Returns: String of characters expN2 in length from expC starting at position expN1.

TAN(<expN>) — Returns: Tangent of angle expN.

TIME() — Returns: System time.

TRIM(<expC>) — Returns: Character string in expC with trailing blanks removed.

UPPER(<character string>) — Returns: The uppercase equivalent of the character string.

VAL(<character string>) — Returns: The numeric equivalent of the character string.

C.3 dBASE PICTURE CLAUSES

TEMPLATE SYMBOLS	
SYMBOL	**MEANING**
#	Only digits, blanks, and algebraic signs.
!	Converts lowercase letters to uppercase.
$	Displays dollar sign rather than leading zeros.
*	Displays * rather than leading zeros.
,	Comma positions.
9	Only numbers in character data. Numbers and algebraic signs for numerical data.
A	Only letters.
L	Only logical-type data.
N	Letters and numbers.
X	Any characters.
Y	Only Y, y, N, or n. Lowercase y or n will be converted to uppercase.

PICTURE FUNCTIONS	
SYMBOL	**MEANING**
^	Scientific notation.
!	Lowercase converted to uppercase.
$	Display with dollar sign.
(	Parentheses around negative numbers.
A	Only letters.
B	Left-justify text in field.
C	Display CR after positive numbers.
I	Center text in field.
J	Right-justify text in field.
L	Display leading zeros.
R	Literals in picture are displayed on screen but not stored as part of the field's value.
S<n>	Limits field width to specified number of characters. Scrolls within field.
T	Trims blanks from field.
X	Display DB after negative numbers.
Z	Display numeric value zero as space.

D ASCII CODES

INTRODUCTION

Character data is stored using the ASCII (American Standard Code for Information Interchange) code. This appendix lists the ASCII codes and their character equivalents.

ASCII VALUE	CHARACTER	CONTROL CHARACTER	ASCII VALUE	CHARACTER	CONTROL CHARACTER
000	(null)	NUL	054	6	
001	☺	SOH	055	7	
002	☻	STX	056	8	
003	♥	ETX	057	9	
004	♦	EOT	058	:	
005	♣	ENQ	059	;	
006	♠	ACK	060	<	
007	(beep)	BEL	061	=	
008	◘	BS	062	>	
009	(tab)	HT	063	?	
010	(line feed)	LF	064	@	
011	(home)	VT	065	A	
012	(form feed)	FF	066	B	
013	(carriage return)	CR	067	C	
014	♫	SO	068	D	
015	☼	SI	069	E	
016	►	DLE	070	F	
017	◄	DC1	071	G	
018	↕	DC2	072	H	
019	!!	DC3	073	I	
020	¶	DC4	074	J	
021	§	NAK	075	K	
022	▬	SYN	076	L	
023	↨	ETB	077	M	
024	↑	CAN	078	N	
025	↓	EM	079	O	
026	←	SUB	080	P	
027	→	ESC	081	Q	
028	(cursor right)	FS	082	R	
029	(cursor left)	GS	083	S	
030	(cursor up)	RS	084	T	
031	(cursor down)	US	085	U	
032	(space)	SP	086	V	
033	!		087	W	
034	"		088	X	
035	#		089	Y	
036	$		090	Z	
037	%		091	[	
038	&		092	\	
039	'		093	]	
040	(		094	^	
041	)		095	_	
042	*		096	`	
043	+		097	a	
044	,		098	b	
045	-		099	c	
046	.		100	d	
047	/		101	e	
048	0		102	f	
049	1		103	g	
050	2		104	h	
051	3		105	i	
052	4		106	j	
053	5		107	k	

ASCII VALUE	CHARACTER	CONTROL CHARACTER	ASCII VALUE	CHARACTER	CONTROL CHARACTER
108	l		158	Pt	
109	m		159	f	
110	n		160	a	
111	o		161	i	
112	p		162	o	
113	q		163	u	
114	r		164	n	
115	s		165	N	
116	t		166	a̲	
117	u		167	o̲	
118	v		168	?	
119	w		169	⌐	
120	x		170	¬	
121	y		171	1/2	
122	z		172	1/4	
123	[		173	!	
124	¦		174	<	
125	]		175	>	
126	~		176	░	
127			177	▒	
128	C		178	▓	
129	u		179	│	
130	e		180	┤	
131	a		181	╡	
132	a		182	╢	
133	a		183	╖	
134	a		184	╕	
135	c		185	╣	
136	e		186	║	
137	e		187	╗	
138	e		188	╝	
139	i		189	╜	
140	i		190	╛	
141	i		191	┐	
142	A		192	└	
143	A		193	┴	
144	E		194	┬	
145	ae		195	├	
146	AE		196	─	
147	o		197	┼	
148	o		198	╞	
149	o		199	╟	
150	u		200	╚	
151	u		201	╔	
152	y		202	╩	
153	O		203	╦	
154	U		204	╠	
155	-		205	═	
156	£		206	╬	
157	Y		207	╧	

ASCII VALUE	CHARACTER	CONTROL CHARACTER	ASCII VALUE	CHARACTER	CONTROL CHARACTER
208	╨		232	Φ	
209	╤		233	Θ	
210	╥		234	Ω	
211	╙		235	δ	
212	╘		236	∞	
213	╒		237	Ø	
214	╓		238	∈	
215	╫		239	∩	
216	╪		240	≡	
217	┘		241	±	
218	┌		242	≥	
219	█		243	≤	
220	▄		244	⌠	
221	▌		245	⌡	
222	▐		246	÷	
223	▀		247	≈	
224	α		248	°	
225	β		249	●	
226	Γ		250	•	
227	π		251	√	
228	Σ		252	^{n}	
229	σ		253	^{2}	
230	μ		254	■	
231	τ		255	(blank 'FF')	

ERROR CODES AND MESSAGES

INTRODUCTION

This appendix lists the dBASE error codes and corresponding error messages.

ERROR CODE	ERROR MESSAGE
232	ALIAS expression not in range
24	ALIAS name already in use
13	ALIAS not found
230	Bad array dimension(s)
38	Beginning of file encountered
176	Cannot clear menu in use
177	Cannot clear popup in use
185	Cannot close database; transaction in process
187	Cannot close index files; transaction in process
89	Cannot erase open file
186	Cannot execute command; transaction in process
174	Cannot redefine menu in use
175	Cannot redefine popup in use
17	Cannot select requested database
201	Cannot write to a database due to incomplete transaction.
188	Cannot write to transaction log file
122	Catalog has not been established
487	Copying production MDX requires free work area
44	Cyclic relation
9	Data type mismatch
131	Database encrypted
26	Database not indexed
216	Display mode not available
211	Duplicate production MDX file
4	End of file encountered
193	Environment not correct for rollback
145	Error in configuration value
192	Error in reading log file
96	Error on line ()
248	Exceeded maximum compiler nesting level
274	Exceeded maximum number of compile time symbol
272	Exceeded maximum number of runtime symbols
141	Fields list too complicated
110	File must be opened in exclusive mode
29	File not accessible
206	File not an MDX file

ERROR CODE	ERROR MESSAGE
194	File not in transaction log
14	Find not successful
46	Illegal value
19	Index file does not match database
113	Index interrupted. Index will be deleted
205	Index TAG already exists
43	Insufficient memory
227	Invalid box dimensions
81	Invalid date
11	Invalid function argument
106	Invalid index number
107	Invalid operator
202	Invalid path or filename ()
123	Invalid printer port
124	Invalid printer redirection
221	Left margin plus indentation must be less than right margin
222	Line number must be between zero and page length
217	Lock table is full
191	Log file not found
196	Log record does not match database record
58	LOG(): Zero or negative
203	MDX file full
235	NDX index may not be DESCENDING
213	No more windows available
45	Not a character expression
37	Not a logical expression
229	Not an array
170	ON PAD already defined for this prompt pad
169	ON SELECTION already defined for this prompt pad
22	Out of memory variable slots
243	PARAMETERS command must be at top of the procedure
125	Printer not ready
252	Procedure not found
289	Production MDX file is damaged
210	Production MDX file not found
143	Query not valid in this environment

ERROR CODE	ERROR MESSAGE
20	Record not in index
5	Record out of range
142	Relation record in use by another
88	REPLICATE(): String too large
197	ROLLBACK database cannot be executed inside a transaction
218	SQL system tables may not be USEd
62	SUBSTR(): Start point out of range
10	Syntax error
209	TAG not found
6	Too many files are open
28	Too many indexes
92	Unable to load COMMAND.COM
129	Unable to LOCK
133	Unauthorized access level
228	Undefined box border
104	Unknown function key
36	Unrecognized phrase/keyword in command
35	Unterminated string
183	Unterminated transaction file exists, cannot start new transaction
12	Variable not found

CASE STUDY/ MAJOR REPORT

INTRODUCTION

This case study/project involves the creation, maintenance, and utilization of a database for Premiere Products. The data to be stored in the database and the structure of the database is given in Figure F.1. (**Note:** The data is already on your data disk.)

SLSREP

SLSRNUMB	SLSRNAME	SLSRADDR	TOTCOMM	COMMRATE
3	Mary Jones	123 Main,Grand,MI	2150.00	.05
6	William Smith	102 Raymond,Ada,MI	4912.50	.07
12	Sam Brown	419 Harper,Lansing,MI	2150.00	.05

CUSTOMER

CUSTNUMB	LAST	FIRST	ADDRESS	BALANCE	CREDLIM	SLSRNUMB
124	Adams	Sally	481 Oak,Lansing,MI	418.75	500	3
256	Samuels	Ann	215 Pete,Grant,MI	10.75	800	6
311	Charles	Don	48 College,Ira,MI	200.10	300	12
315	Daniels	Tom	914 Cherry,Kent,MI	320.75	300	6
405	Williams	Al	519 Watson,Grant,MI	201.75	800	12
412	Adams	Sally	16 Elm,Lansing,MI	908.75	1000	3
522	Nelson	Mary	108 Pine,Ada,MI	49.50	800	12
567	Baker	Joe	808 Ridge,Harper,MI	201.20	300	6
587	Roberts	Judy	512 Pine,Ada,MI	57.75	500	6
622	Martin	Dan	419 Chip,Grant,MI	575.50	500	3

ORDERS

ORDNUMB	ORDDTE	CUSTNUMB
12489	9/02/92	124
12491	9/02/92	311
12494	9/04/92	315
12495	9/04/92	256
12498	9/05/92	522
12500	9/05/92	124
12504	9/05/92	522

Figure F.1 DATABASE STRUCTURE AND CONTENTS FOR CASE STUDY

(continued)

ORDLNE

ORDNUMB	PARTNUMB	NUMBORD	QUOTPRCE
12489	AX12	11	14.95
12491	BT04	1	402.99
12491	BZ66	1	311.95
12494	CB03	4	175.00
12495	CX11	2	57.95
12498	AZ52	2	22.95
12498	BA74	4	4.95
12500	BT04	1	402.99
12504	CZ81	2	108.99

PART

PARTNUMB	PARTDESC	UNONHAND	ITEMCLSS	WREHSENM	UNITPRCE
AX12	IRON	104	HW	3	17.95
AZ52	SKATES	20	SG	2	24.95
BA74	BASEBALL	40	SG	1	4.95
BH22	TOASTER	95	HW	3	34.95
BT04	STOVE	11	AP	2	402.99
BZ66	WASHER	52	AP	3	311.95
CA14	SKILLET	2	HW	3	19.95
CB03	BIKE	44	SG	1	187.50
CX11	MIXER	112	HW	3	57.95
CZ81	WEIGHTS	208	SG	2	108.99

Figure F.1 DATABASE STRUCTURE AND CONTENTS FOR CASE STUDY

Figure F.2 gives pertinent details concerning these database files and fields.

SLSREP

COLUMN	TYPE	LENGTH	DEC. PLACES	NULLS ALLOWED?	DESCRIPTION
SLSRNUMB	Numeric	2	0		Sales rep number (key)
SLSRNAME	Char	15			Sales rep name
SLSRADDR	Char	25		Yes	Sales rep address
TOTCOMM	Numeric	7	2	Yes	Total commission
COMMRATE	Numeric	3	2	Yes	Commission rate

CUSTOMER

COLUMN	TYPE	LENGTH	DEC. PLACES	NULLS ALLOWED?	DESCRIPTION
CUSTNUMB	Numeric	3	0		Customer number (key)
LAST	Char	10			Customer last name
FIRST	Char	8			Customer first name
ADDRESS	Char	25		Yes	Customer address
BALANCE	Numeric	7	2		Current balance
CREDLIM	Numeric	4	0		Credit limit ($300, $500, $800 or $1,000)
SLSRNUMB	Numeric	2	0		Sales rep number (matches SLSRNUMB in SLSREP table)

ORDERS

COLUMN	TYPE	LENGTH	DEC. PLACES	NULLS ALLOWED?	DESCRIPTION
ORDNUMB	Numeric	5	0		Order number (key)
ORDDTE	Date	6	0		Order date
CUSTNUMB	Numeric	3	0		Customer number (matches CUSTNUMB in CUSTOMER table)

Figure F.2 DATABASE FILE AND FIELD INFORMATION

(continued)

ORDLNE					
COLUMN	TYPE	LENGTH	DEC. PLACES	NULLS ALLOWED?	DESCRIPTION
ORDNUMB	Numeric	5	0		Order number (matches ORDNUMB in ORDERS table)
PARTNUMB	Char	4			Part number (matches PARTNUMB in PART table)
NUMBORD	Numeric	3	0		Number of units of the part that were ordered
QUOTPRCE	Numeric	6	2		Quoted price

PART					
COLUMN	TYPE	LENGTH	DEC. PLACES	NULLS ALLOWED?	DESCRIPTION
PARTNUMB	Char	4			Part number
PARTDESC	Char	10			Part description
UNONHAND	Numeric	4	0		Number of units on hand
ITEMCLSS	Char	2			Item class
WREHSENM	Numeric	2	0	Yes	Warehouse number
UNITPRCE	Numeric	6	2		Unit price

Figure F.2 DATABASE FILE AND FIELD INFORMATION

In addition to the columns in Figure F.2, the following extra items must be included on screens and reports:

- The name of the sales rep who represents the customer in the CUSTOMER database file.
- The available credit (credit limit – balance) for any customer in the CUSTOMER database file.
- The name (FIRST and LAST) of the customer who placed the order in the ORDERS database file.
- The description of the part and the unit price in the ORDLNE database file.
- The price variance (unit price – quoted price) in the ORDLNE database file.
- The on-hand value (units on hand * unit price) in the PART database file.

F.1 UPDATES

This project includes dBASE IV programs to allow users to update (add, change, or delete) sales reps, customers, orders, parts, and order lines. Each update screen should display all the items in the corresponding master but should not allow changes to any of the "extra items." (For example, the screen for customers should include the sales rep name, but the user should not be allowed to change this name.)

F.2 REPORTS

For each database file, the project includes a full-detail report listing all the records in the master. Each listing should have appropriate headings and should include the appropriate "extra items." In addition, the following reports are also included:

1. **List of all credit limits.** For each credit limit, list
   a. the number of customers who have this limit,
   b. the number of customers who have the limit and whose balance exceeds the credit limit, and
   c. the average balance for all customers who have this limit.
2. **List of all sales reps.** For each sales rep, list
   a. the number of customers who are represented by the sales rep,
   b. the number of customers who are represented by the sales rep and whose balance exceeds the credit limit, and
   c. the average balance for all customers of this sales rep.
3. **Open orders by customer.** For each customer, list the number, name, and address. In addition, for each part the customer currently has on order, list the part number, description, order number, number of units ordered, and quoted price.
4. **Open orders by part.** For each part, list the part number, part description, and unit price. In addition, for each customer who currently has an order for the part, list the customer number, name, order number, number of units ordered, and quoted price.
5. **Order report.** List full detail about each order. Each order should be on a separate page. The format of the page should be as close to the format of your order entry screen as possible.

F.3 LABELS

The following labels are included in the system:

1. **Sales reps.** There should be mailing labels for sales reps. Each label should contain the sales rep's number, name, and address.

2. **Customers.** There should be mailing labels for customers. Each label should contain the customer's number, name, and address. In addition, the user should be given the following options for printing these labels:
   a. Print labels for all customers.
   b. Print labels for those customers whose balance exceeds the credit limit.
   c. Print labels for customers of a specific sales rep. (The user will have to enter the sales rep number.)
3. **Parts.** There should be labels for parts. Each label should include the part's number, description, item class, warehouse number, and unit price.

F.4 UTILITIES

The system contains the following utilities:

1. **Backup.** Backup all database files and corresponding production index files.
2. **Recover.** Use backup copies to recover live database files and corresponding production index files.
3. **Repair indexes.** Recreate all indexes.

F.5 EXITS

The system includes two Exit options:

1. **Return to dBASE IV.** User will be taken back to the dot prompt.
2. **Exit to DOS.** User will be returned to DOS.

F.6 MENUS

All the programs in the system are tied together with appropriate menus. The main menu is a horizontal bar menu containing "Updates," "Reports," "Labels," "Utilities," and "Exit" options. Each option on the main menu is associated with a pull-down menu. The Reports, Labels, Utilities, and Exit menus are simply lists of all available choices.

The Updates menu contains five choices: "Sales reps," "Customers," "Orders," "Parts," and "Order lines." Thus the user will first select the database file to be updated. Once the user selects one of these options, a pop-up menu will appear asking for the type of update. If the user selects "Customers," for example, the pop-up menu that appears would have three choices: "Add new customers," "Change existing customers," "Delete customers."

GLOSSARY

-> — arrow prefix to identify SELECTed files.
Accumulator — a memory variable used to accumulate an arithmetic total.
Action diagrams — the bracketing of control structures for clarity.
Algorithm — a logical series of steps to solve a problem.
Alphanumeric — any character-type symbol.
Alphanumeric constant — a specific piece of character-type data.
Alphanumeric literal — another term for *alphanumeric constant*.
Archive — to place records in an inactive file.
Argument — the data affected by a function.
Array — a group of elements sharing a common name.
ASCII — a standard code used to represent data in a computer system.
Attribute — a property of an entity.
Backup — to copy a file to prevent data loss.
Batch mode — processing transactions as a group.
Buffer — a portion of memory reserved for file transfer.
Byte — the amount of storage required for one character of data.
Called program — a subprogram activated by another program.
Calling program — a program that activates a subprogram.
Chaining — establishing indexed links among files.
Character — a single symbol; for example, 7, @, or z.
Coding — writing instructions using a programming language.
COMMAND.COM — a file containing a portion of MS-DOS.
Compiler — a program used to reduce source code to machine code.
Concatenation — the combining of two strings with a + sign.
Condition — an expression that evaluates to true or false.
CONFIG.DB — a file containing dBASE IV settings.
CONFIG.SYS — a file containing DOS settings.
Corrupted — refers to a database or index file whose contents have been damaged.
Counter — a memory variable incremented for counting purposes.
CPU — the central processing unit.
Data — information represented in a computer system.
Data dictionary — a tool that is used to store descriptions of the entities, attributes, relationships, and so on, that are associated with a database.
Data integrity — using programming to ensure that the data in the database is correct.
Database — an organized collection of data.
Database management system — a program to store and organize data.
DBMS — a database management system.
Dijkstra structures — the three primary control structures.
Element — one item in an array.

Exclusive mode — a mode where only one user can access a database file.
Field — a piece of data representing an attribute of an entity, such as a customer's name.
Field-access privilege — privilege associated with actions a user may take on a field in the database.
File — a collection of records.
File-access privilege — privilege associated with actions a user may take on a database file.
Filename — a name assigned to a file by the user.
File server — the central computer in a local area network.
First normal form — a table that does not contain repeating groups.
Flat file — an unorganized list of data.
Formatted output — output created with @..SAY commands.
Full-screen editing — the use of blocks and editing keys on the screen.
Function — preset routines available to solve a variety of tasks. Returns a value that can be used by a program or at the dot prompt.
Functional decomposition — the process of top-down design.
Functional dependency — a field is functionally dependent on a second field if a value for the second field uniquely determines a single value for the first.
Hierarchical — a type of DBMS used on mainframe systems.
Horizontal bar menu — a menu in which the options are arranged in a horizontal line.
I-P-O chart — a chart that represents input, processing, and output.
If-then-else — a decision-making control structure.
Index key — the field or combination of fields on which an index is built.
Interactive — programs that respond to user input as it occurs.
Iteration — the repeating of a section of code.
Key field — a field used to index or sort.
Kilobyte — 1024 bytes of data.
LAN — local area network.
Local area network — a configuration of several computers hooked together in a limited geographic area allowing users to share a variety of resources.
Locking — restricting access to a record or file.
Machine language — native instructions to the CPU.
Major key — more important of the two fields that make up an index or sort key.
Menu-driven — systems controlled with menu selections, not commands.
Minor key — less important of the two fields that make up an index or sort key.
Modules — small programs designed to perform one specific function in a system.
MS-DOS — the operating system used with dBASE IV.
Mutually exclusive — when only one option is logically possible in a set.
Nesting — the placing of one control structure within another.
Normalization — the process of eliminating redundancy in files.
Null string — a character literal containing no data.
Numeric constant — a specific numeric value.
Numeric literal — a specific numeric value.
Operating system — a set of programs essential to basic system operation.

Pop-up menu — a menu, with vertically-arranged choices, that appears when the user presses Enter.
Procedure — a program that has been included in another PRG file. Usually used to accomplish some specific task.
Production index file — special file containing all the indexes (up to 47 of them) for a database file.
PROTECT — a utility to provide file security.
Pseudocode — brief statements outlining program functions.
Pull-down menu — a menu, with vertically-arranged choices, that appears automatically when the user highlights the corresponding option in a horizontal bar menu.
Query — a request for data from a system.
Reasonableness — testing whether data is within acceptable limits.
Record — a collection of fields.
Relational model — A data model in which the structure is the table or relation.
Relational operator — operators that are used in comparisons.
Report generator — tool to simplify the creation of reports.
Scope — specifies the records that will be affected by a command.
Screen painter — Tool to simplify the creation of data-entry screens.
Second normal form — a record is in second normal form if it is in first normal form and there are no partial dependencies (dependencies on only a portion of the key).
Selection — using the IF-THEN-ELSE control structure.
Self-documenting — including comments and indentation in a program.
Shared mode — a mode where several users can access a database file simultaneously.
Source file — code to be processed by a compiler.
SQL — a standard programming language used in DBMSs.
Streaming output — output sent to the screen or printer a line at a time. Usually accomplished with ? and ?? commands.
String — a set of alphanumeric characters.
Structure diagram — a means of outlining system relationships.
Subprograms — modules within a system.
Subroutine — a subprogram.
Syntax — the rules of a language.
Table — an arrangement of data in rows and columns.
Tag — name for an index within a production index file.
Template — collection of symbols governing format of data for input and output.
Third normal form — a record is in third normal form if it is in second normal form and if there are no transitive dependencies (dependencies on something other than the key).
Transparent — processes that are not evident to the user.
Value — a specific number, character string, date, or logical entry.
Window — a rectangular portion of the screen that can be manipulated in a variety of ways.
Work area — a section of memory assigned to one DBF file.
Workstation — one computer in a local area network.

INDEX